GLEANINGS
in
JOSHUA

GLEANINGS

in

JOSHUA

By

ARTHUR W. PINK

MOODY PRESS • CHICAGO

PUBLISHER'S PREFACE

These studies in the life and times of Joshua were some of the last expositions to come from the gifted pen of the late Arthur W. Pink. They were originally published in *Studies in the Scriptures,* of which he was publisher and editor. He died July 15, 1952, before the series was completed. Mr. James Gunn of Midland, Ontario concluded the studies. Most of the material in chapters 20-23 was written by him.

THE PUBLISHERS

CONTENTS

Chapter 1

INTRODUCTION

The Significance of Joshua

"I am fearfully and *wonderfully* made: marvellous are Thy works" (Psa. 139: 14). The reference there is to the physical body of man, which is the product of Omniscience. "Thy testimonies are *wonderful*: therefore doth my soul keep (treasure and submit to) them" (Psa. 119: 29). The Maker of man's body is the Author of the Word and each is alike "wonderful", evidencing its Divine source. The human body is made up of two halves: two arms and legs, two eyes and ears, two lungs and kidneys etc.; so also the Word is made up of the two Testaments. Each is a living organism: a single and complete entity, yet with many members. Each of those members is necessary to give completeness to the others, and the cutting off of one results in multilation to the whole. Each of those members has its own function to fulfil and each book in the Scriptures makes its own separate contribution to the sum of Divine revelation. As each physical member is fitted for discharging its own distinctive office, so the substance of each book in the Bible is suited to its own special theme. As there is a real difference between both the texture and purpose of the eye and the ear, so there is between the contents and leading subjects of any two books in the Word.

The analogies drawn between the living and physical body of man and the living and holy Word of God might be considerably extended. The design and functions of some members of our bodies are self-evident even to the layman. But there are others which are understood only by a trained physician. In like manner, the purpose and purport of some of the books of the Bible is more or less apparent to the rank and file of God's people, but the special character and distinctive features of others is discerned only by the Spirit-qualified teacher. That particular parallel may be extended still further: as there are certain glands of the body which still puzzle anatomists, so there are some books of Scripture the theme of which is by no means certain to the most diligent student. After all the centuries that have passed and all the attention that has been devoted to the human body and the Divine Word there yet remains an element of mystery about the one and the other, and only the blatant or the ignorant will deny it.

Now it should be evident that in approaching the study of one of the books of Scripture it must be of considerable help to the student if he can ascertain what is its main design and what is its outstanding topic. As we pointed out in these pages over twenty years ago, in our Introduction to Exodus (now out of print), each book in the Bible has a prominent and dominent theme which, as such, is peculiar to itself, around which everything is made to centre and of which all the details are but the amplification. What that leading subject may be, we should make it our business to prayerfully and diligently ascertain. This can best be discovered by reading and re-reading the book under review,

9

noting carefully any particular feature or expression which occurs frequently in it—such as "under the sun" in Ecclesiastes or "the righteousness of God" in Romans. If other students before us have published the results of their labours it is our bounden duty to closely examine their findings in the light of Holy Writ, and either verify or disprove. Before pointing out the peculiar character and dominant subject of Joshua, let us briefly state that of the books preceding.

Genesis is obviously the book of *beginnings*. Considered historically there is a three-fold beginning recorded: of the heavens and the earth, of the post-diluvian world, of the nation of Israel—in the call of Abram. Viewed doctrinally, it illustrates, as might be expected, the foundation-truth of *election*, for our salvation began in God's eternal purpose. Thus we see here that Noah (alone of the antediluvians) "found grace in the eyes of the Lord" (6: 8), and that Shem (rather than Japheth or Ham) was the one selected to be the channel through which should ultimately issue the Saviour (9: 26). Here we see God singling out Abram to be the father of the chosen Nation. Here we see see God choosing Isaac and passing by Ishmael, loving Jacob but hating Esau. Here we behold God appointing Joseph from the twelve sons of Jacob to be the honoured instrument of saving them all from the famine. The same principle appears again in the passing by of Joseph's older son and bestowing the portion of the firstborn upon Ephraim (48: 13-20). "God hath from *the beginning* chosen you unto salvation" (2 Thess. 2: 13), and that basic truth is illustrated again and again in that book which begins the Scriptures.

Historically the book of Exodus treats of the deliverance and departure of the Hebrews out of Egypt, but doctrinally its theme is clearly that of *re-demption*. That is just what the spiritual mind would expect, for it is by means of the redemptive work of Christ that the Father's eternal purpose is made good. If the first book of the Bible reveals a sovereign God passing by some and choosing others to salvation, Exodus makes known how that salvation is accomplished, namely, by the mighty power of God and through the blood of the Lamb. Moses was bidden to say unto the children of Israel "I am the Lord, and will bring you out from under the burden of the Egyptians and I will rid you out of their bondage, and I will *redeem* you with a stretched out arm and with great judgments" (6: 6)—the first clause showing what redemption is from and the last how it is effected. At the Red Sea they sang "Thou in Thy mercy hast led forth the people which Thou hast *redeemed*. Thou hast guided them in Thy strength unto Thy holy habitation" (15: 13). Between those two passages comes the record of the slaying of the lamb and the efficacy of its blood, while the remainder of the book is devoted to instructions re God's habitation.

The book of Leviticus covers a period in Israel's history of less than two months, for the whole of it (as well as the first ten chapters of Numbers) treats of what occurred between the first day of the second year and the twentieth day of the second month (Ex. 40: 17, Num. 10: 11). As we might expect, being the third book of Scripture, it views the people of God as on resurrection ground—regenerated. It is not so much doctrinal as experimental. The key is hung upon its door: "And the Lord called unto Moses and spake unto him out of the *tabernacle*" (1: 1). It naturally and necessarily comes after Exodus, informing us what we are redeemed for, being the book of Divine *fellowship and worship*. Here we are shown the glorious privileges of the believer, the holy requirements of God and the gracious provisions which He has made to meet them. It proclaims that God will be "sanctified in them that draw nigh Him" (10: 3). Typically it is full of Christ, setting Him before us as our Altar, Sacrifice, and High Priest.

The fourth book of Scripture treats of the practical side of the spiritual life, tracing the history of the believer in the world—for four is the number of the earth. Its key is also hung upon the porch: "And the Lord spake unto Moses in the *wilderness* of Sinai" (1: 1)—the "wilderness" being a symbol of this world in its fallen condition, alienated from God. It records at greater length than Exodus the history of Israel's journeyings and sojournings. Its theme then is the *walk and wanderings* of the believer during this life, depicting his testings and trials in the world. Note well it is preceded by Leviticus, for only as we first commune with God within the veil are we fitted to go out into the world and there walk before Him. Typically it represents the experiences we encounter in this scene of sin and suffering, our repeated and excuseless failures and God's longsufferance. It reveals God maintaining His holy government and yet dealing in grace with His own, destroying unbelieving rebels yet preserving the faithful.

Deuteronomy is the bridge between the four books which precede and the seven which follow it, for the former deal with Israel before they entered Canaan and the latter with their history after settling there. Its name signifies "a second law"—the ten commandments of Ex. 20 being repeated in Deut. 5: the reason for this being, because of their awful sin at Kadesh-barnea, God swore that all the adult Israelites who came out of Egypt (with the sole exception of Caleb and Joshua) should perish in the wilderness (Num. 14). That fearful threat had now been carried out and in Deut. we find Moses (himself on the eve of death) addressing the generation who had grown up in the wilderness. That new generation required to know on what terms they were about to enter Canaan and on what conditions they should hold and enjoy it. The addresses of Moses therefore centred around two things: reviewing the past and giving instructions for the future, pressing upon them the claims of God (10: 12): hence the key words are "remember" (14 times), "hear" (over 30) and "do" (about 100). In its application to us it reveals that whole-hearted *obedience to God* is the grand condition of possessing our possessions.

The book of Joshua records one of the most interesting and important portions of Israel's history. It treats of the period of their estatement as a nation, of which Genesis was prophetic and the rest of the Pentateuch immediately preparatory. The books of Moses would be imperfect without this one: as it is the capstone of them, so it is the foundation of those which follow. Omit Joshua and there is a gap left in the sacred history which nothing could supply. Without it what precedes would be incomprehensible and what follows unexplained. The sacred writer was directed to fill that gap by narrating the conquest and apportionment of the promised land. Thus this book may be contemplated from two distinct but closely related standpoints: first as the end of Israel's trials and wanderings in the wilderness, and second as the beginning of their new life in the land. It is that twofold viewpoint which supplies the clue to its spiritual interpretation, as it alone solves the problem which so many have found puzzling in this book.

As the inheritance which the Lord appointed, promised and gave to Israel, Canaan has rightly been regarded as a type of Heaven, unto which the Church is journeying through this wilderness-world. But Canaan was the scene of fierce battles, and that presents a serious difficulty unto many, though it should not. They point out that Heaven will not be the place of fighting, but of eternal rest and felicity, and then ask, How could Israel's history in

Canaan prefigure our experience on High? It did not, but it strikingly and accurately foreshadowed what Christians must accomplish if they are to enter and enjoy "the purchased possession". The book of Joshua not only exhibits the sovereign grace of God, His covenant-faithfulness, His mighty power put forth on behalf of His people, but it also reveals what was *required from them* in the discharge of their responsibility: formidable obstacles had to be surmounted, a protracted warfare had to be engaged in, fierce foes overcome, before they entered into the actual enjoyment of the land.

If our conception of what constitutes a Christian or the character of the Christian life be altogether lop-sided, little wonder that we have difficulty in rightly applying to ourselves the contents of that book which typically contains so much important instruction for us. If we will confine our viewpoint solely unto the sovereign grace of God in connection with our salvation, and deliberately close our eyes to all that Scripture teaches upon the discharge of our responsibility in relation thereto, then it would indeed be strange if we apprehended how that on the one hand Canaan was a free gift unto Israel, which they entered by grace alone; and on the other, that they had to fight for every inch of it! But when we realise that "eternal life" is both the gift of God (Rom. 6: 23) and a "crown" which has to be won by faithfulness (Rev. 2: 10), that the Christian inheritance is not only purchased by the blood of the Lamb, but is also the "reward" of those who "serve the Lord Christ" (Col. 3: 24), then we should have no trouble in perceiving how the type answers to the antitype.

"Narrow is the way that leadeth unto Life" (Matt. 7: 14) i.e. unto Heaven, unto Glory. There is but one way that "leadeth unto" it, and that is the way of personal and practical holiness (Isa. 35: 8), "without which no man shall see the Lord". That "way" is a narrow one for it shuts out the world and excludes self-pleasing. True, the few who tread it have previously been made partakers of spiritual life, for none of the unregenerate walk therein; nevertheless they must persevere in it to the end, resisting temptations to forsake it and overcoming whatever would impede, if they are to enter Life itself. Salvation is indeed by grace, and grace alone, for human merit has no place therein; yet good works are necessary, because it was to fit us for them that grace is given. In Joshua we have a striking and blessed exemplification of the twofoldness of Truth and the perfect balance of its essential parts. The sovereign grace of God and the discharge of His peoples' responsibility run side by side therein. Canaan was God's free gift unto Israel, yet they had to fight for possession of it—let *that* be carefully pondered, and remember it was typical.

The reader should keep steadily in mind that Israel's entrance into Canaan occurred at the *end* of their trials in the wilderness. Taking that alone, by itself, we have a foreshadowing of our entrance into Heaven at the close of this life (Rev. 14: 13); but viewing Israel's entrance into Canaan in the light of all that is recorded in the book of Joshua, we must regard what precedes as the experiences of the soul prior *to* conversion, and Israel's history there as adumbrating his *new* life. Thus, in Ex. we see the natural man in bondage to sin and Satan; in Leviticus we behold him as one to whom God is speaking, making known His holy requirements; in Numbers he finds himself in a great howling wilderness, which is what the world appears to one who has been awakened by the Spirit; while in Deut. he learns the strictness and spirituality of the Law, which cuts into pieces his self-righteousness and reveals that

Another than Moses must become the Captain of his salvation if ever he is to be estated in the antitypical Palestine.

Let the reader also remember that Israel's entrance into Canaan marked the beginning of a distinct stage in their history, and there we have a figure of the new life of the converted soul. Observe carefully how definitely and clearly this is brought out in the type. It was a *new* generation of Israel (the second and not the adult one that came out of Egypt) which is here in view; that they were under a new leader—no longer Moses but Joshua; that they were inducted into a new sphere—delivered from the wilderness, entering into Canaan. Thus we have a picture of those who have passed through a season of conviction of sin, who have felt the terrors of the Law, and have now been brought to put their trust in Jesus Christ, the antitypical Joshua. Conversion dates the end of the old life and the beginning of the new. As Israel's entrance into Canaan marked the end of their wilderness wanderings, so at conversion the soul experiences the verity of Christ's promise, "Come unto Me and I will give you rest". Likewise, as Israel's entrance into Canaan marked the beginning of their life of conquest, so at conversion we begin that "good fight of faith" which is required before we can enter our Eternal Rest.

Those two aspects of the Christian's rest are brought together in Heb. 4. First, "we which have believed *do* enter into rest" (v. 3). The moment a regenerated, awakened, convicted soul savingly believes in Christ the burden of his sins roll away, and peace of conscience, rest of soul, assurance of acceptance by God, are his. Yet, he is not there and then taken to heaven. No indeed, he is now made conscious of foes, both within and without, of which previously he knew nothing. He is now called upon to mortify the flesh, resist the Devil, overcome the world: not by his own might, but in the strength of the Lord, under the leadership of the antitypical Joshua; and this *in order to* an entrance into the promised inheritance. Thus, second, Heb. 4: 11 bids us "let us labour therefore *to enter* into that Rest". Yes, "labour" is necessary (cf. John 6: 27, 2 Cor. 5: 9): fighting the good fight, finishing our course, keeping the faith is required, if we are to receive the "crown of righteousness" (2 Tim. 4: 7, 8)!

Joshua's Earlier Days

Joshua was born in the land of Egypt and with the sole exception of Caleb he was the only adult Israelite in the great exodus who survived the forty years wanderings in the wilderness and actually entered Canaan. He is mentioned for the first time in Ex. 17: 9, where he is introduced to our notice most abruptly, nothing being told us there of his parentage, early history, or his piety. It was on the occasion when Amalek came and fought against Israel at Rephidim: "Moses said unto Joshua, Choose out men and go fight with Amalek". From that brief statement we gather that our hero had already attracted the notice of Moses, gained his confidence and was therefore a man of valour and competent to be captain over others. The following verse also represents him in a favourable light: "So Joshua did as Moses had said to him": he made no demur, objected not to receive orders from his superior, but obediently complied with his instructions. "And Joshua discomfitted Amalek and his people with the edge of the sword" (v. 13): thus success attended his efforts.

What we have briefly glanced at above supplies a most striking illustration of the law of *first mention*. The initial occurrence of anything in Scripture invariably supplies the key to the later ones, forecasting by means of a broad outline its subsequent usage. In other words, the first time a subject or object, a person or thing, is brought before us in God's Word what is there said of it or him virtually supplies a definition of its meaning, or at least gives us the principal clue to the significance of its later mentionings. Thus it is here. The very first time Joshua is brought to our notice it is as a successful warrior: and note carefully, not slaying innocent people, but in fighting the enemies of the Lord. How this brief allusion in Ex. 17 foreshadowed the great work which lay before him! The immediate sequel confirms this: "And the Lord said unto Moses, Write this for a memorial in a book, and rehearse it in the ears of (not Israel, but) *Joshua*, for I will utterly put out the remembrance of Amalek from under heaven" (Ex. 17: 14)—a plain hint of his future work, as an appointed instrument to execute the Divine vengeance upon His foes.

Personally we believe there is a definite reference unto Joshua in Ex. 23: 20-23, though his name be not specifically mentioned. Those verses contain a Divine prophecy and promise unto Israel, and as is so often the case with similar passages, there is, we conceive, a *double* allusion. "Behold I send an Angel before thee, to keep thee in the way and to bring thee into the place which I have prepared." No doubt the primary reference is to Christ as the Angel of the Covenant, yet subordinately it points, we think, unto Joshua as God's "messenger" or "angel", for he was the one who actually brought Israel into the heritage which God had prepared for them. So too it seems clear that there is a double allusion in "My name is in Him" (v. 21): when the Angel of the covenant became incarnate it was said "His name shall be called Immanuel" (Matt. 1: 23), and when our hero's name was changed from "Oshua" to "Jeho-shua" (Num. 13: 16), the Divine name was incorporated into his! Israel were ordered to "obey his voice" (Ex. 23: 22) and in Josh. 1: 16 they affirmed to him "all that thou commandest us we will do"!

The next reference to him is found in Ex. 24: 13, when in response to Jehovah's bidding Moses went up unto Him in the mount that he might receive from Him the tables of the Law, we are told that "Moses rose up and his minister Joshua, and Moses went up into the mount of God". From this reference we learn the peculiar and honoured position which he occupied even at this early stage in his career: he was the "minister" or assistant of Moses, the personal attendant of that eminent man of God. But there is more in it than that: he was subservient to Moses, yet he was also to complement his work. Moses brought Israel out of Egypt, but Joshua would bring them into Canaan. That the latter was not disconnected from the former is clear from the opening verses of his book, for not only is Joshua there again designated "Moses' minister" (1: 1), but when the Lord gave to him his great commission He expressly bade him "do according to all the law which Moses My servant commanded thee" (1: 7). So in the antitype: Christ was "made under the Law" (Gal. 4: 4).

When Moses left the camp to go unto Jehovah into the mount, his minister Joshua accompanied him, though evidently only a part of the ascent—the attendant being left at some lower level as Moses drew near unto the Lord. In what follows we are furnished with a valuable side-light on our hero's character. Joshua was left alone for "forty days and forty nights" (Ex. 24: 18)! What a testing of his faith, his patience, and his fidelity was that! His response to that severe test shines out the more blessedly when contrasted from the conduct of Aaron in the camp. Ex. 25 to 31 gives a record of the instructions which Moses received, while the opening verses of 32 show us what transpired in the camp. "When the people saw that Moses delayed to come down out of the mount, the people gathered themselvess together unto Aaron and said unto him, Up, make us gods which shall go before us, for as for this Moses . . . we wot not what is become of him" (v. 1). Apparently Aaron shared their fears that they would see Moses no more, for he yielded to their solicitation.

Now in blessed contrast from the unbelief and impatience of the people and of Aaron, Joshua trustfully and perseveringly awaited the return of his master. Thus was he tried and proved, manifested to be "a vessel unto honour, sanctified and meet for the Master's use" before the grand task of conducting Israel into Canaan was assigned unto him. Proof that Joshua had remained in the mount during those forty days and nights is supplied by Ex. 32: 15-18, for there we are informed "And Moses turned and went down the mount . . . and when Joshua heard the noise of the people as they shouted (in their idolatrous and carnal revelry: see v. 6), he said unto Moses, There is a noise of war in the camp. And he said, It is not the noise of them that shout for mastery, neither is it the noise of them that cry for being overcome; but the noise of them that sing do I hear"—observe that though puzzled by what he heard, yet Joshua placed a favourable construction upon it, not suppposing the worst.

When Moses drew nigh unto the camp and beheld the idolatrous and lascivious scene spread before him, he was filled with righteous indignation, and took the golden calf, burnt it in the fire, ground it to powder, strewed it upon the water and made the children of Israel drink. Under his orders the Levites slew about three thousand men and the Lord "plagued the people". After they had been severely chastened and humbled, Moses "took the tabernacle and pitched it without the camp". Then as he entered into the tabernacle the Cloudy Pillar descended and stood at the door of the tabernacle and the Lord talked with Moses. Later "he turned again into the camp, but his servant Joshua, the son of Nun, a young man, departed not out of the tabernacle" (Ex. 33: 11). That is indeed a remarkable statement, yet too brief to warrant inferences. But it at least shows the distinguished favour bestowed upon the honoured servant of Moses, that he, rather than Aaron, was here left in charge of the sacred tent of meeting: whether he was inside it when Jehovah stood at its door we cannot say.

Another brief mention is made of Joshua in Num. 11. On the occasion when Moses gathered the seventy men of the elders of the people and set them round about the tabernacle, the Lord came down in a cloud and spake unto him, and took of the Spirit that was upon him and gave unto the seventy elders, so that "they prophesied and did not cease". Two others of the elders had for some reason remained in the camp, yet the Spirit now rested upon them, so that they too "prophesied" even in the camp. Evidently deeming this irregular, a young man ran and told Moses of the unusual occurrence. "And Joshua the son of Nun, the servant of Moses, one of his young men, answered and said, My lord, Moses, forbid them" (v. 28). That too reveals his character: he did not take it upon himself to rebuke the elders, nor did he request Moses to slay them. It was zeal for his master that promoted his petition, as Moses' reply clearly indicates: "enviest thou for my sake". There was no jealousy or self seeking here on the part of Joshua, but only a concern for the honour of the one he served.

We turn now to that passage which is probably the most familiar to the reader wherein our hero figures. When the Lord gave order to Moses that he send twelve men to "search the land of Canaan", a ruler from each tribe, Oshua was the one selected from the tribe of Ephraim, and it was on this occasion that his name was changed to "Jeho-shua" (Num. 13: 16), or, in its abbreviated form "Joshua": so that he was one of the persons mentioned in Scripture —all of them of eminence—whose name was changed. "Oshua" means "salvation" and "Jeho-shua" he by whom Jehovah will save. We need hardly add that, through the Greek, Joshua is precisely the same as "Jesus"— see Acts 7: 45, Heb. 4: 8. When the twelve spies returned to Moses and made report of what they had seen, though they acknowledged the land was one that flowed with milk and honey, yet its inhabitants appeared to them so formidable and their cities so powerful they declared, "We be not able to go against the people, for they are stronger than we". The immediate sequel was most solemn and sad.

Though Caleb boldly declared "Let us go up at once and possess it, for we are well able to overcome it", his fellow-spies persisted in their "evil report" and the whole congregation wept, murmured against Moses and Aaron, lamented that they had ever started out on their journey and said one to another "let us make a captain and let us return into Egypt. Then Moses and Aaron fell on their faces before all the assembly . . . and Joshua and Caleb . . . rent their clothes". Then it was that our hero (and his faithful companion) evinced his spiritual character and calibre, for we are told that they said unto the whole company of Israel, "The land which we pass through to search it is an exceeding good land. If the Lord delight in us, then He will bring us into this land and give it us . . . Only rebel not ye against the Lord, neither fear ye the people of the land, for they are bread for us: their defence is departed from them, and the Lord is with us; fear them not" (Num. 14: 7-9). Thus we see their confidence in God and their courage, for as the next verse shows they took their lives into their hands in so remonstrating with the people.

It was there that that wayward and stiff-necked generation of Israel filled up the measure of their sin. It was then that Jehovah swore in His wrath that they should not enter into His rest (Psa. 95: 11, Heb. 3: 18). They had said, "Would God we had died in this wilderness" (Num. 14: 2), and now He took them at their word, declaring "your carcasses shall fall in this wilderness, and all that were numbered of you, according to your whole number, from twenty years old and upward, who murmured against Me, doubtless ye shall not come into the land which I sware to make you dwell therein, save Caleb the son of Jephunneh and Joshua the son of Nun. But your little ones, which ye said should be a prey, them will I bring in, and they shall know the land which ye despised" (vv. 29-31). The ten spies who brought an evil report upon the land "died by the plague before the Lord, but Joshua the son of Nun and Caleb the son of Jephunneh . . . lived" (vv. 37, 38), being the only two adults who came out of Egypt which entered into Canaan.

In Numbers 27 we have an account of the ordination of Joshua to office as the future leader of Israel. "And the Lord said unto Moses, Take thee Joshua the son of Nun, a man in whom is the Spirit, and lay thine hand upon him (the symbol of identification), and set him before Eleazar the priest, and before all the congregation; and give him a charge in their sight (as proof of his induction into office). And thou shalt put some of thine honour upon him, that all the congregation of the children of Israel may be obedient (to him). And he shall stand before Eleazar the priest, who shall ask for him after the judgment of Urim before the Lord: at his (Joshua's) word shall they go out and at his word shall they come in, he and all the children of Israel with him, even all the congregation. And Moses did as the Lord commanded him" (vv. 18-22). Thus, to all who feared the Lord and had respect unto His servant Moses, none could henceforth doubt that Joshua was the man appointed to lead Israel after the removal of Moses from this scene.

"Surely none of the men that came up out of Egypt . . . shall see the land . . . save Caleb the son of Jephunneh and Joshua the son of Nun for they have wholly followed the Lord" (Num. 32: 11, 12). That is another statement which throws light upon the spiritual character and calibre of Joshua. When Jehovah declared he had "wholly followed" Him, He did not signify he had lived a sinless life, but that he had trod the path of obedience, faithfully performed his duty and sincerely aimed at the glory of God in it. He had stood firm and fearless in a day of prevailing unbelief and general apostasy. In passing it may be pointed out, at a later date, Caleb did not hesitate to affirm he *had* "wholly followed the Lord" (Josh. 14: 6-8), upon which M. Henry rightly said that "since he had obtained this testimony from God Himself, it was not vain glorious in him to speak of it, any more than it is for those who have God's Spirit witnessing with their spirit they are the children of God, to humbly and thankfully tell others, for their encouragement, what God has done for their souls".

"These are the names of the men which shall divide the land unto you: Eleazar the priest and Joshua the son of Nun" (Num. 34: 17): here we learn that our hero, under the guidance of the high priest (Josh. 14: 1), was to apportion the inheritance among the tribes.· "Joshua, the son of Nun, which standeth before thee, he shall go in thither: encourage him, for he shall cause Israel to inherit it" (Deut. 1: 38). That was surely necessary, for well might he be discouraged after seeing Moses himself fall under the weight of leadership. A part of the encouragement which Moses gave to his successor is recorded in Deut. 3: 21, "I commanded Joshua at that time (namely, when reviewing the overthrow of the powerful monarchs of Bashan and Og), Thine eyes have seen all that the Lord your God hath done unto these two kings: so shall the Lord do unto all the kingdoms whither thou passest", which was as though Moses reminded Joshua, when the Lord begins a work He finishes it—His overthrow of those kings was an *earnest* of the destruction of all who opposed His people. It is blessed to remember that those whom God calls into His service He also grants "encouragement" along the way. So we have always found it.

"And Moses called unto Joshua and said unto him in the sight of all Israel: Be strong and of a good courage, for thou must go with this people unto the land which the Lord hath sworn unto their fathers to give them; and thou shalt cause them to inherit it. And the Lord, He it is that doth go before thee: He will not fail thee, neither forsake thee; fear not neither be dismayed" (Deut. 31: 7, 8). Here was further "encouragement" for Joshua and the final charge which he received from his predecessor. That "charge" was a wise mingling of precept and promise, of calling unto the discharge of duty and of informing him where his strength lay for the performance thereof. It is blessed to see that the apostle did not hesitate to apply unto all the people of God (Heb. 13: 5) this promise made specifically to Joshua "He will not fail thee nor forsake thee"—something which should be carefully noted by those who have so much to say about "rightly dividing the Word of Truth"!

"And Joshua the son of Nun was full of the spirit of wisdom, for Moses had laid his hands on him; and the children of Israel hearkened unto him and did as the Lord commanded Moses" (Deut. 34: 9). This is the final reference to Joshua in the Pentateuch, occurring right after the account of the death and burial of Moses. God may remove His workmen, but He ceases not to carry forward His work. When one of His servants be removed, He raises up another to take his place—not always to *fill* his place, for the work may already be completed (for the time being, at any rate) in that particular section of His vineyard, and if so, the new man may be called upon to break soil elsewhere. This was really the case here. Moses was raised up specifically to bring Israel out of the house of bondage—a stupendous and difficult task— and by Divine enablement he accomplished it. He was Israel's leader through- out their wilderness journeys, but now they were over. An entirely new venture lay before the people of God: their entrance into and taking possession of their heritage, and that called for a new leader.

In the preceding paragraphs we have seen how the new leader of Israel had been duly appointed by God (not chosen by the people!) and then publicly ordained or inducted into his office, for God requires all things, especially in connection with His immediate service, to be done "decently and in order". We have seen too something of the qualifications which Joshua possessed for the work assigned him, for when God calls a man to a work, He endows him suitably for the same, equipping him both naturally and spiritually. Pharaoh might require the Hebrews to make bricks without supplying them with straw, but not so the Lord! Joshua was indwelt by the Spirit (Num. 27: 18), possessed of unusual faith, patience and courage, and "full of the spirit of wisdom"—that being as necessary as any of the others. Finally, we are told above "and the children of Israel hearkened unto him", for God ever works at both ends of the line: when He fits a man to minister, He also prepares a people for him to minister unto.

A General Survey

As Moses sent forth the twelve spies to " search the land of Canaan " before Israel sought to enter into occupation of the same, so we propose to now take a bird's eye view of that book which bears the name of Joshua before examining it in close detail. We shall not give a chapter by chapter summary of its contents, but rather essay a comprehensive sketch of those contents as a whole, pointing out the main design of the book, and some of its leading features. It has already been stated in our Introductory article, that this portion of Scripture treats of the period of Israel's estatement as a nation in that land which Jehovah gave unto their fathers, and that it forms both the capstone of the Pentateuch and the foundation of the Historical books which follow. The design of its penman, under the superintendence of the Holy Spirit, was to describe the conquest of Canaan by the Hebrews and the apportionment of it among their twelve tribes.

It was not Joshua's intention to give an account of his own life, nor even to undertake a description of his principal exploits and achievements : rather was it his purpose to show how the Lord had made good His promises unto the patriarchs. If that dominant fact be kept steadily in mind it will explain fully and satisfactorily the principle of selection and the arrangement of the materials he was guided to use. We can then the better perceive why Joshua recorded what he did, why he related certain incidents in fulness of detail and merely glanced at others, and why whole years are passed over in silence. He was writing with a *definite plan* before his mind, and therefore he related only what was pertinent to his scheme and design, omitting everything which was not relevant thereto. The same principle of selection regulated all the sacred penmen, and it is only as we are able to discern the particular plan of each book that we can properly appreciate what is brought into the picture and what is left out.

It has been far too little realised that the historians of Scripture were much more than journalists narrating interesting events, more than mere chroniclers writing for the sake of gratifying the curiosity of those who should live in a future age, or even of detailing memorable incidents to please their contemporaries. They were *theocratic* historians (a theocracy is a government in which the chiefs of state are the immediate servants of God—there has never been but one), whose object was to trace the progress and development of the kingdom of God on earth : to mark its great epochs and record those events which were, from a *religious* standpoint, of deep importance to their own and future generations. Thus it is with the book that is now to be before us—and equally so with those that follow, for they give not merely the history of Israel, but the history of *God's kingdom in Israel* : discover its plan or theme and the choice or rejection of certain materials becomes patent.

The book opens with the Lord's directions to Joshua, who had already been designated as the successor of Moses, to go over Jordan and take possession of the land which He had sworn to their fathers and to divide it among the people as their inheritance, with the promise that if he faithfully observed the laws given by Moses that God would be with him, and " there shall not a man be able to stand before thee all the days of thy life " (1 : 5). Those opening verses supply the key to the whole book. Joshua's execution of his commission in strict obedience to the Divine directions and God's gracious fulfilment of His promised assistance are the sum of all it contains. The first twelve chapters treat of the conquest of Canaan. They do not contain a detailed account of all the marches and the battles of each campaign : instead, only the outstanding particulars are narrated— those which marked the progress of events, those which brought out most clearly God's miraculous help, and those which demonstrated the necessity and inseparable connection between their obedience and that miraculous help.

Many other things belonging to the Conquest, such as battles, capture of cities, and even long expeditions which had nothing remarkable about them, are therefore mentioned only summarily, so as to give a general view of the whole line of operations with its ultimate success. The time occupied in the conquest was much briefer, everything considered, than might be supposed. Though we cannot calculate the exact length of it, we may its approximate duration. *After* Canaan had been subdued and upon the division of its territory, we find Caleb saying " And now, behold, the Lord hath kept me alive as He said these forty and five years, even since the Lord spake this word unto me (in Num. 14 : 30) while the children of Israel wandered in the wilderness " (Josh. 14 : 10). From that forty-five years we have to deduct the thirty-eight years spent in the Wilderness (Deut. 2 : 14), so that the whole campaign lasted less than seven years.

In chapters 13-21 we have the Dividing of the Land among the several tribes, concerning which it is difficult for a commentator to write profitably at any length. In chapter 22 the two and a half tribes who had assisted their brethren in the Conquest and stood by them in the allotting of Canaan, return to their own possession across the Jordan. Then an interval of several years is passed over during which Israel was settled in the Land, an interval which fell not within the scope of the writer to take notice of, for it furnished nothing suited to his particular theme. Finally, we come to the closing scene of Joshua's life, when he gathered around him the responsible heads of the Nation, rehearsed what God had done for them in giving them such a goodly heritage, and engaged them to renewed pledges of obedience unto Him. Thus the book closes with a recapitulation of Jehovah's fulfilment of the promise with which it opens and a public covenant-engagement of the people to serve the Lord who had driven out the Amorites and the other nations from before them.

After Joshua had received his orders to go up and possess the Land, he at once sent forth two spies. The experiences they met with are described with considerable detail : not because of the interest attaching to their hazardous undertaking and their remarkable escape from a perilous situation, but because what occurred vividly exemplified the promise which the Lord had given to Moses : " there shall no man be able to stand before thee, for the Lord shall lay the fear of you and the dread of you upon all the land that ye shall tread upon " (Deut. 11 : 25)—a promise, which as we have seen, was repeated in substance to Joshua himself. Hence we fine in striking and full accord therewith Rahab acknowledging to the spies, " I know that the Lord hath given you the land and that your terror is fallen upon us and that all the inhabitants of the land faint because of you " (2 : 9). The anxious preparations of the king, his vigorous pursuit of the spies, and their language to Joshua upon the accomplishment of their mission (2 : 24) all served to forcibly illustrate that fact.

Next follows the passage of the Jordan. Its waters though unusually high, were supernaturally divided, so that the people of God passed over dry shod. Let us pause and ask, What was the design of that remarkable event ? God works no trifling miracles : He does not suspend the established order of nature without good reason, nor unless some important end is to be answered by so doing. Wherein lay the necessity for this prodigy ? Israel could have crossed the Jordan by natural means, without the intervention of Omnipotence. Though the river was then too high for fording, especially for the women and children, yet boats could have been built or bridges thrown across it, for the Jordan is neither swift nor very wide, and such a delay had been but a brief one. The reason for this miracle was the same as of all others recorded in Holy Writ : the necessity for it was not physical but moral. The object of all miracles is to reveal the power and grace of God.

The laws of nature which God established at the beginning were amply sufficient to accomplish every physical end : it is only to meet our moral and spiritual needs that they are ever interfered with. Israel might have taken Canaan without any miracle, but in such a case there had been no glorious display unto them of God's all-mightiness, His loving-kindness, His nearness to them. The stupendous marvels which He wrought in Egypt, at the Red Sea, in the Wilderness, and now in Canaan, were designed to teach the covenant people (and the surrounding nations, too) that the gods of the heathen were no gods and could neither do good nor evil. Jehovah was the living and true God : " the Lord of all the earth " (Josh. 3 : 11, 13) ! Those miracles were intended to make them more sensible of the infinite perfections of the One with whom they had to do, and of their complete dependence upon Him. Consequently they were brought into situations from which they could not extricate themselves in order to learn it was the Lord their God who delivered them.

In a variety of ways Israel were made to see that it was not their own valour and strength which delivered them, but rather Jehovah's right hand and mighty arm which secured the victory for them. Canaan did not become theirs so much by their own prowess and conquest as by Divine gift. But there was a special reason why the Lord intervened for them in the extraordinary manner He did at the Jordan, for it was as though He then opened to them the door of that land which He had promised and personally conducted them into it. By that memorable act the Lord pledged to them the subjugation of the whole country. At the same time there was in connection therewith, the public act of Joshua in his new capacity as leader of the people, and thus it gave Divine authority and confirmation to his office in their eyes, and was, in comparison with his predecessor at the Red Sea, a striking verification of that word to him " As I was with Moses, so I will be with thee " (1 : 5).

The circumcising of the people and their celebration of the Passover comes next (chap. 5). There should be no difficulty in perceiving the relevancy and significance of these events at this stage in the book we are now reviewing. They belonged to the Conquest, inasmuch as that very conquest was conditioned upon Israel's punctillious compliance with all that Moses had commanded. After the appearing unto Joshua of the " Captain of the Lord's host," there follows an account of the capture of Jericho. In connection therewith there stand out plainly the same two features which mark the passage of the Jordan : that an unquestioning obedience to God's orders was required from them, and that the victory was His and not theirs. In the conquest of Ai the same lesson is taught, though in reverse : there they were made to taste the bitter consequences which followed upon their disobedience to the Divine injunctions. But we will not now further anticipate what we hope to consider in the articles which are to follow.

At this point a word needs to be said, perhaps, in reply to the attacks made now upon this book by the enemies of the Lord. The ethical character of the contents of Joshua has been viciously criticised by infidels and agnostics. The Israelites have been regarded as a horde of fierce nomads, falling upon and murdering the Canaanites, and stealing the land of a peaceful people. These critics have asserted it is unworthy of the Divine character to represent Him as sanctioning such injustice and ferocity. In reply it needs to be pointed out that, Canaan was Israel's by Divine appointment and gift long before (Gen. 15)—a promise repeated to Abraham's immediate descendants ; and it was in fulfilment thereof that they now received the land. They entered and took possession of Canaan by immediate command from God, who has an absolute right to interfere in human affairs as He pleases. Moreover, it was in the exercise of His righteousness (as well as of His sovereignty) that God now took from the Canaanites the land which they had forfeited by their sins, and by His grace gave to Israel with the distinct understanding that they, too, would be deprived of it if they proved unfaithful and disobedient stewards.

But why should God give instructions for the utter destruction of the Canaanites ? Because of their horrible depravity and gross idolatry : let the reader turn to Lev. 18 : 3, 27, 28 and then see the verses between 3 and 27 for a description of those " abominations," and also remember God did not act in judgment upon them until " the iniquity of the Amorites " had come to the " full " (Gen. 15 : 16). God now glorified His justice by destroying those who refused to glorify Him by a willing obedience. Israel acted not under the impulse of a lust of conquest but as the executioners of Divine wrath—just as the flood, the pestilence, the earthquake are commissioned by Him to cut off those who provoke His holiness. When He is pleased to do so, He makes use of men as His instruments, rather than the elements. " The Assyrian " was the rod of God's anger to cut off nations, though he knew not he was being so employed (Isa. 10 : 5-7). Why then might He not use an elect and godly nation as the conscious instrument of His just vengeance !

Israel was manifestly under God's guidance, and their success must be attributed to His presence and might. Miraculous power attended them and proved that the commission and commands they had received were no fanatical delusions, but the mandates of the Judge of all the earth. He opened a way for them through the Jordan, threw down the walls of Jericho, smote their enemies with hailstones and even stayed the sun in its course. There could be no mistaking the fact that the living God was in their midst. But there was also a special reason why Israel should be the particular executioner of God's vengeance in this instance rather than that the land should be totally depopulated by, say, pestilence. In that case, they could not have felt so sensibly their own weakness and entire dependency on the power of God. In such a case they had soon forgotten *His* agency in giving them the land, and attributed it to secondary causes ; nor would the residue of the Canaanites been left as a continual trial to test their faithfulness in the service of the Lord.

But why should only the Canaanites be singled out for this summary judgment ? Were there not many other idolatrous nations ?—why then should they be exempted ? The righteous government of God extends over all nations, and each is punished when its iniquities are come to the full : not by the same means or to the same extent, but punished as God deems best. But the Canaanites were not only idolaters, but they were guilty of practices which the heathen themselves regarded with abhorrence. Let it also be remembered that this generation of Israel under Joshua was the most pious one in all their history as a nation, and that they burned with the same holy zeal against Achan as against the degenerate Canaanites ; and that later God sorely punished Israel, too, when they turned away from Him. Most important then are the lessons contained in this book. It shows how God intervenes in the affairs of human history. It reveals that He deals with nations as well as individuals—deals with them in mercy or judgment according as they honour or displease Him.

The contents of this book and the lessons which they are designed to teach us are greatly needed by our own generation. First, in counteracting the one-sided " evangelism " of our day, which tells the sinner that all he has to do is to accept Christ as his personal Saviour and Heaven is then his certain portion— ignoring the fact that there is a fight which must be fought and a race to be run before he can be crowned. Second, in rebutting that doleful view that the Christian should expect nothing but frequent and wellnigh constant defeat in his warfare against the world, the flesh, and the devil—overlooking the truth that if he meets the required conditions he may " do all things through Christ strengthening him." Third, in setting before us, by clear exemplifications and striking illustrations, the rules and requirements upon which success is conditioned. Here, as nowhere else in Scripture, are we shown *how* we may be " overcomers." Fourth, in making known the blessed fact—so little apprehended by Christians to-day--that it is both their privilege and birthright to enter into a *present* possession and enjoyment of their Inheritance. O that more of us may do so.

Chapter 2

THE GREAT COMMISSION

Joshua 1:1-9

The Call to Faith

" Now after the death of Moses the servant of the Lord, it came to pass that the Lord spake unto Joshua " (1 : 1). The opening word of this verse, when rightly rendered, supplies to the spiritual mind an indication of the verbal inspiration of the Scriptures. Properly translated it would be " And," and what uninspired writer would ever think of beginning his production with such a connective ! John Urquhart in his " The Bible : its Structure and Purpose " (vol. 1) called attention to this feature, which though a minute detail is one of considerable importance, namely, that many of the books of the O.T. commence with the conjunction " ve." This indicates of course that those which open thus are so closely linked with the ones preceding that they are really *continuations* of them. But, we may say, it does more than that : the employment of " And " at the beginning of quite a number of them signifies that they are not so many books but chapters in the Book. In other words, this binding together of the variousl books by the copulative " And " gives more than a hint of their fundamenta. unity : that one Author composed them, that one Rule of Faith is found in them

Genesis has no " And " at the commencement of its opening verse, for the simple reason that it is the first book or chapter, the beginning. But Exodus opens with this connective " ve "—" and "—rendered there " Now." So does Leviticus, and likewise Numbers. Thereby we are taught that those first books are inseparably united together, and form the first division of the Bible. But, as Urquhart pointed out, " It is a surprise at first glance when we find that Deuteronomy, which is regarded as the completion of the four previous books, is, as a fact, disconnected from them." He might also have dwelt on the fact that such a variation or difference is a designed evidence of Divine superintendence. The very fact that Deuteronomy is regarded (and from one standpoint, rightly so) as the completion of the Pentateuch argues that were the first five books of the Bible nothing more than the uninspired productions of Jews, writing in collaboration, the fifth one had been brought into accord with those which precede it.

The absence of " and " at the opening of Deuteronomy at once intimates that that book is not a supplement to what has gone before, but rather a new beginning, or a new division of the O.T. It looks forward and not backward : a careful study of its contents will verify this. Joshua comes next and it *does* open with " And "—and so does every book which follows until 1 Chronicles is reached ! Thus, Joshua to the end of 2 Kings is annexed to Deut., and the whole forms the second division of the O.T. Having pointed out this feature, let us pause and consider its significance. Why are the first four books of the Bible coupled together ? why the next eight ? and why does Deut. belong to the second group rather than the first ? The answer must be sought in the history of Israel, for that is the theme of the O.T. The first four books give us the history of Israel *outside* the *Land* which was promised them for an inheritance, the next eight treat of

23

their history *in it*. Deut. rehearses the past history of the Nation and restates the Law in view of their approaching possession of.Canaan, informing them how they must conduct themselves therein.

" And after the death of Moses the servant of the Lord " (1 : 1). The removal of Moses from their head was a heavy loss unto Israel. For many years he had been their leader and legislator. It was under him they had been delivered from the cruel bondage of Egypt. It was in answer to his prayers that a way was opened for them through the Red Sea. He was the one who acted as their representative before the Lord and as His mouthpiece unto them. It is true there were times when they distrusted him and murmured against him, yet on the whole they respected and confided in him. A stage had now been reached when it seemed that Israel needed him more than ever, for with practically no fighting experience and possessing scarcely any weapons, they were about to pit themselves against the " seven nations in the land of Canaan " (Acts 13 : 19). Yet he was no longer to be their commander : death took him from them. That was a deep mystery to carnal reason, a most painful providence, a sore trying of their faith. That they felt it keenly is clear : " the children of Israel wept for Moses in the plains of Moab thirty days " (Deut. 34 : 10).

" And after the death of Moses the servant of the Lord, it came to pass that the Lord spake unto Joshua the son of Nun, Moses' minister, saying, " Moses My servant is dead : now therefore arise, go over this Jordan " (vv. 1, 2). The work of God is in nowise hindered by the decease of His servants, no matter how eminent they be in office nor how much used in blessing to His people. Though the workmen be removed, His work goes forward to its ordained completion. " God will change hands to show that whatever instruments He uses, He is not tied to any " (Matt. Henry). That does not mean that God will necessarily supply another pastor for a church when one has died, for His work in that particular place may be finished ; or that when His time arrives for the work of this magazine to end, that He will provide another ; but it *does mean* that He will continue to maintain His Cause upon earth and supply every need of His people. That is certain, and it should both comfort and inspire us with courage in these dark days in which our lot is cast.

It is to be duly noted that Joshua did not push himself forward to fill the breach made by the departure of Moses, but waited until ordered by the Lord to do so. The relation which he sustained to his predecessor is not only one of interest but also of deep importance, not so much so from a historical standpoint as from the typical and doctrinal. This is the point at which we should amplify that statement at some length, but we are afraid to do so lest some of our readers wonder if we are ever going to ' get down to business,' for we have already written three articles without taking up the opening verses of our book. Yet others will say, What does that matter if their contents were instructive and profitable ? We will therefore adopt a compromise, and defer our remarks upon that subject until a little later. Meanwhile perhaps a few may be stimulated to ponder and supply answers for themselves to the following questions : What was the varied relationship of Joshua unto Moses ? and what important truth is illustrated and illuminated thereby ?

" Moses My servant is dead, now therefore arise, go over this Jordan, thou and all this people, unto the land which I do give to them, to the children of Israel " (1 : 2). The appointed time had now arrived for Jehovah to make good the promises which He had made to Abraham and his children long centuries before. All that had been accomplished through Moses was but preliminary thereto, yet supplying a sure earnest that He would continue to show Himself strong on their behalf, so long as they adhered strictly to the covenant which He had entered into with them at Sinai. For that covenant, and the earlier one constituted the basis of all His dealings with Israel : while they kept it, they prospered : when they broke it, they experienced His judgments. It is to be duly observed that this commission which Joshua here received from the Lord was given to him as the head of Israel : it was made not with him alone, but the nation as well : " thou and all this people." This needs to be borne in mind in connection with all that follows.

" Every place that the sole of your foot shall tread upon, that have I *given* unto you, as I said unto Moses " (1 : 3). Here again (see previous verse) the Lord emphasised the fact that Canaan was a sovereign and free gift which He made unto Israel. It was not a portion to which they were in any wise entitled : neither they nor their ancestors had done anything to merit such a heritage, nor would their subsequent prowess in conquering or dispossessing the Canaanites warrant the idea that they had earned it. Thus it is with the eternal inheritance of the spiritual Israel. When they are finally gathered into it, they will with one accord exclaim " Not unto us, O Lord, not unto us, but unto Thy name give glory " (Psa. 115 : 1). And even now while upon earth, they frankly aver, " Not by works of righteousness which we have done, but according to *His mercy* He saved us by the washing of regeneration and renewing of the Holy Spirit, which He shed on us abundantly through Jesus Christ our Saviour " (Titus 3 : 5, 6). They one and all subscribe to that declaration " By grace are ye saved through faith, and that not of yourselves : it is the gift of God ; not of works lest any man should boast " (Eph. 2 : 8, 9).

Nevertheless, though Canaan was a Divine gift unto Israel, yet they did not enter into possession of it without effort on their part : *their* concurrence was required, and thereby their responsibility was enforced ! Unless that fact be clearly recognised we shall be all at sea in applying the type unto ourselves, and seriously, aye fatally, pervert God's " plan " or way of salvation. There is not the slightest excuse for our doing so, for the teaching of Scripture on this subject —both in the type and the antitype—is as clear as a sunbeam. Canaan was first given unto Abraham, and he is " the father of all them that believe " (Rom. 4 : 11), and therefore his case is the norm or model after which ours is patterned. Concerning Abraham himself, all room for doubt as to *how he* obtained Canaan, is removed by Heb. 11 : 8 : "By faith Abraham, when he was called to go out unto a place (which he should after receive for an inheritance), *obeyed*, and he went out, not knowing whither he went." It was by faith-obedience that Canaan became his.

What has just been pointed out and our placing that clause in parenthesis is clearly confirmed by Gen. 12 : 1, " Now the Lord had said unto Abraham, Get thee out of thy country and from thy kindred and from thy father's house, unto a land that I will *show* thee." There was no promise at that time that the land would be made over to him for a possession : it was not until years after that God said to him " I am the Lord that brought thee out of Ur of the Chaldees to *give* thee this land to inherit it." Abraham was first required to break completely from his old life and separate from the world, to submit himself unreservedly to God, to walk by faith, to act in unquestioning obedience to His revealed will, *before* the heritage became his ! Yes, my reader, the call which Abraham received from God made very real and definite demands upon him ; and since he is " the father of us all " (Rom. 4 : 16), each of his children must be conformed to the family likeness. Abraham is a figure or prototype of those who have, by grace, been made " partakers of the heavenly calling " (Heb. 3 : 1).

" By faith Abraham, when he was called to go out into a place which he should after receive for an inheritance, *obeyed*, and he went out, not knowing whither he went "—still less knowing that the land would be given to him. A saving faith is one which heeds the Divine commandments as well as relies upon the Divine promises. Make no mistake about that, dear friends, Christ is " the Author of salvation unto all them that *obey* Him " (Heb. 5 : 9). Abraham obeyed not only in word, but in deed : " he went out." In that he was in marked contrast from the prevaricating one who said " I go, Sir, and went not " (Matt. 21 : 30). Faith and obedience can no more be severed than can the sun and the light, fire and heat. Therefore we read of " the obedience of faith " (Rom. 1 : 5 margin). " Obedience is faith's daughter. Faith hath not only to do with the grace of God, but with the duty of the creature as well. By apprehending grace, it works upon duty : ' faith worketh by love ' (Gal. 5 : 6). It fills the soul with apprehensions of God's love, and then makes use of the sweetness of love to urge us to more work or obedience " (T. Manton).

And now the descendants of Abraham were called upon to act by a similar faith and walk by the same implicit obedience unto God which had marked their progenitor ! The Jordan must be crossed, cities must be captured, battles must be fought, the Canaanites conquered, *before* Israel could enter into possession of and enjoy their inheritance. True, blessedly true, they were not required to perform such feats in their own unaided strength : the might of Omnipotence would work on their behalf. Yet also and equally true was it that God would show Himself strong on their behalf only while they yielded to His authority and conducted themselves according to His orders. The Land was indeed His gift— His free and sovereign gift—unto them, yet they would only obtain possession of the same by their own efforts. There is nothing inharmonious between those two things, any more than there is an inconsistency in the Gospel call, " Ho, every one that thirsteth come ye to the waters, and he that hath no money come ye, *buy* and eat ; yea, come, *buy* wine and milk without money and *without price* " (Isa. 55 : 1)—alas that that repeated " buy " is totally ignored by modern ' evangelism.'

" Every place that the sole of your foot shall tread upon that have I given you, as I said unto Moses. From the wilderness and this Lebanon even unto the great river, the river Euphrates, all the land of the Hittites, and unto the great sea toward the going down of the sun shall be your coast " (1 : 3). As we have pointed out in a previous paper, the contents of this book have a twofold application : an initial and a progressive, to the sinner and to the saint. That is intimated, we believe, by the very position Joshua occupies in the Sacred Canon : it sustains a *dual* relation : coming after, yet being linked to the Pentateuch, and also forming the commencement of the Historical books. That hints strongly at a twofold spiritual significance of its contents. Concerning the land of Canaan Moses said to the Congregation, " Ye are not as yet come to the rest and to the inheritance which the Lord your God giveth you " (Deut. 12 : 9). In contrast from the wanderings in the Wilderness, Canaan was their " rest," but in actual experience their entrance into the Land marked the beginning of years of hard fighting. The moment a sinner believes in Christ peace of conscience, rest of soul is his ; nevertheless, only then begins the fierce battle between the flesh and the spirit.

That rest of soul enjoyed by the Christian when he ceases fighting against God and trusts in the Saviour is an earnest of his inheritance, a foretaste of the perfect and eternal rest awaiting him on high. The initial act of faith in Christ puts him in possession of an inalienable title to " the purchased possession," but his actual entrance therein is yet future. But it is both his privilege and duty to

" possess his possessions " (Obad. 17) even now, to enjoy them by faith and anticipate them by hope. It is his privilege and duty to appropriate by faith and live in the present enjoyment of that rich portion which God has given him in Christ. But the flesh, the world and the Devil will oppose, and seek to keep him out of a present enjoyment of his possession. There is nothing the Devil hates more than to see a saint glorying in God and rejoicing in Christ his Lord, and therefore both directly and by means of indwelling sin, or the allurements and cares of this world, he is ever seeking to deprive him of his rights. But if we mortify the flesh, steadfastly resist the Devil, live a life of faith and walk obediently, we can overcome both self, Satan and the world.

In this connection we need to recall that word of the Lord unto Israel at an earlier date : " I will not drive them out from before thee in one year, lest the land become desolate and the beast of the field multiply against thee : *by little and little* I will drive them out from before thee, until thou be increased and inherit the land " (Ex. 23 : 29, 30), which shows that God does not act arbitrarily, but compassionately with respect to His people. To their short-sightedness it might have appeared a more signal mercy had God exterminated the Canaanites in the first few months after the crossing of its boundary, but that had neither been most for His glory nor their good. There were wild beasts in the land as well as gross idolaters, and even though the latter had been extirpated, Israel were yet too few in number to properly occupy the whole of the country—they must wait for that until they had sufficiently multiplied. Moreover, by driving out the Canaanites from before them " little by little," Israel was kept in a state of constant dependence before the Lord. That is one of His principal designs in all His dealings with people : to wean them from self-reliance and teach them to lean more and more upon Himself.

The spiritual application to the Christian of the above is simple and informative. God has nowhere promised to give him victory over all his enemies at once, and therefore he should not expect it. Nor would it be good for him if He did—pride and self-esteem would be the immediate outcome. " Therefore will the Lord *wait* that He may be gracious unto you " (Isa. 30 : 18). He has many things to say unto us, but we cannot bear them now (John 16 : 12) ; and He has victories to give us, but we are not yet fitted for them. As Israel were not to be discouraged by the slowness of their arms, neither must we be dismayed if victory be not ours at once—still less entertain the thought that success will never be achieved by us. In like manner, the possessing of our possessions, the present entering into and enjoyment of our heritage in Christ, is not attained all in a moment, but it is a progressive experience—" by little and little." Growth in grace is not an instantaneous thing like the new birth, but a gradual one : patience has to have her perfect work.

Perhaps some reader may recall another word of Jehovah's spoken before the Jordan was crossed : " The Lord thy God is He which goeth over before thee : as a consuming fire He shall destroy them and He shall bring them down before thy face ; *so* shalt thou drive them out and destroy them *quickly* " (Deut. 9 : 3). We need hardly say that there is no conflict between this passage and the one in Ex. 23, for there are *no* " contradictions " in the Word of God. All that is needed is a little careful attention to each passage. The " I will not drive them out before them in one year " of Ex. 23 : 29 has reference to the Hivites, Canaanites, and Hittites, as the previous verse shows ; whereas the " them " of Deut. 9 : 3 is the Anakim—see v. 2. Nor does this present any difficulty in the spiritual application : there *are* some enemies which the Christian is enabled to overcome

" quickly," while there are others which continue to try him unto the end of his earthly course.

Divine Assurances

It is scarcely possible to overstate the importance of the book of Joshua. Its contents are an intrinsic part of "the children's bread", which is essential to their well-being. It is of incalculable value to us both doctrinally and practically. Doctrinally it casts clear light on a subject which has deeply exercised the best theologians throughout the centuries, namely, the relation which the Gospel sustains to the Law; yet so far as we are aware, none has ever appealed to this portion of the Word as providing a solution to that problem. Surely it is clear that if we can ascertain what was the precise relations which Joshua bore to Moses, we shall discover the relations which the Gospel sustains to the Law. It has indeed been recognised by many that the relation of those men unto each other indicated in a general way one of the chief distinctions between the Law and the Gospel: that as Joshua rather than Moses was the one who led Israel into Canaan, so it is the merits of Christ and not the works of the Law to which the sinner must look for his justification; but there they stopped. Instead of starting at the beginning and tracing through the subject, they began in the middle and drew a single conclusion.

The very first thing told us about Joshua in the book which bears his name is that he was "Moses' minister" (1: 1), a statement that looks back to Ex. 24: 13. Thus, Joshua is not set before us as antagonistic to Moses, but as his attendant and supporter. Apply that to the antitype and it should at once be evident that it is a serious mistake to regard the Gospel and the Law as being mutual enemies. Perhaps some will object, but is it not derogatory to the Son of God to view Him as subservient to the Law?· Our reply is, What saith the Scriptures? Upon that point there is no room for uncertainty: "When the fulness of time was come God sent forth His Son, made of a woman, made under the Law" (Gal. 4: 4). It was in order to prevent any mistake upon this point, to allay any fears they might entertain about it, that Christ said to His disciples "Think not that I am come to destroy the Law or the Prophets: I am not come to destroy, but to fulfil" (Matt. 5: 17)—to "fulfill" it by rendering thereto a perfect obedience and then to endure, on behalf of His sinful people, its unremitting penalty.

But second, it is quite clear from the book of Deut. that the mission of Joshua was to *complement* that of Moses, to bring to a successful issue what he began. Moses had led Israel out of Egypt and he had been their leader all through the wilderness journeyings, but it was left unto Joshua to induct Israel into their promised inheritance. Here too we find no antagonism between Joshua and Moses, but rather the one augmenting the other. Therein we have a blessed and striking adumbration of the relation which the Gospel sustains to the Law: it is not its adversary but its handmaid, not its destroyer but its fulfiller. Christ has not only honoured and magnified the Law personally, but He secures its being honoured and magnified in the affections and lives of His redeemed: "For the Law was given by Moses, but grace and truth came by Jesus Christ" (John 1: 17). "For what the Law could not do, in that it was weak through the flesh, God sending His own Son in the likeness of sinful flesh, and for sin, condemned sin in the flesh: that the righteousness of the Law might be fulfilled in us" (Rom. 8: 3, 4).

Under Moses the Law obtained not its due because of the weakness of the flesh in those who received it. They declared unto Moses "speak thou unto us all that the Lord our God shall speak unto thee, and we will hear and do" (Deut. 5: 27). Nor was the Lord displeased at such an avowal. So far was He from condemning them for a presumptuous boast, we are told, "the Lord said unto me, I have heard the voice of the words of this people which they have spoken unto thee: they have *well said* all that they have spoken" (v. 28). Nevertheless, there *was* a "weakness" of which they were ignorant, but of which He was cognizant, for He went on to say "Oh that there were such a heart in them that they would fear Me and keep all My commandments always, that it might be well with them and with their children forever!" There we learn what their "weakness" consisted of: they *lacked a heart* for the Lord Himself. That is the lack of the natural man the world over: until he is born again no man has either any filial fear of God nor love for Him, and where those be absent there is neither desire nor sincere effort to keep them.

"The carnal mind is enmity against God: for it is not subject to the Law of God, neither indeed can be" (Rom. 8: 7). Inexpressibly solemn are those words: true of writer and reader alike until a miracle of grace was wrought within him. The carnal mind is not subject to the Law of God nor is it capable of being so: it is utterly *lawless*, determined only on pleasing self and having our own way. The reason for this insubjection of the carnal mind to the Divine Law is that it is "enmity against God": it is alienated from Him, it hates Him—abhorring His ineffable holiness and despising His sovereign authority. But at regeneration the love of God is shed abroad in the heart by the Holy Spirit (Rom. 5: 5): a contrary principle is implanted which opposes that enmity and its reigning power is destroyed. Hence, there is on the part of the regenerated person a radically changed disposition and attitude to the Divine Law, so that he declares "I delight in the Law of God after the inward man. . .with the mind I myself serve the Law of God" (Rom. 7: 22, 25).

Third, not only was Joshua, originally, "Moses' minister", not only did he supplement his ministry and bring his mission to successful completion, but when commissioned by Jehovah to conduct His people into Canaan, he was bidden "Only be thou strong and very courageous, that thou mayest observe to do according to all the Law which Moses My servant commanded thee: turn not from it to the right hand or to the left, that thou mayest prosper whithersoever thou goest. This book of the Law shall not depart out of thy mouth, but thou shalt meditate therein day and night" (Josh. 1: 7, 8). Here again we see that so far from the work assigned Joshua being inimical to that of his predessor, he was enjoined to honour and magnify it. That commission concerned not so much Joshua personally as it did the people entrusted to his charge. If Israel were to "possess their possessions", then under the leadership of Joshua they must regulate their conduct by the Divine Law. God has not regenerated those for whom Christ died that they might live as they please, but that they "might *serve Him* without fear, in holiness and righteousness before Him, all the days of our life" (Luke 1: 73, 75).

Herein lies the triumph and glory of the Gospel: not merely that transgressors are pardoned and sinners delivered from the wrath to some, but that they are "created in righteousness and true holiness" (Eph. 4: 24), given a nature which delights in the Law and sincerely serves it. The Law is written on their hearts (Heb. 8: 10), enshrined in their affections, and under the leadership of the antitypical Joshua their conduct is governed by it. Christ has left them an example that they should follow His steps (1 Pet. 2: 21), and *He* respected, honoured, and fulfilled the Law. True, they do not *perfectly* obey the Law, though they long to and honestly endeavour so to do, and where there is that honest endeavour God accepts the will for the deed. So far from the Law's being set aside, N. T. saints are "under the Law to Christ" (1 Cor. 9: 21), and just so far as they act in accordance with that fact is "good success" theirs in the spiritual life.

Here, then, is the relation between the Law and the Gospel. First, as Moses preceded Joshua, so God employs the Law as an instrument for convicting the sinner of his need of Christ, for "by the Law is the knowledge of sin" (Rom. 3: 20). Second, as Joshua was "Moses' minister", so Christ was made under the Law and satisfied its every requirement, both preceptive and penal, that a perfect righteousness might be provided for His people. Third, as the mission of Joshua supplemented and complemented that of Moses, so when the Gospel of Christ is made the power of God unto salvation to every one that believeth, there is communicated to that soul a nature which loves the Law and is subject to it. Fourth, as the success of Israel in Canaan turned upon their obedience to Joshua, who was to be regulated wholly by the Law of Moses, so the Christian enters into possession of his possessions only so far as he is subject to the Law in the hands of the Mediator. This will be made increasingly evident if we are permitted to continue our meditations upon this book of Scripture.

In our last we dwelt a little on Josh. 1: 1-3. With v. 4 should be compared Gen. 15: 18, Ex. 23: 31, Num. 34: 3-12, Deut. 11: 24. Turning now to v. 5 we have the blessed promises which the Lord made unto Joshua as the basis of the great commission he then received. "There shall not any man be able to stand before thee all the days of thy life: as I was with Moses, so I will be with thee: I will not fail thee, nor forsake thee". In seeking to ponder them in the light of what immediately follows, we need to bear in mind that the terms of the commission were made with Joshua not simply as a private person, but *as leader* of the Nation, that what God required from him He required from them, and that what He promised him He promised them. We saw this when looking at v. 2, wherein Jehovah said unto Joshua "Moses My servant is dead: now therefore arise, go over this Jordan, thou *and* all this people". That "therefore" is most significant and suggestive: so far from the loss of their former leader inclining them to sit down in dejection and despair, it was all the more necessary why they should go forward under their new commander.

"There shall not any man be able to stand before thee". That this promise was made unto the Nation as here represented by Joshua is clear from a comparison with Deut. 7: 24. There we find Moses addressing the whole congregation, assuring it of what the Lord God would do for them when He brought them into the land (see v. 1): "He shall deliver their kings into thine hand, and thou shalt destroy their name from under heaven: there shall no man be able to stand before thee". Thus as Josh. 1: 2 gave the Divine call of duty unto Israel—"arise, go over this Jordan, thou and all this people unto the land which I do give thee"—so in v. 5 we see the Divine encouragement given them unto the discharge of their duty. Moses had to face the haughty monarch of Egypt—then the mightiest kingdom on earth—and confront his wise men and magicians; yet none were able to stand before him. Powerful nations were in possession of Canaan, among them the giant Anakim (Deut. 9: 2), but none shall be able to withstand Joshua and those under him: "as I was with Moses, so I will be with thee".

"There shall not any man be able to stand before thee all the days of thy life: as I was with Moses, so I will be with thee". But was that blessed assurance designed only for Joshua and the Israelites of that day? Is it not recorded also for *our* sakes (Rom. 4: 23, 24). Then are we making practical use of it? Do we frequently remind ourselves of the same? Do we plead it before the throne of grace in time of need and ask God to make it good in our experience? Realising that we are called upon to "fight the good fight of faith", conscious of our weakness and the might of our foes, have we put God in mind of this word? If not, why not? Is not our failure at this point the explanation of many other failures? It is not enough that we should long to enter more fully into our heritage in Christ, we should also appropriate unto ourselves this blessed assurance and beg God to overthrow whatever is standing in the way and hindering us from a present and personal enjoyment of our spiritual portion. We should be daily and confidently entreating Him to teach us to vanquish the Anakim which are usurping our rightful heritage.

Should any doubt the dispensational validity of what we have just pointed out and demur at the idea of Christians today applying to themselves a specific promise made to Joshua thousands of years ago, then all room for a questioning of the same should at once be removed by the final clause of that verse: "I will not fail thee nor forsake thee" (v. 5). Let the reader very carefully observe that that very promise is quoted in Heb. 13 and a most important conclusion drawn from it: "For He hath said, I will never leave thee, nor forsake thee. So that *we* may boldly say, The Lord is my Helper and I will not fear what man shall do unto me" (vv. 5, 6). The very fact that the Holy Spirit moved the apostle to apply unto Christians that promise made unto Joshua is clear proof of its significance for believers in this age. Although the principle of one basic interpretation with many legitimate applications may still be maintained, the promises of God frequently transcend dispensational distinctions. This is particularly true when the promise is restated in another historical context. In such instances the promise definitely pertains to those living in the other era as well and God's children should rightly partake of this needful portion of their bread.

What has just been mentioned ought to be so obvious that it requires no further amplification: but since some of our readers have been wrongly instructed therein, we must labour the point a little further. Are not the needs of believers the same in one age as another? Does not God bear the same relation to them and is He not affected alike unto all of His children—does He not bear them the same love? If He would not fail or forsake Joshua, then He will not us. Are not Christians today under the same everlasting covenant of grace as were the O. T. saints? Then they have a common charter: "For the promise is unto you, and to your children, and to all that are afar off —as many as the Lord our God shall call" (Acts 2: 39). Let us not forget that "Whatsoever things were written aforetime were written for our learning, that *we* through patience and comfort of the Scriptures might have hope" (Rom. 15: 6). Then let this principle be held tenaciously by us: the Divine promises which were made on special occasions to particular individuals are of general use for *all* the members of the Household of Faith.

"I will not fail thee, nor forsake thee" is one of "the exceeding great and precious promises" of God (2 Pet. 1: 4) which is addressed to me now as much as it was to Joshua of old, and therefore is available for my faith to lay hold of and enjoy. Note the use which the apostle made of the same: "So that we may boldly say, the Lord is *my* Helper, and I will not fear what man shall do unto me" (Heb. 13: 6). Those words "so that" point an inference drawn from the promise: a double conclusion is thereby reached—confidence in God and courage against man. That intimates the various and manifold *use* we should make of God's promises. The conclusion drawn by the apostle was based upon the character of the Promiser. and similarly should faith ever reason. Since God is infinitely good, faithful, all-powerful and immutable, we may boldly or confidently declare with Abraham "the Lord will provide" ,Gen. 22: 8), with Jonathan "there is no restraint to the Lord to save by many or by few" (1 Sam. 14: 6), with Jehoshaphat "None is able to withstand Thee" (2 Chron. 20: 6), with Paul "If God be for us, who can be against us" (Rom. 8: 31).

"So that *we* may boldly say, The Lord is *my* helper, and I will not fear what man shall do unto me". Note attentively the change in number from the plural to the singular: general principles are to be appropriated by us in particular, as general precepts are to be taken by us individually—as the Lord Jesus individualized the "*Ye* shall not tempt the Lord your God" of Deut. 6: 16 when assailed by Satan (Matt. 4: 10)! It is only by taking the Divine promises and precepts unto ourselves personally that we mix faith with the same and make a proper and profitable use of them. It is further to be observed that "The Lord is my Helper." etc, is a citation from Psa. 118: 6. In that quotation the apostle teaches us again that the language of the O. T. is exactly suited unto the case of Christians now, and that they are fully warranted in appropriating the same"; "*we* may boldly say" just what the Psalmist did! It was in a season of sore distress that David expressed his confidence in the Lord, at a time when it appeared that his enemies were about to swallow him up; but contrasting the omnipotence of Jehovah with the feebleness of the creature his heart was strengthened and emboldened.

Ah, but does the reader clearly perceive what *that* involved? It meant that David turned his mind away from the seen to the unseen. It means that he was regulated by faith rather than by sight or reason. It means that his heart was occupied with the omnipotent One. But it means much more: he was occupied with the relationship of that omnipotent One unto himself. It means that he recognised and realised the spiritual bond there was between them, so that he could rightly and boldly say "the Lord is *my* Helper". If He be my God, my Redeemer, my Father, then He can be counted upon to undertake for me when I am in sore straits, when my foes would devour me, or when my barrel of meal is well-nigh empty. But that "my" is the language of *faih* and "my Helper" is the conclusion which faith's assurance unhesitatingly drew. Often God so orders His providences and places us in trying circumstances that there may be suitable opportunity for our exercise of faith and that He may be glorified by the same. Nothing honours Him more than the unquestioning confidence of our hearts when everything outward seems thoroughly against us.

Yes, David turned away his eyes from his numerous and powerful enemies unto the omnipotent One, and so should we. God will not disappoint us if we do: He never fails those who really trust Him. Consider another example which illustrates the same principle. On one occasion "the children of Moab the children of Ammon, and with them other besides the Ammonites, came against Jehoshaphat to battle" (2 Chron. 20: 1). The king was quickly informed that "there cometh a great multitude against thee", and we are told that he "feared". But that was not all he did: he "set himself to seek the Lord and proclaimed a fast throughout all Judah". Then in the presence of the whole congregation he prayed and pleaded with Jehovah, concluding with "O our God, wilt Thou not judge them? for we have no might against this great company that cometh against us, neither know we what to do: but our eyes are *upon Thee*" (v. 12). Nor did they look unto Him in vain. Read the sequel —vv. 14-26: without themselves striking a blow, the Lord smote their enemies with such a spirit of confusion that they fell upon one another and completely destroyed themselves.

Divine Injunctions

When Jehovah called Moses to go down into Egypt and make known His demand unto Pharaoh He assured His servant "I will be with thy mouth and teach thee what thou shalt say" (Ex. 4: 12). When Jeremiah was ordained a prophet unto the nations and he shrank from the task before him, God said "they shall fight against thee, but they shall not prevail against thee, for I am with thee, saith the Lord, to deliver thee" (Jer. 1: 19). With such assurances does the Lord fortify the hearts of those whom He commissions to go forth in His name. Similarly, when the risen Redeemer bade His apostles make disciples of all nations and baptise them, He first emphasised the fact that "all power had been given to Him in heaven and in earth", and then comforted them with the declaration "Lo, I am with you alway, even unto the end of the world" (Matt. 28: 18-20). So too when He told Paul to remain at Corinth, He cheered him thus: "Be not afraid, but speak, and hold not thy peace, for I am with thee and no man shall set on thee to hurt thee, for I have much people in this city" (Acts 18: 9, 10).

In like manner did the Lord prepare Joshua for the undertaking to which he was called. First, He gave him the threefold assurance, "There shall not any man be able to stand before thee all the days of thy life: as I was with Moses, so I will be with thee: I will not fail thee, nor forsake thee" (1: 5). The time had arrived when he was to lead the people of Israel across the Jordan and marshal their forces for the conquest of the promised land. On the threshold of that difficult and dangerous task Jehovah had thus encouraged and animated His servant. Great were the obstacles and perils confronting them, but great too were the consolations here vouchsafed him. Highly favoured as was Joshua in being made the recipient of such promises, yet they were not designed to set aside the discharge of his own responsibility: he was not to say within himself, These covenant engagements will certainly be fulfilled, so there is no need for me to be exercised. So far from using them as a couch for him to rest upon, they were designed as a girdle wherewith to gird up his loins for future activities.

"Be strong and of a good courage, for unto this people shalt thou divide for an inheritance the land which I sware unto their fathers to give them. Only be thou strong and very courageous" (1: 6, 7). The Divine assurance received by Joshua was therefore intended as a spur unto energy, as an incentive to the performance of duty, for the quickening of his heart unto the same. The connection between this exhortation and what immediately precedes it inculcates a most important practical lesson: God's promises are not meant to set aside His precepts, but rather are given to encourage us to do with all our hearts and might whatever He has bidden us. Assurances of Divine assistance must never be regarded as nullifying our accountability or as rendering needless the putting forth of our utmost endeavours, but instead, are to be taken as so many guarantees that if we be "always abounding in the work of the Lord" (the discharge of our daily duties), then we may know "that our labour is not in vain in the Lord" (1 Cor. 15: 58).

Those professing Christians who reason, God has promised never to leave nor forsake us and therefore it is quite safe for us to flirt with the world and trifle with sin, do but make manifest the unregenerate condition of their hearts. They who take unto themselves the Divine declaration "He who hath begun a good work in you will perform it until the day of Jesus Christ" (Phil. 1: 6) and then conclude there is no need for them to make their calling and election sure, or desire the sincere milk of the Word that they may grow thereby, render it very doubtful that a good work has been begun in *them*. They who say, God will assuredly fulfill His decrees and draw unto Christ all whom He has ordained unto eternal life, and therefore there is no need for us to be deeply concerned about souls and seek after their salvation, speak not the language of His true children, but wrest the Truth. If our response to God's promises be that of sloth and carelessness, that is proof we have received them carnally and not spiritually. The use or misuse we make of the Divine cordials affords a good index of the state of our hearts.

God had just assured Joshua "as I was with Moses, so I will be with thee". That language was unequivocal and unqualified, yet it was far from signifying that he might take things easily, or simply "stand still, and see the salvation of the Lord"—words which have been grievously misapplied. No, rather were they designed to inspire him to the performance of duty and to let him know that his efforts should not be in vain. "Be strong and of a good courage": that was the first effect which those assurances should work in him, and until they *did* he was not fitted for the task before him. That task entailed the facing of problems and dangers such as were enough to make the stoutest heart to quake, nevertheless, Joshua was to undertake it without trepidation or hesitation. And why so? Because the living God, the omnipotent Jehovah had declared that not a man should be able to stand before him, that *He* would not fail nor forsake him. Then what was there to fear? Had not Joshua good ground, sufficient reason, to be strong and to act valiantly?

Upon entering Canaan powerful enemies had to be faced, for the land was inhabited by races of giants, men who were famous both for stature and strength. They were a fierce and warlike people, strongly armed, for they had "chariots of iron" (17: 16). True, but God had said "Not any man shall be able to stand before thee". Formidable obstacles had to be overcome. The cities of the Canaanites were fortified, described by the ten spies as "great and walled up to heaven" (Deut. 1: 28). That was the language of unbelief's exaggeration, yet they were mighty strongholds which had to be overthrown. Even so, God's "I will not fail thee" was more than sufficient. Again, there was the food problem to be considered. In the wilderness the Israelites had been daily supplied with manna from heaven, but that was now to cease. When the Jordan was crossed that great host of people must quarter on the enemy. Who was to provide for such a multitude? How should they be fed? Was not such a problem enough to make Joshua quail? No, not after he had received such assurances.

Not only were the Canaanites a numerous and powerful foe, but those whom Joshua commanded were a most unpromising people. What trouble they had occasioned his predecessor in the desert! Ever ready to murmur, wanting to turn back to Egypt, stiffnecked, and with no faith in Jehovah. What could Joshua expect from their immediate descendants? How far could he count on their loyalty and co-operation? Was it not more than likely that their hearts would turn from him as those of their fathers so often had from Moses? Even so, God had said "I will not forsake thee". How well suited were those Divine assurances to his situation! In view of them what good reason had the Lord to bid him "Be strong and of a good courage". And in view of the same what sufficient ground had Joshua to go forward in full confidence and valour! So he *would* if he took those promises to heart and mixed faith with them. Ah, it all turned on that. As cause stands to effect so would the laying hold of those promises produce strength of spirit and courageous action. Joshua did receive them by faith, and such was their effect upon him.

What bearing does the above have upon *us* today? In our last we pointed out that the promise of Josh. 1 : 5 belongs to Christians today, and here we must insist that the precept "Be strong and of a good courage" is also addressed to us personally, that God so enjoins *us*. "Quit you like men, be strong" (1 Cor. 16 : 13), "be of good courage" (Psa. 31 : 24) make known the Divine requirements from us. Those are the graces specially needed by believers if they are to overcome their enemies, surmount the obstacles in their path and possess their possessions. Granted, says the reader, but when you bid me "be strong" you do but tantalize me, seeing that is the very thing I desire to be and yet am conscious I am not. But cannot you see the fault is entirely your own: that your weakness and fear is due to your failure to mix faith with God's promises? What more do you want than what God has said to you in Josh. 1 : 5? If God be for you, who can be against you? Look away from yourself, from your enemies, from your difficulties, unto Him who hath said "I will not fail thee, nor forsake thee": count upon Him, and strength will displace weakness and courage fear.

"Only be thou strong and very courageous, *that* thou mayest observe *to do* according to all the Law, which Moses My servant commanded thee" (v. 7). This exhortation is not a mere repetition of the one in the previous verse, but a particularizing of it or an application of the same to a specific duty. The "be strong and of a good courage" of v. 5 was more general, this here relates especially to walking in the way of God's commandments. Resoluteness, fortitude, daring and perseverance were required for the great exploits which lay ahead, yet equally necessary and essential—if less apparent unto some to-day—was strength and courage if Joshua was to be completely *submissive* to the legislation of his predecessor. The world admires most the man who is independent, strikes out along a line of his own, and counts meekness and submission as a mean-spirited thing. It is the free-thinker and the free-liver who is generally admired by the godless, and obedience is despised as something servile. Joshua was now virtually made king in Jeshurun and it called for real courage for Israel's commander-in-chief to take his orders from another, and especially so when the carrying out of the same seemed to be a hazardous matter.

Let the Christian faithfully apply this exhortation unto himself and perhaps he will the better perceive what it involved for Joshua. "Be *thou* strong and very courageous, that (in order that) thou mayest observe to do according to all the Law". Is there not an inseparable connection between the two things: is not courage required in order to obedience? Fellow-Christian, if your character and conduct is to be regulated by the Divine standard, if all the details of your life are to be ordered by God's statutes, what will men think and say of you? Will they not deem you mad? It calls for courage, courage of a high order, for a preacher to scorn all novelties and disdain the contemptuous sneers of his fellows that he is "behind the times" because he declares only the counsel of God. And it calls for real courage for the private Christian to cleave close to the path of obedience when many professors will sneer at his "strictness" and "strait-lacedness". How many are *afraid* of being thought "queer" or "puritanical"! Ah, my reader, it requires resolution and valour to swim against the tide of popular opinion, as it does to differ from "our doctrines" if one sees God's Word requires it.

"That thou mayest observe to do according to all the Law, which Moses My servant commanded thee: turn not from it to the right hand or to the left, that thou mayest prosper whithersoever thou goest" (v. 7). There was the commission which Joshua received from the Lord. He was not to be regulated by his own inclinations nor lean unto his own understanding, he was not to be governed by the principle of expediency nor be seeking to please those under him; instead, he must be actuated in all things by a "thus saith the Lord". For the carrying out of that commission he needed strength and courage, that he might be daring enough to strictly heed the instructions which Moses had left in writing for him. And in order to the exercise of those graces his heart must be constantly occupied with the assuring promises God had given him. So God's servant today must teach His people to observe all things whatsoever Christ has commanded, resting on His promise "Lo, I am with you alway". So too the private Christian must heed that word "whatsoever He saith unto you, do" (John 2: 5), counting on His promise to make his way prosperous.

As another has pointed out, "In Joshua's case, full obedience to the Divine command involved innumerable difficulties, such as besieging fortified cities and fighting against warriors who came to battle in chariots of iron armed with scythes". He who contemplates enlisting under the banner of Christ needs well to sit down and count the cost, for it is no child's play to "follow the Lamb whithersoever He goeth". A merely nominal profession is easy enough to make and maintain after the manner of the times, but to be a real Christian means to deny self, take up the cross and go forth unto Christ without the camp. Through his obedience Joshua made many enemies. When it became known that Jericho had been captured and Ai vanquished, we read of certain kings confederating together to destroy him. Such will be the experience of the obedient Christian. It will be his desire and effort to make no enemies, but if he is faithful to Christ many of his old friends will turn against him, and he probably prove that his foes are found even in his own household. "Woe unto you" if "all men speak well of you".

Joshua's obedience required strength and courage because it involved years of *persevering effort*. Rome was not built in a day, nor was Canaan captured in a twelve month. Long marches, protracted campaigns, much heavy fighting was entailed before Israel fully entered into possession of their heritage. As another has said "The days were not long enough for his battles. He bids the sun stand still and the moon is stayed: and even when that long day has passed, yet the morning sees him sword in hand still. Joshua was like those old knights who slept in their armour. He was always fighting". Such is the life of the Christian: a warfare from end to end. No sooner does he receive pardon from 'Christ than the great conflict begins. Every yard of the narrow way which leadeth unto Life is contested—not a foot will Satan yield to him. When victory has been obtained over one lust, another immediately raises its ugly head. When one temptation has been overcome, ten others more subtle menace him. There is no respite, no furlough is granted. "He that endureth unto the end shall be saved", and none other will. Something more than human strength and prowess is called for.

"Do according to all the Law which Moses My servant commanded thee: turn not from it to the right hand or to the left". As one has well pointed out, "It is the exactness of obedience which constitutes the essence of obedience".

The fact is that if we do not desire and earnestly endeavour to keep *all* of God's commandments we are totally lacking in the spirit of genuine obedience. He who picks and chooses between them is a self-pleaser and not a God-pleaser. The vast majority in Christendom today say, We must not be too precise: but that is too thin a garb to cover their hypocrisy. At heart they want to turn their backs on God's Law altogether, but as an open avowal of such a sentiment would at once expose them, they resort to such cant as, We must not be too nice, too strict, too particular. It is this temporizing and compromising which has brought Christendom into the sorry state that it is now in. An omission here and a human addition there opened the flood-gates of evil. As the Lord will have all our hearts or nothing, so He will accept only an obedience which respects "all His commandments" (Psa. 119: 6), and not one which is partial and discriminating.

Joshua was granted no indulgence, but must adhere rigidly and constantly to the Rule set before him. No matter how contrary to natural wisdom and prudence might be the carrying out of its precepts, no matter how unpopular it should make him with the people of Israel, God required full and coɪtinuous obedience from him. And so He does of us today, and unto those of His nominal disciples who fail to render the same, He asks, "Why call ye Me, Lord, and do not the things whi h I say?" (Luke 6: 46). Yes, "nominal" disciples is all they are, for He Himself declares "that servant which knew his Lord's will and prepared not, neither did according to His will, shall be beaten with many stripes" (Luke 12: 47). It is probable that the apostle had Joshua 1: 7 in mind when he said "by the armour of righteousness on the right hand and on the left" (2 Cor. 6: 9)—righteousness is right doing, acting according to the standard of right, namely, the Law of God. When one said to a Puritan, "Many people have rent their consciences in halves: could you not just make a little nick in yours?" He answered, "No, I cannot, for my conscience belongs to God".

Finally, let us notice that the path of obedience is the path of *prosperity*: "turn not from it to the right hand or to the left, that (in order that) thou mayest prosper whithersoever thou goest" (v. 7). Conformity unto the revealed will of God may entail trial, but there will be abundant compensation. Of course there shall, for the Lord will be no man's Debtor. The path of obedience is the path of blessing: the treading thereof may incur the frowns of men, but what matters that if we have the smile of our Master! True, the prosperity may not immediately appear, for faith has to be tried and patience developed, yet in the long run it will be found that in keeping the Divine commandments "there is great reward" (Psa. 19: 11). So Joshua found it: he adhered strictly to the Divine Law and success crowned his efforts; and that is recorded for *our* encouragement. Let us not forget that "Godliness is profitable for all things: having promise of the life that *now is* and of that which is to come" (1 Tim. 4: 8), yet that promise is conditioned by our keeping of the precepts.

The Primacy of God's Word

We turn now to the closing portion of the great commission which Joshua received from the Lord. We have already seen that it came to him after the death of Moses, and that it was concerned with Israel's conquest and occupation of the land of Canaan (vv. 1-4). We have contemplated the blessed assurances which Jehovah gave unto His servant, for the comforting of his heart and the strengthening of his hands (v. 5). We have pondered the general injunction which God laid upon the new leader of His people (v. 6), and sought to show its meaning and timeliness. We have also noted the particular application which the Lord made of that injunction unto Joshua, in requiring that he should be very courageous in regulating all his actions by the statutes He had given through Moses and placed on permanent record as an authoritative Rule for all who should succeed him, and how that He enjoined implicit and undeviating obedience from him, (v. 7), and endeavoured to indicate the very real and practical bearing all of that has upon our spiritual lives today. In what we are now to ponder, we learn what more was demanded of Joshua in order to ensure a successful realisation of all the foregoing.

"This Book of the Law shall not depart out of thy mouth; but thou shalt meditate therein day and night, that thou mayest observe to do according to all that is written therein: for then thou shalt make thy way prosperous and then thou shalt have good success" (1: 8). Joshua was to be guided and governed wholly by the written Word, which was something unprecedented, unique, No man before Joshua had received orders from God to regulate his conduct by the Words of a *Book*. True, Abram and his household obeyed God's voice in keeping His commandments and His statutes (Gen. 26: 5). Moses too had acted by Divine authority, but each had received his instructions from the mouth of the Lord, But Joshua, and all who succeeded him, must be governed by "this Book of the Law". It is remarkable that Joshua and the Book come before us together, without any introduction, in the same passage: "and the Lord said unto Moses, Write this in a book and rehearse it in the ears of Joshua" (Ex. 17: 14)—the Book was prepared for Joshua; Joshua came to fulfill the words of the Book. The typical significance of that is at once apparent.

Let it be carefully noted that God's Word, from its very first appearance as a book, occupies the same position, namely, the position of unqualified *supremacy*. It was set above Joshua: all his actions were to be regulated by it. Let us also observe that the authority of this Book is quite independent of its quantity or size. "The law of Moses", "Moses and the Prophets", "The Law, the Prophets and the Psalms" (Luke 24: 44) are descriptions of the same Book, differing in the quantity of its matter but not differing in its authority, nor in its relation to the people of God. "Blessed is he that readeth and they that hear the words of this prophecy" (Rev. 1: 3) is a declaration that applies with equal force to the Holy Scriptures in every stage of their compilation, from the opening chapters of "The Book of the Law" till the completion of the Sacred Canon. Let us further remark that in this first title given to the Bible in its earliest form, we have emphasised its leading characteristic: it contains more than good advice or salutary counsel—it is a "Law" binding upon us, a Law clothed with Divine authority, a Rule for us to walk by.

"This Book of the Law" comprised the entire Pentateuch, the first five books (or chapters) of the O.T. It is not "these books of the Law" for all through the O.T. those five books are regarded as a unit. Now it is very rare indeed that we turn aside and pay any attention to the ravings of sceptics and infidels, but on this occasion we will depart from our custom. It is one of the many erroneous allegations of the self-styled "Higher Critics" that the Pentateuch was not written by Moses, but was composed at a very much later date —some say, in the time of king Manasseh; others, not until the days of Ezra. But over against this assertion, stands the fact that a definite "Book" is spoken of all through the O. T., as being constantly appealed to, with directions how it was to be preserved; and it should be of interest to our readers if we briefly outline the references to the same. The first mention of this

"Book" is as stated above, in Ex. 17: 14, and there we see it was written by Jehovah's command, and (in the Heb.) is designated *"the* Book".

"And Moses wrote all the words of the Lord. . .and he took the Book of the Covenant and read it in the audience of the people" (Ex. 24: 4, 7), tells who was its first penman. "Moses wrote their goings out according to their journeys by the commandment of the Lord" (Num. 33: 2), and if we compare Deut. 1: 2, 3 and 2: 14 it will be found that those "journeys" were from the early part of the first year after Israel came out of Egypt until the end of the thirty-eighth. "Moses wrote this Law and delivered it unto the priests, the sons of Levi" (Deut. 31: 9) entrusting it to their custody, and v. 26 of the same chapter informs us he bade the Levites, "take this Book of the Law and put it in the side of the ark of the covenant of the Lord your God, that it may be there for a witness against them". It is clear from v. 19 that copies were made of parts of it at least, but the standard copy was preserved in the side of the ark, which vessel was kept in the holy of holies. From that Standard copy each king of Israel was required to "write him a copy of this Law in a book out of that which is before the priests the Levites" (Deut. 17: 18).

Once every seven years the whole of the Book of the Law was to be read in the hearing of the entire congregation. "And Moses commanded them, saying, At the end of every seventh year, in the solemnity of the year of release, in the feast of tabernacles, when all Israel is come to appear before the Lord their God in the place which He shall choose, thou shalt read this Law before all Israel in their hearing. . .that they may learn and fear the Lord your God and observe to do all the words of this Law" (Deut. 31: 11-13). This was the Book by which Joshua was to be regulated. At a later date, the Spririt moved him to write therein (24: 26), as Samuel also added portions thereto (1 Sam. 10: 25). It was *this* Book David had in mind when he prayed "teach me Thy statutes"; "order my steps in Thy Word" (119: 12, 133). When David drew nigh unto death, he gave this commission unto Solomon: "Keep the charge of the Lord thy God, to walk in His ways, to keep His statutes and His commandments. . .as it is written in the Law of Moses, that thou mayest prosper in all that thou doest" (1 Kings 2: 1-4).

Alas, Solomon failed to heed that injunction, following too much the evil devices of his heart. The decline which began in his reign accelerated and continued many generations, and during that time "this Book of the Law" was lost to the people. In the days of Josiah, the high priest "found the Book of the Law in the house of the Lord" (2 Kings 22: 8), for *He* had guarded and preserved it despite Israel's apostasy, and the godly king himself read "all the words of the Book of the Covenant" in the hearing of a vast assembly (2 Kings 23: 2, 3). Later, we find Ezra doing the same thing (Neh. 8: 1;8, 13: 1). Daniel made reference to this Book; "the curse is poured upon us and the oath that is written in the Law of Moses the servant of God, because we have sinned against Him" (9: 11). While the very last chapter of the O.T. contains this injunction, "Remember ye the Law of Moses, My servant, which I commanded unto him in Horeb for all Israel, with the statutes and judgments" (v. 4); which completes the cycle.

"This Book of the Law shall not depart out of thy mouth" (Josh. 1: 8). No man, however dignified his position, is above the Law of God. Though exalted to be commander-in-chief over Israel, and thereby given great power and authority, Joshua himself must be in subjection to the Divine Law: he was to issue no orders save those which were authorised by the Rule given to him. He was to invent no new statutes or ordinances, but be regulated solely by what was "written". If Joshua was to complete the work which Moses began, then he must maintain the Law which Moses had established. There was no need for him to make new laws: he was already furnished with a Divine and complete Charter, and *that* it was his business to heed and enforce. "To the Law and to the Testimony" he was to be held accountable, and if he spake not according thereto, then there was no light in him (Isa. 8; 20), and those under him would be left in spiritual darkness. Just so far as he executed this commision would the smile of God be upon him and prosperity attend his efforts.

"But thou shalt meditate therein day and night, that thou mayest observe to do according to all that is written therein" (1: 8). Meditation upon the Word of God is one of the most important of all the means of grace and growth in spirituality, yea there can be no true progress in vital and practical godliness without it. Meditation on Divine things is not optional but obligatory, for it is something which God has *commanded us* to attend unto. The order which Joshua received was not restricted to himself, but is addressed to all of God's people. Nor does it by any means stand alone. "Set your hearts unto all the words which I testify among you this day" (Deut. 32: 46). "Ponder the path of thy feet" (Prov. 4: 26); "Consider your ways" (Hagg. 1: 7). "Let these sayings sink down into your ears" (Luke 9: 44), which they cannot do, unless they be frequently turned over in our minds. "Whatsoever things are true, venerable, just, pure, lovely. . .*think on* these things" (Phil. 4: 8).

Meditating in God's Law day and night is one of the outstanding marks of the man whom He calls "Blessed" (Psa. 1: 1, 2). It is a holy art and habit commended in the practice and example of the saints: Isaac (Gen. 24: 62), David (Psa. 119), the mother of our Lord (Luke 1: 19, 51). But though meditation be a duty and a great moral and spiritual aid, it is practised by few. The usual plea proffered by those who neglect it is, I am too busy, my life is so crowded with a multiplicity of duties and concerns, that, alas, I have not the necessary leisure for quiet ruminating. Our first reply is, Then you are acting in theenergy of the flesh and suffering yourself to be little better than a slave. God is no Egyptian taskmaster. Christ's yoke is easy and *His* burden is light and if *your* "burden" be heavy it is a self-imposed one. God calls you to no manner of life which crowds out the needs of your soul and entails the neglect of your eternal interests. "Set your affection on things above, not on things on the earth" (Col. 3: 2) is His unchanging call, and He has given no harsh and unreasonable precepts.

But this plea "I am too busy to engage in regular and spiritual meditation" is an idle excuse, yea it is worse—it is a *deceit* of your evil heart. It is not because you are short of time, but because you *lack a heart* for the things of God! "Where your treasure is, there will your heart be also" (Matt. 6: 21), and that which most occupies our heart will most engage the mind, for our thoughts always follow our affections; consequently the smallest actions, when we have no delight in them, are tedious and burdensome. Is it not money which most absorbs the attention of the miser? The voluptary thinks only of satisfying his senses. The giddy youth is concerned mainly with the pursuit of pleasure. The man of the world devotes his time and energies to acquiring wealth and honours. It is not lack of opportunity but of relish for the Word and a desire to please God which lies at the root of our failure here. Said David "O how love I Thy Law, it is my meditation all the day" (119: 97)—he *evidenced* his love for God's Law by constantly pondering it! To him meditation was not a task but a joy.

You may seek an extenuation by appealing to numerous obligations and heavy responsibilities, but it is invalid before God. You certainly do not hold a more important position than Joshua did, nor are your tasks more numerous and exacting. Well did Matt. Henry point out, "If ever any man's business might have excused him from meditation, and other acts of devotion, one would think Joshua's might at this time. It was a great trust that was lodged in his hands: the conduct of it was sufficient to fill him if he had ten souls, and yet he must find time and thoughts for meditation. Whatever affairs of this world we have on hand, we must not neglect the one thing needful". We cannot expect the God of Truth to be with us if we neglect the Truth of God. Nor is reading it and hearing it preached sufficient: they produce but a transient effect upon us, but *meditating* on some portion of the Word, going over it again and again in our minds, deepens the impression, fastens the truth on our memory, and sets our hearts and hands a-work.

But let us carefully observe that meditation was not enjoined upon Joshua in a general way, but with a specific design: "thou shalt meditate therein day and night, that (in order that) thou mayest observe *to do* according to all that is written therein". His mind was to be exercised upon God's Word with a specific purpose and practical end: not simply to rest in contemplation, but in order to be regulated by its precepts, through a serious inculcating of them upon his heart. Meditation was not to be an occasional luxury, but the regular discharge of a constant duty—"day and night". and this in order to a prompter, fuller and more acceptable obedience. God requires an intelligent, voluntary, and joyous obedience, and if we are really desirous of pleasing and glorifying Him we shall not only familiarise ourselves with His Word, but habitually ponder how its holy precepts may best regulate all the details of our daily lives. "I will meditate on Thy precepts, and have respect unto Thy ways" (119·15)—the latter cannot properly be without the former.

It is easy to persuade ourselves we really desire that our lives may be wellpleasing to God, but what *evidence* can we produce that such a desire is genuine. That which is wellpleasing unto God is made known in His statutes: to what extent are our hearts and minds seriously engaged with them? It is by definitely recalling who is their Author that I am most likely to hold them in greater reverence and esteem, realise they are designed for my good, and bring my walk into fuller accord with them. It is only by repeated and prayerful meditation upon them that I shall perceive their spirituality and scope. For example, that the prohibition of any vice inculcates its opposite virtue: that the thing forbidden is not merely the overt act, but everything leading up to and stimulating the same. It is by meditating on the precepts we come to understand them, that our consciences are impressed by them, that our wills are moved to do them.

"My hands also will I lift up unto Thy commandments, which I have loved, and I will meditate in Thy statutes" (119: 48). The moving cause of David's respect for the Divine commandments was his *love* for them, and that produced two practical effects. First, a "lifting up of the hands", which is an expression of varied significance, but here it means to make a diligent application unto the keeping of them. "Without thee shall no man lift up his hand" (Gen. 41: 44)—attempt to do anything. "Arise, O Lord; O God, lift up Thine hand: forget not the humble" (Psa. 10: 12)—put forth Thine active power for their assistance. "Lift up the hands which hang down" (Heb. 12: 12)—set them to vigorous use. It is, then, a figurative expression which imports a serious and deliberate setting about upon a course of action. "I will lift up my hands unto Thy commandments": I will apply myself diligently to the keeping of them; I will earnestly endeavour to put them into practice; such is my solemn resolution.

Second, and in order to the carrying out of that resolution, "I will *meditate* in Thy statutes". It is not enough to barely approve of them: they must also be performed—see James 1: 22, 1 John 2: 4. If we would seriously address ourselves to a course of obedience, then we must use much forethought and meditation. God's chief complaint against Israel of old was, "My people doth not consider" (Isa. 1: 3). God's statutes must be kept in mind and what they require from us constantly pondered. The longer we hold the Divine precept before the conscience, the more powerfully shall we be affected by it. We complain of our forgetfulness, but fail to take the right course to cure it: the Word is only fixed in our minds by turning it over and over in our thoughts. "Be ye not unwise, but understanding what the will of the Lord is" (Eph. 5: 17): grace does not act as a charm, but sets us a-work, and much care and labour is entailed in obtaining spiritual understanding—*see* Prov. 2: 1-5.

"For then thou shalt make thy way prosperous, and then thou shall have good success". Yes, "then", but *only then*. We must comply with the required conditions. Walking in the path of God's commandments alone ensures success in the spiritual warfare. God's smile of approbation will not be upon us unless we walk as obedient children. Nor shall we possess our possessions and enjoy our heritage except as we conduct ourselves by the Divinely-given Rule. And in order to "observe to *do* according to *all* that is written therein" then we must "meditate therein day and night"! The designed use of this exercise is to bring the heart to a greater detestation of sin and a more diligent care to please God, and thereby we promote both our temporal and eternal welfare. We have dwelt the longer on these verses because they are of incalculable importance to the Christian life. If we would *prosper* as Joshua did, then we must *act* as he did!

The Concluding Charge

"Have not I commanded thee? Be strong and of a good courage: be not afraid, neither be thou dismayed, for the Lord thy God is with thee whithersoever thou goest" (1: 9). This was the concluding part of the charge which Jehovah there laid upon His servant. For the third time Joshua was bidden to be courageous. The natural inference to draw from such repetition would be that he was a timid and cowardly man; but his previous record effectively disposes of such a conclusion. He was one of the twelve selected by Moses to spy out the Land. In his bold dissent from the gloomy report of ten of his fellows, and in his fighting of Amalek (Ex. 17) he had manifested himself as one possessed of valour. Yet God saw fit to press this injunction upon him repeatedly: as Matt. Henry pointed out, "Those that have grace, have need to be called upon again and again to exercise grace and improve it". Though that precept did not imply that Joshua was faint-hearted, it did import he would be faced with situations which called for the exercise of sterling qualities.

But let it be pointed out that there is a moral courage as well as a physical, and not all possessing the latter are endowed with the former. How many who flinched not in the face of the enemy's fire, were afraid to be seen reading God's Word! There is also strength of mind and will, which refuses to be daunted by difficulties and dismayed by failures. Let it also be noted that that threefold call to act valiantly was not a mere repetition. In v. 6 Joshua was bidden to be strong and of a good courage in view of the task before him—which demanded physical prowess. In v. 7 it was an injunction unto personal and moral courage: "that thou mayest observe to do according to all the Law" —to seek not counsel from his fellows, nor fear their criticisms, but to order all his actions by "the Book". It requires more courage to keep to the old paths than it does to follow after novelties. A stout heart is indispensable in order to tread the path of God's commandments.

"Have not I commanded thee? Be strong and of a good courage" (v. 9). It seems to us this was more distinctly a call to the exercise of spiritual courage. In proportion as the child of God becomes aware of his own weakness and insufficiency, he is very apt to be cast down; instead, it should make him look outside himself and lay hold of the strength of Another. Was it not as though the Lord said to His servant: It is indeed unto a great undertaking I have commissioned thee, but let not a sense of thine own infirmities deter thee, for "have not I commanded thee"! It would be a great help unto Joshua if he kept his eye on the Divine warrant. The same One who had issued the precept must be looked unto for enablement to the performance thereof. Christ Himself was borne up under His suffering by a regard to the Divine will: "as the Father gave Me *commandment*, even so I do; Arise, let us go hence" (John 14: 31).

"Have not I commanded thee? Be strong and of a good courage". It is not sufficiently realised that God's commandments, equally with His promises, are addressed unto *faith*; yet a little reflection ought to convince us that such is the case. That which we are required to believe and take for our Rule is the Word of God as a whole, and a heart which has been turned unto the Lord and brought into loving subjection to Him does not delight in one part of it and despise another. The fact is we do not believingly receive God's Word at all, unless we heartily receive *everything* in it: there are precisely the same reasons for our embracing the precepts as the promises. Yea, in one sense, it should be easier for us to be convinced of our present duty than to be assured of the future things promised us. It is by our obedience to the Divine precepts that our faith is to be tested and measured. Faith without works is dead. Faith worketh by love (Gal. 5: 6), and how can I express my love than by doing what God bids me: "he that hath My commandments and keepeth them, he it is that loveth Me" (John 14: 21).

"I have *believed* Thy commandments" (Psa. 119: 66). Have we? Do we clearly understand what is signified and included in that statement? To "believe God's commandments" is to have a ready alacrity to hear God's voice in them, for the heart to be suitably impressed and for our actions to be regulated by them. Faith always has to do with God Himself. It is the work of faith to acquaint us with the character of God and His attributes, and to be duly influenced in our souls by a sense of the same. Faith looks to His majesty as truly as it does to His love, and submits to His authority as truly as it delights in His grace. The precepts as much as the promises bind us to trust in God: the one issues from His lips and requires a response from us as much as does the other. The commandments are an expression of God's will, binding us to our duty, and since they are not addressed unto sense, they must be given unto faith. There can, in fact, be no acceptable obedience unless it proceeds from faith—Heb. 11: 8.

Faith views the commandments as what God demands of me and therefore submits to His authority. As the promises are not really esteemed and embraced by us unless they are received as from *God*, so the precepts do not awe our consciences nor bring the will into subjection to them unless we accept them as Divine fiats binding upon us. If we actually believe God's promises with a living faith, then our hearts are drawn off from carnal vanities, to seek our happiness in what they pledge us. In like manner, when we actually believe God's precepts with a lively faith, our hearts are drawn off from a course of self-will, for we accept them as the only Rule to guide and govern us in the obtaining of that happiness; and thereby we submit ourselves to the Divine authority and conduct ourselves "as obedient children". Nothing produces a real submission of soul but a conscious subjection to a "thus saith the Lord".

Faith receives the commandments as coming from an all-mighty Lawgiver and therefore as One who is not to be trifled with, knowing "There is one Lawgiver, who is able to save and to destroy" (James 4: 12). It is because the unregenerate do not believe in the majesty, authority, righteousness and power of God that they so lightly regard and despise His commandments. But faith realises there is a Day of accounting, a Day of Judgment ahead, and keeps before it the penalty of disobedience. Heb. 2: 1-4 makes it clear that we ought to be as solemnly affected by the Divine Law and the majesty of its Promulgator as though we had been personally present at Sinai. But faith not only recognises the authority of the Divine precepts but their excellency too. It sets too its seal that "the Law is holy, and the Commandment holy, and just and good" (Rom. 7: 12). Nay more, it says with the apostle "I delight in the Law of God after the inward man" (Rom. 7: 22).

When the apostle declared "I consent to the Law that it is good" (Rom.7: 16) he expressed his willingness and desire to be ruled by a perfect Law. A bare assent is not sufficient: there must be a consent too—a readiness to obey. "Consent" is a mixed act, in which the judgment and the will concur. The commandments are not only received as God's, but they are highly valued and embraced as such. The more we are convinced of their excellency, the easier it is to obey them. "The Lord commanded us to do all these statutes, to fear the Lord our God, *for our good always*" (Deut. 6: 24). Satan would fain have us think God's Law is a severe and harsh one; but the Spirit assures us "His commandments are *not* grievous" (1 John 5: 4). God has made an inseparable connection between the precepts and the promises: the latter cannot benefit us if we disregard the former—our peace and happiness depend on complying with the one as much as it does with the other. Our assurance of acceptance with God cannot be greater than the diligence of our obedience: *see* 1 John 2: 4.

"Have not I commanded thee? Be strong and of a good courage, be not afraid, neither be thou dismayed". Let it be duly noted that the Divine precepts are to govern our *inner* man as well as our actions. "Behold, Thou desirest truth in the inward parts" (Psa. 51: 6). God's commands require more than external conformity, including also the state of our hearts, and the spirit in which we obey. Covetousness is as sinful as lying, anxiety as theft, despair as murder, for each is a disobeying *God*. The above command is addressed to us as truly as it was to Joshua, and so too is the promise that accompanies it: "For the Lord thy God is with thee whithersoever thou goest"— with us as "a very present help". How that should encourage us to turn the precepts into believing prayer, looking to the Lord to work in us that which He requireth, and counting upon Him to do so! Then, can we, in the fullest sense say, "I have *believed* Thy commandments".

Here then was an additional reason why the Lord should, three times over, bid Joshua "be strong and of a good courage": "it was not written (not spoken) for his sake alone. . .but for us also" (Rom. 4: 23, 24), and that is why we have spent so much time upon these particular verses. The directions given to Joshua for the conquering of Canaan and enjoyment of the promised heritage, are the instructions *we* must needs follow if success is to be ours in the warfare to which we are called. It is the "good fight of faith" in which we are to engage, and a life of faith consists first and foremost in a life of *obedience* to the Divine statutes, submitting ourselves to the authority of an invisible God, ordering our lives by the Rule He has given us. It consists in a trustful seeking of strength from Him that we may be enabled to do those things which are pleasing in His sight. It consists in a laying hold of His promises as the incentive of our task.

But a life of faith calls for a stout heart, that we may not be daunted by either the difficulties or the dangers of the way. The flesh, the world and the Devil are arrayed against us, seeking our destruction. Nor are we called upon to engage them for a season only—it is a lifelong battle. Nor can we expect to avoid hardship or escape being wounded in such a conflict. Let the young Christian realise, then, that if he is to be a good soldier of Jesus Christ" (2 Tim. 2: 3) he must "be strong and of a good courage", and faint not though the march wearies, and be not dismayed when the enemy gains an advantage over him. He may be bested in the preliminary skirmishes, he may be hard put to it to so much as hold his ground for days together, but if he "endure to the end"—and for *that* fortitude, resoluteness, perseverance, as well as trusting in the Lord, are indispensable—victory is certain.

Chapter 3

THE RESPONSE OF FAITH

Joshua 1:10-18

"Then Joshua commanded the officers of the people", giving to them their orders. Observe that he did not call a conference of the heads of the tribes to ascertain how many of them he could count upon for co-operation, nor to seek their counsel and advice. No, like the apostle, when the Lord's will was made known to him, he could say "I conferred not with flesh and blood" (Gal. 1 : 16). Nor did he, like vacillating Felix, defer the performance of duty unto "a more convenient season". There is an old but wise adage "Strike while the iron's hot": act at once in response to the convictions of conscience or the promptings of the Spirit. Or better, perform your duty immediately it is clear to you. The longer we delay, the more reluctant we are to comply with God's requirements. Delay itself is disobedience. Procrastination evidences a lack of heart for the Divine precepts and an absence of concern for the Divine glory.

It is nothing but a species of hypocrisy for me to tell myself that I am willing to obey God while I delay in doing so, for nothing hinders me but want of heart—where there's a will there's always a way. When there is an earnest bent of heart we shall not linger. When the rebuilding of the walls of Jerusalem proceeded apace we are told *"for* the people had a mind to work" (Neh. 4 : 6). Once a duty is discovered, it should be discharged. Peril attends the neglect of any acknowledged obligation. *"Then* Joshua commanded the officers of the people": he not only complied with God's order, but he did so promptly. There was no absorption with the difficulties confronting him, no inventing of excuses for the non-performing of his task, no tardiness of action, but prompt obedience. *That* is another important secret of success which each of us needs to take to heart.

"Then Joshua commanded the officers of the people". That was his response to the commission he had received: an immediate tackling of the duty nearest to hand. He could say with David, "I made haste, and delayed not, to keep Thy commandments" (119: 60). He resolved upon a course of instant obedience, and promptly put it into execution. He considered that the One who was vested with such sovereignty and power, and who had given him such blessed assurances, was worthy of being loved and served with all his heart and might. Is that the case with you? with me? "Whatsoever ye do, do it heartily, as to the Lord" (Col. 3: 23), and where there is heartiness, there will be no delay. Is it not evident then, my reader, that the readiness or tardiness of our obedience is a good index to the state of our hearts? When we stand debating instead of doing, reasoning instead of "running" (119: 32), something is seriously wrong.

Alas, how different is our obedience from our praying under the pressure of need. When at our wit's end or sorely afflicted and we cry for relief or deliverance, is not our language that of David's "Lord, hear me speedily"

46

(102: 2)? And how disappointed and fretful we are if His answer does not come swiftly. Ah, may we not perceive from what has been before us why it is that His answers are often delayed! If we be so slow in responding to His calls of duty, what right have we to expect the Holy One to be early in responding to our calls for favour? The One who has reason to ask "how long?" (Rev. 6: 10) is not myself, but God. A holy alacrity in God's service is much to be desired. "We are too often in haste to sin; O that we may be in a greater hurry to obey God" (C. H. Spurgeon). Have we not much lost time to make up?

"Then Joshua *commanded* the officers of the people". In so doing he did not act officiously, but was rightly exerting the authority with which God had endowed him. As the servant of Jehovah he was himself subject to the will of his Master, but as the leader of God's people it was both meet and necessary that he should exercise his power and control over them. Therein he has left an example which each genuine minister of the Gospel would do well to emulate. While it be true that they today do not occupy a position which is in all respects analogous to that of Joshua's, yet as those who have been called and commissioned by Christ to preach in His name (John 13: 20) and "rule over" His assemblies (Heb. 13: 17), it behoves them to conduct themselves with becoming dignity and decorum so as to command the respect of those they address.

The true minister of the Gospel is neither a pope nor a mere figure-head. He is to behave neither as a Diotrophes lording it over God's heritage, nor as a sycophant who is subservient to others. There is a happy medium between conducting himself as a blatant dictator and a servile flatterer. There are far too many preachers today who act as though they are begging their hearers to do Christ and His cause a favour, who are so apologetic, fawning and effeminate they have forfeited the respect of real men. "These things speak, and exhort, and rebuke with all *authority*. Let no man despise thee" (Titus 2: 15). "The most effectual way for ministers to secure themselves from contempt, is to keep close to the doctrine of Christ and imitate Him" (M. Henry), and He taught "as One having *authority*" (Matt. 7: 29).

"Then Joshua commanded the officers of the people, saying, Pass through the host and command the people, saying, Prepare you victuals, for within three days ye shall pass over this Jordan, to go in to possess the land which the Lord your God giveth you to possess" (1: 10, 11). It is striking to note the iteration of this word "commanded". First, the Lord declared unto Joshua "Have not I commanded thee!" (v. 9), then he commanded his officers, and they in turn commanded the people: the exercise of Divinely-given authority and the requirement of implicit obedience was essential if success was to be theirs. And those two things are indispensable today if we would have the Lord show Himself strong on our behalf. If the minister of the Gospel be required to "exhort and rebuke with all authority" (Titus 2: 15), those committed to his care are bidden "obey them that have the rule over you" (Heb. 13: 17). God requires from His people a subjection to the ministerial office, as truly as he does to the magisterial in the civil realm (Rom. 13) and to the husband and parent in the domestic (Eph. 5: 22; 6: 1). Discipline must be maintained in the house of God.

"Prepare you victuals". A journey lay ahead, a strenuous campaign was before them, but the one thing enjoined by way of aniticipation was "prepare you victuals". The spiritual significance and application of that unto ourselves is obvious. If we would be strong and stouthearted, and therefore eqip-

ped for our warfare, we must be well fed—nourished up in the words of faith"
(1 Tim. 4 : 6). The "victuals" are furnished us by God, but *we* must "prepare"
them. At no point does God encourage slothfulness. Unless we give good
heed to this injunction we shall not be able to overcome our foes. That word
is addressed as directly to us today as it was unto Israel in the time of Joshua.
We are guilty of flagrant dishonesty if we appropriate to ourselves the promises
"I will not fail thee nor forsake thee. . .The Lord thy God is with thee whithersoever thou goest" (vv. 5, 9), and disregard the precepts "Observe to do according to all that is written. . .meditate therein day and night. . .be strong
and of a good courage. . .prepare you victuals".

   "Prepare you victuals, for within three days ye shall pass over this Jordan"
One had naturally expected that order to be "Prepare you *boats*", for there was
no bridge across the river. There had been none over the Red Sea, yet Israel
had crossed it safely, dryshod, and that without recourse to boats or rafts. As
M. Henry pointed out "He that brought them out of Egypt on eagle's wings,
would in like manner bear them into Canaan". Such was evidently Joshua's
expectation on this occasion. He was fully assured that if he and those under
him rendered obedience to the Divine Will they could count upon God's help:
hence his contemptuous "*this* Jordan"—it would present no difficulty to Omnipotence, nor need it dismay them. "In three days ye shall pass over this Jordan: not "ye may", nor "ye shall attempt to do so": it was the language of
full confidence—not in them, nor in himself, but in the living God. Such must
be the spirit of those who feed and lead God's people today, otherwise they will
depress rather than hearten.

   There is an important typical and spiritual truth contained in that "three
days": it is the number of resurrection. It is only as the Christian conducts
himself as one who is risen with Christ that he can overcome the flesh, the world
and the Devil, and that requires two things from him: the exercise of faith and
of obedience. Faith seeing myself as God sees me, faith viewing myself as one
with Christ in His death and resurrection, faith appropriating His victory over
sin, death and Satan. "Reckon ye also yourselves to be dead indeed unto sin,
but alive unto God in Jesus Christ our Lord" (Rom. 6: 11). That is the
"reckoning" of faith, for feelings have nothing whatever to do with it. It is
taking our stand on the infallible Word of God, irrespective of our conscious
"experience". In the reckoning of the Divine Law the one who trustfully
commits his soul unto Christ has "passed from death unto life", and faith is
to accept that blessed truth on the bare but all-sufficient authority of God.
The believer is legally and vitally united to a risen and triumphant Saviour.

   What has just been pointed out is of first importance. There can be no
real peace for the conscience, no substantial rest of soul, no lasting joy of heart,
until the Christian is assured on the authority of Him who cannot lie that "our
old man is (Gk. "was") crucified with Him" (Rom. 6: 6) and that we are
"risen with Christ" (Col. 3: 1). The believer cannot *walk* on resurrection
ground until it is a settled and glorious fact in his mind that he is *on* resurrection
ground, legally one with his risen Surety, rejoicing that "there is therefore now
no condemnation to them that are in Christ Jesus"; yea glorying in the fact
that the righteousness of Christ has been imputed to his account. When that
is received by faith then "the joy of the Lord is my strength". I cannot
possibly go forward and "fight the good fight of faith" nor expect any success
in overcoming the Canaanites, so long as I doubt my acceptance before God and
fail to realise my union with Christ. That is foundational, and we repeat,
feelings have nothing whatever to do with it.

But something more than the exercise of faith—resting on the declarations of Holy Writ—is required if I am to enter experimentally and practically into the good of my being legally one with Christ, and that is, the rendering of obedience to Him. "He died for all (His people), that they which live (legally) should not henceforth live (practically) unto themselves, but unto Him which died for them and rose again" (2 Cor. 5: 15). "But now we are delivered from (the curse of) the Law, being dead to that wherein we were held, that we should serve in newness of spirit" (Rom. 7: 4)—from a spirit of gratitude and joy. Henceforth the Christian is to "walk in newness of life" (Rom. 6: 4): a new principle is to actuate him—love; a new design is to regulate him—honouring his Master. The self-will which dominated him while unregenerate is to be displaced by seeking to please Christ in all things. *That* is to "walk in newness of life", on resurrection ground.

The antitypical Canaan is ours. It is the "purchased possession", bought by Christ s precious blood. That inheritance is to be enjoyed *now*: by faith, by hope, by fixing our affection upon things above. As we do so, we experimentally "possess our possessions". "The upright shall have good things in possession" (Prov. 28: 10)—not merely in prospect, but in actual possession. But there are powerful foes seeking to keep us from enjoying our heritage! True, but we may obtain victory over them, as Israel did over theirs. We may, we shall, in proportion as faith is in exercise and as we walk obediently. Note the precision and meaning of Joshua s language: "to go in to possess the land which the Lord your God *giveth* you to possess it" (v. 11). God had given Canaan in promise long before (v. 3), but that promise was to be realised by *that* generation according as they submitted themselves to Him. So it is with us: God will give us a present possession if we meet His requirements.

The Lord God had sworn unto their fathers "to give them" the land of Canaan (v. 6), yet that did not preclude strenuous efforts on their part. Hitherto He had furnished them with manna, for there was nothing in the wilderness they could live upon; but now His command was "prepare you victuals", and that was indicative of what was required from *them*—they must discharge their responsibility. The Lord never panders to laziness: it is the one who is out and out for Him who enjoys most of His smile. A protracted conflict had to be waged, and success there in was made dependent upon their implicit compliance with God's orders through Joshua: only thus would He give the land into their possession. That is the central message of this book: unreserved obedience as the condition of God s putting forth His power against our enemies and bringing us into the enjoyment of our inheritance.

"And to the Reubenites, and to the Gadites and to half the tribe of Manasseh, spake Joshua, saying, Remember the word which Moses the servant of the Lord commanded you (12, 13). The reference is to what is recorded in Num. 32. Upon Israel's conquest of the kingdoms of the Amorites and Bashan (v. 33), the two and a half tribes, who had "a very great multitude of cattle" (v. 1), came to Moses and asked "let this portion be given unto thy servants for a possession, and bring us not over Jordan" (v. 5). At first he was very displeased, regarding their request as proceeding from unbelief and from an unwillingness to bear their share in the fighting which lay ahead. But being assured that on permission being granted them to build sheepfolds for their cattle and dwellings for their children, their men-folk would accompany the other tribes and fight with them until Canaan was conquered (vv. 16-19), Moses consented to their proposal (vv. 20-24).

If careful attention be paid to Moses' words on that occasion we see how that incident supplied a striking illustration of what is dominant in this book. Num. 32: 33 says "he *gave* unto them" that portion of country, yet it was not an absolute grant but a provisional one, which turned upon the faithful discharge of their responsibility. If the reader does not like the sound of that statement, if it clashes with his "belief", let him pay extra diligence to what follows, and if needs be *correct* his "beliefs". "Moses said unto them, *If* ye will *do* this thing, if ye will go armed before the Lord to war. . .until the land be subdued before the Lord, *then* afterward ye shall return (to your side of the Jordan) and be guiltless before the Lord and before Israel; and this land *shall be* your possession before the Lord" (vv. 20-22). They agreed: "thy servants will do as my lord commandeth" (v. 25).

Then we are told, "So concerning them Moses commanded Eleazar the priest and Joshua the son of Nun" (v. 28). Accordingly, now that Moses was dead and the Lord's time had come for Israel to enter Canaan, Joshua said unto those two and a half tribes "Remember the word which Moses the servant of the Lord commanded you". In so doing he complied with his commission, for Jehovah had bidden him "observe to do according to all the Law which Moses My servant commanded thee" (v. 7), and this was one of those things (Num. 32: 28)! It was not natural prudence or a spirit of expediency which actuated Joshua to seek their co-operation, still less was it from fear that the remaining tribes would be insufficient for the task confronting them, but obedience to his Master which regulated his action.

Joshua did not take it for granted that the two and a half tribes would now carry out their agreement, but definitely reminded them of the same and held them to it. But note *how* he did so. He did not beg for their compliance as a favour unto himself—I hope you will be willing to serve under *me*. Nor did he appeal on behalf of their brethren—the other tribes will be encouraged if you are willing to help them. Nor did he bid them remember their promise to Moses. No, he pressed upon them the *Word* of God! That is another lesson for the servants of God to heed today: if we would honour Him, we must honour His Word, by enforcing its requirements. "God now *commandeth* all men everywhere to repent" should be their language to the unsaved.

"Remember the word which Moses the servant of the Lord commanded you, saying, The Lord hath given you rest and hath given you this land. Your wives, your little ones and your cattle shall remain in the land. . .but ye shall pass before your brethren armed, all the mighty men of valour, and help them. Until the Lord hath given your brethren rest, as He hath given you, and they also have possessed the land which the Lord your God giveth them; then ye shall return unto the land of your possessions and enjoy it" (vv. 13-15). There are a number of things here on which we can but briefly touch. That word "remember" signifies *heed*, and is invariably a call to obedience. The fact that their portion had *already* been "given", placed an additional obligation on them—gratitude demanded their compliance. As M. Henry reminds us "when God by His providence has given us rest, we ought to consider how we may honour Him with the advantages of it, and what service we may do to our brethren"

Once again we would call attention to the truth here exemplified: we cannot enter into our inheritance without fighting. See how the two aspects combine: the eastern country of the Jordan had already been allotted and given to the two and a half tribes, but *they* must now bear their share in the conquest of Canaan. Nay, they must take the lead in the fighting: "ye shall pass before your brethren armed"—they were to form the 'spearhead' of Israel's army. See the meetness and justice of that arrangement: they had obtained their inheritance *before* any of their brethren, and so they must be in the van. And thus it came to pass: when the Jordan was crossed the two and a half tribes "passed over armed before the children of'Israel, as Moses spake to them" (4: 12). Observe it was "the mighty men of valour" who did so—there were no women in the 'forces'!

"And they answered Joshua saying, All that thou commandest us we will do, and whithersoever thou sendest us we will go. According as we hearkened unto Moses in all things, so will we hearken unto thee: only the Lord thy God be with thee, as He was with Moses" (vv. 16, 17). If we wrote a separate article on these verses, we should entitle it "Joshua's encouragement" and dwell upon the relation between this incident and that which precedes. It is ever God's way to honour those who honour Him. Joshua had promptly complied with his commission and had magnified God's Word, and now He moved those two and a half tribes to willingly serve under him. In his words "Until the Lord have given your brethren rest. . .and they also have possessed the land" (v. 15), he had spoken in unwavering faith as to the outcome, and now the Lord graciously inclined these men to fully co-operate with him.

Those two and a half tribes might have pleaded that their agreement had been made with *Moses*, and that since death cancels all contracts, his decease released them from their engagement. But instead, they averred their unqualified readiness to accept Joshua as their leader and yield to his authority. Their promise to him went beyond what they had pledged unto Moses. Joshua had received the assurance "Be not afraid neither be thou dismayed, for the Lord thy God is with thee whithersoever thou goest" (v. 9), and in His moving those two and a half tribes to loyal subjection unto Joshua, He gave the initial manifestation and earnest of His fulfilment of the same. Their promise to Joshua on this occasion was no idle boast, for as 22: 1-6 shows, they faithfully kept their word. "Only the Lord be with thee, as He was with Moses" (v.17) should be regarded as their prayer for him.

"Whosoever he be that doth rebel against thy commandment, and will not hearken unto thy words in all that thou commandest him, he shall be put to death: only be strong and of a good courage" (v. 18). They suggested that this military edict should be enacted in order to prevent cowardice and disloyalty on the part of others in the army, implying their readiness to co-operate in the enforcing of the same. It is probable that they had in mind the Lord's word unto Moses, "I will raise them up a prophet from among their brethren like unto thee, and will put My words in his mouth, and he shall speak unto them all that I shall command him. And it shall come to pass that whosoever will not hearken unto My words which he shall speak in My Name, I will *require it of him*" (Deut. 18: 18, 19). We know that prophecy received its ultimate fulfilment in Christ, but Joshua was a type of Him. "Only be thou strong and of a good courage" was tantamount to their declaring " We, for our part, will do nothing to weaken thy hands, but on the contrary will do all in our power to make thy lot easier!" Such should ever be the attitude of the Christian unto both magistrates and the ministers of the Gospel.

Chapter 4

A SCARLET CORD

JOSHUA 2:1-24

The Spies

In the second half of chap. 1, the Holy Spirit has recorded the response made by Joshua unto the great commission he had received from the Lord: he complied promptly, he conducted himself according to the Divine Rule, and he acted in faith. The command he issued to his officers (v. 11) showed he had no doubt whatever that the Jordan would be crossed, and his words to the two and a half tribes (v. 15) evinced his full confidence in the Lord's help for the whole campaign. Such language had been both honouring to God and encouraging to His people. We have already seen how the Lord rewarded His servant by constraining the two and a half tribes to accept Joshua as their leader and yield full obedience unto his authority. Those things are recorded for *our* instruction and encouragement: to show that none are ever the losers by trusting in the Lord and rendering obedience to His Word. In what is now to engage our attention we have a further proof of the Lord showing Himself strong on behalf of the dutiful.

The land which Joshua was called upon to conquer was occupied by a fierce, powerful and ungodly people. Humanly speaking, there was no reason to conclude that the Canaanites would render assistance or do ought to make his task easier: rather to the contrary, as the attitude and actions of the kings had shown (Num. 21: 1, 23, 33). When he sent forth the two spies to obtain information about Jericho, he could not naturally expect that any of its inhabitants would render them any help in their difficult task. Yet that is exactly what happened, for those spies received remarkable favour in the eyes of her in whose house they obtained lodgment. Not only was she kindly disposed toward them, but she even hazarded her own life on their behalf. What an illustration was this that "When a man's ways please the Lord, He maketh even his enemies to be at peace with him" (Prov. 16: 7)! Those two men were in the path of duty, carrying out the orders of God's servant, and He undertook for them.

"And Joshua the son of Nun sent out of Shittim two men to spy secretly, saying, Go view the land, even Jericho. And they went, and came into a harlot's house, named Rahab, and lodged there" (2: 1). For some time past the children of Israel had been encamped in the plains of Shittim, which bordered on the Jordan and lay opposite Jericho (Num. 33: 49). And now Joshua sent forth these two spies to obtain information about this enemy stronghold which lay in their path of advance. In so doing, Joshua has been severely criticised by some, who regarded him as here acting according to a carnal policy, that was dictated by unbelief. They argue that he should have trusted the Lord wholly, and that had he done so, he had relied upon Him *alone*, instead of resorting to this device. We do not agree with these faultfinders, for we consider their criticism is entirely unwarranted, arises from their own confusion of mind, and is a most mischievous one.

In the first place, Joshua had a good precedent for acting as he did, for Moses had sent forth spies to view Canaan on a former occasion (Num. 13) and Joshua had been Divinely ordered to regulate his conduct by "this Book of the Law . . . to do according to all that is written therein" (1: 7, 8), and *that* was one of the things recorded therein! But there are those who say that the suggestion to send forth those first spies proceeded from the unbelief of those who proffered it, and that Moses failed to detect their evil motive. That is indeed the view taken by most writers on the subject: but there is nothing whatever in the Word to support it. Moses declared "the saying pleased me well" (Deut. 1: 23), and he made no apology later for his action. The exercise of unbelief appeared in *the sequel*: it was the gloomy report of ten of the spies which expressed unbelief, and the ready credence of that report by the faithless congregation.

Not only is Scripture silent upon any unbelief prompting the sending forth of those twelve spies, but Num. 13: 1, 2 expressly informs us, "And the Lord spake unto Moses saying, Send thou men, that they may search the land of Canaan"! Nor is there the slightest indication that that was a concession on the Lord's part, or His giving up the people unto their hearts' lusts. Joshua, then, had a good precedent, and a written example to guide him in the sending forth of the two spies. Yet, even had there been neither, so far from his action being reprehensible, it was the exercise of wise prudence and the use of legitimate means. It was his duty to 'look before he leaped': to ascertain the lay-out of Jericho, to discover if there was a weak spot in its defenses to learn the best point at which to attack, and make his plans accordingly. In so doing, he was but discharging his responsibility.

There is much misunderstanding to-day about the scope of those words "Trust in the Lord with all thine heart, and lean not unto thine own understanding" (Prov. 3: 5), and only too often fanaticism is confounded with faith. It needs to be clearly insisted upon that the exercise of faith does not preclude the use of all legitimate means, though we are not to rest in the means alone, but rather count upon God's blessing the same. To decline the locking of my doors and the fastening of my windows when there is an epidemic of burglary in the neighbourhood, or to retire for the night and leave a roaring fire in the grate, under the pretext of counting upon God's protecting my property, is not trusting but *tempting* Him: should any disagree with that statement, let him carefully ponder Matt. 4: 6, 7! Faith in God does not preclude the discharge of my performance of duty, both in taking precautions against danger or using proper means for success.

Joshua was no more actuated by unbelief in sending forth those spies than Cromwell was when he bade his men "Trust in God, and keep your powder dry". Faith does not release us from our natural obligations. As yet, Joshua knew not that the Lord had purposed that Jericho would fall without Israel having to fight for it. It was some time later when He revealed to His servant that this stronghold of the Canaanites would be overthrown without Israel's army making any direct assault upon it. The secret will of God was in nowise the Rule for Joshua to order his actions by: he was to do according to all that was "written" in the Scriptures; and thus it is for us: our responsibility is measured by the Word, not by God's decrees, nor the inward promptings of His Spirit. As Israel's leader, it was Joshua's duty to learn all he could about Jericho and its surroundings before he advanced upon it—Luke 14: 31 illustrates the principle for which we are here contending.

"And Joshua the son of Nun sent out of Shittim two men to spy secretly, saying, Go view the land, even Jericho. And they went". In view of his own earlier experience (Num. 13), there is good reason to believe that Joshua made a careful selection on this occasion and chose men of faith, courage and prudence. We are therefore justified in concluding that ere those spies set out on their dangerous venture, they first sought unto the Lord, committed themselves and their cause into His hands, and asked Him to graciously give them success in the same. If such were the case, and it would be uncharitable to suppose otherwise, then they received fulfilment of that promise "It shall come to pass that before they call I will answer, and while they are yet speaking I will hear" (Isa. 65: 24). Ere those two men set out on their mission, the Lord had gone before them, preparing their way, by raising up a brave and staunch friend in the person of her in whose house they took refuge. How often has the writer—and probably the reader too—met with just such a blessed experience!

"And they went and came into a harlot's house, named Rahab, and lodged there". They were Divinely directed to that particular house, though it is not likely they were personally conscious of the fact at the first. God's providence acts silently and secretly, by working in us "both to will and to do of His good pleasure" (Phil. 2: 13). Those spies acted quite freely, by their own volition, yet their steps were "ordered by the Lord" (Psa. 37: 23). The house in which they sheltered was owned by a harlot, named Rahab: not that she was still plying her evil trade, but that formerly she had been a woman of ill fame, the stigma of which still clung to her. As M. Henry pointed out, "Simon the leper (Matt. 26: 5) though cleansed from his leprosy, wore the reproach of it in his name as long as he lived: so 'Rahab the harlot', and she is so called in the New Testament, where both her faith and her good works are praised".

"And it was told the king of Jericho, saying, Behold, there came men in hither tonight of the children of Israel to search out the country" (v. 2). Since it must have been known unto all in Jericho that the hosts of Israel had been encamped for some months on the opposite side of the Jordan, a keen watch had doubtless been kept on all their movements, and the entry of the two spies had therefore been observed. Even when we have committed ourselves and our cause unto God, and are in the path of duty, we have no right to expect that we shall be exempted from trials, and that all will be smooth sailing. So long as Christians are left in a world which lieth in the Wicked one (1 John 5: 19), and is therefore hostile unto true godliness, they may look for opposition. Why so? why does God permit such? that their graces may be tested and developed, evidencing whether they be real or fancied; and if the former, bringing forth fruit to the glory of their Author.

Had He so pleased, the Lord could have prevented the discovery of those spies in Jericho. Had He not done so in the case of the twelve men sent forth by Moses? From Num. 13 it appears that they made an extensive survey of Canaan, and returned to report unto Israel without their enemies being aware of what had occurred. But God does not act uniformly, varying His methods as seems best in His sight. That not only exemplifies His own sovereignty, but keeps us in more complete dependence upon Him, not knowing whether His interposition on our behalf will come in one way or in another, from this direction or from that. No, even though those two men were under His immediate guidance and protection, He permitted their entry into Jericho to become known. Nor were they the losers by that: instead, they were granted a manifestation of God's power to deliver them from a horrible death.

In more than one respect is it true that "the children of this world are in their generation wiser than the children of light" (Luke 16: 8): a case in point is here before us. Does not the wise precaution taken by these Canaanites put most of us to shame! Are not the wicked much keener in looking after their interests than the righteous are? Are not unbelievers much more on the alert against what would be disastrous to their prospects than the saints are? The Christian ought ever to be on his guard, watching for the approach of any enemy. But is he? Alas, no; and that is why Satan so often succeeds in gaining an advantage over him. It was while men slept that Satan sowed his tares (Matt. 13: 25), and it is when we become slack and careless that the Devil trips us up. We must "watch" as well as "pray" if we would not "enter into temptation" (Matt. 26: 41). Let those who have access to Bunyan's works read his "Holy War".

There is yet another line of truth which is illustrated here, and which we do well to heed. A careful and constant watch—by "night" as well as by day! —had evidently been set, yet notwithstanding the same, the two spies succeeded in obtaining an entrance into Jericho! "Except the Lord keep the city, the watchmen waketh but in vain" (Psa. 127: 1) was strikingly exemplified on this occasion. And what is the spiritual application of that unto *us*?—this should ever be what exercises our hearts as we read and ponder God's Word. Is not the answer found in the verse just quoted above: since watchfulness as well as prayer be necessary if we are to avoid temptation, equally indispensable is prayerfulness as well as watchfulness. No matter how alert and vigilant *we* be, unless *God's* assistance be humbly, earnestly, and trustfully sought, all our efforts will be in vain. "Commit thy way unto the Lord, *trust also in Him*, and He shall bring it to pass" (Psa. 37: 5).

Viewing this detail from a higher standpoint may we not also see here a demonstration, of that truth "There are many devices in a man's heart, nevertheless the counsel of the Lord *that* shall stand" (Prov. 19: 21). It was so here: the king of Jericho proposed, but God disposed. He determined to prevent any Israelite from entering his city, but his well-laid plans came to naught. When the Lord sets before us an open door, none can shut it. (Rev. 3: 8), and *He* set before those two spies an open door into Jericho, and it was utterly futile for any man to endeavour to keep them out. Equally true is it that when the Lord "shutteth no man openeth" (Rev. 3: 7), yet God Himself can do so: therefore it is the privilege and duty of His servant never to accept defeat, but seek the prayers of God's people that He would "open to him a door of utterance, to speak the mystery of Christ" (Col. 4: 3).

"And the king of Jericho spake unto Rahab, saying, Bring forth the men that are come to thee, which are entered into thine house; for they be come to search out all the country" (v. 3). If the reader has not already formed the habit of so doing, let him now begin to read such a passage as the one we are considering with the specific object of trying to find something in each verse of practical importance to *himself*—not that which is "deep" and intricate, but what lies on the surface and is obvious to a *thoughtful* reader. Here we may learn an important and needful "lesson" from the action of the king of Jericho. When he was informed that Israel's spies were now in the city, he did not treat the report with either contemptuous scorn or careless unconcern, but believed the same and acted promptly upon it. Well for us if we heed a timely warning and seek to nip a danger while it is still in the bud. If we do not heed the first alarms of conscience, but instead, trifle with temptation, a fall is sure to follow; and the allowance of one sin leads to the formation of an evil habit.

Changing our angle of meditation, let us contemplate the effect upon the two spies of the demand made upon Rahab by the king's officers. If she complied with their peremptory order and delivered her guests into their hands, then—humanly speaking—they could hope for no other treatment than what has always been meted out unto captured spies. Imagine the state of their minds as they listened intently—which doubtless they did—to that ominous command. Remember they were men of like passions unto ourselves: would they not, then, be filled with perturbation and consternation? Up to this point things had gone smoothly for them, but now all seemed lost. Would they not ask themselves, Did we do the right thing after all in taking shelter in this house? Ah, have we not too passed through some similar experience? We entered upon what we believed was a certain course of duty, committed the same unto God and sought His blessing. At first all went well, His smile appeared to be upon us, and then a crisis occurred which seemed to spell sure defeat. Faith must be tested, patience have her perfect work.

Rahab's Defiance

"And the king of Jericho sent unto Rahab, saying, Bring forth the men that are come to thee, which are entered into thine house: for they be come to search out all the country. And the woman took ("had taken") the two men and hid them, and said thus, There came men unto me, but I wist not whence they were. And it came to pass about the time of the shutting of the gate, when it was dark that the men went out: whither the men went, I wot not; pursue after them quickly, for ye shall overtake them" (2: 3-5). This passage has presented some formidable difficulties to not a few of those who have carefully pondered it, and perhaps we can best help our readers by seeking to answer the following questions. First, did Rahab do right in defying the king's authority and betraying her own country? Second, is she to be exonerated in the untruths she here told? Third, if not, how is Heb. 11: 31 to be explained?

"Let every soul be subject unto the powers that be, for there is no power but of God" (Rom. 13: 1). God requires us to render submission to human government: to be obedient to its laws, to pay the taxes it appoints, to cooperate in upholding its authority. Christians especially should set an example as law-abiding citizens, rendering to Caesar that which he has a right to demand from his subjects. Jeremiah 29: 7 makes it clear that it is the duty of God's people to seek the good of the country in which they reside—see the sermon by Andrew Fuller on "Christian Patriotism" which appeared in these pages a year ago. There is but one qualification, namely, when the powers that be require anything from me which is obviously contrary to the revealed will of God, or prohibit my doing what His Word enjoins: where such a case arises, my duty is to render allegiance unto God and not unto any subordinate authority which repudiates His requirements.

The refusal of the three Hebrew captives to worship Nebuchadnezzar's image and Daniel's defiance of the decree of Darius which forbade him praying unto God, are cases in point (Dan. 3: 18, 6: 10). We must never render to Caesar that to which God alone is entitled. "Fear God; honour the king" (1 Pet. 2: 17) indicates our relative obligations: God must be feared at all costs; the king is to be cheerfully and universally honoured so far as that consists with my fearing God. When the religious powers forbade the apostles to preach in Christ's name, they replied "We ought to obey God rather than man" (Acts 5: 29). It was thus with Rahab: there was a clash of interests: loyalty to her king and country, loyalty to God and His servants. In the kind providence of God such a dilemma is rarely presented to a saint today, but if it were, the lower authority must yield to the higher.

It is indeed the duty of a saint to seek the good of that country which affords him both shelter and subsistence, nevertheless he is bound to love God and His people more than his country and fellow-citizens. He owes fidelity to the Lord first, and then to the place he lives in; and he is to promote the welfare of the latter so far as it is compatible with the former. In seeking to estimate the conduct of Rahab, we must carefully weigh Heb. 11: 31, James 2: 25, and especially Josh. 2: 9-11. From her language it is manifest that she was fully convinced the Lord had purposed the destruction of the Canaanites, and therefore she must either side with Him and His people against her country, or enter into a 'hopeless contest against the Almighty and perish under His judgments. By her actions she exemplified what God requires from every truly converted soul; to renounce allegiance with His enemies—however closely related (Luke 14: 26)—and refuse to join with them in opposing His people.

As one who had received mercy from the Lord—for Heb. 11: 31 evidences that sovereign grace had brought her out of darkness into God's marvellous light before Joshua sent those men to reconnoitre—and as one who knew Jehovah had given the land of Canaan unto Israel, it was plainly the duty of Rahab to do all in her power to protect these Israelish spies, even at risk to her own safety. That principle is clearly enunciated in the N. T.: "we ought to lay down our lives for the brethren" (1 John 3: 16). But now the question arises, in view of that being her duty, was Rahab warranted in resorting to falsehoods so as to protect the two men she had given shelter to? Different opinions have been formed of her conduct, and various arguments employed in the attempt to vindicate her. Some of the best commentators, even among the Puritans, pleaded she was guiltless in this matter, and we know of none who plainly stated that she sinned therein.

One of the most difficult tasks which confronts a Christian writer is that of commenting on the offences of God's dear people: that on the one hand he may not dip his pen in the pharisaic ink of self-superiority, and that on the other hand he does not make light of any evil or condone what is reprehensible. He is himself compassed with infirmity and a daily transgressor of God's law, and should be duly affected by a realisation of the same when dealing with the faults of his fellows. Nevertheless, if he be a servant of God, preaching or writing to the saints, then he must remember that "it is required in stewards that a man be found faithful" (1 Cor. 4: 2), and he is most certainly unfaithful if—even from a desire to be charitable—he deliberately lowers God's standard of holiness, minimizes that which contravenes it, or glosses over anything which is culpable. Much grace and wisdom is needed if he is to act in both a spirit of meekness and righteousness, of compassion and fidelity.

It is one of the many evidences of the Divine inspiration of the Scriptures that their Author has painted the conduct of the most eminent characters portrayed therein in the colours of reality and truth. Unlike human biographies, which almost always present a one-sided view—setting forth and extolling the virtues of its subjects and ignoring or toning down their vices—the Holy

Spirit has not concealed the blemishes of the most distinguished saints: the lapses of Noah, Abram, Moses, David being faithfully chronicled. It is true that their sins are not mentioned in the N. T., for the sufficient and blessed reason they were all under the atoning blood of the Lamb; nevertheless, the record of them remains on the pages of the O. T.—left there as a lasting warning unto *us*. Moreover, it is to be borne in mind that the sins of N. T. saints are not to be ignored but to guide those whose task it is to comment thereon.

The prevarications of Rahab unto the king's officers is appealed to by the Jesuits in support of their pernicious dogma "The end justifies the means", that if we aim at a praiseworthy object it is permissible to use questionable or even evil means to attain the same—a principle which has regulated many so-called "Protestants" during the past century, and which is flagrantly flouted before our eyes today throughout Christendom, as seen for example, in the carnal and worldly devices used to attract young people to "religious" services. But "let us do evil that good may come" is a sentiment entertained by no truly regenerate soul, rather is it detested by him; and Scripture plainly declares of such as are actuated by it, that their "damnation is just" (Rom. 3: 8). Bellarmine, the infamous champion of Popery, boldly declared in his work on "The Pontifice" that "If the Pope should err in commending vice or forbidding virtue, the Church is bound to believe vice to be good and virtue to be bad" (Book 4, chap. 5).

Some have pointed out the exceptionally trying position in which Rahab found herself, arguing that considerable latitude should be allowed her therein. We are aware that appeal is often made to that aphorism "Circumstances alter cases", and while we are not sure what its originator had in mind, this we do know, that no "circumstances" can ever obliterate the fundamental distinction between good and evil. Let the reader settle it in his mind and conscience that it is *never* right to do wrong and since it be sinful to lie, no circumstances can ever warrant the telling of one. It is indeed true that all transgressions of the Divine Law are not equally heinous in themselves nor in the sight of God: that some sins are, by reason of certain aggravations, greater than others, even of the same species. Thus, a lie unto God is worse than a lie unto a fellow-creature (Acts 5: 4), a premeditated and presumptuous lie is viler than one uttered upon a surprise by temptation.

It is also true that attendant circumstances should be taken into account when seeking to determine the *degree* of criminality: it would be a far graver offence for writer or reader to utter falsehoods than it was for Rahab, for we should be sinning against greater privileges and light than she enjoyed. She had been reared in heathendom: yet while that mitigated her offence, it certainly did not excuse her. One preacher who occupied a prominent pulpit in London asked the question, "Was Rahab justified in those falsehoods?" and answered in the affirmative, arguing "She must either utter them or else betray the spies, and their lives would have been lost". But that is the reasoning of unbelief, for it leaves out *God*. Had Rahab remained silent before the king's officers, declining to give any information, or had she acknowledged that the spies were on her premises, was the Lord unable to protect them?

We much prefer the brief remarks of Thos. Ridgley's to those of his contemporaries. "She would have been much clearer from the guilt of sin had she refused to give the messengers any answer relating to them, and so had given them leave to search for them, and left the event hereof to Providence". Undoubtedly Rahab was placed in a most trying situation, for as Ridgley went on to point out, "This, indeed, was a very difficult duty, for it might have endangered her life; and her choice to secure them and herself by inventing this lie, brought with it a degree of guilt, and was an instance of the weakness of her faith in this respect". That last clause brings us to the heart of the matter: she failed to fully trust the Lord, and the fear of man brought a snare. He whose angels had smitten the men of Sodom with blindness (Gen. 19: 11) and who had slain the fifty men sent to lay hands on His prophet (2 Kings 1: 9-12), could have prevented those officers finding the spies.

Some have gone even farther than exonerating Rahab, insisting that God Himself *approved* of her lies, appealing to Heb. 11: 31 and James 2: 25 in support. But there is nothing whatever in either of those verses which intimates that the Lord sanctioned her falsehoods. Heb. 11: 31 says nothing more about this incident than that "she had received the spies with peace". James points out that the faith of Rahab was "justified by works"—*not* by her "words"—and then specified *which* "works", namely, her receiving of the messengers and her sending them out another way. But, it may be asked, Did not the workings of providence in the sequel go to show God approved of Rahab's policy? did He not give success to the same? Answer, His providences are no Rule for us to walk by or reason from: though water flowed from the rock which Moses smote in his anger, yet that was no proof God approved of His servant's display of temper. God indeed graciously overruled Rahab's conduct, yet that did not vindicate her.

We frankly acknowledge—though to our shame, that were we placed in a similar situation to the one which confronted Rahab and God should leave us to ourself, we would acquit ourself no better than she did, and probably far worse. Yet that acknowledgement by no means clears her, for two wrongs do not make one right. If God's restraining hand be removed or His all-sufficient grace be withheld, the strongest of us is as weak as water. Therefore none is in any position to point the finger of scorn or throw a stone at her. As Manton tersely summed up the case "Her lie was an infirmity, pardoned by God, and not to be exaggerated by men". It should be remembered that Rahab had only recently been brought to a saving acquaintance with the Lord. Many young converts have but little clear knowledge of the Truth and therefore less should be expected from them than mature saints: they make many mistakes, yet they have a teachable spirit, and as light increases their walk is more and more regulated by the same.

In closing, let us point out one or two lessons which may be learned from what has been before us. First, we may see therein the refutation of a popular and widespread error, namely, that if our motives be right the action is a praiseworthy one. It is quite true that an unworthy motive will ruin a good deed— as, for example, contributing to charity in order to obtain a reputation for benevolence, or in performing religious exercises so as to be seen and venerated by men; yet a good motive can never render an evil act a desirable one. Even though Rahab's design was to protect the lives of two of God's people, that did not render commendable the deception which she practised on the king's messengers. Four things are required to render any action a "good work" in the sight of God: it must proceed from a holy principle, be regulated by the Rule of righteousness, be done in a right spirit—of faith or love; and be performed with a right end in view—the glory of God or the good of His people.

Second, it is recorded—as in Holy Writ are all the failings and falls of the saints—as a solemn warning for us to take to heart. So far from furnishing examples for us to imitate or refuges for us to hide in, they are so many danger-signals for us to heed and turn into earnest prayer. We are men and women of like passions as they were subject to. Native depravity still remains in us as it did in them, even after regeneration. In ourselves we are no stronger than they were and no better able to resist the inclinations of the flesh. What need has each of us then, to pray "hold Thou me up, and I shall be safe" (Psa. 119: 117). And even when we are preserved from outward sins, the flesh obtrudes and defiles our best performances. It was "by faith" that Rahab received the spies with peace, and at risk to herself concealed them on her roof, yet when the officers appeared on the scene her faith failed and she resorted to lying. Our godliest deeds would damn us if they were not cleansed by the atoning blood of Christ.

Third, this incident gives real point to and reveals our deep need of crying "Lead us not into temptation, but deliver us from evil". Indeed, that seems the principal lesson to draw from it : that I may be kept from any such situation, that, conscious of my weakness, I may be preserved from such a temptation as confronted Rahab. We deem it more than a coincidence that in the very midst of preparing this article we heard—the first time in five years—from an old reader in Holland. During the last half of that time, while the enemy was occupying that country, our friend and his wife concealed three Jewesses in their home, and the last ten days before liberation actually had two German billeted with them: yet no discovery was made of their refugees. I know not what my friend had done if they had asked him point blank whether he was sheltering any Jews; but I am thankful not to be placed in such a situation myself.

Had I been in his place, I would have begged the Lord to keep from me any such interrogators and counted upon His doing so. Perhaps we may be pardoned for relating an experience—to the praise of the faithfulness of a prayer-hearing God. Some fifteen years ago when residing in Hollywood, California, we occupied a furnished bungalow. The owner was a typical Jewess, and when we gave notice of leaving she put an advertisement in the local papers and stuck up a prominent sign "To Let" at the foot of our drive. Though she knew we kept the Lord's day holy and held a small service in our room each Sabbath evening, she insisted it was her right to show over the house those who answered the advertisement. We protested strongly, but she would not heed, saying "Sunday" was always her best letting day. We then told her that our God would keep away all applicants on the coming Sabbath, which she heard with derisive scorn.

That Saturday evening my wife and I spread the matter before the Lord and begged Him to cause His angel to encamp round about us, and protect us by keeping away all intruders. During the Sabbath, which was a cloudless day, we continued seeking God's face, confident He would not put us to confusion before our landlady. Not a single caller came to look over the house, and that night we held our little meeting as usual, undisturbed!—one of those present will read these lines, though not until he does so will he know what has been related. Next day our landlady, who owned two similar bungalows, stated it was the first time in her ten years' experience of letting that she had ever failed to let on a "Sunday". Ah, my reader, God *never* fails those who trust *Him* fully. He will protect you if you confidently count upon Him. "Lead us not into temptation, but deliver us from evil".

A Harlot's Faith

Little as Joshua may have raised it, he was Divinely impelled and directed to send forth the two spies to "Go view the land, *even Jericho*" (2: 1). Why so? Because there was one of God's elect residing in that city, and none of His sheep shall perish. Unto that vessel of mercy were they led, in order that arrangements should be made for her protection, so that she "perished not with them that believed not" (Heb. 11: 31). There was then a *needs be* why those two spies should visit Jericho and converse with Rahab, not merely a miltary needs be but one far more vital and blessed. It is still another example of what we have, on several occasions, called attention to, in these pages, namely, that when God works, He always works at *both* ends of the line. As it was in the case of the Ethiopian and Philip the evangelist and of Cornelius and Peter, so it was here. Before those two men set foot in Jericho the Lord had already wrought, signally and savingly, in the heart of Rahab, and now opportunity is afforded for her to confess her faith, to receive a token for good, and to be made a blessing unto others.

The needs be for those spies entering Jericho reminds one of John 4, and there are some striking parallels between what is recorded there and the case of Rahab. First, we are told of the Lord Jesus that "He must needs go through Samaria" (v. 4). That "must" was not a geographical but a moral one. From all eternity it had been ordained that He *should* go through Samaria. There was one of God's elect there, and though she was "alienated from the commonwealth of Israel", being a Samaritan, yet she could not be ignored: "other sheep I have which are not of this fold, them also I *must* bring" (John 10: 16) declared the good Shepherd. There were those in Samaria whom the Father had given Him from before the foundation of the world, and them He *must* save. And, my reader, if you be one of God's elect, even though now unregenerate, there is a needs be put on the Lord Jesus to save *you*. For years you have been fleeing from Him, but when the appointed time arrives, He will overtake you.' You may kick against the pricks, as did Saul of Tarsus, but He will overcome your rebellion and reluctance and win you to Himself.

Second, not only was the one whom Christ was constrained to seek and save in John 4 a woman, and a Gentile, but she was one of loose moral character. Said He to her, "Thou hast had five husbands, and he whom thou now hast is not thy husband" (v. 18). Such too had been this chosen one in Jericho: defiled both in mind and body with idolatry and adultery—"Rahab the harlot". Many of God's elect, though by no means all of them, fall into gross wickedness in their unconverted days: fornicators, idolaters, thieves, drunkards, extortioners: "and *such were* some of you; but ye are washed, but ye are sanctified, but ye are justified in the name of the Lord Jesus and by the Spirit of our God" (1 Cor. 6: 9-11). How illustriously is the sovereign mercy and invincible might of God displayed in the conforming of such unto His image! "Base things of the world, and things which are despised, hath God chosen" And why so? "That no flesh should glory in His presence" (1 Cor. 1: 26-29), that His wondrous *grace* might the more clearly appear.

But grace does not leave its subjects in the condition in which it finds them. No indeed, it appears "Teaching us that, denying ungodliness and worldly lusts, we should live soberly, righteously, and godly in this present world; looking for that blessed hope and the glorious appearing of the great God and our Saviour Jesus Christ" (Titus 2: 12, 13). Saving faith is ever accompanied by evengelical repentance, which mourns over past sins and resolves to avoid a repetition of them in the future. Saving faith ever produces obedience, being fruitful in good works. Those who are the recipients of God's grace are not only grateful for their own salvation, but are concerned about the salvation of others, especially of those near and dear to them by nature. When Christ stood revealed to the Samaritan adulteress, she "went her way into the city and saith to the men, Come see a man, which told me all things that I ever did: is not this the Christ?", and "many believed on Him" (vv. 28, 29, 39). So too Rahab asked for kindness to be shown her father's house, and her whole family found deliverance (Josh. 2: 12, 18). But we are anticipating.

The case of Rahab is worthy of our closest attention, for it exemplifies and magnifies the riches of Divine mercy in many striking respects. Born and brought up in heathendom, belonging to a race that was to be exterminated, her salvation was a signal dislpay of God's dominion, who not only singles out whom He pleases to be the recipients of His favours, but is trammelled by nothing in the bestowal of them. "She was not only a Gentile, but an Amoritess, of that race and seed which in general was devoted to destruction. She was therefore an instance of God's sovereignty in dispensing with His positive laws, as it seemed good unto Him, for of His own mere pleasure He exempted her from the doom announced against all those of her original and traducion" (John Owen). Being the supreme Potentate, God is not bound by any law or consideration other than His own imperial will, and therefore does He have mercy on whom He will have mercy, and whom He will He hardens" (Rom. 9: 18).

In God's saving of Rahab and bringing her into the congregation of His people we may perceive a clear and glorious foreshadowing of the fuller scope of His eternal purpose as it is now made more plainly manifest in this N. T. era. Since Rahab was a Canaanite, she was by nature cut off from the Abrahamic stock and therefore a "stranger to the covenants of promise" (Eph. 2: 12). By her conversion and admission into the congregation of Israel she was obviously both a type and a pledge of the calling of the Gentiles and their reception into the mystical Body of Christ. Thus did coming events cast their shadows before them. In such cases as Rahab and Ruth God gave an early intimation that His redemptive purpose was not confined to a single people, but that it reaches out unto favoured individuals in all nations. Their incorporation by marriage among the Hebrews was a blessed adumbration of the "wild olive tree" being graft in and made a partaker of "the root and fatness of the (good) olive tree" (Rom. 11: 17). Such we believe is, in part at least, the typical and dispensational significance of what is here before us.

But the outstanding feature of this remarkable case is the free and discriminating grace of God toward her. Not only did Rahab belong to a heathen race, but she was a notorious profligate, and in singling her out to be the recipient of His distinguishing and saving favour God made it evident that He is no respecter of persons. By her choice she was given up to the vilest of sins, but by the Divine choice she was predestinated to be delivered from the miry pit and washed whiter than snow by the precious blood of Christ, and given a place in His own family. It is in just such cases as hers that the unmerited favour of God shines forth the more resplendently. There was nothing whatever in that poor fallen woman to commend her to God's favourable regard, but where sin had abounded grace did much more abound, bestowing upon her His unsolicited and unearned favours—the gift of eternal life (Rom. 6: 23), the gift of saving faith (Eph. 2: 8, 9), the gift of evangelical repentance (Acts 5: 31). He is indeed "the God of all grace" (1 Pet. 5: 10), and as such He is a giving and freely-conferring

God, and not one who barters and sells. His bestowments are "without money and without price", imparted to spiritual bankrupts and paupers.

Not only may we behold in Rahab's case the exercise of Divine sovereignty and the manifestation of Divine grace, but we may also pause and admire the wondrous working of God's power. This is best perceived if we take into careful consideration the virtually unparalleled element which entered into it: here the Holy Spirit wrought almost entirely apart from the ordinary means of grace. There were no Sabbaths observed in Jericho, there were no Scriptures available for reading, there were no prophets sounding forth messages from Heaven, nevertheless Rahab was quickened unto newness of life and brought unto a saving knowledge of the true God. The Lord Almighty is not restricted to the employing of certain agencies nor hindered by the lack of instruments: He deigns to use such or dispenses with them entirely as He pleases. He has but to speak, and it is done, to command, and it stands fast (Psa. 33: 9). It is to be duly noted that this woman, who had previously walked in open sin, was regenerated and converted *before* the spies came to her house: their visit simply afforded an opportunity for the avowal and public manifestation of her faith.

It is quite clear from both the Old and N. T. that Rahab was converted before the two spies first spoke to her. Her language to them was that of a believer: "I *know* that the Lord *hath* given you the land. . .the Lord your God He is God in heaven above and in earth beneath" (2: 9, 11)—yea, such assurance puts many a modern professing believer to shame. *"By faith* the harlot Rahab perished not with them that believed not, when she had received the spies with peace" (Heb. 11: 31). Summing up the whole of her conduct on that occasion, Thos. Scott pointed out, "It cannot therefore be reasonably doubted her faith had, before this, been accompanied with deep repentance of those sinful practices from which she derived the name of 'Rahab the harlot'"; with which we heartily concur. But some, who have been poisoned with the errors of dispensationalism, and others who are slaves to the mere letter and sound of the Word, are likely to object, saying *that* is a gratuitous assumption, for the word "repentance" is never found in Scripture in connection with Rahab. For their benefit we will devote another paragraph or two unto this subject.

"Repent ye and believe the Gospel" (Mark 1: 15); "Testifying both to the Jews and also to the Greeks repentance toward God and faith toward our Lord Jesus Christ" (Acts 20: 21). A contrite spirit and a heart acceptance of the Gospel are inseparably connected, so that wherever the one is mentioned the other is presupposed. For example, take the passages recording the Gospel commission: in Mark 16: 16 the emphasis is on "believing", while in Luke 24: 47 it is on "repentance"—the two together explaining the "make disciples" of Matt. 28: 19. The one cannot exist without the other: it is just as morally impossible for an impenitent heart to believe, as it is for an unbeliever to repent. There may indeed be a mental assent to the Truth unaccompanied by any brokenness of heart, as there may be natural remorse where no faith exists; but there can be no saving faith where evangelical repentance is absent. Since the faith of Rahab was a saving one, as Heb. 11 clearly shows, it must have been attended with godly sorrow for sin and reformation of life. There can be no pardon while there is no repentance (Isa. 55: 7, Luke 24: 47, Acts 3: 19) i.e. mourning over and abandoning of our evil ways.

Repentance is a change of mind: one that goes much deeper and includes far more than a mere change of opinion or creed. It is a changed mind, a new perception, an altogether different outlook on things as they previously appeared. It is the necessary effect of a new heart. Repentance consists of a radical change of mind about God, about sin, about self, about the world. Previously God was resisted, now He is owned as our rightful Lord. Previously sin was delighted in, but now it is hated and mourned over. Previously self was esteemed, but now it is abhorred. Previously we were of the world and its friendship was sought and prized, now our hearts have been divorced from the world and we regard it as an enemy. Everything is viewed with other eyes than formerly, and an entirely different estimate is formed of them. The impenitent see in Christ no beauty that they should desire Him, but a broken and contrite heart perceives that He is perfectly suited to him. Thus, while He continues to be despised by the self-righteous phariesees, He is welcomed and entertained by publicans and sinners. Repentance softens the hard soil of the soul and makes it receptive to the Gospel Seed.

Repentance necessarily leads to a change of *conduct*, for a change of mind must produce a change of action: repentance and reformation of life are inseparable. It must have been thus with Rahab: she who had been a harlot, would become chaste, and a life of wanton pleasure would give place to one of honest work. Some may deem our conclusion a 'far-fetched' one, but personally we consider that we are given a plain intimation of her changed manner of life. In Josh. 2: 6 we are told that "she brought them up to the roof of the house and hid them with the stalks of *flax*, which she *had* laid in order upon the roof". As there is not a superfluous nor meaningless word in the Scriptures, why then has the Holy Spirit specified the particular kind of straw which Rahab used to cover and conceal the two spies? Now "flax" was labouriously gathered by the industrious women, laid out on the flat roofs of the houses to dry, and was then used for spinning and weaving. The presence of a quantity of it "laid out" on Rahab's roof was an evidence she was now living a useful life.

But that is not all the presence of the "flax" tells us. If we go to the trouble of searching our concordance and comparing Scripture with Scripture, we discover something yet more praiseworthy. In the last chapter of the book of Proverbs we are supplied with a full-length portrait of "a *virtuous* woman", and one of her features is that "she seeketh wool and *flax*, and worketh willingly with her hands"! Such we are assured was now the character and occupation of this outstanding monument of mercy. Another mark of repentance is a changed esteem of and attitude toward the people of God: formerly their presence irritated, for their piety condemned us; but when the heart be changed by the operations of Divine grace, their company and communion is desired and valued. It was thus with Rahab and the two Israelites: she "received the spies with peace".(Heb. 11: 31) is the Divine testimony. It was not with reluctance and complaint that she accepted them into her abode, but with a spirit of good will, welcoming and giving them shelter. Admire then the blessed transformation which the operations of the Spirit had wrought in her character.

Let us now consider more particularly her faith. First, the *ground* of it. "Faith cometh by hearing, and hearing by the Word of God" (Rom. 10: 17). This does not mean that faith is *originated* by hearing the Word of God, any more than that the shining of the sun imparts sight to the eye. No, faith is bestowed by a sovereign act of the Spirit, and then it is instructed and nourished by the Word. As an unimpaired eye receives light from the sun and is thereby enabled to perceive objects so faith takes in the testimony of God and is regulated thereby. My acceptance of the Truth does not create faith, but makes manifest that I *have* faith, and it becomes the sure ground on which my faith rests. Unto the spies Rahab said, "I know that the Lord hath given you the land, and that your terror is fallen upon us and that all the inhabitants of the land faint because of you. For we have *heard* how the Lord dried up the water of the Red Sea for you when ye came out of Egypt; and what ye did unto the two kings of the Amorites that were on the other side, Jordan, Sihon and Og whom ye utterly destroyed. And as soon as we had *heard* these things our hearts did melt, neither did there remain any more courage in any man, because of you" (vv. 9-11).

How marked the contrast between Rahab and that generation of Israel whose carcasses fell in the wilderness! They not only "heard" of but were the actual eye-witnesses of those wonderful prodigies which Jehovah wrought on behalf of His people. They personally saw Him cleave a way for them right through the Red Sea so that they passed through it dryshod, and then His causing the waters to come together again to the drowning of Pharoah and his hosts. They beheld the solemn manifestation of His august presence on Sinai. They were the daily recipients of a supernatural supply of food from heaven, and drank of water which was made to gush from a smitten rock. But their hearts were unaffected and no faith was begotten within them. They too "heard" God's voice (Heb. 3: 5, 6) but responded not, and therefore were debarred from the promised land: "they could not enter in because of unbelief" (Heb. 3: 19). Ah, my reader, something more than the beholding of miracles or witnessing outward displays of God's power is required in order to beget faith in those who are spiritually dead, as was evidenced again in the days of Christ.

How marked the contrast too between Rahab and the rest of her compatriots! As her words in Josh. 2: 9-11 clearly indicate, *they too* heard the same reports she did of the marvels performed by the Lord's might, yet they produced no faith in them. They were indeed awestruck and terrified by the accounts of the same that reached them, so that for a season there did not remain any more courage in them; but that was all. Just as under the faithful preaching of God's servants many have been temporarily affected by announcements of the Day of Judgment and the wrath to come, but never surrendered themselves to the Lord. God declared unto Israel, "This day will I begin to put the dread of thee and the fear of thee upon the nations that are under the whole heaven, who shall hear report of thee, and shall tremble and be in anguish because of thee" (Deut. 2: 25). That was literally fulfilled in the case of the inhabitants of Jericho, yet it wrought no spiritual change in them, for they were children in whom was no faith, and they had no faith because no miracle of grace was wrought in their souls. Of itself the soundest preaching effects no spiritual change in those who hear it.

Mark the contrast: "By faith the harlot Rahab perished not with them that believed not" (Heb. 11: 31). And why? Because a sovereign God had made her to differ from them (1 Cor. 4: 7). She was blessed with "the faith of the operation of God" (Col. 2: 12). Consequently, she "heard" of the works of the Lord not merely with the outward ear, as was the case with all her fellow-citizens, but with the ear of the heart, and therefore was she affected by those tidings in a very different manner from what they were who heard but "believed not". It is clear from her words "I know that the Lord hath given you the land" that she had both heard and believed the promises which He had made to Abraham and his seed, and perceiving He was a gracious and giving God, hope had been born in her. Behold then the distinguishing favour of God unto this vessel of mercy and realise that something more than listening to the Gospel is needed to beget faith in us. "The hearing ear and the seeing eye, the Lord hath made even both of them" (Prov. 20: 12). Only those "believe the report" to whom "the arm (power) of the Lord is revealed" (Isa. 53: 1). As later with Lydia, so Rahab was one "whose heart the Lord opened that she attended unto the things which were spoken" (Acts. 16: 14).

Solemn indeed is the warning pointed by the unbelieving fellows of Rahab. So far as we are informed, they heard precisely the same report as she did. Nor did they treat those tidings with either scepticism or contempt: instead, they were deeply affected by them, being terror-stricken. The news of God's judgments upon the Egyptians, and their nearer neighbours, the Amorites, made their hearts melt as they feared it would be their turn next. If it be asked, Why did they not immediately and earnestly cry unto God for mercy, the answer—in part, at least—is supplied by Eccl. 8: 11: "Because sentence against an evil work is not executed speedily, therefore the heart of the sons of men is fully set in them to do evil". Space was given for repentance, but they repented not. A further respite was granted during the six days that the hosts of Israel marched around Jericho, but when nothing happened and those hosts returned to their camp, its inhabitants continued to harden their hearts. Thus it is with the majority of our fellows today, even of those who are temporarily alarmed under the faithful ministry of God's servants. ✓

The workings of natural fear and the stirrings of an uneasy conscience soon subside; having no spiritual root, they endure not. Only one in all that city was Divinely impressed by the account which had been received of the Lord's work in overthrowing the wicked. Ah, my reader, God's sheep have ever been few in number, though usually a great many goats have mingled with them, so that at a distance and to a superficial survey it seems as though the flock is of a considerable size. Not only few in number, but frequently isolated from each other, one here and one there, for the children of God are "scattered abroad" (John 11: 52). The experience of David was very far from being a unique one when he exclaimed "I am like a pelican of the wilderness, I am like an owl of the desert. I watch, and am as a sparrow alone upon the housetop" (Psa. 102: 6, 7). God's thoughts and ways are not as ours, being infinitely wiser and better, though only the anointed eye can perceive that. Not only is His keeping power more strikingly displayed, and glorified, by preserving a lone sheep in the midst of goats and wolves, but that solitary believer is cast back the more upon Him.

It is this very *loneliness* of the saint which serves to make manifest the genuineness of his faith. There is nothing remarkable in one believing what all his associates believe, but to have faith when surrounded by sceptics, is something noteworthy. To stand alone, to be the solitary champion of a righteous cause when all others are federated unto evil, is a rare sight. Yet such was Rahab. There were none in Jericho with whom she could have fellowship, none there to encourage her heart and strengthen her hands by their godly counsel and example: all the more opportunity for her to prove the sufficiency of Divine grace! Scan slowly the list presented in Heb. 11, and then recall the recorded circumstances of each. With whom did Abel, Enoch, Noah have spiritual communion? From what brethren did Joseph, Moses, Gideon receive any help along the way? Who were the ones who encouraged and emboldened Elijah, Daniel, Nehemiah? Then think it not strange that *you* are called to walk almost if not entirely alone, that you meet with scarcely any like-minded or any who are capable of giving you a lift along the road.

During the past six years this magazine was sent to quite a number in the different fighting forces, and without a single exception they informed us that they were circumstanced similarly to Rahab. Some were with the British, some with the Colonials, some with the Americans; some were in the navy, others in the army and air force; but one and all reported the same thing— totally cut off from contact with fellow-Christians. The "Studies" were sent to and deeply appreciated by men in both the royal and the merchant navies, but in each instance they were on different ships, surrounded by the ungodly. How easily the Lord could have gathered them together on to one ship! But He did not. And it was for their *good* that He did not, otherwise He had ordered things differently (Rom. 8: 28). Faith must be tried, to prove its worth. Nor is it a hothouse plant, which wilts and withers at the first touch of frost. No, it is hardy and sturdy, and so far from winds and rain dashing it to pieces, they are but occasions for it to become more deeply rooted and vigorous.

The isolation of Rahab appears in that utterance of her's "*I* know your terror is fallen upon *us*". They were but naturally and temporarily affected, she spiritually and permanently so. What she heard came to her soul with Divine power. And again we say, it was God who made her to differ. By nature her heart was no different from that of her companions, but having been supernaturally quickened into newness of life, she received with meekness the engrafted Word. "All men have not faith" (2 Thess. 3: 2) because all are not born again. Faith is one of the attributes and activities of that spiritual life (or nature) which is communicated at regeneration. The firm foundation for faith to rest upon is the sure Word of God, and Divine testimony: by it alone is faith supported and established. Frames and feelings have nothing whatever to do with it, nor is spiritual confidence either begotten or nourished by them. Assurance comes from implicitly receiving the Word into the heart and relying upon it. Such was the case with Rahab: "I *know* that the Lord hath given you the land. . .*for* we have *heard* how the Lord" etc. She received those tidings "not as the word of men, but as it is in truth the Word of God" (1 Thess. 2: 13). Have you done so, my reader?

Observe well how definite and confident was her language. There was no "if" or "perhaps", no dubious "I hope", but instead, a sure and positive "I know". That was the knowledge of a saving faith. It is true that faith and assurance may be distinguished, yet they can no more be separated than can faith and obedience. Faith without works is dead, and faith without assurance is something of which this writer can find no mention in Scripture. We refer, of course, to a *saving* faith. What is that faith? It is taking God at His Word, appropriating it unto myself, personally resting upon the testimony of Him who cannot lie. Now I either am doing so, or I am not. If I am, then I must be conscious of so doing, for I cannot possibly be trusting in God and relying on His promise and yet be unaware that I am so doing. Read through the N. T. epistles and nowhere is there a single passage addressed to saints who questioned their acceptance by God, but everywhere the language is "we *know*" 2 Cor. 5:1, Gal. 4: 9, Eph. 6: 9, Phil. 1: 6, Col. 3: 24, 1 Thess. 1: 4, 1 Pet. 1: 18, 19.

Rahab's faith was not only accompanied with confidence but it regulated her actions. The faith of God's elect is a living, energetic principle, which "worketh by love" (Ga.1 5: 6) and produces fruit to the glory of God. Therein it differs radically from that nominal and inoperative faith of frothy professors, which goes no deeper than a mere mental assent to the Gospel and ends in fair but empty words. That faith which is unaccompanied by an obedient walk and abounds not in good works is "dead, being alone" (James 2: 17). Different far was the faith of Rahab. Of her we read, "likewise also was not Rahab the harlot justified by works, when she had received the messengers and had sent them out another way" (James 2: 25). This does not mean that her good works was the meritorious ground of her acceptance with God, but that they were the evidence before men that a spiritual principle had been communicated to her, the fruits of which vindicated and approved her profession, demonstrating that she was a member of the household of faith. "Had she said 'I believe God is your's and Canaan is your's, but I dare not show you any kindness', her faith had been dead and inactive, and would not have justified her. . .Those only are true believers that can find in their hearts to venture for God, and take His people for their people, and cast in their lot among them" (Matt. Henry).

That is something which needs to be constantly insisted upon in this day of empty profession. A faith which does not issue in conversion is not a saving one, and conversion is a radical change of conduct, a right-about face, a reversal of our former manner of life. Saving faith necessarily involves the relinquishing of what previously occupied the heart, the repudiation of what formerly was trusted in, the abandonment of all that is opposed to the thrice holy God. It therefore involves the denying of self and the forsaking of old companions. It was thus with Abram, who was required to leave his old situation in Ur of Chaldea and follow the call of God. It was thus with Moses, who "refused to be called (any longer) the son of Pharoah's daughter. Choosing rather to suffer affliction with the people of God than to enjoy the pleasures of sin for a season, esteeming the reproach of Christ greater riches than the treasures of Egypt" (Heb. 11: 24-26). It was thus with Ruth, who, in sharp contrast from Orphah went "back unto her people and unto her gods", refusing to forsake Naomi, averring "thy people shall be my people, and thy God my God" (Ruth 1: 15, 16). And it was thus with Rahab. A faith which does not relinquish anything and produce a break from former associations is worth nothing.

Yes, Rahab's faith was a *self-denying* one, and nothing short of that is what the Gospel requires from all to whom it is addressed. Said the Lord Jesus, "Whosoever will come after Me, let him deny himself, and take up his cross, and follow Me" (Mark 8: 34); and again, "Whosoever does not bear his cross and come after Me, cannot be My disciple" (Luke 14: 27). Ah, dear friend, you may profess to "believe John 3: 16", but suffer us to ask, Do you also, do you really, *believe* Luke 14: 27? Be honest with yourself: does your daily walk supply *proof* you do so? The self-denying faith of Rahab appeared in her preferring the will of God to the safety of her country and in sheltering those two spies before the pleasing of her fellow-citizens. Still more conspicuously did it appear in the venturing of her own life rather than betray the messengers of Joshua, who were the worshippers of the true God. Her faith in God and love for His people made her scorn whatever scoffs she might be subject to and the dangers threatening her. A saving faith is ready, whenever God shall call upon us, to part with everything which we hold near and dear in this world. Acts of self-denying obedience are the best and surest evidences of a real spiritual faith.

From the standpoint of natural and temporal considerations Rahab's faith cost her something. It induced her "to renounce all her interests among the devoted Canaanites (i.e. doomed to destruction), to venture her life and expose herself to the imminent danger of the most cruel tortures in expressing her love for the people of God" (T. Scott). Such is the wonder-working power of the Spirit in a human soul, producing that which is contrary to fallen human nature, causing it to act from new principles and motives, making it to prefer sufferings for Christ's sake and to endure afflictions by throwing in its lot with

His people, than to pursue any longer the vanities of this world. Such was the transformation wrought in Saul of Tarsus, who not only bore with fortitude the persecutions which faith in Christ entailed, but rejoiced that he was counted worthy to suffer for His sake. Such too has been the blessed fruit borne by the faith of many a converted Jew since then, and many a Gentile too, especially those in Papish and heathen countries, as the missionary-records abundantly testify. And such in some measure is the case with every converted soul.

In "receiving the spies with peace" Rahab made it manifest that she had a heart for the people of God, and was ready to do everything in her power to assist them. That brief clause summarises all that is revealed in Josh. 2 of her kindly conduct toward the two Israelites. She welcomed them into her home, engaged them in spiritual conversation, made provision for their safety, and refused to betray them. "Her whole conduct manifested a reverential fear of the Lord, an entire belief of His Word, a desire and hope of His favour, an affection for His people, and a disposition to forsake, venture and suffer anything in His cause" (Scott). We believe there is a latent reference to her kindness (as well as Abram's) in Heb. 13, for the word translated "messengers" in James 2: 25 is the one rendered "angels" in Heb. 13: 2: "Let brotherly love continue, Be not forgetful to entertain strangers, for thereby some have entertained angels unawares. Remember them that are in bonds, as bound with them". Alas, that so many today instead of so doing, are almost ready to rend each other to pieces over every difference of opinion.

Yet, as we saw in our last, Rahab's faith—like ours—was not free from defect, for her falsehoods proceeded from one who failed to trust God fully. This illustrates, in a general way, the humbling fact that in our best performances there is a mingling of frailty and folly. But let it be pointed out that in this matter her conduct is far from being recorded as an excuse for us to shelter behind. Rather is it chronicled as a solemn warning, and also to teach us that faith in its beginnings has many blemishes. God bears with much weakness, especially in the lambs of His flock. Those who have faith do not always act faith, but there is often much of the flesh mixed with that which is of the spirit. Very different is *our* case and situation from that of this young convert from heathendom. Rightly did the editor of Matt. Henry's O. T. commentary point out, "Her views of the Law must have been exceedingly dim and contracted: a similar falsehood told by those who enjoy the light of Revelation, however laudable the motive, would of course deserve much heavier censure".

"And she said unto the men, I know that the Lord hath given you the land. . .for the Lord your God, He is God in heaven above, and in earth beneath" (vv. 9, 11). Here we find her making an open avowal of that which the Holy Spirit had secretly wrought in her heart. She acknowledged Jehovah to be the true God, that Israel was the people whom He had loved and owned, and hoped for a place among them. Nothing less is required from the believing sinner today: "If thou shalt confess with thy mouth the Lord Jesus, and shalt believe in thine heart that God hath raised Him from the dead, thou shalt be saved" (Rom. 10: 9). The Lord will not own any cowardly and secret disciples. "Whosoever therefore shall confess Me before men, him will I confess also before My Father which is in heaven. But whosoever shall deny Me before men, him will I also deny before My Father which is in heaven" (Matt. 10: 32, 33). Joseph was not ashamed to confess his God in Egypt, nor Daniel in Babylon, and when Paul stood forth in the midst of the idolatrous crew and soldiers on the ship and told of the reassuring message he had received from the angel of God, he added, "whose I am, and whom I serve" (Acts 27: 23). Then, no matter where we be, let us not be afraid to show our colours and make known whose banner we serve under.

"Now therefore, I pray you, sware unto me by the Lord, since I have showed you kindness, that ye will also show kindness unto my father's house, and give me a true token. And that ye will save alive my father, and my mother, and my brethren, and my sisters, and all that they have, and deliver our lives from death" (vv. 12, 13). Some contracted hearts, in which the very milk of human kindness appears to have congealed, would regard this request of Rahab's as highly presumptuous. Personally, we believe that her soul was so overflowing with gratitude unto the Lord for having saved such an abandoned wretch, that her faith now perceived something of the infinitude of theDivine mercy, and believed that such a God would be willing to show grace to the whole of her family. Nor was she disappointed. Moreover, as Matt. Henry rightly pointed out, "those who show mercy may expect to receive mercy". Thus God promised Ebedmelech, in recompense for his kindness to the prophet, that in the worst of times he should "have his life for a prey" (Jer. 39: 18).

That this request of Rahab's was something more than an expression of the tenderness of nature is evident from the whole of its tenour: that it was the language of faith appears from her assurance that without any doubt Canaan was going to fall before Israel. Her "sware unto me by the Lord" indicates the intelligence of her faith—a solemn oath would clinch the matter. In asking for a "true token", she made request for some pledge of deliverance —the word occurs first in Gen. 9, where God announced that the rainbow would be "the token of the covenant". In supplicating for the deliverance of her whole family, she left us an example which we may well follow. It is right that we *should* desire God to show mercy unto those who are near and dear unto us: not to do so would show we were lacking in natural affection. It only becomes wrong, when we ignore God's sovereignty, and dictate instead of supplicate. It is blessed to observe that He who has said "according unto your faith be it unto you", responded to Rahab's faith (Josh. 6: 22)!

The Scarlet Cord

Rahab's request of the two spies that they should enter into a solemn covenant with her, guaranteeing the preservation of her family from the impending destruction of Jericho (2: 12, 13), placed them in a very awkward predicament, or it is more accurate to say, presents an acute problem which we fear some of our moderns would fail to solve aright. Only a short time before, Israel had received the following commandment concerning their treatment of the Canaanites: "When the Lord thy God shall deliver them before thee, thou shalt smite them and utterly destroy them: thou shalt make no covenant with them, nor show mercy unto them" (Deut. 7: 2). In the light of that express prohibition, what ought the spies to do? The correct answer to that question turns upon the proper application of a real and necessary distinction between the Divine commands—a distinction which has been drawn by well-instructed scribes in all ages—namely, between moral and positive laws: the one being grounded in essential rectitude, the other in sovereignty. The moral nature with which God has endowed us teaches that parents should cherish and care for their children, and that children should revere and obey their parents; but it would not prompt Christians to practice baptism or observe the Lord's supper—those are positive institutions, ad extra.

The things enjoined by God's positive laws depend solely on His sovereign pleasure, there being no other reason for them. But the things enjoined by

His moral precepts are required not only by the authority of His will, but also by that nature and order of things which He has placed in the creation. The former are alterable at His pleasure, being appointed by mere prerogative; the other are perpetual, enforcing as they do the necessary distinctions of good and evil. All the ceremonial laws given unto Israel were of the former order; thou shalt love the Lord thy God with all thine heart and thy neighbour as thyself—the sum of the Ten Words—belonging unto the latter. The former are only of local application unto those who receive them by Divine revelation, the latter are universally binding on all who are possessed of moral accountability. Whenever obedience to a positive law would involve a plain violation of the principles of the moral law, then the inferior must necessarily yield to the superior: though God requires us to believe and do many things which are contrary to our depraved inclinations, yet He never demands from us that which is opposed to the moral nature He has given us.

An illustration of the distinction pointed out above is supplied by the case of David and his men when they were a hungered, and he requested five loaves of the show bread (1 Sam. 21). Ahimelech the priest pointed out that that bread was not for common use, but had been "sanctified unto the Lord", yet after being assured the men were free from defilement, gave the loaves unto David. None other than our Lord tells us that though it "was not lawful" for them to eat the sacred bread, yet they were "blameless" (Matt. 12: 3-6). Thus the positive law which prohibited the priest from giving the hallowed bread for food unto David and his men, yielded to the pressing need of the situation. "The Son of David approves of it, and shows from it that mercy is to be preferred to sacrifice, that ritual observances must give way to moral duties, and that that may be done in a case of urgent providential necessity which may not otherwise be done" (Matt. Henry).

The law laid down in Deut. 7: 2 was, then, a positive one, and neither absolute in its force nor binding in all cases, for justice itself requires that we must ever show mercy unto the merciful and never return evil for good. Now Rahab *had* shown mercy unto the two spies, and at great risk to herself. The instincts of humanity would fill them with kindly feeling toward their benefactress. Gratitude is a law of nature, and the law of nature takes precedence over positive precepts. Thus those two godly Israelites had sufficient moral sensibility and spiritual discernment to perceive that Deut. 7: 2 could not debar them from acting justly and kindly toward her who had ensured their safety. Yet, though their duty was quite clear, that did not warrant them acting hurriedly and rashly. No arrangement should be entered into thoughtlessly, on the impulse of the moment. No definite promise should be made until we have carefully weighed what we are committing ourselves unto, for our word must be our bond. Still less should we enter into any solemn compact without first prayerfully and thoroughly pondering all that is involved in it.

"And the men answered her, Our life for yours, if ye (better "thou", as in v. 20) utter not this our business. And it shall be, when the Lord hath given us the land, that we will deal kindly and truly with thee".(2: 14). Let it be noted that the fulfilment of Rahab's request was suspended upon an "if"! Necessarily so, for those men were entering into a covenant with her—as her "sware unto me by the Lord" intimated: compare 1 Sam. 20: 16, 17; Psa. 89: 3—and a covenant is a mutual compact in which each party agrees to do or grant certain things in return for the other fulfilling certain conditions. That which they agreed upon was qualified by three provisos, the first of which was that she must continue loyal to their interests. Thus we see their circumspection in binding Rahab to this condition. "They that will be conscientious in keeping their promises, will be cautious in making them, and perhaps may insert certain conditions which may otherwise seem frivolous (M. Henry). The Christian should always qualify his promises with "the Lord willing" or "the Lord enabling me".

They solemnly bound themselves for her preservation in the common destruction of Jericho. Their "our life instead of you to die" (margin) not only affirmed that they would be as much concerned about her safety as their own, but signified a definite imprecation of God's judgment on them if they failed in their part of the agreement. "We will *deal* kindly with thee" was an assurance that their words would prove no empty ones, but that there should be an actual performance of what was promised. Observe too how they employed the language of faith: "it shall be when the Lord hath given us the land". There was no doubt in their minds about the issue: instead, they were fully convinced that Canaan was going to be conquered—yet "by the Lord" and as His "gift"! We too should wage the fight of faith with full assurance of the outcome, that the Lord will grant ultimate success, so that each exclaims, "I will dwell in the house of the Lord forever" (Psa. 23: 6). In their "we will deal kindly" they gave proof they were imbrued with no ferocious spirit, and were far from being the blood-thirsty creatures which infidels charge the conquerors of Canaan with being.

"Then she let them down by a cord through the window, for her house was upon the town wall, and she dwelt upon the wall" (v. 15). As soon as she received promise from the spies, Rahab set about assisting them in their escape. It was most convenient for them that her house was so situated, for had it been in the centre of the town there was much more likelihood of their being recognised and arrested; but being on the outer wall, they could be let down by night unseen by unfriendly eyes. Yet let it be pointed out that the convenience was no mere happy co-incidence but *ordered* by the Lord, for of all men He hath appointed "the bounds of their habitation" (Acts 17: 26)—a sovereign God ordained where each of us should be born and reside. But not only was the particular location of Rahab's house of assistance to the spies, it also served to display more evidently the power of God, for it was the wall of the city which "fell down flat" (6: 20) and the preservation of her lone house amid the universal devastation, stood forth as a monument both of His might and of His mercy.

"And she said unto them, Get you to the mountain, lest the pursuers meet you, and hide yourselves three days until the pursuers be returned, and afterward may ye go your way" (v. 16). It is striking to behold the blending together of Divine power and human precaution all through this incident. The grand truth of Divine preservation is typically illustrated, yet that preservation was accomplished *by* the use of means at every point: Rahab's by obeying the orders she received, her house because of the cord in her window, the spies by concealing themselves in the mountain. Let those who teach the "eternal security of the saints" see to it that they present it *with* the safeguards by which God has hedged it about. True, the accomplishment of His eternal purpose of grace is not left contingent upon the acts of the creature, nevertheless He who has ordained the end has also appointed the means by which that end is reached. God has not promised to conduct any one to Heaven without the exercise of his faculties and the discharge of his responsibility. He deals with us throughout as moral agents, and requires us to heed His warnings and *avoid* that which would destroy us (1 Cor. 9: 27).

Committing my soul and its eternal interests into the hand of the Lord by no means releases me of obligation. "He who has fixed the limits of our life, has also entrusted us with the care of it; has furnished us with means and supports for its preservation, has also made us provident of dangers, and that they may not oppress us unawares has furnished us with cautions and remedies. Thus it is evident what is our duty". That, my reader, is a quotation not from the Arminian, J. Wesley, but from the Reformer, J. Calvin!—alas that so many who claim to be Calvinists lack his wisdom and balance of doctrine. The truth of Divine preservation is not designed as a shelter for either laziness or licentiousness. God's promises are made to those who honestly strive against sin and mourn when tripped up by it, and not to those who take their fill thereof and delight therein; for He undertakes to keep His saints *in holiness* and not in wickedness. If God has turned our feet into that way which leadeth unto life, we must continue therein, otherwise we shall never reach our desired destination. Only those who press forward to that which is before reach the Goal.

Saving faith is far more than an isolated act: it is a spiritual principle which continues to operate in those to whom it is communicated. Divine preservation works through Christian perseverance, for grace is given us not to render our efforts needless, but to make them effectual. God does not carry His children to glory in a state of passivity, but works in them both to will and to do of His good pleasure—to hate and fear sin, to desire and strive after holiness; to heed His warnings, to shun the things which would destroy, to *keep* His commandments. The Christian must continue as he began, for Christian perseverance is the maintaining of godly affections and practices. We are indeed "kept by the power of God", yet "through faith" (1 Pet. 1: 5), and therefore so long as the flesh is left in us and we in the world, we are required to attend unto that exhortation "Take heed, brethren, lest there be in any of you an evil heart of unbelief, in departing from the living God" (Heb. 3: 13), for the verses which follow solemnly remind us that many of those who came out of Egypt never entered Canaan!—"they could not enter in because of unbelief" (v. 19).

"And she said unto them, Get you to the mountain, lest the pursuers meet you, and hide yourselves three days until the pursuers be returned, and afterward may ye go your way". Observe how this illustrates and enforces what we have just said above. The spies were under the immediate care of God, they had trustfully committed themselves into His hands, and He would certainly bring them safely back unto Joshua. Nevertheless, they were required to exercise care and caution, and they did so, for v. 22 shows they acted in exact accordance with Rahab's counsels. They might have argued, We cannot afford to waste three days in the mountain, rather does it behoove us to make all possible speed to Joshua and make our report unto him. But that had been only the feverish energy of the flesh: "he that believeth shall not make haste" (Isa. 28: 16)—alas that that wise old proverb "Slow but sure, is sure to do well" is now despised. Nor did those spies, under the plea of trusting God, recklessly disregard the peril of being captured by the pursuers—that had been tempting Him, acting presumptuously rather than believingly. God requires us to conduct ourselves circumspectly, to exercise good judgment.

"And the men said unto her, We will be blameless of this thine oath, which thou hast made us to sware. Behold, when we come into this land, thou shalt bind this line of scarlet thread (or "rope") in the window which thou didst let us down by; and thou shalt bring thy father, and thy mother, and thy brethren, and all thy father's household home unto thee" (vv. 17, 18). If the spies must need take due precautions for their personal safety, equally indispensable was it that Rahab should act in obedience with their orders, otherwise they would be released from their promise and the oath would no longer be binding upon them. Their oath, as pointed out above, was for the confirmation of the covenant they had entered into with Rahab, and a covenant is a mutual compact between two parties, which is rendered null and void if either of them fails to keep his part of the agreement. Now the Gospel itself is a covenant, for in it God offers and promises certain blessings upon our acceptance of His offer and compliance with His terms (Psal 50: 5, Jer. 50: 5) and we are required to be "*mindful* always of His covenant" (1 Chron. 16: 15) and to "*keep* His covenant" (Psa. 25: 10)—for a fuller discussion of this see the March and April articles on "Reconciliation".

The binding of the scarlet cord in her window was for the purpose of *identification*, so that when Israel made their attack upon Jericho they might know which was her house, and spare it. It must be borne in mind that when the spies gave her those instructions they knew not that the Lord was going to work a miracle, and cause the walls of the city to fall down without any assault upon them by Israel. That was not revealed unto Joshua until later (6: 5), illustrating the fact that God's will is made known unto us only a step at a time—He sees the end from the beginning (Acts 15: 18), but He does not permit us to do so (John 13: 7). That cord was the "token" for which she had asked (v. 12), and it enabled the army of Israel to ascertain which was her house—just as the sprinkled blood on the door-posts of the Hebrews in Egypt caused the angel of death to recognise their houses and pass over them, when He went forth to slay the firstborn (Ex. 12: 13); and just as the 144000 who are exempted from judgment are "sealed in their foreheads" (Rev. 7: 3), their identifying mark being that of *obedience* to the Lord (Rev. 14: 1-5), for it is obedience which manifestatively distinguishes the children of God from the children of the devil.

"And it shall be that whosoever shall go out of the doors of thy house into the streets, his blood shall be upon *his* head, and we will be guiltless; and whosoever shall be with thee in the house, his blood shall be on *our* head if any hand be laid upon him" (v. 19). Thus the terms of the covenant or agreement were precisely stated and carefully explained to her before they parted. Those of Rahab's family who were to be preserved from the common destruction must be inside her house, *separated from the wicked*; if they forsook that shelter and mingled with the heathen inhabitants of Jericho, they would perish with them —as Noah and his family had in the flood, unless they had separated from the ungodly and taken refuge in the ark. Typically this teaches the imperative necessity of separation from the world if we would escape from its impending doom. The case of Rahab's family remaining secluded in her house as the condition of their preservation is parallel with Acts 27, where we find that though the angel of God assured Paul "there shall be no loss of life" (v. 21, yet when the sailors were about to abandon it, he cried, "except these abide in the ship, ye cannot be saved" (v. 31), and except Christians maintain separation from this evil world they cannot escape destruction with it.

"And *if* thou utter this our business, then we will be quit of thine oath which thou hast made us sware" (v. 20). Let those who proclaim the grand truth of "the eternal security of the saints" fail not to give due place unto that "if"—the if not of uncertainty from the Divine side, but of enforcing responsibility from the human. Let them carefully ponder the "if" in Rom. 8: 13 and 11: 22; 1 Cor. 15: 2; Col. 1: 23; Heb. 3: 6, 14. Scripture does not teach a mechanical security, but one which is obtained through our use of means and avoidance of dangers. The preservation of Rahab from destruction was conditioned upon her obedience to the instructions of God's messengers and her use of the means they specified. First, she must mention not their business or betray them to their enemies: she must be loyal to them and promote their interests—a figure of love for the brethren. Second, she must place the scarlet cord in the window so that her house might be recognised: we must bear the identifying mark of God's children. Third, she must abide in her house: we must maintain separation from the world.

"And she said, According unto your words, so be it": there was no resentment, no offering of objections. "And she bound the scarlet line in the window" (v. 21), manifesting by her obedience that she was an elect and regenerate soul. Unless you, my reader, are walking in obedience to God, you have no scriptural warrant to conclude you are "eternally secure". The *reward* of her faith and obedience is revealed in other passages. First, she "perished not with them that believed not" (Heb. 11: 31). Second, she "dwelt in Israel" (6: 25): from being a citizen of heathen Jericho, she was given a place in the congregation of the Lord. Third, she became the honoured wife of a prince in Judah, the mother of Boaz and one of the grandmothers of David Matt. 1: 5). Fourth, she was one of the favoured ancestresses of the Saviour (Matt. 1). Thus did God do for her exceeding abundantly above all that she asked or thought: delivered from awful depths of sin and shame, elevated to heights of honour and dignity.

Chapter 5

STANDING AT THE JORDAN
JOSHUA 3:1-6

The Jordan

The long season of preparation had reached its close, and the arduous task confronting Israel must now be tackled. The forty years they had spent in the wilderness requires to be viewed from a twofold standpoint. First, it was a Divine judgment on the adult generation which, after being so graciously brought out of Egypt and so gloriously delivered at the Red Sea, gave way to an evil heart of unbelief, baulking at the prospect of conquering Canaan (Num. 13: 28-33) and resolving to "return into Egypt" (Num. 14: 1-4)—whose carcasses fell in the wilderness (1 Cor. 10: 5, 10; Heb. 3: 8-17). Second, it was a training for the younger generation who were to occupy the land of promise. This has not been sufficiently recognised. During that forty years many sons and daughters had been born, and *they* were given to behold the wonders of the Lord in a manner and to an extent which no other generation ever has. Not only was there a visible display of Jehovah's faithfulness and power before their eyes in sustaining such a vast number by a daily supply of food from heaven, but at the close Moses could say "your clothes are not waxed old upon you and thy shoe is not waxed old upon thy foot" (Deut. 29: 5).

And is not this ever the Lord's way with His people. He does not bid them to trust in Him with all their hearts and lean not unto their own understandings until He has given them clear proof that He is fully worthy of their confidence. He does not call upon them to overcome the world, mortify their lusts and resist the devil, until He has strengthened them with might by His Spirit in the inner man. He does not exhort them to tread that path of "much tribulation" which alone conducts to Glory, without first weaning their hearts from this world, giving a death wound to their love of sin, and vouchsafing them a ravishing earnest of that glory. How gracious is the Lord, and how tender are His ways! He does not quench the smoking flax, but feeds the spark of grace with the oil of His Spirit. He carries the lambs in His bosom (Isa. 40: 11) until they be able to walk. Only a personal and experimental knowledge of Him with whom they have to do will sustain the heart of a saint under the testings and trails to which he must be submitted.

In the same way the Lord deals with and furnishes His servants. It was thus with Joshua's predecessor. When Jehovah first appeared unto him and made known it was His purpose to employ him in leading the Hebrews out of Egypt, he was fearful, and though the Lord declared He would stretch forth His hand smiting Egypt with all His wonders and giving His people favour in the sight of their oppressors, poor Moses continued to raise objections that Israel would not believe him nor hearken to his voice. Then the Lord bade him cast his rod on the ground, and it became a serpent; told him to take it by the tail, and it became a rod in his hand. Ordered him to thrust his hand into his bosom, and he drew it forth leprous as snow; repeating the action and it

76

was made whole (Ex. 4: 1-4). Thus assured Moses went forth on his mission. So it was with the Eleven: before they entered upon their life work and went forth to "make disciples of all nations", they spent three years with Christ (Mark 3: 14)—witnessing His miracles and being instructed by Him.

We have already seen how such was the case with Joshua. First, the Lord had spoken to him after the death of Moses, giving him the most definite and heartening promises for his faith to rest upon (1: 1-6). Then his hands had been strengthened by the ready co-operation of the two and a half tribes whose portion lay on the eastern side of Jordan, vowing "According as we hearkened unto Moses in all things, so will we hearken unto thee" (1: 12-18). Next he had sent forth the two spies to reconnoitre the land and they, having received a most unlooked-for welcome and assistance from Rahab, had returned and said unto Joshua, "Truly the Lord hath delivered into our hands all the land, for all the inhabitants of the country do faint because of us" (2: 24). What more could Israel and their leader want! The Lord had gone before them preparing their way, causing His "terror" to fall upon the inhabitants (2: 9). With what confidence then might Joshua and all the people go forward into their inheritance! And should it not be the same with Christians now? "When He putteth forth His sheep He goeth before them, and the sheep follow Him" (John 10: 4). If our eyes be fixed on Him and our ears respond to His voice there is nothing to be afraid of.

But we must now turn to the sequel: and what does the reader suppose is the *nature* of it? A severe testing of faith? Doubtless that is what many would term it: personally we would prefer to say, A glorious opportunity for exercising faith in the living God. Do not, dear reader, look so much upon painful circumstances and difficult situations as unpleasant trials of faith which have to be endured, but rather thankfully regard them as golden occasions for you to prove afresh the sufficiency of Him who never fails those who fully trust Him. God gives His people grace not only for the comfort of their hearts, but to use for Him. He has placed His sure promises in the Word not merely for us to wonder at, but to turn unto good account. He grants encouragements along the way and strengthens us that we may press forward and do further exploits in His name. He imparts faith unto His people that they may employ it in a manner honouring to Him. Such it appears to us is, in part, the relation between Joshua 1 and 2 and what is now to be before us. Israel was faced with a most formidable obstacle, but in view of what God had wrought for them, there was no ground for dismay.

Above we have said, Such it appears to us is, *in part*, the relation between Josh. 1 and 2 and what is now to be before us. But there is something else, and if we deliberately disregarded it, we should be guilty of handling the Word of God deceitfully and seriously misleading His people. That 'something else' is either blankly repudiated today—by those who turn the grace of God into lasciviousness in failing to insist that grace reigns through righteousness (Rom. 5: 21), teaching us to deny ungodliness and worldly lusts, that we should live soberly, righteously and godly (Titus 2: 11, 12); or is ignored by those who studiously omit everything which would be unpalatable to empty professors, well knowing that if they are to receive their support, such must be bolstered up in their worldliness and carnality. These hirelings harp continually on God's grace, His promises, and nought but faith being required by Him; and woefully fail to lay stress upon God's holiness, His precepts, and obedience being indispensably necessary. Josh. 1 and 2, my reader, contains something more than precious promises and gracious encouragements.

Josh. 1 and 2 also make prominent the *claims* of God and strongly enforces human *responsibility*. Let us refresh the reader's memory. First, the Lord had bidden Joshua "Only be thou strong and very courageous, that thou mayest observe to do according to all the law which Moses My servant commanded thee. This Book of the Law shall not depart out of thy mouth; but thou shalt meditate therein day and night, that thou mayest observe to do according to all that is written therein; for then thou shalt make thy way prosperous". Thus was the leader himself required to render the most complete subjection unto the revealed will of the Lord, and informed that success would hinge thereon. Joshua, in turn, "Commanded the officers of the people" what orders to give unto them. Then he pressed upon the two and a half tribes their obligations, bidding them "Remember the word which Moses the servant of the Lord *commanded* you" (1: 7-13). It was only in the behalf of a people whose hearts were right with Him and who walked in the way of His precepts, that the Lord would show Himself strong. Faith in Him was to be evidenced by obedience unto His commands; no other faith would He own.

It is to be carefully noted that Josh. 3, like Josh. 2, opens with the word "And", which not only shows the three chapters are closely connected, but also tells us we must carry in our minds what has previously engaged our attention. Joshua and the people, as they started forward on their new venture, must be regulated entirely by the instructions which they had already received. So must we be! And if we are to make a right application of this memorable incident unto ourselves, if we are to draw from it the spiritual lessons which it is designed to teach us, then we need to heed what was before us in the previous sections. A most formidable obstacle lay in Israel's path: the river Jordan barred their entrance into Canaan, and we are now to behold how that obstacle was surmounted. If we are to make a personal and practical use of this portion of Scripture, that river which intercepted Israel's progress should be regarded as illustrative of any problem or obstruction which confronts the minister of the Gospel or the ordinary Christian, and then ascertain from this passage what he must do if he is to overcome his difficulty and be enabled to go forward.

"And Joshua rose early in the morning ' (3: 1). Observe well that the Holy Spirit has taken due notice of this! Not only so, but He has recorded the same thing again in 6: 12; 7: 16; 8: 20! In his early rising, as in so many other respects, he foreshadowed the antitypical Joshua, our Saviour: see Mark 1: 35, Luke 4: 42, etc. Joshua's "early" rising shows that he was not slothful, a lover of his own ease, but one whose heart was in his work and who diligently applied himself unto the same. Therein he has left an example for each servant of Christ to follow. The minister of the Gospel is to be no slacker and shirker, but rather "a *workman* that needeth not to be ashamed" (2 Tim. 2: 15). Whether he rises early or (as this writer) finds it more expedient to burn the midnight oil, he is in honour and duty bound to spend at least as many hours in his study each day as does the farmer in his field, the clerk in his office, or the labourer in the factory. He has no warrant to expect God to use him unless he be industrious and denies himself.

"And they removed from Shittim and came to Jordan, he and all the people of Israel, and lodged there before they passed over" (3: 1). Moses had conducted Israel as far as Shittim (Num. 25: 1), and after his death it was from there that Joshua had sent out the two spies (2: 1). They had returned to him with their favourable report, and now we behold the sequel. In his "rising early" Joshua gave proof that he did not shirk the difficult task before him, but was anxious to come to grips with it. The Lord rewarded his diligence by inclining the people to co-operate with him. They might have demurred, saying "What is the use of leaving this place where we have so long been encamped, and moving forward to Jordan itself, where there are neither bridges nor boats for us to cross over it? Instead, they laid hold of the promise "within three days *ye shall* pass over this Jordan (1:11), and went forward in faith and obedience. They knew not *how* the obstacle was to be overcome, and for the moment that was nóne of their business. Their responsibility was to proceed along the path of duty so far as they were able, and count upon God's continuing to keep that path open for them!.

"And it came to pass after three days that the officers went through the host" (v.2). At first thought it seems strange that such a multitude should be left encamped there for this length of time ere a further word was spoken to them, but a little reflection should indicate the Lord's design therein, and then show us the important lesson *we* should learn therefrom. Ponder this incident; visualise the scene before your mind's eye. It was not an army of men only, but a vast congregation of men, women and children, to say nothing of their baggage and herds of animals, and further advance was blocked by the river. Whatever the breadth and depth of the Jordan in recent centuries or today, it is evident that it presented an impassable obstruction in Joshua's time— moreover, it was *in flood* at that particular season (3:15): and yet they were left to gaze upon it for three days, faced with the fact that they had no means of their own for crossing it! Why? What was the Lord's object in this? Was it not to impress Israel more deeply with a realisation of their own utter helplessness?- Was it not to shut them up more completely unto Himself?

And is not that, very often, the chief design of God's providential dealings with us? To bring us to the end of our own resources, to make us conscious of our own insufficiency, by bringing us into a situation from which we cannot extricate ourselves, confronting us with some obstacle which to human wit and might is insurmountable? By nature we are proud and self-reliant, ignorant of the fact that the arm of flesh is frail. And even when faced with difficulties, we seek to solve them by our own wisdom, or get out of a tight corner by our own efforts. But the Lord is graciously resolved to humble us, and therefore the difficulties are increased and the corner becomes tighter, and for a season we are left to ourselves—as Israel was before the Jordan. It is not until we have duly weighed the difficulty and then discovered we have nothing of our own to place in the opposite scale, that we are really brought to realise our impotency, and turn unto Him who alone can undertake for us and free us from our dilemma. But such dull scholars are we that, the lesson must be taught us again and yet again before we actually put it into practice.

Those three days before that unfordable river was the necessary preparation for what followed—the background from which the following miracle might be the more evident to and the more appreciated by Israel. Man's extremity furnishes the most suitable opportunity for God to display His power. And it is not until man is made painfully aware of his extremity that he turns unto the Lord and seeks His intervention. That truth is writ large across the 107th Psalm, which forcible illustrates and exemplifies what we have been seeking to express. "Hungry and thirsty their souls fainted in them. *Then* they cried unto the Lord in their trouble" (vv. 5, 6). "There was none to help: then they cried unto the Lord in their trouble, and He saved them" (vv. 12, 13). "They draw near unto the gates of death: then they cry unto the Lord" (vv. 18, 19). They "are at their wits' end: then they cry unto the

Lord" (vv. 27, 28). They are brought into a desperate situation, to the end of their own resources, and then it is that they—not merely utter a few cold and formal petitions, but—*"cry unto* the Lord", and such a cry is ever responded to by His deliverance.

Ah, my reader, do not close your eyes to the Jordan—the problem, the difficulty, the obstacle—that confronts you, but face it. Do not attempt to minimise it, but take its full measure. Continue contemplating it until you plainly realise your own helplessness to cope with the same, and then trustfully turn unto Him who is capable of dealing with it. Suppose you be a minister of the Gospel, and you yearn for your hearers to be saved: is there not an insuperable obstacle standing in the way of the realisation of your desire? Indeed there is: the stolid indifference and unresponsiveness of your hearers. *That* is the "Jordan" which confronts you: the spiritual insensibility of your congregation—and "Jordan" is the symbol of *death*! Do you fully realise that: that your hearers have no more spiritual life in them than the waters of that river had? That you can no more open their hearts to the reception of the Gospel than Israel could open a path through the Jordan? Are you acting accordingly? Few ministers, few churches today are! When they would have a "revival" they hire an outside evangelist and count on special singing, instead of crying unto the Lord.

"And it came to pass after three days that the officers went through the host. And they commanded the people, saying, When ye see the ark of the covenant of the Lord your God, and the priests the Levites bearing it, then ye shall remove from your place and go after it" (3: 2, 3), For three days the congregation of Israel had been encamped before that river which barred their entrance into the land of promise, thus being obliged to take full stock of that formidable barrier and made fully conscious of their own helplessness. The Jordan is the symbol of death, and it is not until the saint appropriates the solemn truth or has learned from painful experience that death is written upon all his natural powers that he is likely to make any real spiritual progress or enter practically into his fair heritage. *That* was the great lesson which had to be learned by the father of them that believe, before his longing could be realised and fruit borne. Because Sarah was barren he thought to obtain the desired son by Hagar, only to bring trouble upon his household. Not until he truly recognised the natural impotency of himself and his wife did he count upon Him who quickenth the dead: Rom. 4: 17-21.

Thus it was too with the chief of the apostles. "For we would not, brethren, have you ignorant of our trouble which came to us in Asia, that we were pressed out of measure, above strength, insomuch that we despaired even of life. But we had the sentence of death in ourselves that we should not trust in ourselves, but in God who raiseth the dead. Who delivered us from so great a death (Acts 19: 22-41), and doth deliver (from those who then sought his life), in whom we trust that He will yet deliver us" (2 Cor. 1: 8-10). It is God's way with His people to so order His providences that they are "pressed out of measure, above strength", until they are brought to despair of deliverance by their own efforts. Then it is they discover that death is stamped upon all their members and powers and are brought to acknowledge "we have no might. . .neither know we what to do" (2 Chron. 20: 12). Ah, but note they at once added, "but our eyes are *upon Thee*"! It was for that very reason Paul and his companions had "the sentence of death" in themselves—that they "should not trust in themselves, but in God which raiseth the dead".

By nature we are self-confident and by practice to a considerable extent self-reliant. But those qualities have no scope or place in the spiritual life,

having to be completely renounced. Just as we must repudiate our own righteousness before the righteousness of Christ is imputed to us, so we are required
to disown our own wisdom and strength ere the power of Christ works in us and
for us. "Whosoever will come after Me, let him deny himself, and take up his
cross, and follow Me" (Mark 8: 34) is Christ's own unchanging demand. To
"deny himself" is for a man to abandon all trust in himself, to disclaim any
capability of his own, to be emptied of self. In order thereto God often
brings him into situations where he discovers it is utterly vain to look to himself for relief. Until he has found out that all attempts to extricate himself
are futile, he has not learned his utter helplessness, and until he does so he will
not really look outside himself unto the Lord. Israel then were made to feel
their powerlessness during the three days they were encamped before the overflowing Jordan, and that, in order to prepare them to count upon the Almighty.

But let it is also be duly observed that to "deny himself" is not only for
a man to disown his own righteousness, wisdom and strength, but also to
renounce all self-will and self-pleasing. The *whole* of "self" is to be set aside
and "the cross" taken up: that is, the principle of self-sacrifice, is to dominate
and regulate him, and that, in order to "follow Christ". The former are
negative—means to an end: they are preparatives unto a life of obedience or
a practical owning of the Lordship of Christ. We turn to God "from idols"—
the chief of which is *self*—that we should "serve the living and true God" (1
Thess. 1: 9) i.e. that we should be subject to Him, governed by Him. And
that is the important truth set forth here. Israel were now commanded to
turn their gaze away from the Jordan and fix their eyes steadily on "the ark".
And of what or of whom does the ark speak? Of *Christ*, says the reader.
True, yet such an answer is far too general to be of any elucidation. Of Christ
in what relation? Of His person, His work, or His official character? If
of His office, which particular aspect thereof?

It should be evident to any attentive student that the spiritual interpretation of our passage—both doctrinally and practically—turns upon our answers
to those questions. The ark is the central object in this miraculous event,
being mentioned by name in chapters 3 and 4 no less than sixteen times and
alluded to as "it " five times, or a total of twenty-one times, or 7 x 3, which
in the language of Scripture numerics signifies, a complete manifestation of
God. What, then, was the ark, and for what purpose was it made? The ark
was a coffer or chest, made of shittim wood, overlaid both within and without
with pure gold (Ex. 25: 10, 11). It was to be a depository for the two tables
of stone (Ex. 25: 16), and accordingly, when all its sacred furniture was made
and the tabernacle was set up, we are told that Moses "took and put the testimony into the ark" (Ex. 40: 20), where it still abode in the days of Solomon
(1 Kings 8: 9). It is most essential that this fact be carefully noted, if we are
to perceive aright the spiritual meaning of this holy vessel: the ark was made
for the Law, and not the Law for the ark, as is abundantly clearly from Deut.
10: 1-5.

It was for the above-mentioned reason that the ark was called "the ark of
the testimony" (Ex. 26: 33, 34, etc.). The tables of stone on which the
finger of God had written the ten Commandments were termed "the tables of
testimony" (Ex. 31: 18), and from their being deposited in it the ark received
its principal designation, and since the ark was the most important object in
the tabernacle, it was called "the tabernacle of testimony" (Num. 1: 51, 53,
etc.). The tables of stone were designated "the testimony", the ark "the ark
of the testimony", and the tabernacle "the tabernacle of testimony" because

they one and all declared *what God is* and made known the terms on which He would hold fellowship with His people. The Law was a revelation of the righteousness of Jehovah, with its demands upon the faith, love and obedience of His saints. It witnessed immediately to the Divine holiness, yet by necessary implication to the sinfulnes of Israel. The tabernacle was the place of God's habitation where Israel was to meet with Him: not only to receive a knowledge of His will and hold fellowship with Him (Ex. 25: 21, 22) but also having a prominent respect to their *sins* against which the Law was ever testifying, and to use the appointed means of their restoration to His favour and blessing.

It has not been sufficiently recognised by more recent writers that in that Tabernacle of Testimony not only was witness plainly borne unto the ineffable holiness and majesty of the Lord, but also to His gracious condescension and abounding mercy. It testified to the wondrous provisions He had made whereby transgressors of the Law could receive pardon and the defiled be cleansed. In its outer court stood the brazen altar, where sacrifices of atonement were offered. There too was the laver of water for the washing of the hands and feet (Ex. 30: 18-20). Still more significant and blessed, the very ark which enshrined the Law was covered with the mercy-seat (Ex. 25: 21)! That mercy-seat formed Jehovah's throne in Israel, for it was there between the cherubim that He "dwelt" (Psa. 80: 1 etc.), ruling over His people. Thus the ark and its lid, the mercy-seat, testified unto His being "a just God and a Saviour" (Isa. 45: 21): the Law, proclaiming His inexorable justice, the mercy-seat testifying to the provision of His grace for the transgressions of His people— a covering of mercy that they might draw near unto Him and live.

We turn now to take particular note of the fact that in Josh. 3:3 etc. the ark is called "the ark of *the covenant*", the reference being to that compact into which Jehovah entered with Israel at Sinai and which they solemnly bound themselves to keep (Ex. 19: 1-6; 24: 1-8). By the establishment of the Sinaitic Covenant the relation between God and Israel was brought into a state of formal completeness. Under the Abrahamic covenant (Gen. 17: 7, 8 etc.) the Lord had pledged Himself to faithfully bestow upon Abraham's seed every needful blessing, and now that covenant of promise was supplemented by the covenant of Law, which bound that seed to render the dutiful return of obedience which their gracious God justly required from them. The foundation was thus outwardly laid for a near and lasting relationship, resulting in a blessed intercourse between the God of Abraham on the one hand and the dutiful descendants of Abraham on the other. And it was primarily with the design of furthering and securing that end that the ratification of the covenant at Sinai was so immediately followed by instructions for the making and erection of the tabernacle.

The Ten Commandments were *the terms* of the covenant entered into at Sinai (Ex. 34: 28): "He declared unto you His covenant which He commanded you to perform, even ten commandments" (Deut. 4: 13), and it was on the basis of their compliance therewith that God undertook to deal with Israel and make good His promises to Abraham. His readiness to show Himself strong in their behalf was at once evidenced: "and they departed from the mount of the Lord three days' journey; and the ark of the covenant of the Lord went before them in the three days' journey, to search out a restingplace for them" Num. 10: 33). But alas, the very next thing recorded is "the people complained" and "it displeased the Lord" and His chastening hand fell heavily upon them (Num. 11: 1). Then we learn of the opposition made against Moses by his own brother and sister, and the Lord's smiting Miriam with leprosy (Num. 12). That is at once followed by an account of the sending forth of the twelve men to spy out the land of Canaan, the mixed report which they made upon their return, the unbelief and rebellion of the people, with their repudiation of Moses as their leader and determination to return unto Egypt (Num. 13: 1; 14: 5).

The evil conduct of Israel is summed up by the Psalmist in those solemn words "They kept not the covenant of God and refused to walk in His Law (Psa. 78: 10). Their breaking of the covenant at once released the Lord from making good unto *that* perverse generation His declarations unto Abraham, and therefore He told them "your carcasses they shall fall in this wilderness. And your children shall wander in the wilderness. . .after the number of the days in which ye searched the land, forty days, each day for a year, shall ye bear your iniquities, forty years, and ye shall know My breach of promise" (Num. 14: 32-34). They should know to their lasting misery what had produced that "breach of promise" (compare the "if" of Ex. 19: 5!) and the protracted and woeful consequences thereof. The promises Jehovah made unto Abraham and unto Moses would not be fulfilled unto that particular generation because of their unbelief and disobedience; but unto their descendants they should be made fully good. As Joshua himself testified at a later date, "the Lord delivered all their enemies into their hands. There failed not aught of any good thing which the Lord had spoken unto the house of Israel: all came to pass" (21: 44, 45).

The forty years' wandering in the wilderness expired with the death of Moses, and all whose sins occasioned that punishment had also died. It was the new and younger generation over which Joshua was placed, and now a fresh chapter opened in the history of Israel What has been pointed out above explains not only the prominent position occupied by the ark in the crossing of Jordan and in the subsequent events, but why it is there designated "the ark of the covenant". Israel's success, or rather the Lord's showing Himself strong in their behalf, would turn upon *their keeping of* the covenant established at Sinai and their walking in implicit obedience unto God. Israel's crossing of the Jordan with their eyes fixed on the ark signified that they marched into Canaan *led by the Law*!

What has just been emphasised is of something more than mere historical importance: it is recorded for the instruction of God's people in *all* generations, and needs to be turned by them into earnest prayer for Divine enablement. It reveals to us the principal thing which the Holy One requires from us if He is to undertake for us and make a way through whatever "Jordan" may confront us. It makes known the basic principle of God's governmental dealings with His people in every age: the exercise of His power on our behalf is regulated by our submission to Him. God cannot be the Patron of sin, and therefore He will not show Himself strong in the behalf of rebellious subjects. As said before, we must deny self and take up our cross in order to "follow" Christ, and what *that* signifies is made clear to us here in Israel's "following" the ark of the covenant. "He that saith he abideth in Him ought himself also so to walk even as He walked" (1 John 2: 6), and *He* walked in perfect subjection to the Law of God!

The Ark

"And they commanded the people, saying, When ye see the ark of the covenant of the Lord your God, and the priests the Levites bearing it, then ye shall remove from your place, and go after it. Yet there shall be a space between you and it, about two thousand cubits by measure: come not near unto it, that ye may know the way by which ye must go; for ye have not passed this way heretofore" (iii, 3, 4). Keeping in mind the principal things which have already been before us: that this was a new generation of Israel which was about to enter into their heritage; that that heritage prefigured the portion and privileges which should—in this life—be enjoyed by the Christian; that the ark was an outstanding type of the person of Christ; that the particular name by which it is here designated intimates the special character in which Christ is to be viewed and followed by the believer; that Israel's crossing of the Jordan and entrance into Canaan is fraught with the most important practical instruction for us today; let us proceed.

The ark was the sacred chest in which the two tables of stone were deposited, and thus it pointed to Christ as our Lawgiver (Psa. xl, 8; John xiv, 15). The ten commandments were the terms of the covenant which was mutually entered into between Jehovah and Israel at Sinai (Ex. xxxiv, 28), and it was on the basis of their compliance. or non-compliance with that solemn pact that the Lord agreed to deal with Israel and make good His promises to Abraham. Hence the name by which the ark is called throughout Joshua iii and iv. Thus the ark here prefigured Christ as the believer's *Covenant-head,* the meaning of which, though of the first moment, is alas little understood today. It is in the Gospel that Christ is tendered unto us as such, and it is by our complying with its terms that the soul enters into a covenant with Him. "Incline your ear, and come unto Me: Hear, and your soul shall live; and I will make an everlasting covenant with you, even the sure mercies of David" or "the Beloved" (Isa. lv, 3). That is the Gospel offer or proposal, and our acceptance thereof is a "joining ourselves to the Lord, to serve Him and to love the name of the Lord" and is a "taking hold of His covenant" (Isa. lvi, 6).

That which will best enable us to grasp the basic truth which we are here concerned with is the *marriage contract,* for marriage is a covenant voluntarily, lovingly, and solemnly entered into between two parties, wherein each gives himself or herself unto the other, disowning all rivals, pledging unending fidelity, vowing to make the interests and welfare of the other his or her own. Nothing less than is what the Lord requires from man. The evangelist calls upon his hearers to throw down the weapons of their enmity against Him, forsake all illicit lovers, and unite themselves with those who declare, "Come, and let us join ourselves to the Lord in a perpetual covenant that shall not be forgotten" (Jer. l, 5). Thus it was in that wondrous and blessed foreshadowment in Genesis xxiv, where Abraham (figure of the Father) sent forth his servant Eliezer (figure first of the Holy Spirit, yet principally of the evangelist through whom He works) to seek and woo a wife (emblem of the Church collectively and of the believer individually) for his son Isaac—Christ; the whole of which sets before us a most instructive picture of the preaching of the Gospel, both from the standpoint of God's sovereign grace and the enforcing of human responsibility—though, as usual, the latter is ignored by most Calvinistic writers thereon.

As the figure of the evangelist we may note how Eliezer received most specific instructions from Abraham concerning his mission and how that servant obediently complied therewith (Gen. xxiv, 10). Then we observe how Eliezer betook himself unto prayer, asking the Lord to grant him " good speed " and success on his errand (verse 12)—an unmistakably plain intimation that Eliezer is not to be regarded solely as a type of the Holy Spirit. When Abraham's servant encountered the object of his quest he presented her with tokens of his good will (verse 22), and extolled the excellency of his master (verse 35). Then we behold how she was required to make a personal decision: " Wilt thou go with this man? " (verse 58): she had to choose for herself, freely and deliberately. Such a decision, personal and definite, is required from the sinner as the terms of the Gospel are presented unto him, for they are addressed to him as a moral agent, testing and enforcing his responsibility. " And she said, I will go." She was willing and ready to turn her back upon the old life, and forsake her family to become the wife of Isaac. " And she became his wife " (verse 67), and never regretted her decision. And that is the grand type and picture of a soul entering into an everlasting covenant with the Lord Jesus, the eternal Lover of His people —made willing in the day of His power.

In full accord with the striking type of Genesis xxiv we find our Lord Himself speaking of the Gospel-order thus: " The kingdom of heaven is like unto a certain King which made a *marriage* for His Son " (Matt. xxii, 2), upon which Matthew Henry rightly averred, " The Gospel covenant is a marriage covenant betwixt Christ and the believer, and it is a marriage of God's making. This branch of the similitude is only mentioned, and not prosecuted here "; by which he meant that the wedding feast and its guests is what is mainly dwelt upon in the sequel. Concerning the force of the " marriage " figure itself, Thomas Scott aptly said, " The union of the Son of God with man by assuming human nature; the endeared relationship into which He receives His Church and every member of it; the spiritual honours, riches and blessings to which they are advanced by this sacred relation; the comforts they receive from His condescending and faithful love, and from communion with Him; and the reciprocal duties of their relation to Him are all intimated by the metaphor." True, yet, with their accustomed partiality and lack of balance, most preachers have dwelt considerably upon the first four of these analogies, but have been criminally silent upon the " reciprocal duties " which that relation involves, and which we are here insisting upon.

The same lopsidedness is seen again in the explanations given of Matthew xxii, 11: " When the King came in to see the guests, He saw there a man which had not on a wedding garment." Thomas Scott is right in saying, " This denotes that some who are not true believers appear as willing and welcome guests at the Gospel feast and intrude into its most sacred ordinances," but it seems to us he quite missed the point when he added, " It is not material whether we understand the wedding garment to mean the imputed righteousness of Christ, or the sanctification of the Spirit; for both are alike necessary and they always go together." This parable is not treating so much of the Divine side of things, but rather the testing of human *responsibility* and the disclosing of its failures. Verses 3, 5 and 6 exhibit man's obstinacy and enmity, while verse 11 depicts the exposure of an empty profession. " If the Gospel be the wedding feast, then the wedding garment is a frame of heart and a course of life agreeable to the Gospel and our profession of it "

(Matthew Henry). Many take up a profession of the Gospel and claim to be united to Christ without any newness of heart and life. They lack a disposition and conduct suited to Christ and His precepts: they are devoid of habitual and practical holiness. They have no marriage " certificate"!

Now none can enter into and enjoy the heritage which God has provided for His people save those who have personally and experimentally passed from death unto life, who have entered into definite and solemn covenant with Him, and who cleave unto and conduct themselves by the commandments of Christ—the anti-typical Joshua. That is the great and grand truth portrayed here in Joshua iii and iv, and it is because it is such a momentous one, and yet so little apprehended today, that we are labouring it so much in our comments upon this passage. It is at regeneration that the soul passes from death unto life, when by a sovereign act of God's power—wherein we are entirely passive—we are spiritually quickened and thereby capacitated to turn unto Him. This miracle of grace is made manifest by the understanding of its subject being enlightened to perceive his awful enmity against God, by his conscience being convicted of his guilty and lost condition, by his affections being turned against sin so that he now loathes it, by his will being inclined Godwards; all of which issues in a genuine conversion or right-about-face—a forsaking of his wicked ways, an abandoning of his idols, a turning away from the world, and a taking of Christ to be his absolute Lord, all-sufficient Saviour, and everlasting Portion.

Such a conversion—and none other is a saving one—is an entering into covenant with God in Christ, and a being married or united unto Him. Hence we find the conversion of the Corinthians described thus: they " first gave their own selves to the Lord and unto us, by the will of God " (II Cor. viii, 5): that is, they willingly yielded and gladly dedicated themselves unto the Lord—acknowledging the just requirements of His proprietorship and authority, and responding to the claims of His redeeming love as the only suitable acknowledgment of that debt which can never be repaid; and gave up themselves unto His servants to be directed by them; which is ratified in baptism, when we *openly* give up ourselves to be His people. Hence, under a slightly varied figure Paul reminded those who had been thus converted under his preaching, " I have espoused you to one Husband, that I may present you as a chaste virgin to Christ " (II Cor. xi, 2). The apostle had been the instrument in forming a connection between them and Christ like that of the marriage union, the obligations of which are devotedness, fidelity, loving obedience; and unto the preservation and promotion thereof the apostle laboured with a godly jealousy for them.

At regeneration the Spirit vitally unites us to Christ; at conversion we personally and practically give up ourselves unto Him. Conversion is when we accept Christ to be our Husband and Lord, to be cherished and ruled by Him. It is an entering into a covenant-engagement with Him, for Him to be our only God, and for us to be His faithful people. That the covenant relationship *is* a marriage union is clear from Jeremiah xxxi, 32, Hosea ii, 18, 19 (and cf. Jer. ii, 2; Ezek. xvi, 60); and that is why Israel's idolatry was commonly spoken of as (spiritual) adultery—unfaithfulness to Jehovah, going after other gods. Since conversion be our entering into covenant with God in Christ, the great business of the Christian life is to "*keep* His covenant " (Psa. xxv, 10): that is, to be regulated at all times by its terms. Or, since conversion be a marriage union with Christ, the whole aim of the Christian life is to be as a loving and dutiful wife should unto her husband. All of which is summed up in that comprehensive word. "As ye have therefore received Christ Jesus the Lord, so walk ye in Him" (Col. ii, 6): continue as you began, be actuated by the same motives and principles now as when you first surrendered to Him, let your Christian life be a perpetuation of your conversion, be wholly devoted to Him.

What we have endeavoured to set before the reader above as a definition and description of the true and normal Christian life is that which is typically portrayed in Joshua iii and iv. The ark was a figure of Christ; the "ark of the covenant of the Lord your God" pointed to Him as our Covenant-head, the One with whom we entered into a solemn compact and engagement at our conversion, to be henceforth and for ever only His. Israel's *following* of that ark pictured our *keeping* of the covenant, our being in practical subjection to Christ as our Lord and Lawgiver, our being faithful to the marriage relationship, ever seeking to please and promote the interests of the eternal Lover of our souls. Just in proportion as we conduct ourselves *thus* will Israel's experiences become ours. As they submitted unto Joshua's orders, as they obediently followed the ark of the covenant, God put forth His mighty power on their behalf, they entered into a present "rest" (Heb. iv, 3), He subdued their enemies, and a land flowing with milk and honey became their actual portion. And if *such* experiences be not those of the writer, or the reader, it is just because he is failing to conduct himself as Israel did here.

Having entered so fully into an attempt to explain the fundamental principles underlying this incident and the main lessons to be learned from it, there will be the less need to spend much time on its details. "There shall be a space between you and it about two thousand cubits by measure: come not near unto it" (verse 4). That was parallel with the solemn prohibition given unto Irael when the Lord was about to enter into covenant with their fathers, and make known unto them the terms of that covenant: "the third day the Lord will come down in the sight of all the people upon mount Sinai. And thou shalt set bounds unto the people round about, saying, Take heed to yourselves that ye go not up into the mount or touch the bound of it. Whosoever toucheth the mount shall be surely put to death" (Ex. xix, 12). The spiritual application of both unto us is set forth in that word, "God is greatly to be feared in the assembly of the saints and to be had in reverence of all them that are round about Him" (Psa. lxxxix, 7). Or, to express the same in New Testament language, "Let us have grace whereby we may serve God acceptably with reverence and godly fear: for our God is a consuming fire" (Heb. xii, 28, 29).

The natural and local reason why the ark of the covenant should proceed so far in advance was that it could readily be seen by all the vast multitude: had there been no space between it and them, those who followed closely behind it would obscure the view of the others—only those in the first few ranks had been able to behold it. But being borne by the priests half a mile in the van, the ark would be visible to the whole multitude. But typically and spiritually the lessons inculcated were: First, we should ever bear in mind that by nature we are sinners, and as such far removed from the Holy One. Second, that as sinners we are to look off unto Christ as our Sin-bearer, of which the mercy seat or propitiatory (which formed the lid of the ark) spoke. As the uplifted serpent on the pole (emblem of Christ bearing the curse for His people) was visible to all the congregation, so the ark in the foreground. Third, that as saints we need to keep our eyes steadfastly fixed upon Him, "looking off unto Jesus the Author and Finisher of faith" (Heb.

xii, 2), for it is a life of faith unto which He has called us, strength for which is to be found in Him alone.

Fourth, Christ's leaving His people an example that they should "follow His steps," for "when He putteth forth His sheep, He goeth before them and the sheep follow Him" (John x, 4): our duty is to "follow the Lamb whithersoever He goeth" (Rev. xiv, 4). Fifth, the immeasurable superiority of Christ above His people—"that in all things He should have the pre-eminence" (Col. i, 18), He being the Head, we, but members of His body. This must ever be borne in mind by them, for though He be their Kinsman-Redeemer and is not ashamed to call them "brethren," nevertheless He is their Lord and their God, and to be owned and worshipped as such—"that all should honour the Son even as they honour the Father" (John v, 23). Sixth, that we must conduct ourselves toward the Lord our God with proper decorum and not with unholy familiarity. Seventh, that He entered the anti-typical Canaan in advance, to take possession of heaven on our behalf: "whither the Forerunner is *for us* entered" (Heb. vi, 20)—there is both a present and future, an initial and a perfect occupying of our heritage.

"Yet there shall be a space between you and it, about two thousand cubits by measure: come not near unto it, that ye may know the way by which ye must go; for ye have not passed this way heretofore" (iii, 4). Having pointed out some of the probable reasons why the ark was to proceed so far in advance of the people, we must now turn to consider the meaning of the last clause of this verse. Personally, we consider the commentators and sermonizers have quite missed the force of the "for ye have not passed this way heretofore" when they explain it is signifying "For ye are about to march over *unfamiliar* ground." Admittedly the Hebrew, and at first glance this English rendering, appears to decidedly favour such a view, yet a careful weighing of this clause in the light of its whole setting seem to require a different interpretation of it, understanding it to mean "for ye have not marched in this *manner* hitherto." Nor is that by any means a wresting of the text, for though the Hebrew word "derek" be translated "way" in the vast majority of instances, yet it is rendered "manner" eight times—as, for example, in Genesis xix, 31; Isaiah x, 24, 26).

To give as the reason why the children of Israel should follow the ark on this occasion as "because ye are about to tread new and strange ground" seems to possess little or no point, for had not *that* been equally true on most of their journeying across the wilderness! But, it will be asked, to what else is the reference? We answer something entirely different from what had marked their marches previously, as the "heretofore" indicates. The immediate context is concerned with the informing of Israel as to when they were to advance: "when ye see the ark of the covenant of the Lord your God, and the priests the Levites bearing it, *then* ye shall remove from your place and go after it" (verse 3). Hitherto, it was only when the cloud moved that they did so too (see Ex. iii, 21, 22, xl, xxxviii); "whether it was by day or by night that the cloud was taken up, they journeyed" (Num. ix, 21, and cf. xiv, 14). During the whole of the preceding forty years Israel had been led by that supernatural "pillar of cloud," but now and henceforth that cloud was no longer to be with them. It was a visible token of Jehovah's presence, especially granted unto Moses, and with his death it disappeared.

A different arrangement was now made, a new means for recognizing God's will concerning their journeyings was now revealed unto Israel, another symbol of Jehovah's presence should henceforth strike terror into the hearts of His enemies. The ark of the covenant now took, in an important sense, a new position. Formerly, when journeying the ark had been carried in the midst of the host. It had indeed gone before Israel on one previous occasion "to search out a resting place for them" (Num. x, 33), yet the very next verse informs us "and the cloud of the Lord was upon them by day, when they went out of the camp"; and, as we have seen, the immediate sequel was the fatal apostasy of that generation. The cloud had moved above the ark (cf. Lev. xvi, 2), where all the people could see it easily and follow the ark without inconvenience; but now the cloud was no longer with them—the ark becoming their visible guide.. Another indication of this new arrangement appears in the ones who bore the ark. A specific command had been given that the ark should be carried by the sons of Kohath (Num. iii, 30, 31; iv, 15), but here "the priests" were appointed as its bearers.

Thus, in keeping with this new venture by the new generation, a different order of procedure was appointed—"ye have not travelled in this manner before." The first generation of Israel had been a lamentable and utter failure, but there can never be any failure with the Lord God, nor in the accomplishment of His eternal counsels. God always takes care of His own glory and of the full and final blessing of His people according to His purpose; yea, He never suffers them to be divorced or pass out of His own hands. In His wondrous wisdom and amazing grace God has inseparably united the two, and therefore does He make all things work together for the accomplishment of each alike, for He has made His people and their blessing a constituent part of His glory—"Israel My glory" (Isaiah. xlvi, 13). Thus we see how fitting it was that the ark of the covenant went in advance of the twelve tribes on their entrance into Canaan, which the Lord had chosen to be the place where He would make a full display of Himself in the midst of His people. As the Lord had magnified Himself before Pharaoh and his hosts in Egypt and at the Red Sea in connection with Israel's exodus, so now He would magnify Himself in the sight of the Canaanites as He bared His arm on behalf of His people.

This is indeed a marvellous and blessed truth that God has bound up the good of His people with His own manifestative glory, that at the same time that He furthers the one He promotes the other also. It is a truth which ought to exercise a powerful influence upon our hearts and lives, both in strengthening holy confidence and in preventing unholy conduct. It furnishes us with an invincible plea when praying for the prosperity of God's cause on earth or for our own individual fruitfulness: "grant it, O Lord, for the honour of Thy great name." It was on *that* ground Moses, in a sore crisis, presented his petition (Num. xiv, 15-17), so Joshua (vii, 9), Hezekiah (II Kings xix, 19), Joel (ii, 17). But One far greater than any of those prayed "Father, the hour is come, glorify Thy Son, that Thy Son also may glorify Thee" (John xvii, 1). And should not each Christian say, "Father undertake for me, that Thy child may—in his measure—glorify Thee"! Yet this wondrous truth has a bearing on duty as well as privilege. Since my good and God's glory be inseparably united, how careful I should be in avoiding everything which would bring reproach upon His name! How diligent in seeking to tread that path where communion with Him is alone to be had! How zealous in "doing all things to the glory of God" (I Cor. x, 31).

"And Joshua said unto the people, Sanctify yourselves, for tomorrow the

Lord will do wonders among you" (iii, 5). The word "sanctify" is one of the most difficult terms to define that is used in Scripture: partly because of the great variety of objects to which it is applied; partly because it has so many different shades of meaning; partly because doctrinally and experimentally considered there is both a Divine and a human side to sanctification, and few find it easy to adjust those two sides in their minds. With their customary partiality Calvinistic writers and preachers confine themselves almost entirely to the Church's sanctification by the Father (setting her apart from the non-elect by His eternal decree), by the Son (who cleansed her from her sins and adorned her by His merits), and by the Holy Spirit (by her regeneration and daily renewing), and say little or nothing upon the necessity and duty of the Christian's *sanctifying himself*. Whereas Arminian writers and preachers dwell almost exclusively on the human side of things, as the believer's dedication of himself unto God and His service, and his daily cleansing of himself by the Word: Since the days of the Puritans few indeed have made a full-orbed presentation of this important truth.

The first time the term occurs in Holy Writ is Genesis ii, 3, and, as is invariably the case, this *initial* mention at once indicates its essential meaning and content: "And God blessed the seventh day and sanctified it," which obviously means that He separated it from the other six days and set it apart for His own particular use—such is the underlying and root idea in all its subsequent occurrences where *God* Himself is the Agent or Actor. The next reference is Exodus xiii, 2: "Sanctify unto Me all the firstborn: whatsoever openeth the womb among the children of Israel, of man or beast: it is Mine": that was something which the Lord required *from them*, namely, to dedicate and devote the firstborn entirely unto Him. The third occurrence is in Exodus xix: "And the Lord said unto Moses, Go unto the people and sanctify them today and tomorrow, and let them wash their clothes. And be ready against the third day, for the third day the Lord will come down in the sight of all the people upon mount Sinai" (verses 10, 11, and see verse 15). There the word "sanctify" manifestly has reference unto a personal cleansing by the Israelites themselves, to fit them for the approach of the thrice Holy One.

Now it is quite clear that the injunction which Joshua gave unto Israel in verse 5 was of precisely the same import as that which Moses received for the people in Exodus xix. The Lord was about to appear on their behalf, and they were required to be in a meet condition. When God bade Jacob go to Bethel and make there an altar unto Him, we are told that the patriarch said unto his household, "Put away the strange gods that are among you and be clean, and change your garments" (Gen. xxxv, i, 2)—idols and the worship of the Lord do not accord. Unto the elders of Bethlehem the prophet said, "I am come to sacrifice unto the Lord: sanctify yourselves, and come with me to the sacrifice" (I Sam. xvi, 5). In each case the reference was first unto the removal of ceremonial defilement, the putting away of all outward pollution, and then to bringing their hearts into a suitable frame towards the One with whom they had to do, for God has never been satisfied with mere external purification and punctiliousness of formal worship (Isa. xxix, 13, 14). Sacred duties call for diligent preparation on the part of those who would discharge them. Holy things are not to be touched with unholy hands nor approached with hearts filled by the world (Psa. xxvi, 6; I Tim. ii, 8).

Christians are bidden to draw near unto God, "having their hearts sprinkled from an evil conscience [i.e. all known sin forsaken and confessed] and their bodies washed with pure water "—their daily walk regulated and purified by the Word (Heb. x, 22), for we must not insult Him by carelessness and moral unfitness. In order thereto we need to give constant heed to that precept, " Let us cleanse ourselves from all filthiness of the flesh and spirit, perfecting holiness in the fear of God " (II Cor. vii, 1). And be it carefully noted that " cleanse ourselves " is as much a part of the inspired Word of God as is " the blood of Jesus Christ His Son cleanseth us from all sin," and that that latter statement is qualified by (though scarcely ever quoted!) " If we walk in the light as He is in the light." The Holy One requires us to sanctify ourselves both internally and externally, and if we do not, our worship is unacceptable. " If a man purge himself from these [the things which " dishonour "] he shall be a vessel unto honour, sanctified; and meet for the Master's use, prepared unto every good work " (II Tim. ii, 21). " Every man that hath this hope in him *purifieth himself* even as He is pure " (I John iii, 3). How? By mortifying his lusts and cultivating his graces, by daily repentings and renewings of his consecration.

" Sanctify yourselves," then, has been an imperative requirement of God upon His people in all generations. The only difference which the change of covenant has made is that, under the old, their sanctification of themselves consisted chiefly in a ceremonial and external purification, while that of the new is principally a moral and internal one, and where *that* obtains the outward life will be adjusted to our Rule. No servant of Christ declares " all the counsel of God " who fails to press that imperative requirement of God's upon His people, and if he be silent thereon he " withholds " that which is " profitable for them." *We* must " draw nigh to God " if we would have Him draw nigh unto us (James iv, 8), and, as that verse goes on to tell the careless and those with unexercised consciences, in order to draw near unto Him aright we must " cleanse our hands and purify our hearts "! " Who shall ascend into the hill of the Lord? or who shall stand in His holy place? " which in New Testament language means, Who shall be received by God as an acceptable worshipper? The inspired answer is, " He that hath clean hands and a pure heart, who hath not lifted up his soul unto vanity, nor sworn deceitfully " (Psa. xxiv, 3, 4). Alas that so little heed is now given to such verses.

" And Joshua said unto the people, Sanctify yourselves, for tomorrow the Lord will do wonders among you." That was an enforcing of their moral responsibility. It was a call for them to cleanse themselves and dedicate them- selves unto the Lord their God. It was a bidding of them to prepare themselves by prayer and meditation, to recall God's gracious interventions in the past, to ponder His ineffable holiness, awful majesty, mighty power and abundant mercy, and thereby bring their hearts into a fit frame, so that with faith, reverence and admiration they might behold the great work which Jehovah was about to do for them. They must be in a suitable condition in order to witness such a manifestation of His glory: their hearts must be " perfect toward Him "—sincere and upright, honest and holy—if He was to " show Himself strong in their behalf " (II Chron. xvi, 9). Have we not here the explanation why God is *not* now performing marvels in the churches?—they are too carnal and worldly! And is not this the reason why a way is not being made through our personal " jordans "? And why we receive not wondrous and blessed discoveries of His glory—we are not "sanctified" in a practical way nor sufficiently separated from the world.

"And Joshua said unto the people, Sanctify yourselves, for tomorrow the Lord will do wonders among you." Observe the positive and confident language of Joshua: there was no doubt whatever in his mind that their covenant God would perform a miracle on their behalf, and therefore he assured them accordingly. What an example for Christ's servant to follow! He has no right to expect that his flock will wax valiant in fight if their shepherd be full of unbelief and fear. And, too, when urging upon them the duty of self-sanctification, he should fail not to add the encouragement, "the Lord will do wonders," for sure it is that the more we shun that which defiles, and devote ourselves unto God's service and glory, the more will He work mightily in us, for us and through us. It is quite possible that on this occasion Joshua had in mind that word, "And it came to pass when the ark set forward that Moses said, Rise up, O Lord, and let Thine enemies be scattered" (Num. x, 35), for certain Joshua was that when the ark should now advance the waters of the Jordan would recede.

"And Joshua spake unto the priests, saying, Take up the ark of the covenant and pass over before the people. And they took up the ark of the covenant and went before the people" (verse 6). Having directed the people what to do, Joshua now gives instruction unto the priests. Thereby he acted in strict accord with his own personal commission ("do according to all that is written in this book of the Law" (i, 8)—i.e. the Pentateuch), for in preparation of Jehovah's descent upon Sinai Moses had given express charge to the priests as well as to the people (Ex. xix, 22). In the charge here given to the priests we see how their subjection to the revealed will of God was put to the proof, how their faith and courage were tested, and how their reverence for the symbol of the Lord's presence was to be manifested. Corresponding unto them today are the ministers of the Gospel, concerning whom T. Scott well said, "They are especially required to set before the people an example of obedience, patience, and unshakable confidence in God, by abiding in their perilous position or difficult stations which He has assigned them, when others fear to pass that way; and in so doing they may expect peculiar support and protection."

The people were commanded to follow the priests as far as they carried the ark, but no farther, and God's children today are responsible to heed and obey His servants (Heb. xiii, 7, 17) only while they set forth and honour Him of whom the ark was a figure. Namely, Christ; yet not simply as a Saviour, but in the fullness of His threefold office: as our Prophet or Teacher (the Law within the ark), our Priest (the propitiatory upon it), our King and Lord ("the ark of *the covenant*"). But the minister of the Gospel is required to do more than faithfully preach Christ, namely *live* Him: "Be thou an example of the believers in word, in conversation, in love, in spirit, in faith, in purity" (I Tim. iv, 12); "In all things showing thyself a pattern of good works" (Titus ii, 7; and cf. I Thess. ii 10; I Peter v. 3). The minister is to set before his people a godly example. Unless he takes the lead in enduring hardships and facing dangers (not showing more concern for his own ease and safety), then his exhortations unto self-denial and courageous action will have no power upon his hearers.

Chapter 6

CROSSING THE JORDAN
Joshua 3:7-17

The Miracle

"And the Lord said unto Joshua, This day will I begin to magnify thee in the sight of all Israel, that they may know that as I was with Moses so I will be with thee. And thou shalt command the priests that bear the ark of the covenant, saying, When ye are come to the brink of the water of Jordan ye shall stand still in Jordan" (Jos. iii, 7, 8). Before his death it had been revealed to Moses by the Lord that Joshua should be his successor as the leader of His people, and unto that office he had been solemnly set apart (Num. xxvii, 18-23). Moses had also announced unto Israel that Joshua " should cause them to inherit the Land " (Deut. i, 38), and " the children of Israel hearkened unto him, and did as the Lord commanded Moses " (Deut. xxxiv, 9). After the death of Moses the people had avowed their willingness to do whatever Joshua commanded them and to go whither he should send them, and expressed the desire that Divine assistance would be granted him: " the Lord thy God be with thee, as He was with Moses " (i, 16, 17). In the interval the two spies had reconnoitred Jericho at his orders, the people had followed him from Shittim to the Jordan (iii, 1), and had remained there three days. Now the time had come for the Lord to more fully authenticate His servant.

Joshua had duly discharged his duty and now he was to be rewarded. He had set before the people a noble example by acting faith on God's word, had confidently expressed his assurance that God would make good His promise (i, 11, 15), and now the Lord would honour the one who had honoured Him. Joshua had been faithful in a few things and he should be made ruler over many. Devotedness unto God never passes unrecognized by Him. The Lord would now put signal honour upon Joshua in the sight of Israel as He had done upon Moses at the Red Sea and at Sinai. " The Lord said unto Moses, Lo, I come *unto thee* in a thick cloud that the people may hear when I *speak* unto thee, and *believe thee* for ever " (Ex. xix, 9): thus did He honour and authenticate Moses. And here at the Jordan he magnified Joshua by the authority which He conferred upon him, and attested him as His appointed leader of Israel. The result of this is stated in iv, 15, " on that day the Lord magnified Joshua in the sight of all Israel, and they feared [revered and obeyed] him as they feared Moses, all the days of his [Joshua's] life."

But we must be careful lest we overlook something far more glorious than what has just been pointed out. Surely those words, " This day will I begin to magnify thee in the sight of all Israel," should at once turn our thoughts to One infinitely superior to Joshua: that what God did here for His servant was a foreshadowment of what later He did to His Son at this same Jordan. No sooner was our blessed Lord baptized in that river than,

" Lo, the heavens were opened unto Him and he saw the Spirit of God descending like a dove, and lighting upon Him: And, lo, a voice from heaven, saying, This is My beloved Son, in whom I am well pleased " (Matt. iii, 16, 17). Then was *He* " made manifest to Israel " (John i, 31). Then was He authenticated for His great mission. Then did God " begin to magnify Him." Still more wonderful is the type when we observe at what part of the Jordan this occurred: " These things were done in Beth-abara " (John i, 28), which signified " the place of passage " (John i, 28), so that Christ was attested by the Father at the very place where Israel passed through the river and where Joshua was magnified!

Solemn indeed was the contrast. By what took place at the Jordan Israel knew that Joshua was their Divinely appointed leader and governor, and therefore they " feared him . . . all the days of his life " (iv, 15), rendering implicit and undeviating obedience unto his orders: " And Israel served the Lord all the days of Joshua " (xxiv, 31). But after the anti-typical Joshua had been far more illustriously magnified at the Jordan, identified as the Son of God incarnate, and owned by the Father as the One in whom He delighted, what was Israel's response? Did they love and worship Him? Did they fear and obey Him? Very far otherwise: " He came unto His own, and His own received Him not " (John i, 11). Their hearts were alienated and their ears closed against Him. Though He spake as never man spake, though He went about doing good, though He wrought miracles of power and mercy, they " despised and rejected Him," and after a brief season cried " Away with Him, crucify Him." Marvel, dear Christian reader, that the Lord of glory endured such humiliation " for us men and our salvation." Wonder and adore that He so loved us as not only to be willing to be hated of men but smitten of God that our sins might be put away.

" And thou shalt command the priests that bear the ark of the covenant, saying, When ye are come to the brink of the water of Jordan, ye shall stand still in Jordan " (verse 8). What anointed eye can fail to see here again a shadowing forth of a greater than Joshua! Next after this mention of God's beginning to magnify Joshua in the sight of the people, we find him exercising high authority and giving orders to the priests; and almost the first public act of Christ's after the Father had attested and honoured Him at the Jordan is what is recorded in Matthew v—vii. In that sermon on the mount we behold our Saviour doing the very same thing: exercising high authority, as He evinced by His frequently repeated " I say unto you," and issuing orders to His disciples, who, under the new covenant, correspond to the priests under the old; and it is very striking to see how the twofold application of that term and the type appear in that sermon. As we pointed out in our last, the " priests," when bearing the ark of the covenant, were figures of the ministers of the Gospel in their official character, but looked at as those privileged to draw near unto God. The " priests " were types of all the redeemed of Christ (I Peter ii, 5, 9).

Now in the opening verses of Matthew v, it was His servants whom " Christ taught " (verses 1, 2, 13-16), and to whom He issued commandments, for " His disciples " there are to be understood as " apostles "—as in x, i, 2, and xxviii, 16-20. Yet as we continue reading that wondrous discourse we soon perceive that it cannot be restricted unto ministers of the Gospel, but is addressed to the whole company of His people. Therein we learn what is required from the redeemed by the One who is their Lord, possessed of Divine authority: namely, entire subjection unto Him, unreserved conformity to

His revealed will. As the priests of Israel must order their actions by the instructions which they received from Joshua, so must the ministers of the Gospel take their orders from their Divine Master, and so also must the whole company of His redeemed be regulated wholly by the injunctions of the Captain of their salvation. Nothing less is due unto Him who endured such shame and suffering on their behalf; nothing else becomes those who owe their all unto Him who died for them. It is in *this* way that their gratitude and devotion is to be manifested: "If ye love Me, keep My commandments" (John xiv, 13).

"And thou shalt command the priests that bear the ark of the covenant, saying, When ye are come to the brink of the water of Jordan, ye shall stand still in Jordan." What a testing of their faith and obedience was that! The swollen and unfordable river before them, and they ordered to advance unto the very edge thereof, yea, to stand still in it! How senseless such a procedure unto carnal reason! Such too appears the policy and means appointed by God in the Gospel: "For after that in the wisdom of God the world by wisdom knew not God, it pleased God by the foolishness of preaching to save them that believe" (I Cor. i, 21). And the preaching of Christ crucified, my ministerial friends, is entirely a matter of faith and obedience, for to our natural intellect and perceptions it appears to be utterly inadequate to produce eternal fruits. And even when we *have* preached Christ to the best of our poor powers, it often seems that our efforts are unavailing, and we are perhaps sorely tempted to act contrary unto that word, "the weapons of our warfare are not carnal, but spiritual." Seek grace, then, to heed the lesson pointed by the above verse: discharge your responsibility to the utmost extent and trustfully leave the issue with God, as did the priests.

But there is not only a much-needed message contained in verse 8 for the discouraged servants of Christ, but there is one too for the rank and file of God's people, especially those of them who may be sorely tried by present circumstances. Their faith and obedience must be tested—that its reality may appear. Some of the Lord's commandments present less difficulty, for they are embodied in the laws of our land and respected by all decent people. But there are others of His precepts which are most trying to flesh and blood and which are scoffed at by the unregenerate. Nevertheless, our course is clear: there can be no picking and choosing—"whatsoever He saith unto you, do" (John ii, 5). Yes, but when I *have* sought to obey to the best of my ability I find circumstances all against me, a situation beyond my powers to cope with, a "jordan" too deep and wide for me to pass through. Very well, here is the word exactly suited to your case: come to "the brink of the water" and then "stand still in it": proceed to your utmost limits in the path of duty and then count upon the omnipotent One to undertake for you.

"And Joshua said unto the children of Israel, Come hither, and hear the words of the Lord your God" (verse 9). Once more our minds are carried beyond the type to Antitype, who said unto Israel, "My doctrine is not Mine, but His that sent Me" (John vii, 16), and again, "the Father which sent Me, He gave Me a commandment what I should say and what I should speak" (John xii, 49). And therefore the most diligent heed is to be given and the most unquestioning obedience rendered unto Him. "And Joshua said, Hereby ye shall know that the living God is among you, and that He will without fail drive out from before you the Canaanites, and the Hittites, and the Hivites, and the Perizzites, and the Girgashites, and the

Amorites, and the Jebusites " (verse 10). That title, " the living God," is used in the Scriptures to point a contrast with the inanimate idols of the heathen (II Kings xix, 4; I Thess. i, 9), and doubtless was employed by Joshua on this occasion for the purpose of accentuating the impotency and worthlessness of all false gods, who were utterly incapable of rendering aid, still less of performing prodigies, for their deluded votaries; a warning also to Israel against the sin of idolatry to which they ever were so prone. As Joshua owned Jehovah as " the living God " so also Christ acknowledged the One who had sent Him as the " living Father " (John vi, 57).

"And Joshua said, Hereby ye shall know that the living God is among you " (verse 10). Note carefully the statement which immediately follows: " and that He will without fail drive out from before you the Canaanites," etc. We had naturally expected Joshua to say in this connection, God will open a way for you to pass through this Jordan, but instead he gives assurance of the conquest of the " seven nations in the land of Canaan " (Acts xiii, 19). And why? To assure Israel that the miracle of the Jordan was a Divine earnest, a certain guarantee, that the Lord *would continue* to show Himself strong in their behalf. And similarly He assures His people today. " Being confident of this very thing: that He which hath begun a good work in you, will finish it " (Phil. i, 6). Israel's supernatural journey through Jordan was a figure of our regeneration, when we pass from death unto life, and that experience ensures that the living God will *perfect* that which concerneth us " (Psa. cxxxviii, 8). In a word, regeneration is an infallible earnest of our ultimate glorification. But as Israel concurred with God, and were themselves active in driving out the Canaanites, *so we* have to mortify our lusts and overcome the world in order to possess our inheritance.

Yes, replies the reader, but that is much easier said than done. True, yet, not only is it indispensable that we should do so, but if due attention be paid to the passage before us and its spiritual application unto ourselves, valuable instruction will be found herein as to the secrets of success. Not to anticipate too much what yet remains to be considered in detail, let us summarize the leading points so far as they bear upon what was just said above. First, Israel was required to act with implicit confidence in God: so must we, if we are to be successful in our warfare, for it is " the good fight *of faith* " which we are called upon to wage. Second, Israel must render the most exact obedience to God's revealed will: so we can only prevail over our lusts and possess our possessions by walking in the path of His precepts. Third, Israel had to fix their eyes upon " the ark of the covenant ": so we are to be subject unto Christ in all things, and make daily use of His cleansing blood—the propitiatory which formed the lid of the ark. Fourth, " The Lord of all the earth "—God in His unlimited dominion—was the particular character in which Israel here viewed God: so we must rely upon His all-mighty power and count upon Him making us more than conquerors.

"Behold, the ark of the covenant of the Lord of all the earth passeth over before you into Jordan. Now therefore take you twelve men out of the tribes of Israel, out of every man a tribe. And it shall come to pass, as soon as the soles of the feet of the priests that bear the ark of the Lord, the Lord of all the earth, shall rest in the waters of Jordan, that the waters of Jordan shall be cut off from the waters that come down from above; and they shall stand upon a heap " (verses 11-13). In those words Joshua now specifically announced and described one of the most remarkable of the miracles recorded in Holy Writ. The priests were to proceed unto the edge of the water and then stop—that it might be the more evident that the Jordan was driven back at the presence of the Lord. As Matthew Henry wrote, " God could have divided the river without the priests, but they could not without Him. The priests must herein set a good example and teach the people to do their utmost in the service of God, and trust Him for help in time of need." Note how the opening word of verse 11 emphasized yet again that attention was to be concentrated upon *the ark,* which, as we have previously pointed out, was made for the Law and not the Law for it—typifying Christ, " made under the Law " (Gal. iv, 4), magnifying and making it honourable (Isa. xlii, 21).

Remember too that the propitiatory formed the lid of the ark: it was not only a cover for the sacred coffer, but a *shield* between the Law and the people of God. The central thing within it was the Law (I Kings viii, 9), and between the cherubim on its mercy seat Jehovah had His throne (Psa. xcix, 1). That is why all through Joshua iii and iv it is termed " the ark of the covenant," for when Moses went up upon Sinai the second time we are told that " he wrote upon the tables the words of the covenant, the ten commandments " (Ex. xxxiv, 28). It should be carefully borne in mind that even under the old covenant the *promise* preceded the giving of the Law (Ex. iii, 17; xii, 25), yet the fulfilment thereof was not to be without the enforcing of their accountability. In like manner the ten commandments themselves were prefaced by " I am the Lord thy God which have brought thee out of the land of Egypt," manifesting His " goodness " to them and His " severity " upon their enemies—that was the testimony of His character who entered into covenant with them.

It is to be duly noted that the particular designation given to Jehovah in connection with the ark of the covenant in verse 11 is repeated in verse 13, which at once intimates it is one of special weight and significance. This title, " the Lord of all the earth," is not found in the Pentateuch, occurring here in Joshua iii for the first time, its force being more or less indicated by what is said in verse 10 and the nature and time of the miracle then wrought. The reference here is unto God the Father, and signifies His absolute sovereignty and universal dominion—the Proprietor and Governor of the earth which He created, the One whom none can successfully resist. This title occurs in the Scriptures seven times! Twice in Joshua iii, then in Psalm xcvii, 5, Micah iv, 15, Zechariah vi, 5. In Zechariah iv, 14, we behold the three Persons of the Godhead in their covenant characters: " these are the two Anointed Ones [Christ and the Holy Spirit] that stand before the Lord of all the earth." But in Isaiah liv, 5, we see the incarnate Son, " the Lord of hosts is His name, and thy Redeemer the Holy One of Israel, the God of all the earth shall He be called "—a prophetic intimation of the taking down of the " middle wall of partition," when Jew and Gentile alike should own Him as their *God.*

As a reward for Joshua's past faithfulness and in order to equip him more thoroughly for the great task before him, the Lord determined to put signal honour upon His servant so that Israel might assuredly know that as the mighty God had been with Moses so He would be with his successor (iii, 7). That at once turns our thoughts back to Exodus xiv, and it is both interesting and instructive to trace out the many points of contrast and comparison between what occurred at the Red Sea and here at Jordan. Let us consider first those respects in which they differed.

First, the one terminated Israel's exodus from the house of bondage, while the other initiated their entrance into the land of promise. Second, the former miracle was wrought in order that Israel might escape from the Egyptians, the latter to enable them to approach and conquer the Canaanites. Third, in connection with that, the Lord caused the sea to go back by a strong east wind (Ex. xiv, 21); but with reference to this no means whatever were employed—to demonstrate that He is not tied unto such, but employs or dispenses with them as He pleases. Fourth, the earlier miracle was performed at night time (Ex. xiv, 21), the latter in broad daylight. Fifth, at the Red Sea multitudes were slain, for the Lord "made the waters to return upon the Egyptians, so that it covered the chariots and the horsemen: all the host of Pharaoh that came into the sea after them, there remained not so much as one of them" (Ex. xiv, 28); whereas at the Jordan not a single soul perished. Sixth, the one was wrought for a people who just previously had been full of unbelief and murmuring, saying unto Moses: "Because there were no graves in Egypt, hast thou taken us away to die in the wilderness? wherefore hast thou dealt thus with us?" (Ex. xiv, 11); the other for a people who were believing and obedient (ii, 24; iii, 1).

Seventh, with the sole exception of Caleb and Joshua all the adults who benefited by the former miracle perished in the wilderness because of their unbelief, while not a single one of those who were favoured to share in the latter failed to "possess their possessions." Eighth, at the Red Sea the waters were "divided" (Ex. xiv, 21), but here at the Jordan they were not so— rather they were made to "stand upon a heap" (Josh. iii, 13). Ninth, in the former the believer's judicial death unto sin was typed out; in the latter, his legal oneness with Christ in His resurrection, to be followed by a practical entrance into his inheritance. Tenth, consequently, whereas there was no "sanctify yourselves" before the former, such a call was an imperative requirement for the latter (Josh. iii, 5). Eleventh, the response made by Israel's enemies to the Lord's intervention for Israel at the Red Sea was, "I will pursue, I will overtake, I will divide the spoil, my lust shall be satisfied upon them" (Ex. xv, 9); but in the latter, "It came to pass when all the people of the Amorites, which were on the other side of Jordan westward, and all the kings of the Canaanites . . . heard that the Lord had dried up the waters of Jordan . . . that their heart melted, neither was there spirit in them any more" (Josh. v, 1). Twelfth, after the working of the former "Israel saw the Egyptians dead upon the sea shore" (Ex. xiv, 31); after the latter a cairn of twelve stones memoralized the event (Josh. iv, 20-24).

It is surely remarkable that there are as many analogies between the two miracles as dissimilarities. Yet that illustrates a principle which the attentive observer will find exemplified all through Scripture,·and which the young student is advised to make careful note of. "Two" is the number of *witness*— as the Lord sent forth the apostles in pairs to testify of Him. It was the minimum number for such under the Law (John viii, 17), for if the sworn testimony of two different men agreed, this was considered conclusive. Thus two is also the number of comparison and contrast. Hence it will be found that when there are *only two* of a kind, such as the miracles of the Red Sea and the Jordan, there is always a number of marked resemblances and divergencies between them. Some may like to work out for themselves the parallels and oppositions between the Old and New Testaments, Sinai and Sion, the first and second advents of Christ, the respective careers of Moses and Joshua, the ministries of Elijah and Elisha, and so on. The same principle is exemplified where a Greek word occurs but twice: as "*apopnigo*" (Luke viii, 7, 23), "*apokueo*" (James i, 15, 18), "*panoplia*" (Luke xi, 22;

Eph. vi, 11). So too when two parables, miracles, incidents, are placed in juxtaposition.

The following are some of the points of resemblance between these two. (1) In each case the miracle was connected with water. (2) Neither was done in a corner or beheld by only a few, but was witnessed by the whole nation of Israel. (3) Each was preceded by an act required of God's servant—Moses, in the stretching forth of his hand (Ex. xiv, 21); Joshua, in giving command to the people. (4) Each was the removal of a formidable barrier in Israel's path. (5) Each had the design of authenticating Israel's leader (Ex. xiv, 31; Josh. iv, 14). (6) Each presented a severe test unto Israel's faith and obedience (Ex. xiv, 15; Josh. iii, 3). (7) In each case they passed over dry-shod. (8) Both miracles were wrought in silence: neither was accompanied by shouts of triumph, nor was there any sounding of the rams' horns—as, later, in the case of the miraculous fall of Jericho's walls (Josh. vi, 9, 20). (9) Afterward both the Red Sea and the waters of the Jordan returned again to their normal state. (10) Each inaugurated a new period in Israel's history. (11) In both there was a prodigious display of Jehovah's power to the consternation of His enemies. (12) Both miracles were celebrated by songs of praise.

Some of our readers may think that we made a slip in the last point: they will recall the songs of Israel in Exodus xv and ask, But where is there any song of praise celebrating what occurred at the Jordan? Separate celebration there is none, but the two miracles are conjoined and made the special subject of sacred ode, namely in Psalm cxiv, to which we would now direct attention. Many of those who are best qualified to express a considered opinion on the merits of poetry have freely testified that in this psalm the art of sacred minstrelsy has reached its climax: that no human mind has ever been able to equal, much less to excel, the grandeur of its contents. In it we have most vividly depicted the greatest of inanimate things rendering obeisance unto their Maker. As one beautifully summarized it, " The God of Jacob is exalted as having command over river, sea and mountain, and causing all nature to pay homage and tribute before His majesty."

Psalm cxiv is a remarkable one in several respects. First, it is written without any preface. It is as though the soul of its author was so elevated and filled with a sense of the Divine glory that he could not pause to compose an introduction, but rather burst forth at once into the midst of his theme, namely, the wondrous works which were wrought for Israel of old, of which they were the actual eye-witnesses and beneficiaries. Second, in it the rules of grammar are ignored, for in verse two we find the possessive pronoun used without a preceding substantive. The presence of God is concealed in the first verse, for, as Isaac Watts pointed out, " If God had appeared before, there could be no wonder when the mountains should leap and the sea retire— therefore, that these convulsions of nature may be brought in with due surprise, His name is not mentioned till afterwards." Third, this psalm was fittingly made a part of " the Hallelujah " which the Jews of all later generations were wont to sing at their passover supper. Fourth, all that is portrayed in this psalm was typical of the still greater wonders wrought by the redemptive work of Christ.

That psalm celebrates the marvels performed by Jehovah on behalf of His people of old, particularly their exodus from Egypt and His conducting them through the Red Sea and the Jordan. Such glorious acts of God's power and grace must never be forgotten, but owned in gladsome praise. " When Israel went out of Egypt, the house of Jacob from a people of strange language, Judah was His sanctuary, Israel His dominion" (verses 1 and 2). The Lord delivered His people from the house of bondage that they might serve Him and show forth His praises, in the duties of worship and in obedience to His Law. In order thereto, He set up His "sanctuary" among them—first in the tabernacle, then in the temple, finally in Christ His incarnate Son—in which He gave special tokens of His presence. Further, He set up His "dominion" or throne among them, being Himself their Lord, King and Judge. Observe well how that here, as everywhere, privilege and duty, Divine favour and human responsibility, are *united*. God acted graciously. God maintained the rights of His righteousness. As His "sanctuary" Israel was separated unto God as a peculiar people, a nation of priests, holy unto the Lord. As His "dominion" they were a theocracy, governed directly by Him. So *we* have been redeemed that we should "*serve* Him . . . in holiness and righteousness . . . all the days of our life" (Luke i, 74, 75). If we enjoy the favours of His "sanctuary" we must also submit to His "dominion."

"The sea saw, and fled; Jordan was driven back. The mountains skipped like rams, the little hills like lambs" (verses 3, 4). In those words the inspired poet depicts inanimate creation trembling before its Maker. It was because Jehovah was Israel's "sanctuary" and "dominion" that the Red Sea fled before them. Sinai quivered and the waters of Jordan were effectually dammed. The Almighty was at the head of His people, and nothing could stand before Him, or withstand them. "The sea saw": it now beheld what it never had previously, namely, "the pillar of cloud" (Ex. xiv, 19)—symbol of Jehovah's presence; and, unable to endure such a sight, fled to the right and to the left, opening a clear passage for the Hebrews. Jordan, too, as the ark of the covenant entered its brim, was driven back, so that its rapid torrent was stayed, yea, fled uphill. Graphic figures were those of that invincible operation of Divine grace in the hearts of God's elect, when the mighty power of God is so put forth that turbulent rebels are tamed, fierce lusts subdued, proud imaginations cast down, and self-sufficient wiseacres are brought to enter the kingdom of Christ as "little children"!

"What ailed thee, O thou sea, that thou fleddest? thou Jordan, that thou wast driven back? Ye mountains that ye skipped like rams, ye little hills like lambs?" (verses 5, 6). That is the language of holy irony, the Spirit of God pouring contempt upon the unbelieving thoughts of men who foolishly imagine that the Almighty can be withstood, yea, thwarted by the creatures of His own hands. "What ailed thee, O thou sea?": the poet apostrophizes it in the terms of mockery. "Wast thou so terribly afraid? Did thy proud strength then utterly fail thee? Did thy very heart dry up, so that no resistance wast left in thee?" Such an interrogation also teaches us that it behoves us to inquire after the reason of things when we behold the marvels of nature, and not merely gaze upon them as senseless spectators. We have here also a foreshadowing and sure prophecy of the utter impotency of the wicked in the last great day: if the granite cliffs of Sinai were shaken to their base when Jehovah descended upon it, what consternation and trembling will seize the stoutest hearts when they stand before their awful Judge! See verse 7.

Psalm cxiv is by no means the only place where we find celebration made of the miracles witnessed at the Red Sea and Jordan and the other marvels wrought about the same time. The prophet Habakkuk also links together those two wonders, and in language which serves to cast further light upon the Lord's design therein—teaching us the importance and necessity of carefully comparing Scripture with Scripture, if we would obtain a full view of any event or subject, for each passage makes its own distinct contribution unto the whole. In Joshua we behold the Lord acting more in His sovereign grace and covenant faithfulness on behalf of the seed of Abraham, but Habakkuk informs us He was exercising *righteous indignation* against His enemies, who had devoted themselves unto the most horrible idolatry and unspeakable immorality. It was in holy wrath against both the Egyptians and the Canaanites that God put forth His mighty power, when "the iniquity of the Amorites" had come to the "full" (Gen. xv, 16). The whole of Habakkuk iii is exceedingly graphic and solemn, though we must do no more here than make a bare quotation of portions of it.

The Holy One is vividly pictured as manifesting Himself in the whole of that district which lay to the south of Judah, including Sinai, when "His glory covered the heavens and the earth was full of His praise" (verse 3). "He stood and measured the earth" (verse 6) or "caused the earth to tremble," as the Jewish Targum renders it, and as appears to be required by the parallelism of the next clause: "He beheld [merely "looked upon"!], and drave asunder the nations." That sixth verse may be regarded as the "text" which is illustrated by God's control over the forces of nature. "Was the Lord displeased against the rivers? was Thine anger against the rivers? [when He made the lower waters of the Jordan to flee away, and the higher ones to "stand on a heap"]; was Thy wrath against the sea, that Thou didst ride upon Thine horses and Thy chariots of salvation?" (verse 8), when, as an invincible Conqueror, Thou didst carry all before Thee! "The mountains [of Sinai] saw Thee and trembled: the overflowing of the water [Josh. iii, 15] passed by: the deep uttered his voice and lifted up his hands on high" (verse 10)—see Joshua iii, 16—as though in token of submission to and adoration of their Maker. "The sun and moon stood still in their habitation" (verse 11)—see Joshua x, 12, 13. "Thou didst march through the land in indignation, Thou didst thresh the heathen *in anger*" (verse 12).

Returning to Joshua iii. "Behold the ark of the covenant of the Lord of all the earth passeth over before you into Jordan. . . . And it shall come to pass, as soon as the soles of the feet of the priests that bear the ark of the Lord, the Lord of all the earth, shall rest in the waters of Jordan, that the waters of Jordan shall be cut off from the waters that come down from above; and they shall stand upon a heap" (verses 11, 13). "He who is your covenant God with you, has both the right and power to command, control, use and dispose of all nations and all creatures. He is 'the Lord of all the earth' and therefore He needs not you, nor can He be benefited by you: therefore it is your honour and happiness to have Him in covenant with you; all the creatures are at your service, when He pleases all shall be employed for you. When we are praising and worshipping God as Israel's God, and ours through Christ, we must remember that He is the Lord of the whole earth, and reverence and trust in Him accordingly. . . . While we make God's precepts our rule, His promises our stay, and His providence our guide, we need not dread the greatest difficulties we may meet with in the way of duty" (Matthew Henry).

Here we may see yet another reason—beyond those we have previously pointed out—why the sacred ark was carried so far in advance of the people (verse 4), namely, that the whole congregation might have a better and clearer view of the miracle which God was about to perform for them. The host of Israel standing so far in the rear would have a much plainer opportunity of witnessing and adoring the glorious power of their God.

Lessons from the Crossing

Before mentioning some of the different aspects of Truth which are illustrated in Joshua iii, let us look at the miracle there recorded. "And it came to pass, when the people removed from their tents to pass over Jordan, and the priests bearing the ark of the covenant before the people; and as they that bare the ark were come unto Jordan, and the feet of the priests that bare the ark were dipped in the brim of the water, for Jordan overfloweth all his banks all the time of harvest" (verses 14, 15). First, observe well the *time* when this wonder was wrought. It was in the spring of the year, when the river was in spate. At that season the snows on Mount Lebanon (near which Jordan had its rise) melted, when there was an annual inundation of the valley. God selected a month when conditions were such as to form the most suitable background for an illustrious display of His power. He did not defer the crossing of the river until the end of summer, when it had been at its lowest, but chose the month when it was at its broadest and deepest, that His hand might be the more plainly seen. I Chronicles xii, 15, tells us Jordan continued to "overflow" in the days of David.

Next, we would take note of a little detail here which brings out the minute accuracy of Scripture and attests its historical verity, and that in a most artless manner. Joshua iii, 15, tells us it was "the time of harvest." Now the "barley harvest" came first (Ruth i, 22), and after an interval of a month or so the "wheat harvest" (Ruth ii, 21, 23). Now the Jordan was crossed on the tenth day of the fourth month (Josh. iv, 19), or four days before the Passover, which fell in with the barley harvest. From Exodus ix, 31, we learn that the barley ripened at that season, for the plague of hail was only a day or two before the Passover. From that verse we learn that the "flax" crop ripened at the same time, and, since the climate of Palestine differed little from that of Egypt, this, no doubt, was the case in Canaan too. Thus, by a comparison of Joshua iii, 13, and iv, 19, with Exodus ix, 31, we see that Israel crossed the Jordan when both the barley and the *flax* were ripe. What a silent but convincing confirmation does that furnish of the incidental statement that Rahab hid the spies "with the stalks of *flax*" (ii, 6)! This is one out of scores of similar instances adduced by J. J. Blunt in his remarkable book (out of print) *Undesigned-Coincidences* to manifest the veracity of the Word.

"That the waters which came down from above stood and rose up upon a heap very far from the city Adam, that is beside Zaretan, and those that came down toward the sea of the plain, the salt sea, failed and were cut off; and the people passed over right against Jericho" (verse 16). First, the waters were cleft asunder so that those which came down from above—i.e. from the mountains—were invincibly dammed, so that the down-flowing torrent was supernaturally stayed. It was as though an enormous but invisible sluice had suddenly shut off the stream at its source. Second, the huge volume which had already descended was made to turn backward and stand on a heap in a congealed mass—which in our judgment was more remarkable than what occurred at the Red Sea. That solid wall of water must have appeared like some mammoth buttress, yet without any apparent support. Third, the waters which were already in the Jordan valley rapidly drained away into the Dead Sea, leaving the whole of the river's bed dry—"as far downward, it is likely, as it swelled upward" (Matthew Henry). Most vividly did R. Gosse depict this prodigy.

"At any time the passage of the river by such a multitude, with their wives and children, their flocks and herds, and all their baggage, would have presented formidable difficulties; but now the channel was filled with a deep and impetuous torrent, which overflowed its banks and spread widely on either side, probably extending nearly a mile in width; while in the very sight of the scene were the Canaanitish hosts, who might be expected to pour out from their fortress and exterminate the invading multitude before they could reach the shore. Yet these difficulties were nothing to Almighty power, and only serve to heighten the effect of the stupendous miracle about to be wrought. No sooner had the feet of the priests touched the brim of the overflowing river than the swollen waters receded from them; and not only the broad lower valley but the deep bed of the stream was presently emptied of water, and its pebbly bottom became dry. The waters which had been in the channel speedily ran off, while those which would naturally have replaced them from above were miraculously suspended, and accumulated in a glassy heap, far above the city Adam . . . nearly the whole channel of the Lower Jordan from a little below the Lake of Tiberias to the Dead Sea was dry."

"And the priests that bare the ark of the covenant of the Lord stood firm on dry ground in the midst of Jordan, and all the Israelites passed over on dry ground until all the people were passed clean over Jordan" (verse 17). What a test of the priests' faith and obedience was that!—a much more severe one than that required of them in verse 8. There they were only bidden to step into the brink of the water, which at most occasioned but a temporary inconvenience, though since they had to do so *before* any miracle was wrought, it called for unquestioning submission to the Divine will. But here they were required to remain stationary in the centre of the river bed, which to sight was a most perilous situation—with the great mass of the higher waters liable to suddenly rush down and engulf them. But there they patiently abode, for it must have taken many hours for such a huge multitude to pass over on foot. God's servants are not only called upon to set His people an example of implicit confidence in and full obedience to Him, but to take the lead when dangers threaten and acquit themselves courageously and perseveringly. The Lord fully vindicated the priests' obedience, holding back the mighty torrent until after they too crossed to the farther side; thereby denoting that the same power which divided the waters kept them suspended.

Consider now some of the lessons taught us here.

(1) We are shown the fundamental things which God requires from His people. First, they must "sanctify themselves" (verse 5), the essential elements of which are separation from sin and the world, entire consecration of ourselves unto God. Thereby we evince that He has won our hearts. Second, they must obediently follow the ark of the covenant, ordering their actions by it. In the ark was the Divine Law—the articles of the covenant. They must, in resolve and earnest endeavour, be regulated by the will of God in all things, doing whatsover He commanded them. Third, they must steadily and thankfully view the propitiatory which formed the lid of the ark. Here we behold the blessed balance. The ark spoke of the righteous demands of God upon us, the mercy-seat of His gracious provisions for us. Humbly confess your sins to God, and thankfully plead the cleansing blood

of Christ. If we conduct ourselves by those three basic rules all will be well.

(2) What a glorious God do we serve! He is possessed of all-mighty power and infinite wisdom. All the powers and elements of nature are subject to Him and make way for His presence. When He so pleases He can alter all the properties of those elements and change the course of nature. Nothing is too hard for that One who has turned liquid floods into solid walls, who has caused the sun to stand still (yea, to go backward: II Kings xx, 11), who has made flinty rocks to pour out fountains of water, ravens to feed Elijah, iron to swim, fire not to burn. "He turneth rivers into a wilderness and the water-springs into dry ground. . . . He turneth the wilderness into a standing water and dry ground into water-springs. And there He maketh the hungry to dwell" (Psa. cvii, 32-35). And if such a God be *for us*, who can be against us?

(3) Man's extremity is God's opportunity. The Lord waits to be gracious. Often He suffers our circumstances to become critical, yea, desperate, before He appears on our behalf. Here was Israel ready to enter Canaan, and there was the Jordan "overflowing his banks"—a season which to carnal reason seemed the most unfavourable of all. Ah, but it afforded the Lord a most fitting occasion to display His sufficiency. "Though that opposition made to the salvation of God's people have all imaginable advantage, yet God can and will conquer it. Let the banks of Jordan be filled to the brim, filled till they rush over it, it is as easy to Omnipotence to divide them and dry them up, as if they were never so narrow, never so shallow: it is all one unto the Lord" (Matthew Henry). Then let not the Christian reader give way to despair because the conditions in which he finds himself are altogether beyond his power to overcome. Your troubles may have already reached the high-water mark, but when they "overflow" and all appears to be lost, then you may expect the Lord to show Himself strong in your behalf.

(4) We have here an illustration of the grand truth expressed in Romans viii, 28, "For we know that *all* things work together for good to them that love God." Alas, there are times when many a Christian has unbelievingly said with Jacob "all these things are against me" (Gen. xlii, 36), and even though some may not have gone that far, yet few could plead guiltless to having feared that *some* things were against them. Did not the flooded valley appear to be directly against Israel, working for their ill? Yet, in reality, the very overflowing of the Jordan was among the all things contributing to their good, for it furnished an occasion for their God to the more manifestly display His power for them, so that instead of hindering, that inundation actually promoted their good—strengthening their faith in the Lord. How that should reassure the hard-pressed saint today! The very thing or things which are inclining you to give way to despair will yet prove a blessing in disguise, and you will have reason to acknowledge with David "it is *good* for me that I have been afflicted" (Psa. cxix, 71). The dark dispensations of Divine providence, the tribulations you experience, are for the trying and development of your graces.

(5) We have here an exemplification of what is stated in Genesis i, 6-9, where we are told that on the second day "God made the firmament, and divided the waters which were under the firmament from the waters which were above the firmament." By the latter "waters" we understand the reference to be unto something other than the ordinary moisture suspended

in the atmosphere, namely, to those "floods" of Genesis vii, 11, 12. "By the dividing of the waters from the waters [at the Jordan] and the making of the dry land [there] to appear, God would remind them of that which Moses by Divine revelation had instructed them in concerning the work of creation. That, by what they now saw, their belief of that which they there read might be assisted, and they might know that the God whom they worshipped was the same God that made the world and that it was the same power which was engaged and employed for them" (Matthew Henry). Thus this miracle of Joshua iii serves to illustrate the verity of Genesis i, 6-9.

(6) We also behold a striking but solemn type of Christ effecting the work of our redemption. The ark adumbrated Him as the Covenant-head of His people: borne by the priests, signifying that His work was wrought in His official character. The Divine appointment that the ark must go so far in advance of the people (Josh. iii, 4) foreshadowed the blessed but awe-inspiring fact that Christ was *alone* in performing the work of redemption: "there is none to help" (Psa. xxii, 11) was His plaintive cry. Peter declared that he was ready to accompany his Master unto death, but He answered, "whither I go, thou canst not follow Me now" (John xiii, 36). And why? Because Christ was about to endure the wrath of God and experience the awful curse of the Law in the stead of His people. The "Jordan" was not only an emblem of death, but of *judgment*—"dan" meaning "judging" (Gen. xxx, 6). Observe well that in Joshua iii, 15, we are most significantly told that the river fled back to the place of Adam, to intimate that Christ bore the judgment of all our sins, even "original sin"—the condemnation which the first man's transgression brought upon us, as well as the additional guilt of all our own iniquities.

(7) How to act when confronted by difficulty or danger. Though we dwelt upon this at some length in a previous article, yet because we deem it the most important practical lesson inculcated, we make further reference to it now. Perplexing problems, baffling situations, being faced with formidable obstacles are, from time to time, the experience of each Christian: how then is he to conduct himself? Without again enlarging upon the necessity of his taking full stock of the obstacle and of his own inability to remove it, of his refusing to lean unto his own understanding or resort to any carnal expediency, of his being regulated only by the Word of God and walking "in newness of life," we will stress but one feature, the central one: his looking trustfully, expectantly, and perseveringly unto the Lord to make a passage for him through his "Jordan." In a word, to keep the eye of faith steadfastly fixed on the Anti-typical Ark, to grasp firmly His promise, "When thou passeth through the waters, I will be with thee; and through the rivers, they shall not overflow thee . . . for I am the Lord *thy* God: the Holy One of Israel, thy Saviour" or "Deliverer" (Isa. xliii, 2).

(8) For the Christian there is nothing whatever to fear in death, is another truth writ large across Joshua iii. Yet the fact remains that, excepting sin, there is nothing so much dreaded by not a few of God's children: with them a horror of sin proceeds from a spiritual principle, of death from their natural constitution. But death can no more harm a saint than the Jordan did any of the children of Israel, and that for the very same reasons. Christ has vanquished death, as in a figure the ark of the covenant vanquished the Jordan. It was as that sacred vessel entered the brim that its waters fled before it, and in consequence all who followed it passed

through dry shod. So it was Christ's going before His people into death which has rendered it impotent to hurt them, and therefore they exultantly cry, "O death, where is thy sting? O grave, where is thy victory? The sting of death is sin, and the strength of sin is the Law, but thanks be to God which giveth us the victory through our Lord Jesus Christ" (I Cor. xv, 55-57), for He endured the Law's penalty upon our behalf and extracted the fatal sting from death. For the believer death is the portal into the heavenly Canaan.

Activity of the Priesthood

Before we turn to consider the contents of Joshua iv and contemplate the *memorials* that God ordered to mark the Jordan miracle, we should look more definitely at a prominent detail in chapter three which did not receive due attention in the preceding articles, and which supplies an important link between the two chapters, namely, the prominent part played by *the priests* in bearing the ark of the covenant, the "ark of the Lord, the Lord of all the earth," before which the lower waters of the Jordan fled and the upper water "stood upon a heap." Therein we behold the nation of Israel in its primary relations to God. In the books, of Exodus, Leviticus and Numbers we are shown the establishment of God's way with them and the declaration of His will and purpose through Moses, who was both their Divinely appointed commander and mediator, while Aaron was their great high priest. That relationship was reaffirmed in the opening verses of Joshua: "As I was with Moses, so I will be with thee. I will not fail thee, nor forsake thee" (i, 4). Besides that assurance to Joshua personally, as the successor of Moses, there was the necessary continuation of the high priest and the Levitical priesthood in Israel's midst.

The priesthood in their service had charge of the ark and the order of the tabernacle which was erected at Shiloh (xviii, 1), neither of which Joshua nor his armed men were suffered to touch. Each of those great functionaries held their respective appointments directly from the Lord, and the two in their *combined action*—whether in the sanctuary of God or in the camp of Israel—executed the will of Jehovah concerning both His majesty and holiness, which was thus the glory of His people. The priesthood and the tabernacle were indispensable as their way of approach unto God as worshippers, while outwardly the relations of God with Israel, by the ark of the covenant, were manifested in the sight of all their enemies. That was equally true during the ministration of Aaron in the wilderness, or the Levites with Joshua when the waters of Jordan fled, or while marching around the city of Jericho and its walls fell down flat. Just as Moses and Aaron were inseparable in their varied ministrations from the exodus of Egypt and onward, so were the priest and the captain of Israel's hosts at the door of the tabernacle in Shiloh when the land was divided among Israel's tribes (xviii, 10).

Not only were those two distinctive orders and services established by God at the beginning (adumbrated as early as Ex. iv, 14, 15!), but when Aaron died on mount Hor, we are told that "Moses stripped Aaron of his garments and put them on Eleazar his son," and this he did "as the Lord commanded in the sight of all the congregation" (Num. xx, 27, 28). In like manner, when the death of Moses drew nigh on mount Abarim (the "mountain" is ever the symbol of *government*), he besought the Lord "to set a man over the congregation" (Num. xxvii, 16), and the Lord bade him, "Take thee Joshua the son of Nun, a man in whom is the Spirit, and lay thine hand upon him [the figure of *identification*] and set him before Eleazar the priest and before all the congregation, and give him a charge in their sight" (verses 18, 19). The connection, and yet the contrast between them, was intimated thus: "And he shall stand before Eleazar the priest, who shall ask counsel for him, at the judgment of Urim before the Lord: at his [Joshua's] word shall they go out and at his word shall they come in; both he and all the children of Israel with him" (Num. xxvii, 21).

What has just been pointed out serves to explain the fact that in the book which bears his name, Joshua (though the commander-in-chief of Israel) is seen to be subservient unto Eleazar the priest—four times the two are mentioned together, and in each instance Eleazar is given the precedence. This order and those Divine appointments were the basis of the history of Israel under Joshua and the anointed priesthood, with "the ark of the covenant of the Lord your God" which they bore along, for that ark (as was pointed out in an earlier article) was not only the witness of Joshua's *presence* in the midst of His people, but also the symbol of His *relations* with them. God ever takes care of His own glory and yet at the same time promotes the full blessing of His people according to His eternal purpose. He never allows those two things to be separated, or to pass from His own immediate control but works them out together, for He has made their felicity an integral part of His glory. How fitting then that the ark of the covenant should be in advance of the twelve tribes as they went forward into their inheritance and unto the mount (Zion) of God's holiness.

But let us pause for a moment and point out the practical bearing of this upon ourselves. It is indeed a most wonderful and blessed thing that the great God has inseparably connected His own manifestative glory and the good of His own people, yet it is one which should have a moving and melting effect upon our hearts, and cause us to see diligently to it that our lives are duly ordered and made suitable thereto. Without entering into details, let us summarize in two brief statements the obligations which that grand truth devolve upon us. First, we should ever be on our guard against separating our present communion with God from the revealed pathway of His glory. Communion with God can only be had and maintained while we tread "the way of holiness" (Isa. xxxv, 10), for we cannot glorify Him unless we walk in obedience to Him. Second, Christ Himself must be the Object of our eye (Heb. xii, 2) and heart (Song of S. viii, 6): upon Him our affections are to be set (Col. iii, 1, 2), to Him we are to live (Phil. i, 21), for it is *in Him* the glory of God and the present and eternal blessedness of His people meet.

In Psalm lxxviii, 61, the ark is designated "His glory," and when (in token of His displeasure with Israel and of the severance of their communion with Him) God suffered the ark to be captured by the Philistines, the daughter-in-law of the high priest cried, "The glory is departed from Israel" (I Sam. iv, 22). But here in Joshua iii that "glory" advanced at the head of Israel and opened a way for them into Canaan. But every eye was to be upon "the ark of the covenant of the Lord *your* God," who went before them to find a "resting place" worthy of Himself, in which to keep His appointed service and share His delights with His people. Accordingly we find, in the heyday of Israel's prosperity, that Solomon prayed at the dedication of the temple on Mount Zion, "Now therefore arise, O Lord God, into Thy resting place, Thou, and the ark of Thy strength: let Thy priests, O Lord God, be clothed with salvation, and let Thy saints rejoice in Thy goodness" (II Chron.

vi, 41, 42)—which will receive its final and complete fulfilment when the prayer of Christ in John xvii, 24, receives its answer.

Now it was "the priests, the Levites" who were appointed to bear the ark, which, when Israel saw in motion, was their signal for advance—" then ye shall remove from your place and go after it" (iii, 3). As the congregation did so, the first thing which they beheld was the manner in which God gets glory to Himself, namely, by driving back that which intercepted their way, putting forth His mighty power on their behalf as "the Lord your God." That which we are particularly concerned with now is the fact that it was when "the feet of the priests that bare the ark were dipped in the brim of the water . . . that the waters which came down from above stood and rose up upon a heap very far from the city of Adam, that is beside Zaretan; and those that came down toward the sea of the plain, the salt sea, failed, and were cut off; and the people passed over right against Jericho" (Josh. iii, 15, 16). Thereby the priesthood are given a distinguished position on this occasion, and are placed in the forefront in this book because of their consecration and appointment to the service of the sanctuary. Yet their prominence did not derogate from the honour of Joshua as the leader of the people, for *he* is the one who gave direction unto the priests (iii, 6)!

That is very remarkable, and should be duly pondered. When the Lord said unto Joshua, "This day will I begin to magnify thee in the sight of all Israel, that they may know that, as I was with Moses, so I will be with thee," the very next thing was, "And thou shalt *command* the priests that bear the ark of the covenant" (iii, 8). Even when Eleazar, the high priest, comes more distinctively into the forefront in connection with the assigning of the inheritance of the tribes, he does not interfere with the place which God had given Joshua. One of the principal values of these inspired records is the *conjoint action* of Eleazar and Joshua when they could act together. The same feature of the honourable and prominent place accorded the priesthood, and yet Joshua's authority over them, is seen again in chapter six, in connection with the taking of Jericho, for not only did the ark of the covenant go before all the men of war, but that in turn was preceded by "seven priests bearing the seven trumpets of rams' horns," before whose blast the walls fell down; yet it was Joshua who issued orders to these priests (vi, 6).

We have dwelt the longer upon this prominent feature of the book of Joshua (about which we shall have more to say, D.V., as we pass on to the later chapters) not only because it has been largely ignored by those who have written thereon, but also and chiefly, because of the deep importance of the same when considered, first, in connection with the Lord Jesus Christ; and, second, in connection with His people. It has indeed been widely recognized that Joshua is one of the outstanding characters of the Old Testament, who foreshadowed our Saviour, and if we are spared to complete this series we hope to show that he did so in no less than fifty details. But it has been perceived by very few indeed that *Eleazar* was equally a type of Christ, and that the two must be viewed in conjunction in order to behold the completeness of their joint adumbrations. That should be apparent at once from their immediate predecessors, for we need to join together Moses *and* Aaron in order to obtain the Divinely designed prefiguration of the One who was both "The Apostle *and* High Priest of our profession, Christ Jesus" (Heb. iii, 1). Thus it was also with Joshua and Eleazar.

That the history of the children of Israel was a typical one and that it adumbrated the experiences, the provisions made for, and the salvation of the whole election of grace, is too plain for any anointed eye to miss. Their oppression by Pharaoh and their groaning amid the brick kilns of Egypt present an unmistakable picture of our servitude to Satan and bondage under sin, our condition by nature as the consequence of our fall in Adam. Their utter inability to free themselves from the cruel yoke of the Egyptians forcibly portrayed our own native impotency to better our condition. The sovereign grace of God in raising up a deliverer in the person of Moses, was a prophecy in action of the future coming forth of the Divine Deliverer to emancipate His people. The provision of the lamb and the efficacy of its blood to provide shelter from the angel of death on the night of the passover, yet more clearly revealed what is now fully proclaimed by the Gospel. While the overthrow of Pharaoh and his hosts at the Red Sea and Israel's sight of the "Egyptians dead upon the seashore" (Ex. xiv, 30) told of the completeness of our redemption and the putting away of our sins from before the face of God.

The subsequent history of Israel in the wilderness, their testings and trials there, their failures and successes, the gracious and full provision which the Lord made for them, have rightly been contemplated as shadowing forth the varied experiences of the saints as they journey unto their eternal Inheritance. But the typical value of the second half of Exodus and much of the book of Leviticus has been far less generally discerned. The delivering of His people from their enemies was but a means to a far grander end, namely, that they should be brought into a place of favour and nearness unto God; and Exodus xxv-xl and most of Leviticus make known the provisions which God has made for the maintenance of their communion with Him, and this in such a way that the requirements of His ineffable holiness were duly maintained and the obligations of their moral agency and their duties as a redeemed people should be fitly discharged. Their relations with Jehovah were maintained on the one hand, through the Divinely appointed priesthood; and on the other, by their obedience to the Divine commandments. Only thereby could they draw nigh unto the Holy One as acceptable worshippers, and only thereby could they receive from Him the necessary instructions for their guidance.

The typical significance of the book of Joshua, while maintaining and enforcing the truth made known in the foregoing books, supplements and complements the earlier history. Here it is Israel, under God, possessing their possessions, brought into that rest which had been promised their fathers. In regard to this, we prefer to speak in the language of one whom we consider was better qualified to treat upon this subject. "The earthly Canaan was neither designed by God, nor from the first was it understood by His people to be, the ultimate and proper inheritance which they were to occupy; things having been spoken and hoped for concerning it which plainly could not be realized within the bounds of Canaan. The inheritance was one which could be enjoyed only by those who had become the children of the resurrection, themselves fully redeemed in soul and body from all the effects and consequences of sin—made more glorious and blessed, indeed, than if they had never sinned, because constituted after the image of the heavenly Adam. And as the inheritance must correspond with the inheritor, it can only be man's original possession restored—the earth redeemed from the curse which sin brought on it, and, like man himself, be the fit abode of a Church made like, in all its members, to the Son of God.

"The occupation of the earthly Canaan by the natural seed of Abraham was a type, and no more than a type, of this occupation by a redeemed Church of her destined inheritance of glory; and consequently everything concerning the entrance of the former on their temporary possession was ordered so as to represent and foreshadow the things which belong to the Church's establishment in her permanent possession. Hence, between the giving of the promise, which, though it did not terminate in the land of Canaan, yet included that, and through it prospectively exhibited the better inheritance, a series of important events intervened, which are capable of being fully and properly examined in no other way than by means of their typical bearing of the things hereafter to be disclosed respecting that better inheritance.

"If we ask, why did the heirs of promise wander about so long as pilgrims, and withdraw to a foreign region before they were allowed to possess the land, and not rather, like a modern colony, quietly spread, without strife or bloodshed, over its surface, till the whole was possessed? Or, why were they suffered to fall under the dominion of a foreign power from whose cruel oppression they needed to be redeemed, with terrible executions of judgment on the oppressor, before the possession could be theirs? Or why, before that event, also, should they have been put under the discipline of law, having the covenant of Sinai, with its strict requirements and manifold obligations of service, superadded to the covenant of grace and promise? Or why, again, should their right to the inheritance itself have to be vindicated from a race of occupants who had been allowed for a time to keep possession of it, and whose multiplied abominations had so polluted it that nothing short of their extermination could render it a fitting abode for the heirs of promise? The full and satisfactory answer to all such questions can only be given by viewing the whole in connection with the better things of a higher dispensation—as the first part of a plan which was to have its counterpart and issue in the glories of a redeemed creation, and for the final results of which the Church needed to be prepared, by standing in similar relations and passing through like experiences in regard to an earthly inheritance.

"The whole series of transactions which took place between the confirmation of the covenant of promise with Jacob, and the actual possession of the land promised, and especially of course the things which concerned that greatest of all the transactions, the revelation of the Law from Sinai, is to be regarded as a delineation in the type, of the way and manner in which the heirs of God are to obtain the inheritance of the purchased possession. Meanwhile, there are two important lessons which the Church may clearly gather and which she ought never to lose sight of: First, that the inheritance, come when and how it may, is the free gift of God, bestowed by Him as sovereign Lord and Proprietor on those whom He calls to the fellowship of His grace. Second, that the hope of the inheritance must exist as an animating principle in their hearts, influencing all their procedure. Their spirit and character must be such as become those who are the expectants as well as heirs of that better country, which is an heavenly; nor can Christ ever be truly formed in the heart, until He be formed as 'the hope of glory'" (P. Fairbairn, Vol. I of his *The Typology of Scripture,* 1865).

Chapter 7

THE TWO MEMORIALS

JOSHUA 4:1-24

Typical Application

That which is recorded in the book of Joshua fully maintains the Truth presented in the Pentateuch, yet its typical teaching carries us considerably beyond what is there set forth. This is to be expected, especially when we bear in mind (as we must do continually while pondering its contents) that it was the *new* generation of Israel which is here in view. The lesson taught at the supernatural crossing of the Jordan conducts us farther in the unfolding of the Gospel than what was signified at the Red Sea. There, it was the might of God put forth on behalf of His covenant people in the total destruction of that antagonistic power which had held them captive so long and had refused to let them go. Here, it was His vanquishing of that obstacle which barred the way into their inheritance. When Satan's captives are freed at the miracle of regeneration, he does not henceforth ignore them and leave them in peace: though he cannot prevent their entrance into the "purchased possession," yet he is ever assailing them in one form or other as he seeks to keep them from a *present* enjoyment of the same. What is required from us in order to thwart those designs of our Enemy, we are seeking to show in the course of this series of articles.

But it was the Divine side of things, the provisions God made for Israel's entrance into and occupation of the land of Canaan with which we were more concerned in our last. Those provisions were, first, the appointing and qualifying of Joshua to be the leader of Israel, the typical "captain of their salvation." Second, the ark of the covenant, which (we repeat) was both the witness of Jehovah's presence in Israel's midst and the symbol of His relations to them. And third, the priesthood, culminating in their service in "the tabernacle which was pitched in Shiloh." Thus, as we hope to yet show, not only are we required to turn unto the epistles of Paul to the Romans, the Ephesians and the Colossians, in order to find the antitypical truths of what was spiritually adumbrated *of us* by Israel in the book of Joshua, but also to his epistle to the Hebrews. We know of only one other writer who has called attention to that fact, in an article written before we were born, and which appeared in a magazine (*The Bible Treasury*) under the title of "The Book of Joshua and the Epistle to the Hebrews," unto which we gladly acknowledge our indebtedness and of which we made free use.

We are now to take notice of the Divine command which Joshua received, to take twelve stones from the bed of the Jordan, "out of the place where the priests' feet stood firm" (iv, 3), which were made a "memorial" unto future generations, and in addition, the setting up of "twelve stones in the midst of Jordan" (v, 9). At the Red Sea Israel neither left twelve stones in its bed, nor took twelve with them unto the other side. Instead, Pharaoh and his chosen captains, his chariots and his host, God drowned therein, so that Israel sang "The depths have covered them: *they* sank into the bottom as a *stone*" (Ex. xv, 4, 5). "But the children of Israel walked upon dry land in the midst of the sea, and the waters were a wall unto them on their right hand and on their left. Thus the Lord saved Israel that day out of the hand of the Egyptians" (Ex .xiv, 29, 30), and put the song of redemption into their mouths, saying, "The Lord hath triumphed gloriously" (Ex. xv, 1, 13). At the Red Sea Jehovah showed Himself strong on the behalf of that people who had previously found shelter under "the blood of the lamb," and whom He now brought nigh unto Himself—"unto Thy holy habitation" (Ex. xv, 13, 17).

But at the Jordan a further and grander lesson was taught Israel, something which went beyond the truth of redemption by blood and by power, even that of *resurrection*. Fundamental and blessed as is the truth taught us by the cross of Christ, there is something further which is even more vital and glorious, and that is our Lord's victory over the grave. When the apostle throws out that irrefutable challenge, "Who shall lay anything to the charge of God's elect?" his triumphant answer is, "It is God that justifieth, who is he that condemneth? It is Christ that died, *yea rather*, that is risen again" (Rom. viii, 33, 34). It is abundantly clear in I Corinthians xv (see especially verses 3 and 4, 14, 17) that the resurrection of Christ is not only an integral part of the Gospel but its distinctive and outstanding feature; and those evangelists who go no farther than the cross are preaching only half of the Gospel. But more, the saints themselves are greatly the losers if their faith and spiritual apprehensions stop short at the atoning death of Christ, for unspeakably precious as it is to recognize *our* death unto sin in the death of the Surety, still more blessed is it to perceive our federal union with Him and our title to the inheritance in His triumph over death.

At the Jordan the redeemed of God were shown their own passage through death and resurrection by the figure of the twelve stones placed in the Jordan and the twelve stones taken out of it. It was at this point that Israel entered upon a new stage in their history, yet perpetuating all the essential features which had previously marked them as the peculiar people of the Lord—as will be seen when we examine (D.V.) into the new circumcising at Gilgal, the celebration of the passover, and the appearing of the Captain of the Lord's host with drawn sword (chap. 5). Nevertheless, as said above, that which characterized the crossing of the Jordan is in sharp contrast with what took place at the Red Sea. There, instead of the priests bearing the ark of the covenant being seen, it was Israel's enemies which lay there, consumed as stubble by the wrath of the Lord. On the other hand, no Canaanites were in Jordan, not a single foe was overthrown there; yet it was sanctified to the Lord and to Israel by the priests and the ark of the covenant for glory and victory as truly as were the waters of the Red Sea when they returned and engulfed the host of Pharaoh in terrible judgment—that glory and victory quickly appears in the sequel.

As previously pointed out, the river Jordan was not only the emblem of death, but of judgment also, as the word itself signifies—"jor," literally, "spread," and "dan" which means "judging" (Gen. xxx, 6). The use made of this river in New Testament times supplies clear confirmation, for the Jordan was where the Lord's forerunner exercised his ministry, of whom it was foretold "prepare ye the way of the Lord." And *how* did he do so? By preparing a people to receive Him. In what manner? By preaching "Repent ye," i.e.

judge yourselves; and those who did so were (most appropriately) baptized of him in the Jordan "confessing their sins" (Matt. iii, 8); and by that "baptism of repentance unto the remission of sins" (Mark i, 4) they acknowledged that death was their due, and therefore were they (symbolically) placed in a watery grave. There too, the Lord Jesus as the Surety and Sinbearer of His people identified Himself with them by being placed beneath its waters, thereby pledging Himself unto that "baptism" of death (Luke xii, 50) wherein He met the needs of all who truly repent or adjudge themselves worthy of death, when all "the waves and billows" of God's wrath (Psa. xlii, 6) passed over Him.

The good Shepherd entered the river of judgment on behalf of His sheep, making for them a new covenant by His atoning death, delivering thereby from judgment all who follow Him: "this is My blood of the new covenant, which is shed for many for the remission of sins" (Matt. xxvi, 28) He declared only a few hours before the crucifixion, when He instituted the memorial of His death. That was typified by the entrance into Jordan of the ark of the covenant "borne by the priests" and at once the flow of its waters was stayed, so that the people who followed it passed over dryshod, though the ark itself did not come out of the Jordan until it had secured a passage for all the people (iii, 17). Profoundly suggestive and significant are those words "For the priests which bare the ark stood in the midst of Jordan until *every thing was finished* that the Lord commanded Joshua to speak unto the people, according to all that Moses commanded Joshua" (iv, 10). How that reminds us of "Jesus, knowing that *all things were now accomplished,* that the Scripture might be fulfilled, saith, I thirst . . . when Jesus therefore had received the vinegar He said, It is finished, and He bowed His head and gave up the spirit" (John xix, 28, 30). All that the justice of God demanded, all that the Law required ("Moses commanded") had been rendered by the antitypical Joshua.

"And it came to pass, when all the people were clean passed over Jordan, that the Lord spake unto Joshua, saying, Take ye twelve men out of the people, out of every tribe a man, and command ye them, saying, Take you hence out of the midst of Jordan, out of the place where the priests' feet stood firm, twelve stones, and ye shall carry them over with you, and leave them there in the lodging place where ye shall lodge this night" (iv, 1-3), i.e. in Gilgal (verse 19). That those stones were large ones is evident from the fact that they were to be carried upon the "shoulder." The men who carried them had been selected beforehand (iii, 13), ready for this task, that there might be no delay in connection with what lay immediately before the nation —the encamping of that vast multitude for the night in a suitable place, namely, at one which was afterwards called Gilgal, and which some inform us was about mid-way between the river Jordan and the city of Jericho. In the light of Joshua iv, 4, "then Joshua called the twelve men whom he had prepared of the children of Israel," we personally regard that as a foreshadowing of the antitypical Joshua, who at an early stage of His ministry "called unto Him the twelve" (Mark vi, 7).

"And Joshua said unto them, Pass over before the ark of the Lord your God into the midst of Jordan, and take you up every man of you a stone upon his shoulder, according unto the number of the tribes of Israel: That they may be *a sign* among you, that when your children ask their fathers in time to come, saying, What mean ye by these stones? Then ye shall answer them, That the waters of Jordan were cut off before the ark of the covenant of the Lord: when it passed over Jordan, the waters of Jordan were cut off; and these stones shall be for a *memorial* unto the children of Israel for ever" (verses 5-7). The two words we have italicized call attention to the double design which those stones were intended to serve, which will be more intelligible to the reader when he bears in mind that those twelve stones "did Joshua pitch in Gilgal" (verse 20). They were not left flat on the ground but orderly formed into a cairn or monument. The Hebrew word for "pitch" there, Young's Concordance defines as "To cause to stand, raise." Twenty times this verb is rendered "set up" in the Authorized Version. It is the same word which is used in connection with the erection of the Tabernacle when it was complete (Ex. xl, 2, etc.). Thus, those large stones were arranged in such a manner, possibly placed one on top of another monolith-like, so as to attract the attention and invoke the inquiry of those who should afterwards behold them.

That monument of stones was designed first as a "sign" unto Israel. It was a message for their hearts via their eyes rather than ears. It was an enduring sermon in stone. It spoke of the goodness and power of God exercised on their behalf at the Jordan. That word "sign" is a very full one—our Lord's miracles are termed "signs" (John xx, 30; Acts ii, 22). The two wonders which Moses was empowered to work before his brethren were called "signs" (Ex. iv, 1-9), they authenticated him as their Divinely-appointed leader and signified that the power of the Almighty was with him. In Deuteronomy xi, 18, and Judges vi, 17, "sign" has the force of token or representation—of Israel's being regulated by God's Word, and of the Lord's granting success to the commission He had committed to Gideon. In other passages a "sign" was a portent or pledge of something concerning the future —I Samuel x, 1-9; II Kings xix, 29. In each of those senses may "sign" be understood in Joshua iv, 6. That cairn of stones was to signify that Israel had not crossed the Jordan by their own ability, but because of the miracle-working power of God. It was a representation unto them that they had passed through the river's bed dryshod. More especially, it was an earnest and *pledge* of what God would yet do for them.

Second, that monument was designed as a "memorial" that Israel had passed through the river of death, that they were now (typically) on resurrection ground, that *judgment lay behind them*. Israel upon the Canaan side of Jordan adumbrated that blessed truth expressed by our Redeemer in John v, 24, where He so definitely assures His people that each soul who hears His word and believes on the One who sent Him "hath everlasting life, and shall not come into condemnation, but is passed from death unto life." The reason why he shall *not* "come into condemnation" is because in the person of his Surety he has already been condemned and suffered the full judgment of God upon all his sins, and therefore, judicially, as federally united to Christ, he "is passed from death [that death which is the wages of sin] unto life"—that "life" which is the award of the Law, as it was "magnified" by the Saviour and "made honourable" (Isa. xlii, 21). As the ark of the covenant entered the river of death and judgment the flow of its waters was stopped until the ark had secured a safe passage for all who followed it; so Christ endured the unsparing wrath of God that by His atoning death those who were legally one with Him, and who are made voluntary followers of Him, shall be delivered from all future judgment.

In addition to the monument erected on the Canaan side of the river we are told that "Joshua set up twelve stones in the midst of Jordan, in the place where the priests which bare the ark of the covenant stood; and they are there unto this day" (iv, 9). Thus there was a *double* monument to perpetually commemorate Israel's passing through the place of judgment: the one in the midst of the Jordan, the other in their new camping-ground at Gilgal. What anointed eye can fail to see in them the *two signs* and memorials which Christ has instituted to symbolize that, as the result of their faith in His atoning death, His people have not only passed through death and judgment, but are now united to a risen Christ and are "alive unto God"! The meaning of the two ordinances appointed by Christ clearly confirms this, for each of them speaks of both death and resurrection. "Know ye not, that so many of us as were baptized into Jesus Christ were baptized into His *death*? Therefore we were buried with Him by baptism into death, that like as Christ was *raised* from the dead by the glory of the Father, even so we also should walk in newness of life" (Rom. vi, 4, 5; and cf. Col. ii, 12). Christian baptism is designed to symbolize the believer's union with Christ in His death, burial, and resurrection, as well as being his personal profession that he is dead to the world and has resolved to walk in newness of life.

The Lord's Supper also, while it celebrates our passage with Christ through death, yet it is with the added blessedness and triumph of being now on the resurrection side of judgment. Just as the *twelve* stones which had been in Jordan were formed into a *single* cairn in the camp at Gilgal—type of "the Israel of God" (Gal. vi, 16) in its entirety, made into "one body"— was a testimony that the twelve tribes had passed through the unfordable river; so the Lord's supper, partaken of by those who were once lost sinners under condemnation, is a testimony that they have passed over, and being on resurrection ground can look forward not to judgment but to the consummation of their hope and bliss. This is clear from I Corinthians xi, 26, "For as often as ye eat this bread and drink this cup, ye do show the Lord's death *till He come.*" The Lord's supper not only looks back to the cross but forward to Christ's return in glory, and therefore is it designated a "feast" (I Cor. v, 8) and not a fast, and instead of "bitter herbs" (Ex. xii, 8) being eaten, the "wine" of gladness is drunk.

Practical Application

The very fact that God saw fit to devote two whole chapters of His Word unto a description of Israel's crossing of the Jordan is more than a hint that the narration of that memorable incident embodies teaching of much importance and value for His people in succeeding generations. Christians are greatly the losers if they concentrate their attention chiefly upon the New Testament and regard the Old Testament as containing little of vital moment for their souls. If on the one hand the New Testament often illuminates and explains the Old, yet on the other hand there is not a little in the New Testament which cannot be properly understood apart from the Old. In the last two or three articles we sought to indicate the typical and spiritual significance of Israel's passage through the river of death and judgment; on this occasion we propose to point out some of the practical lessons to be learned from the things there recorded. We shall not give a complete exposition of chapter iv, but single out various details for comment, and intimate the many useful truths inculcated by the memorial erected in Gilgal.

"For the priests which bare the ark stood in the midst of Jordan, until everything was finished that the Lord commanded Joshua to speak unto the people, according to all that Moses commanded Joshua: and the people hasted and passed over" (verse 10). There are three things here which are worthy of our observation and admiration. First, the implicit obedience and patient fortitude of the priests. They were the ones who occupied the place both of honour and of danger. They were the ones who bore the ark, before whose presence the waters had "rose up like a heap," held by an invisible Hand. Advancing to "the midst of Jordan," they remained stationary for many hours, until all the vast host of Israel had crossed to the far shore. It was a severe test both of their courage and patience. Therein an example is left the ministers of the Gospel to continue steadfast in their duty, to be a model unto their people of uncompromising fidelity, of undaunted courage, of patient endurance. Second, we see again how that Joshua closely followed the orders he had received from Moses, doing nothing without a Divine command; while the priests, in turn, were required to be regulated by Joshua's orders—the ministers of the Gospel are to be governed solely by Christ.

Third, the deportment of "the people" on this occasion exemplified that which should ever characterize the rank and file of the saints in connection with those who minister unto them in spiritual things. We are told that they "*hasted* and passed over." That denoted their thoughtful consideration of the priests, so that they would not be put to unnecessary delay and strain through their dilatoriness—the slower their movement, the longer the priests would have to stand bearing the ark! The practical lesson is that God's people should do everything in their power to make the spiritual lot of God's servants easier. That can be done by promptly responding to their instructions, by supporting them through earnest prayer, and by being thoughtful of their comfort. That is something which particularly needs to be laid to heart in this day of selfishness and lack of concern for the comfort of others. It is both solemn and blessed to note how *God* took note of this detail, that the Holy Spirit has specifically recorded this thoughtful "haste" of the people. The Lord not only marks *what* we do, but *how* we do it: as in "his princes gave *willingly*" (II Chron. xxxv, 8), "their nobles put their necks to the work of the Lord . . . Zabbi *earnestly* repaired the other piece" (Neh. iii. 5, 20).

"And the children of Reuben and the children of Gad, and half the tribe of Manasseh, passed over armed before the children of Israel, as Moses spake unto them: About forty thousand prepared for war passed over before the Lord unto battle, to the plains of Jericho" (verses 12, 13). Here is a case in point how that one part of Scripture is dependent upon another for its explanation and interpretation. We have to go back to Numbers to discover why *these* particular ones constituted the fighting force of the nation. Those two and a half tribes, who were rich in cattle, desired to have for their portion the fertile lands of Jazer and Gilead, rather than any part of Canaan (verses 1-5). When Moses demurred, they agreed to build sheepfolds for their cattle and fenced cities for their little ones, and then they would go armed before the children of Israel until the remaining tribes had secured their inheritance (verses 16, 17). Moses agreed to their proposal, and they ratified that arrangement; and Moses then gave command to Eleazar and Joshua to see that their promise was made good. Here in Joshua iv we are shown the fulfilment of the same. Those two and a half tribes were the only ones unencumbered with their families and flocks, and thus we see *how suited* they were to be the fighting force, and how graciously God made all things work together for good unto His people.

"On that day the Lord magnified Joshua in the sight of all Israel; and they feared him, as they feared Moses, all the days of his life" (verse 14). Therein we may see how the Lord made good unto Joshua the word He gave him in iii, 7. "Faithful is He that calleth you, who also will do it" (I Thess.

v, 24). That detail has been placed upon imperishable record for the encouragement of every servant of the Lord. Ministers of the Gospel may prosecute their labours with absolute confidence in the promises of their Master: not one of them shall fail. He has said of His Word, "it shall not return unto Me void, but it shall accomplish that which I please, and it shall prosper in the thing whereto I sent it" (Isa. lv, 11); then he need not entertain the slightest doubt about the same. He has declared "all that the Father giveth Me shall come to Me," that they "*shall* believe on Me through their [His ministers'] word" (John vi, 37; xvii, 20); then neither the perversity of human nature nor the opposition of Satan can prevent it. He has promised His servants, "Lo, I am with you alway, even unto the end of the world" (Matt. xxviii, 20), then let them conduct themselves accordingly. Let them also learn from Joshua iv, 14, and its context that the surest way for them to gain the respect and observation of their people is to be diligent in personally honouring and obeying God, and caring for their welfare.

"And the Lord spake unto Joshua, saying, Command the priests that bear the ark of the testimony, that they come up out of Jordan. Joshua therefore commanded the priests, saying, Come ye up out of Jordan" (verses 15-17). That is indeed striking: the priests did not take a step until they were Divinely authorized. There they stood hour after hour, and there they still remained after the vast concourse had passed through and reached the other side in safety! Patiently they waited until leave was given them to move. They did not act on their own impulse or initiative, but meekly waited God's time. "The priests did not quit their station till Joshua, who had commanded them hitherto, ordered them from thence: nor did he thus order them till the Lord commanded him: so obedient were all parties to the Word of God, and so entirely confident of His protection" (Matthew Henry). It is ours to render unquestioning obedience to God, and leave the consequences with Him; nor need we have the least fear or hesitation in so doing—we shall not be the losers, but the gainers. "Them that honour Me, I will honour" (I Sam. ii, 30) is more certain than that night shall follow day, as the writer has often proved.

"And it came to pass, when the priests that bare the ark of the covenant of the Lord were come up out of the 'midst of Jordan, and the soles of the priests' feet were lifted up unto the dry land, that the waters of Jordan returned unto their place, and flowed over all his banks, as they did before" (verse 18). No sooner did the priests with the ark step upon the shore of Canaan than the Jordan resumed its normal flow, or rather its abnormal condition, for it was then in flood. That at once accentuated the miracle which had just been wrought, making it the more apparent that the stopping of its flow was not from any abnormal natural cause, but that it was the will of their Creator which had temporarily suspended the laws of nature, for the display of His glory and the fulfilment of His promise unto His people. As Israel beheld the upper waters which had been invisibly dammed and the lower ones that had stood up in a heap now suddenly acting as formerly, how apparent it would be unto them that it was the presence and power of their covenant God which had wrought so gloriously for them!

Bearing in mind the meaning of "Jordan," the spiritual application of verse 18 is apparent. It was the presence in its midst of the priests who bore the ark which stayed its course: and it is the godly example and faithful ministry of God's servants which, under the Divine blessing to His people, and through their moral influence upon others, which hold back His judgments upon the world. They are the salt of the earth, which prevents the carcass of the unregenerate mass turning into complete putrefaction. But that "salt" has steadily *diminished* during the-last two centuries. As the population of the world has increased, the proportion of the righteous—despite a widespread "profession"—has decreased, and therefore sin has abounded more and more; and so too have the judgments of God. As the entrance of righteous Noah and his family into the ark was the signal for the flood to commence, as the removal of just Lot from Sodom was at once followed by the fire and brimstone from heaven, so the removal of God's eminent servants and saints from the earth (the places of few being filled) has been followed by the Divine judgments which we have witnessed and are still witnessing. Dispensationally, Joshua iv, 18, foreshadowed the awful fact that when the Day of grace is concluded, the world will be completely inundated by the storm of God's wrath.

"And the people came up out of Jordan on the tenth day of the first month, and encamped in Gilgal, in the east border of Jericho" (verse 19). There is nothing meaningless or valueless in the Scriptures. and we are the losers if we ignore or pass hurriedly over its *time marks*. The carnal critic would say, what interest is it unto me which particular day of the month this event occurred; but different far should be the spirit of the believer. But *how* is he to ascertain the significance of this detail? By looking up the marginal references, and if they do not furnish what he needs. by consulting his concordance, where he will find that the first reference to "the tenth day" of the first month (Ex. xii, 2, 3) supplies the key. It was the day when the paschal lamb was selected!—to be slain on the fourteenth (Ex. xii, 6, and see Josh. v, 10). How wonderfully God times everything for His people! "He so ordered things here that Israel entered Canaan four days before the annual solemnity of the passover. and on the very day when the preparation for it was begun, for He would have them enter into Canaan graced and sanctified with that religious feast, and would have them to be reminded of their deliverance from Egypt that, combining the two together, God might be glorified as the Alpha and Omega of their blessing" (Matthew Henry).

"And those twelve stones, which they took out of Jordan, did Joshua pitch [i.e. "erect"] in Gilgal" (verse 20). Probably those large stones were placed on some eminence where there was none other, for they were to be "a monument unto the children of Israel for ever" (verse 7). Some surmise, and we think with considerable probability, that when the Pharisees and Sadducees came to John's baptism and he said unto them "Think not to say within yourselves we have Abraham to our father: for I say unto you, that God is able of *these stones* to raise up children unto Abraham" (Matt. iii, 9) he pointed to the very cairn erected by Joshua. Confirmation of this appears to be furnished by John i, 28, which informs us that he baptized in "Bethabara beyond Jordan," for "Bethabara" means "the house of passage," i.e. the place where Israel passed over the river.

"And he spake unto the children of Israel, saying, When your children shall ask their fathers, in time to come, saying, What meaneth these stones? Then ye shall let your children know, saying, Israel came over this Jordan on dry land. For the Lord your God dried up the waters of Jordan from before you, until ye were passed over, as the Lord your God did to the Red Sea, which He dried up from before us, until we were gone over" (verses 21-23). Normal children have inquiring minds and ought not to be snubbed or even discouraged when they ask their parents questions. Rather should parents seek to improve their curiosity as an opening for instruction, *directing* the same into profitable channels. The very inquisitiveness of little ones affords their elders an opportunity to make known unto them the wonderful works of God, that their minds may be informed and their hearts awed by His perfections. But note well, it is *the father* (the "head" of the home) upon whom the main responsibility devolves, to see to it that his children are taught by him the things of God (Eph. vi, 4). Let him not pass on this task to his wife, still less to "Sunday-school teachers."

"That all the people of the earth might know the hand of the Lord that it is mighty: that ye might fear the Lord your God for ever" (verse 24). God's miraculous deliverances of His own people have a message for all the world, and when He is pleased to sanctify the same unto the unregenerate, they are deeply impressed thereby (Dan. iii, 29; vi, 25-27). The effects produced by the Jordan miracle are recorded in v, 1, which properly ends chapter iv: "And it came to pass, when all the kings of the Amorites which were on the side of Jordan westward, and all the kings of the Canaanites which were by the sea, heard that the Lord had dried up the waters of Jordan from before the children of Israel until we were passed over, that their heart melted, neither was there spirit in them any more, because of the children of Israel." The Canaanites were completely dispirited and cowed, realizing their utter incompetency to successfully oppose a people who had the Almighty for their Friend and Benefactor. But we must now seek to formulate the various lessons which we should learn from the memorial erected at Gilgal to mark the miraculous passage of the Jordan.

First, the wonderful works of God are worthy of treasuring in our memories, and He requires that pains be taken by us to see that they are so. It should be carefully noted that Joshua, even in the midst of a most exacting business, was not permitted to neglect the promotion of the Lord's honour. While superintending the passage through the river's bed of that vast concourse of people, with all their baggage (tents, etc.) and cattle, God bade him see to it that he took a man from each tribe and bid them select the twelve stones which were to be carried to Gilgal (iv, 2, 3). Nor did he demur or ask for a more convenient season.

Second, God's ordering of this memorial is a solemn reminder of how prone our hearts are *to forget* His past interpositions on our behalf. Of Israel we are told they "forgat His works and His wonders that He showed them"; and again, that "they soon forgat His works" (Psa. lxxviii, 11; cvi, 13). Alas, is not the same true of us? Even of the apostles Christ asked, "Do ye not yet understand, neither *remember* the five loaves ye took up?" (Matt. xvi. 9).

Third, because of our proneness to forget, suitable means are to be used in assisting us. We are to make conscience of the fact that God has bidden us *to* "remember all the way which the Lord thy God led thee" (Deut. viii, 2), and that precept should be turned into earnest *prayer* that we may not be negligent therein. We should frequently call to mind our previous experiences of God's faithfulness and tender care of us. This will strengthen the spirit of thanksgiving and cause us to praise God anew. It will deepen our confidence in Him to count upon Him in present emergencies and trust Him for future deliverances. The more we do so, the less shall we fear the experience of death, assured that God will undertake for us as we are called upon to pass through the valley of the shadows, as certainly as He conducted Israel safely through the Jordan (see II Cor. i, 10)!

Fourth, not only God's past deliverances of us are to be treasured up in our memories, but also His mercies unto His people in times gone by. Faith is to look back to what the arm of the Lord hath done "in the ancient days, in the generations of old," and say, "Art not Thou He which hath dried the sea . . . that made the depths of the sea, a way for the ransomed to pass over." And what will be the consequence of such exercise of believing memories? This: "Therefore the redeemed of the Lord shall return, and come with singing unto Zion" (Isa. li, 9-11). Why has God recorded the deliverance of Noah from the flood and of Lot from Sodom but to assure us that "the Lord knoweth how to deliver the godly out of temptation" (II Pet. ii, 5-9). Not only is "what was written aforetime written for our learning and comfort" (Rom. xv, 4), but what God did aforetime is to teach us what He can and will now do for His own. "I remembered Thy judgments of old, O Lord, and have comforted myself" (Psa. cxix, 52).

Fifth, the monument erected at Gilgal teaches us that we should take thought of and seek to make provision for the rising generation. That cairn of stones was erected with the express desire of evoking inquiry from those who should later behold it. God would have the wonders of His power and mercy preserved for posterity. There was to be a permanent witness of what God had wrought for His people; that no impotency or weakness of theirs prevented them reaching the shores of Canaan. It was meant as a sure pledge that God would continue to show Himself strong in Israel's behalf and would overthrow those then in occupation of the land. Thus, we rejoice when readers of this magazine purchase the bound volumes with this design before them. At least one is now thankfully reading those volumes which his mother (now in heaven) purchased from us twenty years ago, when he was unconverted. We cherish the hope that the bound volumes will be read by many long after we are called Home.

Sixth, in the *nature* or character of the two monuments which Joshua was instructed to set up, we see how different are the thoughts and ways of the Lord from those of men. No costly shrine, with useless ornamentations and affected splendour, was to mark the event, but only that which, though impressive, was simple and plain. "Never did triumphant column or arch, with all the magnificence of architecture, form so proper a monument of some celebrated victory as the twelve rude stones from Jordan's channel recorded the miraculous passage of Israel into Canaan under the conduct of the ark of the Lord." Equally true is this of the two signs and memorials which God has appointed for this dispensation. When divested of all priestly and parsonic trappings, how plain and simple, yet how significant and impressive, are the ordinances of baptism and the Lord's supper. The same principle was exemplified by Christ in the choice of His ambassadors—for the most part unlettered fishermen.

Seventh, that monument teaches us that we should recognize and own the corporate *unity* of God's people. It was comprised of twelve stones, taken up by one man from out of each tribe (iv, 2) and erected in Gilgal. That is the more noticeable since two and a half of the tribes had received their inheritance on the eastward side of the Jordan. Yet this cairn on the western shore must have in it not nine or ten, but twelve stones, to signify the oneness of Israel. We behold the same thing again in I Kings xviii, when, centuries later, the division between the northern and southern kingdoms of Israel obtained, and Elijah "took *twelve* stones according to the number of the sons of Jacob, unto whom the word of the Lord came, saying, Israel shall be thy name, and built with them an altar on Mount Carmel" (verses 31, 32), resting by faith on God's Word when what was visible to sight clashed with the same. They were all the elect of God and brethren. So *we* should view God's children, separated as they now are by party partitions and denominational walls, as members of the same Family, and sharing a common interest. Let our hearts embrace and our prayers include the entire household of faith.

Chapter 8

SYMBOLS OF COMMITTAL

JOSHUA 5:1-15

Circumcision

That which is to engage our attention on this occasion, as in the article following, is still concerned with what was preparatory to the real task awaiting Israel, and is found in what, strictly speaking, belongs unto the introductory portion of Joshua, rather than to the body of the book, where Israel's conquest and occupation of Canaan is the distinctive subject. Yet it is in these opening chapters that the Holy Spirit has (in typical form) revealed the fundamental secrets of success in the Christian warfare and their present enjoyment of the heritage which Christ has procured for them. It is therefore all the more needful for us to proceed *slowly* and seek to thoroughly assimilate these initial truths if we are to obtain the richest benefit from them. The first thing absolutely indispensable to Israel's possession of Canaan was their crossing of the Jordan. That, as we have shown, was a figure of the Christian's passing through death and judgment in the person of his Surety and then his entrance into "life." It is only one who is on *resurrection ground* that is qualified to overcome the foes which would prevent him possessing his possessions. Equally essential is it for the Christian to experience in a spiritual and practical way that which marked Israel's history at Gilgal.

"At that time the Lord said unto Joshua, Make thee sharp knives, and circumcise the children of Israel the second time " (v, 2). With those words chapter 5 ought to begin, for verse 1 in our Bibles obviously concludes the preceding one. Here in verses 2-9 the Holy Spirit has recorded what took place in Gilgal, namely, the circumcising of Israel. The narration of that important event is introduced by informing us *when* it occurred—a detail which must not be overlooked when seeking the spiritual application unto ourselves. "At that time," i.e., first when the Lord their God had so signally shown Himself strong in their behalf by performing a miracle of mercy for them. Second, when they had just passed through the river which spake of death and judgment. Third, as soon as they had set foot within the borders of their promised inheritance. Fourth, four days before the passover, as a necessary pre-requisite and qualification for them to participate in that feast. Fifth, ere they began the real task of possessing their possessions—by vanquishing those who would seek to prevent their enjoyment of the same. We shall ponder first the literal or historical meaning of this for the natural Israel, and then its application unto and significance as it respects the spiritual Israel, the Church of Christ.

The " circumcise the children of Israel the *second time* " requires a word of explanation. It should be apparent at once that the reference is not unto a repetition of a painful operation upon those who had previously been circumcised, but rather in contrast from a *general* circumcising of Israel on an earlier occasion. In the light of Josh. xxiv, 14, Ezek. xx, 7, 8 and xxiii, 3 it is clear that during their lengthy sojourn in Egypt the children of Israel

122

departed grievously from the revelation which God had made unto their fathers, and the statutes (Gen. xxvi, 5) He had given them; and judging from the case of Moses' own son (Ex. iv, 24, 25), there is little doubt that the ordinance of circumcision had been generally, if not universally, neglected and omitted by them. The words " God *remembered* His covenant with Abraham, with Isaac, and with Jacob" (Ex. ii, 24, and vi, 5) imply that Israel had *forgotten* it. The express prohibition that none should partake of the pass-over, save those who were circumcised (Ex. xii, 48, 49), and the added state-ment, " Thus *did* all the children of Israel: as the Lord commanded Moses and Aaron, so did they," denotes that circumcision had at last been adminis-tered—probably at the beginning of the " thick darkness which was upon all Egypt " for the " three days " (Ex. x, 21) that preceded the pass-over night.

Verses 4 to 7 (of Josh. v) tell us what it was that required such a wholesale circumcising of the male Israelites—adults as well as children—on this occasion: " Now all the people that came out were circumcised, but all the people that were born in the wilderness by the way as they came forth out of Egypt, them they had *not* circumcised " (verse 5), which in view of Genesis xvii, 9-11, was a startling omission. There has been considerable conjecture as to why Israel had failed to administer this essential rite for so many years. Thos. Scott says, " The reason for this omission is not so manifest." John Gill, " because of their frequent journeying, and the inconvenience of per-forming it being always uncertain when they pitched their tents how long they should remain and when they should remove . . . it was not safe to administer it." But the most popular explanation is that of *sinful neglect*. Yet even though that were the case with the great majority, would not the pious among them have complied? If rank disobedience was the cause, why is there no record of Moses rebuking them for such a grave sin? And why had not Joshua insisted upon it while they tarried in the plains of Moab, instead of waiting till the Jordan was crossed.

Matthew Henry came very much nearer the true explanation, though he states it rather vaguely and with some measure of uncertainty. The real reason, we submit, was what occurred at Kadesh-barnea. It was there the murmuring and unbelief of Israel reached its awful and fatal climax, when they hearkened to the evil report of the ten spies and refused to go forward into the land of Canaan, saying " Let us make us a captain, and let us return to Egypt "; and when Joshua and Caleb expostulated with them " all the congregation bade stone them with stones " (Num. xiv, 1-10). It was then that Jehovah swore in His wrath that they should not enter into His rest (Psa. xcv, 11). It was then that He declared " But as for you, your carcases, they shall fall in this wilderness. And your children shall wander in the wilderness forty years, and *bear your whoredoms,* until your carcases be wasted in the wilderness. All the number of the days in which ye searched the land, forty days, each day for a year, shall ye bear your iniquities forty years, and ye shall know *My breach of promise* " (Num. xiv, 32-34)—their apostasy and breaking of the covenant releasing Him from His engagement to bring them into Canaan. *There* is the key to Joshua v, 5!

When Israel, after repeated provocations, at length consummated their rebellion by despising the promised land and refused to advance beyond Kadesh-barnea, God swore that only two of that generation should enter it, the remainder being condemned to perish in the wilderness. Thus for thirty-eight years (Deut. ii, 14) Israel was in a state of *apostasy,* and during that time their children bore the reproach of the same by being *denied* the "token" or "sign of the covenant" (Gen. xvii, 11)—wrongly termed by men "the *seal* of the covenant," for circumcision never "sealed" anything to anyone saving only to Abraham (Rom. iv, 11). While the awful sentence of Numbers xiv, 32-34, lasted, Israel was a rejected people, and therefore their children were not entitled to bear the mark of covenant-relationship to God. But for the sake of their children, He did not withdraw every token of mercy from that generation, but provided sustenance and guidance throughout their journeys: the daily supply of manna, the pillar of cloud and fire, the erection of the tabernacle, etc., were so many intimations that God's favour would yet return unto Israel, though He had cast off their fathers.

The miraculous passage of the Jordan gave clear proof that Israel was once more *restored* unto the Divine favour, that Jehovah had resumed His covenant relationship with them, that in emerging from the river of death, judgment was behind them; that His sentence upon their fathers had been completed. That miracle showed unmistakably that Jehovah now owned Israel as His people, and therefore were they fit subjects again to receive the sign of the covenant upon their bodies. Circumcision was the token of the Abrahamic covenant (Gen. xvii, 11). That ordinance was the mark by which the natural seed of Abraham was distinguished from all other nations as a people in covenant with Jehovah, and which bound them by a special obligation to obey Him. It was the sign of the promissory part of the covenant which secured to Abraham's seed the land of promise (Gen. xvii, 8). Thus it was fitting that this second generation should *now* be circumcized. Moreover, the restoration of circumcision was to be accompanied by a revival of other institutions which had lapsed in the wilderness—such as the passover feast, for which circumcision was a prerequisite. Upon Israel's entrance into Canaan they came under a stricter discipline than hitherto (Deut. vi, 1; xii, 1, 8).

"At that time the Lord said unto Joshua, Make thee sharp knives and circumcise again the children of Israel the second time." At the very time when Israel had entered that land whose inhabitants their unbelieving fathers had reported to be "strong" and "the cities are walled, and very great," yea. "all the people we saw in it are men of a great stature" (Num. xiii, 28, 32). What a testing of Joshua's faith was this: that all the males of Israel should now, for several days, be thoroughly incapacitated for fighting (Gen. 34, 25)! But God intended it should be made manifest that the camp of Israel was governed by Himself, and not by any worldly policy. "What general ever opened a campaign in an enemy's country in the manner that Joshua did? On such occasions, all attention paid to the exercises of religion is too generally considered as a needless waste of time. Yet if indeed the help of God be the best security for success, and if His anger is more to be feared than the sword of any enemy, it will be found true policy to begin every expedition with repentance of sin, and attendance on the solemn worship of the Lord, and with using every method of securing *His* protection, though to a carnal eye it may appear unfavourable to success" (T. Scott).

"And Joshua made him sharp knives and circumcised the children of Israel" (verse 3). Severe as was this testing of his faith to thus handicap his fighting forces, yet counting upon the Lord's protection, his confidence in Him triumphed over it. We need hardly say that such a vast undertaking was not performed by him in person, but is attributed unto Joshua because the operation was carried out under his order and observation—just as we read that "Jesus made and baptised more disciples than John. Though Jesus Himself baptised not, but His disciples" (John iv, 1, 2). Not only was this command of God's a severe test of Joshua's faith, but of the people's too: their submission would evidence whether they owned the verity of that Divine promise (Num. xiv, 7, 8) which their fathers had disbelieved. Moreover, their submitting unto circumcision was designed as a test of their *obedience,* for their conquest of Canaan was conditioned upon their punctillious compliance with all that God had commanded through Moses (i, 8). Their willing compliance was a fulfilment of the promise which they had made unto Joshua in i, 17. 18, and afforded a further demonstration that *they* were the best of all the generations of Israel—in answer to the prayer of Moses (Psa. xc, 13-17).

"And it came to pass, when they had done circumcising all the people, that they abode in their places in the camp till they were whole. And the Lord said unto Joshua, This day have I rolled away the reproach of Egypt from off you. Wherefore the name of the place is called Gilgal [or "rolling"] unto this day" (verses 8, 9). The commentators are strangely "at sea" concerning the significance of that expression "the reproach of Egypt," most of them regarding it as a reference to the stigma incurred by Israel when they were the slaves of the Egyptians. But surely *that* reproach was for ever rolled away when Jehovah delivered His people from Egypt by a high arm, brought them safely through the Red Sea and there destroyed Pharaoh and his hosts. No, rather is it an allusion to Egypt's taunt of Exodus xxxii, 12. During the thirty-eight years when Israel was *rejected* by God there appeared ground for Egypt's sneer that they would perish in the wilderness; but all occasion for such a reproach had now been removed by the Lord's return unto Israel, and by restoring the token of the covenant He gave intimation that He had resumed His mighty works on their behalf, that they were His people and He their God.

But we must turn now and consider the application of this unto ourselves, for like all the ceremonial rites and institutions of the Old Testament times, circumcision is, antitypically, a real and substantial thing unto New Testament saints. Stating it first in a brief sentence, circumcision respected the *mortification of sin,* the putting off of the filth of the flesh. But that statement calls for explanation and amplification, for the great majority of Christians have very low and defective thoughts on this subject—inherited as they have been from the errors of Rome. Far too many of God's children today suppose that "mortification" signifies a dying to some specific acts of sin, the overcoming of this or that particular corruption. But that is a serious mistake. Watching against, offering stern resistance unto, and obtaining the victory over some particular acts of sin, falls far short of real mortification. That is evident from the fact that none of that is beyond what persons in a state of nature may do, and not a few *have* actually done. Men and women whose hearts know nothing whatever of the power of Divine grace have, nevertheless, succeeded in gaining the mastery over an unruly temper, and of denying their craving for strong drink.

Again, let it be granted that, as the result of a course of strict self-discipline, a Christian has overcome some besetting sin; or, putting it on a higher ground, that by Divine enablement in answer to prayer, he has become dead to some particular lust; nevertheless, the evil nature, the root, the filthy fountain from which such foul streams proceed, the whole body of sin, still remains within! No, Christian mortification consists of something much better, something far greater and grander than anything poor Papists are acquainted with. To be mortified unto sin is a higher and holier mystery than to be delivered from any mere acts of sin. It consists of having union and communion with Christ in *His* death unto sin (Rom. vi, 10, 11). It is the effect and fruit of Christ's death for us, and of Christ's death in us by the power of the Holy Spirit, whereby we live upon and enjoy fellowship with Him in His death, and are made partakers of "the power of His resurrection." As faith is exercised upon Him as our Head, we experience the virtue and efficacy of His death and resurrection in our hearts and lives.

That which was shadowed forth by circumcision, namely the putting off of the filth of the flesh, all believers find the substance of *in Christ,* and the same is made good *in their souls*—in measure here, but perfectly so at death. In order to obtain a complete view of the Christian's circumcision, we need to consider it federally and judicially, then spiritually and experimentally, and then practically and manifestatively. First, then, all believers are *legally* circumcised in Christ. That which circumcision prefigured was the removal of the pollution of sin, and that was accomplished for believers judicially in the death of their Head. Circumcision symbolized the entire mortification of sin, and that is the effect and fruit of Christ's death for His people. " Ye are complete in Him [Christ], which is the Head of all principality and power. *In whom* ye are circumcised with the circumcision made without hands, in putting off the body of the sins of the flesh by the circumcision of Christ" (Col. ii, 10, 11). There we have the blessed fact stated, that in Christ their federal Head His redeemed are already, truly legally circumcised. It is said to be "without hands" to distinguish it from the physical circumcision of the type, and to show that it is the result of no attainment of ours. Colossians ii, 11, is a statement which is addressed to our *faith,* for it refers to something outside of our actual experience, to something which we have in Christ.

The apostle was moved by the Holy Spirit to employ quite a variety of terms to express the same fact. In Romans vi, 2, he said of all believers "we *died* unto sin." In I Corinthians vi, 9, "but ye are *washed,* but ye are sanctified, but ye are justified in the name of the Lord Jesus." In Galatians ii, 20, he declared—as the representative of all saints—" I am *crucified* with Christ." Here in Colossians ii, 11, he affirms, "In whom also ye are *circumcised,*" which signifies that in the sight of God's Law and justice the total pollution and defilement of sin (as well as its guilt and criminality) has been for ever removed. "I have blotted out as a thick cloud thy transgressions" (Isa. xliv, 22). "Thou art all fair My love, there is no spot in thee" (Song of S. iv, 7). ·"And you that were sometime alienated and enemies in your mind by wicked works, yet now hath He reconciled in the body of His flesh, to present you holy and unblameable and unreprovable in His sight" (Col. i, 21, 22). Those scriptures bear witness that Christ and the Church are federally and legally *one*: that God the Father accepts them and views them in the Beloved as both righteous and holy; that He now sees them as without spot or wrinkle or any such thing; that He pronounces them eternally cleansed and blessed.

The faith of many of God's people apprehends the blessed fact that the guilt and condemnation of their actual transgressions was perfectly atoned for by Christ, but the faith of very few apprehends that their evil nature itself and all their corruptions have been made *a legal end of* by the sacrifice of Christ. They recognize by faith that God views them as cleansed from the curse of the Law, that there is "no condemnation" resting upon them; but they fail to perceive that the justice of God regards them as purged from the very presence and defilement of sin in their natures, that there is no filth within them. Yet the latter is just as true of them as is the former. Their "old man was crucified with Christ" (Rom. vi, 6). They were circumcised in Christ, which is described as a "putting off the body of the sins of the flesh." Indwelling sin is called a "body" because it consists of various parts and members, and that "body of sin" has been "put off," yea, "destroyed" or "annulled" as the word used in Romans vi, 6 signifies. Not only so, but the holiness of Christ has been imputed or placed to the account of their souls, so that God Himself declares, "the King's daughter is *all* glorious *within*" (Psa. xlv, 13), and not merely "without"—as covered with the robe of Christ's righteousness.

We say again that Colossians ii, 11, is a Divine declaration (as is Song of Solomon iv, 7, and Psalms xlv, 13, quoted above) which is addressed *to faith*, and is not a description of Christian experience; though in proportion as faith really appropriates it, we experience the comfort and joy of it. Alas that some of our readers are likely to refuse that comfort and joy through suspicion and fear that a belief of the same might lead to carelessness and low views of sin. When God bids His children to "reckon ye also yourselves to be dead indeed unto sin" (Rom. vi, 11)—which means exactly the same as "Reckon ye also yourselves to be circumcised indeed in Christ, in putting off the body of the sins of the flesh"—He certainly is not bidding them do anything which has a dangerous tendency. He exhorts them to so regard themselves because they have good and solid ground *for* doing so. They had a representative being and existence in their Head when He suffered and died to remove both the guilt and the defilement of their sins. Unless we were one with Christ in His death, there could be no pardon or cleansing for us. The saints then are to regard their state before God to be what Christ's is: delivered from sin's dominion, accepted in the Father's unclouded favour.

In our last we pointed out that the circumcising of all the male Israelites at Gilgal was a type of the circumcision of the Church. First, that all believers were *legally* circumcised in Christ: that at the cross the "body [or totality] of the sins of the flesh" was put off, completely and forever removed from the sight of God's law and justice; for such is the blessed meaning and teaching of Colossians ii, 11. God's elect had a federal being, a representative existence in their Head, so that when He died unto sin, they died unto sin; and it is both the duty and privilege of faith to appropriate that truth, and rest upon that fact. Therein we have revealed the Gospel method of mortifying sin—in blessed contrast from the fleshly devices of the Papists. It must flow from our union and communion with the Lord Jesus in His death, and faith's receiving of the virtue and efficacy of it. The fountain of all true and spiritual mortification was opened at the Cross and God is very jealous of the honour of the person and work of His beloved Son, and every departure from Him and it, every attempt of the carnal mind to devise some other remedy for any of the wounds which sin has inflicted upon and within us, is doomed to certain failure. Christ alone must be looked to for deliverance, not only from the guilt of sin, but from its power and pollution; yes, and from its presence too.

But it must now be pointed out that as Christ is the federal Head of His people, so also is He their vital or life-giving Head. As the natural head of the physical body influences all its members, imparting life and motion to them (for when one side of the brain becomes paralyzed, one whole side of the body does too), so Christ imparts life unto and influences the members of His mystical body, the Church. This He does by sending down His Spirit into their hearts, who communicates *to* them what Christ did and purchased *for* them. Thereby they are "circumcised" *spiritually and experimentally*. That brings us to the second branch of our subject. " For he is not a Jew who is one outwardly, neither is that circumcision which is outward in the flesh. But he is a Jew who is one inwardly, and circumcision is that of the heart; in the spirit, and not in the letter; whose praise is not of men, but of God " (Rom. ii, 28, 29). There is much of deep importance in those two verses yet they are little understood today, especially by Dispensationalists and writers on " Prophecy " ; but it would be outside our present scope to give an exposition of them, or even show the apostle's line of argument in that passage; rather we must confine ourselves to that in them which bears directly upon our present theme.

" Circumcision is that of the heart: in the spirit, and not in the flesh." There we are plainly taught that real " circumcision," the circumcision which God most approves, is an *internal* one. Even that is little understood by our moderns, and has no real place in their teaching. We wonder how many of our own readers have any definite and clear-cut conception of what is meant by *spiritual* " circumcision." Very few, we fear. All the more need then for us to take up this subject here, instead of seeing how swiftly we can get through the book of Joshua by merely offering generalizations upon its contents. It should be apparent to all who have read the Scriptures with any degree of attention and care that He who " desires Truth in the *inward* parts " (Psa. li, 6) required very much more from Israel even in Old Testament times than obedience to the outward ordinance of circumcision. The call " Circumcise therefore the foreskin of your heart, and be no more stiffnecked " (Deut. x, 16) is too plain for misunderstanding. It is quite clear from Leviticus xxvi, 41 and the last clause of Jeremiah ix, 26 that the Lord punished Israel because they were " uncircumcised in heart." The same fault Stephen charged upon the Jews of his day (Acts vii, 51).

" Circumcise yourselves to the Lord and take away the foreskins of your heart " (Jer. iv, 4) was His just demand. John Gill acknowledged that " men are exhorted to this " (alas that so many of his admirers refuse to do so), though he rightly added " yet elsewhere He promises to do this for them." God has ever required reality and not simply outward profession, inward and moral purity and not merely external and ceremonial. " O Jerusalem, wash thine heart from wickedness " (Jer. iv, 14). This spiritual circumcision, or cleansing of the heart, is the negative side of regeneration, or as the older writers more aptly expressed it " the privative " side. Strictly speaking there is no English word which accurately defines it, but " privative " is the nearest —that which results in a privation through the absence of something, the withholding or taking of it away. This is one aspect or part of " the great change " which takes place in a person when he is made the subject of a miracle of grace. Since we recently dealt with that in considerable detail, there is the less need to be lengthy on this occasion; but as spiritual circumcision is included in the general term " regeneration," we must not altogether ignore it.

As we emphasised in our articles upon " The Great Change," far too many writers when treating of regeneration confine their attention unto but a single aspect of the same—the communication of a new life or " nature." But *that* contemplates only one angle of it even from the positive side. There is a negative or privative side too. There is travail and pain in connection with a birth. Perhaps the reader will find it easier to grasp what we are saying and the better understand our terms when we remind him that justification has *two* parts to it: a privative and a positive—something removed and something bestowed. The cancellation or removal of the guilt and penalty of all sins is the privative side of justification, for remission (forgiveness) means " sending away." The imputation of the meritorious obedience of Christ to the account of the believing sinner is the positive side, for " justify " signifies to declare a person (not merely innocent, but) *righteous*. The two things are brought together in that lovely type in Zechariah iii, 4, " Behold I have caused thine iniquity to pass from thee "—that is the privative side; " and I will clothe thee with change of raiment " (the " best robe " of Luke xv) is the positive.

Now at regeneration something is *removed*, as well as something imparted: " I will *take away* the stony heart out of your flesh, and I will give you a heart of flesh " (Ezek. xxxvi, 26). Though that be metaphorical language, yet is the figure easily understood. The affections are divorced from evil and united to that which is good. By the miracle of grace, God takes away the love of sin and implants a love of holiness. And how is fallen man's radical and inveterate love of sin removed from him? By the Holy Spirit's illumination, revealing to him the exceeding sinfulness of sin; by His convicting him of the enormity and heinousness of sin, striking his conscience with terror and horror at having waged war against the Almighty; by bringing him to realize that it was *his* sins which caused the Lord of glory to bleed and die. Then it is that the love of sin receives its death-wound in his soul. Then it is he is " pricked in his heart " and cries out in anguish and despair " what shall I do? " (Acts ii, 37). Which is only another way of saying, Then it is that his soul is spiritually and experimentally *circumcised*; when so far as his love of it is concerned, he puts off " the body of the sins of the flesh " (Col. ii, 11).

The work of the Holy Spirit within the saint is many-sided, but its grand design and accomplishment is to make good *unto* him what Christ did *for* him: or to state it in other words, the Spirit imparts to the soul an actual acquaintance and effects with it a spiritual experience of what he has in Christ federally and legally. Christ died unto sin, for He was " made sin [judicially] for us," and His death was the penal death of our sin. Consequently, when the Holy Spirit is given to us He first works death in our hearts: that is, He both slays our self-righteousness, and gives a death-wound to sin in our affections. As the apostle tells us when relating one aspect of his own conversion, " when the commandment came, sin revived, and I *died* " (Rom. vii, 9). That is, when those words " thou shalt not covet," thou shalt not even lust after or desire any unlawful object, was applied in Divine power to his soul, the awful nature and extent of his sin became a living reality in his conscience, and he died to all good opinions of himself. By the spiritual slaying of our self-righteousness and making us loathe sin, the soul is experimentally " made conformable unto Christ's death " (Phil. iii, 10).

" The Lord thy God will circumcise thine heart, and the heart of thy seed [which is to be taken *generally* as " all " and " the world " in the New Testament] *to* love the Lord thy God with all thine heart " (Deut. xxx, 6). There we have the two principal aspects of regeneration or the miracle of grace brought together: the privative side, the circumcising of the heart, when it is made willing to part with its cherished sins, when its affections are severed from all evil. That is in order to the positive side, namely, the heart's being brought to love the Lord with all its faculties and strength. That love to God, John Gill rightly pointed out is " the duty of every man," and thus of the unregenerate: so, contrary to his followers, Gill not only taught " duty faith,' but "*duty* love"! Nevertheless, none performs this duty until God Himself circumcises the heart. Then it is that the soul of the elect is transformed from a natural man into "a new creature" (Gal. vi, 15). That moral change of "putting off the old man with his deeds" (Col. iii, 9) was prefigured by the fact that literal circumcision was required to be performed on the "*eighth day*" (Lev. xii, 3)—the numeral which always signifies a new beginning, and thus of "the new creature."

There is yet another aspect of this subject which calls for careful attention, namely, that circumcision of the Christian which is *practical and manifestative*. What Christ accomplished for His people, His Spirit effects within them, and they are required to make the same apparent in their daily lives and actions. Our federal and legal circumcision in Christ was in order to our vital and experimental circumcision, for by His meritorious work on their behalf the Lord Jesus procured the gift and grace of the Spirit unto His people (Gal. iii, 13, 14). Our inward circumcision by the operations of the Spirit unto His people was in order to the better qualifying us for the discharge of our responsibility and the glorifying of our God. While at regeneration the Spirit gives a death-wound unto sin in the affection of its favoured subject, and while at the same time He implants in his heart an imperishable love of and longing for holiness, yet He does *not* then remove from him the evil principle—"the flesh" remains in his soul unto the end of his earthly pilgrimage. Consequently, there is now a ceaseless conflict within him (Gal. v, 17), and therefore he is henceforth called upon to "fight the good fight of faith": to swim against the stream of his corruptions, deny self, mortify his members which are upon the earth.

The foes against which the Christian is called to wage conflict are mighty and powerful. That evil trinity, the flesh, the world, and the Devil, are relentlessly determined to destroy him. How then is he to successfully engage them in mortal contest? A great variety of answers have been returned to that question, all sort of rules and regulations prescribed; but most of them proceeded from "physicians of no value." It is too generally overlooked that *this* is "the fight of *faith*." The Devil can only be successfully resisted as we remain "steadfast in the faith" (I Peter v, 9). "This is the victory that overcometh the world—our faith" (I John v, 4). And there can be no victory over indwelling sin except by the actings of faith. And faith, my reader, always has to do with Christ: *He* is its grand Object (Heb. xii, 2), its Sustainer (Phil. i, 21), its Strengthener (Phil. iv, 13). That is according to the appointment of the Father, who has determined that His people should be beholden to His beloved Son for everything, that they may ascribe their all unto Him, that they may place the crown of honour and glory upon His Head. Christ is the alone Saviour not only from the guilt and pollution of sin, but likewise from its power and ragings within us.

In this matter of practical circumcision, our mortifying of sin, man's thoughts and ways are as far below God's as in everything else—as far as the earth is below the heavens. Man supposes he must do this in order to obtain that, avoid this in order to enjoy that, abstain from evil so as to enter into good. But he knows not where to obtain strength *for* the doing! Contrastively, God's way is to furnish that which equips for the performance of duty: to bestow freely, that gratitude will respond gladly; to lavish love upon us, that we cannot but love Him in return; to make known what He has made Christ to be unto us, and then bids us walk worthily of such a Saviour. He first makes us "light in the Lord," and then bids us "walk as children of light " (Eph. v, 8). He first makes us saints, then bids us act " as becometh saints " (Eph. v, 3). He makes us holy, then calls us " to be in behaviour as becometh holiness " (Titus ii, 3).

Immediately after Christians are bidden to likewise reckon ye also to have died indeed unto sin, but live unto God in Christ our Lord, they are exhorted " Let not sin therefore reign in your mortal body, that ye should obey it in the lusts thereof " (Rom. vi, 11, 12). Though they have died unto sin legally, sin is far from being dead within them. Though they are no longer " in the flesh " (Rom. viii, 9) so far as their standing before God is concerned, yet " the flesh " is still in them. Though Christ has put away the whole of the guilt and pollution of their sins, He has not yet fully delivered them from its power—that they might prove the sufficiency of His grace, the marvels of His forbearance, and the reality of His keeping power; and that there might be opportunity for the trial, exercise, and development of their graces. But though the evil principle (or " nature ") be not eradicated, the Christian is exhorted " Let not sin therefore reign in your mortal body." In that " therefore " we have an example of the apostle's evangelical method when urging Christians to perform their duty: not in order to obtain some further blessing, but because of what they already have in Christ.

That " therefore " looks back generally over the whole preceding section (from v, 1), but has a more particular reference to vi, 10, 11. The " Let not therefore sin reign " is far more than an appeal for us to exercise our wills: it is a call for faith to make one's own all that standing and state which is ours by virtue of our legal and vital union with Christ. Faith is urged to apprehend and appropriate our sinlessness in Christ by our death and resurrection in Him. *That* is the only right way of approach unto gaining the victory over sin in our daily lives. God will set no premium upon unbelief, but He will honour *faith*. Faith is called upon to recognize and reckon that sin was vanquished by Christ, and therefore it has no right to lord it over us. We are to refuse obedience to its desires and behests. We are to yield no subserviency unto the dethroned adversary of Christ, but strive constantly against every effort it makes to gain the ascendancy over us. And in order unto strength *for* such striving, we are to draw motives and encouragement from the love of Christ, who suffered and died for us. Strength to resist sin comes from faith's eyeing Christ and love's drawing from Him incentives to mortify that which slew Him.

It is " the love of Christ " which is ever to *constrain* the Christian in all things. But I must first be assured of His love for me, before my affections will flow out to Him in grateful submission and service. Any service which issues from fear or is prompted by reward, is either legal or mercenary, and unacceptable to Him. Without a realization of pardoning mercy in the soul, we can gain no victory over indwelling sin. In Christ we are not only dead to sin legally, but victors over it. As faith beholds sin perfectly conquered by Christ judicially, it seeks to have fellowship with Him therein in a practical way. To repudiate long-cherished sins, relinquish beloved idols, is a cutting and painful experience to nature, and therefore is it designated a circumcision and mortifying of our members; yea, so distressing is such work, our Lord likened it unto plucking out a right eye and cutting off a right hand (Matt. v, 29, 30). Yet such is not only a needful and profitable duty, but it becomes a desirable and *longed-for* one by those who truly love the Lord. The more their minds be spiritually occupied with Christ's love, the more are their affections drawn forth unto Him, and the more are their hearts brought to hate sin; and the more we hate sin, the more are we *dying to* it in our affections!

In our last, we pointed out the importance of observing the opening words of Joshua v, 2 when seeking the spiritual and practical application unto ourselves of what God required from Israel at Gilgal. " At that time ": as soon as they had passed through that river which spoke of death and judgment they were required to be circumcised. Likewise it is immediately after the Christian is assured of his union with Christ in death and resurrection that he is enjoined " Let not sin therefore reign in your mortal body." It is by faith's realization of that union we draw motives to resist sin's solicitations and derive strength against it. And as stated in our last we cannot serve God trustfully and joyously unless we are assured we are forever beyond condemnation (Rom. viii, 1), so it must now be added, there can be no progress in the Christian life unless we heed Romans vi, 12. That is amplified in the next verse: " Neither yield ye your members as instruments of unrighteousness unto sin; but (1) yield *yourselves* unto God as those that are alive from the dead and (2) your *members* as instruments of righteousness unto God." Because you have been " made alive," put away all the trappings of death, put off the old man, mortify the lusts of the flesh. Give up yourselves to God without any reserve.

Yet we repeat, obedience unto Romans vi, 12, 13, is possible only as we maintain the assurance of our perfect standing in Christ (verse 11), drawing motives and strength thereform for practical holiness, and by constantly seeking help from Christ by drawing upon His fullness (John i, 16). That is ever the evangelical order, " Be ye kindly affectioned one to another, tender-hearted, forgiving one another, even as God for Christ's sake *hath* forgiven you " (Eph. iv, 32). " Set your affection on things above, and not on things on the earth." Why? " For ye died, and your life is hid with Christ in God ... *mortify therefore* your members which are upon the earth " (Col iii, 1-5). " Put off all these: anger, wrath, malice, blasphemy, filthy communications out of your mouth; lie not one to another." Why? " Seeing that *ye have* put off the old man with his deeds " (Col. iii, 8, 9). " Behold! what manner of love the Father hath bestowed upon us that we should be called the sons of God . . . when He shall appear we shall be like Him; for we shall see Him as He is." And what is the effect of faith's appropriation thereof? This, " And every one that hath this hope in him *purifieth himself* [not merely ought to do] even as He is pure " (I John iii, 1-3).

But, says the Christian reader, notwithstanding my best efforts to keep my heart occupied with Christ and my faith fixed steadfastly on Him, sin daily gets the better of me. And what is the effect upon you? Are you pleased thereby? No, the very reverse; you are cut to the quick. That too is an integral part of practical " circumcision." Not only is every denying of self, every striving against sin, an element of mortification or practical circumcision, but equally so is all godly sorrow, all evangelical repentance, all contrite confession of sin. Blessed are they that " mourn " over their backslidings and falls, for it evidences they belong to those " whose circumcision is that of *the heart,* in the spirit and not in the letter " (Rom. ii, 29)—real and effectual, in contrast from the formal and ceremonial.

The Passover

It is most blessed to observe how Israel conducted themselves upon their first entrance into the promised land, for therein is manifested not the workings of nature but the fruits of Divine grace. After God had wrought so signally for them at the Jordan, they did not rush ahead and seek to immediately possess their inheritance. The miraculous dividing of its waters so that they passed through dryshod, must have greatly disspirited the Canaanites and thus have prepared the way for an easy triumph for the invaders. It had been natural, yea, what all military men would call "good policy" for Israel to have made the most of this terror by striking a heavy blow at once, pressing on with might and main before the enemy could recover himself, and so carry all before them in one swift campaign. But God's people follow not the ways nor employ the devices of the world. They are a "peculiar people": distinct and separate from the unregenerate, acting not by carnal wisdom and expediency, but regulated by spiritual considerations. "He that believeth shall not make haste" (Isa. xxviii, 16) is one of the principles by which they are required to act, for "the race is not to the swift, nor the battle to the strong" (Eccl. ix, 11).

Instead of immediately assaulting Jericho, the children of Israel pitched their tents at Gilgal and tarried there for a season. Exemplary restraint was that, and one which we do well to take to heart in this feverish age of mad speed. This tarrying in the camp at Gilgal was the more noteworthy when we bear in mind the very lengthy interval which had elapsed since their exodus from Egypt, during which they were prevented from reaching their goal and realizing their eager expectation. Yet there was something far more praiseworthy than self-discipline which marked their conduct on this occasion: they had the glory of God before them. They eyed His authority, had respect for His institutions, and acted in faith and obedience to His appointments. That should ever be what marks God's people, collectively or singly. It is neither the first business of the Church to "win the world for Christ" nor of the individual Christian to seek the salvation of his relatives and companions: rather is it to "show forth the praises of Him who hath called us out of darkness into His marvellous light" (I Pet. ii, 9) by our entire subjection to His Word. God has nowhere promised to *use* those who make not conscience of obeying Him in all things.

The appointments of God and not the attaining of their own desires were given the pre-eminence. First, Joshua had, in submission to the Lord's requirement, circumcised all those male Israelites who had been born in the wilderness. We have previously shown that the non-observing of that rite during those thirty-eight years was due to no sinful neglect, but was owing to the apostasy of their fathers at Kadesh-barnea, in consequence of which Jehovah declared "ye shall know My breach of promise" (Num. xiv, 32-34), and therefore were their children denied the token or "sign of the covenant" (Gen. xvii, 11). But the miraculous passage of the Jordan demonstrated that Israel was once more restored to the Divine favour, that He had resumed His covenant relationship with them, that in emerging from the river of death, judgment was behind them; and therefore it was fitting that this second generation should now be given that mark which distinguished them from all other nations as bound by special obligation to serve their God. It was also observed, how that the Lord's commanding Joshua to then circumcise the people presented a real test to his faith and obedience, severely handicapping for a few days his fighting forces; but counting upon God's protection, he confided in Him and triumphed over the trial.

Second, we are told, "And the children of Israel encamped in Gilgal and kept the passover" (v, 10). Appropriately did Matthew Henry point out, "We may well imagine that the people of Canaan were astonished and that, when they observed the motions of the enemy they could not but think them very strange. When soldiers take the field, they are apt to think themselves excused from religious ceremonies (they have not time or thought to attend to them), yet Joshua opens the campaign with one act of devotion after another. What was afterwards said to another Joshua might truly be said to this: 'Hear now, O Joshua, thou and thy fellows that sit before thee are men wondered at' (Zech. iii, 8); and yet indeed he took the right method." And, my reader, if *we* be actuated and regulated by a concern to the glory of God worldlings will wonder at us. It cannot be otherwise, for the natural man acts only from a spirit of self-love and self-will, and his end is self-pleasing and self-advancement. Thus, if he beholds any denying self, subordinating their interests to the honouring of God, he marvels at such conduct. Unless, then, *we* be "wondered at," yea, sneered at and regarded as crazy, it is because we have "left our first love" and become conformed to this world.

Israel's keeping of the passover was, like the circumcising of the people, an act of *obedience* unto the Lord: in fact the one could not be without the other, for it had been expressly laid down that "no uncircumcised person shall eat thereof" (Exod. xii, 48). For that very reason this ordinance had not been observed while the Nation lay under the wrath of God. They *had* kept it on the first anniversary of the event which it commemorated (Num. ix, 5), but not during the next thirty-eight years. God had said "I hate, I despise your feast days, and I will not smell in your solemn assemblies. Though ye offer Me burnt offerings and your meat offerings, I will not accept them" (Amos v, 21, 22)—language which not only applied to the prophet's own day but also had special reference to their sojourn in the wilderness as verse 25 evinces. But now the Lord had resumed His covenant relations with Israel and they had attended to the matter of circumcision; it was in order, yea, requisite, for them to do so. They had been strictly enjoined "Ye shall observe this thing for an ordinance to thee and to thy sons for ever. And it shall come to pass, when ye be come to the land which the Lord will give you, according as He hath promised, that ye shall keep this service." (Exod. xii, 24, 25).

In previous articles we have noted that this particular generation under Joshua was not only vastly better than the one which preceded but also far more spiritual than any that followed it. This was exemplified in the willingness of their adults to be circumcised without any demur. It appears again in what is now before us. The Lord had particularly said unto Moses almost a year after their leaving Egypt, "Let the children of Israel also keep the passover at his appointed season" (Num. ix, 5), as though to intimate, otherwise His command in Exodus xii, 24, had not been complied with. But on this occasion no mention is made of God's reminding them of their duty. We are told "the children of Israel kept the passover" (v, 10). And that is not all which is stated: "on the fourteenth day of the month," which is something more than a mere narration of a historical fact—it tells us that they kept the passover "at his appointed season." Nor is that all: it is added "at even," which was as the Lord required. How the Spirit delights to notice and record the *details* of obedience! The Israelites did not tamper with this

Divine ordinance and change it to a morning observance to suit their own convenience, as a compromising Christendom has done with "the Lord's *supper.*" Unless we conform strictly to the letter of the Divine precept, it is not "obedience" but "will worship."

Israel's act of keeping the passover was not only one of obedience but also of *commemoration*. "And this day shall be unto you for a *memorial,* and ye shall keep it a feast to the Lord throughout your generations. . . . And it shall come to pass when your children shall say unto you, What mean ye by this service? That ye shall say, It is the sacrifice of the Lord's passover, who passed over the houses of the children of Israel in Egypt when He smote the Egyptians, and delivered our houses. . . . It is a night to be much observed unto the Lord " (Exod. xii, 14, 26, 27, 42). This feast, then, was appointed to celebrate the great goodness of the Lord unto His people and their deliverance both from death and from the house of bondage. It was designed to keep before their minds the blessed provision He had made for them in the night of their deepest need, a provision all sufficient. It was to express anew their gratitude unto God for His distinguishing favour: the original "sacrifice" was expiatory, but the memorial of it was eucharistic. It was intended to signalize those perfections of God which had been exemplified on that never-to-be-forgotten night.

The passover had demonstrated in unmistakable manner the *sovereignty* of God, when He had "put a difference between the Egyptians and Israel " (Exod. xi, 7), that is, between the reprobate and His own elect—no lamb was provided for the former! It had manifested the *grace* of God. By nature the children of Israel were no better than the Egyptians, nor in conduct, as is clear from Ezekiel xx, 7, 8; xxiii, 3. It was out of His mere good pleasure and unmerited favour that the Lord exempted Israel from the destroyer (Exod. xii, 23). It displayed the *righteousness* of God, which announced that He "will by no means clear the guilty " (Exod. xxxiv, 7). They were flagrant sinners and "the wages of sin is death": death must do and did its work in their households too when the sacrificial lamb was slain. It revealed the amazing *mercy* of God in providing that substitute. It placated the *wrath* of God: He said to the avenging angel concerning Israel's firstborn "deliver him from going down to the pit: I have found a ransom " (Job xxxiii, 24), illustrating that basic principle "without shedding of blood is no remission." It testified the *faithfulness* of God: "When I see the blood I will pass over you," and He did. It made known His *love,* which had chosen Israel to be His favoured people (Deut. x, 15).

Again, the passover was not only commemorative, but *anticipative*: it memorialized what was past and also foreshadowed what was to come. The institution and ritual of the passover furnished one of the most striking representations of the person and work of Christ to be met with anywhere in the Old Testament. That it was a type thereof is clear from I Corinthians v, 7. "Christ our passover is sacrificed for us." Here then is our authority for regarding the contents of Exodus xii as shadowing forth the cross-work of the Saviour, and it is this which invests that chapter with such deep interest. The passover was the first of those annual "feasts" which God appointed unto Israel, for it sets forth the grand truth of redemption, which is the foundation blessing of believers, the fountain from which all others flow; and the passover was kept upon Israel's entrance into Canaan to signify that their possession of the Inheritance, no less than their deliverance from Egypt, was owing to the merits of the blood of the Lamb. Christ Himself observed it, saying to His apostles "With desire have I desired to eat this passover with you before I suffer" (Luke xxii, 15). In the light of these facts it becomes us to give our best attention to the teaching of Scripture thereon. ✓

Observe first, the *occasion* of its institution. It was at the close of God's judgments upon Egypt. He had declared, "About midnight will I go out into the midst of Egypt, and all the firstborn in the land of Egypt shall die, from the firstborn of Pharaoh that sitteth upon his throne, even unto the firstborn of the maidservant that is behind the mill, and all the firstborn of beasts. And there shall be a great cry throughout all the land of Egypt, such as there was none like it, nor shall be like it any more. But against any of the children of Israel shall not a dog move his tongue, against man or beast: that ye may know how that the Lord doth put a difference between the Egyptians and Israel " (Exod. xi, 4-7). Note carefully the exact wording of verse 5: it was not " all the firstborn *of* the land of Egypt shall die," but " all the firstborn *in* the land of Egypt," and that necessarily included Israel's equally with Egypt's. Yet in verse 7 the Lord said, He would "put a difference" between the Egyptians and Israel " so that the latter should be wholly exempt from judgment. That is what infidels would term " a flat contradiction," but the Christian knows there is none in the Word of Truth. What, then, is the explanation?

Each of those Divine declarations was literally accomplished: all the firstborn in the land of Egypt died, nevertheless the firstborn of Israel were delivered from the angel of death. But how could that be? Surely both could not take place! Yet they did, and therein we have a blessed illustration of the contents of the Gospel. It was the question of *sin* which was here raised and dealt with by God, consequently both parties were equally involved in His righteous judgment. The Israelites were not only sinners by nature, but practice; not only sins of infirmity, but high-handed sins of idolatry (Lev. xvii, 7; Joshua xxiv, 14). Divine holiness can never ignore sin no matter where it be found: when the angels sinned God " spared them not " (II Peter ii, 4). Justice must be satisfied; sin must pay its wages. A reprieve is out of the question. Then must guilty Israel perish? It would seem so. Human wisdom could devise no way of escape. But Divine wisdom did, and without compromising righteousness. How? By means of a *substitute*: sentence of death was executed on an innocent victim, because guilt had been legally transferred unto it. A lamb was provided for Israel, and it died in their stead.

Observe next, *the nature* of this transaction: " it is the Lord's passover " (Exod. xii, 11). Those words bring before us a fundamental aspect of Truth which is much neglected in evangelical preaching. Gospellers have much to say upon what Christ's death accomplished for those who believe on Him, but far less upon what it effected *Godwards*. Yet that is clearly brought out in the first direct mention of the " lamb " in Scripture: " God will provide Himself a lamb for a burnt offering " (Gen. xxii, 8). It was not simply that God would " provide a lamb," but that He would provide *Himself* one! The antitypical Lamb was appointed and supplied to glorify God, to vindicate His throne, magnify His law, satisfy His justice and holiness. The life and death of Christ brought infinite glory to God though not a sinner had been saved thereby. The two leading aspects of Christ's atonement—Godward and usward —were shadowed again in the ritual for the day of atonement: " Aaron shall cast lots upon the two goats: one lot *for the Lord*, and the other for the scape-goat " (Lev. xvi, 7, 8)—Israel's substitute, which bore away their sins into a place uninhabited. Christ must first be " the Lord's passover," accepted by

Him, before He could be " our passover " (I Cor. v, 7)—received by us.

Consider now *the substance* of God's gracious provision for Israel, namely, " the lamb." Though we cannot dwell upon details, we will furnish a broad outline for the benefit of young preachers. How well fitted was a lamb to be an emblem of the Saviour is at once apparent: so gentle and innocent, so mild and harmless, neither hurting others, nor seeming to have the capacity to resent an injury; useful in life (its fleece), valuable for food when killed. (1) The passover lamb was taken " out from the sheep " (Exod. xii, 5). " I will raise them up a Prophet from among their brethren." (Deut. xviii, 18). Christ, according to His humanity, was " made of the seed of David." " Forasmuch then as the children are partakers of flesh and blood, He also Himself likewise took part of the same " (Heb. ii, 14). (2) It was taken from the flock (not on the first, but) " the tenth day of the month " (verse 3). The Son of God did not become incarnate as soon as sin entered the world, but when " the fulness of time was come " (Gal. iv, 4), after forty centuries of human history had passed: after man had been *fully tested* (10 is the number of his responsibility) and his *probation* (which 40 signifies) was completed—10 × 10 × 40.

(3) " Your lamb shall be without blemish " (Exod. xii, 5, and cf. Lev. xxii, 21, 22). Nothing but a perfect sacrifice could satisfy an infinitely perfect God. One who had any sin in him could not make atonement for sinners. But where was such a one to be found? Nowhere among the fallen sons of men. That lamb " without blemish " pointed to the immaculate purity of Christ (Heb. vii, 26, 27; I Peter i, 19). (4) " A male of the first year " (verse 5): it was not to be too young or too old, but was to die in the fullness of its strength. So Christ died neither in childhood nor in old age, but in the prime of manhood —He was cut off " in the midst of His days " (Psa. cii, 24). (5) " And ye shall keep it up until the fourteenth day of the month " (verse 6). For four days the lamb, separated unto sacrifice, was kept tethered, apart from all others, during which time it could be fully inspected to perceive its flawlessness. Antitypically that may be taken two ways: on the principle of " a day for a year " (Num. xiv, 34; Ezek. iv, 6)—before His public ministry began (which lasted between three and four years) the Father bore testimony to the perfection of the Lamb (Matt. iii, 17); taking it literally, during His last four days Christ was under the closest scrutiny of men, and even His judge confessed " I find no fault in Him."

(6) The lamb must be slain: " The whole congregation of Israel shall kill it in the evening " (verse 6). That is very striking. It was not Moses and Aaron, or the Levites, who slew it, but the entire people as represented by the heads of every household. Nor was it only the chief priests and elders who were responsible for the slaying of Christ, for when Pilate decided the issue as to whether Barabbas or Christ should be released, he did so on the popular vote of the common people, who *all* cried " crucify Him " (Mark xv, 6-15). In like manner it was the sins of each believer individually (Gal. ii, 20) and of the Church corporeally (Eph. v, 25) which necessitated the death of Christ. It is also very remarkable to observe that though many thousands of lambs were slain that night, it was said " Israel shall kill *it*," not " them "! " There was only one before God's mind—the Lamb of Calvary " (Urquhart). (7) Its blood must be applied: " Thou shalt take the blood and sprinkle it on the two sideposts," etc. (verse 7). Mental assent to the Gospel without a personal receiving of Christ avails not to deliver from judgment: there must be an appropriation of Christ, " faith in His blood " (Rom. iii. 25). A Saviour accepted, not a Saviour provided, actually saves.

(8) The sprinkled blood gave security. " When He seeth the blood . . . the Lord will pass over the door, and will not suffer the destroyer to come in " (verse 23). And why? Because death had already done its work *there*! God's eye was not on the house or its inmates, but on the atoning blood. (9) " And the blood shall be to you for a token " (verse 13), i.e. " a token for good (Psa. lxxxvi, 17). It was to assure their hearts, as the " token " given to Rahab (Joshua ii, 12) was a guarantee of her preservation. God would have the hearts of His people in perfect peace, even while hearing the cries of the stricken Egyptians. No harm should befall them, and no fear distress while they rested on His sure promise! It is most important for the believer to distinguish between the foundation of his security and the basis of his peace: that which provided safe refuge from judgment was the slain lamb and its sprinkled blood; that which afforded a sure stay for the heart was the Word of One who cannot lie. (10) " Ye shall eat the flesh in that night " (verse 8). This was God's gracious provision for those within the house. Eating speaks of fellowship. It is Christ as the Food of His people, feeding by faith upon Him for strength and sustenance of soul.

(11) It must be " roast with fire " (verse 8). " Fire " here, as throughout, speaks of the wrath of a sin-hating God. The " roasting " of the lamb was a solemn figure of Christ suffering what was due to His people when He passed under and endured the awful wrath of God as He was " made a curse " (Gal. iii, 13). It is that which explains the deeper meaning of His cry " I thirst ": it was the effect of agony of soul as He endured the fierce heat of God's wrath. " Not sodden [boiled] at all with water " tells us nothing was allowed to hinder the direct action of " fire " on the Sinbearer: God " spared not His own Son " (Rom. viii, 32). (12) " With bitter herbs " (verse 8) or remorse of conscience. The Christian cannot have " fellowship with His sufferings " without remembering it was *his* sins which made them needful. (13) " And thus shall ye eat it: with loins girded . . . and staff in your hand " (verse 11). Fellowship with Christ can only be had as we maintain our pilgrim character. (14) " Not a bone of it shall be broken " (verse 46 and see John xix, 33-36)

All the leading features of redemption were more or less shadowed forth by the passover, and therein God would keep those things in the minds and before the eyes of Israel by their annual memorial of the same. But not only did the passover furnish a vivid portrayal of the Gospel, it was also a *means* for Israel's good, a gracious provision for their bodily needs. Before another day dawned they were to leave Egypt and start out for the promised land, and by feeding on the lamb strength was supplied for the journey which lay before them. Thus it is with the Christian: he must feed on Christ in order for strength as he passes through this wilderness, for the world supplies no nourishment for the soul. So it was at Gilgal (Joshua v, 10): as the passover had been the prelude to Israel's deliverance from Egypt and the commencement of their wilderness history, so it was made introductory to their new experience in Canaan: it was a blessed reminder that while they walked according to the Divine precepts, they might count upon God's mighty power. As their feeding on the lamb in Egypt supplied energy for their wilderness journey, equally needful was its strength for the warfare in which they were about to engage.

" And they did eat of the old corn of the land on the morrow after the passover, unleavened cakes and parched corn in the selfsame day " (Joshua v, 11). Once more we would observe how the Holy Spirit delights to take notice of and place on record the details of the saints' obedience. It had been expressly commanded that the pascal lamb must be eaten with "unleavened bread" (Exod. xii, 8), and strict compliance was here made with that order. They did not say, as long as it is *bread*, what else matters? but subjected their wills to God's. Throughout the Scriptures "leaven" is emblematical of corruption and evil, and therefore it had been a horrible incongruity and most unsuited to use leavened bread at a feast wherein the immaculate purity of Christ was set forth in the lamb "without blemish." The least tampering with the Divine ordinances alters their significance, mars their beauty, and is an act of presumption on man's part. If they be not kept in the letter of them, they certainly are not in their spirit, for true love seeks to please its object in all things.

"In the first month, on the fourteenth day of the month at even ye shall eat unleavened bread, until the first and twentieth day of the month at even. Seven days shall there be no leaven found in your houses: for whosoever eateth that which is leavened, even that soul shall be cut off from the congregation of Israel" (Exod. xii, 19). Thus, when it is said in Joshua v, 10, that when the children of Israel encamped in Gilgal they "kept the passover" we are to understand that for a whole week they observed the same. As Matt. Henry pointed out, "They kept the passover in the plains of Jericho as it were in defiance of the Canaanites that were round about them and enraged against them, and yet could not give them any disturbance. Thus God gave them an early instance of the performance of that promise, that when they went up to keep the feasts, their land should be taken under the special protection of Divine Providence: Exodus xxxiv, 24, 'Neither shall any man desire the land.' He now 'prepared a table before them in the presence of their enemies' (Psa. xxiii, 5)."

"And they did eat of the old corn of the land on the morrow after the passover, unleavened cakes, and parched corn in the selfsame day" (v, 11). A supply of food was already to hand when they entered Canaan: probably in granaries abandoned by its inhabitants as they took refuge in the walled city of Jericho. The Lord is no Egyptian taskmaster, requiring His people to make bricks without supplying them with straw. Now that "the feast of unleavened bread unto the Lord" was to be eaten seven days (Lev. xxiii, 6), an abundant quantity of grain was available for them. It is blessed to observe that before they used any of it for their own comfort, it was made into unleavened cakes in their worship of Jehovah. Thus did they act on the basis of that essential precept, "Honour the Lord with thy substance, and with the *firstfruits* of all thine increase" (Prov. iii, 9). And as the Lord Jesus has taught us, "seek ye first the kingdom of God and His righteousness" (Matt. vi, 33). He is to be given the pre-eminence by us in all things, and accordingly as we honour Him, so will He honour us.

This supply of corn upon Israel's first entrance into Canaan was *an earnest* of that promise which God had made through Moses: "It shall be when the Lord thy God shall have brought thee into the land which He sware unto thy fathers, to Abraham, to Isaac and to Jacob, to give thee great and goodly cities which thou buildest not, and houses full of good things, which thou filledst not, and wells digged, which thou diggedst not, vineyards and olive trees, which thou plantedst not" (Deut. vi, 10, 11); the complete fulfilment whereof is recorded in Joshua xxiv, 13. Typically, the "old corn of the land," equally with the manna, spoke of Christ (John xii, 24), yet in a very different character. The manna—"a small round thing" (Exod. xvi, 14), which lay on the ground and was Israel's wilderness food—was an emblem of Christ in His humiliation; but the old corn of Canaan pointed to Christ in His exaltation. The Christian needs to meditate and act faith on Christ not only as he is presented to us in all His moral perfections in the four Gospels, but also upon His official glories as they are set forth in the Epistles, particularly does he need to be occupied with Him as portayed in Hebrews as our great High Priest and Intercessor.

In the earlier articles of this series we laid considerable emphasis on the fact that the spiritual value and the practical *use* which *we* should make of the book of Joshua is, that we should see unfolded therein the principles by which the Christian is to enter into a present possession and enjoyment of his inheritance, and the secrets of successfully fighting the good fight of faith and the spiritual warfare to which he is called. We sought to make plain what are some of those basic principles and essential secrets as they are illustrated and exemplified by the historical incidents recorded in the first four chapters of this book, and before turning from the first two sections of chapter v, let us stress the truth that two more of them are here intimated as foreshadowed in the circumcising of the Israelites and their keeping of the passover. The Christian must be diligent in mortifying his lusts if he would walk in newness of life, and equally necessary is it that he feed daily on Christ—considered both as the sacrificial Lamb and as the great High Priest—in order to obtain strength to overcome the flesh, the world and the Devil. Practically, the corn of Canaan is a portion of our Inheritance which faith is to *now* appropriate.

"And the manna ceased on the morrow after they had eaten of the old corn of the land; neither had the children of Israel manna any more; but they did eat of the fruit of the land of Canaan that year" (verse 12). "To show that it did not come by chance, or by common providence as snow or hail does, but by the special designation of Divine wisdom and goodness; for as it came just when they needed it, so it continued as long as they had occasion for it, and no longer" (M. Henry). The practical lesson which we are to draw therefrom is, that we are not to expect extraordinary supplies when they can be had in an ordinary way: God works no unnecessary miracles. It is blessed to remember that the Lord had not discontinued the manna when the people despised it (Num. xi, 6), nor even when He severed His covenant-relation with that evil generation; but had mercifully continued to give it for the sake of their children, who had now grown up and entered Canaan. Here ends the first main Division of the book: i, 1-9 is the Introduction; i, 10 to v, 12, concerns the passage of the Jordan; v, 13 to xii, the conquest of Canaan.

"And it came to pass, when Joshua was by Jericho, that he lifted up his eyes and looked, and behold, a Man over against him with His sword drawn in His hand: and Joshua went unto Him and said to Him, Art Thou for us, or for our adversaries?" (verse 12). Though this verse begins a new section of the book, yet it opens with the word "And"—not simply to preserve the continuity of the narrative, but especially to link this incident with what immediately precedes. God has promised to honour those who honour Him, and Joshua had done so in the circumcising of the people and in the strict observance of the passover and the feast of unleavened bread; and now the Lord bestows a signal favour upon His servant. How much we lose by failing to render unto our God that full and implicit obedience which is His due! "He that hath My commandments and keepeth them, he it is that loveth Me; and he that loveth Me shall be loved of My Father, and I will love him, and will *manifest* Myself to him" (John xiv, 21) declares the Saviour. That is exactly what He was here doing unto obedient Joshua! It is of His spiritual manifestations to the soul we deprive ourselves by disobedience.

"And it came to pass, when Joshua was by Jericho, that he lifted up his eyes and looked." Probably he was here engaged in reconnoitring the walled city with a view to determining his best plan of campaign against it, for as Israel's leader that was his obvious duty; nor would the firm expectation that the Lord should show Himself strong on behalf of His people discharge him from the performing of it. Even when we are fully assured that God is for us and will undertake for us, it is required that we act as rational creatures, use all proper means and precautions, and put forth our best efforts. To refuse doing so on the pretext of relying wholly on God to do all for us is not faith but presumption. Though Christ was about to supply a miraculous draught of fishes, yet He bade Peter "Launch out into the deep and let down your nets" (Luke v, 4). True, we must not lean unto our own understanding nor rely on our own strength, yet both the one and the other are to be exercised by us. It was, then, while Joshua was in the path of duty, discharging his responsibility, that the Lord met with him! Only while similarly engaged are *we* warranted in expecting His help.

"And it came to pass, that when Joshua was by Jericho, that he lifted up his eyes and looked." The doubling of the verb seems to intimate a two-fold significance about Joshua's action—a natural and a spiritual: that after viewing the enemy's citadel, he supplicated the Lord. The *usage* of the verbs confirms this. The "lifted up" his eyes in a natural way, taking a comprehensive survey of things, occurs in Genesis xiii, 10, 14; while it is found in a spiritual sense in "unto Thee, O Lord, do I lift up my soul" (Psa. xxv, 1); for "looked" see Genesis viii, 13 and Exodus ii, 25. "And behold, a Man over against him, with His sword drawn in His hand." This represented a real test to Joshua's valour. God had bidden him "Be strong and of a good courage" (i, 6), and now he is put to the proof. There is nothing whatever here to intimate that Joshua beheld this Man in a vision, but rather that He appeared before him objectively and tangibly. Even though He had a "drawn sword in His hand," Israel's leader did not panic and flee, but boldly advanced "unto Him." We should harbour no fear while in the path of duty, but count upon the Divine promise "The Angel of the Lord encampeth round about them that fear Him, and delivereth them."

On the other hand Joshua did not rashly draw his own sword and engage this Man in conflict. Instead, he inquired, "Art Thou for us, or for our adversaries?" which challenge intimates Joshua recognized that this Stranger was no Israelite. A moment later he was to discover this Person was more than "a Man." Previously the Lord had *spoken* unto Joshua (i, 1; iii, 7; iv, 1, 15), but had made no visible manifestation of Himself unto His servant until now. Observe well how God suits the revelation of Himself unto His saints according to their circumstances and needs: to Abraham in his tent He appeared as a Traveller (Gen. xviii, 1, 2, 13), to Moses at the backside of the desert in a bush (Exod. iii, 1, 2), to Joshua at the beginning of his campaign as " a Man of war" (cf. Exod. xv, 3). In the celebrating of the passover Christ had been prefigured as the Lamb slain (verse 11); here in verse 13, with drawn sword in hand, He appeared as "the Lion of the tribe of Judah" (Rev. v, 5). It was one of the pre-incarnate appearings of the Son of God. in human form, which brings before us a most blessed yet profoundly-mysterious subject, concerning which the reader will probably welcome a few details.

In respect to Their Godhead, each of the three Divine Persons is equally invisible: the Triune God is seen alone in Christ. The invisibility of the Divine Being to mortal eyes is clearly taught in Old and New Testament alike. " There shall no man see Me, and live " (Exod. xxxiii, 20), "no man hath seen God at any time " (John i, 18), "dwelling in the light which no man can approach unto: whom no man hath seen nor can see " (I Tim. vi, 16). That raises the question, How are we to understand those passages in the Old Testament where it is said " Jacob called the place Peniel [the face of God]: for I have seen God face to face, and my life is preserved " (Gen. xxxii, 20), "and they saw the God of Israel " (Exod. xxiv, 10). In many passages it was not only that God was seen in vision or symbol, but corporately and actually. As, for example, by Moses: " If there be a prophet among you, I the Lord will make Myself known unto him in a vision and will speak unto him in a dream. My servant Moses is not so, who is faithful in all Mine house. With *him* will I speak mouth to mouth, even apparently, and not in dark speeches; and the similitude [" form " or " likeness "] of the Lord shall he behold " (Num. xii, 6-8). Those are what infidels term " contradictions."

The New Testament makes it known that another Person of the same essence as the Father has had for His office the making known of God unto His people: " the only begotten Son, which is in the bosom of the Father, He hath declared Him " (John i, 18), " he that hath seen Me," said Christ, " hath seen the Father " (John xiv, 9), " Who is the Image of the invisible God " (Col. i, 15 and cf. Heb. i, 3). The intimate communion between the two Persons appears in Exodus xxiii, 20, 21: " Behold I send an Angel before thee, to keep thee in thy way, and to bring thee into the place which I have prepared. Beware of Him, and obey Him, provoke Him not; for He will not pardon your transgressions: for My name is in Him." Observe how such language is used there by one Person about another Person as precludes our identifying Him as a single Person; yet both are certainly Divine. Thus, we must not exclude Jehovah the Father wholly from these communications to the Old Testament saints and attribute all the messages unto the Son immediately. We are to admit the presence of the first Person *per se* (by Himself), as well as the second: two Persons with Divine attributes, employing the name of Jehovah in common, the one the Sender, the other the Sent—the latter communicating directly with men.

In each instance the theophanic manifestation was made by God the Son, sometimes in the form of an angel, at others in the form of man. It is the same person, whether called " the God of Abraham, Isaac and Jacob," " the God of Israel " or " the Angel of the covenant." Those mysterious appearances were so many intimations that the Son even then personated the character of the Mediator, under which He would yet reveal Himself openly. It was God the Son who thus appeared to Hagar (Gen. xvi, 7), Abraham (Gen. xviii, 1), Jacob (Gen. xxxii, 24-30), Israel (Judges ii, 1), Gideon (Judges vi, 12-18), Manoah (Judges xiii, 21). In Malachi iii, 1, " the Messenger " or "Angel of the covenant " is called " The Lord of His temple." Those theophanies not only disclosed a personal distinction in the Godhead, but show the pre-existence and Deity of our Redeemer. That the Jehovah who manifested Himself again and again unto Israel in the wilderness was none other than the Mediator, is unequivocally established by I Corinthians x: " for they drank of that spiritual Rock that followed them and that Rock was *Christ.* . . . Neither let us tempt Christ, as some of them also tempted, and were destroyed of serpents " (verses 4, 9). See also Hebrews xi, 26.

The appearings of the Son of God to men in human form—sometimes in vision (Ezek. i, 26; Dan. x, 5, 6), sometimes in prophecy (Psa. lxxxix, 17; Dan. vii, 13), sometimes tangibly (Gen. xxxii, 24; Joshua v, 13)—were so many anticipations of the Word becoming flesh, and were in order to acquaint the Church with the Person of her Head by providing a blessed intercourse between them. They were endearing manifestations of Christ to His saints (and to none other!) of His love, that " His delights [even then] were with the sons of men " (Prov. viii, 31). It is most blessed to observe how many and varied ways the Lord Jesus took to display His personal love unto His people by vision and open revelation, by type and tangible similitude, in the early ages of the world, until the time that He became incarnate and tabernacled among men. They were all designed to prepare the minds of His people for His becoming the Son of man and furnishing the supreme proof of His love for them in New Testament times. He graciously adopted such methods to indicate how much He longed for the fullness of time when He should put away their sins and bring in an everlasting righteousness for them.

" And He said, Nay, but as Captain of the host of the Lord am I now come. And Joshua fell on his face to the earth and did worship and said unto Him, What saith my Lord unto His servant? " (verse 14). Joshua now discovered it was far more than " a Man " who stood before him, and therefore did he prostrate himself before Him and humbly sought His will. Had this Visitor been only an angel, he had rebuked Joshua for worshipping him (Rev. xix, 10; xxii, 8, 9); but this Person accepted it, thereby evincing His Deity! This faithful servant of His now had a special visit from his Lord to inaugurate the great enterprise on which he was about to engage, namely, the putting of the inhabitants of Canaan to the sword. It was the sign and token that complete victory should be Israel's, a guarantee that success should be granted their warfare. This " Man over against him, with drawn sword in His hand " had come as no idle Spectator of the conflict, but to command and direct every movement of their battles. " As Captain of the host of the Lord am I now come ": at the head of the angelic hierarchy stands the Angel of the Lord, " the Captain of our salvation " (Heb. ii, 10).

" And the Captain of the Lord's host said unto Joshua, Loose thy shoe from off thy foot, for the place whereon thou standest is holy. And Joshua did so " (verse 15). Here was further proof that the One speaking to Joshua was infinitely above the highest celestial creature, for the arch-angel's presence had not rendered the very ground whereon he stood sacred. It was in fact none other than the august Person before whom the seraphim veil their faces and cry, " Holy, holy, holy is the Lord of Hosts " (Isa. vi, 3 and cf. John xii, 41). It will be noted that the token of reverence required from Joshua was identical with that demanded of Moses by " the God of Abraham, the God of Isaac and the God of Jacob " at the burning bush (Exod. iii, 5, 6). That order for the removing of his shoes not only linked together the two incidents, but supplied a further assurance of God's promise to His servant " as I was with Moses, so I will be with thee: I will not fail thee, nor forsake thee " (Joshua i, 5). What an encouragement for faith was that! Who could stand before the Captain of the Lord's host? What was there for Israel to fear under such a Leader! Note how the Spirit again registers Joshua's obedience to the command to remove his shoes: " And Joshua did so." Nothing is too small for God's notice. Our every act is recorded by Him—how solemn! how blessed!

Chapter 9

VICTORY AT JERICHO

Joshua 6:1-27

A Closed City

We have now arrived at what is perhaps the most interesting and instructive incident recorded in this book, namely, the fall of Jericho, which appears to have been the principal stronghold of the Canaanites. Up to this point everything had been more or less preliminary and preparatory: now the real task before them must be faced and tackled: the Canaanites must be dispossessed if Israel were to occupy their goodly heritage. They had already received very great encouragement in connection with the Jordan, where the Lord had so signally undertaken for them by the might of His power. Having attended to the important duty of circumcision and having kept the feast of the passover, they were now fitted and furnished to go forward. What a parable was that of the beginning of the Christian life! Having been made the subject of the miracle of regeneration, plucked as a brand from the burning, the sinner saved by Divine grace now enters upon a new life—one as radically different in character as Israel's after they left the wilderness behind. Having obediently submitted to the ordinance of baptism and fed on the antitypical Lamb, the believer is not to settle upon his oars, but is called upon to engage in spiritual warfare and glorify God as "a soldier of Jesus Christ" (II Tim. ii, 3), serving under His banner and doing exploits, overcoming his foes and entering into a present possession of his inheritance.

Jericho was a frontier town and key city. It was a powerful fortress barring Israel's ingress. Its capture was indispensable before any progress could be made by Israel in conquering and occupying the land of Canaan. It was the enemy's leading fastness, which doubtless they considered to be quite impregnable, and the destruction of it would not only be a great encouragement unto Israel, but must still further dismay the remaining Canaanites. In its overthrow we perceive how different are the ways of God from man's, and with what ease He accomplishes His purposes. Here we behold how futile are the efforts of those who oppose Him, and how worthless the refuges in which they vainly seek shelter. In this memorable episode we are taught how the people of God are to act if they would have Him show Himself strong in their behalf: how that carnal scheming and worldly methods are given no place; but instead, faith, obedience, courage, patience, must be exercised, if they would obtain the victory over their foes. In what is here to be before us we see not Israel acting on the defensive, seeking to protect themselves from the attacks of others, but rather, under Divine orders, taking the initiative and assuming the offensive, which tells us there is an *active side* to the Christian warfare as well as a passive one—something which is too often forgotten by many of us.

We must not lose sight of the close connection between what is now to be before us and that which engaged our attention in the preceding article.

144

There we beheld Joshua alone by Jericho, apparently reconnoitring that fortress and noting its formidable strength—compare our remarks on chapter iii, verses 1 and 2, where Israel was required to take full stock of the flooded river which barred their entrance into Canaan. While so engaged, Israel's leader was suddenly confronted with a mysterious Personage " with His sword drawn in His hand " who, upon being asked. " Art thou for us, or for our adversaries? " replied, " Nay, but as Captain of the host of the Lord am I now come " (v, 14). Just as Jehovah had appeared to Moses at the burning bush before he entered upon his great task of leading the children of Israel out of the house of bondage and Moses received assurance that God had " come down to deliver them out of the hand of the Egyptians and to bring them out of that land, unto a land flowing with milk and honey " (Exod. iii, 8), so Joshua was then given promise that an all-sufficient Leader would take charge of Israel's host and conduct them to complete victory. That we *should* link together Exodus iii, 1-10, and Joshua v, 13-15, is intimated by the fact that on each occasion the appearing of the Lord was marked by the command, " loose thy shoe."

As stated in our last article, the second main division of the book of Joshua commences at chapter v. verse 13 (that section which has for its theme The Conquest of the Land), and therefore it behoves us to pay extra close attention to its *opening* verses. The incident described therein is not only introductory to what follows in the next six chapters, but it furnishes the key to their right interpretation. The appearing of the Angel of the Lord unto Moses at the burning bush had a deeper design than the strengthening of his heart, being a symbolical representation of the people of God then in " the iron furnace " (Deut. iv, 20), the " furnace of affliction " (Isa. xlviii, 10), and that the Lord Himself was present with them in it: " in all their affliction He was afflicted, and the Angel of His presence saved them " (Isa. lxiii, 9, and cf. Matt. xxv, 36; Acts ix, 11). But in Joshua v, 13-15, the Lord is viewed as no longer suffering in and with His people, but stands forth as their Captain, to command and lead them in battle. It was plain intimation that this was not Israel's quarrel, in which they should seek Divine assistance; but Jehovah's own quarrel, and Israel was but a division of *His* " host." The wars of Israel are expressly called " the wars of the Lord " (Num. xxi, 14). Israel's destruction of the Canaanites was no private vengeance, but Divine, because their iniquities were now " come to the full " (Gen. xv, 16; Lev. xviii, 25-28).

Far more was involved here than appears on the surface, and it is only by carefully comparing Scripture with Scripture that we can discover what was really taking place behind the scenes. The dispossession of the Canaanites from their native land should cause us no uneasiness, for it was no unrighteous act on Israel's part: rather were they made the instrument of God's holy judgment upon those who had persisted so long in their abominations that nought remained but their extermination. We need to look above the human side of things here, and contemplate them in the light of that expression, " the wars *of the Lord*," for that is what they were. It was more than human forces which were involved on both sides, namely, Divine and infernal. Jehovah Himself was now waging war upon Satan and his hosts. The Canaanites were devoted to idolatry and necromancy, using divination, being enchanters, witches, charmers, consulters with familiar spirits; and as Moses had announced, " because of these abominations the Lord thy God doth drive them out before thee " (Deut. xviii, 9-14)! As the apostle also informs us,

" the things which the Gentiles sacrifice, they sacrifice to *demons*, and not to God " (I Cor. x, 20). God, then, was here waging war upon the powers of darkness, and, as was evident at the Red Sea, none could withstand *Him*.

The subject is admittedly mysterious, yet sufficient light is cast upon it by the Word of God to enable us to perceive something of its real character. When man apostatized from God, he became the captive of the Devil; and when Christ came here to effect the redemption of His enslaved people, He had first to conquer their Captor. The Gospels make it clear that Christ's conflict was far more than one with men who hated Him, namely, against the Prince of this world—it was Satan who " entered into Judas " and moved him to perform his dastardly work. The " strong man armed " kept his palace, and his goods were in peace. But when " a Stronger than he came upon him," He overcame him and took from him all his armour in which he trusted, and " divideth his spoils " (Luke xi, 21, 22, and cf. Isa. liii, 12); " that through death He might destroy him that had the power of death " (Heb. ii, 14); " having spoiled principalities and powers, He made a show of them openly, triumphing over them in 'Himself " (Col. ii, 14). Likewise His soldiers are bidden to " Put on the whole armour of God, that ye may be able to stand against the wiles of the Devil "; the reason given being, " For we wrestle not against flesh and blood, but against principalities, against powers, against the rulers of the darkness of this world, against wicked spirits in the heavenlies " (Eph. vi, 10, 11)! How little is this realized!

" Now Jericho was straitly shut up, because of the children of Israel: none went out, and none came in " (Joshua vi, 1). This at once arrests our attention. They were not willing to issue forth and fight against Israel in the open. The fear of the Lord was upon them. What Jehovah wrought for His obedient people at the Jordan had struck terror into their souls. They were made to realize that One was with them who could not be withstood. " And it came to pass, when all the kings of the Amorites which were on the side of Jordan westward, and all the kings of the Canaanites which were by the sea, heard that the Lord had dried up the waters of Jordan from before the children of Israel, until we were passed over, that their *heart melted*, neither was there spirit in them any more because of the children of Israel " (v, 1). Consequently, their hope now lay in the height and strength of the walls of Jericho. There they sheltered, yet in a spirit of uneasiness. When there is an ungrieved Spirit in the midst of God's people, not only are *they* made the subjects of His quickening, fructifying and comforting influences, but those that are *without* are awed by His power! It is the absence of His restraint which explains the present lawlessness of society.

" Now Jericho was straitly shut up." The attentive reader will observe that the margin has it, " did shut up and was shut up." It is an expressive emphasis in the Hebrew like " dying thou shalt die " (Gen. ii, 17) and " in blessing I will bless thee " (Gen. xxii, 17). All the passages of ingress and egress were closed: the heavy gates barred, the inhabitants shut in by the massive walls. But what could *such* measures avail them? What are bolts and bars unto Him who can make the iron gate of a city " open of his own accord " (Acts xii, 10), and cause " all the doors " of a prison to be opened when He pleases (Acts xvi, 26)? Verily, " except the Lord keep the city, the watchman waketh but in vain " (Psa. cxxvii, 1). How little is that apprehended by this materialistic generation, who give little or no thought at all unto the agency of God in human affairs! What a rude awakening awaits them at the moment of death, and in the Day to come, when it shall be made to appear before an assembled universe that any other refuge than Christ Himself in which sinners sought shelter, stood them in no better stead in the hour of trial than Jericho did the Canaanites!

Jericho was one of those well-secured cities of Canaan of which it is said, "The cities were walled and very great" (Num. xiii, 28) and which to the carnal spies appeared utterly unassailable (Deut. 1, 28). It was therefore a *challenge to faith*—just as was Jordan. God did not work that first miracle before Israel's faith was put to the proof, but *afterward*. The priests bearing the ark were required, at the Divine command, "When ye are come to the brink of the water of Jordan ye shall stand still in Jordan" (iii, 8), and it was not until they had complied with that order that the Lord wrought so wondrously for them: "And as they that bare the ark were come unto Jordan, and the feet of the priests that bare the ark were dipped *in* the brink of the water . . . that the water which came down from above stood and rose up in a heap" (verses 15 and 16). So it was at Jericho. The Captain of the Lord's host had declared He would undertake for Israel, yet here was this citadel barred against them! Its gates were not opened by Divine hand, nor was its king panic-stricken so that he surrendered to them. No; "Jericho was straitly shut up." *That* was what confronted outward sight! So it is in our experiences today. "According unto your faith be it unto you": it is in response to *that*, God works.

"And the Lord said unto Joshua, See, I have given into thine hand Jericho, and the king thereof, and the mighty men of valour" (vi, 2). Very blessed is that. The Lord graciously made free with His servant, and before the campaign opened assured him of the complete success of the same. But let us not fail to call to mind that which had immediately preceded this favour, for there is an inseparable moral connection between them, which it behoves us to note. Joshua himself, the priests, and the whole nation had exercised an exemplary obedience to the Divine will and had manifested a real concern for the Divine glory—in circumcising the men and in celebrating the passover feast. It is ever God's way to make free with us when everything is right between Him and our souls. Thus we have illustrated and exemplified here yet another effect that always follows when there is an ungrieved Spirit in the midst of a company of saints. Not only does He awe those who are without, but Divine communications are freely vouchsafed unto those who are within! That ought to be a normal and regular experience, and not an occasional and extraordinary one. As the Lord Jesus declared, "He that hath My commandments and *keepeth them*, he it is that loveth Me; and he that loveth Me shall be loved of My Father, and I will love him and will *manifest* Myself to him" (John xiv, 21).

Above, we have said that this confronting of Jericho "straitly shut up" was a challenge to faith, and that God acts "according to" our faith. But faith must ever have a foundation to rest upon, and here one was afforded the same. That word "See, I have given unto thine hand Jericho," was instructive and emphatic. "See" was a definite call to view things with the eye of the spirit rather than that of the body: contemplate this obstacle by faith and not by carnal reason. Just as at the Red Sea the word was, "Stand still, and *see* the salvation of the Lord, which He *will* show you today . . . the Lord shall fight for you" (Exod. xiv, 13, 14). Yet they saw not that "salvation" or deliverance *outwardly* until they had, in faith and obedience, complied with the Divine order, "speak unto the children of Israel that they go forward" (verse 15). They were required to "see" God's promised deliverance by faith before it was accomplished unto outward sight! It was the same thing here: "See, I have given into thine hand Jericho." Have you, my reader, *thus* "seen" that blessed One of whom previously you had only "heard" (Job. xlii, 5)? Have you *thus* "seen Him who is invisible" (Heb. xi, 27)? Have you thus "seen" your final and complete victory over sin and death? Have you thus *seen* that place which your Redeemer has gone to prepare for you? That is what faith is: "the *substance* of things hoped for, the *evidence* of things not seen" (Heb. xi, 1)!

Instructions for Conquest

"And the Lord said unto Joshua, See, I have given into thine hand Jericho, and the king thereof, and the mighty men of valour" (Joshua vi, 2). That gracious declaration was not only a challenge unto the exercise of faith, and an evidence of God's bounty, but it was also designed to subdue all the workings of self-sufficiency. The proud flesh remains in all God's people, and the best of them are prone to take unto themselves that credit and praise which belong alone unto God. But that "See [take note of, keep steadily in mind, that] *I have given* into thine hand Jericho" was meant to exclude all boasting. It was not only a word to encourage and animate, but also one to *humble*, signifying that the success of this venture must be ascribed unto the Lord Himself, apart from whom "*we* can do nothing" (John xv, 5). Victory over our enemies must never be ascribed to our own prowess: rather are we to aver, "Not unto us, O Lord, not unto us, but unto Thy name give glory, for Thy mercy, for Thy truth's sake" (Psa. cxv, 1). Jericho was Israel's by Divine donation, and therefore its capture was to be attributed wholly unto the God of all grace. "What hast thou that thou didst not receive? Now if thou didst *receive*, why dost thou glory, as if thou hadst not received it?" (I Cor. iv, 7). What need there is for that truth to be pressed today upon a boastful and vainglorious Christendom!

When the people of Lystra saw the healing of the cripple, they sought to render Divine homage unto Barnabas and Paul, which, when they beheld, "rent their clothes and ran in among the people crying and saying, Sirs why do ye this thing? we also are men of like passions with you" (Acts xiv, 14, 15). O for more of that self-effacing spirit. How dishonouring it is unto God to have so many professing Christians eulogizing worms of the dust and using such expressions as "He is a great man," "a remarkable preacher," "a wonderful Bible teacher." What glory doth the Lord get therefrom? None. No wonder the unction of the Spirit is now so generally withheld! Moreover, nothing is so apt to destroy a preacher's usefulness as to puff him up with flattery; certainly nothing is so insulting to the Spirit and more calculated to cause Him to withdraw His blessing than such idolatrous man-worship. How much better to say, "Such a preacher is highly favoured of the Lord in being so gifted by Him." "The pastor was much helped by God in his sermon this morning." "Every good and every perfect gift is from above, and cometh down from the Father of lights" (James i, 17), and therefore it behoves us to thankfully acknowledge the Giver and freely render unto Him undivided praise for every blessing which He vouchsafes us through His servants, whether it comes in an oral or written form.

"And the Lord said unto Joshua, See, I have given into thine hand Jericho, and the king thereof, and the mighty men of valour." Taking that verse as a whole, we may perceive the Lord's concern for His own honour.

He is very jealous of the same, saying "My glory will I not give unto
another" (Isa. xlii, 8). Let us not forget that Herod was eaten up of worms
"because he gave not glory to God" (Acts xii, 23)! It was to prevent Israel's
committing this sin the Lord here made this affirmation unto their leader.
It was in order that His people might freely own, "He hath done marvellous
things: *His* right hand and His holy arm hath gotten Him the victory" (Psa.
lxxx, 1). How often the Scriptures record such statements as these: "today
the Lord hath wrought salvation [deliverance] in Israel" (I Sam. xi, 14); "So
the Lord saved Israel that day" (I Sam. xiv, 23); "The Lord wrought a
great salvation for Israel" (I Sam. xix, 5); "The Lord wrought a great
victory that day" (II Sam. xxiii, 10); "By him [Naaman] the Lord had given
deliverance unto Syria" (II Kings v, i). Alas, how little is such language now
heard! David had been taught this God-honouring and self-abasing truth,
as is shown by his words "Blessed be the Lord my strength, who teacheth my
hands to war, my fingers to fight" (Psa. cxliv, 1). Such should be the
acknowledgment made by us in connection with our spiritual warfare and
every success granted us in the Christian life.

"And ye shall compass the city, all ye men of war, and go round about
the city once. Thus shalt thou do six days. And seven priests shall bear
before the ark seven trumpets of rams' horns: and the seventh day ye shall
compass the city seven times, and the priests shall blow with the trumpets.
And it shall come to pass, that when they have made a long blast with the
rams' horns, when ye hear the sound of the trumpet, all the people shall
shout with a great shout; and the wall of the city shall fall down flat, and the
people shall ascend up every man straight before him" (verses 3-5). In view
of the preceding verse, that may strike some of our readers as a very strange
requirement. If the Lord had definitely given Jericho into the hands of
Joshua, why were such elaborate preparations as these necessary for its overthrow? Let those who feel the force of any such difficulty weigh attentively
what we are about to say. In reality, those verses exemplify and illustrate a
principle which it is most important for us to apprehend. That principle may
be stated thus: the disclosure of God's gracious purpose and the absolute certainty of its accomplishment in no wise renders needless the discharge of our
responsibilities. God's assuring us of the sureness of the end does not set aside
the indispensability of the use of means. Thus, here again, as everywhere,
we see preserved the balance of Truth.

So far from the Divine promises being designed to promote inactivity on
our part, they are given as a spur unto the same, to assure us that if our
efforts square with the Divine Rule, they will not be in vain. The gracious
declaration that God had given Jericho into the hand of Israel did not discharge them from the performance of their duty, but was to assure them of
certain success in the same. That principle operates *throughout* in the accomplishment of the Divine purpose. The truth of election is not revealed in
order to license a spirit of fatalism, but to rejoice our hearts by the knowledge that the whole of Adam's race is not doomed to destruction. Nor are
the elect mechanically delivered from destruction apart from any action of
theirs, for though they be "chosen to salvation," yet it is "*through* sanctification of the Spirit and belief of the Truth" (II Thess. ii, 13)—unless the
Truth be embraced by them no salvation would be theirs, for "he that believeth not shall be damned." Likewise the revealed truth that Christ will
yet "see of the travail of His soul and be satisfied" (Isa. liii), that "all that
the Father giveth Him *shall* come to Him" (John vi, 37), does not render

needless the preaching of the Gospel to every creature, for that preaching is the very means which God has appointed and which the Holy Spirit makes effectual in drawing unto Christ those for whom He died. We must not divide what God has joined together.

It is the sundering of those things which God has connected—wherein He has made the one dependent upon another—which has wrought so much evil and caused so many useless divisions among His people. For example, in the twin truths of Divine preservation and Christian perseverance. Our assurance of glorification in no wise sets aside the need for care and caution, self-denial and striving against sin on our part. There is a narrow way to be trodden if Life is to be reached (Matt. vii, 14), a race to be run if the prize is to be secured (Heb. xii, 1; Phil. iii, 14). We are indeed "kept by the power of God,' yet " through faith " (I Peter i, 5) and not irrespective of its exercise; and faith eyes and makes use of the Divine precepts equally with the Divine promises, and heeds God's admonitions and warnings as well as appropriates His comforts and encouragements. God has nowhere declared that He will preserve the reckless and presumptuous. He preserves in faith and holiness, and not in carnality and worldliness. Christ has guaranteed the eternal security of a certain company, but He was careful to first describe the marks of those who belong to it: " My sheep hear My voice, and I know them, and they follow Me, and *they* shall never perish " (John x, 27, 28), but no such assurance is given unto any who disregard His voice and follow a course of self-will and self-pleasing. God's promise of Heaven to the believer is far from signifying that he will not have to fight his way there.

The appointed means must never be separated from the appointed end. Strength for the body is obtained through the mouth, and health is not maintained without observing the rules of hygiene. Crops will not be produced unless the ground be prepared and sown. Yet in connection with spiritual matters we need to be particularly careful that we employ only those methods and use none but those means which God has appointed. " If a man also strive for masteries, yet is he not crowned except he strive *lawfully* " (II Tim. ii, 5). For *us* to determine the methods and select those means which appeal most to us when engaged in the service of God is presumptuous, a species of self-will, laying us open to the charge of " Who hath required *this* at your hand? " (Isa. i, 12); and for us to ask God's blessing upon the same is only seeking to make Him of our mind. Let us not forget the solemn warning pointed by the death of Uzzah, when the Lord God made a breach in Israel because they " sought Him not after the due order " (I Chron. xv, 13). We must keep closely to God's " due order " if we are to have His approbation. That was one of the outstanding lessons here taught Joshua. He was not left free to follow his own devices, but must adhere strictly to the plan God gave him, following out His instructions to the very letter if Jericho was to fall before Israel.

How passing strange those instructions must have appeared! How utterly inadequate such means for such an enterprise! How futile would such a procedure seem unto carnal reason! " No trenches were to be opened, no batteries erected, no battering-rams drawn up, nor any military preparations made " (Matt. Henry). Who ever heard of a mighty fortress being completely demolished in response to a company of people walking around it? Ah, God's ways are not only very different from man's, but they are designed to stain his pride and secure the glory unto Himself. The leader and lawgiver of Israel was preserved in a frail ark of bulrushes. The mighty giant of the Philistines was overcome by a sling and a stone. The prophet Elijah was sustained by a widow's handful of meal. The forerunner of Christ dwelt in the wilderness, had his raiment of camel's hair and a leathern girdle, and fed upon locusts and wild honey. The Saviour Himself was born in a stable and laid in a manger. The ones whom He selected to be His ambassadors were for the most part unlettered fishermen. What striking illustrations are these that "that which is highly esteemed among men is abomination in the sight of God" (Luke xvi, 15)! Yet how needful it is to keep this principle before us!

Had Joshua called a council of war and consulted with the heads of the tribes as to what *they* deemed the best policy to adopt, what conflicting advice he had most probably received, what various methods of assault had been advocated. One would have reasoned that the only way to subdue Jericho was by the starving out of its inhabitants through a protracted siege. Another would have counselled the use of ladders to scale its walls by men heavily mailed and armed. A third would have argued that heavy battering-rams would be more effective and less costly in lives to the attackers. While a fourth would have suggested a surprise attack by secretly tunnelling under the walls. Each would have leaned unto his own understanding, and deemed *his* plan the best. But Joshua conferred not with flesh and blood, but received his commission direct from the Lord, and therein he has left an example for all His servants to follow. The minister of the Gospel is responsible to Christ: he is *His* servant, called and commissioned by Him, and from Him alone must he take his orders. He has no authority except what Christ has given him, and he needs no more. Joshua did not refer the instructions he had received from God to the judgment of the priests and elders and ask their opinion on the same, but instead acted promptly upon them, counting upon the Divine blessing, however his fellows might regard them.

"When the Lord effects His purposes by such means and instruments as we deem *adequate*, our views are apt to terminate upon *them*, and to overlook *Him* 'who worketh all things after the counsel of His own will.' To obviate this propensity, the Lord sometimes deviates from the common track and works by methods or instruments which in themselves appear not at all suited to produce the intended effect; nay, sometimes have no real connection with it (Num. xx, 6-9; Ezek. xxxvii, 1-10; John ix, 4-7). But it is our duty to use only those means which the Lord appoints or allows, to submit to His will, and depend upon His blessing; and with patient waiting and self-denying diligence, to expect the event: and we shall thus succeed as far as is conducive to our real good. He takes peculiar pleasure in leading men's attention to His own truths and ordinances, in exercising their faith and patience, in inuring them to submit their understandings implicitly to His teaching and their wills to His authority, and in securing to Himself their praises and thankful acknowledgements. In promoting true religion, especially, He works by means and instruments which the proud, the learned, and the wealthy of this world generally despise. The doctrine of a crucified Saviour, God manifested in the flesh, as the only foundation of a sinner's hope of acceptance, and the only source of sanctifying grace; preached by ministers, frequently of obscure birth and moderate abilities, and destitute of the advantages of eminent learning or eloquence; sometimes even homely in their appearance and address" (Thos. Scott).

Looking more closely now at the instructions which Joshua received from the Lord on this occasion, we see that once more " the ark " was given the place of honour, being made central in the order of the procession. First were to proceed the " men of war," then came the ark with seven priests in front of it with " trumpets of rams' horns," and behind it came all the body of the people. The ark was the recognized symbol of Jehovah's presence, and its being carried before the congregation was to intimate the victory was *from Him.* Very much indeed turns upon our realization of the Divine presence—both as a restraint upon the flesh, and a stimulant to the spirit. When assured that the Lord is not only for us but *with us,* fear gives place to holy confidence. Deeply important is it for the servant of Christ not only to adhere strictly to the terms of His commission, but also to rest upon His blessed promise, " Lo, I am with you alway, even unto the end " (Matt. xxviii, 19, 20). Equally necessary for the rank and file of God's people to lay hold of that word, " I will never leave thee, nor forsake thee." Joshua had received personal assurance of this by the appearing to him of the " Captain of the Lord's host " (v, 13-15), and by the prominence accorded the ark: the whole congregation were given a visible reminder of the same fact. All were to move with their eyes fixed upon the Captain of their salvation, for none could stand before Him.

But the ark was also the repository of the tables of stone, on which were inscribed the ten commandments. It therefore denoted that Israel now marched as subject to the Divine Law, for only as they acted in obedience to its terms could success be expected. As was pointed out in our articles on the crossing of the Jordan, Israel marched into Canaan *led by the Law:* so here we are shown their conquest of the land depended upon their compliance with its requirements. But more: the presence of the ark here intimated that the Law was the minister of vengeance to the Canaanites: their cup of iniquity was now full and they must suffer the due reward of the same. Here the Law was " the minister of death " as the sequel demonstrated: see verse 21.

Seven Days of March

In our last we considered the instructions which Joshua received from the Lord concerning Jericho; now we are to observe how the same were carried out. "And Joshua the son of Nun called the priests, and said unto them, Take up the ark of the covenant, and let seven priests bear seven trumpets of rams' horns before the ark of the Lord. And he said unto the people, Pass on, and compass the city, and let him that is armed pass on before the ark of the Lord " (Josh. vi, 6, 7). It is therefore quite evident from these verses that Joshua understood God's promise " I have given into thine hand Jericho, and the king thereof, and the mighty men of valour " (verse 2) as meaning that, if His directions were faithfully and exactly executed, but *only* in that case, would the city be supernaturally overthrown. That promise was to assure Joshua that the Canaanites would be unable to successfully defend their city, and that the Lord would make it manifest that *He* had delivered it up to Israel; nevertheless they must act in full subjection to His revealed will.

This incident of the capture of Jericho is one which should be carefully pondered and taken to heart by all the people of God today, especially so by His servants, for if it be so it will supply a grand tonic to faith, and effectually counteract that spirit of gloom which now so widely obtains. Alas, the majority of professing Christians are far more occupied with what are called "the signs of the times" than they are with the One in whose hand all "times and seasons" are (Acts i, 7). They are walking by sight, rather than by faith; engaged with the things seen, rather than with those which are unseen. The consequence is that many of them are cast down and dispirited over present conditions, and only too often the preacher is apt to regard the situation as hopeless. But *that* is to be of the same temper as the unbelieving spies, who said "We be not able to go up against the people: for they are stronger than we" (Num. xiii,'31), magnifying the difficulties which confronted them and yielding to a spirit of defeatism.

If the minister of the Gospel be occupied with the smallness of his congregation, and their unresponsiveness to his preaching; if he dwell unduly upon the lack of interest on the part of the young people, and listens to the prophets of gloom, who ever give the darkest possible interpretation to things, then he may well be dejected. But if his thoughts be formed by and his own soul fed upon the Word of God, then he will discover that there is no cause whatever for dismay. Scripture nowhere teaches that God is seeking to convert the world, rather does it declare that He is visiting the Gentiles "to take out of them a people for His name" (Acts xv, 14). When giving instructions to His servants, Christ bade them "take no anxious thought," for He would have their hearts at rest, trusting in the living God to supply their every need; and also said "Fear not *little* flock, for it is your Father's good pleasure to give you the kingdom" (Luke xii, 22, 32). He ever sought to strengthen their confidence in the invincibility of God's purpose, declaring "all that the Father giveth Me, *shall come* unto Me" (John vi, 37).

Instead of perplexing his mind with useless speculations about the ten toes of Daniel's colossus, the business of the minister of the Gospel is to faithfully carry out the commission which he has received from his Master (Matt. xxviii, 19, 20). Instead of wasting time upon the newspapers and listening in to the wireless in order to ascertain the latest threats of the Kremlin or menaces of the Vatican, let him give more earnest heed to that injunction "Study to show thyself approved unto God, a workman that needeth not to be ashamed, rightly dividing the Word of truth" (II Tim. ii, 15). Instead of being so absorbed with the activities of Satan's emissaries, let him mix faith with that heartening assurance of the Most High, "For as the rain cometh down, and the snow from heaven, and returneth not thither, but watereth the earth and maketh it bring forth and bud, that it may give seed to the sower, and bread to the eater: so shall My Word be that goeth forth out of My mouth: it shall not return unto Me void, but it *shall* accomplish that which *I please,* and it shall prosper whereto I sent it" (Isa. lv, 10, 11).

The Word of God is not outdated: "heaven and earth shall pass away but My words shall not pass away" (Matt. xxiv, 35). Then preach that Word in its purity, in its fullness, with implicit confidence in its sufficiency. The Gospel of Christ is not obsolete, but is still "the power of God unto salvation to every one that believeth" (Rom. i, 16). Then proclaim it, realizing that the curse of God rests on all who preach any other (Gal. i, 8). Do you reply, I *have,* in my poor way, sought to preach the Gospel as faithfully and earnestly as I know how: but so far as I can see, it has been fruitless, and I am thoroughly discouraged. Then take heed, we beg you, to the incident which is here before us. Get down on your knees right now and beg God to bless this article unto you. Fervently implore Him to open your heart to receive the same. Ponder afresh those words "*by faith* the walls of Jericho fell down, *after* they were compassed about seven days" (Heb. xi, 30). Surely then "all things are possible to him that believeth" (Mark ix, 23)!

It requires no forced or fanciful effort of ours to show that Israel's conquest of Jericho adumbrated the victories won by the Gospel, when it is faithfully preached and the blessing of God attends the same. As was pointed out in our last, Jericho was one of the leading strongholds of the enemy: "the cities are walled and very great" (Num. xiii, 28). Probably Jericho was the most powerfully fortified of any of them, and as such it presented a formidable obstacle unto Joshua and his fellows. Nevertheless, it fell before them in response to the punctual observance of the orders which they had received from the Lord. It was in manifest reference to this that the apostle declared, "For the weapons of our warfare are not carnal, but mighty *through God* to the pulling down of strongholds" (II Cor. x, 4). How blessedly and unmistakably was that demonstrated under his own ministry! How gloriously was the same made evident in the days of Luther! How frequently has the same truth been made to appear in various parts of the earth since then. And *you,* my brethren in the ministry, have the same glorious Gospel to preach, and the same mighty God to look unto to bless your labours!

Do you reply, But I am no Joshua, no Paul, no Luther? Then we remind you of the apostle's self-abasing and God-honouring words to those who were glorying in the flesh. "Who then is Paul, and who is Apollos, but ministers by whom ye believed, even as the Lord gave to every man. I have planted, Apollos watered, but *God* gave the increase. So then neither is he that planteth any thing, neither he that watereth; but God that giveth the increase" (I Cor. iii, 5-7). The men whom God has most used throughout the ages were those who rated themselves as *nobodies!* But you say, I feel so weak and ill-equipped —God grant that such is your sincere language, for if the contrary were the case, if you deemed yourself an able and well-qualified man, you are no servant of Christ's. Listen again to Paul, who with all his gifts and graces contemplated the tasks before him in this spirit and attitude: "who is sufficient for these things?" (II Cor. ii, 16.)

Writing to those same saints and looking back to the days of his evangelistic labours among them, the apostle declared "I came to you not with excellency of speech or of wisdom, declaring unto you the testimony of God. For I determined not to know anything among you save Jesus Christ and Him crucified. And I was with you in weakness, and in *fear,* and in much trembling" (I Cor. ii, 1-3). Self-diffidence is no disqualification for Christ's service. It was not Paul that was "great," but rather that the weapons he used when engaging the forces of evil were "mighty through God"! And what were those "weapons"? Prayer, "the Sword of the Spirit, which is the Word of God" (Eph. vi, 17), and faith in the One who had commissioned him. Note that we put *prayer* first. Does not the example of the supreme Preacher (Mark i, 35; Luke vi, 12, 13) require us to do so? Did not the Twelve declare, "We will give ourselves continually to [1] prayer and [2] to the ministry of the Word" (Acts vi, 4)? Then do thou the same. Concerning *faith,* we refer the reader again to Hebrews xi, 30. Now fellow preachers, the same three "weapons" are available *to us,* and we need no others for the glorifying of Christ and the execution of His commission.

Note well, ye preachers, our last sentence. We did not say that no other weapons are needed in order for you to be eminently "successful" in your work, or that your use of the same will ensure prompt "visible results." *That* must not be made your chief concern nor immediate end: and if you make it such, a jealous God is most likely to blow upon rather than bless your efforts. Your paramount care and principal design must be the *glorifying of God* (I Cor. x, 31): to make known His excellency, to enforce His just claims upon the creatures of His hands, to bid men throw down the weapons of their warfare against Him, and be reconciled to Him. If you be a real servant of God's He has sent you forth to *magnify Christ:* the salvation of sinners is but secondary and subordinate thereto. God would have a universal testimony borne unto the matchless worth of the person and work of Christ—the Gospel is a "witness" (Matt. xxiv, 14) to His perfections. God would have proclaimed far and wide the amazing fact that His own beloved Son "became obedient unto death, even the death of the cross" (Phil. ii, 8), being wholly devoted unto the will of His Father.

It is of first importance that we should be quite clear upon the *nature* of the Gospel: it is "the Gospel of God . . . *concerning His Son,* Jesus Christ our Lord" (Rom i, 1, 3). In the Gospel is made known the Saviour's personal dignities: that He is the Lord of glory, the Prince of life, the King of kings, the Creator and Upholder of the universe. In the Gospel is revealed His amazing condescension and humiliation: how that in obedience to the Father's word He voluntarily and gladly took upon Him the form of a servant and was made in the likeness of sin's flesh, tabernacling for a season in this scene. In the Gospel is exhibited His holy and unique life: performing the work which the Father had given Him to do. In the Gospel is displayed His official glories, as Prophet, Priest and Potentate. In it is told forth His grace unto sinners: dying the Just for the unjust. In it is declared how that He magnified the Divine Law and made it honourable, superlatively glorifying the Father thereby. In it we are informed how that God rewarded His incarnate Son by raising Him from the dead, and seating Him at His own right hand on high. Our business, fellow preachers, is to proclaim that Gospel in its purity and fullness, that God may be glorified, and His Son magnified.

Our commission is crystal clear. It is no other than this: "Speak unto them, and tell them: whether they will hear, or whether they will forbear" (Ezek. iii, 11). Our business is to declare "all the counsel of God" and keep back nothing that is profitable unto souls (Acts xx, 20, 27). Our marching orders are the same as Jonah's (iii, 2) and of Deuteronomy iv, 2: "Preach unto it [the city] the preaching that I bid thee." "Ye shall not add unto the Word which I command you, neither shall ye diminish ought from it." Only by so doing will God be glorified and our souls cleared from the awful charge of infidelity. But if we *do so*—and only by Divine grace, earnestly and constantly sought, can we—we may safely *leave* "results" with the Lord of the harvest. Nay more, we may rest in full confidence on the promise "them that honour Me, I will honour" (I Sam. ii, 30). But it must be left *with Him* as to when and how He "honours." In the Day to come He will say "Well done, good and faithful servant." Even now "we are *unto God* a sweet savour of Christ, in them that are saved *and* in them that perish" (II Cor. ii, 15)!

But let us now take a more definite look at the instructions given to Israel's priests in Joshua vi, 6. Observe carefully a significant omission therein, which silently but decidedly confirms what has been said above. Joshua did not announce to them the promise which he had received from the Lord in verses 2 and 5, but simply gave them their marching orders, without any assurance that success would certainly attend their efforts! In this, as in almost all things, Joshua was a type of Christ, who, although receiving promise from His Father (in the everlasting covenant) of the sure success of *His* undertaking (cf. Isa. liii, 10-12), yet when commissioning His servants, gave them specific commandments but said not a word about their labours being fruitful!— see Matthew xxviii, 19, 20; Mark xvi, 15, 16; Luke xxiv, 46-49; John xx, 21-23; Acts i, 7, 8. So here: the priests were told what to do, and that was all. Unquestioning and unreserved obedience to their orders was what was required from them: nothing more, nothing less. They were, first, to "take up the ark of the covenant"; second, to "bear seven trumpets of rams' horns"; and third, to go "before the ark of the Lord." Let us now point out the typical significance of the same.

The ark of the covenant was the symbol of the Lord's presence with them, as their "Leader and Commander" (Isa. lv, 4). In like manner, Christ has assured His servants "Lo! I am with you alway, even unto the end of the world" (Matt. xxviii, 20). That is to be realized by faith, and not by sense. The minister of the Gospel is to go forward to the fight in the blessed consciousness that he is not alone: he is to act with full assurance that the Captain of his salvation is *with him*. What a difference it will make if he steadily bear the same in mind! Let him act accordingly. Let the known presence of Christ serve both as a bridle upon the flesh, and as a spur to his zeal. The priests "bearing the trumpets" at once identifies them as adumbrating ministers of the Gospel sounding forth their imperative message. "Cry aloud, spare not, lift up thy voice like a trumpet, and show My people their transgressions" (Isa. lviii, 1). "I set watchmen over you, saying, Hearken to the sound of the trumpet" (Jer. vi, 17). "Blow ye the trumpet in Zion, and sound an alarm in My holy mountain" (Joel ii, 11). The apostle made use of this figure when he said "If the trumpet give an uncertain sound, who shall prepare himself to the battle" (I Cor. xiv, 8).

The sounding of the trumpets by the priests on this occasion had a two-fold design: to strike terror into the hearts of the Canaanites: to inspire with courage and confidence the people of God. And that is the twofold work of Christ's servants. First, to solemnly declare the revealed wrath of God against all ungodliness and unrighteousness of men (Rom. i, 18): to announce His war against those who continue in sin: to boldly declare "he that believeth not shall be damned." Thus did the supreme Gospeller: Matthew xi, 23, 24; John iii, 18, 36! Second, to strengthen the hearts of God's people: "And if ye go to war in your land against the enemy that oppresseth you, then ye shall blow an alarm with the trumpets, and ye shall be remembered before the Lord your God, and ye shall be saved from your enemies" (Num. x, 9). "And it shall be when ye are come nigh to the battle, that the priest shall approach and speak unto the people, and shall say unto them, Hear, O Israel, ye approach this day unto battle against your enemies: let not your hearts faint, fear not, and do not tremble, neither be ye terrified because of them; for the Lord your God is He that goeth with you, to fight for you against your enemies, to save you" (Deut. xx, 2, 4). Thus is the preacher to encourage the saints in their conflict with the flesh, the world, and the devil.

"And Joshua the son of Nun called the priests and said unto them, Take up the ark of the covenant, and let seven priests bear seven trumpets of rams' horns before the ark of the Lord. And he said unto the people, Pass on and compass the city, and let him that is armed pass on before the ark of the Lord" (Josh. vi, 6, 7). Lack of space prevented the completion of our remarks upon these two verses in our last. There we dwelt at length upon the former one, and sought to show that Israel's priests, on this occasion, shadowed forth the ministers of the Gospel, and how that the appointed (spiritual) weapons of their warfare are made "mighty through God to the pulling down of st100g-holds" (II Cor. x, 4). Care needs to be taken against carnalizing that expression an l interpreting it in a manner unwarranted by the Analogy of Faith. It is not the Gospel converting people *en masse* (in a body)—"Glasgow for Christ," "C icago for Christ," as Arminian slogans express it—but the delivering of *individual* souls from that powerful "refuge of lies" in which the natural man is entrenched. The meaning of II Corinthians x, 4, is explained in the next verse:

"Casting down imaginations [or "reasonings"] and every high thing that exalteth itself against God, and bringing into captivity every thought to the obedience of Christ" (II Cor. x, 5). The heart of the natural man is stoutly opposed to God, being filled with enmity against Him. It is fortified by the love of sin against every appeal unto holiness. The unregenerate are so inured and hardened by habit and practice that the Holy Spirit declares "Can the Ethiopian change his skin or the leopard his spots? then may ye also do good, that are accustomed to do evil" (Jer. xiii, 23). Their wills are enslaved, so that they "will not come to Christ" (John v, 40). They are steeled against both the terrors of the Law and the attractions of the Gospel. Furthermore they are the captives of the devil (Luke xi, 21; II Tim. ii, 26), and are unable to emancipate themselves. Naught but a miracle of grace can free them, and the means used by the Spirit in accomplishing that miracle is the preached Word, effectually applied to the heart by His power. Then is the proud rebel humbled into the dust before God, delivered from the dominion of sin and Satan, transformed into a loving and loyal subject of Christ.

In the seventh verse of Joshua vi, instructions were given to the people. On this occasion they were to accompany the priests! When crossing the Jordan the priests went "before the people" (iii, 6), and stood alone "in the midst of Jordan" until "all the people had passed over" (iv, 10). *There* they foreshadowed our great High Priest, who "by Himself" opened a way through death for His people (see Chapter Six). But *here* the priests typified the servants of Christ, as engaged on their evangelistic labours. Con-sequently the hosts of Israel must now *accompany them*. What a word is that for the rank and file of the people of God today! Only too often has the minister of the Gospel to go forth alone. He does not receive that moral and spiritual support to which he is entitled, and which he so much needs. No wonder so many faithful preachers are discouraged when the prayer-meetings are so thinly attended, and when so few are holding up their hands at the throne of grace! O that it may please God to use this paragraph in stirring up professing Christians to be more definite and fervent in praying for all godly ministers. Only a preacher knows what difference it makes to have the assurance that the hearts of his people are *with* him!

"And it came to pass, when Joshua had spoken unto the people, that the seven priests bearing the seven trumpets of rams' horns passed on before the Lord, and blew with the trumpets: and the ark of the covenant of the Lord followed them" (verse 8). Observe, first, how precise is the *time-mark* here of the priests' action: they did not move forward until the people had taken their allotted position according to the instructions they had received from their leader. There was to be *conjoint* action: the priests accompanied by the people—exemplifying what we have said in the above paragraph. Second, since there is nothing meaningless or superfluous in Holy Writ, note how the Spirit has again emphasized the rude nature of the priests' "trumpets." No less than five times in this chapter are we told that those employed on this occasion were made of "rams' horns"—a cruder or meaner material could scarcely be imagined. They were in designed and striking contrast with the "trumpets of silver" which were normally used in the camp of Israel (Num. x, 1-10). It was God pouring contempt on *the means used*—those which were despicable in the eyes of men—that Israel's pride might be stained and Himself glorified, for His strength is ever made perfect through weakness.

Bearing in mind that Israel's priests here foreshadowed the true servants of Christ, their using trumpets of rams' horns is deeply significant, albeit, very distasteful to that pride of heart which glories in the flesh. It not only emphasized the feebleness of the means used by God in accomplishing His purpose of grace, namely, that it hath pleased Him "by the foolishness of preaching to save them that believe" (I Cor. i, 21), but also indicated the *type of men* God deigns to employ as His mouthpieces. When our Lord chose the men who were to be His apostles and ambassadors, He selected not those who occupied eminent stations in the world, nor those who had passed through the schools of learning, but unlettered fishermen and a despised tax-gatherer—*that* was the antitype of "the rams' horns" in contrast with "the trumpets of silver"—men of lowly origin, despised by those who are great and wise in their own eyes! To effect the mightiest of all works, God employs what is to the mind of the natural man the most inadequate means, in order that *His* wisdom and power may be the more apparent. The Gospel does not depend for its success on human wisdom—a fact lost sight of by the churches today.

That same flesh-withering truth is clearly expressed in I Corinthians i, 26-31, though few have perceived it. The immediate design of the apostle in I Corinthians i and ii was to show that the great and grand change wrought in the hearts of believers is not to be ascribed to any wisdom or power possessed by the preacher (who is but a channel through which God condescends to work), but is to be attributed wholly to the Divine grace in making his message effectual. The Corinthians were glorying in *human instruments,* setting up one against another (see i, 12), and the apostle shows how utterly baseless and foolish was such glorying. He pointed out that it was not the learning of Paul nor the eloquence of Apollos which could convert a soul, but that God must, from beginning to end, accomplish the same. This he demonstrates by describing the *type of instruments* which He makes to be vehicles of blessing unto sinners. "For ye see your calling, brethren [i.e. ye perceive from your own calling out of darkness into God's marvellous light], that not many wise men after the flesh, not many mighty, not many noble" —"are employed" (by God) is a far better and more pertinent supplement than "are called."

"But God hath chosen [for His servants] the foolish things of the world to confound the wise; and God hath chosen the weak things of the world to confound the things which are mighty; and base things of the world, and things which are despised, hath God chosen; and things which are not [nonentities, nobodies] to bring to naught the things that are." Thus, verses 26-28 are to be connected with the whole context, and not simply with verses 24, 25. In them we behold again "the trumpets of rams' horns"—God employing instruments which appear utterly inadequate to carnal reason. *That interpretation* is clearly confirmed by "*that* no flesh should glory in His presence," for the Corinthians were not glorying in themselves, but in their *ministers* (i, 12; iii, 4)! It is clinched by the next words: "But *of Him* [and not by Paul, or Apollos, or any worm of the earth] are ye in Christ Jesus" (verse 30). Thus, Paul was showing that it was not through learned philosophers nor highly trained rabbins that the Corinthians had heard the Gospel of their salvation, but rather through those whom both the one and the other regarded with contempt. If further corroboration be needed, verse 31 supplies it!

God is jealous of His honour and will not share it with another. It pleases Him, as a general rule, to select for His instruments those who have no glittering accomplishments: rather, plain, simple, homely men. It is not silver-tongued orators through whom He most shows forth His praises, but by those who have nothing more, naturally, to commend them unto their hearers than that which resembles the "rams' horns"! His most eminent servants have not been those of royal blood, noble birth, or high station, but taken from the lower walks of life. Luther, the principal agent used by God in the mighty Reformation, was the son of a miner. Bunyan was but a tinker, yet his book *Pilgrim's Progress* has been translated into more languages, had a much wider circulation, and been used in blessing to a far greater number of souls, than all the writings put together of the learned Owen and Goodwin! Spurgeon had neither university nor college training, nor was he a graduate of any seminary! Though after God's call to the ministry, each of them studied hard and long to improve himself! In proportion as the churches have made an idol of education and theological learning in their ministers, has their spirituality waned: that is a *fact*, however unpalatable it may be.

There is a third thing in verse 8 which claims our notice, namely, that the seven priests bearing the seven trumpets of rams' horns "passed on before the Lord." This is generally understood to mean that they preceded the ark, but that can scarcely be its significance, unless we are ready to conclude there is needless tautology here, for the same verse ends by declaring "and the ark of the covenant of the Lord followed them." What then is imported by they "passed on before the Lord"? It is very much more than a bare historical detail, which has no relation unto us today—alas that so few search for the present application *to themselves* of all in the Bible. There is that here which the servants of Christ need to observe and take to heart: something of vital importance and blessedness. That brief statement reveals to us the inward condition of the priests. It expressed their attitude unto Jehovah, and the Spirit of Truth delighted to record the same. Man looketh on the outward appearance but God looketh on the heart; and the hearts of Israel's priests were engaged with Him, and they comported themselves accordingly. By carefully comparing Scripture with Scripture we may ascertain the meaning of this clause.

In Genesis v, 24, we are told that "Enoch walked *with* God." In I Samuel ii, 21, that "the child Samuel grew *before* the Lord." In Deuteronomy xiii, 4, that Israel were bidden to "walk *after* the Lord their God." While in Colossians ii, 6, Christians are exhorted "As ye have therefore received Christ Jesus the Lord, so walk ye *in* Him." In those four prepositions we have an outline of the whole privilege and duty of the saint in his relation to God. To "walk with God" is only possible unto one who has been reconciled to Him, for "Can two walk together except they be agreed?" (Amos iii, 2). Thus it is expressive of holy *communion* with God. To go or walk "before the Lord" is to conduct ourselves in the realization that all our actions are being scrutinized by Him: "For the ways of man are before the eyes of the Lord, and He pondereth all his goings" (Prov. v, 21). Thus it is expressive of holy *fear*. To walk "after the Lord" is to live in complete subjection to His revealed will: "And the king stood in his place and made a covenant before the Lord, to walk after the Lord, and to keep His commandments, and His testimonies, and His statutes, with all his heart and with all his soul" (II Chron. xxxiv, 31). There it is expressive of unreserved *obedience*. To "walk in Christ" is expressive of *union*, like a branch in the vine, and signifies to live by His enablement, strengthened by Him, "rooted and built up in Him" as Colossians ii, 27, explains it.

But the one passage which more expressly explains these words of the priests passing on "*before* the Lord" is Genesis xvii, 1, when He said unto Abraham "I am the Almighty God: walk before Me, and be thou upright." That was said, first, by way of *rebuke*, right after his impatient and carnal conduct with Hagar. Second, that was said for his instruction and encouragement: to show him that there was no occasion for taking matters into his own hands. The Lord now made known Himself to Abraham as "The Almighty"—*El Shaddai*—the fully competent One, able to supply all his need, without the patriarch resorting to any fleshly devices. In view of which Abraham was bidden to "walk before Me and be thou upright": that is, count upon My infinite resources. Thus, when it is said that Israel's priests "passed on before the Lord," the meaning is that they acted in complete *dependence* upon God's all-sufficiency, confidently counting upon His undertaking for them. In the light of Proverbs v, 21, it signifies too that they moved forward in God's *fear*, conscious that His eye was upon them, and therefore they dared not depart from the orders which He had given them.

Let every preacher who reads this article endeavour to recognize that *this* too has been recorded for *his* learning, his guidance, his encouragement. Let him seek to realize, first, that he is beneath the all-seeing eye of his Master: that his actions are "before the eyes of the Lord, and He pondereth all his ways." Let him bear that in mind while he is out of the pulpit: that the One to whom he must yet render an account of his stewardship takes note whether he is an idler and slacker, or one who faithfully devotes his time to prayer and *study*, and not only to "sermon preparation." And, second, let him view by faith the all-sufficiency of the One before whom he walks, refusing to depart from His instructions, confidently counting upon Him fulfilling His purpose by and through him. Let him constantly call to mind that He is none other than "the Almighty," the self-sufficient Jehovah. No other provider, no other protector is needed. It was because Abraham forgot *that* that he stooped to fleshly devices; and when *we* forget it, we are very apt to depart from His rule and resort to carnal methods. It is distrust of God which lies behind the fleshly and worldly devices now so commonly employed in the churches.

"And the armed men went before the priests that blew with the trumpets, and the rearward came after the ark, the priests going on, and blowing with the trumpets" (verse 9). Here our attention is directed away from the priests unto the remainder of the children of Israel, and they are divided into two companies—those who went before, and those who followed behind the ark of the covenant. The ones taking the lead consisted of the fighting force, who were to advance when the walls of Jericho fell down and slay those within the city. This arrangement originated not in the mind of Joshua, for at no point was he required to lean unto his own understanding. The Lord had previously given orders through Moses that the fighting men of the tribes of Reuben and Gad should "go armed before the Lord to war . . . until He had driven out His enemies from before Him" (Num. xxxii, 20, 21). It was in obedience thereto that Joshua here acted. As the margin more correctly renders, it was the "gathering host" of Israel who made up the rearward. In that twofold division we may find a hint that only a few of the Lord's people are possessed of a courageous spirit and prepared to show a bold front to the enemy.

"And Joshua had commanded the people, saying, Ye shall not shout, nor make your voice to be heard, neither shall any word proceed out of your mouth until the day I bid you shout; then shall ye shout" (Josh. vi, 10). Here. is the third item in the instructions which Joshua gave to "the people." First, they had been bidden to "compass the city"; and second, the armed men among them to "pass on before the ark of the Lord" (verse 7); now they are enjoined to maintain strict silence as the long procession wended its way around Jericho. Very precisely and emphatically was this order worded: its threefold prohibition reminding us of the repeated interdiction of Proverbs iv, 14, 15, "Enter not into the path of the wicked, and go not in the way of evil men. Avoid it, pass not by it, turn from it, and pass away." There is no excuse for ignorance of the Divine will: the things which God forbids us doing are as plainly stated in His Word as those which He requires of us.

No explanation was given the people, but simply the bare command: sufficient for them that so God required. Pondering it in the light of Scripture, several reasons for it and significations of it may be suggested. First and more generally, this injunction for the people to preserve complete silence constituted a test of their obedience—made the more real by their not being told why such an imposition was necessary. For the mouths of such a vast multitude to be sealed during the entire march around the city was no small test of their subjection unto the revealed will of Jehovah. Second and more specifically, such decorous silence well became them on this occasion. Why so? Because God was in their midst, and *He* is "greatly to be feared in the assembly of His saints, and to be had in reverence of all them that are about Him" (Psa. lxxxix, 7)—a verse which many preachers today need to press upon their congregations, among whom much irreverence obtains in the house of prayer. If the seraphim veil their faces before the Lord, how reverent should be *our* worship!

The "ark of the covenant" was the symbol of the Lord's presence, and its being in Israel's midst on this occasion required that they conduct themselves with the utmost propriety. God was about to speak loudly to the Canaanites in judgment, and it was therefore fitting that every human voice should be stilled. There is "a time to keep silence, and a time to speak" (Eccles. iii, 7). When Pharaoh and his hosts were pursuing the children of Israel, and they were confronted by the Red Sea, they were told, "The Lord shall fight for you, and ye shall hold your peace" (Ex. xiv, 14). The case was a parallel one here: Jehovah was about to lay bare His mighty arm and show Himself strong on behalf of His people, and it was meet that they should be still before Him, in reverent expectation of the event. It was a case of "hold thy peace at the presence of the Lord God, for the day of the Lord [when He acts in an extraordinary manner] is at hand" (Zeph. i, 7); "Be silent, O all flesh, before the Lord; for He is raised up out of His holy habitation" (Zech. ii, 13). The profound silence observed by Israel's hosts added impressively to the gravity and solemnity of their procession.

Again; Israel's being forbidden to open their mouths on this occasion supplied another illustration and exemplification of the difference which marks the ways of God from man's. We are aware that some are likely to regard that statement as a trite platitude, yet *they* are probably the very ones who most need to be reminded of it here, for they are the least affected and influenced by it. God's work is to be done *in His appointed way*: but instead of that, much of what now pretends to be "His work" is being done in the *world's* way. God works silently, whether it be in creation, providence, or grace. Vegetation makes no noise in the process of its growth. God's government, both of individuals and nations, is wrought secretly. The miracle of regeneration is not perceptible to our senses, though its effects and fruits soon become apparent. So it is in His dealings with our souls: the Lord is not in the wind, nor in the earthquake, nor in the fire, but in the "still small voice" (I Kings xix, 11, 12). We too should go about our appointed tasks in the same calmness: "a meek and quiet spirit" is of "great price" in His sight (I Peter iii, 4).

Third, the silence required of "the people" on this occasion supplied another important line in the typical picture furnished by this incident—though one which certainly will not appeal to many in present-day Christendom. Israel's capture of Jericho unmistakably pre-figured the victories achieved, under God, by the Gospel. The priests blowing with the trumpets of rams' horns pictured the servants of God preaching His Word. The forbidding of "the people" to open their mouths signified that the rank and file of Christians are to have no part in the oral proclamation of the Truth—they are neither qualified for nor called to the ministration of the Word. Nowhere in the Epistles is there a single exhortation for the saints as such to engage in *public* evangelism, nor even to do "personal work" and seek to be "soul winners." Rather are they required to "witness for Christ" by their *daily conduct* in business and in the home. They are to "show forth" God's praises, rather than tell them forth. They are to let their light shine. The testimony of the life is far more effectual than glib utterances of the lips. Actions speak louder than words.

How vastly different was the typical scene presented here in Joshua vi from that which is now beheld in the so-called "evangelism" of our day! Here everything was orderly, decorous and reverent. "The people" in the rear: "the ark of the covenant"—symbol of the Lord's presence—in the midst: the "seven priests" blowing with their trumpets: the "armed men" in front. The absolute silence of all the hosts of Israel—so utterly different from the war cries to which they were accustomed—must have deeply impressed the citizens of Jericho. But not only is there the marked absence of that dignified silence, gravity, solemnity and reverence, which befits all gatherings that are professedly engaged in Divine worship, but modern "evangelism" is characterized by that which is noisy, vulgar, and carnally exciting. How different the self-advertised "evangelists" of this decadent age from the supreme Evangelist, who "suffered not the demons to speak, because they knew Him," and who said to the cleansed leper "See thou say nothing to any man" (Mark i, 34, 42)!

"So the ark of the Lord compassed the city, going about it once" (verse

Read also
Page 288,
290

11). And what follows? Therefore its walls at once fell down? No; "and they came into the camp and lodged in the camp." Then they had all their trouble for nothing! No indeed. But nothing happened: they were no forwarder, but just where they were previously! That is estimating things *by sight,* and is an erroneous conclusion. Much had happened. That which is of supreme importance had been accomplished. *God* had been honoured and glorified! How so? By the implicit obedience of Joshua, of the priests, of the congregation of Israel. O that both ministers and laymen were more thoroughly convinced that nothing honours God so much as our *obedience.* "To obey is better than sacrifice" (I Sam. xv, 22)—the most lavish offering is unacceptable to God unless it be made by one whose will is subject to His. Attending meetings, contributing generously to His cause, busying ourselves in what is wrongly termed 'Christian service," is worthless—yea, a species of hypocrisy —if we be not walking in the path of the Divine precepts.

Unless what has just been said be laid to heart by both the public servants of God and private Christians, the most important lessons of this incident will be missed. As was pointed out in our last, the preacher who most honours Christ is not the one who produces the largest "visible results," but he who sticks the closest to His commission and preaches the Word most faithfully. So with the saints. The Christian housewife who discharges her God-given duties in the home and the domestic in the kitchen who conscientiously performs her menial tasks are as pleasing and glorifying to Christ as the most self-denying missionary in the foreign field. What is the one outstanding excellence in the Saviour's life and work which the Holy Spirit has emphasized more than any other? Is it not that His meat and drink was to do the will of Him that sent Him (John iv, 34)! That there was no limit in His subjection to the Father's authority, that He "became obedient unto death, even the death of the cross" (Phil. ii, 8)! Say not that nothing was accomplished by Israel here, but admire their God-honouring obedience, and seek to emulate them.

"And Joshua rose early in the morning, and the priests took up the ark of the Lord" (verse 12). Nothing escapes the all-seeing eye of the One with whom we have to do. In human estimation this may appear a very trivial detail, nevertheless it is one which the Holy Spirit delighted to notice and place upon imperishable record. Why so? Because it marked the diligence, fidelity and zeal of those servants of the Lord. Why so? Because they also inculcated yet another lesson which ministers of the Gospel need to heed. They are expressly bidden to study and show themselves "approved unto God, workmen who needeth not to be ashamed" (II Tim. ii, 15). Slackness and slothfulness ill become those who claim to be the ambassadors of Him who rose up "a great while before day" (Mark i, 35) and "early in the morning He came again into the temple" to teach the people (John viii, 2). That searching question of His, "what do ye more than others?" (Matt. v, 47), is capable of many legitimate applications—not least to *the preacher.* Does he spend fewer or more hours per day in his study than do those who work for their daily bread!

"And seven priests bearing seven trumpets of rams' horns before the ark of the Lord went on continually, and blew with the trumpets; and the armed men went before them, but the rearward came after the ark of the Lord, the priests going on and blowing with the trumpets" (verse 13). The Hebrew word for "trumpet" (*shophar*) has its first occurrence in Exodus xix, 16, 19, where its loud blast was used to awe the nation at Sinai: highly significant is the fact that it is mentioned just fourteen times here in Joshua vi: 7×2, or the number of perfect witness. The word for "rams' horns" (*yobel*) is the one used throughout Leviticus xxv, where twenty times it is rendered "jubilee," so that as an alternative to "trumpets of rams' horns" it would be equally permissible to say "trumpets of jubilee." In the year of jubilee all slaves were released and given their freedom, and all alienated estates were restored to their original owners. In view of the oft-repeated "ye shall return every man unto his possession" (Lev. xxv, 11, 13, 27, 28) and "the land of your possession" (verse 27) we perceive the significance and appropriateness of the sounding of "trumpets *of jubilee*" as Israel now began to possess their inheritance.

In that *double* meaning and purpose of the priests' "trumpets of rams' horns" we have clearly intimated the nature of that twofold work to which God has appointed His servants. Those trumpets had a mission and a ministry both unto the Canaanites and to Israel: the one were to be awed and affrighted, the other to be cheered and comforted. By faithfully preaching the holiness of God, the demands of His Law, the sinfulness of sin, and the reality of its awful wages, the minister of the Gospel is to strike terror into the hearts of the ungodly (II Cor. v, 10), urging them to "flee from the wrath to come." Unto those who give evidence that they have forsaken their wicked ways and believed the Gospel, it is his privilege and duty to strengthen their faith and gladden their hearts by announcing to them the liberty which they have in Christ and the nature of that glorious inheritance which He purchased for them. In other words, to proclaim the grand jubilee tidings, so that assurance and joy may be the present portion of the redeemed. It is in the Epistles that the blessed contents of the Gospel are most fully unfolded to the saints.

"And the second day they compassed the city once, and returned into the camp" (verse 14). A careful reading of the context shows that while Divine assurance had been made unto Joshua himself that the Lord had given Jericho into his hand, yet he made no mention of this when giving orders to either the priests, the people, or the armed men: all were to act in what the world terms "blind obedience"—without any promise of reward. It is also to be duly noted that while Joshua had been informed by God how many days and times the enemy's stronghold must be encircled before its walls should supernaturally collapse (verses 3-5), he kept this knowledge to himself, leaving all under him in ignorance of *how long* this strange method of procedure was to be continued. The absence of such information made an additional demand upon the faith and obedience of Israel on this occasion. After making one complete circuit of the city, the holy ark of Jehovah being carried aloft in their midst, and all the host had returned to their camp *without* any tangible result, it is much to their credit that they repeated the whole performance a second time. Yet still there was not the slightest sign of God's appearing on their behalf!

How striking then are the closing words of verse 14: "so they did six days"! After a second and third encompassing of Jericho, without any apparent success, little wonder had the people complained and said, What is the use of prolonging this business? Admire then their persistency. How different was this generation from their forefathers in the wilderness, who so quickly became discouraged and murmured against their leader!—and never possessed their heritage! In contrast, their sons vowed unto Joshua, "All that thou commandest us we will do, and whithersoever thou sendest us we will go" (i, 16), and faithfully did they keep their word. This too has been recorded for *our* instruction and for our encouragement. Was there not a time, fellow-minister, when Christ made Himself known and you asked "Lord, what wouldest Thou have me do?" Did He not in His condescending grace answer "Son, go work today in My vineyard"? When you received His call to devote the whole of your time and talents to His service, did you not promise to spend and be spent in the same? Then be not weary in well doing, for in *due season* ye shall reap, if ye faint not..

However impetuous be our spirit, the Lord is never in a hurry, and we are required to wait *His* leisure. Every dispensation of God has its prefixed period: as the mercy itself, equally so the timing of the mercy, is wholly in God's hand. "The vision is yet for an appointed time, but at the end it shall speak, and not lie: though it tarry, wait for it; because it will surely come, it will not tarry" (Hab. ii, 3). It is not at our beck and call: we can neither hasten nor retard the Almighty. "He that believeth shall not make haste" (Isa. xxviii, 16), but continue steadfast in the performance of duty. We must neither fail through discouragement, nor adopt means of our own in order to speed the issue. Two things are required of us: adhering strictly to the directions which God has given us, trustfully and hopefully waiting His blessing on the same. Patience must have her perfect work. Thus it was with Israel here. They fainted not because the walls of Jericho fell not the first or second, nor even the fifth or sixth day; nor did they take matters into their own hands and resort to another method. Rather did they "Wait on the Lord, and keep His way" (Psa. xxxvii, 34).

"Rest in the Lord, and wait patiently for Him" (Psa. xxxvii, 7) was the grand lesson inculcated by this incident. Confide in the Lord's goodness, count upon His power, submit fully to His authority, or there will be no waiting *for* Him. Israel must have implicit trust in the One who had given them their instructions through Joshua. And so must *we*. We are to wait in obedience as servants, and in expectation as believers. A desirous expectation concerning the future must be subordinated to a meek submission to God's will in the present. "Wait on the Lord, and *keep His way*, and He shall exalt thee to inhabit the land" (Psa. xxxvii, 34). It is failure to "wait on the Lord"—through giving way to the feverish flesh—which causes us to depart from "His way"! Those who are in too great a hurry to acquire things take "short cuts" which God has not appointed; but such who act in unholy haste are sure to repent at leisure. But if we patiently tarry for God's time, then we shall confine ourselves to those means which He has assigned. Let preacher and layman alike lay hold of that promise, "they shall not be ashamed [or "confounded"] that *wait for Me*" (Isa. xlix, 23).

"And it came to pass on the seventh day, that they rose early about the dawning of the day, and compassed the city after the same manner seven times: only on that day they compassed the city seven times" (verse 15). What a demand upon their faith, obedience, and patience was this! After their apparently fruitless effort of marching around Jericho once a day for no less than six days, now they were required not only to do the same on the seventh day, but to then repeat the performance no less than seven times more! And note well those words "after the same manner." There was to be no change of procedure: seeming failure did not warrant them in adopting *other* measures: they must adhere strictly to the Divine directions unto the end. What a needful lesson is there pointed for us! Not only was their testing protracted, but it became increasingly severe. Once a day for six days had been unavailing; and six times more on the seventh day passed without any

Divine intervention; yet still they persevered! What cause for shame that *we* become discouraged so easily and faint so quickly!

A brief word needs to be said about the repeated occurrence of the number *seven* here: the seven priests, the seven trumpets, the seven days, and the seven encirclements of Jericho on the seventh day cannot be without some design and significance. The best comment we have seen thereon is John Owen's: "The compassing of the city once every day for six days, and the entrance into it on the seventh, had respect unto the work of the creation. For God was now entering into His *rest* with respect unto His *worship*, in a new way of settlement and solemnity, such as He had not erected or made use of from the beginning of the world. Hence He frequently calls it 'His rest' (Psa. xcv, 11; cxxxii, 8, 14; Heb. iii, 11; iv, 3, 11). And it was a type of the new creation, with the rest of Christ thereon, and of believers in Him. Therefore would God give here a resemblance of the first work of the labour of the six days, and the reward they received on the seventh."

The Obedience of Faith

"And it came to pass on the seventh day that they rose up about the dawning of the day, and compassed the city after the same manner seven times: only on that day they compassed the city seven times" (Josh. vi, 15). Israel was now put to a more exacting test than hitherto: once a day they had marched around Jericho for six consecutive days, but on the seventh they must do so no less than seven times. That illustrates a principle in the ways of God. In His dealings with His people the Lord develops their graces by submitting them to a variety of trials, which are harder and harder to bear. Was it not thus with "the father of all them that believe" (Rom. iv, 11)? First, Abraham was called upon to leave his native land, and go forth not knowing whither. Then, after receiving promise from God of a son, his wife for many years remained barren. Finally, when the son was given and grown, the patriarch was bidden to offer him for a burnt offering. Do not expect your path to become easier, but rather that trials will be more severe. Why so? That the sufficiency of God's grace may be known.

Seek to visualize the course followed by Israel on this occasion: project yourself in spirit among them: remember they were "men of like passions" with you. For six days they had apparently made fools of themselves before the eyes of the Canaanites, and they did so unmurmuringly. Six times more they repeated the process, yet without any Divine intervention or the slightest outward sign of success! The powerful walls of Jericho stood as firm as ever! What was the use of making still another journey around them when twelve had produced no tangible results? But they made no demur, nor declined such a seemingly senseless waste of time and energy. Instead, they carried out their orders. That is the most remarkable example of united obedience recorded in the Scriptures—emphasized here by the Spirit's telling us twice in this verse that "they compassed the city seven times." Admire then the grace of God which wrought so gloriously in and through them. He it was who subdued their corruptions and made them willing in the day of His power. Though trials increase in severity, so increased grace is given to bear them!

Here, as ever in Scripture, we should discern a blessed conjunction of the Divine and the human, and the latter concurring with the former. God wrought secretly by imparting to them the inclination and the impulse; they exercising the same by obedient action. Though a much more severe test was made of them on this seventh day, it is expressly recorded that "they rose early about the dawning of the day." *That* is the spirit in which to approach our tasks and perform our duties: with earnestness and enthusiasm, and not reluctantly and tardily. The more unpleasant the task, the sooner should it be tackled and disposed of. The harder be the duty, the more energetically should it be discharged. "Whatsoever thy hand findeth to do, do it with thy might" (Eccles. ix, 10). This is not the time for the Christian to take his ease: he must "labour" before he enters into his rest (Heb. iv, 11). He is not called to picnic, but to "fight the good fight of faith," and that implies strong opposition, and calls for the putting forth of all that is within us, if victory is to be ours.

"And it came to pass at the seventh time, when the priests blew with the trumpets, Joshua said unto the people, Shout, for the Lord hath given you the city" (verse 16). Note well *when* that promise was made to Israel. Not until they had fully discharged their duty, not until their obedience and patience had been severely tested, only after they had completed twelve circuits of the city, were they assured that God would deliver it into their hands. Does not that fact suggest that we make too much of the promises, or rather too little of the precepts to which they are attached? There has been a deplorable lack of balance at this point on the part of many preachers and writers. Comforting passages have been taken from their setting, and promises severed from the conditions by which they are qualified. The consoling of saints rather than the honouring of God is too often the aim of the pulpit. The manifestation of "good works" (Matt. v, 16) and the bearing of "much fruit" in our lives (John xv, 8) are what most glorifies the Father.

"And it came to pass at the seventh time, when the priests blew with the trumpets, Joshua said unto the people, Shout." Previously they had been enjoined to preserve strict silence (verse 10). They were not to shout at their own caprice or pleasure, but only as and when their leader bade them—they must be completely subservient to *his* orders. Now the time had come for them to give one loud concerted shout. Why so? To indicate the victory was sure. But this latter command was a harder one than the former. The injunction to maintain a decorous silence was but a test of their morale; but this order for them to give a grand and general shout made a very real demand upon their faith and obedience, for it was to be made while the fortress still stood intact before them! Easy enough to shout *after* the victory; but this was to be given in assured anticipation of the same. It was *faith's* shout of conquest. It had been prophetically announced by Balaam, when he was moved to say of Israel, "the Lord his God is with him, and the shout of a king is among them" (Num. xxiii, 21).

"And the city shall be accursed ["devoted"—margin] even it and all that are therein to the Lord: only Rahab the harlot shall live, she and all that are with her in the house, because she hid the messengers that we sent" (verse 17). This brings before us the dark side of the picture: with the sole exception of Rahab and her family all within Jericho were doomed. They were accursed, being idolaters and flagrantly wicked. As such they were "devoted to the Lord," that is, set apart unto destruction, to the praise of the glory of His justice. "The Lord hath made all things for Himself: yea, even the wicked for the day of evil" (Prov. xvi, 4). True, God hath made a difference between them according to His purpose of election, yet, whether this one was "chosen to salvation" (II Thess. ii, 13) or that one was "before of old ordained to this condemnation" (Jude iv), both alike were created for the Divine glory. In the former, God makes manifest the riches of His mercy; in the latter, He displays the purity of His holiness and the verity of His righteousness. God's burning hatred against sin and His power to execute vengeance on all accursed to Him were solemnly demonstrated here at Jericho.

"And ye, in any wise keep yourselves from the accursed thing, lest ye make yourselves accursed when ye take of the accursed thing, and make the camp of Israel a curse and trouble it. But all the silver and gold, and vessels of brass and iron, are consecrated unto the Lord: they shall come into the treasury of the Lord" (verses 18, 19). Their being forbidden to enrich themselves by any of the spoils of war was a further testing of Israel's obedience. Thereby they were taught not to set their hearts upon worldly wealth, nor heap up an abundance of it for themselves. As Matthew Henry pointed out, "God had promised them a land flowing with milk and honey, not a land abounding with silver and gold, for He would have them live comfortably in it that they might serve Him cheerfully, but not covet either to trade with distant countries, or to hoard for after time." There was a special reason for this prohibition being laid upon Israel here (for we do not find it repeated subsequently) namely, that Jericho was the *first fruits* of Canaan, and therefore it was most fitting that it should be entirely devoted unto the Lord, and its treasures consecrated unto Him.

It is to be duly noted that Joshua was not acting on his own initiative nor was he prompted by his own understanding when he proscribed the possessions of the Canaanites, for Moses had given express orders, "The graven images of their gods shall ye burn with fire: thou shalt not desire the silver and gold that is on them, nor take it unto thee, lest thou be snared therein: for it is an abomination to the Lord thy God. Neither shalt thou bring an abomination into thine house, lest thou be a cursed thing like it; but thou shalt utterly detest it, and thou shalt utterly abhor it" (Deut. vii, 25, 26). There we see once again how Joshua was in all things, like his Antitype, regulated by Divine Law. Let us also point out how that this prohibition supplied yet another line in the typical picture which the capture of Jericho presents to us: when success attends the efforts of Christ's servants, they must be particularly on their guard against taking any credit unto themselves: *all* the glory must be ascribed to God alone!

"So the people shouted when the priests blew with the trumpets. And it came to pass when the people heard the sound of the trumpet, and the people shouted with a great shout, that the walls of Jericho fell down flat, so that the people went up into the city, every man straight before him, and they took the city" (verse 20). Here was the grand reward of Israel's courage, obedience and patience. Looking at it from one viewpoint, it must be said that the walls of Jericho fell down by the alone act of *God,* for no human hand or power contributed to it in the least. Yet from another viewpoint, the miracle may be justly attributed unto Israel: "*By faith* the walls of Jericho fell down after they were compassed about seven days" (Heb. xi, 30). From yet another angle it is equally permissible and correct to say that Jericho fell in response to their implicit *obedience.* Nor is there the slightest inconsistency in those three statements: far from being contradictory, they are complementary if preserved in the above order. Though He certainly is not restricted thereto, yet God is pleased, generally, to work in response to the faith and obedience of His people.

It is a very serious mistake to suppose that faith is restricted to a resting upon God's promises: it is equally to be exercised in complying with His precepts. Trusting God is only one part of faith's work. It is far too little recognized that conforming to God's revealed will is also required of faith. Faith always has to do with *God:* He is its Object and His Word is its Rule and Regulator. It was by faith that Noah and his family were delivered from the flood, yet it was because he took to heart the warning God gave him, and being moved with fear complied with His directions and "prepared an ark to the saving of his house" (Heb. xi, 7). It was by faith that Abraham received the land of Canaan for an inheritance, yet in order thereto, when he was called to leave his home he "obeyed and went out not knowing whither he went" (Heb. xi, 8). The man after God's own heart did something more than confide in Him: "I have *believed* Thy commandments" (Psa. cxix, 66) he declared. The Divine commandments, equally with the Divine promises, were the objects of his faith. Are they of *your* faith, my reader?

"By faith the walls of Jericho fell down, after they were compassed about seven days" (Heb. xi, 30). For the benefit of the many young preachers who take this magazine we propose to sermonize that verse, and at the same time summarize what has been before us in Joshua vi. Let us consider *the daring* of their faith. When Israel crossed the Jordan, they, as it were, burned all their bridges and boats behind them. It was not only the "armed men," but the whole congregation which was involved. Flight was impossible, and there was no fortress in which to shelter, nor even houses to which they could retire. They were now in the enemy's territory, completely exposed to him. To advance unto Jericho and to march quietly around its walls (within which were "men of valour"—verse 1) seemed a perilous undertaking, for what was to hinder the Canaanites from shooting at them, or casting down rocks upon them? It was truly an adventure of faith, and it is adventuresome faith which God delights to honour. Unbelief is hesitant and timorous, but daring faith is confident and courageous. "The wicked flee when no man pursueth: but the righteous are bold as a lion" (Prov. xxviii, 1). O to be strong in the Lord, and in the power of His might.

There are three degrees of faith. There is a faith which *reposes* on the truth of the Gospel, when the weary and heavy-laden sinner comes to Christ and rests his soul upon His atoning sacrifice. There is a faith which *reckons,* counting upon the veracity and fidelity of God to fulfil His promises and undertake for us (Rom. iv, 21; II Tim. i, 12). There is also a faith which *risks,* which dares something for the Lord. That kind of faith was exemplified by Moses when he ventured to confront the king of Egypt, and make known to him Jehovah's demands. This daring faith was manifested by David, when with naught but a sling and some pebbles he went forth and engaged the mighty Goliath. It was demonstrated by Elijah, when single-handed he contested with the hosts of Jezebel's false prophets on Mount Carmel. We see it again in Daniel, when he dared to be cast into the den of lions rather than comply with the idolatrous edict of Babylon's king; and when his three fellows refused to be intimidated by the fiery furnace. We behold it again and again in the ministry and journeys of the apostle Paul, who shrank not from perils of every conceivable kind, that he might preach the unsearchable riches of Christ.

In the sequel to each of the above cases, we behold how God *honoured* those trusting and brave hearts. God may indeed severely try, but in the end it will be seen that He never confounds or puts to shame those whose eyes are fixed steadfastly upon Himself, seeking His glory. It is venturesome faith which He ever delights to reward. When those who carried the man sick of the palsy were unable to get near Christ because of the press, and therefore broke through the roof and lowered the sufferer, so far from charging them with impudence or presumption "when Jesus saw their faith" He owned the same by healing the sick man (Mark ii, 5). When Peter essayed to walk unto Him upon the sea, Christ rebuked him not for his rashness, but because his faith wavered. Luther would not be deterred by his friends from going to Worms, saying he would do so though every tile on its houses were a devil. George Muller feared not to count upon God to feed and clothe his two thousand orphans, refusing to make an appeal (direct or indirect) for funds. How such examples shame the churches today! How few are prepared to risk anything in the Lord's service!

Consider next *the obedience* of Israel's faith—here the most prominent feature of all. Joshua himself, the priests, the armed men, the body of the people, carried out all their directions to the letter. The method prescribed and the means appointed not only appeared to be utterly inadequate to reason, but senseless; nevertheless they were strictly complied with. To do nothing more than walk around the powerful walls of Jericho and for the priests to blow upon their trumpets of rams' horns, seemed a childish and ridiculous performance, yet that was what they had been bidden to do. Unquestioning submission to God's revealed will, an exact carrying out of His instructions. employing none other than those means which He has assigned, is what God requires from us, both in the performance of our daily duties and in that which pertains more especially to His worship and service. We are forbidden to lean unto our own understandings or resort unto our own devices. God has plainly declared His mind unto us in the Holy Scriptures, and they are to be the alone Rule and Regulator of all our actions. Implicit obedience unto the Lord is absolutely essential if we are to have *His* blessing upon our efforts.

Reader, the Divine commandments and precepts often appear strange unto fleshly wisdom. How absurd did God's order appear to the great Naaman when he was bidden to bathe his leprous body in the Jordan; yet there was no healing for him until he complied with the same. How contrary was it to all human ideas for God to send His prophet to be fed for many months by a widow who had naught but a handful of meal and a little oil; yet under Him, it proved amply sufficient. What a testing of Simon's submission when Christ told him to let down the nets for a draught: they had toiled all night and taken nothing, yet said the apostle "nevertheless at Thy word I will let down the net" (Luke v, 5). How unreasonable it must have seemed to the Twelve when Christ bade them tell the vast multitude to sit down and only five loaves and two little fishes were in sight! And how unreasonable does it now appear unto the majority of preachers and members to heed the call to cast away all the fleshly and worldly devices which have been brought into the churches, substituting fasting and prayer, and counting upon God to bless the preaching of His own Word.

"The obedience of faith" (Rom. xvi, 26). Weigh well those words. Too often has it been affirmed that obedience is an effect or fruit of faith. Obedience is an essential *element* of faith: the one can no more be separated from the other than can the light and heat of the sun. Where there is no true obedience, there is no real faith Godwards. The Gospel requires obedience as truly as it does reliance, for it bids the rebel sinner throw down the weapons of his warfare against God, to repent of his wickedness, and to surrender to the Lordship and yoke of Christ. In II Peter ii, 21, the Gospel is designated "the Holy Commandment," and in II Thessalonians i, 8, we are told that Christ will yet take vengeance upon them "that *obey not* the Gospel of our Lord Jesus Christ" which goes on to give the solemn answer to that searching question "What shall the end be of them that obey not the Gospel of God?" (I Peter iv, 17), namely, they "shall be punished with everlasting destruction from the presence of the Lord." The Gospel does far more than issue an invitation to "receive Christ as a personal Saviour" or offer pardon to all who do so; it first makes known the holy requirements of God for us to forsake our evil ways and submit ourselves to the just claims of Christ.

Christ "became the Author of eternal salvation unto all them that obey Him" (Heb. v, 9): not simply those who trust in Him. In like manner, the Holy Spirit is by God "given to them that obey Him" (Acts v, 22). As we began, so must we continue, and be able to say with David "Teach me good judgment and knowledge, for I have believed Thy commandments" (Psa. cxix, 66). The commandments neither sway the conscience nor incline the affections until they be received as from God. "As the promises are not believed with a lively faith unless they draw off the heart from carnal vanities to seek that happiness which they offer to us; so the precepts are not believed rightly unless we be fully resolved to acquiesce in them as the only rule to guide us in the obtaining of that happiness, and to adhere to them, and to do them" (Manton). To "*believe* God's commandments" is to hear His voice in them, to submit to His authority, to have our hearts and actions governed by His revealed will in them. If we heed not God concerning our present duties, we do but deceive ourselves when we imagine we are trusting Him with respect to future privileges. We must consent to the commandments as good and blessed in themselves. and love them as issuing from our Father.

The Discipline of Faith

"By faith the walls of Jericho fell down, after they were compassed about seven days" (Heb. xi, 30). In our last we contemplated the daring and obedience of Israel's faith on this memorable occasion, and now we turn to observe the *discipline* of it. We have reference to Joshua vi, 10, where we learn that the people were commanded, "Ye shall not shout, nor make any noise with your voice, neither shall any word proceed out of your mouth, until the day I bid you shout." That injunction constituted a very real test of their morale. For all that host of Israel to preserve strict silence as they journeyed around Jericho's walls was a severe restraint upon their natural inclinations—the more so that no explanation for the same was furnished them. There are times when to preserve silence is far harder than for us to express what is on our minds. The tongue is an unruly member, yet God requires us to control the exercise of it, and there are occasions when to be mute is a manifestation of grace which is honouring to Him. Such was the case when fire from the Lord devoured the presumptuous sons of Aaron, and their father "held his peace" (Lev. x, 3), and when David was sorely chastised by God and he was "dumb, and opened not his mouth" (Psa. xxxix, 9).

How often are the sinews of faith cut by the injudicious and un-friendly criticisms of those who pose as our Christian friends, who so far from encouraging us to adhere strictly to our Rule, would have us conform to this world! How often is the servant of Christ hindered by the God-dishonouring counsels and carnal suggestions of church members when he seeks to employ none but spiritual weapons! How much mischief is wrought by those who are perpetually talking about the difficulties confronting us! The soldiers of Christ must be trained: faith must be disciplined: each one in the ranks of the Lord's hosts must learn there is "a time to keep silent and a time to speak" (Eccles. iii, 7). The children of Israel must neither make any sally upon this garrison of the Canaanites, nor employ the customary war-cries of assailants, but, instead, preserve a solemn silence as in sacred procession they encompassed the city. That might have conveyed the impression that they were lacking in spirit and zeal, thereby rendering them increasingly despicable in the sight of their enemies, yet that was the manner in which they were required to conduct themselves. God delights to make use of contemptible instruments and means, that the glory may be His alone.

We turn next to consider the *patience* of their faith, which was con-spicuously evidenced here. The walls of Jericho did not fall down the first day nor the sixth that Israel marched around them, but only "after they had been compassed about seven days." Nor did they fall the first time they were encompassed on the seventh day, but not until after seven circuits had been made on that day. No less than thirteen journeys around them were completed before the power of God was displayed. Why so? To test their patience as well as their courage and obedience. They must be kept waiting on the Lord. "As promised deliverances must be expected in God's way so they must be expected in God's time" (Matthew Henry). Israel were required to carry out the orders they had received, to persevere in the performance of duty, and leave the issue with the Lord. The race is not to the swift, nor the battle to the strong, but to those who are steadfast and persistent. "It is good [though we may not think so at the time] that a man should both hope and quietly wait for the salvation [deliverance] of the Lord" (Lam. iii, 26).

Observe how one Scripture throws light upon another: Hebrew xi, 30, does not tell us that Israel encompassed Jericho seven times on the seventh day, nor does Joshua vi inform us that they did so "by faith." As pointed out previously, neither the priests nor the people received any assurance from Joshua that success would attend their efforts: they are seen there simply complying strictly and patiently with the instructions they had been given. But in Hebrew xi the Holy Spirit discloses to us that they acted *in faith*. But how could that be, seeing they had no promise to rest upon? We wonder if that question presents any difficulty to the reader. We hope not, for it is a mistake to suppose there can be no faith in God unless we have some definite word from Him to warrant it. So far as Scripture acquaints us, when Abraham was told to sacrifice Isaac upon the altar, he received no promise that he would be restored to him again; nevertheless, it was "by faith" he offered Isaac "accounting that God was able to raise him up, even from the dead" (Heb. xi, 19). David had no promise that he would slay Goliath, yet he had full confi-dence that God would enable him to do so. Daniel had no guarantee of deliver-ance from the lions, yet he "believed in his God" for protection from them (vi, 23).

Faith has to do with a *known God,* with One who is a living reality to the soul, with One who can be counted upon to undertake for us. It is God in His revealed character, as made known to us in His Word, God in Christ in covenant relation to us, who is the Object of faith. True, a definite promise makes it easier to act faith, yet is not the Promiser greater than the promises, as the Giver is to all His gifts! And when we are unable to locate a promise which precisely meets our particular case, that should not deter us from having implicit confidence in God Himself. When David was guilty of the terrible sins of adultery and murder, there was no sacrifice under the law available for such crimes, but he had recourse to the known mercy of God (Psa. li, 1)— the infinite mercy of an infinite God; nor was he confounded. So with Israel before Jericho. They had for years been supernaturally fed in the wilderness, and unfailingly guided by the pillar of cloud and fire. They had witnessed the miracle-working power of Jehovah acting on their behalf in opening a way for them through the Jordan. And now they confidently counted upon His showing Himself strong in their behalf in overthrowing this mighty citadel.

Yes, it was "by faith," in the daring and obedience of faith, they acted, trusting God to work for them. But He was pleased to put their faith to a severe proof: they were required to exercise "the patience of hope" (I Thess. i, 3), to persevere in the course God had appointed, expecting Him to honour the same. Yea, to repeat their performance again and again, and still without the least sign of their efforts being rewarded. Why so? To make it the more evident that the conquest of Canaan was of the Lord and not of them. Each fruitless journey around the city made it increasingly apparent that their enemies were to be overcome not by their power but by God's. What a lesson is there here for each of us. "My soul, wait thou only upon God, for my expectation is from Him" (Psa. lxii, 5). "Therefore will the Lord wait, that He may be gracious unto you . . . blessed are they that wait for Him" (Isa. xxx, 18). But is it not at that very point most of us fail the worst? How easily we become discouraged if our efforts do not meet with prompt success, or if our prayers be not speedily answered! How impatient is the flesh!

"For ye have need of patience, that, after ye have done the will of God, ye might receive the promise" (Heb. x, 36). Indeed we have, for each of us is very prone to say of the Lord, as his mother said of Sisera, "Why is His chariot so long in coming, why tarry the wheels of His chariot" (Judges v, 28). Speaking to His disciples, the Lord Jesus declared, "Men ought always to pray, and not to faint" (Luke xviii, 1). How much we need to take that word to heart! How often have we "fainted" when victory was almost in sight! We become discouraged when our "Jericho" does not fall the first or second time it is encompassed. Most of us find it much harder to *wait* than to believe, yet we prove by painful experience that our fretful impatience accomplishes no good nor speeds the desired event a single moment. Let us be more definite and earnest in begging the Holy Spirit to work this grace of patience in us, and to be "watching thereunto with all perseverance" (Eph. vi, 18), assured that "in due season we shall reap, if we faint not."

Consider for a moment *the assurance* of their faith—a striking proof of which was given by them in what is recorded in Joshua vi, 20. There we are told, "So the people shouted when the priests blew with the trumpets, and it came to pass, when the people heard the sound of the trumpet, and the people shouted with a great shout, that the wall fell down flat." Twice over in that verse does the Holy Spirit record that which was so honouring to the Lord. During all their circuits of the city, they had been bidden to maintain a complete silence, but when their obedience and patience had been fully tested, they were ordered to "shout," for said their leader "the Lord hath given you the city" (verse 16). But mark it well, that shout must be made while the powerful walls still stood intact! It was therefore a shout of faith, of confidence in God, of full assurance that He would appear in their behalf and recompense their "patient continuance in well doing." That shout signified their strong persuasion that victory was certain. That is what assurance consists of: an unshakable belief that God will make good His Word, a steadfast reliance that He will reward those that seek Him diligently (Heb. xi, 6).

That concerted and loud shout of Israel *before* the actual event was one of confident expectation. By such assurance God is greatly glorified. Though Abraham was about a hundred years old and his wife's womb dead, when he received promise of a son he was "fully persuaded that what God had promised He was able also to perform" (Rom. iv, 21). When the son of the woman of Shunem died, so strong was her faith that, though none had previously been restored to life, she confidently expected her son to be revived (II Kings iv)—her actions in verse 21 and her words in verse 23 evince the same. Of our Lord's mother it is said, "Blessed is she which believed that there shall be a performance of those things which were told her from the Lord" (Luke i, 45). To the distressed mariners Paul said, "Be of good cheer, for I believe God, that it shall be even as it was told me" (Acts xxvii, 25). What examples are these of the heart's full reliance upon God while outward appearances were quite unpromising! When Moffatt, the missionary who had laboured for years among the Bechuanas without seeing a single seal to his ministry, received a letter from friends in England who wished to make him a present, asking him to specify what it should be, he answered, "A communion set"! Months after, when it arrived, more than a dozen converted natives sat down with him to remember the Lord's death. Say not "How wonderful" but "How deplorable I do not trust Him more fully."

Take note of the *renunciation* of their faith. Israel's being forbidden to seize the spoils of war, and being told that the silver and gold must be "consecrated unto the Lord" (verses 18, 19), teaches us that real faith takes no credit unto its subject, but ascribes all the honour of its performances unto the Giver. Faith precludes all boasting and self-congratulation (Eph. ii, 8, 9). Faith belongs to those who are "poor in spirit." So far from promoting Laodicean self-esteem, it humbles us into the dust, causing us to look away from self unto God. It is a self-emptying grace, moving us to stretch forth the beggar's hand. Consequently, it takes no praise to itself, but gives the whole unto its Bestower. Its language is "Not unto us, O Lord, not unto us, but unto Thy name give glory, for Thy mercy, for Thy truth's sake" (Psa. cxv, 1). Blessedly was this exemplified by Abraham. When the Lord gave him the victory over Chedorlaomer, and the king of Sodom invited him to take the spoils unto himself, Abraham answered, "I have lifted up my hand unto the Lord, that I will not take from a thread to a shoelatchet . . . lest thou shouldest say, I have made Abraham rich" (Gen. xiv, 22, 23)!

Finally, behold the *triumph* of faith. "And it came to pass, when the people heard the sound of the trumpet, and the people shouted with a great shout, that the wall fell down flat, so that the people went up into the city, every man straight before him, and they took the city" (verse 20). Nothing can stand before faith: the most formidable obstacles give way to it. "All things are possible to him that believeth" (Mark ix. 23) as the whole of Hebrew xi clearly shows. The language of an expectant faith is, "Through God we shall do valiantly, for He it is that shall tread down our enemies" (Psa. lx, 12), because faith looks away from self, with all its infirmities and limitations, unto the Almighty. "This is the victory that overcometh the world: our faith" (I John v, 4): when it is in exercise, the world can neither enthral nor intimidate, for it elevates the heart above the creature. Israel's capture of Jericho is recorded for the encouragement of the saints of all generations, and our lengthy consideration of the same will have been in vain unless it has put new life into us as it has demonstrated afresh the invincibility of God's purpose, the sufficiency of His power, and His readiness to put it forth on the behalf of those who render implicit obedience to His revealed will and count upon His rewarding the same.

"And they utterly destroyed all that was in the city, both man and woman, young and old, and ox and sheep and ass, with the edge of the sword" (verse 21). For several centuries the longsuffering of God had waited because "the iniquity of the Amorites was not yet full" (Gen. xv, 16). Forty years previously, in the first year of the Exodus, the Lord had solemnly threatened them, bringing the sword of Israel to the borders of Canaan, and then withdrawing His hand for a time, giving them a further respite. But the period of waiting was now over. That united shout from Israel was the sign that the Lord would tarry no longer, that the day of His wrath was come. All the guilty inhabitants of Jericho were made a solemn and awful sacrifice to the Divine justice. "The Canaanites were ripe for destruction, and the Lord was pleased, instead of destroying them by a pestilence, a famine, an earthquake, a devastating fire from heaven, to employ the Israelites as the executioners of His vengeance, both for their warning and instruction, and for that of all who read these records. Had an angel been commissioned to slay them (as one did Sennacherib's army: Kings xix, 35), who would have charged Him with iniquity or cruelty? In all public calamities infants are involved and tens of thousands die with great agony every year.

"Now either God is not the agent in these calamities, which opinion—though often implied in man's reasonings on these subjects—is not far from atheism; or they must consist with the most perfect justice and goodness. What injustice then could there be in ordering the destruction of a guilty race by the sword of His people? Or what injustice can be charged on them while executing His express commission, as ratified by undeniable miracles? It is evident that the hand of God would be far more noticed in these uncommon events than if He had destroyed His enemies by the ordinary course of second causes. The malignity of sin, with the indignation of God against sinners, and His power and determination to inflict condign punishment on them, would be far more conspicuous and impressive. In short, every man who by reading the account of these awful judgments, in any age or place, has been led to a deeper sense of the evil of sin, and warned to repent and seek mercy from the Lord, will to eternal ages glorify the Divine wisdom and goodness, in the very dispensations which embolden the blasphemies of the impenitent and unbelieving" (Thomas Scott). "Behold therefore the goodness and severity of God" (Rom. xi, 22): the latter is as truly a Divine perfection as is the former.

In verses 22-25 we see how the promise given to Rahab in ii, 14, 19, was made good: "By faith the harlot Rahab perished not with them that believed not, when she had received the spies with peace" (Heb. xi, 31). Therein we behold the mercy of God unto those who really turn to and believe in Him. The inhabitants of Canaan had heard of Jehovah's drying up the waters of the Red Sea, and of Israel's destroying of Sihon and Og, but Rahab alone believed "that the Lord hath given you the land" (ii, 9, 10). She evidenced her faith by receiving the two spies with good will, and sheltering those servants of God from their foes at the hazard of her own life (illustrating the principle that faith ever requires self-denial), and by a strict compliance with their instructions. The blessed consequence and sequel was that she " perished not with them that believed not." The preservation of her house, which was " upon the town wall " (ii, 15), was as manifest a miracle as was the falling down of all other parts of it, and typified the eternal security of those who trust in the Lord.

Let us now briefly epitomize some of the many important lessons inculcated and illustrated by the contents of Joshua vi. 1. Closed doors and high walls are no insuperable obstacle when God be for us and with us: Acts xii, 10 (verse 1). 2. Faith is to behold that which is invisible to sight and reason: John viii, 56; Hebrews xi, 1 (verse 2). 3. Divine promises do not render needless the discharge of responsibility (verse 3). 4. God pours contempt on human pride by appointing means which are contemptible in the eyes of the world (verse 4). 5. Encouragements (verse 5) are not to be bandied about promiscuously, but given to the diligent and faithful (verse 16). 6. The " ark," in which was the Law and the " trumpets of jubilee " which announced the Gospel, tells, of the preacher's twofold work (verse 6). 7. The rank and file of God's people are required to support and hearten His ministers (verse 7). 8. The Lord's presence with them (Matt. xxviii, 20) is what is to animate and regulate His ministers (verse 7). 9. The position of honour is reserved for the ark and the priests: Hebrews xiii, 7, 17; I Thessalonians v, 12, 13 (verse 9). 10. Muffle not the Gospel trumpet and let it give forth no uncertain sound: I Corinthians xiv, 8 (verse 9). 11. We must be " swift to hear, slow to speak ": James i, 19; I Peter iii, 15 (verse 10). 12. All murmuring against God and unwarrantable criticisms of His servants must be suppressed (verse 10).

13. God takes note of and appreciates thoroughness, the completing of each task assigned (verse 11). 14. Punctuality, diligence, whole-heartedness, must ever characterize the servant of Christ (verse 12). 15. Though no visible results appear, the priests must blow their trumpets " continually " (verse 13). 16. Patience and perseverance are called for in the discharge of all our God-given duties (verse 14). 17. The more trying and difficult the task, the more earnestly should we set ourselves to it (verse 15). 18. When success is delayed, our efforts are to be increased and not diminished (verse 15). 19. We must not be discouraged over the lack of early success, but let patience have her perfect work (verse 15). 20. God's promise is to be faithfully relied upon during the time when there is no indication of its fulfilment (verse 16). 21. Though saints as such have no commission to speak in public, yet their mouths are to utter the Lord's praise (verse 16). 22. It is implicit confidence in Himself which the Lord ever delights to honour—" when " (verse 16). 23. The whole world lieth in the Wicked One and is under the wrath of God (verse 17). 24. We bring trouble upon ourselves when we set our affection on earthly things (verse 18). 25. God never confounds those who trust and obey Him (verse 18). 26. The most unlikely means are used by God in the doing of great things (verse 20). 27. Eternal destruction is the portion of all out of Christ (verse 21), eternal security of those who trust Him (verses 22, 23). 28. Build not again the things you have destroyed or renounced: Galatians ii, 18 (verse 26; cf. Psa. lxxxv, 8).

Chapter 10

SIN, DEFEAT, JUDGMENT
Joshua 7:1-26

Humiliation at Ai

The seventh chapter of Joshua presents to us a drastically different scene from those which have engaged our attention in the previous chapters, yea, so startling is the contrast that we are reminded of that old adage, "Truth is stranger than fiction." Up to this point everything had gone smoothly and blessedly for Israel, but now their progress is suddenly halted. Hitherto we have witnessed them, under God, going from strength to strength and glory to glory. Strict obedience to the Divine commands had marked their every movement; here, the very reverse obtained. They had duly attended to the essential matter of circumcision and had kept the appointed passover feast. On His part, the Lord had wrought wondrously for them, bringing them through the Jordan dryshod and overthrowing the principal fortress of the enemy without a blow having to be struck by Israel. But a startling contrast now confronts us: immediately following the memorable victory at the formidable Jericho, Israel suffer humiliating defeat at the much weaker town of Ai. A member of the tribe of Judah had committed a grievous crime, and the whole nation suffer in consequence. As there was a serpent in Eden and a Judas among the apostles, so there was an Achan in the midst of an obedient Israel.

A series of sad failures are set before us in the passage we are about to consider. The whole nation is thus depicted, "The hearts of the people melted and became as water" (vii, 5). That dejection of God's people was occasioned by the cowardice shown by three thousand of their armed men, who had "fled before the men of Ai," thirty-six of them being slain as the enemy chased them (verse 5). That had been preceded by the remiss conduct of Joshua himself, who, instead of seeking counsel from the Lord, had acted upon the carnal advice of his spies (verse 4). The men whom Joshua had sent out to reconnoitre Ai so far forgot their place that, upon their return, instead of making a simple report, they presumed to inform their commander-in-chief of the policy which *they* deemed it best for Israel to follow on this occasion (verse 3). But before all this, the anger of the Lord had been kindled against Israel by the sin of Achan at Jericho (verse 1). *That* was what explained all which followed: the cause of which they were the consequences. One decayed apple will soon infect a whole box of sound ones; or, to change the figure for a more Scriptural one," A little leaven leaveneth the whole lump." (I Cor. v, 6).

In the light of history there is nothing at all unusual in the sad failures mentioned above, for poor human nature is "as unstable as water" (Gen. xlix, 4). Yet in view of the fact that this generation was far and away the best which Israel ever had, and that Jehovah Himself was their Captain (v, 15) in the conquest of Canaan, it does seem strange that such a deplorable lapse now occurred. How are we to account for the Divine permission, yea, foreordination of the same? From the general teaching of Scripture, may we not

177

say that the Lord suffered this grievous defection for such reasons as these? First, to teach all succeeding generations of His people that they are never in greater danger of yielding to the pride of their hearts than when the Lord's power has been most signally displayed on their behalf. Second, to exemplify the basic truth that, if we are to enjoy a continuation of God's governmental blessing, we must remain steadfast in our subjection to His holy will. Third, to set before His saints a lasting warning that the Holy One is jealous of His glory, and will not condone sin in His own people. Fourth, to emphasize that nothing can be concealed from Him: that the most secret actions of an individual fall beneath His observation (Prov. xv, 3).

How ominous is the initial " But " of vii, 1—the first chapter of our book opening thus: sad intimater of what follows, and well suited to point the contrast with the closing verse of chapter vi. There we read, " So the Lord was with Joshua and his fame was noised throughout all the country "; now we are told, " But the children of Israel committed a trespass . . . for Achan . . . took of the accursed thing, and the anger of the Lord was kindled against the children of Israel." The contrast is a double one: the Lord was *with* Joshua, but here His anger was kindled *against* Israel. The consequence of the former was that Joshua's fame was proclaimed abroad; the sequel of the latter is that he was humiliated and lies on his face before the ark (vii, 5). How often are the brightest prospects dimmed and the most promising projects hindered by sin! It was so with king Saul, and later with Solomon. Thus with Israel's progress in the conquest of Canaan: victory at Jericho gives place to defeat before Ai. How this shows us that a time of success is when we most need to be on our guard, and "rejoice with trembling " (Psa. ii, 11). The moon never suffers an eclipse except at a time when it is at the full! Grace is needed by us to use the grace God gives us and to save us from turning His blessings into curses.

Here, then, is another most important practical lesson for us to lay to heart in connection with the possessing of our possessions and the present enjoyment of our spiritual heritage. When God has vouchsafed light from His Word and opened up to us some passage, beware lest we become conceited and attribute the same to our own perspecuity. When victory is granted over some lust or deliverance from a powerful temptation, boast not, but rather endeavour to become more watchful. When God gives the pastor souls for his hire and prospers his labours, humbling grace must be diligently sought that he may not cherish the spirit of Nebuchadnezzar and say, " Is not this great Babylon that I have built for the house of the kingdom by the might of *my* power! " (Dan. iv, 30). Remember that solemn warning, " But Jeshurun [Israel] waxed fat and wicked: thou art waxed fat, thou art grown thick, thou art covered with fatness: *then* he forsook God " (Deut. xxxii, 15). We need to be much on our guard and fight against the Laodicean self-sufficiency and self-glorying of this evil day. Unless we be kept " little in our own sight " (I Sam. xv, 17) and " poor in spirit," the overthrow of some Jericho in our experience will be followed by an ignominious defeat before an Ai!

" But the children of Israel committed a trespass in the accursed thing: for Achan, the son of Carmi, the son of Zabdi, the son of Zerah, of the tribe of Judah, took of the accursed thing." This awful trespass was committed within the very environs of Jericho, immediately after God had miraculously caused its walls to fall down flat. In connection with the destruction and sacking of that city, specific instructions had been given to Israel that they must neither spare any lives nor take any of the spoils unto themselves (vi, 17-19). The spiritual lesson for us therein is that "the good fight of faith" in which the Christian is called to engage consists of a mortifying of the flesh, the denying of self, and the renouncing of this world in our affections. It was far more than a bare theft of which Achan was guilty, namely, the heinous act of sacrilege, a taking of that which was "consecrated to the Lord"! It is to be carefully noted that the Holy Spirit has furnished us with the genealogy of the offender, and since there is nothing meaningless or unimportant in the Word of Truth, it behoves us to attend to this detail. Achan was the immediate descendant of "Zerah," and *he* was the son of Judah's whoredom (Gen. xxxviii. 15-30). What a solemn example of the sins of the fathers being visited upon the children!

Significant indeed is the name of this disturber of the nation's peace and prosperity, for Achan means "Trouble." It is both solemn and striking to note how the Holy Spirit has phrased His allusion to Achan's sin: He does not say "one of," but rather "the children of Israel committed a trespass in the accursed thing." God regarded them as a unit, and hence what one individual is considered the sin of the nation. This is borne out by what follows, for the whole congregation was affected thereby; "and the anger of the Lord was kindled against [not simply "Achan" but] the children of Israel." We have a parallel in the local church of the New Testament: "whether one member suffer, all the members suffer with it" (I Cor. xii, 26), an example of which is furnished in v, 1-7, of the same epistle. Israel had been plainly warned that if any one of them took of the accursed thing, they would "make the camp of Israel a curse, and trouble it" (Joshua vi, 18), yet that solemn warning deterred not the selfish and rebellious Achan. Until the walls of Jericho fell, all kept strictly to rank, but upon their fall they went "every man straight before him" (vi, 20). Thus the moment discipline was relaxed this reprobate cared only for himself.

"And Joshua sent men from Jericho to Ai, which is beside Beth-aven on the east side of Bethel, and spake unto them saying, Go up and view the country" (verse 2). Joshua did not rest on his oars, but proceeded to the task which lay before him, sending out scouts to examine the next place to be captured. After such a notable victory, he did not deem himself entitled to sit down and take things easy, or give himself to feasting; but believed in the policy of striking while the iron is hot. The best time to hoist sail is when the wind is blowing, so that advantage may be taken of the same. Thus it is spiritually. When favoured with a breeze from Heaven (John iii, 8), it is a propitious season for religious enterprise. Yet observe that the zeal of Joshua was tempered with prudence: he did not rush blindly ahead, but wisely took a preview of what was next to be done. It is the feverish energy of the flesh which impells professing Christians to act hurriedly and rashly, instead of "sitting down first" and "consulting" whether they be sufficiently equipped for the task which they assay (Luke xiv, 31). There is a happy mean between recklessness and a caution which degenerates into apathy.

Ai was a place of sacred memories, for in Genesis xii, 8, we are told of Abraham that he removed "unto a mountain on the east of Bethel and pitched his tent [emblem of being a "stranger and pilgrim" there], having Bethel on the west and Hai [same as "Ai" in Joshua vii] on the east; and there he built an altar to the Lord [symbol of his being a worshipper] and called upon the name of the Lord." But now this territory was occupied by the wicked and marked out for destruction. It was because of their abominable idolatry and immorality that the Lord used Israel as His instrument of judgment upon the Canaanites (Lev. xviii, 24, 25; Deut. xviii, 10-12). Evidence of this is found in the names mentioned in Joshua vii, 2, for "Beth-aven" signifies "House of vanity" or "iniquity." Incidentally we may note an example of the minute accuracy of Scripture in the topographical reference there: "Go *up* and view the country," said Joshua, while the Holy Spirit informs us in Genesis xii, 8, that Abraham "removed unto a *mountain* on the east of Bethel"—which means "The House of God." Ah, my reader, there are no "contradictions" in Holy Writ, but, instead, the most perfect harmony throughout; but only the reverent and diligent student perceives that.

"But the children of Israel committed a trespass in the accursed thing, for Achan . . . took of the accursed thing, and the anger of the Lord was kindled against Israel. *And* Joshua sent men from Jericho to Ai . . . saying, Go up and view the country." The two verses are linked together, and thereby a solemn lesson is pointed. It is evident that Joshua was ignorant of the perfidy of Achan, and therefore was quite unaware that the anger of Jehovah was kindled against Israel. It is a very serious thing to provoke the Lord, and thereby forfeit His providential smile. Yet how few of the "churches" today are conscious that the anger of the Lord is kindled against them! Kindled against them for the self-same reason that it was here against Israel, namely, for having trafficked in "the accursed thing." Dispensationalists may deny it, and say *that* occurred under "the Dispensation of Law," but there is no parallel in this "Dispensation of Grace." Therein they betray their crass ignorance, and, it is much to be feared, their unregeneracy—hearts which know not the Holy One. The case of Ananias and Sapphira (Acts v; Rev. ii, 14-16 and 20-23) and a quenched Spirit in our midst clearly give the lie to their assertions.

"And the men went up and viewed Ai. And they returned unto Joshua, and said unto him, Let not all the people go out, but let about two or three thousand men go up and smite Ai; make not all the people to labour thither, for they are but few" (verse 3). In carrying out Joshua's orders those men acted commendably, but in taking it upon them to advise their general, their conduct was most reprehensible. It was nothing but downright impudence for those subordinates to tell Joshua what he should do. Had he asked for their suggestions it had been a different matter, but to proffer them unsought was a piece of impertinence. It appeared to be the language of kindness, prompted by consideration of others—to save the great bulk of the nation from a needless waste of energy. Yet, plausible as were their words, it was carnal counsel they gave: as much so as Peter's "Pity Thyself, Lord," which seemed to emanate from deep solicitude for Him, when in reality it issued from Satan (Matt. xvi, 22, 23). The same answer which the Redeemer returned unto the apostle was due these spies: "thou savourest not the things that be of God, but those that be of men." They were leaning on the arm of flesh, filled with a sense of self-sufficiency.

These men who returned from their reconnoitring were inflated with pride. Their language was that of presumption, engendered by previous success. They began to entertain the idea that they belonged to a great nation, and none could stand before them. They contemptuously regarded Ai as an easy prey, as their "for they are few" indicated. What need for the whole of the army to journey thither: a small company of *our* men will suffice. There was no dependency upon the One who had wrought wonders for them. Instead, they felt that a couple of battalions could do wonders, and that there was no need for Israel to put forth all their strength. Alas, how like unto them God's servants and people often are today. When the Lord is pleased to exercise His power in the saving of souls, preaching appears to be an easy matter, and the minister is tempted to spend less time and labour in the preparation of his sermons. And when God grants a saint victory over some powerful lust, he is apt to feel there is less need to pray so earnestly. But such a spirit is disastrous. Only as we continue sensible of our weakness shall we seek strength from Above. Take warning from this incident and strive against pride and presumption, especially when God has granted some success.

"Let not all the people go up: but let about two or three thousand go up and smite Ai; make not all the people to labour thither, for they are but few" (verse 3). How different was that conceited boast from the language of the first spies: "Truly the Lord hath delivered into our hands all the land" (ii, 24)! Let not victory lead to negligence. We have no right to count upon the Lord's doing all for us unless we make full use of the means that He has appointed. All of Israel were required to assemble at Jericho: none was left behind in his tent, none suffered to remain at a distance as a mere spectator. It might appear to them as a needless waste of "man-power," but God required it; and gave success to their obedience. *There* was the precedent for them to follow. But the dictate of carnal wisdom intervened. Ai appeared to be an inconsiderable place and no great force required to reduce it. Self-confidence promised an easy conquest, so the greater part of the army might be spared. Instead of regarding it as a blessed privilege for the whole nation to behold the Lord showing Himself strong in their behalf, these men said, "make not all the people to labour thither" or to be a "weariness," as the word is eight times rendered elsewhere—just as at the close of the Old Testament a degenerate Israel said of God's worship "what a *weariness* is it!" (Mal. i, 13).

"So there went up thither of the people about three thousand men" (verse 4). Very solemn indeed is that, for it shows us what the most honoured of God's servants are when left to themselves. We say not "the most eminent," for that savours far too much of the flesh; but rather the "most favoured." Whatever privileges we have enjoyed, or nearness to God has been granted us, we are still entirely dependent upon Him for a *continuance* of preserving grace. If that be withheld from any one of us for a single hour, we shall miserably fail and sin. The upholding Spirit was now withdrawn from Joshua for a season (why so, will be pointed out later), and therefore he acted as a natural man would and followed the carnal policy advanced by his underlings. Instead of rebuking their pride with "Let not him that girdeth on his harness boast himself as he that putteth it off" (I Kings xx, 11), he adopted their fleshly policy, This was the more lamentable and excuseless because express instructions had been given him, "he shall stand before Eleazer the priest, who shall ask counsel for him after the judgment of Urim before the Lord: at *His* word shall they go out and at his word shall they come in" (Num. xxvii, 18-21).

Alas, the evil leaven of Achan's trespass was at work "leavening the whole lump," secretly yet surely defiling all his fellows. Failing to ask counsel of the Lord, Joshua was now deprived of spiritual perception, and so discerned not the carnality and evil of the plan set before him. He should have realized at once that it was at direct variance with the Divine pattern given him at Jericho. *There* everything was done in complete obedience to the revealed will of God, in full dependence upon Him, and yet without the slightest neglect of means or human instrumentality—the entire congregation took their assigned places and parts. But *here* there was no inquiring of God's mind, no reliance on His intervention, and a small part only of the "armed men" were deemed sufficient to perform the work of the whole. Thus the greater part would be idle and the congregation itself deprived of the grand privilege of witnessing the mighty works of their God. When Jericho fell, the whole nation saw by whose Hand its powerful walls were demolished, and could give Him the glory. Thus, the plan adopted now by Joshua was a breaking in upon the Divine design.

How solemnly does that point the injunction "Cease ye from man whose breath is in his nostrils, for wherein is he to be accounted of?" (Isa. ii, 22). What a warning is there here for the pastor to give no heed to the carnal advice of his church officers, and to say with David "My soul, wait thou only upon God" (Psa. lxii, 5). Emulate the apostle who "conferred not with flesh and blood" (Gal. i, 16). It matters nothing what others think and say of you so long as you have the Divine approbation. No matter how plausible may be the suggestions proffered, take orders from none save your Master. At the beginning of the campaign Joshua had given commandment that the Reubenites, Gadites, and half the tribe of Manassah should "remain in the land" and not enter into possession of their inheritance on the other side of Jordan "until the Lord have given your brethren rest" (i, 12-15), thereby insisting that the whole of the twelve tribes should present a united front before the enemy until victory was complete. But the plan now followed introduced disunity. It is the following of fleshly methods which generally brings divisions among the people of God. Later, the Lord said to Joshua "Take *all* the people of war with thee" (viii, 1). He had to return to the Divine plan before there could be any success!

The sad failure of Israel before Ai is one which calls for the most careful and prayerful study. Not only because it points, in a general way, a warning which needs to be taken to heart by all of God's people, especially so by His servants, but more particularly because of the book in which it is recorded and the grand truth which is there illustrated. As we proceed from chapter to chapter it needs to be definitely borne in mind that the theme of Joshua is Israel's entry into and conquest of Canaan, and that this typified the Christian's occupation by faith of his heavenly heritage. In the earlier articles of this series we emphasized that fact considerably, frequently pointing out the principles which must regulate the saints if they are to actually "possess their possessions" (Obad. xvii) in *this* life. Alas that so few of them *do* enjoy their inheritance—because of their failure to act by the same. We need not now enumerate and describe these principles: suffice it to say that they are all summed up in, unremitting submission to the revealed will of God. While Israel followed that course, all went well for them; but as soon as they departed therefrom, disastrous was the consequence. And that is written for *our* learning (Romans xv, 4). O that a teachable spirit may be granted both writer and reader.

"The upright shall have good things in possession" (Prov. xxviii, 10). The upright are they who walk with their eyes fixed on God, in subjection to His authority, and in dependence on His grace. While they maintain that character they have the "good things" purchased by Christ not merely in promise and prospect, but in present "possession," enjoying real and blessed foretastes of their eternal portion. But when self-will and self-pleasing obtrude, they are made to eat the bitter fruits of their folly. And hence it is that in the book we are now studying we are shown, both in the crossing of the Jordan and the capture of Jericho, the blessed effects of Israel's obedience unto the Lord; and on the other hand, we have faithfully set before us—in the shameful defeat at Ai—the evil results which inevitably followed Israel's disobedience. In the one we are taught some of the secrets of *success*, or the things which must be attended to by us if we are to have the mighty power of God working in our behalf; while in the other is made known what are the certain precursors of the Lord's displeasure and of our being overcome by our enemies. The one is as necessary for our instruction as is the other.

It would be stating the same thing in a slightly different form and from another angle if we said, The principal subject developed in the book of Joshua is a showing unto God's people *how their enemies are to be conquered,* for Israel had to vanquish and dispossess the Canaanites before they could occupy their land. In like manner the Christian must overcome the Devil, the world, and the flesh before he can experimentally enjoy his heavenly heritage. Israel's warfare against the seven nations of the land was a figure of the believer's conflict with his spiritual foes. The grand lesson which is set before us in the type is that our foes can be subdued by none but the Lord, and that He will fight for us only so long as we are in complete subjection to Him and maintain entire dependence upon Him. "For *if* ye shall diligently keep all these commandments which I command you to do them, to love the Lord your God, to walk in all His ways, and to cleave unto Him. *Then* will the Lord drive out all these nations from before thee" (Deut. xi, 22, 23). Blessedly was that exemplified at Jericho; but the converse was demonstrated at Ai: the former is chronicled for our encouragement; the latter is narrated as a solemn warning for us to take to heart.

The first thing for us to heed—as we observe that the defeat of Ai followed immediately after the victory at Jericho—is the startling fact that the people of God are never in greater danger of giving place to pride and presumption than when God has signally blessed and prospered them. Never does a believer need to act more warily and in full dependence upon the Lord than when his graces are in lively exercise and his heart in an exhilarated frame. Unless he does so, self-confidence will creep in, and more reliance will be placed upon inherent grace than upon the One from whose fullness we need to be continually receiving "grace for grace." No matter how strong be our faith, joyful our heart, energetic our grace, we must still look up for fresh supplies and renewings in the inner man, for without such our graces will no longer act, no, not for a single hour. Only as we remain in the place of conscious weakness are we really strong. Only as the empty hand of a beggar continues to be extended, shall we receive "the supply of the Spirit of Jesus Christ" (Phil. i, 19). Alas, how often do we give the Lord occasion to complain, "I spoke unto thee in thy prosperity, but thou saidst [by thy self-sufficient attitude] I will not hear" (Jer. xxii, 21).

The hidden cause of Israel's defeat at Ai was the sin of Achan, who had secretly committed a grievous trespass against the Lord (Joshua vii, 1), and as the sequel shows, it is a very solemn and serious matter to provoke Him. In this case His displeasure was evinced by his leaving Israel to act in their own wisdom and strength, and that could issue in nought but disaster. Here we have illustrated the important truth that so long as there be an ungrieved Spirit in the midst of an assembly, He directs its counsels and moves its officers and members to work in a wise and becoming manner; but when He is slighted, then His gracious operations are suspended, and they are left to act in the energy of the flesh—to the dishonour of the Lord, and to their own undoing and sorrow. Thus it was here. Out of the hidden root of Achan's offence grew the more obvious causes of the Ai defeat. Pride and presumption were at work. Ai was regarded with contempt, as an easy prey (verse 3); but to their own overthrow. Learn from this, my reader, that it is a fatal mistake to underestimate the strength of our enemies! It is only as we truly realize that our spiritual foes are too powerful for us to vanquish that we shall really seek help and strength from the Lord.

Alas, Joshua accepted the counsel of those who belittled Ai: "So there went up thither of the people about three thousand men" (vii, 4). And what was the inevitable outcome of such carnal self-confidence? This: "they fled before the men of Ai." What a spectacle! Behold attentively the consequence of leaving the place of humble dependency! Mark well what happens when we follow our own devices. Left to themselves, the courage of these men of war wholly deserted them. It is only as we take unto us "the whole armour of God" that we are "able to withstand in the evil day, and having done all to stand" (Eph. vi, 13). If instead we lean upon the arm of flesh, it is certain to fail us. Sad it is to see those three thousand Israelites panic-stricken before the heathen, especially as the record of the same follows right after the final statement of chapter vi: "So the Lord was with Joshua and his fame was noised throughout all the country." How the ignominious defeat of his soldiers would reflect upon the name and fame of Israel's commander! Sadder still is it to know that *our* sinful failures not only injure ourselves and those people of God with whom we are connected, but that they also bring dishonour upon our Redeemer. Should not the realization of *that* make us work out our salvation "with fear and trembling"?

"And the men of Ai smote of them about thirty and six men, for they chased them from before the gate even unto Shebarim, and smote them in the going down" (verse 5). How forcibly does this incident illustrate what was repeatedly pointed out in the earlier articles. Israel's success in conquering Canaan depended entirely upon the Lord's showing Himself strong in their behalf, and that turned upon their unqualified obedience to Him. As Matthew Henry rightly pointed out, the check which they here received "served to let them know they were still upon their good behaviour." Success was to come from God and not their own valour, yet that success was bestowed only so long as they adhered to the pattern which He had given them. One essential feature in that pattern was that the unity of Israel must be preserved —a united front was to be presented to the enemy; consequently "all the men of war" and "all the people" of Israel were bidden to march against Jericho (vi, 3, 5). But in connection with Ai the spies counselled Joshua quite otherwise: "make *not all* to labour thither" (vii, 3). He acceded: "there went up thither about three thousand"; and now we see them in flight, some of them slain, and the remainder chased to "Shebarim," which most significantly means "*breaches*"!

Next we are shown the effects which this disgrace had upon the congregation. When they learned of the retreat and heard that some of their brethren had been slain, "the hearts of the people melted and became as water." And well they might. Had not Joshua previously assured the nation, "Hereby ye shall know that the living God is among you, and that He will without fail drive out from before you the Canaanites" (iii, 10)? Now that He was no longer leading them to victory, but suffering them to be overcome by their foes, they had reason to be thoroughly dejected. As Matthew Henry well remarked, "True Israelites tremble when God is angry." Here again we may note yet another striking contrast. When Jehovah had put forth His mighty power on Israel's behalf in the drying up of the Jordan, we are told that "all the kings of Canaan," when they heard of it, "their heart melted, neither was there spirit in them any more" (v, 1). But here the hearts of *Israel* melted and became as water (vii, 5)! Nevertheless, even then, God was working in mercy unto Israel. By that painful and humiliating providence He was about to bring to light the hidden things of darkness, give His people an opportunity to dissociate themselves from the trespass of Achan and punish the culprit. ✓

"And Joshua rent his clothes and fell to the earth upon his face before the ark of the Lord until the eventide, he and the elders of Israel, and put dust upon their heads" (verse 6). It is to be duly noted that nothing is here said of Joshua berating the soldiers for their cowardice, or of his expostulating with the people for their faint-heartedness. He did not prate about "the fortunes of war" and tell them there was no need to be dismayed, nor did he make any effort to raise their spirits. Rather did he realize the exceeding gravity of the situation and refuse to say "Peace, peace" when he knew that something was radically wrong. The "elders"—the responsible heads of the nation—also recognized that the defeat was owing to the Lord's being provoked, and they too abased themselves before Him. The rending of their clothes was a symbol of perturbation and lamentation (Gen. xxxvii, 24; II Samuel i, 11), the putting of dust on their heads betokened distress and grief (I Sam. iv, 12; Job ii, 12). How very different was *their* conduct from the foolish and fatal "optimism" that is now so rife, and which is nothing else than a declining to face realities, a refusing to recognize the fact that the Lord is displeased and is withholding His blessing.

When things go seriously wrong, either with the individual Christian or with the local church, diligent and solemn examination is called for. When the providential frown of God be upon us, and we ignore the same or "seek to make the best of a bad job," we are only inviting still heavier chastisements. We are bidden to "hear the rod" (Micah vi, 9, and not to disregard or steel our hearts against it; and the first thing required of us in order to ascertain its message is to humble ourselves before the One who wields it, for "the meek will He guide in judgment, and the meek will He teach His way" (Psalm xxv, 9). When God afflicts us we ought to afflict ourselves. "The day of the Lord [any season when He displays His displeasure and acts in judgment] is great and terrible, and who can abide it? Wherefore also now saith the Lord, turn ye even to Me with all you heart, and with fasting and with weeping . . . for He is merciful and gracious" (Joel ii, 12, 13). For thirty years past that is what God has been saying—by His providences—to the whole of Christendom, and particularly to our nation. But alas, it has to be said of us, as of Israel of old, "Thou hast stricken them, but they have not grieved . . . they have refused to receive correction: they have made their faces harder than rock" (Jer. v, 3).

"And Joshua rent his clothes and fell to the earth upon his face before the ark of the Lord." It is to be carefully observed that not only did he now humbly take his place in the dust, but he did so before that sacred coffer which was the symbol of the Lord's throne and presence in Israel. Most suitably was that posture and position selected, for the holy ark had been grievously slighted! Both in the crossing of the Jordan and the march around Jericho, the ark had, by Divine orders, been accorded the place of honour, as it was borne aloft by the priests, signifying unto Israel thereby that victory for them depended upon their covenant God being duly magnified and counted upon. His glory shone forth unmistakably as, by His almighty power, He had made a way for Himself and His people. It was Joshua's sad failure in not giving the ark its proper place, which was the immediate cause of Israel's humiliation at Ai. Not only had Israel's unity been broken by his heeding the boastful suggestion of the spies, but the guidance and help of the ark was dispensed with, and thereby Jehovah had been affronted! It was, we believe, in the conscious realization of this, that Joshua now lay on his face before it.

Once before, and only once, had Israel suffered defeat at the hands of the 'heathen, and it is by comparing the two together that fuller light is obtained upon the incident now before us. Both that reverse in the wilderness and this one in the land issued from the same cause: the pride of self-confidence. The earlier defeat occurred just after the crisis at Kadeh barnea, when the nation succumbed to unbelief, refusing to follow the counsel of Caleb and Joshua, and listening to the God-dishonouring report of the ten spies. After hearing the Divine sentence that all of them should perish in the wilderness, mourning and confessing their sin, they went to the opposite extreme, and in blatant self-sufficiency declared "We will go up unto the place which the Lord hath promised." Moses at once rebuked them: "Wherefore do ye now transgress the commandment of the Lord; but it shall not prosper. Go not up, for the Lord is not among you, that ye be not smitten before your enemies. But they presumed to go up to the hill top; nevertheless *the ark* of the covenant of the Lord, and Moses, *departed not* out of the camp. Then the Amalekites came down . . . and smote them" (Num. xiv, 41-45). Thus history repeated itself: in their mad assurance, the three thousand went to Ai without the ark and suffered defeat.

"And Joshua rent his clothes and fell to the earth upon his face before the ark of the Lord." That act and attitude of his not only expressed an humbling of himself beneath the mighty hand of God, an unsparing self-judgment for his failure, but it also betokened a spirit of *hope*. Does the reader ask, How so? Because that which formed the lid of the ark was the "mercy-seat," where forgiveness could be obtained on the ground of propitiation. Nor do we regard it as a straining of the verse to introduce this idea here: rather does it appear to us to be required by the Spirit's having informed us that Joshua continued thus "until the eventide." Very blessed indeed is that if it be remembered that the God of Israel had appointed, "thou shalt offer upon the altar two lambs of the first year, day by day continually: the one lamb thou shalt offer in the morning, and the other lamb thou shalt. offer *at even*" (Exodus xxix, 38, 39). Then does not Joshua's remaining before the ark until the time of the evening sacrifice confirm the thought that he did so in the expectation of receiving "an answer of peace," of obtaining mercy through the Lamb! Let the reader compare I Kings xviii, 36; Ezra ix, 4, 5; Daniel ix, 21!

Ere passing from this verse its central figure needs to be contemplated from yet another angle. Does not Joshua's "falling to the earth upon his face" *foreshadow* once more the Divine Saviour! When we remember that the root cause of the Ai calamity, which Joshua was here lamenting, was the trespass of Achan in "the accursed thing," must we not recognize in Joshua's humiliation thereat a striking and solemn prefiguration of the Redeemer's anguish in Gethsemane? When entering upon the climax of His sufferings and the Surety of His people was about to be "made a curse" for them before God, we are told that He "fell on His face, and prayed" (Matt. xxvi, 39).

And the very next thing which Joshua here did was *to pray* (verse 7). If it be objected that Joshua was acknowledging his own sad failure, we answer, That only brings out more pointedly the type, for in Gethsemane the Holy One is seen as the Sinbearer, the iniquities of His people being laid upon Him. Yet in all things He has the pre-eminence: very different indeed was *His* prayer in the Garden from that of Joshua's on this occasion, for the types instruct us not only by comparison but also by way of contrast—as in Israel's eating of the manna, and later dying; not so with those who eat the Bread of Life (John vi, 49, 50).

"And Joshua said, Alas, O Lord God, wherefore hast Thou at all brought this people over Jordan, to deliver us into the hand of the Amorites to destroy us?" (verse 7). Here begins one of the prayers of the Old Testament, which, like those contained in the New, vary considerably both in tenor and tone. It is therefore well for us to inquire, What is prayer? That question may be answered in many ways, according as it be considered from various angles. Thus, prayer is a communing with God, an adoring of Him. Prayer is offering praise to Him, a thanking Him for all His mercies. Prayer is also the making known of our needs unto God, and a looking to Him for the supply of the same. Likewise it is an acknowledging of our sins before Him, and seeking His forgiveness and restoration. Further, it is a taking on our spirits the burdens of others and making intercession on their behalf. But here in Joshua vii we have something quite different from any of those aspects of prayer which, though an humbling one, is nevertheless one which all saints at some time or other in their lives need to avail themselves of. On this occasion we behold Joshua overwhelmed, heavily burdened, deeply perturbed, and we hear him pouring out his heart before God without restraint. It is *our* privilege and duty to do so in similar seasons, though endeavouring to avoid his faults. It will bring relief to an oppressed spirit.

There was no eloquent phrasing, no pleading of the Divine promises, no expressing of any definite petition in Joshua's prayer; but instead an unstudied and spontaneous unburdening of himself before the Lord. If it be examined in a critical and carping spirit, it will be easy to detect its faults and condemn it for its incoherency and inconsistency. But whatever defects this prayer possessed, it must not be overlooked that it obtained a hearing from God! It will therefore be well for each of us to ponder Joshua vii, 7-9, in the light of the title of Psalm cii: "A prayer of the afflicted when he is overwhelmed and poureth out his complaint before the Lord." Upon these words an exceptionally favoured and honoured servant of God wrote: "You and I may be in various cases of affliction: we may at times be overwhelmed with the same: it will be well with us if we act as the Psalmist here doth. I never in the whole of my life got any good by carrying my affliction, or speaking when overwhelmed with sorrow to anyone else; no, let it be with a saint of ever so great a degree in the school of Christ. When I have poured out my complaint before the Lord, I have. Blessed be His name for it."

A Penitent Leader's Prayer

In our last we contemplated Joshua, after Israel's humiliating defeat at Ai, on his face before the ark of the Lord. There he lay, with rent garments and dust upon his head, in a posture of self-judgment and abasement. Not until the hour of the evening sacrifice did he open his mouth to God, and then he might have said, " I poured out my complaint before Him, I showed Him my trouble " (Psalm cxlii, 2). Those words present to us an aspect of prayer all too little dwelt upon by preachers and writers. It is wrong to think that we should approach God only when our hearts are composed and in a spiritual frame. It is our privilege to come to the throne of grace for "*mercy*" and to sob out our griefs when deeply distressed. David tells us he did so "When my spirit was overwhelmed within me" (Psalm cxlii, 3). It is for our relief that we tell out our woes to One who is "touched with the feeling of our infirmities." When none other can enter into our case or assuage our grief, we should present ourselves before the Divine footstool as objects of compassion, remembering that "the Lord is very pitiful and of tender mercy" (James v, 11), and therefore He will not break the bruised reed or quench the smoking flax.

When it lies in his line of duty for an expositor to comment upon a recorded instance of an outpouring of heart by a troubled soul, his task is neither an easy nor a pleasant one; for not a little scum rises to the surface when the spirit reaches boiling point. The Hebrew word for "complaint" in Psalm cxlii, 2, does not mean fault-finding, but signifies, rather, that which causes pain and anguish, as in Job vii, 13, and ix, 27. We may indeed complain *to* God and unburden ourselves before Him, yet we ought never to complain *of* Him or murmur at any of His dealings. But where shall we find one clothed with flesh and blood who is guiltless in this respect? Where indeed! Only in Him who, amid "strong crying and tears," said, "Nevertheless, not My will, but Thine be done." If one of our "complaints" be examined in a captious spirit it will not be difficult for another to find in it expressions which are inadvisable. Let us not then scrutinize this prayer of Joshua's in a pharisaic spirit, but rather let us approach it with that word before us, "He that is without sin among you, let him first cast a stone" (John viii, 7). On the other hand, we must not gloss over the faults nor deliberately condone what is reprehensible in it.

Not a little of human infirmity was discovered by Joshua's language on this occasion, and though that be easily accounted for, yet it must not be rendered an excuse for justifying *our* failures. As is so often the case with us, especially when deeply perturbed, there was a strange mingling of the flesh and the spirit seen in the prayer which is now to engage our attention. While some of its expressions cannot be approved, yet it should be borne in mind that Joshua was not here murmuring against any direct dealing of the Lord with himself, but was venting his sore distress over what had just befallen his nation, and was deeply grieved at the reproach which the same must bring upon the name of the Lord. While those considerations might modify his fault, yet they by no means absolve him. The truth is that Joshua too was a sinner saved by sovereign and amazing grace, and that fact was made to appear clearly in this incident. Let us then admire once more the impartiality and fidelity of the sacred historians in narrating this blemish in Joshua's conduct, and behold therein another proof of the Divine inspiration of the Scriptures, which painted each character in the colours of truth and reality, concealing not the defects of its greatest heroes.

The temporary breakdown of Joshua in heeding the presumptuous counsel of the spies, instead of seeking guidance from the Lord through the high priest (Num. xxvii, 21), and in slighting the ark instead of according it the place of honour, was now further betrayed by his mouth and the hard thoughts which he entertained against God. "And Joshua said, Alas, O Lord God, wherefore hast Thou at all brought this people over Jordan, to deliver us into the hand of the Amorites, to destroy us? would to God we had been content, and dwelt on the other side Jordan! " (Joshua vii, 7). In this failure of so honoured a character as Joshua let both writer and reader see his own deep need of walking humbly before God and clinging to Him in conscious weakness. An object lesson is here set before us of how quickly faith fails its possessor when it be not sustained ·by its Author and Giver. The trouble was that Joshua's heart was no longer occupied with the plain and sure promises he had received from God. And why? Because he was walking by sight, viewing things with the eyes of carnal reason. He rashly concluded from the setback at Ai that it was the harbinger of total defeat. Unbelief is unable to see things in their proper perspective and proportions: thirty-six men and not the whole of the three thousand had been slain!

It was not without good reason that the apostle was moved by the Spirit to say to those who were partakers of the heavenly calling, "Take heed, brethren, lest there be in any of you an evil heart of unbelief" (Heb. iii, 13). There is a very real danger of our doing so, and we need to be ever on our guard against it, walking circumspectly. Even the faith of him who is designated " the father of all them that believe" (Romans iv, 11) failed, for when there arose a famine in the land, instead of trusting God to supply all his need (as Elijah did), he "went down into Egypt to sojourn there" (Gen. xii, 10). That breakdown in Abraham's faith was due to the same cause as that of Joshua's! He was out of communion with God. First, he had left Bethel (" the house of God "), where he had built an altar to the Lord, and then he journeyed "toward the south" (Gen. xii, 8), i.e. Egyptwards. And thus, as we have seen with Joshua, instead of inquiring of the Lord, he had hastily adopted the carnal policy of his underlings. Disaster followed, and now a spirit of unbelief possessed him. Learn, then, dear reader, that faith will only be preserved in a healthy condition as we maintain close communion with God through those means of grace which He has appointed.

"Alas, O Lord God, wherefore hast Thou at all brought this people over Jordan to deliver us into the hand of the Amorites, to destroy us?" Very sad indeed is it to hear Joshua now using the very language which had been employed forty years previously by that generation of Israel whose carcasses fell in the wilderness. Of them it is recorded that they "murmured in their tents and said, Because the Lord hated us He hath brought us forth out of the land of Egypt, to deliver us into the hand of *the Amorites, to destroy us*"; the explanation of such despondency being, as Moses charged them, "in this thing ye did not believe the Lord" (Deut. i, 27, 32). And now Joshua is guilty of expressing the same unbelief. This is the more lamentable since he (together with Caleb) had rebuked the scepticism of the congregation, saying, "Rebel not ye against the Lord, neither fear ye the people of the land, for they are bread for us: their defence is departed from them, and the Lord is with us; fear them not" (Num. xiv, 9)—that was the language of confidence in God. But as faith in Him will make the weak and timid strong and courageous, so will unbelief fill the stoutest heart with terror.

Observe how inconsistent and incoherent is the language of unbelief. Joshua acknowledged that it was the Lord who had brought Israel over Jordan, and then asked if He had done so only for them to be destroyed at the hands of the heathen. It is ever thus. Though the wise of this world look upon the children of faith as a company of credulous simpletons, yet really "the shoe is on the other foot." Nothing is so reasonable as to believe the Bible, for it is the Word of Him who cannot lie. But none so imposed upon and irrational as those who reject a revelation from heaven that is attested by "many infallible proofs": to scorn what is authenticated by unimpeachable evidence is a mark of madness and not intelligence. And when a child of God gives way to unbelief his spiritual understanding becomes deranged, and the conclusions he then draws are faulty and absurd. Behold another example of this in the case of David, when he "said in his heart, I shall now perish one day by the hand of Saul" (I Sam. xxvii, 1). How could he possibly do so, when God Himself had assured him of the throne? He, too, had failed to ask counsel of the Lord, and now that he talks with his own deceitful heart he utters the language of a fool.

What need is there for the Christian to cry, "Lord, I believe, help Thou mine unbelief." And if that prayer be sincere, so far from his excusing unbelief, he will mourn over it; so far from regarding it as an innocent infirmity for which he is to be more sympathized with than blamed, he will strive against its evil workings. We have no patience with those who well-nigh exalt the carnal fears and doubts of God's people into spiritual graces and evidences of humility and "deep experience." Any teaching which makes light of the distrust of God, or which causes His children to pity themselves for their failures and falls, is to be condemned and shunned. To call into question the Divine promises is to make God a liar, and that is a heinous offence by whomsoever committed. As faith honours God, so does unbelief dishonour Him. Faith is said to glorify God (Romans iv, 20), and therefore unbelief is a failing to render to Him the glory which is His due. Unbelief in His people is the sin against which God has most proclaimed His displeasure. Moses and Aaron were excluded from Canaan because of their unbelief (Num. xx, 12). The father of John the Baptist was stricken dumb for not believing what God had revealed (Luke i, 20). Christ chided His disciples for nothing so much as He did for their unbelief (Matt. viii, 26; Luke xxiv, 25). "Lord, increase our faith" must be our daily request.

"Would to God we had been content, and dwelt on the other side Jordan!" Surely this cannot be the language of one who was on his face before the ark of the Lord! Ah, my reader, no fictitious history had contained such an unthinkable anomaly as that. Nevertheless it is true to life, as many a saint discovers by sad experience. Just previously "the Lord was with Joshua, and his fame was noised throughout all the coast" (vi, 27); here disgracing himself, by complaining of the Lord's dealings with Israel. Then in the posture of self-abasement, and now uttering the language of self-will. For how many of God's own people do those words of Jacob's concerning Reuben apply: "Unstable as water" (Gen. xlix, 2). Humbly seeking for light from the Word, and puffed up with conceit when it is granted. Praying for more patience, and fretful when the Divine providences are working it in us (James i, 2). Intrepidly contending, single-handed, against eight hundred and fifty false prophets (I Kings xviii), and immediately after fleeing in terror from the threats of a woman (I Kings xix, 2, 3). Ephraim was not the only one like "a cake not turned" (Hosea vii, 8)—baked on one side, dough on the other. Oh, what a compound of inconsistencies and contradictions is the Christian as the flesh lusteth against the spirit and the spirit against the flesh! Oh, the long-suffering of the Lord!

The best of God's children (if there be any best!) are frequently affected with fits of unbelief and chillings of love. Today they find themselves earnestly proposing and resolving to do those things which are good, but tomorrow they may discover their zeal has somewhat abated, so uncertain and inconstant are their affections. Now hopeful, anon despondent; now singing God's praises, anon their harps upon the willows; now walking obediently in the path of the Divine precepts, anon straying off into bypath meadow. None differ so much from them as they often differ from themselves! Nay, in the very graces for which they are eminent, how have they failed! Moses was the meekest man upon the earth, yet in what a froward passion was he when he struck the rock twice and "spake unadvisedly with his lips"! Peter was the most zealous and courageous of the apostles, yet he yielded to sinful fear in the presence of a maid. Some will glorify God in one condition, but dishonour Him in another. They may conduct themselves becomingly while God keeps them low, and then become fretful against Him when they are exalted. On the contrary, others who tread softly in a time of prosperity are filled with murmuring when the cold winds of adversity smite them.

"Would to God we had been content, and dwelt on the other side Jordan!" Alas, what is man? What is a saint when left to himself? What will not his inbred corruptions produce unless Divine grace suppress them! How the evil leaven was working! How horribly Joshua himself was affected by Achan's sin! Yet that in no wise excused his own unseemly language. Joshua was here taking direct issue with the Most High, openly quarrelling with His dispensations, complaining at His providential dealings. And has the writer and the reader, even after becoming a Christian, never been guilty of the same black offence? Ah, have we not cause to hang our heads in shame? And should not the remembrance of past risings up of a rebellious spirit cause us to beg God to subdue our iniquities and bring our will into fuller subjection to His? Instead of marvelling at the sad language of Joshua, see in it a portrayal of our own wayward hearts and our deep need of crying "Hold Thou me up" (Psalm cxix, 117).

"Would to God we had been content, and dwelt on the other side Jordan!" Most assuredly that was not the utterance of "a sound mind," least of all as now issuing from one who had recently passed through such an experience as Joshua's: he had just witnessed a whole generation of his nation *discontented* with the wilderness, repeatedly lusting after the fleshpots of Egypt. It was the height of folly to express such a wish. Moreover, it was not at all a matter of "contentment": they had left the wilderness at the command of God, and not because they were dissatisfied with it. Mark well the sad process which preceded that frenzy. First, a severance of communion with God, then giving way to an evil heart of unbelief, then quarrelling with God's providential dealings, and now bereft of spiritual sanity, for surely it was nothing less to prefer the wilderness to Canaan! But is it not ever thus when fellowship with the Lord is broken and unbelief actuates us? The barren wilderness is a figure of this perishing world, and when a Christian is out of touch with Christ and a spirit of distrust possesses him, he is infatuated with the things of earth and, unless Divine grace restores him to his senses, becomes more attached to them than the things which are above.

"O Lord, what shall I say!" It seems to us that these words mark a return to sanity. The wild outburst of the preceding verse is checked. It is almost as though he now felt ashamed of his rash utterances as he began to realize to whom he was speaking. Yet he is still quite disturbed and scarcely knows how to express himself. "O Lord, what shall I say, when Israel turneth their backs before their enemies!" (verse 8). Israel was beloved of him, yet he could think of nothing to say on their behalf which excused their cowardly defeat. Nevertheless he *should* have known how to answer his question. The Lord does not act capriciously, nor does He "afflict willingly nor grieve the children of men " (Lam. iii, 33), but only as they give Him occasion; and therefore Joshua ought to have humbly begged the Lord to make known to him the reason for His afflicting judgment. Should he not have asked, " O Lord, why doth Thine anger burn against Thy people? wherein have we provoked Thee? " When they were defeated in battle by the Philistines, the elders of Israel inquired, " Wherefore hath the Lord smitten us today? " (I Sam. iv, 3). When there was a famine in the land for three years, " David inquired of the Lord " (II Sam. xxi, 1), and He at once made known the cause of the same.

What has just been pointed out presents a lesson which we do well to heed. " As I live, saith the Lord, I have no pleasure in the death of the wicked; but [rather] that the wicked turn from his way and live " (Ezek. xxxiii, 11). Much less has the Lord any pleasure in smiting His own people. Yet He must maintain His own honour, and deal with them according to His holiness as well as His grace. And *they* must " hear the rod " if they would profit from it and " be partakers of His holiness " (Heb. xii, 10, 11). Closing our eyes to the providential signs God gives us of His displeasure will not improve matters; nor will wringing our hands in despair when things go wrong get us anywhere. While on the one hand God has said, " My son, despise not thou the chastening of the Lord," yet on the other He bids us " nor faint when thou art rebuked by Him " (Heb. xii, 5). What then should we do and say? Humble ourselves beneath His mighty hand and pray " give me to understand wherein I have erred . . . show me wherefore Thou contendest with me " (Job vi, 24; x, 2) that I may put right what is wrong, and once more have Thy smile upon me. Such an inquiry, if it be sincere and humble, will not be in vain.

" O Lord, what shall I say when Israel turneth their backs before their enemies! " Let us apply those words to ourselves. What should be the believer's reaction to the sad state which the religious world is now in? As he beholds the awful declension of the outward cause of Christ on earth, and realizes that the Spirit has been quenched, what ought he to do and say? First, solemnly examine himself and his ways, and seek to ascertain how far his *own* sins have contributed to the present absence of the Lord's blessing from the churches. During " the desolations of Jerusalem " Daniel sought the Lord, and he tells us " I made my confession and said . . . *we* have sinned and committed iniquity " (ix, 2-5, etc.). Let each of us do likewise. Second, we should be deeply affected by the present situation and mourn before God because of the reproach which prevailing conditions in Christendom cast upon His name: see Psalm cxix, 53, 136; Jer. ix, 1. Third, we should turn the exhortation of Revelation iii, 2, into earnest prayer, and beg the Lord to " strengthen the things which remain that are ready to die," and revive His work in the midst of the years. Fourth, we should plead before Him the promise " When the enemy shall come in like a flood, the Spirit of the Lord shall lift up a standard against him " (Isaiah lix, 19). " Who can tell if God will not turn and repent, and turn away from His fierce anger that we perish not? " (Jonah iii, 9).

" For the Canaanites and all the inhabitants of the land shall hear, and shall environ us round, and cut off our name from the earth: and what wilt Thou do unto Thy great name? " (verse 9). Here the supplicant becomes more intelligible, for the first half of this verse is to be regarded as a plea, being tantamount to asking the Lord to remember that Israel were the sheep of His pasture, and therefore to spare them from falling a prey to the wolves. Then Joshua pointed out the danger Israel were now in, thereby taking the place of weakness; next, he looked to the love and pity of the Lord: Israel's name, which is dear to Thee, will be blotted out if the heathen completely destroy them—which was an indirect appeal to the promises God had made to the fathers (Gen. xv, 18, etc.). Finally, he points out the reproach which would be cast upon God were the Canaanites to triumph completely. Thus when we penetrate beneath the surface agitations of Joshua, we see that at heart it was concern for the Divine glory which had prompted this prayer! He could not endure a prospect which reflected upon the fidelity and power of their covenant God. Herein he foreshadowed the antitypical Joshua. He. too, when in deep trouble of soul, had asked "What shall I say? Father, save Me from this hour?" No, rather, "Father glorify *Thy name*" (John xii, 27. 28)! Let that be *our* plea, and it will prove a prevailing one.

Divine Inquisition

Joshua vii presents to our notice that which is very different from what is found in the preceding chapters. It opens with the ominous word "But," which solemnly prepares for what follows. First, the heinous sin of Achan, which, though the nation knew it not at that time, caused the Lord to burn in "the fierceness of his anger" against Israel (verse 26). The evil effects of Achan's offence and the consequences of Jehovah's displeasure soon appeared. The spies whom Joshua sent out to reconnoitre Ai were left to the exercise of their carnal reason. The result was that when making their report they presumptuously took it upon them to advise their leader how to act. Regarding Ai as an easy prey, they intimated there was no need for the whole nation of Israel to journey thither, that a single battalion of *their* men would suffice. Thereby they suggested a departure from the pattern which the Lord had given His people both at the Jordan and at Jericho, and introduced disunity. Instead of seeking counsel from the Lord, Joshua adopted their foolish plan. The ark of the covenant was left behind in the camp, and three thousand only were sent against Ai. The outcome was disastrous. A spirit of cowardice possessed them, and they fled from the Canaanites, thirty-six of them being slain.

The whole congregation was thoroughly dismayed: "the hearts of the people melted, and became as water." Quite unaware of the root cause of Israel's ignominious setback, Joshua and the elders of the nation rent their clothes, put dust upon their heads, and fell to the earth on their faces before the slighted ark of the Lord. There they remained "until the eventide," when the second of the daily sacrifices was presented. At that hour Joshua addressed himself unto the Lord, pouring out his distressed heart before Him. In view of the circumstances, it is not to be wondered at that the infirmities of this honoured servant of the Lord were made manifest on this occasion. As is usually the case with us at such times, there was a strange mingling of the flesh and spirit, in the supplication of Joshua. While some of his utterances are not to be condoned, still less echoed, yet it should be borne in mind that he was not complaining at any of the Lord's dealings with him personally, but was deeply perturbed at what had befallen God's people. Though his opening expressions were unseemly, his closing ones evidenced that his heart beat true to Jehovah and that it was the honour of *His* name which so greatly concerned him. We shall now consider the response which his prayer met with from God.

"And the Lord said unto Joshua, Get thee up; wherefore liest thou thus upon thy face?" (vii, 10). Before considering those somewhat puzzling words, let it be attentively observed that God did not refuse His servant a hearing, even though considerably infirmity had marred it. Blessed be His name, "He knoweth our frame, He remembereth that we are dust" (Psalm ciii, 14), and in His tender mercy "A bruised reed shall He not break, and smoking flax shall He not quench" (Matt. xii, 20). Joshua had exclaimed, "O Lord, what shall I say, when Israel turneth their backs before their enemies? For the Canaanites and all the inhabitants of the land shall hear, and shall environ us round, and cut off our name from the earth; and what wilt Thou do unto Thy great name?" (verse 9). In those words he had virtually confessed his own failure. used the language of godly sorrow, and had evinced a deep concern for the glory of God. Well for us if such elements be present in our lispings before the throne of grace. The holy but gracious One never repulses those in whom such a spirit is found. On the ground of the evening sacrifice (the slain lamb!) Jehovah met with this soul who manifested a "broken and contrite heart" (Psalm li, 17). How that should encourage failing yet penitent believers today!

"And the Lord said unto Joshua, Get thee up; wherefore liest thou thus upon thy face?" Care needs to be taken in the interpreting of this verse. If it be detached from its context we are almost certain to err and jump to a wrong conclusion, regarding it as an expression of the Lord's displeasure. But if due attention be paid unto its opening "And," and note carefully both what precedes and what immediately follows, we should have no difficulty in arriving at its general tenor. It is not God's way to condemn those who take their place in the dust before Him: rather is His controversy with them who refuse to do so. Nevertheless, though He pardons, He does not gloss over our faults: see Psalm lxxxv, 8; John v, 14. As the prayer of Joshua had been a mixed one, so with the Divine response. God did not turn a deaf ear to it, nor did He ignore His servant's petulance, but gently reproved him. It was both a mild rebuke and a word of instruction. "Wherefore liest thou *thus* upon thy face?" Why so distressed and dejected? There is other work for thee to do. But before performing it, he must be directed by his Master. Up to now Joshua was in complete ignorance of Achan's offence—the root cause of the disaster.

"Israel hath sinned, and they have also transgressed My covenant which I commanded them: for they have taken of the accursed thing, and have also stolen, and dissembled also, and they have put it even among their own stuff" (verse 11). That too needs to be pondered, first, in the light of its setting. As we do so, it will be seen that an important and blessed practical truth receives exemplification: "the secret of the Lord is with them that fear Him" (Psalm xxv, 10). If we really seek God's honour and glory, we shall not be left long in ignorance of the best way to recognize and promote it. So it was here: the Lord now informed Joshua what it was which lay behind Israel's defeat at Ai. In like manner, if our seeking unto Him be sincere and earnest—whether it be an individual or an assembly—God will soon reveal to us what it is that has been withholding His blessing upon our efforts. "Israel hath sinned": there has been no failure on *My* part. I have not changed, but am just as willing and ready as ever to undertake for My people; but *they* have choked the channel of blessing. Thus it ever is. We speak of God's hiding Himself, when in fact we have departed from Him. It is always man that does the turning away, thereby depriving himself of the Divine strength, protection and prosperity.

In the above words of Jehovah unto Joshua it is most noticeable how He set forth and stressed the enormity of Achan's crime: one detail being added to another until no less than six items are specified in the terrible indictment.

First, the general charge is made "Israel hath sinned," followed by the fearful accusation "they have also transgressed My covenant which I commanded them," which greatly aggravated their sin. Observe that the charge is preferred against the whole nation, and not simply against a single individual: "Israel," "they," for in the sight of God they were a corporate and federal unit: as the local church of this Christian era is a moral unit before Christ: see I Corinthians xii, 20, 26; v, 6. This feature received additional emphasis in the reference to "the Covenant," for that had been made with and solemnly entered into by the whole congregation (Ex. xxiv). Next we behold how the Divine Law was brought to the fore: "They have taken of the accursed thing," which was a definite violation of the explicit prohibition of Deuteronomy xiii, 17—"there shall cleave naught of the cursed thing to thine hand." Yet more: "and have also stolen," thereby adding considerably to the heinousness of the offence, for it was a direct breach of the eighth commandment in the Decalogue.

"And have also *stolen*" emphasized another reprehensible feature of the crime—it had been committed surreptitiously and with previous design. It was not that Achan had been suddenly overcome by an unexpected temptation, but that he acted with deliberation, stealthily and secretly, his deceitful and wicked heart persuading him that he would thereby escape the cognizance of the Most High. Horrible impiety is it when we entertain the idea that we can impose upon Omniscience. The more secret our wickedness be, the more does it evince the heart's depravity and industry therein, planning and scheming how to bring the sin to pass with the least danger and shame to ourselves. It was thus with David when he plotted the death of Uriah (II Sam. xi, 14, 15). So too had Ananias and Sapphira arranged in private to impose a fraud upon the Holy Spirit (Acts v, 2-7). How we should pray to be preserved from secret sins! They are particularly heinous because of the premeditation and dissimulation which is used in their commission. "And dissembled also," which made his case that much blacker. When Israel met with shameful defeat at Ai, and the whole nation was plunged into grief, Achan played the part of a hypocrite, pretending to be innocent of causing the same—instead of confessing his iniquity. Finally, "And they have put it even among their own stuff," instead of bringing it into the "treasury of the Lord" (vi, 19).

"Therefore the children of Israel could not stand before their enemies, but turned their backs before their enemies, because they were accursed; neither will I be with you any more, except ye destroy the accursed thing from among you (verse 12). Weigh attentively that statement my reader, for it casts a flood of light upon the reason why the visible cause of Christ is in its present lamentable condition. What took place at Ai has been and is being duplicated in thousands of churches and assemblies the world over. Instead of enjoying the Lord's blessing, His frown is upon them; instead of overcoming the Enemy, they are humiliated before him. How many a minister of the Gospel has to the best of his ability faithfully preached the Word, yet to no effect, unless it be to considerably reduce the size of his congregation! How many a one, fearing that he was a "misfit," has resigned his charge and has accepted a call to another part of the Lord's vineyard, only to discover after a short time there that conditions are just as heartbreaking as those in his previous sphere! A spirit of deadness rests upon his church: the prayer meeting is cold, and thinly attended, preaching is burdensome. His most earnest appeals seem to hit the wall and return upon him. The power of the Spirit is markedly absent: souls are not converted, nor even convicted.

The above verses makes known one of "the ways of the Lord" or one of the principles which regulate His governmental dealings in time. When a company who profess to be in covenant relationship with Him violate its terms and flagrantly transgress His commandments, then His blessing is withheld from them. No matter how zealous and active they may be, God prospers not their efforts. They may go out as of yore against the foe, but the Lord fights not for them. They are left to themselves, and soon their nakedness and shame is made manifest. God will not be trifled with. To the church in Pergamos the Son of God declared "I have a few things against thee," and after specifying what they were, added, "Repent, or else I will come on thee quickly, and will fight against thee with the sword of My mouth" (Rev. ii, 14-16). Likewise did He threaten the church in Thyatira, "I will kill thy children with death, and all the churches shall know that I am He who searcheth the reins and hearts, and I will give unto every one of you according to your works" (Rev. ii, 23).

Alas that the majority of the churches today know nothing of that solemn fact. Alas that they have received so little instruction upon the holiness which must obtain in the assembly if the presence of Christ is to be enjoyed there. Alas that "the accursed thing" has not only been suffered a place, but "they have put it even among their own stuff." Alas that they know not the Holy One has a controversy with them over this very thing. Alas that they are ignorant of the fact that their spiritual poverty and powerlessness, their being humiliated before the world, is due to the Divine judgment upon their sins. Alas that they are completely unaware of the Divine sentence "neither will I be with you any more, except ye destroy the accursed thing from among you." Paul had to rebuke the Corinthian assembly because they tolerated moral evil in their midst, and bade them "Purge out therefore the old leaven, that ye may be a new lump" (I Cor. v, 1-7). "Except *ye* destroy" was the enforcing of Israel's responsibility.

How unmistakably the defeat at Ai and God's solemn words to Joshua make it evident that such a promise as that given in Deuteronomy xx was *not* an absolute one. There God had given instruction, "And it shall be, when ye are come nigh unto the battle, that the priests shall approach and speak unto the people, and shall say unto them, Hear, O Israel, ye approach this day unto battle against your enemies: let not your hearts faint, fear not, and do not tremble, neither be ye terrified because of them; For the Lord your God is He that goeth with you to fight for you against your enemies, to save you" (verses 2-4). Neither in those words, nor in anything preceding or following, was there any proviso. It has the appearance of an absolute promise, without any qualification. Taken by itself, it was so; but taken in conjunction with other passages in Deuteronomy, it was not so—as the event at Ai, and the later experiences of Israel demonstrated. Scripture needs always to be compared with Scripture in order to arrive at the full meaning of any single verse. If we are too lazy to do the necessary searching in order to locate other qualifying or amplifying passages, then the fault is entirely our own if we be left in ignorance of the signification of any statement of Holy Writ. The whole book of Deuteronomy needs to be read through if we are to rightly understand such a passage as the one in the twentieth chapter.

Our purpose in calling attention to Deuteronomy xx, 2-4, in connection with our study of Joshua vii, is to show how easy it is to wrest God's Word, and to utter a warning and protest against the careless and dishonest manner in which it is now so often handled. Such passages as Deuteronomy vi, 16-18 and xi, 8, 9, require to be kept steadily in mind when reading Joshua and the books which follow, for they supply the key to much that is recorded in them. And in connection with the promise in xx, 2-4, particularly do we need to set side by side with it such statements as "For *if* ye shall diligently keep all these commandments which I command you to do this day, to love the Lord your God, to walk in all His ways, to cleave unto Him, *Then* will the Lord drive out all these nations from before you" (xi, 22, 23) and "It shall come to pass if thou shalt hearken diligently to the voice of the Lord your God, to observe to do all His commandments which I command thee this day . . . that the Lord thy God will set thee on high above all nations of the earth" (xxviii, 1); but if they obeyed not, His curse would certainly fall upon them (xxviii, 15). It is handling God's Word deceitfully to stress its promises and ignore their qualifying conditons: to quote John viii, 32, and omit verse 31, to cite John x, 28, and be silent upon verse 27. Hebrews iii, 6, 14, are just as necessary for us as viii, 10-12. God has indeed promised to show Himself strong in the behalf of those whose hearts are perfect towards Him; but nowhere has He declared that He will fight for the self-willed and disobedient.

"Up, sanctify the people, and say, Sanctify yourselves against tomorrow for thus saith the Lord God of Israel. There is an accursed thing in the midst of thee, O Israel. Thou canst not stand before thine enemies, until ye take away the accursed thing from among you" (verse 13). This was the sequel to the "wherefore liest thou thus upon thy face?" (verse 10); this was the duty concerning which the Lord was now instructing His servant. It was not simply "Arise!" but "Up"—bestir thyself now unto the duty which I enjoin thee. "Sanctify the people": this was ever the order when the nation was about to witness some outstandingly solemn or glorious transaction. Thus it was immediately before God gave the Law at Sinai (Exodus xix, 10). Thus it was following the murmuring at Taberah, when the Lord "came down" and talked with Moses (Num. xi, 18). Thus it was on the eve of Jehovah's wondrous intervention for them at the Jordan (Joshua iii, 5). In each case the call was for the people to be sanctified, that is, for them to be formally and reverently assembled before the Lord. Joshua was also to bid them "sanctify yourselves against tomorrow," which signified, duly prepare yourselves for the solemn and searching ordeal which the Lord has appointed: spare no pains in seeing to it that you are in a meet condition for the approach of the Holy One.

Continuing the Lord's response to Joshua's prayer subsequent to the humiliating repulse at Ai. After informing him that Israel had sinned grievously, and therefore His blessing had been withheld from their efforts, the Lord bade His servant, "Up, sanctify the people" (verse 13). Before we consider the immediate and historical application of those words, let us observe how they supplied yet another line to the typical picture of the Saviour which is set forth in this book. As we have passed from chapter to chapter the readers' attention has been directed to quite a number of things in which Joshua foreshadowed the Lord Jesus. A further detail now appears in this injunction for him to sanctify the people, for it prefigured Christ as the Sanctifier of His Church: "Wherefore Jesus also, that He might sanctify the people with His own blood, suffered without the gate" (Heb. xiii, 12). And what was the moral condition of His people when He did so? Precisely the same as Israel's was here: defiled, under the curse of the Law, "the fierceness of God's anger" being upon them (vii, 26 and cf. Eph. ii, 3). To deliver them therefrom, the antitypical Joshua suffered the full penalty of their sins, and set them apart

unto God in all the acceptableness of His meritorious sacrifice. Mark also
the time when this occurred: as it was immediately following upon Joshua's
"falling to the earth upon his face" (vii, 6) that he was bidden to "sanctify
the people," so it was a few hours after His prostration on the ground in
Gethsemane that Christ sanctified His people at the cross!

Turning from the spiritual and mystical signification of the order Joshua
received to its literal and historical meaning, we understand by God's "sanctify the people" that he was to formally and reverently convene the nation
in orderly array before the Lord. That injunction was probably the exact
equivalent of one received by Israel's prophet at a later date, "Sanctify a fast,
call a solemn assembly, gather the people, sanctify the congregation, assemble
the elders, gather the children" (Joel ii, 15, 16), for it is clear from what
follows here that all Israel were required to take their place before the Divine
tribunal. "Sanctify the people, and say unto them, Sanctify yourselves against
tomorrow, for thus saith the Lord God of Israel, There is an accursed thing
in the midst of thee, O Israel, thou canst not stand before thine enemies until
ye put away the accursed thing from among you" (vii, 13). It is striking and
interesting to note how that the Lord here *repeated* what He had just said in
the previous verse, both in charging them with their being an accursed thing
in Israel's midst and that because of it they could not stand before their
enemies. Such reiteration not only evinced how heinous was their crime in
the eyes of the Holy One, but also gave point unto the call for the people to
"sanctify yourselves"—not "for the morrow" but *against* it. They were to
duly anticipate in their consciences the Divine inquisition which would then
be held, when the guilty would be unerringly identified and severely punished.
Thus, "Sanctify yourselves" was tantamount unto "Prepare to meet thy God,
O Israel" (Amos iv, 12).

"Sanctify the people, and say unto them sanctify yourselves against
tomorrow." The same demand had been made at Sinai, and what is recorded
of it casts light upon the import of it here: they were to wash their bodies
and clothes, and abstain from their wives" (Exodus xix, 14, 15). Thus,
"sanctify" here has the force of *purify:* "For if the blood of bulls and goats
and the ashes of a heifer sprinkling the unclean, sanctifieth to the purifying
of the flesh" (Heb. ix, 13 and cf. II Tim. ii, 21). Under the law "sanctification" or "separation and consecration to the Lord, was secured by a process
of cleansing. By a comparison with Joel ii, 15, 16, and its context (verses 12,
13, 17) it is clear that, in addition to ceremonial purification, Israel were here
enjoined to cleanse themselves *morally.* "Sanctify yourselves" would therefore imply and include a solemn call to self-examination, humiliation, and
supplication; and that in turn would necessitate a separating of their minds
from all other cares and concerns, that they might give themselves un-
distractedly and earnestly unto those solemn duties. Such acts of devotion can
only be suitably performed as the thoughts and affections are detached from
the daily business and worries of this world. As they had been required to
sanctify themselves before they received the Law, so now they were ordered
to do so when about to witness a most fearful enforcing of its penalty.

Possibly some will be inclined to ask, Since a single individual only had
committed this offence, or at most with the connivance of his family (vii, 21),
what reason or propriety was there in calling upon *all* the people to employ
themselves in solemn self-examination? How could those who knew they were
innocent of perpetrating a serious crime, sincerely engage in such a task?
Those who are truly jealous of the glory of God and who are painfully con-

scious of the fact that "in many things we all offend" (James iii, 2) will have no difficulty in meeting such an objection. The name of the Lord had been grievously sullied by the enemy's triumph at Ai, and His saints could not but bitterly mourn over it. Furthermore, the whole nation had been put to shame when their soldiers had fled before the Canaanites; yea, the nation was yet in imminent danger while exposed to "the fierceness of God's anger" (verse 26), and therefore it was most fitting that there should be an humbling of the entire congregation before the Lord—as the example of Joshua and their elders (verse 6) had intimated. Moreover, as Matthew Henry pointed out, "The sins of *others* may be improved by *us*, as furtherances of our sanctification, as the scandal of the incestuous Corinthian occasioned a blessed reformation in the church: II Corinthians vii, 11." Every time a saint is overtaken in a fault, it should give point unto his fellows of that warning "let him that thinketh *he* standeth, take heed lest he fall" (I Cor. x, 12).

Ere passing on, one other question needs to be noticed: if the "sanctify the people" unto Joshua foreshadowed Christ's sanctification of His Church, then *what* was spiritually connoted by his bidding the people "sanctify yourselves"? There was a double sanctification: one by Joshua and one by themselves! That twofoldness of Truth appears again and again in connection with God's people. As believers on the Lord Jesus Christ they *are* saved (Acts xvi, 31), yet they are bidden to work out their own salvation (Phil. ii, 12 and cf. I Tim. iv, 16). They are new creatures in Christ, yet exhorted to put on the new man (Eph. iv, 24). They are now clean, and yet need to have their feet washed. They are complete in Christ (Col. ii, 10), yet are bidden to grow in grace and add to their faith virtue, and to virtue knowledge, etc. (II Peter i, 5). Every believer has been "perfected forever" (Heb. x, 14), yet confesses that he is not already perfect (Phil. iii, 11). The one refers to what they are in Christ, the other to what they are in themselves. Unless the Christian reader learns to draw that distinction, much in the epistles will seem almost a meaningless jumble, if not a series of contradictions. There is a tremendous difference between how the believer appears in the sight of God, and how he looks in his own eyes and those of his fellows. He stands before God in the infinite value of Christ's righteousness, while in his actual experience he is warring against the world, the flesh and the devil, and is often worsted by them.

"Sanctification" is still more complex, for a *threefold* distinction is necessary in order to bring into view its leading features, namely, our federal, personal, and practical holiness. By our fall in Adam we lost not only the favour of God but the purity of our nature, and therefore we need to be both reconciled to Him and sanctified in our inner man. The former is secured by the work of Christ; the latter is effected by the operation of the Holy Spirit. The former is judicial; the latter is vital. Christ is the covenant Head of His people, and since He is the Holy One, all in Him are representatively holy. He is their holiness as truly as He is their righteousness: "But of Him are ye in Christ Jesus, who of God is made unto us wisdom, and righteousness, and sanctification, and redemption" (I Cor. i, 30). He is "made unto them" sanctification in precisely the same way as God "made Him to be sin for us" (II Cor. v, 21), namely, by legal reckoning, by imputation. But that is not all: believers are not only sanctified federally and legally but personally and vitally in themselves. In consequence of their covenant union with Christ, the Holy Spirit is sent to quicken them into newness of life, to indwell them, to abide with them forever. This is their "sanctification of the Spirit" (II Thess. ii, 13).

The *fruit* of the believer's sanctification in Christ and of the Spirit's indwelling are, in various ways and degrees, made manifest in their daily lives, which is what we term *practical* sanctification. A principle of holiness is imparted at regeneration, and the workings and effects of the same soon appear in the conduct. Sanctification of the Spirit produces a real and radical change in its favoured subject, and so transforms his behaviour "as becometh the Gospel of Christ." That which has been wrought within every believer is manifested without, by an obedient walk in the paths of holiness as marked out in the Word. Thereby evidence is given that they have been created "by God in righteousness and true holiness" (Eph. iv, 24). It is on the basis of their federal and vital oneness with Christ that exhortations unto practical holiness are addressed to them: "he that saith he abideth in Christ, ought himself also so to walk even as He walked" (I John ii, 6). And it is by virtue of the Spirit's sanctification that such exhortations are exactly suited to the new nature He has wrought in them: "Let it not be once named among you as becometh saints" (Eph. v, 3). Those whom the Spirit has made "saints" (i.e. "sanctified ones") are to conduct themselves *as such* (Romans xvi, 2). The nation of Israel had been set apart unto the Lord, and that call, "sanctify yourselves," was the equivalent of saying, Act accordingly. To us the word is, "Let us cleanse ourselves from all filthiness of the flesh and spirit, perfecting holiness in the fear of God" (II Cor. vii, 1; and cf. I Peter i, 15).

"Sanctify yourselves against tomorrow, for thus saith the Lord God of Israel, There is an accursed thing in the midst of thee, O Israel: thou canst not stand before thine enemies until ye take away the accursed thing from among you." "The Lord did not point out the criminal immediately, but He left the matter in ambiguity for some time, and at last brought it to light gradually: that both magistrates and people might learn to do their duty, and to keep a vigilant eye over one another; and that the delay and process might make the transaction more solemn, and excite the more careful self-examination and sanctification of themselves by every method appointed under the law" (T. Scott). Similarly did the Saviour say unto His apostles, "Have not I chosen you twelve, and one of you is a devil?" (John vi, 70). vi, 70). Later He informed them that one of them would betray Him, though still without actually naming the one who would be guilty of such horrible perfidy; which resulted in each of the eleven asking: "Lord is it I?" Such ought to be the first concern of each of us, once it becomes evident that the light of God's countenance is no longer shining upon the company of saints with whom we are in fellowship: bowing before a heart-searching God and asking, Am I responsible for the withdrawal of Thy favour? Where such a spirit obtains among the members it will not be long ere the One who is jealous of the honour of His house makes known the cause of His displeasure.

"In the morning therefore ye shall be brought according to your tribes: and it shall be that the tribe which the Lord taketh shall come according to the families thereof; and the family which the Lord shall take come by households; and the household which the Lord shall take shall come man by man" (verse 13). First, the opening words of this verse teach us that once an evil be known there must be no delay in dealing with it—true alike whether it respects an assembly or where only a single individual be concerned. The honour of God and our own welfare alike demand prompt action when any "accursed thing" be involved. To procrastinate in such a case is like playing with fire. Delay in such a matter is a sure sign our hearts are not right with God. By all means investigate thoroughly and make sure that God *has been* publicly slighted, and then be not tardy in dealing with the offender. Next, we should note the Lord's insistence upon what Joshua had previousiy disregarded, namely, the *unity* of Israel. In heeding the counsel of the spies and detaching three thousand from the body of the nation (verse 3), he acted contrary to the pattern God gave him in the crossing of Jordan and taking of Jericho. "*Israel* hath sinned," God declared, and now He required that the whole of the tribes should share in the shame of Achan's offence—as later He gave orders "Take all the people of war" against Ai (viii, 1).

"In the morning therefore ye shall be brought according to your tribes, and it shall be that the tribe which the Lord taketh shall come according to the families thereof." The culprit had not been named, and before he was identified there must be a searching investigation. Very solemn indeed was the procedure followed. Most probably the whole congregation was assembled before the tabernacle. The word "brought" is the one generally used in connection with offering of the sacrifices (Lev. i, 2, 10)—"bring," therefore, has the force here of the people being presented for the Lord's inspection. Doubtless it was the "princes" or heads of each tribe which came, respectively, before Joshua and Eleazar. Three times over in this verse we have the expression "which the Lord shall take." We naturally inquire, what is signified thereby? In what way or by what process did He do so? If Scripture be compared with Scripture it seems clear that the Lord here distinguished between the innocent and the guilty by means of the Urim and Thummim in the high priest's breastplate. When Joshua was first set apart unto his office, orders were given that "he shall stand before Eleazar the priest, who shall ask counsel for him after the judgment [decision or verdict] of the Urim before the Lord" (Num. xxvii, 21). Under certain circumstances the will of God was made known via the urim and thummim, and evidently Eleazar "asked counsel" for Joshua by them on this occasion.

Of Saul it is said that "when he inquired of the Lord, the Lord answered him not, neither by dreams, nor by urim, nor by prophet" (I Samuel xxviii, 6) —proof of His having abandoned the apostate king. Thence we gather that by means of the urim and thummim prophetic guidance was at certain times obtained from God. This is further borne out by Ezra ii, 63, when Nehemiah forbade the rejected children of the priests eating of the most holy things, he added "till there stand up a priest with urim and thummim"—through which the Divine mind will again be revealed. From these passages the late Dr. Bullinger drew the following deductions: "The Urim and Thummim were probably two precious stones, which were drawn out as a lot to give Jehovah's judgment. 'The lot is cast into the lap [Hebrew "bosom"] but the whole judgment thereof is of the Lord'(Prov. xvi, 33)—bosom is here put for the clothing or covering over it: cf. Exodus iv, 6, 7; Ruth iv, 16 . . . Thus, those two placed in the 'bag' and one drawn out would give the judicial decision, which would be 'of the Lord.' Hence, the breastplate itself was known as 'the breastplate of judgment' (Exodus xxviii, 15). because by that Jehovah's judgment was obtained when it was needed. Hence, when the land was divided 'by lot' (Num. xxvi, 55) Eleazar the high priest must be present. (Num. xxxiv, 17; Joshua xvii, 14)."

Both words are in the plural number, though (as is often the case in the Hebrew) probably it is what is known as "the plural of majesty"—used for the purpose of *emphasizing* the importance of a thing or the dignity of an object. It is likely that the "urim" was a single stone or object and the "thummim" another, though we cannot be certain. The English equivalent for those words is "light" or "lights" and "perfections"; in the Septuagint they are rendered by "delosis" and "aletheim," meaning "manifestation and truth." As the high priest thrust his hand into the bag of his breastplate (note "doubled" in Exodus xxvii, 16), possibly the bringing forth of the "urim" indicated the Lord's *yes* and the "thummim" His *no*, or vice-versa. In the instance we are now considering, most likely the appearing of the urim signified the bringing to light of the guilty; whereas the issuing of the thummim announced the "perfection" or sincerity of the innocent. Thus, as the head or heads of each tribe stood before Eleazar he would draw out the thummim until the turn of Judah arrived, as indicated by the urim. The same process was followed after the guilty tribe had been identified: the heads of its leading "families" standing before the Lord's representative, and when the particular family was identified, the same with its "households," until the culprit himself stood unmasked before all.

"And it shall be, that he that is taken with the accursed thing shall be burnt with fire, he and all that he hath: because he hath transgressed the covenant of the Lord, and because he hath wrought folly in Israel" (verse 15). Solemn indeed was the transaction which we have endeavoured to picture above, fearful the trial of all who took part in it. A threefold reason may be suggested for the leisurely nature of this inquisition. First, it manifested the calmness and thoroughness of the Judge of all the earth: He is ever a God of order, departing not therefrom when sitting in judgment. Second, the terribleness of their ordeal would impress upon Israel the reality of the holy covenant which God had made with them, and demonstrate before them again the majesty of the Divine Law—seen in arresting the waters of Jordan, overthrowing the walls of Jericho, and now equally so in taking vengeance on the transgressor. Third, in affording the guilty one further space for repentance: but alas, his heart was hardened and he refused to come forward and own that *he* was the cause of the whole trouble. The dreadful sentence that he should be "burnt with fire" does not necessarily signify he was to be roasted alive—vii, 25, seems to clearly show otherwise. If it be asked, Why burn them and their possessions if they were already dead from stoning? To express still more vividly the Divine detestation, and that nothing whatever of the accursed thing should remain.

Judgment

"So Joshua rose up early in the morning, and brought Israel by their tribes" (vii, 16). Here we behold his willingness and readiness in obeying the command he had received (verse 14). However painful the task, there was no delay. In iii, 1, we saw God's servant rising early to engage in a pleasant duty; here, there was equal alacrity when a distressing one was to be performed. Though a sore trial to flesh and blood, yet Joshua's heart was in this work; for he yearned to have the Lord's honour vindicated, and for the nation to be restored to His favour. Therein we have a further adumbration of the antitypical Joshua, of whom we read that after announcing "behold, the hour is at hand, and the Son of man is betrayed into the hands of sinners," at once added "Rise, let us be going" (Matt. xxvi, 45, 46). Yet here, as everywhere, the Saviour had the pre-eminence. There was no "rising early in the morning," for there was no retiring to rest for Him that night! Through all the hours of darkness He was hounded from pillar to post: from Gethsemane to appear before Annas, then sent from him to Caiaphas, from him to Pilate, from him to Herod, from him back to Pilate, from him to the cross: all the while on foot, His body a mass of bleeding wounds, without His eyes closing in slumber! Nevertheless, He *advanced* unto those who thirsted for His blood (John xviii, 4), ready to be led as a lamb to the slaughter.

"So Joshua rose up early in the morning, and brought Israel by their tribes, and the tribe of *Judah* was taken." This must have come as a most painful shock to that tribe as a whole, as well as to Joshua himself. Wondrous things had been foretold of Judah. It was to be the royal and ruling tribe (Gen. xlix, 10). The Lord had laid honour on it by supernaturally endowing one of its men for special skilled work in connection with the furnishing of the tabernacle (Exodus xxxi, 3-5). Of it sprang the illustrious Caleb (Num. xiii, 8). Judah was the tribe which took the lead when the nation was on march across the wilderness (Num. x, 14). His was to be the largest portion of Canaan (Deut. xxxiv, 2). And here their name was disgraced! Nor was this the first time, as a reference to Genesis xxxviii, 2, 15 and 16 will show—Achan being a direct descendant of the Zarah or Zerah of Genesis xxxviii, 30, in Joshua vii. 18. "This was an allay to their dignity and might serve as a check to their pride. Many there were who were its glories, but here was one that was its reproach. Let not the best families think it strange if there be those found in them and descended from them that prove their grief and shame. Since Judah was to have the largest lot in Canaan, the more inexcusable is one of that tribe if, not content to wait for his own share, he break in upon God's property" (Matthew Henry).

Achan remained obdurate even now that it was made known that the guilty one belonged to the tribe of Judah. As he had not confessed his offence when Israel was repulsed at Ai and the hearts of the people melted and became as water (verse 5), so now he maintained silence, yea, continued doing so when his own "family" was singled out (verse 17) and when his particular "household" was identified (v. 18). But in a few more moments he was to receive proof of that Divine declaration "Be sure your sin will find you out" (Num. xxxii, 29). He was also on the point of learning "he that covereth his sins shall not prosper" (Prov. xxviii, 13). To "cover sin" is a keeping of it within our own bosom, a refusing to bring it out into the light by a frank confession of the same unto God. *Pride* restrains many therefrom: they have such a high esteem of themselves that even though guilty they are too self-opinionated to own their sins. With others, *unbelief* is what hinders: they who have no faith to be assured that God will cover repented sins, vainly attempt to do so themselves even while remaining impenitent. *Fear and shame* are what cause the majority to hide their sins. Sin is such a hideous monster that they will not own it as theirs. But whatever be the cause, they "shall not prosper."

"And he brought the family of Judah: and he took the family of the Zarhites, and he brought the family of the Zarhites man by man; and Zabdi was taken; he brought his household man by man: and Achan, the son of Carmi, the son of Zabdi, the son of Zerah, of the tribe of Judah was taken" (verses 17, 18). It should be borne in mind that all of the innocent were under a cloud of suspicion until the culprit himself was definitely recognized. Moreover, it was expedient for the benefit of future generations that no stigma should rest upon the guiltless. "The tribe, family, parentage of the offender were specified with exactness, that the infamy might not rest on the reputation of any other of the same name" (T. Scott). Achan "was taken" means that he was now identified by the "urim," singled out by the unerring judgment given through the high priest. It was now made manifest before the whole congregation that the Divine justice had seized him. When the secret sins of men are brought to light God should be owned in it, and the perpetrator should acknowledge with the brethren of Joseph: "God hath found out the iniquity of thy servants" (Gen. xliv, 16). "For there is nothing covered. that shall not be revealed; neither hid, that shall not be known" (Luke xii, 2).

"And Joshua said unto Achan, My son, give, I pray thee, glory to the Lord God of Israel, and make confession unto Him, and tell me now what thou hast done, hide it not from me" (verse 19). Here again we must look beyond Joshua unto the One spoken of in Acts xvii, 31, "Because He hath appointed a day in which He will judge the world in righteousness by that Man whom He hath ordained." God Himself will judge, yet not immediately, but mediately through Christ. So here: Achan was bidden to give glory to the Lord God, but Joshua at once added, "tell *me* what thou hast done, hide it not from *me*"! The expression "my son" was not here a term of tenderness or kindness (as it usually is with us), but a form of address used by one of eminence or authority unto an inferior, as Saul termed David "my son" (I Samuel xxiv, 16) and Joab designated Ahimaaz, the son of Zadok, "my son" (II Samuel xviii, 22); conversely, a superior was owned as "father" (II Kings v, 13; vi, 21). Nevertheless, it is striking to note how mildly Joshua addressed Achan: "This is an example to all not to insult over those who are in misery, though they have brought themselves into it by their own wickedness, but to treat even offenders with the spirit of meekness, not knowing what ourselves should have been and done if God had put us into the hands of our own counsels" (Matthew Henry).

"And Joshua said unto Achan, My son, give, I pray thee, glory to the Lord God of Israel and make confession unto him" Very striking and blessed is that: the honour of Jehovah was what was uppermost in His servant's heart and mind—as it ever was with the anti-typical Joshua (John viii, 50; xii, 23). But how could Achan's confession give glory to God? In many ways. It testified to the Divine omniscience in detecting and exposing his profane and stealthy conduct, picking him out from that vast multitude as the guilty one. It acknowledged God's holiness in abhorring his wickedness, thereby setting to his seal that "He is of purer eyes than to behold evil, and canst not look on iniquity" (Habakkuk i, 13). It witnessed to His justice, that God was righteous in being so displeased with him. It owned His veracity: that "the soul that sinneth it shall die" (Ezek. xviii, 4). What is the glory of God but the sum of His perfections? It is by those perfections that He is made known to us both in the written and personal Word. And therefore to glorify Him is for us to recognize, acknowledge and be suitably affected by the Divine attributes; as conversely we are guilty of slighting Him when denying, either in word or act, His perfections. When we trample upon His Law we repudiate His authority. When we defy Him, we disclaim His power. When we think to conceal sin from Him, we disown His omniscience.

"My son, give, I pray thee, glory to the Lord God of Israel, and make confession unto Him." It is all too little realized by any of us that this is one of the ways appointed by God in which we glorify Him. In connection with the confessing of sin we are too apt to confine our thoughts unto the clearing of our conscience and being restored to fellowship. In other words, we are too much wrapped up in ourselves and too little occupied with the excellencies of the One we approach. A truly contrite soul will eye the dominion of God, acknowledging His right to rule over us and our duty to live in entire subjection to Him, and will bemoan his insubordination. He will eye God's righteousness and own that "His Law is holy, and the commandment holy and just and good" (Romans vii, 12), and therefore that he is without excuse in breaking it. He will eye His long suffering, which has granted him space to repent, instead of cutting him off in the commission of sin. He will eye the abundant mercy of God, which has opened a way for his pardon without compromising His holiness, laying hold of the promise: "If we confess our sins, He is faithful and just to forgive us our sins, and to cleanse us from all unrighteousness" (I John i, 9). Failure to confess sin is not only to deprive ourselves of comfort, but is to withhold from God that which is His due.

Acceptable confession is very much more than an exercise of our lips: unless it issues from groanings within, our words are worthless and ineffectual. And there will be no inward groaning until we realize the sinfulness of our sins and are duly affected thereby. We shall never confess sin with a true sense of its infinite evil until we consider its contrariety to the nature and will of God, and perceive how it reflects dishonour upon the Divine perfection, particularly as it is a contempt of His authority and a direct opposition to His purity. Nor shall we ever confess our sins with brokenness of heart and confusion of face, until we are sensible of the vile ingratitude of them, as they are committed by those who are under the strongest obligations to the contrary. There will be no confession of sin with self-abhorrence until we recognize that it is aggravated by the light and privileges, the goodness and mercy, the exhortations and warnings, against which we have transgressed, for they greatly heighten our iniquities (Ezra ix, 10-15). To affect our minds and consciences with the heinousness of sin, so as to be kept humble and filled with self-abasement, we need to meditate frequently upon what it cost Christ to make atonement for the same. The sincerity and fervour of our confession evince the depth of our hatred of sin.

"And Joshua said unto Achan . . . tell me *now* what thou hast done, hide it not from me." That "now" was a word of reproof and reproach because the offender had remained silent so long. Achan had delayed until it was impossible any longer to conceal his guilt—his confession being wrung from him by the preceding process. The earlier confession be made, the more God is honoured, and the sooner will peace be restored to the conscience; but, better late than never. It is the fool who procrastinates; the apostate who defiantly refuses to do so. Fearfully solemn is that warning: "Give glory to the Lord your God before He cause darkness and before your feet stumble upon the dark mountains, and while ye look for light. He turn it into the shadow of death and make it gross darkness" (Jer. xiii, 16). Note that to "make confession" and "hide it not" are equivalent terms, and that not to confess is tantamount to a denial (John i, 20). Joshua's "tell me now *what* thou hast done, hide it not from me" makes known unto us what confession of sin is to consist of, namely, a frank and full acknowledgment of the offence, without any attempt at concealment or self-extenuation, however humiliating it may be. By so doing we bear witness that God's prohibition was a righteous one and that His punishment (or chastisement) is just.

"And Achan answered Joshua and said, Indeed I have sinned against the Lord God of Israel, and thus and thus have I done" (verse 20), which was

no more a proof of his genuine contrition than was King Saul's acknowledgment, " I have sinned and transgressed the commandment of the Lord"
(I Samuel xv, 24), or the remorseful avowal of Judas, " I have sinned in that
I have betrayed the innocent blood" (Matt. xxvii, 4). In what follows we
are shown that confession of sin must be in detail. "When I saw among the
spoils a goodly Babylonish garment, and two hundred shekels of silver, and a
wedge of gold of fifty shekels weight, then I coveted them, and took them;
and behold, they are hid in the earth in the midst of my tent, and the silver
under it" (verse 21). The temptation entered through the eye, and that excited
the concupiscence of his corrupt heart: as the prophet said in a different
connection, "mine eye affecteth my heart" (Lam. iii, 51). How needful it is
that we emulate the holy example of Job, who declared: "I have made a
covenant with mine eyes" (xxxi, 1). How earnestly should we cry unto God
daily "Turn away mine eyes from beholding vanity: quicken Thou me in Thy
way" cxix, 37)—make me to view things as *Thou* dost, and to esteem or
disesteem them according to the teaching of Thy Word. Had Achan regarded
those objects with the eyes of faith, he had looked upon them as "accursed
things," for so had God pronounced them!

"I saw . . . then I coveted them." Having viewed them with the eyes
of unbelief, he lusted after them. What a solemn warning for each of us
to heed! Covetousness has in it a far greater degree of malignity and is
more highly provoking to God than is commonly thought. Colossians iii, 5,
declares that covetousness "is idolatry," for it is a bestowing upon the
creature that respect and love which is due alone unto the Creator. When
we mortify not our inordinate desire, we cherish a viper within our own
bosom, for it gnaws at the very roots of contentment and gratitude (Heb.
xiii, 5). When our desire exceeds the present portion God has allotted us, we
are no longer satisfied with the same and are unable to enjoy and give thanks
for it. "I coveted . . . them, I took them": thus he followed precisely the
same order as did Eve (Gen. iii, 6, and cf. James i, 14, 15). "And behold
they are hid in the earth in the midst of the tent." There we behold both the
"deceitfulness of sin" and the anxiety it brings. "No sooner had he got
possession of his plunder than it became his burden! . . . so differently do the
objects of temptation appear at a distance to what they do when apprehended
and when the infatuation ceases" (T. Scott). They who yield to a spirit of
covetousness "pierce themselves through with many sorrows" (I Tim. vi,
8-10).

"So Joshua sent messengers, and they ran unto the tent." The members
of the congregation were as desirous and zealous to have Jehovah's honour
vindicated as was their leader. "And behold it was hid in his tent and the
silver under it. And they took them out of the midst of the tent, and brought
them unto Joshua and unto all the children of Israel" (verses 22, 23). This
was done in order that conclusive evidence of Achan's guilt should be laid
before the eyes of the whole nation, and thereby was brought to light the
hidden things of darkness. By that procedure a solemn warning was given
the people (and us) of the utter futility of any attempt to conceal anything
from the eyes of Him which are "in every place, beholding the evil and
the good" (Prov. xv, 4). "And poured it out before the Lord" (verse 23): that
is, either at the feet of His representative, the high priest, or more probably
immediately before the ark of the covenant. The accursed things were not
poured out "unto the Lord" for His acceptance, but *before* Him for His
destruction—they were never brought into His treasury for use in His service,
but totally destroyed, as the sequel shows.

" And Joshua *and all Israel* took Achan, the son of Zerah, and the silver, and the garment, and the wedge of gold, and his sons and his daughters, and his oxen and asses and his sheep, and all that he had, and they brought them into the valley of Achor " (verse 24). Here was unity of action. The whole nation was required to dissociate itself from the trespass and take part in punishing the culprit. For any not to concur therein would be to condone the sin—just as when any church members refuse to take part in a similar action. Achan, and all pertaining to him were taken outside the camp—compare " take away from among yourselves " (I Cor. v, 2)! Note how what followed gave force to, and shows an additional reason for, the " sanctify yourselves " of verse 13. For those who are themselves erring creatures to sit in judgment upon one of their fellows calls for unsparing self-judgment. Ere a church is in a meet condition to enforce a holy discipline it is required that its officers and members humble themselves before God and clear their own consciences, by confessing every known sin and pleading the cleansing blood of Christ. Only then can they act in godly fear and trembling. Only then will " he that is without sin among you let him first cast a stone " no longer prevent them performing a necessary but painful duty.

" And Joshua said, Why hast thou troubled us? the Lord shall trouble thee this day. And all Israel stoned him with stones, and burned them with fire, after they had stoned them with stones " (verse 25). " By this severity against Achan the honour of Joshua's government—now in the infancy of it—was maintained; and Israel, at their entrance upon the promised Canaan, were minded at their peril, the provisos, and limitations of the grant by which they held it " (Matthew Henry). It is worthy of note that at the opening of the tabernacle worship we behold an instance of the severity of Divine judgment upon the two sons of Aaron (Lev. x, 1, 2), so here upon their entry into Canaan, and similarly at the dawn of Christianity in connection with the death of Ananias and Sapphira (Acts v) we have examples of the same thing: designed no doubt to increase godly fear, promote dutiful circumspection, and prevent general wickedness. Such solemn demonstrations before the eyes of the people would render it the less easy for them to forget that their God was " a consuming fire " unto those who provoked Him

" The severity of the punishment must be estimated by the relation of Achan's crime to the whole plan of the conquest of Canaan. If the destruction of Canaan was indeed the execution of Divine vengeance, it must be kept entirely clear of all human motives, lest men should say that Jehovah had given His people license to deal with the Canaanites as seemed best for themselves. The punishment of Saul (I Samuel xv, 21-23) and the repeated statement in Esther ix, 10, 15, 16 (notwithstanding the king's permission in viii, 11), ' but on the spoil laid they not their hand.' are illustrations of the same principle " (Ellicott). In addition, it is to be borne in mind that Achan deliberately transgressed the plain commandment of Deuteronomy xiii, 17, that he acted in contempt of the awful curse which Joshua had just previously denounced (vi, 17-19), that he defied Jehovah at a time when His presence was so conspicuously manifest among His people, that his crime was not only one of theft but sacrilege (converting to his own use what was devoted to the Lord), and that his offence resulted in the people of God being put to shame in the sight of the heathen.

Our remaining space permits us to do no more than briefly point out that the above incident shadows forth most of the principal features of the Last Assize. (1) It is then there will be a full and final display of God's perfections and the Divine glory will shine forth conspicuously. (2) As "all Israel" here, so all mankind there, will stand before the antitypical Joshua. (3) As the tribe of Judah was marked off from the others, so will the goats then be separated from the sheep. (4) The hidden things of darkness shall then be brought to light. (5) As the innocent were cleared before the guilty were charged, so the righteous will be vindicated before the unrighteous are condemned. (6) As Achan made no attempt to deny his guilt or demur at his punishment, so the damned will concur with the justice of their sentence. (7) As all Israel united in the stoning of Achan's family, so the saints "will judge the world" (I Cor. xvi, 2). (8) As the guilty were "burned with fire" *after* their death, so everlasting fire will be the portion of the lost. (9) As there was a permanent "memorial" unto the grace of God (Joshua iv, 9), so unto His holiness (Joshua vii, 26): the redeemed will for ever exemplify God's love, the reprobate His wrath.

Lack of space prevented our adding a word at the close of our last on the concluding verse of Joshua vii, so to it we now turn. "And they raised over him a great heap of stones unto this day. So the Lord turned from the fierceness of His anger. Wherefore the name of that place was called the valley of Achor [Trouble], unto this day." Three things are to be noted: the memorial to solemnly remind Israel of Achan's sin, the Lord's reconciliation, and the name given to the place of execution and appeasement. As the twelve stones taken out of Jordan were permanently pitched in Gilgal (iv, 20-23) to perpetuate the memory of the miracle which the Lord had so graciously wrought there, so a great heap of stones was raised to mark the spot where the vengeance of the Holy One fell upon the one who had so grievously offended Him. That heap of stones was designed to serve as a terrible warning against the crime of sacrilege, to rebuke those who imagine themselves secure in secret sins, and to furnish a witness of what an awful thing it is to be a troubler of God's people.

There is an instructive emphasis in the "*so* the Lord turned from the fierceness of His anger," teaching us that the assemblies of His people must exercise a strict and holy discipline (for the honour of His name) if they are to escape His governmental judgments and chastenings. Cast into its positive form that statement would read, when Israel, had put away "the accursed thing" and dealt faithfully with the disturber of their peace, they were restored again to God's favour. Two further references are made in the Scriptures to this place, and very significant and blessed they are. Unto backsliding Israel the Lord declared His purpose to recover and restore her, saying, "I will give her her vineyards from thence, and the valley of Achor for a *door of hope*" (Hosea ii, 15): our putting away of the offensive thing—by repentance and reformation—affords ground for hoping that God will renew His favours unto us. "And Sharon shall be a fold of flocks, and the valley of Achor [where things are put right with God] a place for the herds to lie down in, for My people that have *sought Me*" (Isaiah lxv, 10)—a promise which should be spiritualized and pleaded by each wayward but contrite saint.

Chapter 11

THE CONQUEST OF AI

Joshua 8:1-35

Encouragement and Direction

"And the Lord said unto Joshua, Fear not, neither be thou dismayed: take all the people of war with thee, and arise, go up to Ai: see! I have given into thy hand the king of Ai, and his people, and his city, and his land" (viii, 1). In the preceding verse we are told "the Lord turned from the fierceness of His anger," and while there can be little or no doubt that Joshua would—after the matter of Achan had been dealt with—*infer the same,* yet he had not been given any token from Him that such was the case; but now he received from God a word of cheer, a word of instruction, and a word of promise for faith to lay hold of. "When we have faithfully put away sin, that accursed thing which separates between our God, then, and not till then, we may expect to hear from God for our comfort; and God's directing us how to go on in our Christian walk and warfare is a good evidence of His being reconciled to us' (Matthew Henry): that is, fellowship with Him is now restored. Note well that commentator's "and not till then": no purveyors of "smooth things" were the faithful and practical Puritans, nor did they entertain their hearers and readers with matters of no spiritual profit.

The Lord's word "arise" intimates that, following the stoning of Achan and his family, Joshua again took his place on his face, or at least on his knees, before the Lord, seeking consolation and counsel from Him. Israel's progress in their conquest and occupation of Canaan had been rudely interrupted, and though the hindering cause had been put away, yet Joshua dare not attempt any further advance until His Master gave fresh indication of His will. This teaches us that, after a sin has been unsparingly judged by us—be it the case of an individual Christian, or that of an assembly—there must be a humble and definite waiting upon God for guidance as to what He would have us do next. His "fear not, neither be thou dismayed" shows that the offence of Achan and its disastrous consequences had been a sore and unexpected blow to Joshua, making him almost ready to faint. "Corruptions within the church weaken the hands and dampen the spirits of her guides and helpers, more than opposition from without; treacherous Israelites are to be dreaded more than malicious Canaanites" (Matthew Henry).

That word, "fear not, neither be thou dismayed," was designed not only for Joshua personally, but for the whole of the congregation. Israel had failed lamentably at their first assault upon Ai, had been deeply humiliated, and in consequence "the hearts of the people melted and became as water" (vii, 5), and though they had obeyed the Divine command of vii, 15 in utterly destroying the culprit and all that he had, yet they were in real need of an intimation that they had been restored to God's favour, and could count upon His leading them again to victory. Equally requisite is it that the penitent and humbled Christian should lay hold of this or some similar reassuring word.

209

When iniquities have prevailed against him (Psalm lxv, 3) and the enemy has humiliated him, he is prone to be "swallowed up with over-much sorrow" (II Cor. ii, 7) and suffer Satan to keep him in the slough of despond, which is not only needless and foolish, but dishonouring to God. If he has sincerely and contritely forsaken his sins, then he should confidently reckon upon God's mercy (Prov. xxviii, 13) and appropriate His promise "He is faithful and just [to Christ's atoning sacrifice] to forgive us our sins and to cleanse us from all unrighteousness" (I John i, 9).

The word of comfort or reassurance was followed by one of instruction: "take all the people of war with thee, and arise, go up to Ai." Therein Joshua and the people under him received definite directions from the Lord what they must next do. Joshua was now to turn from the throne of grace and make for the field of battle, as the believer has to leave the place of secret prayer and go forth to conflict in the world. Linking the two words together, the Lord was bidding His servant not to be dismayed by the previous repulse at Ai, but to be strong and courageous. In like manner, He calls upon the restored backslider to renew the contest with his enemies. If at first you don't succeed, try, try again. Quit not the fight because you have been worsted, nor even if you were wounded. Though you were blameable for the failure, having confessed the same to God, resume the struggle. *That* is a part of what is included in "perseverance in grace" or "the final perseverance of the saints." "Rejoice not against me, O mine enemy; when I fall, I shall arise" (Micah vii, 8). In its application to us individually the "take all the people of war with thee" means, See to it that all your powers and graces are exerted in a concerted effort.

"See, I have given into thy hand the king of Ai, and his people, and his city, and his land." That was spoken from the Divine purpose: it was not "I will," but "I have given." It was God "calling those things which be not as though they were" (Romans iv, 17), as when He told the aged patriarch with barren wife, "I *have* made thee a father of many nations." And as that word to Abraham was addressed unto his *faith*, so was this one here to Joshua. "See, I have given into thy hand the king of Ai" signified, Regard it as an accomplished fact, behold the victory with the eye of your spirit as one already achieved. It is thus that the soldiers of Christ are to wage their spiritual warfare fully persuaded of the happy outcome. As the beloved, yet often hardpressed, apostle expressed it. "I therefore so run, not as uncertainly; so fight I, not as one that beateth the air" (I Cor. ix, 26)—having no doubt whatever of reaching the goal, nor of vanquishing his enemy. It is "the good fight of *faith*" to which we are called, but if we be regulated by our reason or feelings it soon becomes a fight of unbelief. This "see" (by faith) of viii, 1, was similar to that of Exodus xiv, 13 and Joshua vi, 2 .

Ere passing on to the next verse let it be pointed out that the one we have just been pondering contains a timely message for the pastor, especially if he be discouraged and disheartened by the absence of any apparent success or fruit for his labours. First, he should search himself before God and test both his message and method by the Word, to see if he has in any way grieved the Holy Spirit and thereby prevented His blessing upon his ministry. Should such prove to be the case, his sin must be unsparingly judged and abandoned. If after diligent self-examination no hindering cause is revealed, then let him take these words of the Lord as spoken immediately to himself: "Fear not, neither be thou dismayed"—it is fear which causes dejection and dismay! Then let him say, "What time I am afraid, I will trust in Thee" (Psalm lvi, 3), or better. "I will trust and not be afraid" (Isaiah xii, 2). "Take all the people of war with thee": earnestly solicit the prayerful co-operation of the saints, and, whether you have that or no, be sure to take unto thee "all the armour of God." Further, eye by faith such promises as Isaiah lv, 11; Matthew xxviii, 20, for only thus will your fears be quietened.

"And thou shalt do to Ai and her king as thou didst unto Jericho and her king: only the spoil thereof and the cattle thereof shall ye take for a prey unto yourselves: lay thee an ambush for the city behind it" (Joshua viii, 2). No mercy was to be shown the enemy, no truce made with him, but all the inhabitants were to be "utterly destroyed" as in the former instance (vii, 21). This teaches us that the Christian must adopt an uncompromising attitude toward every form of evil, even abstaining from the very appearance of it (I Thess. v, 22). On this occasion Divine permission was given Israel to appropriate the spoil and the cattle unto themselves. The cattle upon a thousand hills are the Lord's (Psalm l, 10), and He disposes of them as He pleases. In connection with Jericho Israel were forbidden to take anything unto themselves, the whole being "consecrated unto the Lord" (vii, 18), thereby intimating that He has a special claim upon "the firstfruits" (Exodus xxiii, 19; Prov. iii, 9), for that initial restriction was not again enforced. The grant here made may be regarded as a gracious reward for their obedience in vii, 25, thereby exhibiting the folly of covetous Achan—we never lose by waiting *God's* time, and only bring trouble upon ourselves if we attempt to anticipate it.

The method by which Ai was to be taken was quite different from the one used against the first stronghold of the Canaanites, which shows us, among other things, that God does not work uniformly. Thomas Scott pointed out that "Jericho had been taken by a miracle . . . in order to teach the people to depend on God, and give Him the glory of all their successes. But they seemed to have inferred that they might despise their enemies and indulge themselves. They were therefore, in the next instance, instructed that diligence, self-denial and the exercise of all their powers, both of body and mind, were required in order to secure success." While fully agreeing with those remarks, yet they do not, we think, fully explain the case. Though God be absolute sovereign, so that He ever acts freely, yet His ways with men are not capricious, but generally accord with their own behaviour. Because of their rash conduct in the first attack on Ai, Israel had missed God's best, and must now be content with His second best, is how we prefer to express it. The root cause of their failure was the flagrant offence of Achan, but more immediately it was due to the conceit of the spies and the folly of Joshua in acceding to their carnal suggestion.

"So Joshua arose, and all the people of war, to go up against Ai; and Joshua chose out thirty thousand men of valour, and sent them away by night. And he commanded them, saying, Behold, ye shall lie in wait against the city, even behind the city: go not very far from the city, but be ye all ready" (verses 3, 4). To how much trouble had Israel now put themselves in order to overthrow Ai! Ah, my reader, it requires no little pains in order to return to the path of blessing once we have departed from the same! In various ways God makes us feel the folly of leaning unto our own understanding or acting in self-will, and shows us something of what we bring upon ourselves by missing His best. Observe too how precisely the Lord corrected Israel's failures, making them reverse their former policy. When the spies returned from the reconnoitring of Ai, they said unto Joshua, "Let not all the people go up, but let about two or three thousand men go up and smite Ai." That was in direct variance with the pattern which God gave to Israel in vi, 3, and to which He now required them to return—"take *all* the people of war with thee" (viii, 1). The closing words of the spies "for they be few" in vii, 3 showed they regarded Ai with contempt, as an easy prey, and the proposal that a single battalion of *their* fighting men would suffice was manifestly the language of conceit.

The Lord countered their pride by appointing a much more humbling method for capturing Ai than the one used in the overthrow of Jericho. There, Israel's army had marched openly around the walls of that fortress; here, where a smaller and weaker city was involved, the humiliating strategy of a secret ambush was assigned in order for an attack from the rear. In the latter case, Joshua had failed to spread before the Lord the suggestion of the spies and seek counsel of Him, and disastrous was the consequence. The result was that he had to spend many hours "on his face" before the ark ere an explanation of Israel's repulse was vouchsafed him; and later, he had to bow again before the Lord ere instructions were given for the new plan of campaign (viii, 1). The servant of God must not follow his own devices, but rather act according to the Word of his Master, for only then is he justified in counting upon His blessing. It is blessed to observe that however humbling the means which God now required to be used, both Joshua and those under him complied with the instructions God gave them. Having received an answer of peace from the Lord and an intimation of His will for them, they acted promptly in carrying out of the same.

"So Joshua arose, and all the people of war, to go up against Ai." That was not only an act of obedience, but, we doubt not, should also be regarded as one of faith—in response to Jehovah's "See! I have given into thy hand the King of Ai." Should any one be disposed to ask, "But since the Lord had made such an announcement, why was it necessary for Joshua and the whole of his army to go to so much trouble?" he would betray his ignorance both of God's sovereignty and of man's accountability. God's predestination of the end does not render needless our use of means: rather does the former include the latter, and is realized by the same. When the Lord informed Hezekiah through one of His prophets that He would "add unto his days fifteen years" (Isaiah xxxviii, 5), that certainly did not imply that the king might henceforth dispense with food, drink and sleep; any more than God's assurance to Paul that there should be "no loss of life" of the ship's contingent rendered it the less imperative to abstain from recklessness and to use means for their preservation (Acts xxvii, 22-24, 31). God's gracious assurances unto His people are not designed to promote indolence, but instead to stimulate and to encourage diligence, knowing that "our labour is not in vain in the Lord" (I Cor. xv, 58).

While it be true that unless God gives the victory no efforts of ours can possibly achieve it, nevertheless it is our bounden duty to make every effort. Though the fall of Ai was certain, yet Israel were called upon to discharge their responsibility. God's promises to us are not given to induce slothfulness, but to be a spur unto obedience to His precepts. Faith is no substitute for diligent and zealous work, but is to act as the director of the same. Hope is not to absolve us from the discharge of our obligations, but is to inspire unto the performing of the same. It is because victory *is sure* in the end that the soldiers of Christ are called upon to fight: that assurance is to be their incentive, from which they are to draw their energy. The genuine exercise of faith has a powerful influence both upon the Christian's efforts to mortify the old man and to vivify the new. This is clear from Romans vi, 11, and what follows: we must by the reckoning of faith account ourselves legally one with the Lord Jesus Christ in His death and resurrection before we can expect any success in subduing our lusts or developing our graces (v. 13). Faith is indeed the victory "that overcometh the world" (1 John v, 4), yet as the previous verse clearly shows, it is a faith which is operative in the keeping of God's commandments.

Thus, while Israel were called upon to exercise faith in the Divine assurance of success, yet they were also required to adhere strictly to the strategy which God appointed. Very definite were the orders Joshua gave unto the thirty thousand men who were to fall upon the city from the rear: "Ye shall lie in wait against the city, behind the city: go not very far from the city, but be ye all ready" (v, 4): they were told where to go, what to do, and how to comport themselves. Equally explicit are the instructions of the Christian in connection with the waging of his spiritual warfare, and the measure of his success will very largely be determined by how closely he sticks to them. Thus, after bidding believers "Be strong in the Lord, and in the power of His might" (which can only be by the exercise of faith upon Him), the apostle bade them "Put on the whole armour of God, that ye *may be able to stand* against the wiles of the Devil" (Eph. vi, 10, 11), which plainly imports that unless they heeded his injunction they would fall before the enemy's artifices. This is the more noticeable, because after enforcing his exhortation by informing us of the formidable forces which are under Satan's control (v. 12), he repeats, "Wherefore take unto you the whole armour of God, that ye may be able to withstand in the evil day, and having overcome all [margin] to stand" (v. 13). God has provided the armour, but *we* have to "take unto" us and "put on" the same; and not merely a part of it, but "the whole."

In our last we pointed out that in Joshua viii, 1, the Lord gave unto His servant a word of cheer, a word of instruction, and a word of promise. His "fear not, neither be thou dismayed" was to graciously reassure Joshua's heart after the dishonourable repulse Israel had met with upon their first assault on Ai—the reasons for their defeat having been shown. In its wider application, it was a message of comfort to the whole nation, after their elders had duly humbled themselves before the Lord, that they must not be unduly cast down nor suffer Satan to induce them to give way to a spirit of despair. The word of instruction was an intimation of the Divine will of what was now required from Joshua and those under his command: "take all the people of war with thee, and arise, go up to Ai." Therein their presumptuous conduct in vii, 3 was denounced, and an order was given for them to return to the Divine pattern which they had received in vi, 3. The word of promise was addressed unto their faith: "See! I have given into thy hand the king of Ai, and his people, and his city, and his land." *That* was spoken from the standpoint of the certainty of the Divine counsels, and faith was to receive it without question.

The word of instruction received amplification in the second verse: Ai and its inhabitants were to be utterly destroyed. In this instance Israel were given permission to take the cattle as a spoil unto themselves. Finally, the strategy to be followed was made known: an "ambush" was to be laid for the city from its rear. Next we are told, "So Joshua arose, and all the people of war, to go up against Ai; and Joshua chose out thirty thousand men of valour, and sent them away by night" (viii, 3). That is to be regarded as an act not only of obedience but of faith too, or rather as "the obedience of faith" (Romans i, 5, margin). It is a great mistake to suppose that faith in God renders needless our discharge of duty or the use of all lawful means: instead, it is to energize unto the one and to look unto God for His blessing upon the other. Confidence in

God does not produce passivity, nor will the diligence which it evokes issue in self-confidence. True faith ever produces good works, yet those works are performed in a spirit of dependence upon the Lord. It is written: "The way of man is not in himself" (Jer. x, 23), but it is written again: "This is the way, walk ye in it" (Isaiah xxx, 21). Thus does Scripture always guard Scripture!

"And he commanded them, saying, Behold, ye shall lie in wait against the city behind the city: go not very far from the city, but be ye all ready" (viii, 4). Though victory was Divinely guaranteed, that did not preclude the discharge of their responsibilities. Faith in God was to operate in the performing of His commandments. Accordingly, Joshua issued very definite orders to those thirty thousand of his soldiers, telling them where to go and how to conduct themselves. As we said at the close of our last article, equally explicit are the instructions given to the Christian in connection with his spiritual warfare, and the measure of his success therein will very largely be determined by how closely he adheres to the same. It is to be noted that the force which was to lie in wait behind the city was "sent away by night" (verse 3), and thus its members were deprived of their rest, calling for self-denial on their part. *That* is the first and chief task appointed the believer: as Israel had to overcome and dispossess the Canaanites ere they could enter into their inheritance, so we have to get the victory over the flesh, the world and the Devil before there can be any present possessing of our possessions and enjoyment of the same. Before Christ can be followed, *self* has to be "denied," and the *cross* (self-sacrifice) accepted as the regulating principle of our lives (Matt. xvi, 24).

That to which we have just called attention receives confirmation in I Corinthians ix, 24-27, where Paul says, first, "Know ye not that they which run in a race run all, but only one receiveth the prize? So run that ye may obtain," likening the Christian life unto the running of a race—which calls for rigorous training, vigorous exertion, and patient endurance. Then he informs them what is required, and is essential, in order to succeed therein: "And every man that striveth for the mastery is temperate in all things": that is, he puts a bridle upon his appetites, is abstemious in the use of comforts, and exercises a strict self-control at every point. Next, the apostle made mention of his own life, which exemplified what he had just said, and which sets before us an example to follow: "*I therefore* so run, not as uncertainly"—I myself practise such self-discipline as being absolutely necessary in order to ensure success. I conduct myself in such a manner and order my life in such a way that the outcome is not left in any doubt. I run within the lines marked out—keeping to the prescribed path of duty; pressing on till the goal is reached, exerting myself to the utmost unto the end.

Then, slightly varying his figure, and coming closer to what Joshua viii has in view, the apostle added: "So fight I, not as one that beateth the air"—I conduct myself, and so observe the rules of the contest, that there can be no uncertainty that I shall be "more than conqueror through Him that loved us." Paul daily denied himself, mortified his lusts, and consequently he knew that the crown of life was thereby ensured. He did not waste his energies or spend his strength for naught. All his efforts were directed to the grand purpose of subjugating the desires of the flesh and bringing all his members into subjection to God. Alas, how many professing Christians today *are* wasting their energies upon tasks which God has never assigned them! Then in verse 27 he frankly stated the awful alternative: if I fail to make my body the servant of my soul, by yielding its members unto God (Romans vi, 19) and fighting against the lusts of the flesh and temptations of Satan, then eternal disgrace will be my portion. Finally, let it be carefully noted that the apostle *continues* his exhortation to self-denial and caution in the tenth chapter (as its opening word indicates) from the case of Israel, who doubtless felt, as they stood on the other side of the Red Sea, that all danger was past and their entrance into Canaan was certain; yet, because of yielding to evil lusts, they were destroyed in the wilderness (verses 1-15).

Thus we see how that the principles which were to regulate Joshua and his men were the same as those which are to govern Christians in connection with their spiritual warfare. "The two Testaments, like our two eyes, mutually enlighten and assist each other" (A. Searle). They were to proceed with the utmost confidence in God, yet with entire submission to Him. They were to act faith in His sure promise, and at the same time render implicit obedience to His precept. They were to go forward fully assured that Jehovah had given Ai into their hands, nevertheless they must adhere strictly to the strategy He had specified. So, though told "the God of peace shall bruise Satan under your feet shortly" (Romans xvi, 20), we are definitely bidden to resist him steadfast in the faith (I Peter v, 9). Our confidence is "that He which hath begun a good work in us will finish it" (Phil. i, 6), nevertheless, in the very next chapter we are exhorted "work out your own salvation with fear and trembling" (verse 12). Mighty foes and powerful forces are arrayed in the fight, but the ultimate issue is not in doubt: "forasmuch as ye *know* that your labour is not in vain in the Lord" (I Cor. xv, 58).

Unto the thirty thousand who were to lie in ambush behind the city Joshua had said, "go not very far from the city, but be ye all ready"—awake, alert, prepared promptly to make the most of any favourable opportunity which should be presented to them. Such must be the demeanour and spirit of the soldiers of Jesus Christ: "be sober, be vigilant" precedes the call to resist our adversary "steadfast in the faith" (I Peter v, 8, 9). Then Joshua added, "And I, and all the people that are with me, will approach unto the city: and it shall come to pass when they come out against us, as at the first, that we will flee before them" (verse 5). How different was this policy from their boldly walking around the walls of Jericho! How humiliating to proud flesh to have to turn their backs upon the Canaanites! Surely it is obvious from such a course of procedure that Israel had *missed* God's best! True, the enemy was routed and utterly destroyed, and his city reduced to ashes, yet the method which the Lord here called upon Israel to adopt made it but too plain that they only entered into His second best for them.

"For they will come out after us till we have drawn them from the city; for they will say, They flee before us, as at the first: therefore we will flee before them" (verse 6). Those words expressed a deduction which Joshua drew from what the Lord had said to him in verse 1, for since His announcement that He had given the king of Ai and his people and his city into Israel's hand was accompanied by instructions for them to lay an ambush for the city from the rear (verse 2), it logically followed that the success of such strategy depended upon the army of Ai being lured out of it. Yet in the light of the whole context it is clear that we have here something more than a mental inference, namely *faith's conclusion*. Joshua was warranted in having the utmost confidence in the successful outcome of this plan, because he was employing the means which the Lord had appointed, and was resting on His promise in verse 1, and therefore counted upon His *blessing* the same by drawing forth the forces of the enemy and thus leaving their city unprotected. This has been placed upon record for *our* learning and encouragement, particularly for ministers of the Gospel: if they adhere strictly to the methods and means God has appointed, and they look to Him for His blessing on the same, then whatsoever He has purposed shall assuredly be accomplished thereby.

From the above we see how that we should profit from past experiences, especially those wherein disaster overtook us. Note how in the fifth verse Joshua had declared, "they will come out against us *as at the first."* That knowledge was now put to good use, and by availing himself of the same Joshua turned a previous defeat into a success. As Joshua perceived what course the king of Ai would follow, so Christians are told concerning their great adversary, "we are not ignorant of his devices" (II Cor. ii, 11)—nor are we of the various allurements and snares of the world, and least of all of the treachery and wickedness of our own hearts. Great care needs to be taken and honesty exercised upon this point, for while on the one hand the Word makes it very plain that Satan tempts and assaults the saints, on the other hand we are all too prone to father upon him our own sinful brats. It may not always be easy to decide whether a solicitation unto evil originated with our own lusts or the Devil, yet this is sure, that he can gain no advantage over us without our own consent, and therefore whenever we yield to his seductions the fault and guilt are *ours*, and instead of blaming Satan we must unsparingly condemn ourselves and confess the same to God.

This is obviously the principal practical lesson for us to draw from this detail of verse 6: that our knowledge of the enemy's policy and tactics should be turned to good account, or otherwise we fail to profit from God's exposure of the same in the Word of Truth. "For we are not ignorant of his devices": from what is revealed in Holy Writ, from what we observe by carefully noticing the falls of our fellows, and from what we learn from our personal experience, we are cognizant of his favourite methods, baits, subtleties, and lines of approach; and such knowledge *increases* our responsibility to be ever on our guard, to take measures to counteract the same, and, as Joshua here did, turn them to our advantage. To be forewarned is to be forearmed. and when we know beforehand from which direction the attack upon us is most likely to take place, we can not only forestall the same, but turn it to good account. The favourite devices of Satan are to prejudice unbelievers against the Truth. and so engulf them in the pleasures of the world that they lose sight of the interests of their souls and the inestimable importance of the world to come, to mar the believer's testimony for Christ, and to destroy the peace of Christian assemblies by fomenting a spirit of strife and jealousy.

Ere passing on from this point, let us remind the young preacher that he may gather a wealth of suitable material from the Scriptures themselves should he desire to make a sermon on "Satan's devices." In such case he should. of course, concentrate mainly on those which were employed upon Eve in Genesis iii, and those upon our Lord in Matthew iv. Without furnishing a complete list, he may supplement them from the following. Satan seeks to puff up (I Chron. xxi, 1), to stir up to rebellion against the Divine providences and encourage hard thoughts of God (Job i, 11; ii, 7-9), to produce a spirit of cowardice and induce us to betray Christ, as in the case of Peter (Luke xxii, 31), to consort and bargain with the open enemies of Christ and lead us to betray Him (John xiii 2), to drive to despair and self-destruction (Matt. xxvii, 5), to foster the spirit of covetousness and attempt to impose upon the Holy Spirit (Acts v, 3), to tempt to marital infidelity (I Cor. vii, 5). to undue severity (II Cor. ii, 6-11), to corrupt our minds from the simplicity which is in Christ (II Cor. xi, 2), to pose as an angel of light and transform his ministers as the ministers of righteousness (II Cor. xi, 14, 15), to deny the

Truth (II Tim. ii, 25, 26), to intimidate (I Peter v, 8), to slander God's servants and saints (Rev. xii, 10).

"Then ye shall rise up from the ambush, and seize upon the city: for the Lord your God will deliver it into your hand" (verse 7). Joshua was still addressing the thirty thousand of his men who were to lie in wait behind Ai until the opportune moment arrived for them to fall upon it. That would be when the main force of Israel had made a frontal approach in order to tempt its defenders to come out against them, and on their being thus drawn out into the open Israel would pretend to flee, inducing them to pursue and leave their homes defenceless. "*Then* ye shall rise up," seizing the favourable opportunity without delay. The success of the plan required the full *co-operation* of Joshua's men. Not all of them were appointed to the same stations or allotted the same tasks, but each was required to play his part faithfully. Had those who were to accompany Joshua refused to turn tail when the men of Ai advanced upon them, those who formed the ambush had their long wait in vain; and unless *they* acted promptly in occupying the soldierless city, then Joshua's plan had failed. Hence it was that Joshua had bidden them, "be ye all ready," that they might immediately avail themselves of the great advantage which his ruse offered them.

The spiritual application to us of the above is obvious. The Lord's people are called upon to act together in their spiritual warfare. Not all are assigned positions of equal honour, nor are they given the same tasks to perform, yet they must supplement one another and act in conjunction if the interests of their Master's cause are to be furthered, and if they are not to be humiliated before the common enemy. Unless the pastor has the full co-operation of his church officers, he is placed at a most serious disadvantage, and unless the rank and file of the members co-operate with both, little success will crown their efforts. Nor is it sufficient for one local church to fulfil its spiritual functions: there must be *mutual accord* and concerted action on the part of the several battalions of Christ's soldiers if the enemy is to be defeated. Is it not the deplorable absence of such united effort on the part of God's people that explains the comparative impotency of modern Christianity? While a spirit of jealousy and discord prevails, and factions and schisms so largely obtain, corporeate fellowship is impossible, and where there is no fellowship there can be no united front presented before the powers of darkness, and therefore no Ais captured to the glory of God.

Let us now observe and admire the blessed *balance* of Truth as exemplified in the passage which is now before us. In the last three or four verses which have engaged our attention, it is the human-responsibility side of things which is manifestly in view, the several duties which the different parts of Israel's army were called upon to perform, and perform them they *must* if success was to attend their efforts. Nevertheless, Joshua was most particular in guarding the Lord's glory, and in letting his men know that it was *the Divine blessing* upon their efforts which would make them prosperous. This is clear from his words: "Then ye shall rise up from the ambush, and seize upon the city, for the Lord God will deliver it into your hands." *There* was the Divine-grace side of things! The two things are not contradictory but complementary, as in "the hand of the diligent maketh rich" and "the blessing of the Lord it maketh rich" (Prov. x, 4, 22). Both are consistent: the one reveals the primary cause, the other the subordinate and instrumental one. Neither will be effectual without the other. The sluggard looks for prosperity without diligence; the self-sufficient or practical atheist, from diligence alone:

but the balanced Christian, from the blessing of God in the exercise of diligence. That wise combination keeps him both active and humble, energetic, yet dependent on God. "Except the Lord build the house, they labour in vain that build it" (Psalm cxxvii, 1), yet if they build not there will be no "house"!

Ambush

"And it shall be, when ye have taken the city, that ye shall set the city on fire: according to the commandment of the Lord shall ye do. See I have commanded you" (Joshua viii, 8). In those words Joshua completed the orders given to thirty thousand of his men who were to lie in ambush behind Ai. He had already assigned the position they were to occupy. He had bidden them to be all of them ready to strike the blow while the iron was hot. He had explained the part which the major portion of his army would play, making their own task much easier. He had assured them the Lord God would deliver the city into their hands. And now he informed them how they must make a thorough job of and complete the task allotted them. Only half of it was accomplished when the city was captured: it must be reduced to ashes. This teaches us that there is to be no relaxing in the performance of duty when God has granted our efforts a measure of success, but a continuing to render full obedience unto *all* His commandments. Much easier said than done, declares the reader. True, we reply, but enabling grace is available if we seek it wholeheartedly. When the Lord is pleased to prosper our labours, instead of a complacent slackening on our part, it should serve as a spur and encouragement to attempt yet greater things in His name.

Observe the time-mark again: "*when* ye have taken the city, that ye shall set the city on fire." There was to be no tardiness in executing the orders given them. Each of us should be able, by Divine grace, to aver, "I made haste, and delayed not to keep Thy commandments" (Psalm cxix, 60). When our duty is clear it should be performed with alacrity. The more unpleasant it be, the sooner it is done the better. Least of all can we afford to trifle with sin or indulge our evil lusts: no quarter must be shown our enemies—Ai must be completely destroyed! The revealed will of God is to be complied with without any reservation on our part. As full obedience was here required from Joshua's men, not only to take the city, but to destroy it, nothing less is required from the soldiers of the Lord Jesus. There was a needs be for these men to carry out their part of the plan promptly, for the sight of the smoking houses would not only dismay and panic the king of Ai and his forces (verse 20), but was to serve as a signal to Joshua that his "ambush" had made themselves masters of the city, and therefore that he and his company might turn round and fall upon their pursuers. Thus we see that tardiness on our part acts as a hindrance to our brethren!

"Joshua therefore sent them forth; and they went to lie in ambush, and abode between Bethel and Ai, on the west side of Ai" (viii, 9). It speaks well for the spirit and loyalty of these men that they made no objection to their leader's orders: that in view of the disaster which overtook their brethren on a former occasion (vii, 4, 5), they raised no demur. Nor did they complain at being deprived of their rest through being sent away "by night" (verse 3). It is also to be recognized that the position assigned unto *them* was the real post of danger, for, isolated as they would be from the main body of Israel's army, they ran the imminent hazard (humanly speaking) of being discovered by the enemy, and cut off and annihilated by them. It therefore says much for their courage, too, that they promptly complied with Joshua's orders. From the Divine side of things we may perceive again that when God works He always works at *both* ends of the line: having assured Joshua of the certainty of victory, the Lord also wrought in these men, "both to will and to do of His good pleasure," by inclining them to fulfil their mission faithfully. Incidentally, we may observe the minute accuracy of Scripture, as seen in the topographical harmony between this verse and Genesis xii, 8, Bethel and Ai being in close proximity.

"But Joshua lodged that night among the people" (verse 9). He did not accompany the thirty thousand, for there was other important work to engage his attention. It was his evident duty to be with the principal body of his force, that he might maintain their morale, for only a day or two previously their hearts "had melted and become as water" when tidings of the initial failure reached them (vii, 4, 5). He would therefore seek to inspire them with confidence and courage, and turn their minds from the defeat unto the Lord's promise. Not only must discipline be enforced, but there were duties to be discharged which he could not suitably delegate to others, for he had to supervise all the arrangements which needed to be made for the morrow. Yet there is something more here. There is no reason to believe that Joshua had ever done otherwise: nowhere else is such a statement made. Why, then, this particular emphasis: "Joshua lodged *that* night among the people"? We believe it is because the Holy Spirit looked forward to the Antitype. The Lord Jesus was the homeless Stranger here, and "had not where to lay His head," spending His nights upon the mountain side (John vii, 53, and viii, 1). So far as we are aware, the Gospels record but one exception: the last night but one before His crucifixion Christ lodged with His friends at Bethany (Mark xiv, 3, and cf. xiv, 10 with John xiii, 3)!

"And Joshua rose up early in the morning, and numbered the people, and went up, he and the elders of Israel, before the people to Ai" (verse 10). As there was to be no slackness on the part of those whom he had sent away to ambush Ai, so there was no lazing or giving way to self-indulgence by their commander, but the setting before his men a pattern of alacrity and intenseness. "Those who would maintain their spiritual conflicts must not love their ease" (Matthew Henry). The pastor should set his members an example of earnestness, diligence, and zeal. There was no neglecting of his duty on Joshua's part, no treating casually the approaching engagement. All was done decently and in order, in preparation for the forthcoming march. By his "numbering of the people" we understand his marshalling of the host in their proper ranks, seeing to it that each man was in his correct place under his own tribal standard. Then he *and* the tribal heads took the positions of command. Pastors must have the co-operation and support of their church officers, and they in turn inspire the rank and file with courage and unselfishness. It is to be observed that the "elders" were here accorded a position of *honour,* for those who humble themselves before God (vii, 6) are in due time exalted by Him.

"And all the people, even the people of war that were with him, went up and drew nigh, and came before the city, and pitched on the west side of Ai: now there was a valley between them and Ai" (verse 11). The whole fighting force of Israel, having been duly mustered, left the camp at Gilgal, where the women, children, and other non-combatants would remain until the return of the army. Once again we mark the geographical accord of the statement that they "went *up*" with Genesis xii, 8, where, quite incidentally, we are told that Bethel and Ai were situate in a mountainous region. They "drew nigh and came before the city," which was in fulfilment of the agreement Joshua had entered into with the thirty thousand (verse 5)—foreshadowing the fidelity of the Captain of our salvation to fulfil His engagements and make good His promises. It is blessed to see how the Lord overcame the fears of Joshua's followers (vii, 5) and wrought in them a willingness to accompany their leader —which is to be regarded as a part of His gracious answer to the prayer of vii, 7-12! The statement that "there was a valley between them and Ai" is not without spiritual significance—they lined up their forces on *high* ground, and Christians must regard themselves as "partakers of the *heavenly* calling" (Heb. iii, 1) and conduct themselves accordingly if they would be successful in the good fight of faith.

"And he took about five thousand men and set them to lie in wait between Bethel and Ai on the west side of the city" (verse 12). No hurried assault was made upon the enemy by Joshua, but first an orderly disposition of his forces was arranged. It seems strange that some of the commentators should boggle over this verse and be in doubt as to whether or not the five thousand men here spoken of were drawn from the thirty thousand, or were another company, for to us the narrative makes it quite plain that they were a separate force which was now assigned to another position. Joshua's design therein was evident, for his project served a twofold purpose: it cut off Bethel sending any reinforcements to Ai, and it prevented the forces of Ai escaping in that direction when Joshua turned round and fell upon them. It was what strategists would term a *flanking* movement. Therein we behold the *thoroughness* of Joshua's preparations, notwithstanding the Divine promise which he had received—"I have given into thine hand the king of Ai," etc. (verse 1)—he took every possible precaution and spared no effort on his part to ensure victory. In other words he made the fullest possible use of all the means at his disposal. And we are required to do likewise.

"And when they had set the people, even all the host that was on the north side of the city, and their liers in wait on the west of the city, Joshua went that night into the midst of the valley" (verse 13). After their uphill march from Gilgal, Joshua decided that his forces should remain stationary until the morning—another illustration of the important principle. "he that believeth shall not make haste." But though he had risen up early that morning there was no taking of his ease by Joshua that night. No furloughs are granted the soldiers of Jesus Christ, for their enemies take none. Our spiritual warfare calls for incessant alertness. How Joshua spent that night we are not told. Some think it was to make a reconnaissance—to ascertain the lay of the land, its roads, etc.—but that was hardly likely by night. Others suppose he spent the time in prayer, asking God's blessing on the forthcoming fight, yet advance no reason why he should leave the camp in order to do so. In any case it was a bold act on his part to venture alone so near unto Ai—an act in accord with the Lord's words to him in i, 9. Turning from the type to the Antitype, we have here what confirms our remarks on verse 9. Our Lord's last night before the great conflict was spent alone in "the valley" of *humiliation*—from Gethsemane to Pilate's judgment hall!

"And it came to pass, when the king of Ai saw it, that they hasted and rose up early, and the men of the city went out against Israel to battle, he and all his people, at a time appointed, before the plain; but he wist not that there were liers in ambush against him behind the city" (verse 14). From the opening words of this verse it seems clear that whatever Joshua had done that night in the valley it was now *visible* to those in Ai as soon as day broke, and that it at once attracted their attention: something which appears to have constituted a challenge to them—reminding us again of our Lord, who so far from hiding from His enemies boldly "went forth" to meet those who had come to apprehend Him (John xviii, 4). Their "rising up early" indicates their bloodthirstiness and eagerness for the fray, doubting not that an easy conquest would be theirs; possibly they thought to spring a surprise upon Israel by a dawn attack. Alas, how often *are we* surprised and overcome through failure to be constantly upon our guard. It is while Christ's servants "sleep" that the enemy sows his tares (Matt. xiii, 25). There is some difficulty in determining the meaning of "went out against Israel to battle . . at a time appointed": possibly it signifies the same hour as when they were successful against Israel on a former occasion (vii, 5), deeming it a "lucky" one.

"But he wist not that there were liers in ambush against him behind the city." That appears quite a commonplace statement, yet in reality it is far otherwise. The success of Israel's strategy depended upon their men in ambush being undetected, and that in turn depended upon the secret operations of God upon and within the king of Ai. It seems well-nigh impossible that no less than thirty thousand should remain concealed within so short a distance of the city, and not merely for a few minutes, but for forty-eight hours. It was a *miracle*, as truly so as the sun's remaining stationary at the command of Joshua—the tenth chapter. It was due to the power of Jehovah, who prevented the king of Ai from sending out scouts and discovering the hostile force in his rear. "The king's heart is in the hand of the Lord as the rivers of water: He turneth it whithersoever He will" (Prov. xxi, 1)—sometimes to act wisely, at others foolishly; sometimes to deal kindly with His people (Ezra vi, 22), at others to hate them, as in the case of Pharaoh. What is before us in our present passage supplies a striking illustration of the dominion of God over all and His full control of the wicked, preventing this heathen monarch from taking the most elementary precautions for the safeguarding of his city and people.

What has just been pointed out is far too little attended unto today even by the people of God, that the almighty Governor of the world exerts a *restraining influence* upon the wicked, and that for the good of His people. Yet Scripture records many specific examples of the same. Thus when Abraham sojourned in Gerah, and from fear denied that Sarah was his wife, her honour was (humanly speaking) placed in the utmost jeopardy, for the king of that place sent and "took her," yet "had not come near her," for, as God said to him, "for I also withheld thee from sinning against Me: therefore suffered I thee not to touch her" (Gen. xx, 1-6). Had not the Lord, secretly but effectually, interposed, Abimelech had grievously wronged Sarah. Ah, my reader, how often hath thy gracious God withheld the wicked from touching thee—burglars from breaking into thy house, etc. Again we say, the restraining operations of the Most High are all too little perceived by us. Another notable instance is that of Balaam. He was hired by the king of Moab to curse Israel, and it is clear from the Divine narrative that he was anxious to do so, that he might earn "the wages of unrighteousness." But the Lord prevented him, so that he had to acknowledge, "How shall I curse whom the Lord hath not cursed. . . . He hath blessed, and I cannot reverse it" (Num. xxiii, 8, 20).

When Jacob was recounting the wrongs he had suffered at the hands of Laban, his father-in-law, who had deceived him and changed his wages ten times, he added. "But God suffered him not to touch me" (Gen. xxxi, 7), and received a further proof thereof in the immediate sequel (verse 29), when the Lord again held Laban back from venting his anger upon him. The brethren of Joseph hated him, and "conspired against him to slay him" (Gen. xxxvii, 18), but Jehovah interposed and thwarted their designs. Nor is this restraining power of God limited to individuals, but is exerted upon whole communities and nations. Thus we are told: "The terror of God was upon the cities that were round about them, and they did not pursue after the sons of Jacob" (Gen. xxxv, 5). Centuries later the Psalmist was moved to make reference to that phenomenon, "When they were but a few men in number; yea, very few, and strangers in it. When they went from one nation to another, from one kingdom to another people, He suffered no man to do them wrong" (Psalm cv, 12-14), bridling their lusts and causing the wolf to dwell with the lamb and the leopard to lie down with the kid. "Neither shall any man desire thy land when thou shalt go up to appear before the Lord thy God thrice in the year" (Exodus xxxiv, 24). When the menfolk were no longer present to defend their farms, God restrained the covetous desires and designs of the surrounding heathen.

We consider that what has been alluded to in the last two paragraphs casts much light upon the incident which is here before us, that it was due to the restraining operations of God that the king of Ai failed to send out scouts in all directions ere he led forth the whole of his army from the city, and left it defenceless. Instead, "they hasted and rose up early, and the men of the city went out against Israel to battle" (verse 14). Infatuated by his previous success, filled with self-confidence, he rushed forward to complete disaster. Thus it was with Pharaoh and his hosts when they pursued the Israelites through the Red Sea and perished therein. Before God destroys the wicked, He first gives them up to a spirit of madness. Should these lines be read by a Christless soul who is yet in his sins, we beg him to pause and heed the solemn warning which is here presented to him. Let not his previous immunity from Divine judgment fill him with a false sense of security: "they are most in danger who are least aware of it" (Matthew Henry). The king of Ai was blind to his own interests—are not *you* the same? He failed to take the most obvious precautions—are not *you* guilty of similar folly: hastening unto eternity and utterly unprepared to meet your God? O "seek ye the Lord while He may be found, call ye upon Him while He is near" (Isaiah lv, 6). "Today if ye will hear His voice, harden not your heart" (Psalm xcv, 7, 8).

"And it came to pass, when the king of Ai saw it, that they hasted and rose up early, and the men of the city went out against Israel to battle, he and all his people, at a time appointed, before the plain; but he wist not that there were liers in ambush against him behind the city" (Joshua viii, 14). In Scripture those words, "it came to pass," are something more than a formal manner of prefacing a narrative or introducing an incident, signifying the accomplishment of the Divine foreordination, that it occurred precisely as God had decreed, for He has predestined the actions of the wicked equally with those of the godly. Exactly what it was that they "saw" we know not, but they failed to investigate it, and, being regulated by their senses rather than by reason, precipitately rushed forward to death. Infatuated by his previous success (vii, 5), unconscious that he was fighting against the Almighty and flinging himself upon the thick bosses of His bucklers (Job xv, 26), the king issued forth to what he confidently believed would be an easy victory, yet only to fulfil God's purpose (Eccles. iii, 1). Upon further reflection, we are now satisfied that that is the meaning of the clause which has puzzled the commentators—" at a time appointed," i.e. of God, for He has fixed the hour of every man's death (Job vii, 1).

" And Joshua and all Israel made as if they were beaten before them, and fled by the way of the wilderness" (viii, 15). They pretended to be filled with terror, and instead of making a firm stand against these Canaanites they gave ground, and probably fled in some disorder toward the wilderness. Yet however distasteful and degrading it was for the main body of Israel to feign themselves cowards, it was necessary for them to do so if their plan was to succeed. In like manner, there are times when some Christians are required to act a humble part, perhaps a humiliating one, if the task which is assigned others of their brethren is to be duly accomplished. All cannot occupy positions of equal honour in the church, any more than can all the servants of a king's household be equal—scullery maids are as essential as lords in waiting. In the days of David there were some who girded on their swords and accompanied him to the battlefield, while there were others who were required to remain behind and guard the provender; but it is blessed to observe that when the spoil was to be divided he gave orders, " as his part is that goeth down to the battle, so shall his part be that tarrieth by the stuff: they shall [take] part alike " (I Samuel xxx, 24).

" God hath set the members every one of them in the body, as it hath pleased Him. . . . And the eye cannot say to the hand, I have no need of thee; nor again the head to the feet, I have no need of you. Nay, much more those members of the body which seem to be more feeble, are necessary. . . . Now ye are the body of Christ, and members in particular" (I Cor. xii, 18, 21, 22, 27). In our remarks upon Joshua viii, 9, we pointed out how admirable was the self-sacrificing, obedient, and courageous spirit displayed by the thirty thousand: how that they murmured not at being deprived of their rest through being sent away " by night," or at the dangerous post assigned them. Equally praiseworthy was the conduct of this force which accompanied Joshua. They might have asked, Is it for *this* that thou hast brought us from Gilgal? Have we had a long uphill march only to turn tail as soon as the enemy advance toward us? Or, Since the Lord has delivered Ai into our hands [verse 1], what need is there for us to play so ignominious a part and cut so sorry a figure before the heathen? Instead, they meekly complied with their orders and loyally supported their leader.

But in that to which we have just called attention we should recognize the secret power of God at work, overcoming their natural scruples and inclining them to co-operate fully with their brethren, and thus fulfil His will. This too should be regarded as a part of His gracious answer to the prayer of Joshua vii, 6-9. How wondrously He acts when we truly humble ourselves before Him and are concerned for the honour of His name! He makes things work smoothly, yea, work together, when He shows Himself strong in our behalf. Yet how often we miss perceiving the same through failing to observe closely His providences and connect the same with our previous cries unto Him for help. For the sake of our more hyper-Calvinistic readers it may be well for us to point out here that there is nothing more " inconsistent " in admiring the virtues of these men of Israel while ascribing the same unto the gracious operations of God than there was in the apostle's telling the Colossians that he " rejoiced " in their orderliness and the " steadfastness of their faith " (ii, 5), when he knew full well that God was the Author of those spiritual fruits. Because there are no official powers or authorities " but of

God," that does not preclude our rendering "honour to whom honour is due" (Romans xiii, 1, 7)!

"And Joshua and all Israel made as if they were beaten before them, and fled by the way of the wilderness." Once again there is something more here than that which is of historical interest, or even of practical instruction for our hearts. Little as it may appear at first glance, yea, utterly incongruous as it may sound, Joshua's conduct on this occasion—when considered in the light of the immediate sequel—plainly and strikingly foreshadowed Him who though He was rich yet for our sakes became poor, that we through His poverty, humiliation and suffering might be rich. "What Joshua did in this strategem is applicable to our Lord Jesus, of whom he was a type. Joshua conquered by yielding, as if he had himself been conquered: so our Lord Jesus, when He bowed His head and gave up the spirit, seemed as if death had triumphed over Him, and as if He and all His interests had been routed and ruined; but in His resurrection He rallied again, and gave the powers of death a total defeat; He broke the serpent's head by suffering him to bruise His heel. A glorious strategem"! (Matthew Henry). How wonderful are the ways of God, who not only set the sun in the heavens, gave to the lamb its characteristics, appointed the fruit-bearing vine to be a figure of Christ, but also shaped Old Testament events so as to prefigure His person and work!

"And all the people that were in Ai were called together to pursue after them: and they pursued after Joshua, and were drawn away from the city" (verse 16). This too was "of the Lord," and it should be marvellous in our eyes. Therein we behold the success which God gave to Joshua's ruse, when his men made a feint as though they were beaten; or rather to his obedient compliance with the orders he had received from the Lord. Not only had the king of Ai gone out with the whole of his military force—sallying forth with the exultant cry : "They flee before us, as at the first" (verse 6)—but when Israel was seen in flight the non-combatant citizens were summoned to join in their pursuit; thereby rendering still easier the task assigned the thirty thousand. It is obvious that without the Divine blessing on this plan such a considerable body of men could no more have remained concealed than could Jacob's device in Genesis xxx, 37-43, have prospered. "See how the prosperity of fools destroys them, and hardens their hearts to their ruin" (Matthew Henry). Because God had used the king of Ai on a former occasion to chastise Israel, he and his people were puffed up with conceit.

Note carefully the precise expression used here by the Holy Spirit: the inhabitants of Ai were "drawn away from the city." Those words set forth another of the secret operations of the Most High in His government of this world. In our last, we called attention to the *restraining* influence which He exerts upon men; here His *impelling* power is seen. To His people He says, "I have loved thee with an everlasting love, therefore with lovingkindness have I *drawn* thee" (Jer. xxxi, 3), yet not with physical force, but a moral suasion which overcomes their native enmity and frees the will from the dominion of sin. "I drew them with cords of a man, with bands of love" (Hosea xi, 4): not by external force, such as is used on brute beasts, but by cogent arguments, tender inducements, constraining motives and obligations, such as are suited to work on the understandings, affections and wills of rational creatures; the same being rendered effectual by the supernatural power and application of the Spirit. Such Divine drawing is absolutely essential in order to the saving of sin's slaves and the freeing of Satan's captives, for as the Lord Jesus so plainly declared, "No man can come to Me except the Father which hath sent Me *draw* him" (John vi, 44)—a truth so repugnant to the proud heart of the natural man, that when Christ uttered it, "From that time many of His disciples went back and walked no more with Him" (John vi, 65, 66).

Not only does the Word of Truth make known this drawing power of God upon His elect, but it reveals Him putting forth the same upon the non-elect, though in their case He presents a very different set of reasons and inducements before their minds. "I will harden Pharaoh's heart that he shall follow after thee" (Exodus xiv, 4)—impelling Egypt's king to' pursue His people unto the Red Sea. So too with the other kings of Canaan: "For it was of the Lord to harden their hearts that they should come against Israel to battle, that He might destroy them utterly" (Joshua xi, 20). Unto Barak Deborah announced that the Lord God of Israel had declared: "I will draw unto thee to the river Kishon Sisera, the captain of Jabin's army, with his chariots and his multitude; and I will deliver him into thine hand" (Judges iv, 7). "I will bring them against My land, that the heathen may know Me" (Ezek. xxxviii, 16) in the power of My fury (verse 18). "I will also gather all nations, and will bring them down into the valley of Jehoshaphat" (Joel iii, 2). So it was with the Aites: the Hebrew word rendered "draw away" in viii, 16, is translated "pluck" in Jeremiah xxxii, 24, "pull out" in Jeremiah xii, 13, "be rooted out" in Job xviii, 14.

"And there was not a man left in Ai or Bethel that went not out after Israel: and they left the city open, and pursued after Israel" (verse 17). Further proof was this that the king of Ai had been given up to a spirit of madness, employing every male at his disposal to pursue Israel, leaving none to guard the city or secure his own retreat in case of emergency. It is hard to conceive a greater piece of folly unless it be that of Pharaoh, who, after witnessing such manifest demonstrations of the power and wrath of Jehovah upon Egypt, should, immediately after the death of all the firstborn, pursue Israel, and then attempt to march through the Red Sea. The one equally with the other was blinded by pride and obstinacy. Yet observe well that those in verses 17 "went out" of their own volition! Thus does Scripture uniformly present together the *two* sides of man's free agency and God's invincible operations, without any philosophical explanation of the "consistency" of the two things. God "draws" irresistibly, yet without the slightest violation upon man's will or the least impairment of his accountability. If we deny either the one or the other, then we flatly repudiate what is clearly revealed in Holy Writ.

What has just been alluded to is certainly profoundly mysterious, yet that is no valid reason why we should reject it, for if we believe only that which we can fully understand our creed will be a very small one. Even our conscious-ness bears witness that we act voluntarily, and the ungodly will themselves, at times, admit that a "higher power" constrained them to follow such and such a course; nor do they feel that they were reduced to "mere machines" in so being. Viewing the contents of verse 17 in connection with the warfare of the saint, we are there shown that the hand of every man of this world is, spiritually speaking, *against him*. Many of them are indeed kind-hearted, generous, and benevolent unto a Christian in temporal things; but (all unconscious to them-selves) they are antagonistic to his *eternal* interests. Their influence is entirely earthly, and never heavenly. What was the attitude of the world toward Christ? Without a single exception, hostile. Pharisees and Sadducees, priests and scribes, politicians and the common people, the Roman soldiers, and even the crucified malefactors, reviled Him, until a miracle of grace transformed one of them into a worshipper. If we were more like Christ we should experience more of the world's enmity and persecution.

"And the Lord said unto Joshua, Stretch out the spear that is in thy hand toward Ai; for I will give it into thine hand. And Joshua stretched out the spear that he had in his hand toward the city" (verse 18). He had waited for a further word from Jehovah before taking this action. As it was at Jericho, so here at Ai: each stage of the process in the capturing and destroying of the city must be ordered by the Lord. Thus it was with Moses in every project in which he engaged. So also with the apostles, teaching us that the servant of Christ must not do anything without His authorization. It is indeed blessed to observe here that Joshua's hand was the *first* one to be outstretched against Ai. Is not the lesson for us therein plain? It is when the antitypical Joshua stretches forth His hand on our behalf that the best time has come for us to act. The need for the Lord to inform Joshua *when* to stretch forth his hand is obvious, for it served as a signal to those in ambush, and *that* required to be precisely timed—when the men of Ai had left the city—so that they might swiftly seize their opportunity.

The Lord did not fail His servant, but at the crucial moment gave him the word of command: "Stretch out the spear that is in thy hand." That action was not only designed as a signal to his men in ambush, but, as verse 26 makes clear, by the same He directed the whole engagement, until complete victory was achieved. Now was drawing near the hour of Joshua's triumph, for he was on the point of leading Israel to conquest, of which his outstretched spear was the symbol. That too was a foreshadowing of our blessed Saviour. It seems evident from verses 22 and 24 that throughout the contest Joshua must have occupied some position of eminence. from which he gave orders to his troops, and therein he was a figure of Christ on high. The last night but one before the fight, lodging among the people (verse 9), as did Christ with His friends at Bethany. The next night alone in "the midst of the valley" (verse 13)—the symbol of deep humiliation (Isaiah xl. 4; Luke i, 52). as our Lord spent His in Gethsemane and the judgment halls of the Jews and Romans. Then fleeing before the foe as if beaten (verse 15), as Christ, in apparent defeat, was put to death by His enemies. Now assured by God of victory (verse 18), as He has promised to make Christ's foes His footstool.

In concluding this article we propose to consider more closely the lines of typical teaching in Joshua viii. In the course of our comments we have indicated some of the practical applications to be made of its contents. and have pointed out the several respects in which Joshua again foreshadowed our Lord. But now we must inquire. What contribution to the particular theme of this book is made by the capturing and destroying of Ai: what are the principal lessons there for us concerning the Christian's warfare? That question is more easily asked than answered. We must acknowledge we have experienced more difficulty here than when pondering what was before us in Joshua iii and vi. But that is to be expected. First, because Israel here was only enjoying God's second best, and where *that* be the case His showing Himself strong on our behalf is curtailed, and acts of folly on our part raise, as it were, a cloud of dust, which prevents our perceiving so clearly the workings of God. Second, because the *human* side of things is more prominent. At first the babe is carried. but the time arrives when it must learn to use its own feet: so with the saint, who has to develop his graces and subdue his lusts.

Both in the crossing of the Jordan and the capturing of Jericho, the Lord did all for Israel, working miracles on their behalf; but in connection with Ai much more was required *from them*. Thus it is in the spiritual life. Regeneration is a miracle of grace, wherein we were entirely passive; but in order to our growth in grace and spiritual progress, all our faculties have to be called into action. The "lambs" Christ carries in His bosom (Isaiah xl, 11), but the "sheep" are required to follow Him (John x, 27). Immediately after conversion the power of God is so put forth that usually the believer experiences a season of peace from the assaults of Satan and the stirrings of his inward corruptions. But soon he becomes conscious of the serpent's enmity and is made painfully aware of the powerful enemies within his own heart; and the fight of faith gradually becomes fiercer, and he meets with some humiliating falls in the contest. Yet we can discern the wisdom of God therein, promoting our good. If He continued to do all for us without our active concurrence, and if nothing but victory was our uniform experience, we should quickly become proud and self-sufficient—as was the case with Israel after Jericho! But under Divine chastenings, and through His instructions, we are taught how to turn former defeats into successes—by using the means appointed and counting upon God's blessing the same.

Worship in Victory

"And the king of Ai he hanged on a tree until eventide. And as soon as the sun was down, Joshua commanded that they should take his carcase down from the tree, and cast it at the entering of the gate of the city, and raise there a great heap of stones, that remaineth unto this day. Then Joshua built an altar unto the Lord God of Israel in mount Ebal . . . an altar of whole stones" (Joshua viii, 29-31). It can scarcely be doubted that there is a designed contrast between those two events. In the former we see the ignominy of Ai's king, here we behold the worship of the King of kings. The one marked the grave of a malefactor, the other recognized the claims of the Holy One. Great indeed is the contrast between the dead body *under* the stones and the accepted sacrifice *upon* the altar of stones. That bore witness to the carrying out of the curse of the Law, on this was inscribed its precepts. The former was at "the gate" of Ai (the place of judgment—Amos v, 10), the latter was in a mount. That was intended as a solemn warning unto evil-doers, this was for the instruction of those who desired to do well.

"*Then* Joshua built an altar unto the Lord God of Israel in mount Ebal." Everything connected with the incident prefaced by that statement is of deep importance and interest, calling for our closest attention. A further word upon the Spirit's time-mark. This act of worship followed immediately upon the destruction of Ai and all its inhabitants. We should naturally expect that after Israel's capturing of Jericho and Ai they had continued to advance, proceeding to the further occupying of Canaan. Now that they had made themselves masters of its frontier towns, it would appear the only sound policy to forge ahead while their terror was upon the foe, and penetrate into the very heart of his country. Instead, a long and difficult journey was taken unto mount Ebal, that a solemn religious ordinance might be observed. In the midst of their military campaign a lengthy pause was made in order that Jehovah might be honoured. "The camp of Israel was drawn out into the land not to engage the enemy but to offer sacrifice, to hear the Law read, and to say Amen to the blessings and curses. It is a remarkable instance of the zeal of Israel for the service of God and for His glory" (Matthew Henry).

The offering of burnt offerings and peace offerings to Jehovah upon this occasion was an acknowledgment of His blessing upon their arms, and a rejoicing before Him in the successes which His power and goodness had vouchsafed them. At Rephidim Israel had been taught that victory over Amalek was obtained by the hands of Moses being lifted up toward the throne of heaven, and as a monument thereto he erected an altar, naming it " Jehovah-nissi," which signifies "the Lord my banner" (Exodus xvii, 15). So here, as the captain of their salvation, Joshua had not only "stretched out the spear that he had in his hand" (viii, 18), but had kept it raised and extended until victory was complete (verse 26), and now he expressed his gratitude by erecting this altar to mark the same. That is clearly evident from the opening "then" of verse 30. Yet his act on this occasion imported something more. As yet Israel had conquered but a very small section of Canaan, and here they journeyed upwards of another hundred miles, and upon reaching mount Ebal Joshua built this altar. It was therefore a remarkable act of *faith,* a claiming of the whole land for the Lord—men only *build* on land which is their own! Thus, instead of waiting until Israel's victory was complete, Joshua anticipated the same in a sure and certain hope!

This is the first time that any "altar" is mentioned in the book of Joshua, and there are some very striking parallels between it and the one mentioned in Exodus xx, 24. Both were erected upon a mount; both of them at the express command of the Lord, and not merely by the spiritual impulses and promptings of Moses and Joshua. Both of them were designed to magnify the Divine Law, and to exemplify the grand fact that grace reigns through righteousness. On both of them were sacrificed burnt offerings and peace offerings (Exodus xxiv, 5). The one was shortly after Israel's supernatural exodus from the house of bondage and crossing of the Red Sea, the other soon after their miraculous crossing of the Jordan and entrance into the promised land. In the course of these articles we have frequently emphasized the fact that in his actions Joshua (as one of the outstanding types of Christ) was constantly regulated by the written Word of God. That had again received illustration in viii, 29, for the taking down of the carcase of the king of Ai was required in Deuteronomy xxi, 23. Equally so was that principle exemplified here in viii, 30, for the building of this altar was in compliance with the injunctions given through Moses.

In the book of Deuteronomy many instructions were given the children of Israel near the close of their sojourn in the wilderness as to how they must conduct themselves upon their entrance into the land of promise. Therein we find that which explains the incident recorded in the closing verses of Joshua viii. It had been said unto them, " Therefore it shall be when ye be gone over Jordan, that ye shall set up these stones, which I command you this day, in mount Ebal; and thou shalt plaister them with plaister. And there shalt thou build an altar unto the Lord thy God, an altar of stones: thou shalt not lift up any iron tool upon them. Thou shalt build the altar of the Lord thy God of whole stones: and thou shalt offer burnt offerings thereon unto the Lord thy God; and thou shalt offer peace offerings, and shalt eat there, and rejoice before the Lord thy God. . . . These shall stand upon mount Gerizim to bless the people . . . and these shall stand upon mount Ebal to curse" (Deut. xxvii, 4-7, 12, 13).

The "altar" was *the meeting-place* between God and men. In its construction it was of the most simple and unpretending character, no place being allowed for the exercise of human art. This may appear strange when we remember that both rich materials and elaborate skill *were* expended upon the tabernacle and its internal furnishings—the outer-court vessels alone excepted. But when we call to mind the purpose of the altar and its leading object, the difficulty vanishes, and the propriety of its extreme plainness at once appears. It was there the Holy One and the fallen creature transacted concerning sin and salvation: that the alien might be reconciled, the guilty pardoned, the cleansed one have fellowship with the Lord. Therefore did He appoint that man should there be reminded of his utter unworthiness and impotency as he came before the One who deigned to meet with him. His curse rested on the ground for man's sake (Gen. iii, 15), and by no effort of his can man remove it. For the altar to be made of ornamented plates of costly metal would have misrepresented the object for which it was designed, and disposed man to forget his vile condition. So, in the general direction for the formation of altars, God ordained it should be a rude mound of earth, or of unpolished stones (Exodus xx, 24, 25; and cf. I Kings xviii, 31, 32).

The altar, then, must be of *God's* workmanship, unbeautified by man's skill, so that he could not glory in his own production. That chosen meeting place of God with man as a sinner must be such as would convey the impression of a direct contact between the God of heaven and the earth which He had made—on a "mount," but the altar naked, simple, unadorned; thereby emphasizing His own condescension and the poverty of the sinner. The leading idea designed to be set forth by the materials of the altar was confirmed by its *name*. Departing from the common usage of antiquity, Scripture employs a term which vividly enunciates both the humbling element on man's side and the grace on God's. That name is *misbeach*, which means *place of slaughter*, for it was thither the victim was brought and slain. And thus, from the beginning, God taught His people the solemn fact that there could be no communion between Himself and fallen creatures save by the shedding of blood; that the sentence of death must be executed upon the guilty. Later, when a stationary altar was appointed for the sanctuary, it was ordered to be made not of gold and silver, but of wood overlaid with brass.

"Then Joshua built an altar unto the Lord God of Israel in mount Ebal, as Moses the servant of the Lord commanded the children of Israel. As it is written in the book of the Law of Moses: an altar of whole stones over which no man hath lifted any iron. And they offered thereon burnt offerings unto the Lord and sacrificed peace offerings" (viii, 30, 31). In addition to what has been said above, it should be pointed out that the "altar" prefigured our Lord Jesus Christ. He is the sole meeting place between the thrice holy God and guilty sinners. "Neither is there salvation in any other: for there is none other name given among men whereby we must be saved" (Acts iv, 12). None comes unto the Father but by Him. They who look to the merits of the apostles or the mediation of Mary to give them access to God, and their prayers and works acceptance before Him, are miserably deluded; and it is but charity to tell them so. Christ Himself is at once the antitypical Altar, Sacrifice for sin, and acceptable Offerer. While those three things may be distinguished, both in shadow and substance, they must not be separated, for they all meet in Him. As it is "the altar that sanctifieth the gift" (Matt. xxiii, 19), so the dignity of Christ's person gives infinite value to His offering. Furthermore, He is our "Altar" (Heb. xiii, 10) to whom we bring our sacrifices of praise (Heb. xiii, 15), and presents the same, perfumed by His merits, unto God (Rev. viii, 3, 4).

The pile of stones on mount Ebal was not gathered to be thrown in judgment *at* sinners, but for an altar on which was to be offered a sacrifice *for* sinners. Very express was the prohibition concerning the stones of the altar: "Thou shalt not lift up any iron tool upon them. Thou shalt build the altar of the Lord thy God of whole stones." Those unpolished but whole stones set forth both the humiliation and perfection of the Saviour, as He appeared respectively to men and to God. To the natural eyes of Israel He possessed "no form nor comeliness," and when they saw Him, they perceived no beauty in Him that they should desire Him. But in the sight of the Father He was "a precious corner-stone," and in Him He delighted. Nothing was to be hewn off the life of Christ, for it was perfect. None of His actions needed any modification. Yea, as Exodus xx, 25, declared, "If thou lift up thy tool upon it, thou hast *polluted it.*" Not a single deed of Christ's could be bettered, and if one had been missing from His entire life the whole had been spoilt. Much the same thing was borne witness to here as was symbolically shadowed forth in our Lord's coat, which was "*without seam,* woven from the top throughout" (John xix, 23).

More noteworthy than either the time when the altar was erected or the materials of which it was composed was the place where it was set up, namely mount Ebal. There were two mountains to which Israel were now brought—Gerizim and Ebal—and we should naturally have expected to find the altar on the former, for it was there the blessings of the Law upon the obedient were pronounced (Deut. xi, 29), whereas it was on the latter that its curses were published. But "as for God, His way is perfect" (II Samuel xxii, 31), and everything was ordered here so as to foreshadow the most terrible yet most blessed event of all history. The vicarious offering sacrificed on Ebal prefigured the Head of the Church entering the place of the curse, yea, being made a curse for His members. So that what we have here is very similar to —and equally unexpected and precious as—the altar on mount Sinai (Exodus xxiv, 4) (see our "Glorious Sinai" article in the April issue). A reference to Deuteronomy xxvii, 4-7, shows the analogy between the two is yet more complete: the Lord gave orders that after the offering of sacrifice they should "*eat there* [of the peace offering] and *rejoice* before the Lord thy God," as their fathers before them had done on Sinai (Exodus xxiv, 11). How remarkably did Divine grace shine forth there! Who had thought of *rejoicing* on the mount of the curse!

"And he wrote there upon the stones a copy of the law of Moses, which he wrote in the presence of the children of Israel" (verse 32). That also was in obedience to Deuteronomy xxvii, 8, and was equally remarkable. That altar was built as a monument of the Divine mercy to Israel's victories, yet it was not an account of their triumphs but a copy of the Ten Commandments that was inscribed upon it! The grand practical lesson for us therein is that the best way to remember God's mercies is not to forget His Law. As Gurnall well said, "God counts those mercies forgotten which are not written in legible characters in our lives." For Israel, that writing of the Decalogue upon the stones of the altar was a reminder to them that they were taking possession of Canaan not only on the ground of the promise to Abraham but also according to the terms of that Law which they solemnly covenanted themselves to keep (Deut. xi, 29-32). The two things must not be separated: in presenting their offerings upon the altar, they spoke to God; in the writing of the Law upon its stones, He spoke to them, enforcing His holy claims upon them. Christ died to deliver His people from the penalty of the Law, but not from obedience to its precepts.

On Deuteronomy xxvii, 8, John Gill rightly said, "The Law being written on stones denotes *the duration* of it, which continued not only during the times of the Old Testament dispensation, and to the times of John, and had its fulfilment in Christ, but *still continues*; for though Christ has redeemed His people from the curse and condemnation of it, yet it is in His hands as a rule of direction to them, as to their walk and conversation. Nor is it made void by any doctrine of the Gospel, and nothing more strongly enforces obedience to it than the Gospel. The moral law is immutable, invariable, and eternal in its nature, and it is in the matter of it." Alas, that so many of Mr. Gill's admirers have departed so far from his teaching thereon. Thomas Scott also said, "We must rest our hope on the atonement of the great Redeemer, and keep the holy Law of God continually before us as the rule of our grateful obedience." We only deceive ourselves if we suppose that our praise unto God is sincere for the gift of His Son, unless we also delight in His Law and serve the same (Romans vii, 22, 25). God will not be bribed by the worship of rebels (see I Samuel xv, 22; Psalm cvi, 12, 13).

Ere giving a brief exposition of the verses that follow, let us further admire the striking and blessed prefiguration of Christ in what has been before us. No less than three times has the Holy Spirit recorded the Divine prohibition that the altar must be built of unhewn and unadorned stones—in Exodus xx, 25; Deuteronomy xxvii, 5; Joshua viii, 31—so carefully did He guard the glory of Christ. In sharp contrast with us, who, though "living stones," yet need much shaping, there were no rough or sharp edges in the character of Christ; no polishing of His life was required to render it well pleasing to the Father, So much did He resent anything which *marred* a type that when the sons of Aaron offered "strange fire" upon the altar they were immediately consumed by fire from heaven (Lev. x), and when the ark was set upon a cart instead of on the shoulders of the priests, judgment fell upon Uzzah (II Samuel vi). God was exceedingly jealous of the honour of His beloved Son, bidding Moses, again and again, to make all things in the tabernacle according to "the pattern" which He showed him (Exodus xxv, 9, etc.), for everything therein pointed to, and set forth the person and perfections of the Mediator. The writing of the Law on the stones of the altar tells of Christ's sustaining the honour of the Law, that in Him alone is it "established" (Romans iii, 31).

"And all Israel, and their elders, and officers, and their judges, stood on this side of the ark and on that side before the priests the Levites, which bare the ark of the covenant of the Lord; as well the stranger, as he that was born among them: half of them over against mount Ebal; as Moses the servant of the Lord had commanded before, that they should bless the people of Israel" (verse 33). A most solemn and auspicious assembly was this, when the whole nation, with their responsible heads, were gathered before the Lord. The "ark *of the covenant*"—mentioned here for the last time in Joshua—was brought out of the tabernacle on this momentous occasion. The original tables of the Law were preserved therein, and now its statutes had been written on the stones of the altar. That which here took place is to be regarded as a solemn ratification by the *new generation* of Israel of the covenant entered into by their fathers at Sinai. The sanctions of the Law were now proclaimed in the hearing of the whole congregation, and by their repeated "Amen" (Deut. xxii, 15, 16, etc.) all Israel consented to the terms of the covenant. The mention of "the stranger" here anticipated the gathering of the Gentiles into the Church.

It must have been an exceedingly impressive sight as the entire congregation of Israel assembled in the valley between those two mountains. There had been nothing like it since their solemn gathering on Sinai forty years previously: in fact what took place here was virtually a repetition of what had occurred there—Israel solemnly *covenanting* to keep God's Law. As the former had been preceded by wondrous displays of God's grace and power on their behalf, so it had been here; and thus, in each instance, submission and obedience to Him was to be an expression of their love to Him and gratitude for His favours. Such is precisely the place which the Law is to have with the Christian. Because the Lord Jesus has borne his sins and reconciled him to God, he is to express his thankfulness by receiving God's Law at His hand (I Cor. ix, 21) and thereby respond to His injunction: If ye love Me, keep My commandments " (John xiv, 15).

The scene which is set before us in the closing verses of Joshua viii is equalled only by that which is exhibited in Exodus xxiv. The events described therein are parallel in every way, the latter being explained by the former. In each there is a public assembling of the whole congregation of Israel before the Lord. In each a federal engagement is solemnly entered into. Each was transacted upon a mount, where an altar was erected, the Divine Law prominently honoured, and the people ate before Jehovah. The difference between them is that in the former it was the first generation of Israel which had recently emerged from Egypt that was concerned; while in the latter it was the first generation of those who had shortly before entered Canaan. The claims of Jehovah were now made known unto this new generation in a striking and impressive manner, and they were required to aver their recognition of those claims and affirm subjection to the same. First an altar had been erected and sacrifices offered thereon. Most appropriately had "the peace offering" a place, for a portion of it was for the Lord and a portion of it was eaten by the offerer (Lev. vii, 32, 34), for a covenant is a *mutual* engagement between two parties, and thus the Lord and His people here communed together.

Upon the stones of that altar the Decalogue was written. *Typically*, that set forth the fact that the Law had been magnified by Christ (Isaiah xlii, 21). In His teaching He had fully maintained its authority (Matt. v, 17), in His life He rendered perfect obedience to it, and in His death He endured its awful penalty. *Practically*, we are there taught that the redeemed are to receive the Law from the Redeemer. Christ did not keep the Law for His people in order that they might be freed from its holy requirements, but to honour God therein and leave them an example that they should follow His steps. In order thereto, He has not only brought them under the deepest possible obligations of gratitude unto Himself, bidding them to express their love unto Him by keeping His commandments, but has also procured for them the priceless gift of the Holy Spirit, who puts His laws into their hearts and writes them upon their minds (Heb. x, 16): that is, implanting a *love* for them, and *impressing* them with their importance, authority, and spirituality. And therefore it is that the truly regenerate delight in the Law of God after the inward man, and with their minds serve the same (Romans vii, 22, 25).

It is to be duly noted that in the Holy Spirit's description of the company convened on that auspicious occasion express mention is made of "as well *the stranger* as he that was born among them" (Joshua viii, 33), which, as previously pointed out, anticipated the time when the Gentiles would also be brought into the congregation of the Lord. The various references made to "the stranger" in the law of Moses have not received anything like the attention they should by Christian commentators. Provision was made for "the stranger," upon his circumcision, to partake of the passover feast; yea, it was enacted: "One law shall be to him that is homeborn, and unto the stranger that sojourneth among you" (Exodus xii, 48, 49); yea, even the cities of refuge were available to him equally with the Israelite (Joshua xx, 9)! Commandment was given unto Israel that "the stranger that dwelleth with you shall be unto you as one born among you, and thou shalt love him as thyself" (Lev. xix, 34). As he shared Israel's privileges, so he had to share their obligations also, by entering into covenant with God (Deut. xxix, 11, 12), and therefore if he blasphemed the name of the Lord the same penalty was inflicted upon him as upon a guilty Hebrew (Lev. xxiv, 16).

"And afterwards he read all the words of the Law: the blessings and cursings, according to all that is written in the book of the Law. There was not a word of all that Moses commanded, which Joshua read not before all the congregation of Israel, with the women, and the little ones, and *the strangers* that were conversant among them" (Joshua viii, 34, 35). Thus the entire assembly came under the sound of the just requirements of their Benefactor and Governor. As Deuteronomy xxvii informs us, as each of the solemn curses of the Law was uttered by the Levites "with a loud voice" (not an apologetic whisper!), it was required that "all the people should answer and say, *Amen*" (verses. 14, 15), thereby solemnly concurring therewith. As Matthew Henry pointed out, "It was (1) a profession of their faith in the truth of them. (2) An acknowledgment of the equity of them. (3) An imprecation upon themselves as strongly obliged them to have nothing to do with those evil practices upon which the curse was here entailed." What an example was this occasion of the importance of the public reading of lengthy sections of God's Word, and that its most unpalatable portions must not be omitted! The reading of the Law to "the strangers" again intimates that *the Gentiles* are under it. No further mention of "the ark" is found in Joshua, for the covenant had now been ratified by the second generation of Israel.

Israel had marched into Canaan led by the written Law of God (Joshua iii, 11-17), for the ark of the covenant was the Divinely appointed chest in which were deposited and preserved the tables on which the Lord's own finger had inscribed that Law which Israel had covenanted to keep. The same Law had been borne around the walls of Jericho (vi, 4), being the minister of vengeance unto the idolatrous Canaanites. That same Law had now been written on the stones of the altar on Ebal (viii, 32), thus becoming *the Law of the Land*. Was not this God's very object in enabling Israel to conquer Canaan: that He should have not only a people in obedience to Him, but a country in which the blessedness of their obedience should be exhibited before the surrounding nations? Beyond question, for Moses declared, "I have taught you statutes and judgments, even as the Lord my God commanded me, that ye should do so in the land whither ye go to possess it. Keep therefore and do them; for this is your wisdom and your understanding *in the sight of the nations*, which shall hear all these statutes, and say, Surely this great nation is a wise and understanding people" (Deut. iv, 5, 6; and cf. I Kings x, 8, 9). As Jehovah reminded their descendants centuries later, "Ye are My witnesses" (Isaiah xliii, 10; and cf. Mal. iii, 12).

Chapter 12

HONOR AMIDST DECEPTION

JOSHUA 9:1-27

Enemy Reactions

"And it came to pass, when all the kings which were on this side Jordan, in the hills, and in the valleys, and in all the coasts of the great sea over against Lebanon, the Hittite, and the Amorite, the Canaanite, the Perizzite, the Hivite, and the Jebusite, heard thereof; that they gathered themselves together to fight with Joshua and with Israel, with one accord" (ix, 1, 2). At first glance there appears little pertinency or propriety in mentioning this detail immediately after what was described in the closing verses of chapter viii. But careful readers will observe that this passage begins with the word "and," and those who have followed us through the previous articles of this series should know by now what use to make of it. It calls for thoughtful attention to what immediately precedes, so that the force of the connection may be the better perceived by us. And that not merely so as to fix in our minds the order of events, but more especially that we may ascertain the spiritual lessons which are pointed thereby. The book of Joshua contains very much more than a mere historical record of Israel's conquest and occupation of the land of Canaan, namely a shadowing forth of that spiritual warfare unto which Christians are called.

Believers in Christ are not only "witnesses" unto Him (Acts i, 8)—showing forth His praises, reflecting the moral perfections of His character, disciples, "they which follow the Lamb whithersoever He goeth" (Rev. xiv, 4)—but they are also soldiers of Jesus Christ (II Tim. ii, 3), and as such it is especially to the book of Joshua that they should turn for instruction, inspiration, warning, and encouragement. What then are the lessons we should draw from that which is recorded in ix, 1, 2? Two, according as we recognize the twofold link between those verses and their context—with that which immediately precedes and with what is rather more remote. In other words, this coming together of the kings of Canaan, and their agreeing to join forces in making a mass attack upon Israel, is to be regarded first as it is related to that which has just been before us in the closing verses of chapter viii, namely the magnification of the Decalogue on mount Ebal and the covenant which was made by the new generation of Israel with Jehovah; and then with the whole of chapters vi-viii, where the overthrow of Jericho and Ai is narrated. The force of the opening "and" is borne out by the "heard thereof" at the close of verse 1. It is *the enemy's* reaction to those events which is here in view.

Brief though their record be, those two verses present to our notice that which is of deep importance, and something which should be particularly heeded by ministers who desire to be faithful to their calling. The Holy Spirit's mention of this federating of Canaan's kings to fight against Joshua and Israel, immediately after describing what had taken place on the mountains of

234

Ebal and Gerizim, is obviously designed to supply us with a typical illustration and solemn exemplification of man's hostility to the Law of God. No sooner did it reach the ears of these kings that Joshua had built an altar on Ebal and had inscribed on its stones the Divine Decalogue—which was henceforth to be the Law of the Land—than they made common cause against God's people and determined to use force, as the "heard thereof" (verse 1) plainly intimates. To acknowledge the rights and authority of the Most High, and submit themselves unto His revealed will, is something which the unregenerate both resent and oppose. They desire to be lords of themselves and are resolved to go their own way. The language expressed by the actions of all of them, and by the mouths of many, is that of the self-willed and arrogant Pharaoh: "Who is the Lord that I should obey His voice?" (Exodus v, 2). They are determined to please themselves.

Here is the very essence of human depravity. Sin is a revolt against God, a refusing to be in subjection to Him. Sin is not only a determining to follow our own inclinations, but it is a fighting against our Maker and Governor. The carnal mind is enmity against God. Unspeakably solemn is that declaration, and one which is most repugnant to human susceptibilit es. Nevertheless, it is a fact which cannot be gainsaid. Proof thereof is furnished in the clause immediately following: "for it [the mind of the natural man] is not subject to the Law of God; neither indeed can be" (Romans viii, 7). Nothing more plainly evinces the inveterate hostility of the unregenerate unto God than their insubordination and opposition against the Divine Law. Few indeed will openly *admit* that they hate God, and fewer still are *aware* of that awful fact, for sin is very deceitful (Heb. iii, 13), and blinds the judgment (Eph. iv, 18). Nowhere is that more clearly demonstrated than throughout the entire realm of idolatry. If men were pleased with the true God, they would not have manufactured so many false ones. They desire a God and a system of religion which are suited to their depraved inclinations. Millions who bow not before an image of wood or stone nevertheless believe in a God which their own sentiments and imaginations have devised, and against *him* (or it) they have no enmity!

But let the true and living God be apprehended as His character is set forth in the Scriptures, and that enmity will soon be more evident. Let Him be known as the Divine Potentate who shapes one vessel unto honour and another unto dishonour, entirely as He pleases; as the ineffably Holy One who cannot look on evil, and hates all workers of iniquity; and as the righteous Judge of all, who will by no means clear the guilty; and the fallen creature's hatred of such a One will appear in its true colours. Let Him give to such creatures His Law, and require unqualified obedience thereto, and they at once rebel. If God would forgo His sovereign rights, their opposition would be subdued; if He would lay aside His sceptre men would cease fighting against Him. But because He declines to do so, the will of the creature is opposed to the will of the Creator, and he refuses subjection to His throne. Conclusive proof that the sinner's nature is diametrically the opposite of God's is seen in his deadly opposition to the Divine government. The moral law is both a revelation of its Author's character and an expression of His will, and man's repudiation of it exhibits the contrariety of sin to holiness.

What has just been pointed out was unmistakably and most solemnly demonstrated when the Lawgiver became incarnate and dwelt here upon earth, for the ill will of religious and irreligious alike was active against Him. Not only was He despised and rejected by men, but as He plainly declared "they hated Me without a cause" (John xv, 25). Nor did they make any attempt to cloak their malice. While He healed the sick and provided the multitude with loaves and fishes, their hostility was held in abeyance; but when He pressed upon them the claims of His lordship, defined the terms of discipleship, and made known the character and requirements of His kingdom, their resentment soon flared up. Not only did He come unto His own and "His own received Him not," but "His citizens hated Him and sent a message after Him saying, "We will not have this One to reign over us" (Luke xix, 14). Let it not be forgotten that it was as "*the King* of the Jews" Christ was crucified! "The kings of the earth set themselves, and the rulers take counsel together, against Jehovah and against His Christ, saying, Let us break their bands asunder and cast away their cords from us" (Psalm ii, 2, 3); and cf. Acts iv, 25-27)—chafing at the Divine Law, refusing subjection to the Divine authority.

Thus, in the gathering of the kings of Canaan "to fight with Joshua and with Israel" immediately after the promulgation of the Divine Law upon the mountains of Ebal and Gerizim, we have both a solemn adumbration of what took place in the hours immediately preceding our Lord's crucifixion, and an illustration of man's opposition to the Law. Up to this point the Canaanites had been on the defensive, but in Joshua ix, 1, 2, we see them preparing to take the offensive, and make a united attack on God's people. The kings there mentioned were of varied nationalities and interests, and occupied widely scattered territories, but here we behold them sinking their differences and federating together "with one accord"! Just as the priests and scribes, the Pharisees and Sadducees united in opposing the incarnate Lawgiver. And just as it is today, for both "dispensational" Arminians and "antinomian" Calvinists make common cause in repudiating the Decalogue as the Christian's rule of life. So will every true servant of Christ discover. Let him give to the Law that place in his ministry which it has in the Scriptures, let him be faithful in discharging his Divine commission (and remember "all the counsel of God" includes very much more than what are termed "the doctrines of grace"!), and press upon unbelievers and believers the claims of Christ's kingship, and the strictness and spirituality of the Decalogue, and he too will be despised and reviled.

In our last we pointed out that the word "And" at the beginning of Joshua ix has a double force: intimating that what now follows is to be linked with, first, what is recorded in the closing verses of Joshua 8, namely the magnification of the Divine Decalogue on mount Ebal and the renewing of the Mosaic covenant by this new generation of Israel; and second, with the whole of chapters vi-viii, which narrate their conquests, under God, of Jericho and Ai. In other words, the contents of Joshua ix make known to us the enemy's reactions to those incidents. As the events were twofold, so were his reactions. First, we are informed that as soon as the kings of Canaan "heard thereof" they "with one accord" agreed to unite themselves together "to fight with Joshua and with Israel." Up to this point they had acted on the defensive, but now they saw that *their own* interests were threatened, they determined to make a mass attack upon Israel. "The varied expressions here used [in ix, 1] include the inhabitants of the land to the utmost western and northern borders" (T. Scott). It was not an immediate attack that was planned, but a consulting together how best to put a stop to Israel's progress and secure their own territories.

Verily, "there is nothing new under the sun." A "League of Nations" or federating together of different peoples to "pool" their resources is no modern invention, but as old as human history. Here was a banding together of rival kings to make common cause in opposing the people of God. They entered into an agreement "at top level" to support and assist each other, and ultimately to assail Israel—which they did, as Joshua xi, 1-5 shows. For the time being they were willing to sink their individual differences and combine together. Nor was this the first time that such a thing had happened. As far back as Abraham we are told that "It came to pass in the days of Amraphel king of Shinar, Arioch king of Ellasar, Chedorlaomer king of Elam, and Tidal king of nations; that these made war with Bera king of Sodom and with Birsha king of Gomorrah, Shinab king of Admah, and Shemeber king of Zeboiim, and the king of Bela, which is Zoar. All these were joined together in the vale of Siddim, which is the salt sea" (Gen. xiv, 1-3), which may well be designated "the Western bloc of nations' against the "Eastern power and its satellites." At a later date we find still another "consulting together with one consent" of a number of nations, and a federating of themselves against Israel (see Psalm lxxxiii, 4-8).

That which is recorded in Joshua ix, 1, 2, should be of real practical value unto those who are engaged in fighting the good fight of faith. There is real wisdom in that old adage, "To be forewarned is to be forearmed." It is often a very real help to have reliable information of what effects a certain action produces upon the foe. Here we are shown the nature of such immediately upon Israel's solemn renewal of their covenant with Jehovah. The lesson in plain: it is when God's people are most conscious of their obligations, when most determined by grace to discharge the same, when most zealous in fully consecrating themselves unto the Lord, that the ire of Satan breaks out the fiercest. As we have pointed out, up to this point these Canaanitish kings had remained quiescent, but now they planned aggression. Naturally speaking, it seems strange that they were not actually hostile from the beginning, opposing Israel's crossing of the Jordan, for they had received notice of their approach (Joshua ii, 9, 10). Nor had these kings made any attempt to go to the relief of Jericho when that city was seriously threatened by those under Joshua's command.

But notice what these kings *did not do*. They did not surrender themselves unto Israel. They did not consider themselves outnumbered, and cast themselves on Joshua's mercy. Even after they learned of the miraculous crossing of the Jordan and the falling of Jericho's walls, they did not capitulate. Nor do the enemies of the Christian. No matter how marked or extensive the victory God grants us, we must not conclude that the worst of the fight is now over. Satan in his activities is the nearest approach to "perpetual motion" found in any creature. He never accepts defeat or quits the field. One had thought he must recognize the utter futility of assailing Immanuel, but he did not. And though completely worsted and routed in his attempt, it was only "for a season" (Luke iv, 13) he left Him. Why then should any of His followers expect to be exempted! The same is true of "the flesh," with all its evil lusts. Indwelling sin never surrenders to the new nature, nor ceases its attacks upon it. Nay, the farther a Christian advances into an experiential entrance into and enjoyment of his spiritual heritage, the fiercer the conflict becomes, and the more determined and concentrated the efforts of his enemies to thwart him.

It is striking to see how the Holy Spirit has particularized *the diversity* of the kings described in ix, 1: some were from the mountains, some from the valleys, and yet others from the sea coasts; yet though so widely scattered they federated together against Israel. That illustrates the fact that the spiritual enemies of God's people are of many kinds and types, that every form of worldliness—its most refined and elevated as well as its coarsest and lowest—is a menace to them. Equally so are their own evil lusts varied and numerous: self-will, pride, unbelief, slothfulness, cowardice, impatience, discontent, and a host of others, have to be resisted and mortified. How the unanimity of those heathen tribes should shame Christians because of their divisions! And how their banding together against Israel ought to arouse the believer to the realization that *all his graces* must work actively together—faith strenthening hope, love animating both—in waging the fight to which he is called. If it appears strange that these kings had been quiet so long, to carnal reason it seems the more so that they should now plan an offensive after God had so signally shown Himself strong on the behalf of His people. But behind the scenes the Lord was saying, "Assemble yourselves, O ye people, and ye shall be broken in pieces" (Isaiah viii, 9). Thus will it yet be with the enemies of His Church.

But we must now turn to and consider the second reaction of the Caananites unto the recent conquests of Israel. This is quite different from the former one, and is described in Joshua ix, 3-7. Here we are informed, "And when the inhabitants of Gibeon heard what Joshua had done unto Jericho and to Ai, they did work wilily, and went and made as if they had been ambassadors, and took old sacks upon their asses, and winebottles old and rent, and bound up; and old shoes and clouted upon their feet, and old garments upon them; and all the bread of their provision was dry and mouldy. And they went up to Joshua unto the camp at Gilgal, and said unto him and to the men of Israel, We be come from a far country: now therefore make ye a league with us." In x, 2, we are told that "Gibeon was a great city, as one of the royal cities . . . greater than Ai, and all the men thereof were mighty"; nevertheless, they were afraid of Israel. Herein we behold the sovereignty of God: His "terror" (Gen. xxxv, 5) fell not upon the kings mentioned in the preceding verses, yet it *did* upon the Gibeonites! Yet God was not acting arbitrarily or capriciously: He had His own wise reasons for making the Gibeonites an exception.

"And when the inhabitants of Gibeon *heard* what Joshua had done unto Jericho and Ai" (verse 3). This is all of a piece with what is recorded in ii, 9, 10, where Rahab had said to the spies, "I know that the Lord hath given you the land, and that your terror is fallen upon us. . . . For we have *heard* how the Lord dried up the water of the Red Sea for you when ye came out of Egypt; and what ye did unto the two kings of the Amorites that were on the other side Jordan, Sihon and Og, whom ye utterly destroyed." Here is a further example of the same thing, which serves to demonstrate the consistency and truthfulness of this history. Spiritually considered, it illustrates this principle: that the unbelieving world do not remain in ignorance of the mighty works of God, which renders their unbelief the more inexcusable and adds to their guilt. The miracles of Christ were not wrought in a corner, but openly and publicly, so that even His enemies were obliged to acknowledge the reality of them (John xi, 47), and Herod, too, was informed of the same (Luke xxiii, 8). The same is true today, both of the providential interpositions of the Most High in the affairs of nations, and the supernatural operations of the Holy Spirit in His elect.

Whenever there is a definite and striking display of the Holy Spirit's power, some of the unregenerate are impressed and attracted thereby, and seek to join themselves unto the objects of the same. We behold an instance of that in connection with Abraham. He experienced an effectual call from God, which produced a supernatural effect, for it was against nature that he should leave his home, abandon the land of his fathers, and go forth "not knowing whither he went." It was a peculiarly distinctive work of God of which he was made the subject, for the Lord Himself tells us, "I called him *alone*" (Isaiah li, 2). Nevertheless, we find that both his father and his nephew were so impressed by the change wrought in Abraham and his determination to make a complete break from his old manner of life, that they accompanied him as he left Chaldea (Gen. xi, 31)—though the former died before Canaan was reached, and the latter was far from happy therein. Likewise, when the children of Israel left Egypt, in order to go unto their inheritance, "a mixed multitude went up also with them" (Exodus xii, 38), and had an evil influence upon the people of God (Num. xi, 4). It was the same again when those in captivity availed themselves of the edict of Cyrus that they might return to Palestine, for after they did so, and the Law of Moses was restored, we read that they separated from Israel all the mixed multitude" (Neh. xiii, 3)!

In this dual reaction of the Canaanites unto the mighty works which Jehovah had wrought in their land—their determining to use force against Israel, and under the pretence of friendship to seek union with them—we have exemplified the two principal characters assumed by the arch-enemy of God and His people and the methods employed under them. The Devil is depicted in the Scriptures both as the roaring lion and the subtle serpent. As the lion, he uses force and seeks to terrorize; as the serpent, he employs cunning and endeavours to poison and corrupt. In the former character he acts more openly, and assaults from without; in the latter, he works more secretly, aiming to defile from within. Against our first parents he appeared as the lying and beguiling serpent, but in employing Cain to murder righteous Abel, we behold the power and cruelty of the lion (I John iii, 12). Thus it was in connection with what we have here. In stirring up the kings of Canaan to fight with Joshua, Satan was relying upon the use of arms; but in moving the Gibeonites to cloak their character and pose to be what they were not, so that Israel might be deceived into making a league with them, we behold his craftiness, purposing to introduce his leaven into the meal.

We often point out in these pages that God does not work according to a stereotyped plan, but that infinite variety marks His operations. The same is true, in a lesser degree, of the Devil—who is ever a marked imitator. He too acts not uniformly. If one plan or method fails he always has another in reserve, as the whole history of Christendom has repeatedly demonstrated. He altered his tactics with Christ: first seeking to slay Him while a babe, then almost posing as an angel of light when tempting Him, and then as the dragon of darkness (Luke xxii, 53) he bruised His heel. So too with the followers of the Lord Jesus: first openly and directly persecuting, then flattering and fawning upon, and then corrupting by unholy alliances. The opposition and cruelty of Nero and other Roman emperors failing, the patronage of Constantine and the making of Christianity the state religion succeeded in accomplishing Satan's design; just as centuries later the spirituality and power of the great Reformation under Luther was curtailed when the German princes gave support to it because of the political liberty which it promised them. No wonder the apostle declares that—with the Word of Truth in our hands— "we are not ignorant of Satan's devices" (II Cor. ii, 11), and with the records of the last nineteen centuries before us there is still less excuse for our being unacquainted with his strategy.

That which is narrated in Joshua ix, 3-6, of the dishonest Gibeonites gives us a typical picture of graceless professors seeking to "join' the people of God. They knew there was no likelihood of their desire being realized if they presented themselves before Israel in their true character, so they resorted to guile in order to deceive them. "They did work wilily, and went and made as if they had been ambassadors" (verse 4). It must not be overlooked that while Satan is very subtle *the flesh also* is exceedingly artful, fully capable of playing many parts in order to gain its own ends. Behold how it moved Jacob to cover himself with a hairy skin and masquerade as Esau, king Saul to disguise himself when he went to the witch of Endor (I Samuel xxviii, 8), the wife of Jeroboam feigning herself to be another when she visited the prophet Ahijah, whose eyes were set by reason of age (I Kings xiv, 1-6), and the wolves in sheeps' clothing of Christ's day. In his second epistle Paul warned the Corinthians against "false apostles, deceitful workers, transforming themselves into the apostles of Christ" (xi, 13), and Jude complained that ungodly men had "crept in unawares" into the assemblies of the saints (verse 4). The churches are full of such today.

Those Gibeonites posed as "ambassadors," men not only of peaceful design but of importance, fitted to enter into an official engagement with Israel and make a covenant with them. Such is the character assumed by thousands of hypocrites who apply for church membership. They pretend to be fully qualified to be taken into fellowship among the Lord's people, claiming that the peace of God is in their hearts. These Gibeonites pretended to have journeyed from a far country and attired themselves accordingly. They "took old sacks upon their asses, and wine bottles old and rent, and bound up; and old shoes and clouted upon their feet, and old garments upon them; and all the bread of their provision was dry and mouldy." Very thorough were they in this work of imposture, well made up for the part they were playing—even in conforming to Israel's peculiar ways by using "asses" rather than horses. In like manner, empty professors will often go to considerable trouble in their efforts to impose upon the people of God, affecting an outward change in their conduct and laying claim to inward graces which they possess not. They pose as being "poor in spirit," convicted of sin, and hungry for the bread of life, and prate about their unworthiness.

Not only does this incident point a solemn and urgent warning for the churches of Christ to be much on their prayerful guard against taking hypocrites into their membership, but it also intimates how the individual Christian needs to be aware of his danger in being imposed upon by his *inward enemies,* for his lusts not only assume a great variety of forms, but often pretend to be his friends. He knows, both from Scripture and his own experience, that "the flesh lusteth against the spirit," but often he fails to realize that even his corruptions are capable of posing as virtues, and would fain persuade him that they are kindly disposed and have good designs toward him. It is not merely that his evil lusts become less active for a season, and even appear to be asleep, but that they seem to have undergone a change for the better, and now assume the garb of piety. For example, it is easy for a Christian—if he fails to weigh everything in the balances of the Sanctuary and rigidly test his motives by Holy Writ—to persuade himself that his natural self-will is now a holy zeal for God, or that his impatience is really spiritual earnestness, or that his slothfulness is a holy caution.

The "flesh" or sinful nature takes upon itself many plausible guises, and those carnal enemies which are actually very near to us—yea, a part of our very selves—often pretend to have come from "a far country" (Luke xix, 12), that is, from heaven itself, just as the Gibeonites presented themselves before Israel as having come from a great distance. In other words, what we sometimes regard as heavenly graces are nothing but our native corruptions dressed up to deceive us. Particularly is this the case with *mock humility* and lowliness. The Gibeonites appeared not in the attractive apparel of purple and fine linen, but in rags and tatters! Likewise will our very pride take on a deceptively modest appearance and pose. One may, from the teaching of God's Word, be intellectually convinced of the total depravity of man, yea, be thoroughly persuaded of *his own* sinfulness and unworthiness, without his heart being in the least affected and bowed in contrition before God. He may even imagine that he has made considerable progress in the work of mortification, and become *complacent* in the belief that he is increasingly "denying ungodly and worldly lusts," and perceive not that such complacence is a sure sign that pride is at work.

Oh, how powerful and terrible is the "deceitfulness of sin" (Heb. iii, 13). If Joshua himself was imposed upon by these hypocritical Canaanites, how carefully and cautiously do we need to carry ourselves, and seek to profit from this incident. Make no mistake here, my reader: the *real* Christian has many "Gibeonites" within his own breast to contend with! In addition to what has been pointed out above, let us add that one may be not only absorbed with his good works, but even *well pleased with* the knowledge and sense which he has of his own corruptions. Truly "the heart *is* deceitful above all things." Who can know it? Yet if we be sincere and diligent in examining ourselves, in comparing the workings of our hearts with the searching and holy teachings of God's Word, daily viewing ourselves in *its* mirror, we shall perceive more of its "wiliness." True humility is never engaged with itself, still less is it pleased therewith; but rather mourns over its paucity and the constant opposition produced by the workings of pride. True humility delivers from self-importance and self-exaltation, and keeps us from posing as "ambassadors"—wanting to have the pre-eminence.

The Gibeonites

In our last we dwelt upon the twofold reaction of the Canaanites to the notable victories which the Lord gave Israel at Jericho and Ai, namely the determination of the kings to employ massed force (Joshua ix, 1, 2), and the deception which the Gibeonites practised upon them (ix, 3-6), which illustrates the dual character in which Satan opposes the people of God and the methods he employs therein—as the roaring lion seeking to devour, as the subtle serpent using guile. Both Scriptural and ecclesiastical history demonstrate that the latter is far more dangerous and successful than the former. When open persecution fails either to exterminate or intimidate the faithful, Satan resorts to his secret wiles, which only too often corrupt their testimony. Nor is the reason for this hard to discover. Not only is the former method much more easily detected, but fierce opposition casts believers upon the Lord for enabling strength and fortitude, and thus proves a blessing in disguise to them, whereas they are very apt to be less on their guard against Satan's sly artifices, and if pride persuades them that they are too well established in the Truth to be misled by error or taken in by hypocrites, they more easily fall victims of his snares.

What has just been pointed out receives forceful exemplification in the incident we are pondering. By God's enablement Joshua and his men made short work of the combined efforts of the kings and their vast armies (xi, 1-12), but, as II Samuel xxi, 1, shows, the descendants of these Gibeonites were long a thorn in Israel's side. But the fault was entirely their own: due (as we shall see) to their unwatchfulness and self-sufficiency. It was a solemn example of that which our Lord had in mind when He said, "The kingdom of heaven is likened unto a man which sowed good seed in his field, but while men slept, his enemy came and sowed tares among the wheat" (Matt. xiii, 24, 25). In His interpretation, Christ stated that "the good seed are the children of the kingdom, but the tares are the children of the wicked one" (verse 38). That is precisely what happened here. Let it be carefully noted that the enemy did not introduce among the wheat darnel or thistles, but "tares," which are a spurious imitation of the wheat, and so closely alike in appearance that the one cannot be distinguished from the other until the time of harvest. So these Gibeonites came not in their true characters, but posed as those who had come from a far country.

As stated in our last, a threefold view may be taken of these Gibeonites. First, as the world extending its patronage to corporate Christianity, seeking to destroy its distinctive testimony and heavenly character by an amalgamation with the state. In the light of that severe indictment, "Ye adulterers and adulteresses, know ye not that the friendship of the world is enmity with God?" (James iv, 4), we see that the proposal for such an unholy alliance and glaring infidelity unto God must be promptly refused Second, as hypocrites applying for membership in the local church. In view of the Divine prohibition, "Be ye not unequally yoked together with unbelievers: for what fellowship hath righteousness with unrighteousness? and what communion hath light with darkness? and what concord hath Christ with Belial? or what part hath he that believeth with an infidel?" (II Cor. vi, 14, 15), how it behoves each Christian assembly to examine prayerfully and carefully the qualifications of each one seeking fellowship therewith! Third, as our evil lusts pretending to be what they are not, to have undergone a change for the better, so that they would fain persuade the unguarded that they are to be numbered among his graces. That which we are now to consider shows how inexcusable is our being imposed upon.

"And they went to Joshua unto the camp at Gilgal, and said unto him, and to the men of Israel, We be come from a far country: now therefore make ye a league with us" (ix, 6). Incidentally, this reference to Gilgal makes it clear that Israel had made the long journey unto Ebal (viii, 30) for the express purpose of obeying the Lord's injunction in Deuteronomy xxvii, 4, 5, etc., that they remained there but a short time, and then returned to their original camp. But there is far more in it than that: the fact that Israel succumbed to this temptation at *this* particular place rendered their failure the more inexcusable. That will be evident from the sequel. "Gilgal" is mentioned for the first time in our book at v, 9, and there we learn that it was the place where "the reproach of Egypt" was rolled away, when the male members of that new generation were circumcised. In other words, it was there that they received the outward mark and sign that they were separated from all other nations in covenant relation with Jehovah (Gen. xvii, 9, 10), set apart to His service. It was also the place where they "kept the passover" (v, 10), for it is only those who submit to God's ordinances and walk according to His precepts who can really enjoy communion with Him.

What has just been pointed out shows the need for looking up the marginal references of each passage, and seeking to ascertain the meaning of the proper nouns in Scripture—if we are too dilatory or in too much of a hurry to do so, we are sure to be the losers. It also supplies the key to the more specific typical signification of this incident. Circumcision connoted dedication unto God and was the Old Testament's figure of mortifying the lusts of the flesh (Jer. iv, 4; Deut. x, 16)—the two things which Satan hates in the Lord's people above everything else and which he opposes at every turn, for they are what distinguish them from the world, and promote God's glory. That which the Devil is most anxious to destroy is the testimony of the saints as a peculiar people, devoted unto God, walking with Him in separation from the ungodly (Romans xii, 1, 2). They are to conduct themselves as "strangers and pilgrims" (I Peter ii, 11) in this scene. Through Balaam Jehovah had declared "the people shall dwell alone, and shall not be reckoned among the nations" (Num. xxiii, 9, and cf. Deut. xxxiii, 28). Through these Gibeonites—for it is ever his way to use human instruments (his "ministers—II Cor. xi, 14, 15)— the enemy was making an attack upon Israel's consecration, inducing them to ignore God's injunction of separation by a union with the heathen.

Thus, in the light of the special theme of Joshua, the outstanding lesson for us here is that a vital aspect of the believer's spiritual warfare consists of the imperative need for maintaining his consecration to God and persevering with the work of mortification, ever being on the alert against the wiles of the Devil to hinder him therein. But more: he must be on his most diligent guard against the *workings of pride* while engaged in this very work. That also is clearly implied in this incident. After their arduous journey to Ebal and full obedience to God there, they *had* returned to Gilgal, yet it was *here* they suffered themselves to be deceived by the craft of Satan! Alas, how deceitful are our hearts! How prone we are to be elated with the very things Divine grace works in and through us. If we are gratified with our consecration, pleased with our self-denial, puffed up with our obedience, or proud of our prayerfulness and increasing dependence upon God, we are headed for disaster. "Pride goeth before destruction; and a haughty spirit before a fall" (Prov. xvi, 18), and pride was certainly at work in Israel at this time. Oh, how much we need to heed these injunctions, "Be not high minded, but fear" (Romans xi, 20) and "rejoice with trembling" (Psalm ii, 11)!

It is true that God had said unto Israel, "When thou comest nigh unto a city to fight against it, then proclaim peace unto it. And it shall be, if it make thee answer of peace, and open unto thee, then it shall be that all the people that is found therein shall be tributaries unto thee, and they shall serve thee" (Deut. xx, 10, 11)—a passage which must be kept in mind when reading Deuteronomy xx, 16, 17, and one which shows that even here, in holy wrath, God "remembered mercy." But *that* was an entirely different matter from what is now before us. There was nothing whatever in the case of these Gibeonites which justified Joshua in ignoring the plain injunction, "Take heed to thyself lest thou make a covenant with the inhabitants of the land whither thou goest, lest it be for a snare in the midst of thee" (Exodus xxxiv, 13). There is nothing that the Lord abominates more than unholy mixtures. "Thou shalt not sow thy vineyard with divers seeds . . . thou shalt not plough with an ox and an ass together . . . thou shalt not wear a garment of divers sorts, as of woollen and linen together" (Deut. xxii, 9-11) plainly states the principle, and Revelation iii, 15, 16, demonstrates His abhorrence of our repudiation of the same, for "Laodiceanism" is a union between the world and the professing Church.

"And the men of Israel said unto the Hivites, Peradventure ye dwell among us, and how shall we make a league with you?" (verse 7). No doubt it was the responsible heads of the congregation who took the lead in making answer to these disguised Canaanites, who had come with the express purpose of telling lies, to tempt the people of God and lead them into sin. Three things are evident from their words. First, they were well instructed in the Law, for they realized it would be wrong to accede to this suggestion. Second, they were then occupying the ground of faith: "dwell *among us*" was as though the whole of Canaan was already in their possession! Third, they did not immediately and impulsively grant their request, but voiced the language of distrust. It is those very things which made the sequel graver. It pays to be wary, yea, suspicious of impostors, if we are not to be deceived by glib tongues. "Put not your trust in princes" (Psalm cxlvi, 3), and in a day like ours, "Take ye heed every one of his neighbour, and trust ye not in any brother" (Jer. ix, 4). We are sure to suffer if we disregard such warnings.

The careful reader will have observed that these "inhabitants of Gibeon" (verse 3) are designated "Hivites" in verse 7, and, assured that there is nothing superfluous in Holy Writ, he will endeavour to ascertain *why* this detail has been placed on record. It cannot be without reason and significance that the Spirit has here told us that these deceivers belong to the Hivites, and therefore it is our duty to discover His design therein. That may require a little trouble on our part (for the meaning of much in the Word is withheld from those who fail to search it diligently), but if it serves to cast light on this incident, it is worth it. The only way to discover the Spirit's design is to use the concordance and look up other passages, particularly in the earlier books, where "the Hivites" are mentioned. Nor have we far to seek. In Genesis xxxiv we learn how the sons of Jacob answered Shechem and his father (who was a "Hivite" —verse 2) "*deceitfully*" verse 13), and by a treacherous ruse succeeded in slaying them and spoiling their city (verses 14-29). Here then was the biter bit: the descendants of those who had so wickedly deceived the Hivites were now in turn deceived by them!

In the preceding article we called attention to the fact that while the terror of the Lord had *not* fallen upon the kings of ix, 1, yet it *had* upon the Gibeonites, and that while we may behold therein an illustration of His sovereignty, who makes one to differ from another as He pleases, yet He acts not capriciously therein. Let us now amplify that statement. There was nothing arbitrary in the Lord's dealing with these Hivites, rather was He treating with them according to the principles of His government. Though at times His mills grind slowly, yet none the less surely. Centuries previously the sons of Jacob had wickedly tricked the Gibeonites, and now God suffered their descendants to reap the consequences of such deception. Thus what is here before us is a clear case of what is termed "poetic justice." But though God was righteous in permitting Israel to be imposed upon, that in no wise interfered with their accountability or excused their slackness. Joshua and the princes of the congregation acted quite freely, and, as verse 14 clearly intimates, were to blame because they sought not directions from the Lord. God's *Word*, and not His secret will, is the rule of our responsibility.

"And they said unto Joshua, We are thy servants" (verse 8). This was the language of deference, signifying inferiority and expressing their willingness to perform any tasks assigned them. That was the bait to entrap Israel: We can be useful and do the rough work for you. But Joshua was not satisfied with their indefinite statement. He was on his guard, but not sufficiently so. "And Joshua said unto them, Who are ye? and from whence come ye?" It was at this very point that he failed. Instead of conferring with them he should have gone apart and sought counsel from the Lord (verse 14). He was evidently in doubt, and "whatsoever is not of faith, is sin" (Romans xiv, 23). Even the wisdom of this world warns us, "When in doubt, do nothing." But the Word of God proffers the believer far better advice than that: "If any of you lack wisdom, let him ask of God, that giveth liberally to all" (James i, 5). It is always the height of folly for us to parley with the enemy. Moreover, in thus interrogating them Joshua was but *tempting* these Gibeonites to tell further lies! Remember that, my reader, and go very slow in asking souls, "Are you saved?" or "How did you like the magazine I loaned you?" lest you be guilty of giving occasion to your friend (in order to "save his face") to utter a falsehood.

"And they said unto him, From a very far country thy servants are come, because of the name of the Lord thy God, for we have heard the fame of Him and all that He did in Egypt, and all that He did to the two kings of the Amorites that were beyond Jordan, to Sihon king of Heshbon and to Og king of Bashan, which was at Ashtaroth" (verses 9, 10). The Gibeonites had already lied unto the princes of Israel (verse 6 and cf. 15), and now that the further questioning of Joshua had given them an opportunity to declare their true characters, they only used it for an occasion to add to their guilt. Originally they had stated, "We be come from a far country" (verse 6), now they said, "From a very far country," illustrating the solemn fact that one lie generally leads to another and still worse one. How earnestly we need to pray, Remove from me the way of lying" (Psalm cxix, 29)! It is very humiliating but salutary to note that the Lord deemed it requisite to enjoin His own children, "Wherefore putting away lying, speak every man truth with his neighbour" (Eph. iv, 25). Exaggerating is lying, so also is the making of promises which we have no real intention of keeping. Do you really *mean it* when you say to certain ones, "I am so glad to meet you"? We may *act* a lie as well as utter one.

A careful examination of the tale told to Joshua by these Gibeonites reveals how everything in it was designed to appeal unto Israel's *pride*. First, they claimed to have come from a very far country, which was to flatter Joshua that he was now being courted by those from so great a distance. That very feature was part of the temptation which fanned the egotism of Hezekiah and led to *his* undoing, for he was "glad" when the king of Babylon made friendly overtures unto him, and showed his messengers all his treasures, for when God's servant took him to task, he said: "They are come from a far country unto me" (Isaiah xxxix, 3). Beware, my reader, of all those who fawn upon you, and remember that "the Lord shall cut off all flattering lips" (Psalm xii, 3). Second, their repeated "thy servants" emphasized their readiness to take an inferior and subordinate place, and be subservient to Israel. Third, they intimated that so great was the fame of Joshua's God that, even so remotely situate. they had "heard" of His wondrous works. This too was said for the purpose of ingratiating themselves with Joshua, as though they too desired to come under Jehovah's protection.

One Hebrew scholar tells us that their words "From a very far country are thy servants come *because of* the name of the Lord thy God" may be translated "*unto* the name of the Lord thy God": that is, willing to be proselytes to Judaism, desirous of embracing Israel's religion—the added "*for* we have heard the fame of Him" seems to confirm that rendering, and thus a strong appeal was thereby made to Israel's piety. They appeared to be deeply impressed by the wonders which God had wrought, and therefore sought friendship with Israel. For this purpose they had undertaken a very fatiguing journey, which evidenced their willingness to be tributary unto them. Their story had been carefully thought out and was "all of a piece," for while they made reference to their knowledge of what Jehovah had done in Egypt and to the kings of the Amorites, they were careful to make no mention of the supernatural crossing of the Jordan, nor of Israel's recent victories at Jericho and Ai—for tidings of them would not yet have reached "a very far country"! Thus we are shown how far hypocrites will go in order to gain the friendship of God's people.

Joshua's Failure

In our last article (upon the early verses of Joshua ix) we saw how that Israel's supernatural crossing of the Jordan and the victories which the Lord gave them at Jericho and Ai had struck terror into the hearts of the Gibeonites. Consequently, those Canaanites who resided in that part of the land which Israel must very soon reach determined, by means of a piece of trickery, to outwit the hosts of God, and thereby preserve their own lives. They decided to pose as those who dwelt in "a far country"—that is, beyond the bounds of Canaan itself—and who wished to enter into a league of peace with the Hebrews. Accordingly, they attired themselves in tattered garments and came to Israel's camp at Gilgal. They told a plausible tale, saying that the fame of Jehovah had reached their ears—thereby intimating their desire to come under His protection and become proselytes to His religion. They apologized for their sorry appearance, explaining that it was due to the long and fatiguing journey they had come. It was a subtle appeal to Israel's pride that tidings of the wonder-working power of their God had gone so far abroad that even these remote strangers were acquainted with the same, and therefore sought union with His favoured people. In reality it was a tempting of Israel to act at direct variance with an injunction from Jehovah which expressly forbade their doing any such thing.

These Gibeonites belonged to the tribe of the Hivites (ix, 7), and the renowned Hebraist, John Gill, tells us that "The name Hivites signifies *serpents*"! They certainly acted here in complete accord therewith, conducting themselves "wilily" (ix, 4), telling downright lies, and succeeding in thoroughly deceiving Joshua and his princes. Yet Israel ought not to have been imposed upon by them. Even from a natural standpoint their conduct was excuseless. Only recently they had themselves resorted to a subtle strategy in the taking of Ai, and therefore it now behoved them to be doubly on the alert lest they be paid back in their own coin. The men of Israel were indeed suspicious, for they said, "Peradventure ye dwell among us, and how shall we make a league with you?" (ix, 7). Evidently they remembered those words, "When the Lord thy God shall deliver them before thee, thou shalt smite them and utterly destroy them: thou shalt make no covenant with them, nor show mercy unto them" (Deut. vii, 2). Nor was Joshua himself satisfied with the first account they gave of themselves, as his "Who are ye? and from whence come ye?" (verse 8) evidenced. Yet the suspicions of both the one and the other were soon lulled to sleep.

"And they said, From a very far country thy servants are come, because of the name of the Lord thy God" (ix, 9). It is to be noted that though Joshua had specifically asked them, "Who are ye? and from whence come ye?" in their reply they neither declared their nationality nor named the place of their birth. Thus, typically considered, their credentials were unsatisfactory at the *vital* point, for it is the spiritual birth of those applying for fellowship that the churches need to inquire most closely into. "We have heard . . . all that He did in Egypt . . . and to the two kings of the Amorites that were beyond Jordan" (verse 10), intimating that a deep impression had been made upon them thereby. "Wherefore our elders and all the inhabitants of our country spake to us, saying, Take victuals with you for the journey, and go to meet them, and say unto them, We are your servants, and therefore now make ye a league with us" (verse 11). Thus they pretended that their senate had been formally convened and had unanimously appointed their ambassadors to enter into this covenant with Israel—i.e. they were vouched for by reliable authorities, so that Joshua need have no fear of being imposed upon by charlatans.

If the tale told by these Gibeonites was really true, and they *had* come from "a very far country," then the extreme measures which Jehovah had commanded His people to take with the inhabitants of the land (Deut. vii, 1, 2) would not have to be executed against *them*. This is clear from Deuteronomy xx, 15, 16, where a very definite distinction was drawn between the two cases: "Thus shalt thou do [offer "peace" unto it (verses 10, 11)] unto all the cities which are *very far off* from thee, which are not of the cities of these nations. But of the cities of those people which the Lord thy God hath given thee for an inheritance, thou shalt save alive nothing that breatheth. But thou shalt utterly destroy them: the Hivites, and the Amorites," etc. Yet these Gibeonites were *not* the inhabitants of another country, but belonged to the tribe of the Hivites (Joshua ix, 7), and as Genesis x, 15, 17, makes known, "the Hivite" was an immediate descendant of the accursed Canaan (Gen. ix, 25). "This our bread we took hot for our provision out of our houses on the day we came forth to go unto you; but now, behold, it is dry, and it is mouldy. And these bottles of wine, which we filled, were new; and, behold, they be rent; and these our garments and our shoes are become old by reason of the very long journey" (verses 12, 13).

Their repeated "behold" or "see" was an appeal to Israel's *senses*. The present condition of the food and clothing of these Gibeonites was appealed to in corroboration of the account which they had given of themselves. But there was no more reason why Israel should be deceived through their eyes than their ears. Had they walked by faith instead of sight, it would have been impossible. For *faith* always has to with God and is regulated by His Word. Faith is the expression of a spirit of dependence upon Him, and that, in turn, issues from the realization of our own insufficiency. It was doubly inexcusable that Israel were imposed upon *here,* for they were in "the camp at Gilgal" (ix, 6), where the tabernacle of the priesthood resided, and therefore the place where the mind of the Lord could be obtained if they sought Him in the way of His appointment. That way had been plainly made known unto Joshua, for through Moses God gave orders to him, "He shall stand before Eleazar the priest, who shall ask counsel for him after the judgment of Urim before the Lord: at his word shall they go out, and at his word they shall come in, both he, and all the children of Israel with him" (Num. xxvii. 21). It was the failure of Israel, and especially of Joshua on this occasion, to avail themselves of God's gracious provision that rendered their conduct so blameable.

In like manner, there is no excuse for a Christian's being deceived by appearances, or left in ignorance concerning God's will as to his path of duty. The Lord has made ample provision for his instruction. It is our holy privilege to go unto the antitypical Eleazar and ask counsel of Him, and the great High Priest of the spiritual Israel will, through the Urim and Thummim (which signify "lights and perfections") of His Word, lead us in a plain path. "Trust in the Lord with all thine heart, and lean not unto thine own understanding; in all thy ways acknowledge Him" are His requirements, and if we meet them—by His grace, which He is ever ready to give unto those who humbly seek it (James iv, 6)—then His sure promise is, "and He *shall* direct thy paths" (Prov. iii, 5, 6). As another has aptly expressed it, "This is the polar-star of a child of God—faith in his Father's providences, promises, and grace. Let the eye look upward, and all will be light (Matt. vi, 22; cf. Psalms xxxii, 8; xxxiv, 5). To "trust in the Lord with all our heart" is to make Him our entire and exclusive confidence. To "lean not unto our own understanding" is to renounce our own wit and wisdom and refuse to rely upon the proud dictates of reason. To "acknowledge God in all our ways" is to own His proprietorship and supremacy, to ask counsel of Him, to seek His glory, and to be conformed unto His will. Comply with those conditions and Divine guidance is guaranteed—His Spirit will bring to our mind the verse which is exactly suited to our case, and cause us to be regulated by the same.

But alas, instead of trusting in the Lord with all our hearts we are prone to put our confidence in anyone or anything else. How lamentably we fail in looking alone unto God in each fresh trial and emergency, and counting upon His supplying our every need. It is just because we are so slow in casting all our care upon Him and so reluctant to draw strength from Him day by day, and hour by hour, that we stand in need of this very exhortation. Equally so with the one which immediately follows. The understanding has indeed been given us by God, and it is our duty not only to exercise the same, but diligently to cultivate it. Nor will anything else so sharpen and refine it as will the study of and meditation upon the Scriptures. Nevertheless, it must not be *depended upon,* for the mind has been degraded by the fall and darkened by indwelling sin, and therefore is, at best, an unsafe guide. Even in a regenerated man, a prophet of God, it proved a mistaken counsellor (II Samuel vii, 2-5). As a fallen creature, it is still the tendency of a believer to lean unto his own understanding—to his foolish notions and false fancies; to make a god of reason. Just in proportion as we yield to that tendency are we remiss in acknowledging God in all our ways. If we be regulated by natural prudence much trouble shall we make for ourselves, for God will justly suffer us to reap the consequences of our folly. It was at these very points Israel failed in the incident we are now considering.

"And the men took of their victuals, and asked not counsel at the mouth of the Lord" (ix, 14). Here was the crux of the whole matter. Israel failed sadly: failed to give the Lord His proper place; failed to avail themselves of His gracious provision to make known His will via the high priest. And the cause of their failure is here plainly revealed, for the two halves of this verse are inseparably connected. By "the men took of their victuals" we are not to understand that they sampled the same by eating thereof, for obviously there was no need to do that with *mouldy* bread. No, it signifies that they took it into their hands for a closer inspection in order to confirm what the Gibeonites had told them. In other words, they walked by sight and relied upon the testimony of their senses. They acted naturally and not spiritually. Instead of seeking guidance from the Lord through His servant, as they were in duty bound to do by His Word, they confided in their own wisdom, relied upon their own judgment, and thus a looking unto God was precluded. They "asked not counsel at the mouth of the Lord": had they done so there had been no need for them to test the food of these Gibeonites! Had they done so they had not been deceived by them! The whole blame rested upon themselves.

This was Israel's *second* failure after their entrance into Canaan, and in neither of them was Joshua guiltless. The previous one occurred in connection with their first assault on Ai. Those who had reconnoitred the place had said unto Joshua, "Let not all the people go up, but let about two or three thousand men go up and smite Ai; make not all the people to labour thither, for they are but few" (vii, 3). Flushed by their victory at Jericho, possessed by a spirit of self-confidence, they too much lost sight of the fact that the capture of Jericho was due not to the brilliance of their strategy or the valour of their arms, but to the miracle-working power of Jehovah. They now deemed themselves to be invincible and were assured that the taking of the remainder of Canaan would be a simple task. They therefore felt that a single battalion of *their* soldiers would be sufficient to capture that town—even though there were "twelve thousand men" in it (viii, 25). And their leader, instead of seeking counsel from the Lord, foolishly adopted their suggestion. As may well be anticipated, God blew upon their carnal policy and suffered their proud hearts to be humiliated. They were put to shame before their enemies, fled in panic, and the whole congregation of Israel was thoroughly dismayed (vii, 4-6).

We would naturally think that if there were another failure on the part of Joshua and Israel it would be quite dissimilar from the former one, arising from a different cause. Surely, after having had their eyes opened to see the reason for their first defeat, they would now be doubly on their guard against a repetition of the same. Alas, human nature is slow to learn and profit from its failures. Even the father of the faithful *repeated* his initial fault, for though he did wrong in going down into Egypt to sojourn there, and committed a yet worse offence in denying his relationship to Sarah, and though he was there put to shame by Pharaoh for his deception (Gen. xii, 10-20), yet he was guilty of the selfsame thing when he went and sojourned in Gerah (Gen. xx, 1, 2)! The same was true of poor Peter: as it was a spirit of cowardice which led to his denial of Christ, so he yielded to the same weakness at Antioch, separating from the Gentile believers when certain ones came from Jerusalem, "*fearing* them which were of the circumcision" (Gal. ii, 12). In each case it was "the fear of man" that ensnared him (Prov. xx, 25), and as that verse clearly intimates, such ensnaring is the consequence of our not "trusting in the Lord." Thus it was too in the incident we are now pondering: Joshua relapsed into his former fault.

In the very next *test* presented to Israel and their leader, they failed in the same way as they did in connection with Ai. Instead of consulting the Lord, they used their "common sense." As the result, Israel and Joshua too were deceived by the plausible story told by the Gibeonites, and misled by their appearance and the condition of their victuals. And this too has been recorded for *our* instruction: "For whatsoever things were written aforetime were written for our learning" (Romans xv, 4). Yet it is not the mere reading of them that is required: if we are really to profit therefrom, we must examine each incident closely, pondering each detail carefully, and taking it home unto ourselves. The failures of eminent saints have not been chronicled either to encourage slackness on our part or to discourage us, but rather to illustrate and demonstrate that though the spirit be willing yet the flesh is weak, and especially to give point to that exhortation, "Wherefore let him that thinketh he standeth take heed lest he fall" (I Cor. x, 12). If after some painful disillusionment we say, "I believe I have learned my lesson this time," it is a sure sign we have *not* done so if we now proudly assure ourselves, "I shall not be deceived again in *that* way."

That which supplies such solemn warning to us in the cases alluded to above is that in each instance the failure was not committed by a young and inexperienced disciple, but was the lapse of a mature saint; for Abraham, Peter and Joshua had long walked with God. He that hath ears to hear, let him hear—heed! But, more particularly, that which is now engaging our attention is to be viewed in the light of the book in which it is found, and the special theme which is developed therein. As we have so often stated, the book of Joshua sets forth in both a typical and practical manner the spiritual warfare of the saints, and their present entrance into and enjoyment of their spiritual heritage. And in it the Holy Spirit has described not only Israel's victories but their defeats also, and a prayerful study of the same makes known to us both the secrets of success and the causes of failure in fighting the good fight of faith. It is only as we keep these facts steadily in mind as we pass from chapter to chapter and from one episode to another, and faithfully make a personal application of the same unto our own hearts and lives, that we shall really be advantaged by the same. Let us then observe carefully the *nature* of Joshua's failure on this occasion.

It was more of a negative than a positive one. In nowise was it an act of deliberate disobedience or defiant pitting of his own will against the Lord's. Where *those* elements exist, the offence is very much graver, and the resulting chastisement from God will be much sorer. What Joshua did here was not by studied premeditation, but was more of a case of being "overtaken in a fault" (Gal. vi, 1). That in nowise excused him, yet we must not regard him as being guilty of something worse than what he actually did. Both in vii, 3, 4, and here (ix, 14, 15) he acted too impulsively and precipitately. Instead of waiting upon the Lord and seeking direction from Him, in each instance he acted "on the spur of the moment," and on the ground of mere nature, walking by sight instead of by faith. What point this gives to the Divine injunction, "He that believeth shall not make haste" (Isaiah xxviii, 16)! If we act in too big a hurry to pray over anything and work in the energy of the flesh, we displease the Lord, hinder His cause, and bring trouble upon ourselves. The principal lesson taught us in this incident is that, in order to fight the good fight of faith successfully, we must maintain the place of dependence upon God and be constantly seeking wisdom from above.

"And asked not counsel at the mouth of the Lord" (verse 14), and therefore acted in independence of Him—possibly because he regarded this as too trivial a matter to take unto God. But there also we must not lean unto our own understanding: "In everything by prayer and supplication, with thanksgiving, let your requests be made known unto God" (Phil. iv, 4)—big as well as little, the least matters as well as the greatest. What a holy privilege! But "prayer and supplication" is very much more than perfunctorily offering up a petition unto heaven: it is a definite waiting upon God, a diligent seeking from Him. It involved time and trouble for Joshua to ask counsel of the Lord: for it required him to go unto the high priest and inquire His mind through him. As we read in Judges xx, 27, 28, The children of Israel inquired of the Lord [for the ark of the covenant of God was there in those days and Phinehas. the son of Eleazar, the son of Aaron, stood before it in those days] saying, Shall I yet again go out to battle against the children of Benjamin my brother, or shall I cease? And the Lord said, Go up, for tomorrow I will deliver them into thine hand"—and cf. I Samuel xxiii, 9, 12. Observe how frequently "the man after God's own heart" inquired of Him: I Samuel xxii, 10; xxiii, 2. 4; xxx, 8; II Samuel ii, 1, 5, 19. Beautiful too is the picture set forth in Ezra viii, 21.

"And Joshua made peace with them, and made a covenant with them, to let them live, and the princes of the congregation sware unto them" (verse 15). This is not recorded to Joshua's honour, but it manifests the inflexible fidelity of the Divine historian. Scripture is impartial in relating the blemishes of its most famous characters. Joshua ought to have said to these Gibeonites what a loyal servant of God said to the adversaries of Judah and Benjamin: "Ye have nothing to do with us" (Ezra iv, 3). In order to maintain a testimony unto the holiness of God, His people are required to walk in separation from the world; but here we behold Joshua entering into an alliance with those who were under the Divine curse. That is the grand aim of Satan: to destroy the witness of the saints as those who are called to walk apart from the ungodly. Alas, that they so often permit him to succeed! What communion has light with darkness? What concord is there between a people in covenant relation with the Holy One and those who are idolaters? None whatever. Therefore let the former be much on their guard at this point, conduct themselves accordingly, strenuously resist every temptation from Satan to compromise. Finally, let us remember that the Christian is never to "make peace" with his inward enemies, but must ceaselessly fight against them.

It was said by James Durham, the Puritan, "It is hard to know, in spiritual exercises, whether it be more difficult to attain some gracious frame or to maintain it when it is attained, whether more seriousness is required for making peace with God, or for keeping it when made." That observation is confirmed both in the teaching of God's Word and the experience of His children: as it is easier in natural things to squander than acquire, so spiritually to retain is as hard a task as to obtain. In Psalm lxxxv, 8, we read, "I will hear what God the Lord will speak: for He will speak peace unto His people, but let them not turn again to folly." Alas that we should need such an injunction as that. When a child has burned his fingers he is afraid of the fire, and when a believer has dishonoured the Lord, and brought trouble upon himself by foolish conduct, he ought to be doubly on his guard against a repetition thereof. Yet only too often, instead of decreasing self-confidence and walking softly before the Lord, he relaxes his efforts to mortify pride, becomes careless in the use of God's appointed means for maintaining fellowship with Himself in the paths of righteousness, and therefore falls again into the same sin.

The very fact that believers are here dehorted "let them not turn again to folly" intimates their proneness to do so. Yet that is so far from making any allowance for the same, it expressly forbids it. Moreover, what immediately precedes renders a repetition of the fault the more excuseless. When the Lord has so graciously "spoken peace to His people," that is, has pardoned their transgressions and allayed their consciences, a spirit of gratitude should cause them to be more careful in avoiding everything which would displease and grieve Him. As Matthew Henry rightly pointed out, "The remission of sins past is not a permission for sins to come, but a great bridle and restraint to it." Peace is spoken by God unto those who turn from sin, and therefore we have a clearly implied warning here that if we return thereto peace will depart from us. Just so far as we really value God's peace will we diligently endeavour to avoid whatever destroys it. Sin is a breach of the Law (I John iii, 4), Godward it is an "offence" (Romans v, 17) or affront, selfward it is folly or acting contrary to our interests, "forsaking our own mercies" (Jonah ii, 8).

All sin is foolish, but backsliding is doubly so, and it is because of our corrupt tendency unto it that such a caution as the above requires to be taken to heart by all of us. The more so because of sin's insidiousness—ever ready to trip us up if we are the least bit off our guard. As pointed out at the close of our last, sin is by no means always premeditated. Joshua's failure in the making of a covenant with the Gibeonites was no deliberate act of disobedience, but was more a case of being "overtaken in a fault" (Gal. vi, 1)—through hurried action, instead of seeking counsel from the Lord. To be "overtaken in a fault" is a very different thing from resolving and contriving the same: the one is inadvertent, the other planned. It is ever to be borne in mind that the Christian has no inherent strength of his own: he stands by faith (Romans xi, 20), and faith is directly opposed to self-confidence. Therefore it is that, unless he maintains a constant prayerful vigilance and self-discipline, he is ever in danger of a sudden surprisal from the force of temptation, or being overborne by the heat of his passions.

Joshua had not only failed in a similar way previously, but he had been rebuked for it by the Lord, and convicted of his folly (vii, 10, 11). The repetition of such failure has been recorded by the Holy Spirit to bring home to us *our* weakness and fickleness. If one so highly favoured of God as he who had so signally honoured Him by the general tenor of his character and conduct was capable of these momentary lapses, then how much do both writer and reader need to heed that exhortation "Be not high minded, but fear." The sad fact is that a believer may not only fall into sin, but—unless he preserves a spirit of entire dependence upon the Lord—he may, through the infirmity of the flesh, fall into *the same sin*. Samson (who was a believer— Heb. xi, 32) did so, first by marrying a Philistine woman (Judges xiv), which was expressly forbidden by the Divine Law, and later by consorting with a Philistine harlot (Judges xvi), for which he paid dearly. Jehoshaphat committed a great sin in joining affinity with the wicked Ahab (II Chron. xviii, 1-3) and was reproved for the same (xix, 2); yet in xx, 35, we find him relapsing into the same sin. When *we* are guilty of similar folly, it should lead us to deeper repentance, though not to despair.

"And Joshua made peace with them, and made a league with them, to let them live: and the princes of the congregation sware unto them. And it came to pass at the end of three days after they had made a league with them, that they heard that they were their neighbours, and that they dwelt among them" (ix, 15, 16). As Gill pointed out, "The league seems to have been made the same day they came. The Gibeonites were no doubt in haste to have it confirmed, lest they should be discovered; and Joshua and the princes of Israel took no pains and gave themselves no great trouble to inquire about them, but made peace with them at once." And now the deception of the one and the folly of the hasty action of the other were discovered. With rare exceptions, lies are quickly exposed. Only truth wears and lasts. Impostures are speedily found out, as Jacob's by his father Isaac, Jeroboam's wife's by the prophet (I Kings xiv, 1-6), that of Ananias and Sapphira (Acts 5). Then how utterly vain must be every attempt to impose upon Him unto whom "all things are naked and opened"! It is impossible to deceive Omniscience by masquerading before Him in the garb of a hypocritical profession, nor will His people be deceived thereby if they carefully weigh them in the balances of the Scriptures.

The terrible times in which we are living call for a further word on this practical subject. "The lip of truth shall be established for ever; but a lying tongue is but for a moment" (Prov. xii, 19). Then how important it is to eye eternity in all our words—doubly so in the case of preachers! The profession of the Truth may indeed occasion present inconvenience and trouble from men, but it shall receive an eternal reward from God. On the other hand, the preacher who, for momentary gain and popularity, represses the Truth and is a purveyor of lies shall reap a harvest of everlasting shame and woe. But that verse applies to all of us. As Matthew Henry tersely expressed it, "Those that make a lie their refuge, will find it a refuge of lies." Falsehoods and deceits are not only evil in themselves, but a foolish expedient, for they expose the perpetrator to speedy detection, which renders him suspect and distrusted in everything. Even though his fellows should fail to disprove him. unless he sincerely repents, "He that speaketh lies shall perish" (Prov. xix, 9). Nothing makes us more like the Devil than this, for he was a liar from the beginning (John viii, 44). How earnestly we should pray, "Remove from me the way of lying" (Psalm cxix, 29)!

"And it came to pass at the end of three days after they had made a league with them, that they heard that they were their neighbours, and that they dwelt among them" (verse 16). That may well be viewed from another angle. Not only is it a fact that, as a general rule, deceptions are quickly discovered, but it is equally true that, where the heart beats true to Him, God will not long suffer His people to be imposed upon. They are children of the day and not of the night, and therefore there is no reason why they should stumble over any obstacles in their path. As their Master declares, "I am the light of the world: he that followeth Me shall not walk in darkness, but shall have the light of life" (John viii, 12). But to *follow* Christ means very much more than "believing" in Him: it signifies to commit ourselves unreservedly to His government, to walk in His precepts, to emulate the example which he has left us. And in the main, and with few deviations, that is exactly what Joshua and Israel *had done* since their entrance into Canaan. They had been obedient to Jehovah, complying with His revealed will in all things. And though they had temporarily failed to seek counsel from Him, and in consequence had been beguiled by the Gibeonites, yet because the main course of their lives was pleasing to God, He soon allowed them to learn their mistake. How gently the Lord deals with us!

"And the children of Israel journeyed, and came unto their cities on the third day. Now their cities were Gibeon," etc. (verse 17). This is explanatory of the foregoing verse and, by implication, shows us how unnecessary was Israel's precipitate action—had they withheld their judgment and decision but a very short time, they would have learned that these Gibeonites had by no means come from a very far country. By "the children of Israel" here, we are not to understand the entire congregation—for the camp still remained at Gilgal (x, 17)—but rather their fighting-men with the responsible heads of the tribes. Most probably they had advanced this distance in order to investigate the report they had received. It should be pointed out that this was not the "third day" from setting out on their journey—for it was but a night's march from Gilgal to their cities (x; 9)—but from the time when they first "heard" that the Gibeonites were their neighbours. Definite confirmation of this was now before them, for here were "their cities." The Holy Spirit's emphasis here by the repetition of "the third day" intimates that this is a detail which the reader should duly ponder. A further word thereon.

It should be carefully noted that in John viii, 12, Christ did not simply say that the one who followed Him should have light, but "the light of life," and this is exactly what is typically portrayed here in verses 16 and 17, for "at the end of three days" brings us (symbolically speaking) on to resurrection ground. Joshua and his fellows had acted by sight instead of faith, and here the Spirit supplies demonstration of that fact. They had conducted themselves on the ground of mere nature, being regulated by their senses, and not as quickened souls whose privilege it was to enjoy unbroken communion with God and be guided by Him. They had, for the moment, relapsed into carnality, but now "on the third day" they were back on resurrection ground and given to see things in a true light. So the Christian has, by God's grace and power, been brought from death unto life, and is henceforth called upon to "walk in newness of life" (Romans vi, 4) and to "put on the new man" (Eph. iv, 24), which means to act as one who is a new creature in Christ, to be governed by heavenly principles. If he fails to do so, then he will lack discernment and wisdom for his path, and be left to his erring natural judgment. Only so long as his eye be "single" to God's glory will he be full of light.

"And the children of Israel smote them not, because the princes of the congregation had sworn unto them by the Lord God of Israel" (verse 18). Here is further evidence that the rulers in Israel were back again on resurrection ground—in communion with the Lord, conducting themselves as regenerated men. The fear of God was upon them, and they acted accordingly! Had they now been walking according to the flesh, they had argued that "circumstances alter cases," that because the Gibeonites had lied to them they were now automatically released from keeping their part of the compact. The carnal mind would reason that a covenant was surely not binding when one of the parties entering into it had acted under false pretences. But no such corrupt principles regulated these princes. Their word was their bond. "Though we have been imposed upon, we must not think ourselves at liberty to retaliate: solemn engagements made, even to our own hurt, must be conscientiously adhered to" (Thos. Scott). Two wrongs never make one right, and for a child of God to descend unto the sinful level of worldlings is doubly heinous. The deception practised by these Canaanites did not excuse Israel's hasty action: they had been foolish in so rashly committing the nation, and now they must suffer the consequences of the same.

"And the congregation murmured at the princes" (verse 18). The fault was entirely their own that Israel's leaders had been ensnared by such a piece of trickery, and though by grace they had respect unto the Lord's honour and refused to perjure themselves, yet they were made to feel the evil results of failing to "ask counsel at the mouth of the Lord" (verse 14). There is no previous mention of "murmuring" on the part of any of the Israelites; but now their unity was disturbed! This was no casual incident, but a Divine providence, designed to speak loudly unto those who had ears to hear. It was a Divine chastisement, an outward mark of the Lord's displeasure—yet how mild a one! The immediate reason for this "murmuring" is fairly obvious: the soldiers were chagrined at being withheld from seizing and plundering these cities; nevertheless, had not Joshua and the princes offended against the Lord in acting on their own judgment instead of waiting upon Him for directions, His restraining hand had prevented such an exercise of the carnal cupidity of the rank and file of the people, and no spirit of discontent and division would have been shown. Though God judicially pardons our failures, in His governmental ways He often makes us to eat the fruits of our folly.

"But all the princes said unto all the congregation, We have sworn unto them by the Lord God of Israel: now therefore we may not touch them" (verse 19). It is blessed to behold the harmony and unanimity of the princes, that none of them were weakened by the opposition which was encountered. It was not only their own word which was involved, but their word under Divine oath, and to violate *that* would both perjure themselves and grossly discredit their God in the estimation of the heathen. It can hardly be doubted that the congregation itself must have known of their oath, but charity requires us to believe that they had temporarily forgotten it. By way of illustration we may see in this murmuring of the congregation against these princes that, when either religious or political leaders are actuated and regulated by holy and lofty principles, it must not be expected that those under them will appreciate and seek to further their motives, but rather will criticize and oppose. Blessed it is to see how these princes stood their ground, fearing God and not the people. And the Lord honoured them therein, for no further murmurings against them are mentioned—the Lord subduing the people's lusts!

An Honored Oath

"This we will do to them; we will even let them live, lest wrath be upon us, because of the oath which we sware unto them" (ix, 20). In the preceding verses we saw how Israel had been deceived by some of the Canaanites, who, pretending to be from a very far country, posed as ambassadors authorized to treat with Joshua and enter into a treaty of peace for their people. Those impostors had not only prepared a very plausible tale, but were carefully made up in keeping with the part they played, appearing in tattered garments and with mouldy bread as evidences of the long journey they had taken. Instead of seeking counsel at the mouth of the Lord, Joshua and the responsible heads of the nation walked by sight and relied upon their senses (verse 14). Instead of deferring their decision and taking the trouble to carefully investigate the claims of the Gibeonites, Israel hurriedly entered into a covenant with them to spare their lives. Instead of making them a conditional promise, the princes solemnly ratified the agreement by oath (verse 15). All of this should be regarded by us as a pointed warning to avoid precipitate action, and as showing the wisdom of heeding that injunction, "He that believeth shall not make haste" (Isaiah xxviii, 16).

Within three days the folly of Israel was made manifest, for upon penetrating a little deeper into Canaan they came to the cities of the Gibeonites (verses 16, 17). It is to be duly noted that Israel's discovery of the trick that had been played upon them was not made by any spiritual discernment of theirs—which had assuredly been the case had a "single eye" been maintained to God's glory (Matt. vi, 22)—but by external means. Moreover, though the Lord did not allow them to be deceived for any length of time, He made evident, even if in a comparatively mild and gentle way, His displeasure against the princes through His providential dealings with them. The "murmuring" against them by the congregation, though "very natural under the circumstances," should be regarded as a Divine *chastisement*—God's suffering the people to voice their discontent, instead of working in them a spirit of acquiescence. Thus, for the moment, the harmony of Israel was disturbed and their unity seriously threatened. But it is good to see that, with one accord, the princes feared God rather than men, and, so far from desiring amity at any price, recognized that "the wisdom which is from above is first pure, then peaceable" (James iii, 17).

Instead of yielding to the desire of the rank and file of the people, who obviously wanted to avenge themselves upon the Gibeonites, and plunder their cities, all the princes stood their ground, and said, "We have sworn unto them by the Lord God of Israel: now therefore we may not touch them" (verse 19). Matthew Henry pertinently remarked that they "did not apply themselves to Eleazar for a dispensation, much less did they pretend that no faith is to be kept with heretics—with Canaanites; no, they were strangers to the modern artifices of the Roman Church to elude the most sacred bonds and even to sanctify perjuries." No, they were determined to honour the engagement into which they had entered. Happy the nation whose leaders and governors abide by their obligations. The *testing* of these princes was a very real one, but though their fidelity should occasion a mutiny of the people, they refused to go against their consciences. There can be little room for doubt that it was their unanimity which God used to pacify the murmuring congregation, teaching us that the best way to suppress discontent by the governed is for there to be a solid and firm front presented by the governors. Yet it was no mere policy of expediency which regulated these princes, but rather the fear of God and their determination not to dishonour Him.

"Thou shalt not take the name of the Lord thy God in vain; for the Lord will not hold him guiltless that taketh His name in vain" (Exodus xx, 7). There is the original and fundamental law concerning oaths, and with it should be linked, "Thou shalt fear the Lord thy God, and serve Him, and shalt swear by His name" (Deut. vi, 13). An oath, then, is a solemn appeal to the dread name of Jehovah, which, by awakening the spirit of the swearer to a consciousness of the awe-inspiring presence and cognizance of the Most High, gives all its sanctity and power to it. Properly speaking there are four things in an oath. First, a formal asseveration of the truth—which should always be spoken even though no oath be taken. Second, an acknowledgment of the presence of the thrice Holy One, who is solemnly called upon as a Witness in confirmation of the statement that we make. Third, an invocation, whereby we request God to testify unto our conscience that what we swear to is nothing but the truth (Romans ix, 1). Fourth, an imprecation, in which the swearer calls upon God to be the Revenger of all lies, binding himself to Divine punishment if he swear falsely. Since an oath be the invoking of God, it is an act of *worship*, an ascribing glory and owning Him as Judge.

It is therefore evident that the violation of an oath is a sin of the first magnitude, for it is a breach of the third commandment, a taking of God's name in vain, which He will not hold guiltless. As Leviticus xix, 12, informs us, to commit perjury in the name of God is an act of profanity. From such awful considerations it follows that an oath is to be feared (Eccles. ix, 2), and that once made it is binding (Num. xxx, 3)—a solemn example of which is seen in the case of Jephthah (Judges xi, 25). Consequently, it is not to be entered into lightly, nor should one be taken at all except in matters of real importance, and then only in the gravest spirit and manner. There are times, as Deuteronomy vi, 13, shows, when it becomes our duty to appeal unto God by solemn oaths, for deciding matters which cannot be adequately settled without one (Heb. vi, 16). It is to be observed that, when occasion required and men were warranted in the taking of an oath, such obtained centuries *before* the giving of the Law at Sinai. Thus Abraham swore to Abimelech (Gen. xxi, 23, 24), and required an oath to be taken by his servant when seeking a wife for Isaac (Gen. xxiv, 8, 9). Jacob swore to Laban, and Joseph to his father. Since these instances had no respect unto the legal institutes of Moses, they lead us to conclude that there would be nothing in the Gospel to forbid such a practice in this Christian era—again and again Paul confirmed his testimony by calling on God as Witness (II Cor. i, 23; Gal. i, 20).

"This we will do to them: we will even let them live, lest wrath be upon us, because of the oath which we sware unto them" (verse 20). One of the distinguishing marks given of those who shall abide in the Lord's tabernacle (enjoy intimate communion with Him) and dwell in His holy hill (spend eternity in heaven) is, "He that sweareth to his own hurt, and *changeth not*" (Psalm xv, 1, 4): that is, who will not go back on his oath no matter what temporal loss might be involved. On the other hand, "perjured persons" are classed with murderers of fathers and mothers, whoremongers, slave-dealers, etc. (I Tim. i, 9, 10). Very far were these princes from now treating their engagement with the Gibeonites as "a mere scrap of paper"—the Kaiser, Hitler and Mussolini brought down Divine wrath upon themselves and their people by just such perfidy. It is exceedingly solemn to observe that this was one of the crimes which characterized Israel during the closing days of their Old Testament history—see Zechariah v, 4; Malachi iii, 5; II Chronicles xxxvi, 11-13—"until the wrath of the Lord arose against His people, till there was no remedy" (II Chron. xxxvi, 16). Only so long as Britain honours her treaty obligations—no matter what sacrifices be involved—is there any hope of "remedy" for its people.

"And the princes said unto them, Let them live; but let them be hewers of wood and drawers of water unto all the congregation; as the princes had promised them" (verse 21). These princes were twelve in number, one at the head of each of Israel's tribes (Num. i, 15, 16, 44). That God was pleased with their sparing the lives of the Gibeonites is clearly evidenced from the sequel, for the very next chapter records how He gave them the most glorious victory in all their wars. Furthermore, we find that, centuries later, He severely avenged the wrong which Saul did unto the descendants of this tribe, manifesting His sore displeasure against that king's injuring of them in violation of this very league (II Samuel xxi, 1)—mark how David, the "man after God's own heart," honoured *his* oath to Jonathan in this connection, exempting Mephibosheth, Saul's grandson, from the just avengement (verse 7). Though the lives of these Gibeonites were spared, their liberty was taken from them, and they were made bondmen—not only tributaries, but under the yoke of servitude. To be "hewers of wood and drawers of water" would not only be wearisome employment, but regarded as a very low and menial one (cf. Deut. xxix, 11).

From what has been before us in the above incident, as well as from its sequel, we may perceive how that we are never the ultimate losers by fearing the Lord and honouring His name. Folly was committed by Joshua and the princes in so hastily concluding a league with the Gibeonites, and it was too late to rectify it: nevertheless, God overruled the same to His own glory and the benefit of His people, providing both Himself and them with useful servants. God can, and in His own wondrous way often does, turn our mistakes into advantages. That way will not be as good and glorious as His first best for us, yet it will not be without blessing. The same incident also teaches us the needlessness of taking things into our own hands and seeking to anticipate the Divine appointment. The congregation suffered no injury by restraining their desire to seize and plunder the cities of the Gibeonites mentioned in ix, 17, for if the reader will consult Joshua xviii, 25-28, he will find that in the end, when the land came to be divided, the first three cities there mentioned were obtained by them, and the fourth in Joshua xv, 2. It is never to our detriment to wait the Lord's time!

"And Joshua called for them, and he spake unto them, saying, Wherefore have ye beguiled us, saying, We are very far from you: when ye dwell among us?" (verse 22). Let us duly observe and admire the blessed restraint which Israel's leader here placed upon himself. Though these Gibeonites were now entirely at his disposal, he used not his power tyrannically. Nor did he give way to an outburst of temper because of their chicanery, and harshly denounce them as base liars. Instead, he mildly reproved them for their fraud and gave them opportunity to explain their conduct. As Matthew Henry rightly pointed out, " A just cause needs not anger to defend it, and a bad one is never made the better by it." The Lord forbids us rejoice (malignantly) when our enemy falls (Prov. xxiv, 17), and severely chastised the Edomites because they had "spoken proudly in the day of Judah's distress" (Obad. 12). This was the sin of Shimei, scorning his humiliated sovereign (II Samuel xvi, 5-9), for which he paid with his life (I Kings ii, 9, 10) How very differently was the Lord Jesus dealt with when *He* was arraigned before His judges! In Joshua's mild treatment of the Gibeonites we may behold blessedly shadowed forth "the meekness and gentleness of Christ" (II Cor. x, 1). ✓

"Now therefore ye are cursed, and there shall none of you be freed from being bondmen, and hewers of wood and drawers of water for the house of my God" (verse 23). Those words do not signify that Joshua now pronounced a curse upon them, but rather that it would henceforth be made to appear that they belonged to an accursed posterity. In a previous article we pointed out that the reason why these Gibeonites are designated "" Hivites " in ix, 9, was to intimate that they were the descendants of Canaan (Gen. x, 5-7), and here we have set before us an illustration of the sentence pronounced upon him because of his father's sin. By the spirit of prophecy Noah had declared, "Cursed be Canaan; a servant of servants shall he be unto his brethren" (Gen. ix, 25). The curse, then, consisted of *servitude,* and here we behold one part of its fulfilment in these Gibeonites being made the manual servants of Israel. How mysteriously yet wondrously does God order His providences unto the fulfilment of His Word, guiding the princes to select or determine this particular form of punishment upon these men! In Joshua's *confirmation* of the sentence of the twelve princes we have a striking adumbration of Christ making good His promise to the twelve apostles, " Whatsoever ye shall bind on earth shall be bound [ratified] in heaven " (Matt. xviii, 18).

"And they answered Joshua, and said, Because it was certainly told thy servants, how that the Lord thy God commanded Moses to give you all the land, and to destroy all the inhabitants of the land from before you, therefore we were sore afraid of our lives because of you, and have done this thing" (verse 24). Let us first notice that in this part of their reply they bore witness to

God's having made good one of His promises to Israel and fulfilled a prophecy made through Moses, to the effect that such reports would reach their ears of the irresistible power of Israel's God, and the fame of His wondrous works on their behalf, that the inhabitants of Canaan would be filled with dismay and their hearts sink within them. " I will send My fear before thee and will destroy all the people to whom thou shalt come " (Exodus xxiii, 27). " This day will I begin to put the dread of thee and the fear of thee upon all nations " (Deut. ii, 25), Jehovah had declared, thereby fulfilling the prediction of Exodus xv, 14 : " The people shall hear and be afraid, sorrow shall take hold of the inhabitants of Palestina.'" Such terror would fill them that their spirits would sink completely and they would be panic-stricken at the prospect before them. Such was the case here.

"There shall no man be able to stand before you : for the Lord your God shall lay the fear of you and the dread of you upon all the land that ye shall tread upon, as He hath said unto you " (Deut. xi, 25). God would strike such terror into the Canaanites, and make them so conscious of their impotency, that He would render the same subservient to the success of His people. Rahab had, previously, avowed the accomplishment of this, acknowledging that tidings of Jehovah's miracle-working power had reached them, that " your terror is fallen upon us, and that all the inhabitants of the land faint because of you " (Joshua ii, 9). In like manner will God yet make good every prophecy He has made and every promise that He has given. It is therefore to be duly noted that these Gibeonites freely testified that the nation of Israel was now acting according to the commandment of the Lord their God, and not from a spirit of personal blood-thirstiness and greed. They made no attempt to justify the lies which they had told, but frankly owned that they were in dread of losing their lives, and that the principle of self-preservation had moved them to resort to such a device.

"And now, behold, we are in thine hand : as it seemeth good and right unto thee to do unto us, do " (verse 25). That was tantamount to saying, We are fully in thy power and entirely at thy disposal, and readily submit ourselves to thy discretion. Their foregoing statement evinces that they had not only " heard " but also *believed* that God's promises to His people and threatenings to His enemies would certainly be fulfilled. They realized God's word was inviolable and His power invincible, and therefore nothing remained but for them to cast themselves upon His clemency. In their " as it seemeth good and right unto thee to do unto us, do " unto Joshua, one can see they hoped for the best : treat with us according to the laws of justice and kindness, and especially act consistently with the league made and the oath taken. It is in precisely such a spirit and attitude that sinners are to come before God in Christ—convicted of their sins, convinced of the verity of God's threatenings, casting themselves upon His good pleasure, hoping in His mercy, submitting unreservedly to His will, ready to take His yoke upon them.

"And so He did unto them, and delivered them out of the hand of the children of Israel, that they slew them not. And Joshua made them that day hewers of wood and drawers of water for the congregation, and for the altar of the Lord " (verses 26, 27). How blessedly the anti-typical Joshua was there foreshadowed! Though the guilt of these men was established, and though they belonged to an accursed race, yet he spared their lives, and that on the ground of a covenant made by oath! Thus he did what was both good and right ": yea, he went beyond what they " asked or thought," showing them favour and conferring honour upon them, by appointing them to minister unto the ' altar of the Lord "; and thus they would be taught the worship of the true God and delivered from idolatry. It is striking to note that the only ones who *acknowledged* what they " heard " about the Lord (ii, 10 ; ix, 24) were *delivered* from His judgments. The descendants of these Gibeonites—termed " Nethinim " or " devoted persons "—had a place of honour in the service of the temple centuries later (I Chron. ix, 2 ; Ezra viii, 20 ; Neh. vii, 60).

Chapter 13

VICTORY AT GIBEON

Joshua 10:1-43

Peacemaking

As its opening verse shows, the tenth of Joshua is closely connected with chapters vi, viii and ix, and this needs to be duly heeded by us if we are to discover and appropriate the spiritual lessons which it has for the Lord's people today—which should ever be one of our principal quests when reading God's Word. In chapters vi and viii we have an account of Israel's conquest of the cities of Jericho and Ai, but in the ninth something quite different is presented. Following the fighting at Ai there came a lull, and the capitulation of the Gibeonites unto Israel without any strenuous efforts on the part of the latter. It is often thus in the experience of Christians. When they have been particularly active in engaging the enemy and a notable victory has been obtained, the Lord grants a brief season of rest and comparative quietness. Yet they are not to conclude therefrom that the hardest part of their conflict is now over, so that it is safe for them to relax a little. What we are about to ponder indicates the contrary, and warns us that Satan does not readily admit defeat. Not only was Israel's warfare far from being ended, but a more determined and concerted resistance was to be encountered. Instead of having to meet the force of a single king, the massed armies of five of them had now to be defeated. The same thing appears in the history of our Saviour: the farther His gracious ministry proceeded, the greater and fiercer the opposition met with. Sufficient for the disciple to be as his Master.

Proceeding from the general to the particular, we observe that the opening verses of Joshua x *confirm* the typical application which we made of the concluding portion of the preceding chapter. At the close of our last we pointed out that what is there recorded of the Gibeonites adumbrated sinners surrendering themselves unto Christ, or, to use an expression which was freely employed by the Puritans, their "making peace with God." More recently, some have taken decided exception to that expression. It is affirmed that the sinner can do nothing whatever *to* make peace with God, and that it is quite unnecessary for him to essay doing so, seeing that Christ has "made peace" through the blood of His cross. But that is to confound things which differ, confusing what Christ purchased, and when the same is actually applied unto us. The question—and a most important one too—is, What does God require from the sinner in order for him to become a personal partaker of the benefits of that legal "peace" which Christ made with God? To which some make answer, Nothing but faith—simply believing that Christ has fully atoned for all our sins and relying upon the sufficiency of His sacrifice. But that is only half the answer, the second half, for it leaves out an essential requirement which must precede believing.

"Repent ye, and believe the Gospel" (Mark i, 15), "Testifying both to the Jews, and also to the Greeks, repentance toward God, and faith toward our

261

Lord Jesus Christ" (Acts xx, 21). It is very clear from these passages that repentance is as necessary as faith. Nay, we go farther, and declare that an *impenitent* heart is incapable of exercising a saving faith. Christ complained to Israel's leaders, "Ye repented not afterward, *that* ye might believe in him" (Matt. xxi, 32)—they responded not to the ministry of His forerunner because they had no realization of their sinful and lost condition. Those "dispensationalists" who state that repentance is required only of the Jews evince their ignorance of the most elementary truths of Scripture, for in "the great commission" Christ ordered His servants "that repentance and remission of sins should be preached in His name among *all* nations, beginning at Jerusalem" (Luke xxiv, 47), and His apostle announced that God "now [in this Christian era!] commandeth all men *everywhere* to repent" (Acts xvii, 30). Of course He does, for such a call is the pressing of His holy claims upon those who have ignored the same—who have disregarded His authority, slighted His law, and lived entirely to please themselves. It is because so little repentance has been preached that Christendom is now crowded with empty professors.

Repentance is a taking sides with God against myself. It is the laying aside of my awful enmity against Him. It is the privative side of conversion, for there must be a turning from something before there can be a turning unto God. Repentance consists of a holy horror and hatred of sin, a complete heart-forsaking of it, a sincere confessing of it unto God. True repentance is always accompanied by a deep longing and a genuine determination to abandon that course which is displeasing to God. It is impossible, in the very nature of the case, that a soul could seek God's pardon with any *honesty* while he continued to defy Him and persist in what He forbids. Thus, repentance is the sinner's making his peace with God—the throwing down of the weapons of his rebellion, ceasing his warfare against Him. Nor is there anything in the least degree "legalistic" or meritorious about this, for repentance or making peace with God neither atones for our vile misconduct of the past nor moves God to be gracious unto us. Repentance no more *purchases* salvation than does faith, yet the one is as indispensable as the other. The wicked is required to "forsake his way . . . and return unto the Lord" before He will have mercy upon him and abundantly pardon (Isaiah lv, 7, and cf. I Kings viii, 47-50; Acts iii, 19).

"Now it came to pass, when Adonizedek king of Jerusalem had heard how Joshua had taken Ai, and had utterly destroyed it; as he had done to Jericho and her king, so he had done to Ai and her king; and how the inhabitants of Gibeon had *made peace* with Israel. and were among them; that they feared greatly" (Joshua x, 1, 2). Once more we would note the very varied effects upon different ones of what they had "heard" of Israel's exploits, and how some of them attributed their successes unto Jehovah, while others did not so. Rahab (ii, 9-11) and the Gibeonites (ix, 9) were examples of the former, and the kings of ix, 1, and this Adonizedek of the latter. The king of Jerusalem, despite his high-sounding name, gave God no place in his thoughts; yet he was thoroughly alarmed at Israel's progress. His fear was cumulative. He was rendered uneasy at the tidings of Jericho's overthrow, still more so at the news of the destruction of Ai; but when he and his subjects learned of the Gibeonites having concluded a league of peace with Joshua, "they feared greatly"—most probably because he had counted on *their* considerable support in resisting these aggressors.

We would also attentively heed the Spirit's emphasis here on the time-mark: "It came to pass, *when* Adonizedek . . . heard." There is nothing meaningless or superfluous in the Scriptures, and it is by noting such a detail as this that we often obtain the key which opens to us the spiritual significance of what follows. In this instance the immediate sequel was the banding together of four others with the king of Jerusalem against Gibeon, and in the light of the closing verses of chapter ix, the typical force of this is not difficult to perceive. It is when sinners renounce the service of their former master, and the friendship of the world, in order to make their peace with God and join interests with His people, that they must be prepared to encounter persecution from the ungodly. That is why the Saviour bade all would-be disciples of His to sit down first and "count the cost" (Luke xiv, 28-33), and His servant warned believers, "Marvel not, my brethren, if the world hate you" (I John iii, 13). In Adonizedek's determination to slay the Gibeonites we have adumbrated the inveterate enmity of the serpent against the Redeemer's "seed." Previously, while Satan keepeth his palace, "his goods are in peace" (Luke xi, 21), but when he *loses* any of his captives, his rage against them knows no bounds.

Ere passing on let us ponder one other detail in our opening verse, namely Israel's "*utter* destruction" of Jericho and Ai, for a most important lesson is inculcated by that adjective. In its application to the spiritual warfare of the Christian it tells us that we must be ruthlessly thorough in the work of mortification. No half measures are to be taken against the things which hinder the present possession of our heritage. There must be no compromising with our lusts, no trifling with temptation, no flirting with the world. True, inward corruptions will strongly resist our onslaughts upon them, as the men of Ai did when Israel came against it. For a time the king of Ai had the better of the contest, so that Israel were dismayed; but they did not abandon the fight, instead they humbled themselves before the Lord, and He graciously undertook for them. Not that they were released from the discharge of their responsibilities, so that they could *passively witness* His operations on their behalf. No, indeed. They were required to perform their duty and employ different tactics. Accordingly, as they implicitly followed His instruction, the Lord prospered them and Ai was "utterly destroyed": in other words, complete victory was theirs.

But the overthrowing and destroying of Ai proved to be neither an easy nor a pleasant task to Israel, for in the course thereof they passed through both a humiliating and distressing experience. So it is in that work of unsparing mortification to which the Christian is called. Our Lord likened it unto the plucking out of a right eye and the cutting off of a right hand (Matt. v, 29, 30). By such language He intimated the difficulty and severity of the work He has assigned us. The "eye" represents that which is dearest to the natural man, and the "hand" what is the most useful to him. The plucking out of the one and the cutting off of the other signify that we are to exercise the most rigorous denying of self, that however precious an idol or profitable any unrighteous course may be unto the carnal nature, they must be sacrificed for Christ's sake. No matter how unwelcome it proves to the flesh, its lusts are not to be spared; for unless they be brought into subjection to God, the soul is gravely imperiled. By Divine grace this difficult task is not impossible. The "utter destruction" of Ai, then, is recorded both for our emulation and for our encouragement. Yet remember that, though a brief lull may follow such a victory, the surrender of our remaining enemies is not to be looked for; rather must we expect a yet more determined resistance from them, seeking to prevent any further spiritual advance by us.

" They feared greatly, because Gibeon was a great city, as one of the royal cities, and because it was greater than Ai, and all the men thereof were mighty " (verse 2). We believe the Holy Spirit's design in giving us these particulars about the Gibeonites was at least threefold: to magnify the grace of God in subduing them unto Himself, to account for the subsequent actions of Adoni-zedek, and to cast light upon the typical significance of the sequel. In view of what we are here told about the Gibeonites, it is the more remarkable that they had not only made peaceful overtures unto Joshua, but had offered no demur at taking upon them the yoke of servitude and becoming hewers of wood and drawers of water unto Israel. Therein we should discern a people, hostile to Him by nature, " made willing " in the day of God's power, and the might of His grace in bringing them to submit readily to the most exacting and pride-abasing terms. Such is the nature of the miracle of conversion in every case: the slaying of man's awful enmity against God, the humbling of his haughty heart, the bending of his stubborn will, the bringing of him to a complete surrender unto the lordship of Christ, making him an " obedient child " (I Peter i, 14).

" They feared greatly, because Gibeon was a great city, as one of the royal cities, and because it was greater than Ai, and all the men thereof were mighty " (verse 2). Gibeon was not only a formidable frontier town but also the capital of that section, and such a city and territory yielding so tamely to Israel much alarmed the king of Jerusalem. Not only had he lost what he probably counted upon as being a powerful ally, but he feared that other cities would follow suit, so that he now began to tremble for his own skin. If so powerful a people had capitulated without striking a blow, who could be expected to take a resolute stand against Joshua and his men? Not only was he much alarmed, but greatly chagrined and incensed against the Gibeonites, and so resolved upon their destruction (verses 4, 5), which indicates the third design of the Spirit here. The "greater" the trophy which grace secures for Christ, the more "royal" his status, the fiercer will be the opposition which he meets with from his enemies. That is why those whom the Lord makes the ministers of His Gospel are the chief marks of Satan's malice. But let them not be dismayed thereby. Not only is it a high honour to suffer for Christ's sake, but the opposition a faithful preacher encounters is a good sign that God is using him to make inroads into the Devil's kingdom.

" Wherefore Adonizedek king of Jerusalem sent unto Hoham king of Hebron, and unto Piram king of Jarmuth, and unto Japhia king of Lachich, and unto Debir king of Eglon, saying, Come up unto me, and help me, that we may smite Gibeon: *for* it hath made peace with Joshua and with the children of Israel " (verses 3, 4). It will be remembered that the Canaanitish kings whose territories lay farther to the north and the west had previously decided to federate themselves against Israel (ix, 2), and by this time would probably be engaged in mustering their forces for a combined assault upon them. But the tidings of Gibeon's alliance with Joshua so intimidated and enraged these five kings, whose cities were nearer the point which Israel had then reached, that they decided to anticipate the plan of their remoter fellows by falling upon Gibeon. It is likely that the king of Jerusalem reckoned upon Joshua having his hands so full in making his arrangements and deploying his forces to meet the impending attack of the northern and western armies of the Canaanites that he would be unable to come to the relief of the Gibeonites. It therefore appeared to be a favourable opportunity and a safe venture for these five kings to fall upon those whom they regarded as their renegade countrymen; yet in so doing they but accelerated their own destruction.

Verse 2 opens by saying, "That *they* feared greatly," yet the preceding verse mentions no one save the king of Jerusalem, and so we would expect it to read that "*he* feared greatly." While it is likely that the plural number is designed to include his subjects, it is also highly probable that the "they" looks forward to the four kings mentioned in the next verse, and it intimates *why* they were willing to respond to Adonizedek's call. Thus we behold again how widespread was the terror inspired by the news of Israel's victories. Not only was this a further fulfilment of what the Lord had announced in Exodus xxiii, 27, and Deuteronomy xi, 25, but we may perceive therein a shadowing forth of what takes place under the proclamation of the Gospel. As we pointed out above, the hearing of what the mighty arm of Jehovah had wrought reacted very differently in them than in others. There was the same opportunity for those kings to make their peace with Joshua as the Gibeonites had, and their fatal refusal to do so supplies a solemn illustration of the fact that the Gospel is "the savour of life unto life" to those who believe and are saved, but "the savour of death unto death" to those who reject it and are lost (II Cor. ii, 15, 16). Nor is *fear* sufficient to move a sinner to throw down the weapons of his warfare against God, as appears not only from the case before us, but also from that of Pharaoh and of Felix who "trembled" as he listened to Paul speaking on "judgment to come" (Acts xxiv, 25).

Not only was Adonizedek unwilling to humble himself and make peace with Joshua, but he was determined that none of his near neighbours should do so, and in his persuading them to follow his policy we have a sad instance of a strong character being able to influence others to evil. To be a personal transgressor is bad enough, but to be a ringleader in wickedness evinces a high degree of depravity and is doubly damnable. Adonizedek's "Come up unto me, and help *me*" is to be understood in the light of "that *we* may smite Gibeon," thereby signifying that it was a duty devolving equally upon all of them. At first one wonders what they thought would be gained by such a course: would it not be more prudent to husband their forces for self-defence when the army of Joshua should invade their section? Probably their purpose was to make an object lesson of Gibeon and thereby intimidate other cities from following their example. But the inspiring motive which prompted the prime mover is clearly seen in *the ground* of his appeal unto his fellows: "For it [Gibeon] hath made peace with Joshua and with Israel," and as the closing words of verse 1 add, "and were among them." Thus it was something more than an instinct of self-preservation which moved them to act, namely a malignant spirit against those who had united themselves with the people of God. Thereby they had alienated themselves from their original associates and evoked their wrath.

Declaration of War

The typical teaching of the Old Testament is one of its most striking and blessed features. It not only demonstrates the Divine authorship thereof, by causing the shadows to outline so accurately the coming substance, but supplies valuable instruction for the student of the New. We are sometimes reminded that "In the Old Testament the New is contained, and in the New Testament the Old is explained," but there is a danger lest we draw the inference that the latter has largely displaced the former. This is so far from being the case that the former casts considerable light on the latter, and supplies the keys which unlock many of its details. Rather are the two Testaments like the two eyes of our body—both necessary in order to complete vision, the one complementing the other. Not only are we largely dependent upon the prophets for an understanding of the predictions made by Christ and through His apostles, not only is there much in the historical books which supplies vivid illustrations and exemplifications of the practical teaching and precepts of the Epistles, but the ordinances and ceremonies of Judaism foreshadowed and help to open unto us many aspects of Gospel truth. We have sought to give prominence to this in our progress through the book of Joshua, showing that in numerous ways its central character prefigured the Lord Jesus, that Israel's experiences in the conquest of Canaan adumbrated the Christian's spiritual warfare, and that both solemn and precious evangelical pictures are to be found therein.

During the past century there were those who rendered a valuable service unto Christendom by the stress they laid upon the importance and worth of the Old Testament types, and how that many incidents recorded in its historical books set forth " the way of salvation." Yet it is much to be regretted that they were so partial in their selection, and that their emphases on certain particular aspects of the way of salvation were often so disproportionate. It is indeed blessed to point out how that Rahab was delivered from destruction and obtained a place among the people of God by the exercise of *faith,* and how that the Cities of Refuge are a blessed representation of that *security* which is to be found in Christ for those who are pursued by the Law; but it is equally striking to behold, and necessary to insist on if the balance of truth is to be preserved, that the Gibeonites *making peace* with Joshua provides just as real and striking a " Gospel picture " as do the former. There are some of the types which more especially magnify the grace of God; there are others which exemplify His holiness. In the one is displayed His benevolent overtures; in the other, the claims of His righteousness. Sometimes it is the freeness of the Divine mercy which is stressed, at others the responsibility of the sinner is pressed.

Those who have read critically our last six articles on the Gibeonites (Joshua ix) may have concluded that we were guilty of contradicting ourselves, for we began by viewing them as illustrating the character and conduct of empty professors and hypocrites applying for union with God's people, yet ended by regarding them as types of repentant sinners coming to Christ and making their peace with God. It was not a case of our forgetting what we had first pointed out, nor is there anything inconsistent therewith in our latter remarks. There is a fullness in God's Word which pertains not to the writings of men, and many and varied are the "applications" which may be legitimately made of a single passage in it. In Genesis xxii Isaac is first a type of Christ, in his subjection to his father's will and his readiness to be offered in sacrifice; but later he is a figure of the sinner—the ram taking his place and dying in his stead! From Exodus xvi many striking *comparisons* can be drawn between the manna and Christ as the bread of life, yet in John vi we find Him making some very definite *contrasts* between them. Some of the characters in Scripture portray both the unsaved and backslidden believers, nor is there anything incongruous in their so doing. So it is with the Gibeonites: they need to be regarded in two different relations, in accordance with the marked change in their early and later conduct.

We must distinguish between the Gibeonites as they were moved by Satan to act dishonestly and tempt Israel and as they were subsequently moved by the Holy Spirit to surrender unto Joshua and made willing to take his yoke upon them. In his natural condition the sinner is a hypocrite, and even when he is brought sincerely to seek after Christ not a little carnality is mingled with his efforts. There is a very marked difference to be observed between the wily conduct of the Gibeonites in ix, 3-6, and their frankness and meekness in ix, 24, 25, and equally so should there be between the "applications" which the expositor makes of them. What follows in chapter x *confirms* the accommodation we made of the closing verses of chapter ix. No sooner had the Gibeonites made their peace with Joshua than the rage of the enemy was stirred against them. Thus it is in the experience of a saved sinner. If he be truly converted—gives Christ His rightful place in his heart and life, making a thorough break from the world—it is not long before he discovers that so far from his former companions congratulating him, or being ready to emulate him, they now turn against him and become antagonistic, persecuting him in some form or other, seeking to bring about his downfall rather than encourage him.

But we must take a yet closer look at those who *opposed* the Gibeonites. Five kings of the Amorites combined together to destroy them: they were not only fellow Canaanites but close neighbours. Thus we regard them as something more than a figure of the Christian's foes in general, namely as pointing more definitely to those whom, at first, he does not suspect of being inimical to him. When a young convert has broken from the ungodly he is more or less prepared for the enmity of the profane world, but not so of the professing world: rather does he expect that those who bear the name of Christ will be his friends. Alas, he has to discover (in principle at least, and often literally) that "a man's enemies are the men of his own house" (Micah vii, 6)—quoted by our Saviour in Matthew x, 36. This is yet another lesson that the Christian has to learn in connection with his spiritual warfare, and a particularly painful one it is. But sufficient for the disciple to be as his Master, for we are told of our Lord that "neither did His brethren believe in Him" (John vii, 5) and that His kinsmen regarded Him as crazy, saying "He is beside Himself" (Mark iii, 21); while it was one of His apostles who betrayed Him.

What has just been pointed out was clearly adumbrated by those who assailed the Gibeonites. First, as already remarked, they were near neighbours, fellow Canaanites. Second, they dwelt in the *mountains* (x, 6), and it is ever to be borne in mind that there are no meaningless details in God's Word. To inform us that these kings resided in the mountains is only another way of saying that they occupied high ground, that theirs was an elevated position. Sad to say, it is often those who hold a similar place in the religious realm who are the least friendly toward the Lord's little ones. Desiring to have the pre-eminence, they are merciless unto any who refuse to be subject to them—as the Sanhedrin hounded Christ to death and forbade His ambassadors to preach in His name. The mountains are also a symbol of *pride* (Isaiah xl, 4) with which every Diotrephes is filled (III John). Third, the same feature appears again in the high-sounding names of these kings (x, 3), for Adonizedek, the prime mover, means "lord of righteousness"; Hoham, "Jah (God) protects"; Piram, "wild" or "fierce"; Japhia, "high" or "elevated"; Debir, "speaker"—suitable cognomens for pretentious professors!

Adonizedek, the king of Jerusalem, sent a message unto the four kings saying: "Come up unto me, and help me, that we may smite Gibeon" (x, 4). Very soon after the Gibeonites had entered into their friendly league with Israel they found the most powerful forces of southern Canaan arrayed against them. They had done them no wrong, but rather had shown their fellows the wisest and best course to adopt. Yet this was the very thing which the arch-conspirator most dreaded (verses 1, 2). Incidentally, we may note how, at that early date, Jerusalem exerted more or less of a dominating influence in the land of Palestine, for not only was it its king who took the lead in this movement, but his city was to be the gathering centre for the others. Yet apparently he had not sufficient confidence in his own forces to act alone, so sought the co-operation of four of his fellows. Had it been merely a matter of coming to *his* aid, it is to be doubted whether they would have responded, for they were more or less rivals. Human nature and tribal bigotry being the same then as now, it would be *self-interest* which moved them to accede, and since Gibeon was "as one of the royal cities" (verse 2) they coveted a share of its spoils.

But let us observe next *the ground* of Adonizedek's appeal unto his fellows: "*for* it hath made peace with Joshua and with the children of Israel" (verse 4). That which so incensed him was their union with the people of God. It is to be duly noted that this is the third time their "making peace" is mentioned (ix, 15; x, 1), and the setting in which the phrase occurs leaves us in no doubt as to its precise import. It connotes a change of relationship and the complete reversal of the old order of life. Spiritually speaking, it is our response to the Gospel call "be ye reconciled to God" (II Cor. v, 20)—cease your enmity against Him. The very expression occurs in "Let him take hold of My strength, that he may *make peace with Me*" (Isaiah xxvii, 5). It is a complete surrendering of ourselves unto God. It is identical with conversion, which is a thorough right-about-face. Genuine repentance is always accompanied by reformation of conduct. The wicked must abandon his course of self-will and self-pleasing and "return unto the Lord" (from whom he departed in Adam's apostasy) if his sins are to be pardoned (Isaiah lv, 7, and compare Prov. xxviii, 13).

The Scriptures are full of what is deliberately and fatally omitted from the false "evangelism" of our day, which blatantly announces that nothing is required from the sinner except faith in Christ. But an impenitent heart cannot savingly believe, nor is there any forgiveness for those who are determined to continue in a course of carnality and worldliness. "Put away the strange Gods which are among you, and incline your heart unto the Lord God" (Joshua xxiv, 23)—idols must be abandoned before He can be loved and served. "Repent ye therefore, and be converted" is the Divine demand. Observe well what immediately follows: "*that* your sins may be blotted out" (Acts iii, xix). The same order occurs again in Mark iv, 12: "Lest at any time they should [1] be converted, and [2] their sins should be forgiven them." That is the order of *human responsibility*. "We . . . preach unto you that ye should [1] turn from these vanities [2] unto the living God" (Acts xiv, 15). Again, Paul declared that his business was to turn men "from darkness to light, and from the power of Satan unto God" (Acts xxvi, 18), and note well that *precedes* "that they may receive forgiveness of sins." Likewise must a Christian "cast off the works of darkness" ere he can "put on the armour of light" (Romans xiii, 12).

"Therefore the five kings of the Amorites . . . gathered themselves together, and went up, they and all their hosts, and encamped before Gibeon, and made war against it" (verse 5). That is set over against the "made peace" of the preceding verse, teaching us clearly that to make our peace with God signifies to cease fighting against Him. It also shows that, when we do so, those who are opposed to Him will turn against us, and that no matter how circumspectly we conduct ourselves. It is the desire of a Christian to live amicably with all men, but he soon has cause to say with the Psalmist, "I am for peace: but when I speak, they are for war" (Psalm cxx, 7). The enemies of the Lord will not leave alone those who wear His yoke and are joined to His people. In uniting with Israel the Gibeonites had alienated themselves from their heathen neighbours. The four kings offered no objection to Adonizedek's plan, but willingly made common cause in seeking the destruction of their fellows. What a sidelight that casts upon the character of the Canaanites! How it serves to demonstrate their fitness to be the objects of Jehovah's judgment! It is also to be noted that all of these five kings were Amorites, and these were the ancient enemies of God's people (Num. xxi, 21-23).

In those days it was not the custom of an invading army to make an immediate attack upon a city, but rather to surround it and weaken its inhabitants by a process of starvation—cutting them off from all further supplies from without. Ancient cities were surrounded by high and thick walls and protected by powerful gates, and to make a direct assault at first would prove a costly undertaking. Accordingly we read that the hosts of these kings "encamped before Gibeon." They were evidently quite sure of themselves and had no doubt of success. Probably they thought it unlikely that Joshua would go to the trouble of honouring his league with the Gibeonites, and, in any case, that the camp of Israel was too far distant for their fighting men to come up to the relief of the beseiged city; and therefore that the task would prove a simple one. But like many others before and since, they were to prove that "the race is not to the swift, nor the battle to the strong" (Eccles. ix, 11). Like Pharaoh of old, these kings had left the Lord out of their reckoning! And they too discovered that nothing more surely provokes Him against evil-doers and hastens their destruction than for them to make war against those who have entered into a covenant with Him.

But why should God permit this unprovoked attack? Why did He suffer the Gibeonites to be so menaced? Since they had made their peace with Him, why did He not cause the rest of the Canaanites to be at peace with them? For a variety of reasons. First, to impress upon them their *own origin*. They too were "clay of the same lump," and in the evil conduct of their invading fellows they had a solemn reminder of what *they* were by nature. By this painful method the Lord was saying to them, "Wherefore remember, that ye being in time past Gentiles in the flesh . . . having no hope, and without God in the world" (Eph. ii, 11, 12). It was naught but sovereign grace which made them differ from those who sought to slay them. It is a salutary exercise of heart for us to heed that Divine injunction, "look unto the rock whence ye are hewn, to the hole of the pit whence ye are digged" (Isaiah li, 1). Such a look will remove pride from us; such a realization will keep us in our proper place—in the dust before God. The Gibeonites belonged to the same accursed race as these five kings, and it was only God's distinguishing mercy which prevented them from sharing their doom. Seek to remember that, Christian reader, when you are being persecuted by the world, and ask yourself *who* it is that has delivered you from being among the persecutors!

Many other answers may be returned to our question as to why God permitted the Gibeonites to face such a situation. It was to *test their faith* and make it evident unto them whether or not they now regretted the radical step they had recently taken. Would they tell themselves what fools they had been to antagonize their former companions, or were they prepared to endure afflictions for the Lord's sake? Those who heed Christ's exhortation to first sit down and "count the cost" before enlisting under His banner will *not* "think it strange" when the fiery trial comes upon them. Again, it was to make them realize that they were living in a hostile world, as sheep in the midst of wolves. Sooner or later each believer is made to prove that unwelcome fact. "Marvel not, my brethren, if the world hate you" (I John iii, 13). It *did* your Master, and the more faithful you be to Him the more fellowship will you have with His sufferings. Again, this trial was designed to cast them back the more upon the Lord: to wean them from any hankering they had to maintain communion with those who were strangers to Him. Finally, it afforded an opportunity to prove God's sufficiency: His compassion, fidelity, power.

And *how* did the Gibeonites react to the peril threatening them? They did not repudiate their alliance with Israel and apologize to Adonizedek for what he would regard as their perfidy. They did not put their trust in the strength of the city's walls; nor did they, on the other hand, regard their predicament as hopeless, and despairingly await their end. Instead, "the men of Gibeon sent unto Joshua to the camp to Gilgal, saying, Slack not thy hand from thy servants; come up to us quickly, and save us, and help us: for all the kings of the Amorites that dwell in the mountains are gathered together against us" (verse 6). Either they had advance tidings of the impending attack, and in order to save time dispatched messengers unto Joshua, or the cordon which their enemies had thrown around the city was not so complete as to prevent some of their number issuing forth on their mission. Very blessed is it to behold their conduct on this occasion. They appealed to the one who had recently shown them mercy and spared their lives. They had full confidence in him, neither questioning his willingness to come to their aid nor doubting his ability to rescue them.

In appealing to Joshua for help they disavowed their self-sufficiency. So far from proudly entertaining the idea that they were capable themselves of repulsing the enemy, they looked to Joshua for deliverance. Though by nature all the men of Gibeon were "mighty" (verse 2), they relied not on their own skill and valour, but humbled themselves by applying elsewhere for assistance. Note this well, dear reader, if you would be victorious in the fight of faith. Recognize that the forces confronting you are far too formidable for your own wisdom and might. Take the place of dependence and look to the antitypical Joshua. It is in conscious weakness that our strength lies (II Cor. xii, 10). There is no other way of becoming strong in the Lord and in the power of His might than by utterly discounting our own fancied competency. "To them that have no might He increaseth strength" (Isaiah xl, 29). On the other hand, woe is denounced on those who trust in chariots" (Isaiah xxxi, 1). Trust in the Lord and thou shalt not be confounded.

Deliverance

"God is our refuge and strength, a very present help in trouble" (Psalm xlvi, 1). In the heyday of youth, "while the evil days come not" those words mean comparatively little unto us. As the sunshine of prosperity is enjoyed our minds do not dwell upon the shelter provided for the storm. Nevertheless, God has ordained that sooner or later each of His children will be devoutly thankful that such a verse is in His Word, and give them to prove experientially the verity and preciousness of it. Then it is, but only then, we discover that "trouble" is a *blessing* in disguise—as the dark clouds pour down showers which refresh the parched earth. It is true that trouble does not always issue in conscious and manifest blessing, but in such case the fault is ours. Many of the troubles which people impiously ascribe to "bad luck" or "misfortune" are brought upon themselves by hurried decisions or foolish conduct. But if the Christian will place the blame where it belongs, confess to God the sinful failures which have occasioned his trouble, and beg Him graciously to sanctify the same unto him, his prayer will be answered, and he too will learn that the Divine Workman can bring good out of evil.

It is very blessed to observe the climacteric emphasis in Psalm xlvi, 1. First, what God is in Himself: "our refuge and strength"—the One to whom we may turn for succour and shelter; the One whose grace is sufficient for every need. Second, what He is unto His people in trouble, namely a real "help," for He is no "fair weather friend," but One who may confidently be counted upon in the day of adversity and affliction. Third, this is amplified thus: He is not only a "help," but a *present* one: not one who is far distant, but by our side—"closer than hands or feet." And to make it still more emphatic and impressive "a *very* present help," added the Psalmist—as Spurgeon expressed it, "more nearly present than the trouble itself." For, mark it well, it is not merely that the Lord is a very present help "in time of trouble" as so many misquote it, but "in trouble" itself. Thus His assistance may be counted upon with absolute certainty. He is a very present help in trouble to enable us to bear it, to sustain us under it, to comfort us in it, to bring us through it, yea, to sanctify the same unto us. Thus have His people, in all ages, abundantly proved. He was "a very present help in trouble" unto Jacob when He subdued the enmity of Laban and Esau, to Joseph in Egypt, to the widow of Zaraphath, to Daniel in the lions' den. And He is the same today!

No matter how cautiously we plan or discreetly we act, there is no escaping trouble in some form or other, for man is "born unto trouble as the sparks fly upward" (Job v, 7). How can it be otherwise: myself a fallen and erring creature, dwelling in a world which lieth in the wicked one? But let not that fact sour or dismay you: rather use it for obtaining personal proof of the validity and value of the Divine assurances. Trouble is sent not to drive us from God, but to draw us to Him. Emulate the Psalmist: "In the day of my trouble I sought the Lord" (Psalm lxxvii, 2)—not took matters into his own hands, seeking to put right what was wrong, for that ends in making bad matters worse. The believer's duty and privilege is clear: to appropriate and plead that precious promise, "Call upon Me in the day of trouble: I will deliver thee, and thou shalt glorify Me" (Psalm 1, 15). Follow not the vain policy of the world in attempting to forget your trouble or drown it in pleasure, or grit your teeth and make the best of a bad job. No, make the living God your recourse: count upon His lovingkindness and tender pity, bear in mind His mighty power and infinite resources, so that nothing is too hard for Him.

Does the reader say, I *have* called upon the Lord again and again, but He has not removed my trouble or even mitigated it? Nor has He promised to do so. But in Psalm i, 15, He says, "I will deliver thee," and is not that the same thing? No, certainly not; rather is it something much better. There is something worse, something to be far more dreaded, than "trouble," namely the sinful way in which we are so prone to act while under it. The promise is "Call upon Me in the day of trouble: I will deliver *thee*"—not "from it," but *from thyself*. Call upon Me humbly, trustfully, perseveringly, and I will "deliver thee"—from open rebellion against Me, from a suicide's grave, from sinking into utter despair. But more, "and thou shalt glorify Me," by meekly and patiently enduring what I have appointed thee, by leaning harder upon Me, and by thus improving the trouble. This is both our duty and privilege: "glorify ye the Lord *in the fires*" (Isaiah xxiv, 15). To glorify Him should ever be our aim, whether in health or on a bed of suffering. Let not the afflicted saint give way to self-pity and regard himself as "the victim of circum-stances," but seek grace to rise above and be victor over them. "Wait on the Lord, be of good courage, and He shall strengthen thine heart" (Psalm xxvii, 14).

Trouble is not always in consequence of our wrongdoing or injudicious conduct. So far from it, it may be caused by fidelity to Christ, thereby stirring up against us the enmity of Satan. Such was the case of the Gibeonites. A short time after they had made peace with Joshua, entered into a league with him, and he had appointed them to be servants "for the altar of the Lord," five kings of the Amorites determined to destroy them, and "they and all their hosts . . . encamped before Gibeon, and made war against it" (Joshua x, 5). Whereupon we are told, "And the men of Gibeon sent unto Joshua to the camp to Gilgal, saying, slack not thy hand from thy servants; come up to us quickly, and save us, and help us: for all the kings of the Amorites that dwell in the mountains are gathered together against us" (verse 6). Most commendable was such an action. In the hour of their need they turned unto the one who had so graciously spared their lives and entered into a covenant with them: they confided in his sympathy and counted upon his ability and willingness to come to their aid. Thus it is that Christians should ever do with the antitypical Joshua—"casting all your care upon Him, for He careth for you" (I Peter v, 7).

That appeal of the Gibeonites unto Joshua may be typically regarded as the prayer of believers unto the Lord. Considered thus, it contains valuable instruction for us. First, observe the place which they took: "thy *servants*" they acknowledged themselves to be. Such language breathed a spirit of dependence, disowning any might or sufficiency of their own. This is what becomes *us* as we approach the mercy seat—taking the place of confessed weakness, coming as empty-handed beggars. Second, they acquainted Joshua with the desperateness of their situation, spreading their case before him. Such is ever our privilege: to unburden our hearts unto Him who alone can afford us real relief. Third, they made known their request: "save us, and help us." Logically those clauses should be reversed, but a burdened and agitated heart pays little attention to its phrasing when dire calamity prompts the cry for deliverance. Fourth, this appeal was couched in terms of urgency: "slack not thy hand . . . for all the kings of the Amorites . . . are gathered together against us." That was not the language of dictation or of impatience, but a cry of distress, and an appeal unto the relation which now obtained between them and Joshua, for subservience is entitled to protection.

But there was one word in their appeal which perhaps some of our readers would deem unsuitable for use in a prayer unto God: "Come up *quickly*" begged the Gibeonites. Let God's Word determine, for to it we must ever turn for instruction and guidance. Before referring thereto let us bear in mind that the situation in which those men were placed was no ordinary one, but rather were they in extremity, so that unless effectual help reached them promptly it would be too late. Thus we are not about to turn unto the Scriptures for something which will supply us with a general rule to direct us on all occasions, but rather to ascertain whether there are any prayers to God recorded therein which intimate that it is permissible for His people to employ the language of importunity when, to them, their case appears desperate. Undoubtedly there are, not only in a single passage but in many. "Bow down Thine ear to me; deliver me speedily" (Psalm xxxi, 2), cried David. And again, "Make haste to help me, O Lord my salvation" (Psalm xxxviii, 22): he entreated that the help might not be long in coming. "But I am poor and needy: make haste unto me, O God" (Psalm lxx, 5): a desperate case calls for timely aid.

God's time is always the best time, yet when we are sorely pressed we *may* beg Him to act on our behalf without delay. "Hear me speedily, O Lord: my spirit faileth" (Psalm cxliii, 7). When our case is critical we may plead its urgency. "O my God, make haste for my help" (Psalm lxxi, 12). Such a cry was evoked by the sore pressure of affliction, and it shows that if real necessity justifies it we may be urgent with God, though never out of wilfulness. At a time when the enemy had come in like a flood and the cause of God was languishing, and His people were in sore straits, we find that Asaph prayed, "Let Thy tender mercies speedily prevent ["meet"] us, for we are brought very low" (Psalm lxxix, 8): thus in dire distress it is permissible for us to ask for speed on God's part. What is still more pertinent to this particular point is the example of our Saviour, for in the Messianic Psalms we find that He cried, "O Lord, My strength, haste Thee to help Me" (Psalm xxii, 19, and cf. xl, 13). "I am in trouble; hear Me speedily" (Psalm lxix, 17). And again, "In the day when I call answer Me speedily" (Psalm cii, 2).

"So Joshua ascended from Gilgal, he, and all the people of war with him, and all the mighty men of valour" (verse 7). Joshua did not send a messenger to the hard-pressed Gibeonites telling them that they must fight their own battles or proffer the excuse that his hands were already too full for him to intervene on their behalf. Nor did he raise an objection against the hard journey which such an undertaking would involve. Not thus would he mock those who were looking to him for deliverance. Instead, he responded promptly and readily to their pressing request. Therein we see again how blessedly Joshua prefigured the Saviour. As we read through the four Gospels, we find that the Lord Jesus never failed to answer an appeal for help, whether that appeal came from Jew or Gentile, rich or poor, saint or sinner. He was just as willing to heal the servant of the Roman centurion as He was the mother-in-law of His apostle, and to grant the request of the poor leper as to raise Lazarus. Nor did He refuse to give an interview unto Nicodemus because he sought Him by night, or turn a deaf ear to the dying thief when He was experiencing the pains of crucifixion. And, my reader, He is the same today as He was yesterday: vastly different in the position He occupies, but *unchanged* in His readiness to succour the needy.

Though we are very familiar with what has just been pointed out, and freely acknowledge the preciousness of the same, yet every one of us needs to be reminded of it, especially when we are hard pressed. Not only are we ever prone to give way to an evil heart of unbelief, but when sore trouble comes upon us we are likely to be so occupied with *it* as almost to lose sight of our blessed Lord. One reason why He sends or permits the trouble is that we may be drawn closer to Him, and prove more fully His sufficiency to help us, no matter what straits we may be in. As He never turned a deaf ear to any cry of distress during the days of His flesh, nor refused to undertake for anyone who sought His help, neither will He do so now that He is seated at the right hand of the Majesty on high. As He promptly delivered Peter when he cried,

"Lord save me, I perish," so will He still thrust forth His mighty hand and rescue any believer who, fearful that he may be drowned in a sea of troubles, calls upon Him for relief. The Gibeonites did not appeal in vain to the captain of Israel in their emergency, nor will the Christian if he trustfully petitions the antitypical Joshua.

"So Joshua ascended from Gilgal, he, and all the people of war with him, and all the mighty men of valour." This shows that he had "learned his lesson" or had profited from his previous failure (vii, 3-6), for now he employed at least the major part of his forces and accompanied them in person. We say "at least the major part of his forces," for it is most unlikely that he would leave the camp, with all the women and children, entirely undefended. Thus this is probably one of the many instances in Scripture where the word "all" is *not* to be taken absolutely, without qualification, but would here signify battalions of the men of war from all the tribes. Herein we see Joshua fulfilling his covenant engagement, for when those Gibeonites threw in their lot with the people of God they came under His protection—compare Ruth ii, 12. And a courageous enterprise it was—very different from the former ones. On earlier occasions, at Jericho and at Ai, it was but a single enemy which he had to engage, but here it was the massed forces of no less than five kings which he had now to encounter, and they had the great advantage of being stationed in the heights unto which he must ascend. Typically, Joshua was here a figure of the good Shepherd going forth to rescue His imperilled sheep, and in the "all the people of war with him" we behold the plenitude of Christ's resources (Matt. xxviii, 18).

"And the Lord said unto Joshua, Fear them not: for I have delivered them into thine hand; there shall not a man of them stand before thee" (verse 8). We are not told that Joshua "asked counsel of the Lord" on this occasion, nor is it at all likely that he did so. There is no need for any to inquire what be God's will for him when his path of duty is clearly marked out before him, as was the case here. They having owned his dominion and submitted to his yoke, Joshua was now under definite obligation to go to the assistance of the Gibeonites—as the government is to safeguard its loyal subjects. Nevertheless, it is more than probable that Joshua's heart was lifted up to God as he prepared for his arduous and dangerous undertaking, seeking wisdom from Him and making request for Him to grant him success in the same. Not only is this to be inferred from all that is recorded of the general tenor of his pious life, but had Joshua now gone forth in a spirit of independence and self-sufficiency, we can scarcely conceive of the Holy One, under such circumstances, vouchsafing him such a word as this. In appearing unto Joshua at this time the Lord intimated His approval of Israel's sparing the lives of the Gibeonites (ix, 18-20) and of their venturing to deliver them from their enemies, and accordingly He gave him this message of encouragement and assurance.

"Fear them not." Very gracious was this. The Lord would have the heart of His servant in perfect peace from the outset, and thus be the better prepared for the forthcoming battle. Fear is due to unbelief, through being occupied with the puny might of those who are arrayed *against* us, instead of our faith being fixed upon the almightiness of the One who is *for* us. But the Lord did more than barely exhort His servant to banish from him the spirit of trepidation, giving him an all-sufficient reason why tranquillity of mind should now possess him: "*for* I have delivered them into thine hand." Thus, here too, we are taught that perfect peace of heart is the fruit of the mind's being stayed upon Jehovah. "I will trust, and not be afraid, for the Lord Jehovah is my strength" (Isaiah xii, 2): the latter is ever the consequence of the former—

when we resolve to make Him our confidence, none will affright us. In His
" there shall not a man stand before thee " there was a *renewing* of the original
promise which the Lord had made unto Joshua in i, 5. "God hath spoken
once; *twice* have I heard this; that power belongeth unto God " (Psalm lxii, 11)
—alas, most of us are so dull of hearing that the message has to be repeated
much oftener than "twice" before we *really* believe it.

"Joshua therefore came unto them suddenly, and went up from Gilgal
all night " (verse 9). First, we should observe that the assurance which the
Lord had just given Joshua was not perverted by him into an excuse for slackness on his part, but very much the reverse. Instead of reasoning that since
victory was certain there was no need to exert himself and his men unduly,
rather were they thereby stimulated to self-sacrificing effort. He did not wait
until the morning before starting out on the hard and hazardous mountain
climb, but, setting aside his own comfort, journeyed all through the night.
Second, therein we behold the merciful response which he made unto the
urgent request of the Gibeonites, "Come up to us quickly, and save us."
He delayed not, but promptly hastened to their relief. As Matthew Henry
pointed out, "If one of the tribes of Israel had been in danger, he could not
have shown more care and zeal for its relief than here for Gibeon, remembering
then, as in other cases, that there must be one law for the stranger that was
proselytized, as for him that was born in the land. Third, he came upon the
enemy "suddenly," when they were least expecting it, probably before day
had broken and ere they had made their dispositions and taken their places,
thereby throwing them into instant confusion and consternation.

"And the Lord discomfited them before Israel, and slew them with a great
slaughter at Gibeon, and chased them along the way that goeth up to Beth-
horon, and smote them to Azekah, and unto Makkedah " (verse 10). If more of
the servants and soldiers of Christ were willing to lose a night's sleep in His
cause, particularly in efforts to help their distressed brethren, we should
oftener behold the Lord baring His mighty arm, showing Himself strong on
their behalf. Observe how jealous the Holy Spirit ever is in guarding the
Divine glory! Joshua was unquestionably an able strategist and those under
him were "mighty men of valour," and no doubt they acquitted themselves
well on this occasion; yet that also was of God, and therefore the honours must
be ascribed unto Him. Not only spiritual gifts, but physical powers, natural
aptitudes, mental endowments, military skill and success, are all bestowed upon
men by their Maker—"what hast thou that thou hast not received?" This is
not sufficiently recognized by us: if it were, there would be less of idolatrous
hero worship.

Miracles

The spiritual ignorance and scepticism of the day in which we are living
calls for a clear and unhesitating setting forth of the teaching of God's Word
upon this subject. It is the duty of every preacher and Sabbath-School teacher
to bring before the rising generation what Holy Writ reveals thereon. Without
any drawing upon the imagination, yet by the use of vivid and picturesque
language, it is one which can be made deeply interesting to the young. Broadly
speaking, the miracles of the Bible are of two kinds or classes: manifest and
supernatural judgments of God upon the wicked; gracious and mighty interpositions of God on behalf of His people. Of the former we may instance the
destruction of Sodom and Gomorrah by fire from heaven; of the latter, the
opening of a way through the Red Sea so that Israel passed through dryshod.

Briefly, we would define a miracle as a supernatural event brought about by a special act of Divine providence, an extraordinary display of God's power. It is an event occurring in the natural world, which is apparent to the senses and of such a nature that it can be rationally attributed only to the immediate act of God. As a special and more obvious interposition of God, a miracle differs from His common or ordinary providences.

The objection made by infidels against miracles, that they are contrary to nature and its established order, is quite pointless, for it entirely leaves out of consideration the fact that they are due to the direct intervention of One who is superior to those laws and can alter the mode of their operation whenever it pleases Him. The various ways and means by which God governs the universe demonstrate both His freedom and His sovereignty. Matter is ruled by forms, bodies by souls, inferior bodies by celestial, the visible world by invisible angels, angels and souls immediately by God. Nor do the same things always keep the same track or follow the same course. In Moses' time the flowing sea stood up as a wall and the flinty rock flowed as a river. In Joshua's day the glorious sun was halted in his race and remained quite stationary for a whole day. In Elijah's life the iron swam, and in Daniel's the fire did not burn. During Christ's ministry there were numerous excesses of nature, actings by prerogative, displays of the Divine glory. Such variety in the motions of nature exhibits the perfect freedom and superintendence of nature's Lord.

Whatever philosophical difficulties miracles may present to unbelief, the explanation which the Bible gives of them is far more rational and satisfactory than any that human wisdom can supply. The theories and hypotheses advanced by atheists are incredible and irrational, for they are at once unphilosophical and unscientific. But once the living God be postulated as their Author, One who is eternal and almighty, infinite in wisdom and goodness, supernatural works are to be expected. To say that miracles are "impossible" is absurd and the acme of arrogance, for the one who makes such an assertion virtually assumes himself to be possessed of omniscience—endowed with all knowledge. To *deny* that they exist is, if possible, still worse, for it is a deliberate closing of the eyes to that which confronts us on every side. *Creation* is a miracle, for it immeasurably transcends the capabilities and even the understanding of the natural man. The combined wit and resources of all physicists and scientists in the world could not *create* so much as a single blade of grass. No wonder the Lord asks puny man, "Where wast thou when I laid the foundations of the earth? declare, if thou hast understanding" (Job xxxviii, 4).

The *sustentation* and preservation of creation is a miracle. None but the One who gave them being could provide for and maintain such an innumerable multitude of creatures. Even if the wise of this world *were able* to bring into existence a blade of grass, they could not keep it alive a single day if deprived of the soil, and denied the water and sunshine which God provides. The *regulation* of the created system is a miracle. Man may tamper with the clocks in his "daylight-saving" schemes, but he cannot make the sun rise an hour earlier or set an hour later. He may sinfully fret and fume at the weather, but he can no more alter or modify it by any of his devices than he can change the tides of the sea. *Providence* is a continuous miracle, supplying the needs of not only a billion human beings, but myriads of animals, the birds of the air and the denizens of the deep. "Thou openest *Thine* hand, they are filled with good. Thou hidest Thy face, they are troubled" (Psalm civ, 28, 29)—so dependent is the world on its Maker's bounty. Man may attempt to "ration," but when God calls for a famine he is helpless before it.

Strictly speaking, a miracle is something more than an unusual occurrence or mysterious prodigy, for the effects of the electric telegraph had been such unto those who lived a thousand years ago, but today they are explainable by natural laws. Contrariwise, the more fully a real miracle be comprehended the more evident it is that such a phenomenal effect is above all the powers of nature, and must be attributed to an immediate act of God's intervention. Nor are we justified in regarding such interventions as anarchical infractions of nature's order, but rather as the interposition of the Divine will, directing events unto the outworking of His purpose, every miracle being wrought in strict accord with His decrees. As the Westminster Confession so admirably expresses it, " God in His ordinary providence maketh use of means, yet is free to work without [Hosea i, 7], above [Romans iv, 19], and against [II Kings vi, 6; Daniel iii, 27] them at His pleasure." It must not be thought that the Creator has brought into existence a system or instituted such laws as tie His own hands. No, " Whatsoever the Lord pleased, that did He in heaven, and in earth, in the seas, and all deep places " (Psalm cxxxv, 6).

Great care needs to be taken how we employ such expressions as " nature " and " the laws of nature," for they were coined by those who had no knowledge of or faith in the living God, and are commonly used by men who would exclude the thought of God's immediate presence and power in the universe. But the Scriptures teach us to see the hand of *God* operating directly in all that is attributed to " natural causes " by the sceptics. The Christian rejects the idea that the universe is naught but a vast machine which works involuntarily, necessarily and uniformly. Instead he acknowledges a present God in providence as well as creation. As he admires the flowers which spring from the tiny seeds, renewing the original grace and beauty of the parent plant, he traces the immediate influence of the Creator, as truly and as much as in making Aaron's rod to bud (Num. xvii, 8). Nor is the vegetating of the seed any less a Divine work and marvel because it is multiplied by millions and repeated year by year for successive ages. What unbelief terms " the course of nature " is but the agency *of God*. He is operating on the right hand and on the left, constantly maintaining and directing all things, though men discern Him not. Without Him " not a sparrow falls to the ground."

That the so-called " laws of nature " *are* being continually modified in their action by the intervention of Divine will appears plainly in the marked differences in the weather from year to year. Though Lewis be situated so far to the west, this writer has witnessed snow lying on the ground during July! That is, of course, very exceptional, but it illustrates what has just been said, as do also the frequent falsifications of the " weather prophets," even of those who claim that it " runs in cycles." The same thing is exhibited in the longevity of different individuals: not only do no two centenarians give the same recipe for the attaining of old age, but many of them have been of frail physique and delicate constitution, and if naught but physical properties and laws determine the event, then the strongest should live the longest and the weakest die early. The material world abounds in such exceptions. " Cut off a snail's head and it will grow out again; cut off a crab's head, but it will not grow out again. Cut off a crab's claw and it will grow out again, but cut off a dog's leg and it will not grow out again " (Roget: *Physiology*).

Why such marked variations in the seasons? Why such disparity in the health and mentality of members of the same family? Why those differences in the operation of the very same properties and laws of animal substance? " It is as easy for God to turn nature out of its settled course as it was to place it in the station it holds and the course it runs " (Charnock). Verily, " He hath done whatsoever He hath pleased " (Psalm cxv, 3). Rightly did R. Haldane argue, " To affirm that a suspension or alteration of the laws of nature is impossible is to confer on them the attribute of Deity, and to declare they are supreme; and having no superior, precludes the existence of God as well as miracles, or it represents Him as subordinate to His own laws " (*Evidence and Authority of Revelation,* Vol. I). We say again that what is called " the course of nature " is nothing but the *direct agency of God,* the exercise of His will, wisdom and power. " Nature " would cease to move were its Maker to withdraw His energy from it. It can no more operate of itself than it could produce itself. Those laws by which God usually conducts the government of the material creation were originally adjusted by Him, are now preserved by His power and are deviated from whenever He pleases.

" And it came to pass, as they fled from before Israel and were in the going down to Beth-horon, that the Lord cast down great stones from heaven upon them unto Azekah, and they died: they were more which died with hailstones than they whom the children of Israel slew with the sword " (Joshua x, 11). It will be recalled that when the Gibeonites made their peace with Joshua and entered into a league with him, five kings of the Amorites gathered their armies together and made war upon their capital. They sent to Joshua an urgent appeal for help, which he answered at once by marching at the head of his men through the night. Coming upon the Canaanites unexpectedly, and probably before they had made their dispositions and appointed sentries, they threw them into consternation. Moreover, " the Lord discomfited them before Israel, and slew them with a great slaughter," thereby signifying His approval of Israel's sparing the lives of the Gibeonites by now giving them the most glorious victory in all their wars. As the remaining Amorites fled the Lord employed against them the artillery of heaven, which demonstrates how hopeless is the case of those who have Him for their enemy.

In casting down the great stones of hail upon the Amorites we may observe what a *variety of means* God uses in executing His will. In overwhelming the antediluvian world He employed a deluge of rain; in the destruction of Sodom, fire from heaven; in the overthrow of Pharaoh and his hosts at the Red Sea, by removing the wheels of their chariots and drowning them. Therein we behold His sovereignty exemplified, as it is too in ministering unto His people. This was not the first time God made the hail a messenger of judgment, for He did so in the seventh plague upon Egypt (Exodus ix, 22-26). Many of the premillenarians believe that " hail " will be one of the weapons again used by God in His judgments on the earth (Rev. xvi, 21). This awful visitation on the Canaanites had been foretold: " Hast thou seen the treasures of the hail, which I have reserved . . . against the day of battle and war?" (Job xxxviii, 22, 23)—Job was probably written before Joseph's birth.

There are three things which were singular and striking about the hail in Joshua x. First, its great size; second, its force and efficacy—being like bullets from a machine gun, slaying men outright. Occasionally we have read of hail of unusual dimensions, which did great damage to crops and cattle, but not of it effecting such wholesale slaughter of human beings as on this occasion. Third, its *discrimination*—none of the Israelites being killed! This is the feature which most evidently evinced the miraculous nature of this hail. Though Joshua's men must have been in close combat with the Canaanites and more or less mixed up with them as they pursued them, none of the deadly missiles fell on God's people. This was even more remarkable than what occurred under the seventh plague, for whereas the Lord then sent it throughout all the land of Egypt, none fell in Goshen (Exodus ix, 26); but here it fell all round the Israelites, yet without one of them being harmed—illustrating that word, " A thousand shall fall at thy side, and ten thousand at thy right hand; but it shall not come nigh *thee* " (Psalm xci, 7).

There is probably an allusion to this miracle and others of a similar nature in Psalm xviii, 13, 14, both passages speaking of " The Lord discomfited them ... and chased them," and mentioning the hail. There was no escaping His wrath. Hopeless is the plight of all who provoke Him. When the appointed hour of His vengeance arrives, none can deliver himself. Thus will it be with everyone who mocks Him and persecutes His people. They shall discover, to their eternal undoing, that it *is* " a fearful thing to fall into the hands of the living God." That more died from the hailstones than Israel slew with the sword made good God's word unto Joshua, " Thine eyes have seen all that the Lord your God hath done unto these two kings: so shall the Lord do unto all the kingdoms whither thou passest Ye shall not fear them: for the Lord your God He shall fight for you " (Deut. iii, 21, 22). And to Him may the Christian look in his spiritual warfare, and " if God be for us, who can be against us?"

The opening verses of Psalm xliv supply a striking and blessed commentary upon what has been before us. " We have heard with our ears, O God, our fathers have told us, what work Thou didst in their days, in the times of old. How Thou didst drive out the heathen with Thy hand, and plantedst them; how Thou didst afflict the people, and cast them out. For they got not the land in possession by their own sword, neither did their own arm save them: but Thy right hand, and Thine arm, and the light of Thy countenance, because Thou hadst a favour unto them." This was a God-honouring acknowledgment. Canaan was His gift unto Israel, and *He* put them in possession of it. Their warriors, indeed, were not inactive, but it was the light of His countenance which inspired them with valour. God was the Conqueror of Canaan. Without *His* power working in and for them, all their efforts had been in vain. By employing the artillery of heaven against the five kings the Lord made this the more evident.

And what is the application which we are to make of the same? First, give unto the Lord the honour which is due to Him, and freely ascribe our victories unto Him. Whatever success be ours, it is wholly due to the might and goodness of God. Without His blessing all our endeavours would be useless. Second, recognize and own His sovereign *grace* to be the fount from which proceed all His actings on our behalf; " because thou hadst a favour unto them." Third, make known to our children the miracle-working power of God, especially what He has wrought for us. Fourth, count upon Him undertaking for us: He is the same almighty God and Saviour now as then! What we read of in Scripture and have heard from our fathers should strengthen faith, encourage prayer, stimulate hope: " Thou art *my* King, O God: command deliverances for Jacob " (Psalm xliv, 4). Thou art my sovereign Lord, my sure Defence against all enemies, my all-sufficient Redeemer. Intervene on my behalf, confound my foes, grant me the victory. Thou hast but to speak and it is done, to " command " and it standest fast.

"And the Lord discomfited them before Israel, and slew them with a great slaughter" (Joshua x, 10). Therein we behold a solemn exemplification of Christ's utterances in Matthew xviii, 6, "But whoso shall offend one of these little ones that believe in Me, it were better for him that a millstone were hanged about his neck, and that he were drowned in the depth of the sea. Jehovah had previously acted in accordance with that principle in connection with Egypt, for it was because Pharaoh oppressed and afflicted the Hebrews so sorely that his land and people were visited by the ten great plagues. And now the five kings of Canaan had provoked the Most High by their assault upon Gibeon (verses 4, 5), for its inhabitants had made peace with Joshua and with the children of Israel, entering into a league with them, and thereby coming under the Lord's protection. As pointed out in a previous article, the Gibeonites are to be regarded as young converts, and in seeking their destruction the Amorites had affronted God Himself, for as the prophet assured His people, "he that toucheth you toucheth the apple of His eye" (Zech. ii, 8, and cf. Acts ix, 1, 4). Many of those Amorites had fallen beneath the sword of Israel, but a still greater number died under the great hailstones which the Lord cast upon them from heaven (verse 11). In whatever direction they fled the vengeance of God overtook them, for as Isaiah xxviii, 21, informs us, the Lord acted in "wrath" with them.

A great number of the Canaanites had fallen, but the remnant of their armies continued in flight. Joshua was reluctant that complete victory should be prevented by failing daylight, and though he and his men had marched all through the preceding night (verse 9) in hastening to the relief of the sorely menaced Gibeonites, so that he could spring a surprise attack upon their invaders, and though they had been engaged in fighting and pursuing the retreating foe over the mountain passes, yet he was loath to call a halt before his task was completed. We therefore behold him, next, supplementing his self-sacrificing diligence by a remarkable display of faith: "he said in the sight of Israel, Sun, stand thou still upon Gibeon; and thou, Moon, in the valley of Ajalon" (verse 12). From the natural standpoint that appears like the act of a madman, and even from a spiritual aspect it seems to be the height of presumption. Yet it was neither the one nor the other: rather was it the exercise of full confidence in a miracle-working God. Faith must not be judged by the standards of carnal reason.

But, it may be asked, must not faith have something solid to rest upon, some word of God's to lay hold of and direct it? Generally, yes; but not necessarily something specific in every instance. For example, when David committed his fearful sin in connection with Uriah, no provision was made for such a case, nor had he any promise from God which he could plead. What then did he do? Psalm li informs us. He cast himself upon the *known character* of his God. No sacrifice was appointed under the law for murderers, and therefore the guilty one here acknowledged, "Thou desirest not sacrifice; else would I give it" (verse 16). What then? "According unto the multitude of Thy tender mercies blot out my transgressions" (verse 1) was his plea. And Psalm xxxii, 5, shows it prevailed! Again, when Daniel was cast into the lions den, so far as the Scripture informs us he had no definite word from God of deliverance, yet he *was* delivered and that "*because* he believed in his God" (vi, 23)—without any specific promise to appropriate to his case, Daniel's faith confided in the power and sufficiency of his God to extricate him from his perilous position; and the Lord did not confound him. Of course not! It is always safe to trust Him.

In the present instance there is little room for doubt that Joshua had an extraordinary impulse or impression made on his heart by the Holy Spirit, for that alone will satisfactorily account for so pious a man asking God to do this unprecedented thing, as it alone explains why He granted such an unheard-of request. It may be objected that nothing is here said of Joshua making any request. Neither are we told in I Kings xvii that Elijah made request of the Lord that there should be a drought, yet James v, 17, informs us that he *did*: "he prayed earnestly that it might not rain: and it rained not on the earth by the space of three years and six months." But further, let it be duly noted, we are informed that "Then spake Joshua to the Lord in the day when the Lord delivered up the Amorites before the children of Israel" (verse 12). Surely that confirms the thought expressed at the opening of this paragraph, that Joshua acted here in response to an extraordinary impulse from above, as was not infrequently the case with eminent servants of God during the Old Testament era.

"Then spake Joshua to the Lord in the day when the Lord delivered up the Amorites before the children of Israel, and he said in the sight of Israel, Sun, stand thou still upon Gibeon, and thou, Moon, in the valley of Ajalon." The two things, it will be noted, are here joined together, and their order intimates their relationship. The inspired record here is too brief to justify dogmatic assertions. To us it appears that Joshua asked God's permission so to command the sun, or that while he communed with Him he received commission to do so. As Matthew Henry pointed out, "The prayer had not been granted by the Divine power, if it had not been dictated by the Divine grace. God wrought this faith in him and then said 'According to thy faith,' and to the prayer of faith 'be it unto thee.' It cannot be imagined, however, that such a thing as this should have entered into his mind if God had not put it there. A man would have a thousand projects in his head for the completing of the victory, before he would have thought of desiring the sun to stand still; but even in the Old Testament saints 'the Spirit made intercession according to the will of God.' What God will give, He inclines the hearts of His praying people to ask, and for what He will do, He will be inquired of (Ezek. xxxvi, 37)."

Not only was Joshua's ordering of the sun to stand still a glorious exhibition of his faith and implicit confidence in God, but it also manifested his *zeal* in the service of God. This appears more plainly if we bear in mind what has already received our notice, namely that he had engaged in a tiring uphill march all through the previous night, and then had been employed in fighting from early dawn till late that day, for the terms of this double command to the celestial luminaries intimate that the sun was then near the hour of its setting, and the moon of rising. Yet instead of now welcoming a respite, and an opportunity to rest himself and his men, his heart longed for the prolongation of the hours of daylight, so that he might complete his task and utterly exterminate the enemy. How blessedly he here typed out the One who declared by the Spirit of prophecy "the zeal of Thine house hath eaten me up" (Psalm lxix, 9)! In its practical application unto ourselves this detail makes it evident that there must be unwearied efforts put forth by us in our spiritual warfare and that we are not to rest satisfied with partial victories, but must continue fighting until complete success is ours. No doubt Joshua and his men found "they that wait upon the Lord shall renew their strength" (Isaiah xl, 31), and so shall we, if we do likewise.

"He said in the sight of all Israel, Sun, stand thou still upon Gibeon."

To express himself thus before all his army evinced how strong was the assurance of his faith. Joshua was not afraid that the Lord would put him to confusion before the people. Confident that God had inspired his cry, he doubted not that it would be answered. It was to the Almighty, the creator of the sun and moon, that he looked, and with Him all things are possible. Doubtless, he counted too on Jehovah's special favour unto His covenant people. Moreover, He had said, "I have delivered them into thine hand" (verse 8), and therefore the remaining Amorites must not be allowed the opportunity of escaping under the shelter of nightfall. Looking higher: what anointed eye can fail to see in his action here a striking adumbration of Christ as the miracle-worker, who, by His many wonders and signs, gave proof that He was not only the promised Messiah, but none other than God, manifest in flesh. How vividly does Joshua's staying the planets in their courses remind us of that One who had such command over the elements that His disciples marvelled saying, "What manner of man is this, that even the winds and the sea obey Him!" (Matt. viii, 27).

"And the sun stood still, and the moon stayed, until the people had avenged themselves upon their enemies" (verse 13). This is one of the favourite passages which infidels scoff at. Wise in their own conceits, they affirm that for such a thing to happen as is here recorded is contrary to science and philosophy. We do not propose to waste any time in replying to them. It was long ago pointed out by Bishop Watson, "The machine of the universe is in the hand of God, and He can stay the motion of any part, or of the whole, with less trouble than any of us can stop a watch." If a human engineer can slow the speed of an express train by putting on the brake, and bring it to a complete standstill by cutting off the steam, what cannot the Divine engineer do with any ponderous body which He has Himself set in motion. The sun is but an instrument, made by God to perform His good pleasure. That He is in no wise dependent upon or limited by it is clear from the fact that light existed and the earth was clothed with vegetation *before* the sun was made (Gen. i)! By the miracles of Joshua x, 13, and Isaiah xxxviii, 8, the Most High demonstrated that the daily rising and setting of the sun is *not* from a blind instinct of nature, and that He controls its course: "which commandeth the sun, and it riseth not" (Job ix, 7).

"And the sun stood still." Here, as in many other passages, we are taught that the Lord God has a superintendence over all the creatures of His hand. He sends forth His imperious commands not only unto angels and men (Daniel iv, 35), but to the birds of the air (I Kings xvii, 4) and to the wild beasts (Daniel vi, 22), yea, to inanimate things. He issues His edicts to the clouds and to the light of the sun, and they promptly submit and obey. He addresses the light as though it were a rational creature: He commands it not to shine and it shines not. The host of heaven, as well as the inhabitants of the earth, are entirely at His disposal. The whole course of nature moves or stands still at the mere will of its Maker. As the sun stood still at His word through Joshua, so at His fiat it went backward in the days of Hezekiah (Isaiah xxxviii, 8), and it is by *His* orders that the same sun, at any time, withdraws its genial beams and is muffled up with dark vapours. "With clouds He covereth the light; and commandeth it not to shine by the cloud that cometh bewixt" (Job xxxvi, 32).

Those who profess to believe in an omnipotent God do but betray their crass folly when they attempt to reason, and conclude that He either cannot or does not exercise His power in other ways than those known to our very limited experience. It is true that the sun rises and proceeds in a natural course, yet only by Divine commission. Though nothing in nature be more constant than the rising of the sun, God can suspend its motion whenever He likes. He who at first commanded it to rise can easily countermand it. What is swifter in motion than the sun? All creatures upon earth are but slugs in comparison; the eagle of the air but a snail. Yet God can stop it instantly. When He sends forth His prohibition it cannot stir a foot till He removes that prohibition. It shone not for three days upon Egypt (Exodus x, 22). Since He can stop the sun from shining what cannot He do! Great indeed is God's power: equally great is His goodness, which causes the sun to shine upon the evil and unthankful when it is in His power to withhold it. How little is that realized by the world! O that men would praise the Lord for His goodness and for His wonderful works unto the children of men.

Nothing is more "natural" than the succession of the four seasons; nevertheless, there is so great diversity and such marked inequality between summer and summer and winter and winter (even in the same part of the earth) that it is obvious to all enlightened minds that each is controlled and regulated by a new and particular providence of God. It was indeed wonderful that when a blind beggar cried, "Son of David, have mercy on me," *Jesus stood still,* and commanded him to be called," and healed him (Mark x, 48, 49). Behold there "the Sun of righteousness" stayed in His course by the appeal of a poor sinner! There are some who think the action of Joshua in this amazing incident foreshadowed Christ at His second coming when He saves Israel, appealing to Zechariah xiv, 7: that in the day of the Lord's battle with the nations "it shall come to pass that at evening time it shall be light," upon which, at present, this writer has no definite opinion, either pro or con; having learned from long experience to be very chary of prophetical speculations. Sufficient for him to know that whatever the Lord has purposed, promised, or threatened concerning His future dealings with the earth will certainly come to pass.

Rather would we dwell upon the *practical* message which this miracle has for us today. The Christian's confidence in the Lord ought to be greatly strengthened by a pondering of the same. Though God no longer halts the sun in its course, yet He *does* many remarkable things in answer to the believing supplications of His people. When George Muller was crossing the Atlantic to fulfil an important preaching engagement, his ship was delayed by a dense fog off the coast of Newfoundland. Said he to the captain, "I have never yet been late for an appointment: let us go to prayer." The fog lifted almost immediately and the ship arrived in port on time! When entering our train from Chicago to Pittsburgh (April 1931) we encountered a Christian lady in distress. The porter had wrongly put her into an *express,* which would carry her hundreds of miles beyond her destination; and the ticket collector informed her that there was no possibility of the train halting at her village. The writer and his wife reminded her that nothing is too hard for God. We had special prayer, and were able to assure her that the Lord would *stop the train.* Some hours later she was told to get ready, and it stopped for a few seconds. Some of our readers in Pennsylvania will recall this incident, for they saw the letter of thanks which Mrs. Pink received, telling of how the experience had brought her to trust more fully in a miracle-working God.

"And the sun stood still, and the moon stayed, until the people had avenged themselves upon their enemies. Is not this written in the book of

Jasher"? (verse 13). The book of Jasher is generally thought to be the same as "the book of the wars of the Lord" mentioned in Numbers xxi, 14. A further reference is made to it in II Samuel i, 18. Apparently it was a book in which were chronicled outstanding events in the fighting of Israel. The fact that this miracle was recorded in such a book during the lifetime of Joshua not only indicates the deep impression which this phenomenon had made upon the minds of the people but attests its verity. As at a later date Israel sang, "Saul hath slain his thousands, and David his tens of thousands," so they would recite this memorable deed of Joshua's which had an effect upon the whole frame of nature, producing an alteration therein. What is still more important, this miracle is referred to in the inspired writings of the prophets: "The sun and moon stood still in their habitation" (Hab. iii, 11). As a miracle is of Divine causality—an event wrought in the external world by the immediate power of God—so miracles are authenticated by Divine testimony—usually by at least "two witnesses."

Remarkable as was this event, it by no means stands entirely alone in a class by itself. We have already alluded to Exodus x, 22, and Isaiah xxxviii, 8, and would further compare the statement that "the stars in their courses fought against Sisera" (Judges v, 20), and also the star which miraculously moved and led the wise men from the East to the house where the infant Saviour then was (Matt. ii). But let us also point out the *mystical* interpretation which may be legitimately made of what has been before us. As God controls the movements of the sun, causing it to shine brightly or to be overcast with dark clouds, so it is with spiritual light. Those parts of Africa and Asia upon which the Sun of righteousness shone so blessedly during the first three centuries of this Christian era have since been under the black dominion of Mohammedanism, and such lands as Italy and Spain, which were favoured with the glorious light of the Gospel in the days of Paul, have long languished under the darkness of popery. On the other hand, heathen lands are now being evangelized. God orders *spiritual* light and darkness as truly as the natural.

What most impresses us in connection with this miracle is the clear demonstration which it affords of the supremacy of God and His absolute control of all creatures. There was no power in Joshua nor any extraordinary dispensation committed him to exert such an influence upon the whole frame of nature as to produce so great an alteration therein. No, it is clear that he had a Divine warranty to speak that which he knew Jehovah Himself was about to effect. He first addressed himself to Him in prayer, then received assurance from Him, and then at his word the heavenly bodies remained stationary for many hours. Therein we behold how the living God is both the alpha and omega, the first cause and the last end, the wise contriver and the sure moderator of everything, to His own glory, according to the counsel of His own will. Thus will faith perceive the wisdom, goodness and power of God in every event. Anything short of that is virtual atheism, which gives God no place in His dominion over the world. Writing on Joshua x, 13, John Gill said, "How this is to be reconciled with the Copernican system or that with this, I shall not inquire." Wise man not to pretend to understand what has not been Divinely revealed. Wiser still in refusing to allow the theorizings of a Prussian astronomer to cast doubt on what He *has* made known, or to suggest an interpretation which "harmonizes" the same with the hypothesis of "science falsely so called" (I Tim. vi, 20).

Makkedah

"And the sun stood still, and the moon stayed, until the people had avenged themselves upon their enemies" (Joshua x, 13). Therein demonstration was made of the absolute supremacy and invincible might of Jehovah. Three great miracles were wrought that day by the Lord on behalf of his people, for they are explainable by naught but Divine causation. First, there had been the great hailstones that God had cast down from heaven, and which were remarkable for their magnitude, their efficacy and their discrimination—more of the Amorites dying from them than by the sword of Israel, and so directed that none of the latter were even injured by them. Second, the sun standing still in mid heaven, and remaining so for "almost a whole day." Third, the staying of the moon in her course, for it is to be noted that Joshua (as the type of Christ) had addressed her *directly*: "Sun, stand thou still upon Gibeon, and thou, Moon, in the valley of Ajalon" (verse 12)—evidently he did not believe that the two bodies acted so automatically in conjunction that it was unnecessary to give distinct command unto the latter, for in such case he would have spoken only to the sun. It was therefore a different and additional miracle that the moon also "stayed," as is further evident by the Holy Spirit's separate mention of each in verse 13.

It is exceedingly solemn to observe that these extraordinary displays of God's power were *judgments* upon the Canaanites, and that like the great deluge in the days of Noah, the destruction of the cities of the plain by fire from heaven, and the fearful plagues upon Egypt, the miracles of Joshua x were interpositions of Jehovah for the express purpose of destroying the wicked. This presents to us an aspect of the Divine character which, in the vast majority of pulpits, has been deliberately ignored and suppressed for the past fifty years, until the Deity of Holy Writ is now, even in Christendom, "the unknown God." Those miracles make it clearly evident that God's holiness is as real as His grace, His justice as His mercy, His wrath as His love; and they require to be given equal prominence in the preaching of those who profess to be His ministers. They *were so* by the Divine Preacher: neither prophet nor apostle spoke so plainly or so frequently as did Christ upon the fearful portion awaiting the lost: such expressions as "the wrath of God," the "damnation of hell," "the furnace of fire [where] there shall be wailing and gnashing of teeth," the "worm that dieth not and the fire that is not quenched," were upon His lips much oftener than "the love of God."

It is the lamentable and patent dishonesty of so many pulpits during the past two or three generations that is so largely responsible for the moral corruption of our nation today. Of old the Lord complained of those in Israel "whose lips should keep knowledge," that "ye have not kept My ways, but have been *partial* in the Law" (Mal. ii, 9), and thus has history repeated itself. Instead of declaring "all the counsel of God" (Acts xx, 27), unfaithful men dwelt only on those portions of the Truth which made for their own popularity, deliberately omitting whatever would be unpalatable to their unregenerate hearers. Such a one-sided portrayal was made of the Divine character that the Most High was not held in awe; the moral law was relegated unto the Jews, so that sin became to be regarded lightly; and the soothing opiate that God loves everybody took away all fear of the wrath to come. Thousands of thinking men forsook such an effeminate ministry, and those who continued under it were lulled soundly asleep. The children of the former, for the most part, grew up entirely godless; while those of the latter believed in a "god" which is the figment of a sickly sentimentality. And, my reader, where there is no reverence of God and respect for His Law, there will never be genuine regard for human law.

In consequence of such widespread perfidy on the part of the "churches," and the disastrous effects thereof upon the community, an insulted and incensed God is now dealing with Christendom, not in grace, but in judgment! Never was an error so plainly exposed as "Dispensationalism" has been during our lifetime. So far from the "silent heaven" of Sir Robert Anderson and his school, the heavens have been thundering loudly. Instead of this Christian era differing from all previous ones, by an exemption from open displays of God's anger, it has been, and still is, marked by such with increasing frequency and severity. True, the Day of Salvation has not yet expired, the way of deliverance from the everlasting burning is still available for every individual who accepts the free offer of the Gospel; nevertheless, God has a controversy with those who have slighted His authority and ignored the claims of His righteousness. It is an obvious fact that His judgments have fallen the heaviest upon those parts of the earth which have enjoyed the most spiritual light but deliberately closed their eyes to it. He has ceased using the "still small voice" of winsomeness, and has been speaking loudly in the earthquake and the fire (I Kings xix).

"And there was no day like that before it or after it, that the Lord hearkened unto the voice of a man: for the Lord fought for Israel" (verse 14). Those words supply definite confirmation of our remarks upon verse 12, that these miracles were wrought by God in answer to the supplication of His servant— he had at first addressed himself unto the Lord in private, and then, in the hearing of Israel, to the luminaries of heaven. Therein we behold the amazing condescension of the Most High, that he deigns not only to listen to the voice of His creatures, but also to respond to their appeals. It should be pointed out that, as so often in Scripture, the language of this verse is relative and not absolute—both before and since then God has often listened to the voice of man, but not to the extent of altering the movement of the whole planetary system. In this extraordinary instance we may perceive how, once more, the Lord made good His promise to Joshua in iii, 7, and, as the man whom He delighted to honour, further "magnified him in the sight of all Israel." The final clause of the verse tells us why Jehovah so acted on this occasion—to make it still more evident that He was the Captain of Israel's armies, and that when He laid bare His mighty arm none of their enemies could stand before Him. These supernatural phenomena must have made a deep impression upon the surrounding nations, especially those given to the study of astronomy.

"And Joshua returned, and all Israel with him, unto the camp to Gilgal" (verse 15). This verse is by no means free of difficulty, for in view of what is recorded in verses 17-20 it would appear that both Joshua and his men remained for some time in the vicinity of Gibeon; while verse 21 is still more definite—"and all the people returned to the camp to Joshua at Makkedah." Moreover, as Scott pointed out, "It is most unlikely that Joshua would march his army twenty or thirty miles in the midst of victory"—especially after marching all the previous night and being so strenuously engaged that supernaturally prolonged day. The absence of the word "Then" at the beginning of the verse precludes the necessity of our understanding it to mean that they returned *immediately* unto "the camp to Gilgal"; and since identically the same statement is made in verse 43, we regard this in verse 15 as being said by way of anticipation and not as something then accomplished. Ultimately they returned there: to acquaint the congregation with their victory, to render public thanks to God, and to resume and complete their preparations for the northern campaign (xi, 1-7). Note well the "all Israel with him," which was yet another miracle—not one had been killed by the hail or slain by the Canaanites!

"But these five kings fled, and hid themselves in a cave at Makkedah" (verse 16). These were the same kings mentioned in verse 3, who had determined upon the destruction of Gibeon. That very morning they had proudly stood at the head of their armies, only to see them utterly routed and almost annihilated, not only by the sword of Israel but also by the artillery of heaven. The tables had indeed been turned with a vengeance, as the opening " But " of the verse is designed to emphasize. Instead of seeking to rally the remnants of their armies and leading their men in a final stand, they were panic-stricken, and ignominiously took to their heels in an attempt to preserve their own lives. They must have realized that more than human forces were arrayed against them, and, filled with terror, they sought to escape the avenger. Doubtless they cherished the hope that the darkness which was due would aid their escape, and they must have been utterly dismayed by the supernatural prolongation of the daylight. They had travelled quite a distance from Gibeon, but the relentless chase of those who sought their death still continued (verse 10).

The "cave" incidents recorded in the Scriptures are of considerable variety. The first one noticed was the place of unmentionable degradation on the part of Lot and his daughters after their merciful deliverance from Sodom (Gen. xix, 30-38). The next is where Abraham honourably purchased the field of Ephron, wherein was a cave which became the burial place of his wife Sarah (Gen. xxiii, 17, 19), as another was the temporary sepulchre of Lazarus (John xi, 38)—not so the Saviour's, whose holy body was laid in a new tomb "hewn out in the rock" (Matt. xxvii, 60). In the cave of Adullam, David and his loyal followers found asylum from the murderous designs of Saul. At a later date another cave provided shelter for fifty of the Lord's prophets, when Obadiah hid them from the wicked Jezebel (I Kings xviii, 4), to which allusion is made in Hebrews xi, 38. The final reference is in Revelation vi, when in the great day of the Lamb's wrath—of which Joshua x provided a faint adumbration, for in that day too the heavenly bodies shall be affected—the kings of the earth and the great men shall hide themselves in the dens and in the rocks of the mountains, and shall say unto them, "Fall on us, and hide us from the face of Him that sitteth on the throne and from the wrath of the Lamb" (verses 12-17).

"And it was told Joshua, saying, The five kings are found hid in a cave at Makkedah" (verse 17). We may perhaps connect this verse with the fifteenth, and understand by its language simply that Joshua had *planned* to return at once unto Gibeon. Before actually carrying out his design, apparently, he determined to make sure that vengeance had been executed upon the ringleaders of the unprovoked attack upon Gibeon. The fact that Joshua was here told that these kings were "found" suggests that he had given instructions to make search, and ascertain whether the five kings were among those captured, or if their corpses could be identified upon the field of battle. Whether it was some of his own men who had succeeded in locating the fugitives, and now acquainted Joshua with their hiding place, or Canaanitish traitors who had observed their taking refuge in this cave, and desired to ingratiate themselves with Joshua by turning "informers," we know not. The bare fact alone is stated: their attempt at concealment had failed. It is to be borne in mind that they were endeavouring to escape not only the sword of Israel, but the vengeance of God—for "the Lord fought for Israel" (verse 14) —and concealment from *Him* was impossible.

"And Joshua said, Roll great stones upon the mouth of the cave, and set men by it for to keep them" (verse 18). Observe the collectedness of Israel's leader even in the heat of battle. Instead of being elated and excited by the tidings he had just received, or perturbed because it conflicted with his intention of returning forthwith to Gibeon, he calmly gave orders which would effectively prevent the escape of the kings, securing them in the cave until such time as would be convenient for them to be brought before him and dealt with as they deserved, for the next two verses indicate that information had also just been received that Israel's task on this occasion had not yet been completed. "The kings escaped the hailstones and the sword, only to be reserved to a more ignominious death; for the cave in which they took shelter became first their prison and then their grave" (T. Scott). Very similar was this to the case of Pharaoh, who survived the ten plagues upon the land of Egypt, that he might be a greater and more notable memorial of God's wrath and power. Both instances supply illustrations of that solemn declaration, "The Lord knoweth how . . . to reserve the unjust unto the day of judgment to be punished" (II Peter ii, 9).

"And stay ye not, but pursue after your enemies, and smite the hindmost of them; suffer them not to enter into their cities: for the Lord your God hath delivered them into your hand" (verse 19). When directing the battle against the King of Ai it appears that Joshua stood on some eminence where he could be seen by his men and from which he issued his orders (viii, 18, 26). But on this occasion they were in a mountainous section of Canaan where the terrain was much more broken, which precluded such a policy. It is clear from verse 10 that after the principal engagement the Amorites fled in several directions. Possibly the main body of those who took to their heels had been slain, and Joshua concluded that the death-dealing hail had accounted for the remainder, and had therefore commenced preparations for the return to their head-quarters. But the information he had recently received caused him to change his plans, and to issue the above order. His "stay ye not" implies that there had been a pause, and he now gave this word to stimulate his men unto a final effort. Well as they had done, and weary as they might be, this was no time to relax or to sit down congratulating one another.

Note the argument made use of by Joshua as he here encouraged those under him to redouble their efforts and finish the work required of them: "for the Lord your God hath delivered them into your hand." It may well be that they were reluctant to act so ruthlessly, and that there was some doubt in their mind about pursuing so merciless a policy. Having completely defeated them in battle, and seen a still greater number killed by the hailstones, should not the remaining survivors be shown clemency? But neither Joshua nor those under him were free to please themselves in this matter: "when the Lord thy God shall *deliver them before thee*, thou shalt smite them, and utterly destroy them; thou shalt make no covenant with them, nor show mercy unto them" (Deut: vii, 2—repeated in verses 16-23). That Divine command was a general and not a universal one, being limited as to time ("when") and qualified by Deuteronomy xx, 10, 11. On each occasion the task of Israel's army was to be regulated by that Divine mandate. That it must be so in *this* instance was made unmistakably clear by Jehovah's words to Joshua in verse 8, "I have delivered them into thine hand," and therefore they must slay the Amorites without pity or respite.

"And it came to pass, when Joshua and the children of Israel had made an end of slaying them with a very great slaughter, till they were consumed, that the rest which remained of them entered into fenced cities" (verse 20). The closing words of this verse make it clear that, notwithstanding the extremely heavy losses which the Amorites had sustained, some of them succeeded in making good their escape. That some of them *would do so* was intimated by Joshua's "smite the hindmost" in the preceding verse. It was too late then to round them all up: only the laggards in the rear could be overtaken. So it is in the spiritual warfare of the Christian: even after his greatest victories, some of his enemies still survive. In view of God's dealings with Israel we need not be surprised at this, for at a later date He told them: "I also will not henceforth drive out any from before them of the nations which Joshua left when he died: that through them I may *prove* Israel, whether they will keep the way of the Lord to walk therein, as their fathers did keep it, or not" (Judges ii, 21, 22).

"And all the people returned to the camp to Joshua at Makkedah in peace: none moved his tongue against any of the children of Israel" (verse 21). That "*all* the people returned to the camp" shows that none of the Israelites had been slain by the enemy. So it is spiritually. Whatever buffetings the believer endures, none of his graces can be destroyed by Satan. That the men of Israel returned to the camp to Joshua in peace shows how the saint should conduct himself when he has been granted success over his foes, namely, seek and enjoy communion with the antitypical Joshua. That none moved his tongue against them demonstrates how fully the fear of God had fallen upon the Canaanites: so awed were they that none dared to curse their victors, or utter a word of reproach against them.

Let us remind the reader once more that Israel's conquest and occupation of the land of Canaan present to us a typical picture of the Christian's warfare and present enjoyment of his spiritual inheritance. That warfare is many-sided, and constitutes one of the principal parts of the "service" in which the Lord requires His people to be engaged, and which renders all their other actions unacceptable unto Him while it be disregarded. Alas that we are living in a day of such gross darkness and crass ignorance that comparatively few, even in Christendom, have any scriptural concept of the kind of enemies which the saint is called upon to conquer, or the nature of that work in which he ought to abound. The worst of his foes is neither the world nor the Devil, but rather "the flesh." It is not external temptations but *inward lusts* that constitute his gravest menace and greatest danger. It is the *subduing* of those "fleshly lusts, which *war against* the soul" (I Peter ii, 11), the resisting of his inbred corruptions, which the believer is to be constantly occupied with, for while they be neglected all his other efforts to please God are in vain. "From whence come wars and fightings among you [Christians]? come they not hence, even of your lusts that war in your members?" (James iv, 1).

It is the mortification of their lusts and the cultivation of their graces which is the lifelong task that God has set before His children. The greater part of the New Testament consists of the epistles, which are addressed directly to the saints, and they will be searched in vain for any exhortation which bids them preach to others, engage in evangelistic activities, or do "personal work." On the other hand, those epistles will be found to abound in such injunctions as, "Neither yield ye your members as instruments of unrighteousness unto sin: but yield yourselves unto God, as those that are alive from the dead, and your members as instruments of righteousness unto God. ... Let us therefore cast off the works of darkness, and let us put on the armour of light" (Romans vi, 13, xiii, 12), "Having therefore these promises, dearly beloved, let us cleanse ourselves from all filthiness of the flesh and spirit, perfecting holiness in the fear of God" (II Cor. vii, 1), "That ye put off concerning the former conversation the old man, which is corrupt according to the deceitful lusts; and be renewed in the spirit of your mind; and that ye put on the new man, which after God is created in righteousness and true holiness" (Eph. iv, 22-24), "Be diligent that ye may be found of Him in peace, without spot, and blameless" (II Peter iii, 14).

There is the scriptural answer to the oft-raised question, What can I do for the Lord in return for all He has done for me? How can I best express my gratitude for His wondrous mercy? By keeping "thy heart with all diligence" (Prov. iv, 23), for true godliness is not so much a thing of the head, or of the hand, but of *the heart*. Therein lies the "sphere of his service." There he will discover more than enough to keep him diligently engaged the remainder of his days: to transform a barren wilderness, or rather a neglected field (Prov. xxiv, 30, 31), into a garden for his Master to delight in; to root out the weeds and burn up the thorns and thistles, and to replace them with fragrant flowers and luscious fruits; for only then will he be able to say, "Let my Beloved come into His garden, and eat His pleasant fruits" (Song iv, 16). But alas, pride and the restless energy of the flesh cause him to be occupied with the gardens (souls) of his fellows, instead of working out *his own* salvation with fear and trembling. It is much easier to preach unto others than to gain the mastery over sinful self. It is greatly to be feared that many a Christian has cause to say, "They made me the keeper of the vineyards; but mine own vineyard have I not kept" (Song i, 6).

"Mortify therefore your members which are upon the earth: fornication, uncleanness, inordinate affection, evil concupiscence, and covetousness" (Col. iii, 5). Here is the duty enjoined, the great task assigned. The tense of the verb expresses continued action, that which is to be our daily concernment and practice, and not merely by fits and starts. The evil lusts here named are termed "members" because indwelling sin is compared with an organism—"the old man" (Eph. iv, 22), "the body of this death" (Romans vii, 24). In addition to our natural bodies, there is a body of corruption, which wholly compasses the soul—"the body of the sins of the flesh" (Col. ii, 11). "Your members which are upon the earth" is added to prevent our supposing that the reference is to a mortifying of our physical bodies, for external macerations are of no avail. It is our depraved nature which uses these lusts, as the natural body does its members. Sin is very much alive in the Christian, for the flesh or evil nature is ever opposing the spirit (Gal. v, 17), and he is called upon to employ no half measures in resisting the same. Corrupt propensities are to be dealt with unsparingly, sinful desires sternly denied, evil thoughts rejected with abhorrence.

Dangerous enemies are not to be handled gently, and sin is to be shown no mercy, but is to be so striven against that we earnestly seek to slay it. "Mortify" means put to death, destroy. Extinguish all lustings after earthly and carnal things which are opposed to the spiritual and heavenly life which we have in and from Christ. Yet the term is not to be understood absolutely, in the sense of slaying so as to deprive of the being of sin; but rather to render it useless. In Romans iv, 19, we read of Abraham that "he considered not his own body now *dead*," yet it was not so absolutely; but its natural vigour was greatly abated. Hence Hebrews xi, 12, speaks of his being "as good as dead." As Owen well expressed it, "To mortify signifies a continued act, in taking away the power and force of anything, until it ceases to be dead unto some certain ends or purposes." The flesh cannot be subdued without our doing violence to its affections, and the figurative expression of "mortifying" is used to denote the painfulness and troublesomeness of the task. But however unpleasant the duty, we only make more pain for ourselves if it be neglected. Neglect weakens and wastes indwelling grace, for it is impossible for sin and grace to be strong in the soul at the same time.

Now it is *this* aspect of our spiritual warfare which is in view in Joshua x, 17-27. In the slaying of those five kings we have shadowed forth the Christian's obligation to mortify his lusts and render impotent the sin which indwells him. There are several respects in which those kings typed out the believer's corruptions. First, they belonged to an alien race, being Amorites: so, too, the lusts of the flesh are not a part of man's original nature. Second, they sought to slay the Gibeonites, who were a figure of young converts: in like manner, the flesh is hostile to the spirit. Third, they were defeated by the men of Israel: thus also is the saint frequently given the victory over his temptations. Fourth, they hid in a cave: after their temporary defeat, our lusts cease their raving and we are granted a respite. Fifth, they were then rendered helpless by Joshua's orders (verse 18), as our passions are when Christ rebukes them and bids them be still. Sixth, they were taken out of their concealment and brought before Joshua, teaching us that Christ alone can deal effectually with our enemies. Finally, the captains of Israel were bidden to place their feet upon the necks of these kings, after which they were slain.

In the preceding articles on Joshua x we have already covered, from the historical standpoint, the first five of the above points, and we must now consider more distinctly their typical significance ere turning to the final ones. The great work of mortification in which God calls His people to engage consists of a constant endeavour to subdue the ragings of indwelling sin, in order that they may serve and glorify Him. Sin is an active principle, ever inclining us to evil—"warring against" the new nature (Romans vii, 23), hindering us from that which is good, drawing off the heart from holy duties or distracting us in them; and therefore it is to be steadfastly resisted. Complete exemption from its power is not attainable in this life, but its influence over us may be greatly diminished. Mortification is to be extended unto every internal disposition which is evil, as well as unto our external acts, refusing to hearken to their solicitation and denying them that food on which they could feed (Romans xiii, 14), vigorously opposing them as water is cast upon fire. We are to aim at extirpating not only those gross sins which are condemned by men, but even those which are condoned and admired by the world.

When the five kings had met with a summary defeat at Gibeon, they "fled, and hid themselves in a cave" (x, 16). Similar is the experience of the believer when the Lord has granted him a notable victory or a blessed season of revival in his soul: his heart rests sweetly on Christ and inward peace is now his portion. Nevertheless, though quiet, his enemies have not ceased to be, and therefore he needs to make close inspection within, and deal with what will again cause him trouble if it be left to itself. Thus we are told that Joshua was informed, "The five kings are *found* hid in a cave" (verse 17), which implies that a diligent search had been made for them. Israel's leader then gave orders for great stones to be rolled upon the mouth of the cave, and men set before it "for to keep them" (verse 18). Such is our responsibility: to use every means appointed by God for the subduing and suppression of our lusts, and preventing their breaking forth into renewed activity. Said the apostle, "I keep under my body, and bring it into subjection" (I Cor. ix. 27). Said the Psalmist, "I have refrained my feet from every evil way, that I might keep Thy Word" (cxix, 101).

"Then said Joshua, Open the mouth of the cave, and bring out those five kings unto me out of the cave. And they did so, and brought forth those five kings unto him out of the cave: the king of Jerusalem, the king of Hebron, the king of Jarmuth, the king of Lachish, and the king of Eglon" (x. 22, 23). The opening word of those verses is both important and significant, for it not only indicates the connection between them and verse 21, but also serves to intimate and introduce a prophetic picture of things to come. First, there had been "a very great slaughter" of the Lord's enemies (verse 20), as there will be at the close of this world's history (II Thess i. i, 7-9; Rev. xix, 11-15). Second, "all the people returned to the camp to Joshua at Makkedah" (verse 21)—a blessed foreshadowing of the entire Church being gathered around the antitypical Joshua after their warfare is accomplished. Third, "none moved his tongue against any of the children of Israel" (verse 21): in like manner will the supremacy of Christ and His redeemed be recognized and owned in the great day to come (I Cor. vi, 2, 3, Rev. ii, 26). Fourth, Joshua did not personally fetch these kings out of their hiding place, but called upon others to bring them before him: so before Christ "shall *be gathered* all nations" (Matt. xxv, 32)—by "the holy angels" of verse 31, the "reapers" of Matthew xiii, 30.

Those kings had thought more of their own skins than of the welfare of their men. They had fled for their lives and sought refuge from their pursuers. But in vain—impossible to evade the vengeance of God. Their place of concealment was soon discovered, and at the time which best suited Joshua they were brought before him and dealt with as they deserved—those who foment war rarely escape the worst of its consequences. No further respite was allowed them: these kings, who had determined the destruction of the peaceful Gibeonites, must now appear before Israel's commander. Awful and solemn moment was that: an illustration of what shall take place at the final assize, when the wicked will have to stand before and be judged by the great Joshua. They who made lies their refuge shall then be exposed. They who sought shelter in a nominal profession and mingled with the people of God shall then be openly discovered. None can be concealed from the eyes of Omniscience, none escape His tribunal. "Thine hand shall find out all Thine enemies" (Psalm xxi, 8), and then will they prove what a fearful thing it is to "fall into the hands of" the One they opposed.

In Joshua's requiring the kings to be brought before him, the Christian is taught that he must (in prayer) bring all his foes—be they inward lustings or outward temptations—to the Saviour, for it is not by his own strength he can vanquish them. Next, "Joshua called for all the men of Israel, and said unto the captains of the men of war which went with him, Come near, put your feet upon the necks of these kings." And we are told, "They came near and put their feet upon the necks of them" (verse 24). Very striking is this, and most important the spiritual instruction contained therein. Being dealt with in this manner betokened that these kings were in complete subjugation unto the people of God. And *that* is the attitude which faith is to take unto all its enemies, regarding them as foes already defeated—not by himself, but by his victorious Head; and, as a member of His body, sharing therein. Christ has gloriously prevailed over sin and Satan, and it is the Christian's privilege to appropriate the same unto himself. Has not God promised him, "Thou shalt tread upon the lion and adder: the young lion and the dragon shalt thou trample under feet" (Psalm xci, 13)? That is realized each time the saint treats with contempt and abhorrence the evil solicitations of Satan and his agents.

What we have just said ought to be the constant and uniform experience of the believer. That it is not so is due in part to his failure to plead daily the promise of Psalm xci, 13, and count upon the Lord making it good more fully unto him. God has "put all things under His [Christ's] feet" (Eph. i, 22), which is explained by, "Thou hast put all things *in subjection* under His feet ' (Heb. ii, 8); and by Joshua's bidding his captains place their feet upon the necks of these defeated kings we are thereby shown that our Saviour would have His people bring into subjection their spiritual enemies and share in His triumph over them. He would have them plead before God the efficacy of His sacrifice, and beg Him to grant them a deeper acquaintance experientially of its cleansing virtues. Is it not written, "they overcame him [the Devil] by the blood of the Lamb" (Rev. xii, 11)? And so shall we, if we trust in its sufficiency—not only to put away our sins from before God, but also to enable us to prevail over them in our present warfare. Christ has made believers "*kings* and priests unto God" (Rev. i, 6), then let them earnestly seek grace to act as such, having dominion over themselves, ruling their spirit (Prov. xvi, 32; I Cor. vi, 12).

"And Joshua said unto them, Fear not, nor be dismayed, be strong and of good courage: for thus shall the Lord do to all your enemies against whom ye fight" (verse 25). The ultimate and complete victory of the believer is infallibly certain. "The God of peace shall bruise Satan under your feet shortly. The grace of our Lord Jesus Christ be with you" (Romans xvi, 20). The juxtaposition of those two things should be carefully noted, the second one intimating that the first statement is made for the express purpose of quickening us to fight the good fight of faith. The issue of that fight is not left in the slightest doubt. The members of Christ's body must be partakers of the victory of their Head. In emphasizing the prediction of Genesis iii, 15, too little attention has been given to the promise of Romans xvi, 20. Christians have to do with a foe that was completely defeated at the cross, for through death Christ annulled him who had the power of death (Heb. ii, 14) and spoiled principalities and powers, triumphing over them (Col. ii, 15). Those consolatory declarations are made to encourage us to resist the Devil, regarding him as a foe already conquered, as one who has no claims upon us, as one whom at the close God will tread under our feet; and the extent to which we *appropriate* "the [available] grace of our Lord Jesus Christ" will be the measure in which we shall tread him underfoot *now*.

"And afterward Joshua smote them, and slew them, and hanged them on five trees: and they were hanging upon the trees until the evening. And it came to pass at the time of the going down of the sun, that Joshua commanded and they took them down off the trees, and cast them into the cave wherein they had been hid, and laid great stones in the cave's mouth, which remain until this very day" (verses 26, 27). The mightiest of those who have rebelled

against God and persecuted His people will yet be treated with the utmost
ignominy and summary judgment. Hanging them upon trees demonstrated
that they were accursed of God (Gal. iii, 13). "Though hand join in hand, the
wicked shall not be unpunished. Their wisest counsels prove a snare to entangle
them, their most valiant and vigorous exertions expose their weakness and
end in disgrace and dismay, their choicest blessings are changed into a curse,
and their secret retreats become their prisons or their graves! Kings and
mighty captains, who are disobedient to God, will at last be treated as arch-
rebels, to be distinguished only by the deepest infamy and heaviest vengeance;
and all the Israel of God will join the triumph of the Captain of their salvation in trampling upon the necks of their proudest opposers, exclaiming,
' So let all Thine enemies perish, O Lord ' (cf. Psalm cxlix, 6-9) " (Thomas Scott).

Challenged

One or two details in the closing verses of chapter x, which lack of space
prevented a consideration of in our last issue, must be noticed here. First, it
is blessed to observe that all which is recorded from verse 28 onwards manifests
how fully the faith expressed by Joshua in verse 25 was vindicated. There he
had encouraged the captains of his men of war, for as they placed their feet
upon the necks of the five conquered kings of the Amorites, he boldly said
unto them, "Fear not, nor be dismayed, be strong and of good courage: for
thus shall the Lord do to *all* your enemies against whom ye fight." What
implicit confidence in the living God did he there display! There is nothing
in the context to show that Israel's leader had received a recent assurance
from his Master to that effect: rather do we consider that his heart was resting
upon that word he had long ago received through Moses—"Thine eyes have
seen all that the Lord your God hath done unto these two kings [namely Og
king of Bashan, and Sihon of the Amorites, who opposed Israel in the wilderness and were overthrown]: so shall the Lord do unto *all* the kingdoms whither
thou passest " (Deut. iii, 21).

There can be no doubt that that promise became the "sheet anchor" of
Joshua when he came to be elevated to the position of commander-in-chief of
Israel's forces. He had "mixed faith" with the same (Heb. iv, 2) and it became
the stay of his soul until his arduous and dangerous task had been completed.
He had already received more than one definite "earnest" of the Lord's
making good that word: Jericho and Ai had fallen before them, and the
five kings of the Amorites had been utterly routed. But much heavier fighting
now lay before them. They had barely made a beginning, and far more yet
remained to be accomplished. But Joshua had no doubts, no fear of the outcome. His trust was in the Lord of hosts, and he was not afraid to commit
himself *before others*. Fully assured of the Divine fidelity, he boldly avowed
his confidence therein before and unto his brethren. What an example for
Christian leaders to follow! "My soul shall make her boast in the Lord: the
humble shall *hear thereof,* and be glad " (Psalm xxxiv, 2). The confident
language of those who are well acquainted with the Lord is an inspiration
to those of their brethren of less experience. They who have proved the Lord's
goodness should give free expression thereto that others may be confirmed in
their trust of a faithful God. Thus it was here with Joshua.

"And the Lord delivered Lachish into the hand of Israel, which took it
on the *second* day" (x, 32). That detail marks a difference from the other
Canaanitish towns captured by them. Libnah (verse 30), Eglon (35), Hebron
(37) and Debir (39) were apparently mastered in a single attack; but not so

Lachish. Spiritually, that teaches the Christian that some of his lusts are more powerful than others, and require a longer and more determined effort on his part to subdue them. And, too, an initial failure to enter into possession of a particular portion of our inheritance must not deter us from making a second effort to do so. Ellicott pointed out that it appears from other scriptures too that Lachish was a fortress of considerable strength. When Sennacherib king of Assyria " came up against all the fenced cities of Judah " (II Kings xviii, 13), although he personally " laid siege against Lachish, and all his power with him " (II Chron. xxxii, 9), yet he had to abandon his attempt to reduce it (II Kings xix, 7, 8). At a later date, when Nebuchadnezzar invaded Judah in the reign of its last king, *Lachish* was one of the two places which were the last to be conquered: " for these defenced cities remained of the cities of Judah " (Jer. xxxiv, 7).

Our reason for here calling attention to the above historical fact is twofold. First, because it supplies a striking illustration of the Divine inspiration of the Bible from its minute accuracy and consistency. Those three passages, though lying so far apart, agree in showing that Lachish was a city of considerable strength and one which was more than ordinarily difficult to capture. It is one of innumerable evidences of the authenticity or genuineness of Holy Writ, which by silent testimony bears witness to its perfect harmony. This argument, drawn from unmistakable *coincidence without design,* will have greater weight with those best qualified to weigh evidence. In the mouths of three independent witnesses (Joshua, the writer of II Chronicles and Jeremiah) the truth of what they wrote is hereby established, for their separate allusions unto Lachish are unstudied and without collusion, yet are they thoroughly consistent and concordant. Second, because by comparing Joshua x, 32, with those latter passages we learn that Israel succeeded where such mighty warriors as Sennacherib and Nebuchadnezzar failed, which teaches the valuable lesson that under God His people are able to achieve what the natural man cannot!

"And all these kings and their land did Joshua take at one time, because the Lord God of Israel fought for Israel " (x, 42). Another indication of the Divine authorship of the Bible are those words. There is no magnifying of the human instrument, no paying homage to a national hero, but, instead, a placing of the glory where it rightfully belongs. This is but one of a score of similar passages in which we may perceive the Holy Spirit's jealousy of the Divine honour, wherein Israel's successes are attributed unto Jehovah's showing Himself strong in their behalf. This He does in a variety of ways, for when the Lord fights *for* His people He fights *against* their enemies. In the case of Pharaoh and his army, He filled them with a spirit of madness, so that they rushed headlong to their destruction; in others, He instilled a spirit of fear so that they fled when no man pursued them (II Kings vii, 6, 7), and then is made good that word, " The flight shall perish from the swift...and he that is courageous among the mighty shall flee away naked in that day, saith the Lord " (Amos ii, 14-16). A true humility in Christ's servants today will recognize and readily acknowledge the same principle when their labours are made to prosper.

" And Joshua returned, and all Israel with him, unto the camp to Gilgal " (verse 43), which seems to intimate that during the lengthy campaign in which they had been engaged none of the Hebrews were slain, but that their complete force returned safe and sound to their headquarters. It is not without reason that the Holy Spirit mentions by name the place where their camp was situated, for it points at least three most important and valuable lessons for us. First, Gilgal was, spiritually speaking, the place of self-judgment and conscious weakness (see our Joshua articles 27 and 28), for it was there that the Israelites were circumcised (iv, 19; v, 2, 3), and that should ever be the place unto which the Christian has recourse *after his victories*, for only as he preserves a sense of his own nothingness will his strength be maintained. Second, Gilgal was the place of Divine fellowship: "the children of Israel encamped in Gilgal, and kept the passover" (v, 10): only as communion with God is maintained may we count upon Him granting us further success in the fight of faith. Third, Gilgal was the place where the tabernacle was erected (vi, 6), where the priesthood officiated, where sacrifices were offered, and where the Lord manifested his presence.

We would fain believe that when Joshua and all his men returned to Gilgal that, before acquainting their families with the details of how graciously and wondrously the Lord had wrought for them in their battles, they first offered sacrifices of thanksgiving unto Him, and rendered public praise for the notable successes which He had vouchsafed them. The least they could do was to acknowledge Him who was the Bestower of their conquests. And the same is true of us, my readers: the only fitting way in which we can celebrate our spiritual triumphs is to give the whole of the glory of them unto their Author, as that is likewise the best preparative for the further fighting which lies before us. We are diligent and earnest in making supplication unto the Lord when we are hard pressed by the foe, and we should be equally explicit and fervent before Him when He has granted us deliverance. He requires us to make known our requests *with thanksgiving* (Phil. iv, 6), and it is more and more our conviction that one chief reason why so many of our requests are refused is that we fail to appreciate sufficiently those He *has* granted. God will not set a premium upon ingratitude.

But even though the Christian returns to the place of self-abasement after his victories, enters into sweet communion with the Lord and duly acknowledges His favours, he must not expect that henceforth all will be plain sailing for him. It was not so with Joshua and Israel, for the very next thing we read after their return to Gilgal is, "And it came to pass, when Jabin king of Hazor had heard those things, that he sent to Joab king of Madon, and to the king of Shimron, and to the king of Achshaph. . . . And they went out, they and all their hosts with them, much people, even as the sand that is upon the sea shore in multitude, with horses and chariots very many. And when all these kings were met together, they came and pitched together at the waters of Merom, *to fight against Israel*" (xi, 1-5)! Here is a throwing down of the gauntlet with a vengeance. Hitherto the Canaanites had acted on the defensive, for it was Israel who assaulted Jericho and Ai, and the attack of the five kings had not been against Joshua, but the Gibeonites; but now they took the offensive, fiercely challenging Israel's right to remain in Canaan.

There is an old saying that "Any fool can make money, but it takes a wise man to *keep* it." Certainly it requires much diligence and care for the Christian to retain what he has acquired spiritually, to maintain the progress he has made, to consolidate that portion of his heritage which he has entered into, for the great enemy of souls will strive hard to deprive him thereof. He challenged our first parents in Eden while in their sinless condition, for it was abject misery unto him to see them happy. This principle runs all through Genesis. When God prospered Abraham in Canaan and his flocks and herds increased, such strife arose between his herdsmen and Lot's that they could no longer dwell together in peace. Later, the Philistines filled with earth the wells which his servants had dug (xxvi, 15), and when Isaac's men dug new ones the men of Gerar objected, challenging their right to the same, and striving with them (xxvi, 20, 21). When Jehovah made known His purpose that Rebekah's elder son should serve the younger, she had the effrontery to contest His decision (xxv, 23; xxvii, 6, etc.). When by means of dreams it was made known that the rest of his brethren should be subservient to Joseph and pay him homage, they determined to prevent the fulfilment thereof.

Even Joseph challenged the desire of his dying father to bestow his principal blessing upon Ephraim (xlviii, 17). When the Hebrews were peacefully settled in Goshen "there arose up a new king over Egypt, which knew not Joseph" (Exodus i, 8), who was jealous of and fiercely assailed them. And all these things have been recorded for *our* instruction, to teach us to expect that attempts will be made to dispossess us of our rightful portion. Yea, we find that Satan blatantly and impiously assaulted the Holy One, challenging Him to supply proof of His deity—since you be the Son of God, "command that these stones be made bread." So too during His public ministry: again and again he stirred up the priests and Pharisees to demand by what authority He did this and that. Such opposition is epitomized in the parable of the wheat and tares: no sooner had Christ sown the good seed in the field than His right thereto was challenged by Satan's sowing darnel therein.

The Devil sought to rob the apostles of their portion, as is clear from the words of Christ: "Satan hath desired to have you, that he may sift you as wheat" (Luke xxii, 31)—His use of the plural pronoun shows that more than Simon was involved. How long was it after Pentecost before the enemy stirred up Saul of Tarsus to persecute the primitive Christians and encompassed the death of Stephen? No sooner had Peter been Divinely sent unto Cornelius and a blessed work of grace commenced among the Gentiles, than there was determined opposition and an attempt made to bring the same to an end by denying Peter's rights to evangelize the Gentiles. The Book of Acts records instance after instance of attacks made upon the peace and prosperity of one church after another. What force do all the above examples give to our need of taking heed of that exhortation "*hold fast* that which is good" (I Thess. v, 21), for the flesh, the world and the Devil will combine in seeking to get us to relinquish the same. Because of the corruptions of our hearts, the temptations of Satan, the allurements of the world, we are in real danger of letting go what is more precious than rubies. Having bought the Truth, we must resolutely see to it that we "sell it not" (Prov. xxiii, 23).

It is not without good reason that the Lord has bidden His people to "hold fast the profession of our faith without wavering" (Heb. x, 23), and never was it more imperative that they attended to that injunction. We must, despite all opposition and persecution, continue in and press forward along that narrow way which leads unto life, for only he that endures unto the end shall be saved. No matter how fiercely you be assailed, surrender not your ground, but steadfastly maintain your profession. That "hold fast" presupposes inducements to compromise and renounce. It signifies the putting forth of our utmost endeavours to remain steadfast. "Hold that *fast* which thou hast, that no man take thy crown" (Rev. iii, 11). Adhere firmly thereto in faith and with a good conscience: never was it more needful to do so. The character of these times demands unfailing loyalty and unswerving devotion to Christ and to all He has committed to us. "Know ye not that they which run in a race run all, but one receiveth the prize? So run, that ye may obtain " (I Cor. ix, 24)—it is not the *start* but the *end* which determines the fitness to wear the crown.

Thus it will be seen, once again, that the passage before us contains lessons of deep importance for the Christian, particularly regarding his spiritual warfare and present enjoyment of his heritage. The children of Israel had made quite a little progress in their conquest of Canaan, but now they were very seriously challenged as to their occupancy. A most formidable attempt was being made to dispossess them, yea, utterly to vanquish them. In chapter x, only five kings united in their attack upon Gibeon, but here there was a federation of all the remaining kings of Palestine. The vastness of the forces deployed by them appears in "even as the sand that is on the sea shore," and with them were "horses and chariots very many" (verse 4). Ah, my reader, Satan will not readily admit defeat! He did not in connection with Job, but renewed his assault again and again. "When the unclean spirit is gone out of a man, he walketh through dry places, seeking rest, and findeth none. Then he saith, I will return. . . . Then goeth he, and taketh with himself seven other spirits more wicked than himself, and they enter in and dwell there: and the last state of that man is worse than the first" (Matt. xii, 43-45)!

The believer must be prepared for such challenges being made to him, for if Satan opposed our invulnerable Head it is not to be expected that he will leave alone the vulnerable members of His mystical body; and though at the command of Christ he departed from Him, it was only "for a season." So it is with us. We may be enabled by grace so to resist the Devil that he will flee from us (James iv, 7), yet we may be sure that it will not be long before he returns and resumes the conflict. Nor are his efforts confined to individual saints: he assaults their assemblies too, as the New Testament and all ecclesiastical history of this Christian era shows—how many churches' candles have been put out by him because of lack of watchfulness on their part, or through failure to take a firm stand against him! That word of the apostle to the church officers at Ephesus needs to be laid to heart by all holding a similar position today: "Take heed therefore unto yourselves, and to all the flock, over the which the Holy Ghost hath made you overseers, to feed the church of God, which He hath purchased with His own blood. For I know this, that after my departing shall grievous wolves enter in among you, not sparing the flock. . . . Therefore watch" (Acts xx, 28-31).

These paragraphs are not being written merely to fill up space, but in the endeavour to supply young believers with a timely warning, to put them on their guard against the onsets of their adversary. To be forewarned is to be forearmed, and though we may not be ignorant of Satan's devices, yet all of us need to be frequently reminded of them. At no one point does he more often assail than in seeking to take from us what is ours. In Matthew xiii, 19, our Lord solemnly pointed out that the wicked one is able to catch away that which was sown in the heart, yet the fault is our own if we suffer him to do so. He will endeavour to rob us of some Divine promise which we are trying to rest upon, by denying our personal title to the same. He will challenge our warrant to some particularly helpful portion of the minister's sermon, saying that it pertains not to us. He will call into question our right to peace of conscience and joy of heart. He will oppose us when reading the Word or engaged in prayer. In short, we must expect to be challenged by him at every point, and seek grace steadfastly to resist him.

In concluding this article let us take note that Joshua xi opens with the word "And," which intimates that this formidable federation of the Canaanites took the field against Israel while they were at Gilgal (x, 43), which is one reason why we have entitled this meditation "Challenged." There is nothing which more enrages Satan than to behold the saints taking the place of conscious weakness before the Lord, or enjoying blessed communion with God as they feast with Him upon the Lamb; yet there is never a time when it is so certain that he will meet with no success as he attempts to vent his enmity against them, for it is impossible for him to injure any who "dwelleth in the secret place of the most High," for of such it is declared, he "shall abide under the shadow of the Almighty," and therefore can he confidently affirm "I will say of the Lord, He is my refuge and fortress: my God; in Him will I trust." For the promise to him is "Surely He shall deliver thee from the snare of the fowler" Psalm xci, 1-3). Those who live a life of fellowship with God are assured of His protection, and may therefore preserve a holy serenity of mind, assured that He will repel their foes and defend them. Nevertheless, as Scott pertinently pointed out, "The believer must never put off his armour, or expect durable peace, till he closes his eyes in death."

Chapter 14

THE FINAL CONQUEST

Joshua 11:1—12:24

A Challenge Met

Before developing the central theme suggested by the verses which are now to be before us, let us offer a few comments upon their setting. "And it came to pass, when Jabin king of Hazor had heard those things, that he sent" a message to many of his fellow kings, and they, with their armies, met together to fight against Israel (xi, 1-5). It has been pointed out by another that "Jabin seems to have held in northern Palestine a similar position of power and influence to what Adonizedek king of Jerusalem did in the south." If the reader refers back to x, 1-5, he will find that that king had done precisely the same thing, except that his assault was made not directly against Israel, but upon the Gibeonites who had made peace with them. It is a trite remark to say that "history repeats itself," nevertheless it is one which casts an unfavourable reflection upon fallen human nature, for it is tantamount to acknowledging that one generation fails to profit from the faults of those who preceded them and avoid the fatal pits into which they fell. What proof that all are "clay of the same lump (Romans ix, 21), and that "As in water face answereth to face, so the heart of man to man" (Prov. xxvii, 19).

"When Jabin . . . had *heard* these things." Once more we meet with this important word: compare ii, 10; v, 1; ix, 1, 9; x, 1; and note the various reactions of those who received such tidings. It is true that "faith cometh by hearing, and hearing by the word of God" (Romans x, 17), yet it is also a fact that "The hearing ear, and the seeing eye, the Lord hath made even both of them." (Prov. xx, 12). True alike both naturally and spiritually, for morally man is both deaf and blind to the things of God (Matt. xiii, 13, 14), and therefore the voice of mercy is disregarded and the sinner perceives no beauty in Christ that he should desire Him. To his need and to the remedy he is alike insensible. Until a miracle of grace is wrought within him, his imagination is darkened and his heart closed against God. That is why multitudes that hear the Gospel with the outward ear profit not, and those who *are* saved under it and receive it into their hearts do so solely because *God* has made them to differ from their unbelieving fellows. Jabin "had heard" of the destruction of Jericho and Ai, but instead of trembling threat he hardened his heart. Thus do sinners rush madly to destruction, notwithstanding the repeated warnings they receive from the deaths of their godless fellows.

That which is recorded in the beginning of Joshua xi looks back to and is the sequel of what was briefly noticed by us in ix, 2. That was preliminary, a consulting together, and probably a determining and promising how strong a force each king was prepared to contribute unto the common cause. *This* was the materialization of their plans and the actual taking of the field by their armies.

Up to that point the Canaanites had acted more or less on the defensive, but upon hearing of the overthrow and burning of Ai they determined to take the offensive. First, the various kings mentioned in xi, 1-3, considered that now *their own interests* were seriously threatened it was time to unite their forces and make a massed attack upon Israel. Second, the king of Jerusalem and his satellites agreed to fall upon the Gibeonites. The latter was the first to be carried into execution, and, though it met with failure and the utmost disaster, Jabin and his confederates (which appears to have included all the Canaanites to the utmost western and northern borders) were undeterred, and instead of casting themselves upon Israel's mercy determined to destroy them in battle.

This "league of nations" or uniting together of several kings and making common cause was no new thing even at that early date, for Genesis xiv, 1-3, reveals that centuries before there had been what might well be designated "the western bloc of nations" assailing "the eastern power and its tributaries." But this movement was to meet with no more success than had the concerted measures taken by Adonizedek. "And they went out, they and all their hosts with them, much people, even as the sand that is upon the sea shore in multitude, with horses and chariots very many" (xi, 4). A real challenge was now made to Israel's further occupancy of the land, and a most terrifying sight must it have presented to the natural eye. This vast assembly was not only far more numerous than any force which Israel had previously encountered, but it was much more formidable and powerful, being provided with a great number of horses and chariots, whereas Israel's army was on foot (Deut. xvii, 16): note the absence of the mention of *horses* in Genesis xxiv, 35; xxvi, 14; Job i, 3— they are seen first in Egypt (Gen. xlvii, 17).

As a protest against the slavish literalism which now exists in certain circles, and as a demurrer against those who insist that the words of Revelation vii, 9, "a great multitude, which no man could number," mean exactly what they affirm, a few words require to be said upon our being told that the assembled hosts of the Canaanites were "even as the sand that is upon the sea shore in multitude." One had supposed that any person of average intelligence and education would at once perceive that such language is hyperbolical, and therefore not to be understood according to the strict letter of it. Such a rhetorical figure is frequently used in Scripture for the purpose of producing a vivid impression. Thus, in the days of Moses the Lord declared He had multiplied Israel "as the stars of heaven for multitude" (Deut. i, 10). When the Midianites assailed Israel it is said, "they came as grasshoppers for multitude; for both they and their camels were without number" (Judges vi, 5) and "as the sand by the sea side for multitude" (vii, 12). The Philistines who gathered themselves together against Saul are described as "the sand which is on the sea shore in multitude" (I Samuel xiii, 5). When God's judgments were on Israel He declared, "Their widows are increased to Me above the sand of the seas" (Jer. xv, 8). Nineveh is said to have multiplied its merchants "above the stars of heaven" (Nahum iii, 16).

Thus, "as the sand which is upon the sea shore" is a proverbial expression to signify a great number. Before such massed armies Israel might well be affrighted, especially since they were at such a disadvantage, entirely on foot. In the light of Judges iv, 3, it is highly probable that the chariots commanded by Jabin were of iron, and, as was customary of those used by the ancients in warfare, armed with terrible scythes, to cut down men as they drove along. Doubtless such a host would be fully assured of an easy victory, but they were to discover, as others both before and since have done, that "the race is not to the swift, nor the battle to the strong" (Eccles. ix, 11). The size and might of this assembly only made its overthrow the more notorious and demonstrated more evidently that it was the Almighty who fought for Israel. Since they were the aggressors, Israel were fully justified in destroying them. In like manner will God in the day of judgment have abundant cause to cast into hell those who have rebelled against Him and strengthened themselves against the Almighty (Job xv, 25).

We entitled the preceding article "Challenged" and concluded by pointing out that the last verse of Joshua x shows us Israel at Gilgal—the place of conscious weakness and of communion with God—and that while there the enemy could not harm them. In substantiation of that statement, we quoted the opening verses of Psalm xci, "He that dwelleth in the secret place of the most High shall abide under the shadow of the Almighty" (verse 1). Without attempting to indicate the typical allusions of that figurative language, or entering into any niceties of exposition, suffice it to say that spiritually it signifies that they who live in close fellowship with God are in the place of safety and security. No evil can reach them there, or, as Spurgeon expressed it, "the outstretched wings of His love and power cover them from all harm." "I will say of the Lord, He is my refuge and my fortress: my God; in Him will I trust" (verse 2). *That* was the inference the Psalmist drew from that fact, the application he made to himself of that blessed promise. Confiding in the Lord, resting on His word, he knew that he was fully protected from all the storms of life and the malice of his foes. No matter how many, how powerful, how relentless his enemies, he was resolved to trust in Him who was his covenant God, his all in all.

"Surely He shall deliver thee from the snare of the fowler, and from the noisome pestilence. He shall cover thee with His feathers, and under His wings shalt thou trust: His truth shall be thy shield and buckler. Thou shalt not be afraid for the terror by night; nor for the arrow that flieth by day" (verses 3-5). In those words we are permitted to hear the Psalmist's holy soliloquy, assuring himself that, regardless of what form the enemy's attack should take or when it came, he had an unfailing shield in the Lord, and therefore there was nothing for him to fear. And that is just as true today, my reader, as it was three thousand years ago. He who unreservedly places himself in the hands of God is perfectly secure in the midst of all dangers—infallibly so in connection with his soul, and reasonably so in regard to his body—and therefore should he enjoy full serenity of mind when his godless fellows are filled with alarm and terror. But let it be carefully noted that verse 1 is the foundation on which rests all that follows. It is only as close communion with God be maintained that the soul will be able to confide in and rely upon Him in seasons of stress or peril. While we dwell in the secret place of the most High, the most skilful deceiver cannot beguile nor the most formidable foe harm us.

The greater the dangers menacing God's people, the greater support may they ask for and expect from Him. The more entirely their hearts be fixed on Him as their strength and deliverer, the more certainly shall their spiritual enemies be subdued by them. See this most strikingly exemplified here in Joshua xi. "And when all these kings were met together, they came and pitched together at the waters of Merom, to fight against Israel. And the Lord said unto Joshua, Be not afraid because of them: for to morrow about this time will I deliver them up all slain before Israel" (verses 5, 6). First, let us observe that Jehovah here made good the word that He had given through Moses: "When thou goest out to battle against thine enemies, and seest *horses, and chariots,* and a people more than thou, be not afraid of them: for the Lord thy God is with thee . . . to fight for you against your enemies, to save you " (Deut. xx, 1, 4). How this reminds us of the declaration, " He is faithful that promised " (Heb. x, 23)! One of the titles which Deity has taken unto Himself is " The faithful God " (Deut. vii, 9). How safely then may He be relied upon! None ever yet really trusted Him in vain.

" And the Lord said unto Joshua, Be not afraid because of them: for to morrow about this time will I deliver them up all slain before Israel." Very striking indeed is that statement and most blessed. Does the reader perceive its real force as he weighs its connection with what immediately precedes? Surely it is apparent: the challenge made by the Canaanites was not simply against Israel, but against Israel's *God!* It is like what we find in the opening chapters of Job, where something very much more than a satanic attack upon that patriarch is in view. The evil one dared to assail *Jehovah Himself*, for when He asked him, " Hast thou considered My servant Job, that there is none like him in the earth, a perfect and an upright man, one that feareth God, and escheweth evil?" we are told that " Satan answered the Lord, and said, Doth Job fear God for nought? Hast not Thou made an hedge about him, and about his house, and about all that he hath on every side? Thou hast blessed the work of his hands, and his substance is increased in the land " (i, 8-10). That was a maligning of the Divine character, for it was tantamount to saying that Job worshipped God not for what He was in Himself, but merely for what He had bestowed upon him.

What we have just pointed out is made yet plainer in Satan's next words: " But put forth Thine hand now, and touch all that he hath, and he will curse Thee to Thy face "—so far from adoring Thee because of Thy personal perfections, Job merely renders a mercenary service for what he gets from Thee. Base insinuation was that: Job is Thy dutiful servant not because he has any love for Thee or genuine regard to Thy will, but from selfish principles, and *that* reflects no credit on Thee. It was an impugning of the Divine character, a blasphemous challenging of God's own excellency. As the sequel shows, the Lord accepted the challenge, and by so doing made fully evident the adversary's lie, for after he had been allowed to slay his sons and seize his possessions, the Lord gave Job the same commendation as before: " a perfect and an upright man, one that feareth God, and escheweth evil, and still he holdeth fast his integrity, although thou movedst Me against him " (ii, 3). Thus did God glory over the baffled Devil and upbraid him for his failure, for Job was equally loyal to Him in adversity as in prosperity. Still Satan was not satisfied: " all that a man hath will he give for his life . . . touch his bone and his flesh, and he will curse Thee to Thy face " (ii, 4, 5). And again he was proved a liar, for the patriarch declared, " Though He slay me, yet will I trust in Him " (xiii, 15).

Though the circumstances were different, the same principle was really involved here in Joshua xi—the Devil's enmity against and opposition to God. For it was the Lord who had given Canaan unto Abraham and his seed, and He it was who had brought them into it. Palestine was Israel's by right of Divine donation. But now the occupancy of their inheritance was hotly challenged. All those kings with their armies were determined to destroy them. The gauntlet was thrown down: let it be put to the issue was the language of their actions. The Lord promptly accepted the challenge, and let it be known unto Israel that " he that toucheth you toucheth the apple of His eye " (Zech. ii, 8). Blessed figure of speech was that: telling not only of the inherent weakness and tenderness of the Lord's people, but intimating their nearness and dearness unto Himself. God strongly resents any affront done to them, and will severely punish those who seek to harm them. Therefore did the Lord immediately assure Joshua that there was no reason for him to be dismayed by this imposing force of the enemy: they were but flinging themselves upon "the thick bosses of *His* bucklers" (Job xv, 26), rushing headlong to their destruction, as would be made to appear on the morrow. So likewise, in the end, will all the works of the Devil be destroyed.

A most important truth is exemplified in all that has been pointed out above, yet one that is little apprehended by God's people today, namely that Satan's assault upon them is really an attack upon their Lord—upon them only because of their relationship to Him. That is illustrated again in Acts ix, for when He arrested Saul of Tarsus on the road to Damascus, as he was "breathing out threatenings and slaughter against the disciples of the Lord," He said, "why persecutest thou *Me?*"—it was the Devil who was impelling Saul, as it was Christ and not merely His disciples against whom he was venting his animosity. And thus it is now. As God suffered Satan to afflict Job so sorely, not because that patriarch had given occasion to be severely chastised, but in order that his integrity might the more plainly appear and the Divine character be vindicated, so He still permits the adversary both to tempt and buffet His people, that their steadfastness (in varying degrees, but always from a total apostasy) may redound to His own glory. As we are told in I Peter i, 7, "That the trial of your faith, being much more precious than of gold that perisheth, though it be tried with fire, might be found unto praise and honour and glory at the appearing of Jesus Christ"—not only, and not principally, *theirs,* but primarily and pre-eminently *God's.*

The practical value of this important truth scarcely requires to be pointed out. Since it be the Lord Himself rather than His redeemed against whom the venom of the serpent is ultimately aimed, how secure are the saints in His hand! Secure, because His own personal honour is involved in their preservation. He has given definite assurance that "This is the Father's will which hath sent Me, that of all which He hath given Me I should lose nothing, but should raise it up again at the last day" (John vi, 39), that they shall "never perish, neither shall any man pluck them out of My hand" (John x, 28), and therefore if the Devil were to bring about the eternal destruction of a single one of them Christ would be eternally disgraced. But such a calamity is utterly impossible, for though Satan be mighty, the Son of God is almighty. Upon that fact, in full persuasion of the everlasting preservation of every soul who has fled to the Lord Jesus for refuge, may each believer rest with implicit confidence. Here, then, is yet another important lesson taught the believer in this invaluable book of Joshua concerning his spiritual warfare, namely that the contest is, ultimately, between Satan and his Saviour, and therefore the issue cannot be in the slightest doubt: as surely as Joshua and the children of Israel overcame and vanquished all the Canaanites who came against them, so will Christ and His Church triumph gloriously over the Devil and his angels.

But further. It is the believer's privilege to realize, especially when fiercely assaulted and sorely pressed by the foe, that the outcome of the fight in which he is engaged rests not with him, but with the Captain of his salvation, and therefore to Him he may turn at all times for succour and for victory. What the Lord said here unto Joshua the Christian should regard as being said unto himself: "Be not afraid because of them." Those who are now arrayed against the Christian and who seek his destruction shall soon themselves be destroyed. "The God of peace shall bruise Satan under your feet shortly" (Romans xvi, 20), and meanwhile, as the apostle immediately added, "The grace of our Lord Jesus be with you. Amen." But just as that assuring word spoken to Joshua was addressed unto his *faith* and could be enjoyed only by the exercise of that grace in the interval before its fulfilment, so serenity of mind while menaced by his foes can only be the believer's as he by faith appropriates that promise unto himself. Then let his triumphant language be, "Behold, God is my salvation; I will trust, and not be afraid" (Isaiah xii, 2). In proportion as he does so will he be warranted in resting on that declaration, "Surely He *shall deliver thee* from the snare of the fowler, and from the noisome pestilence. He shall cover thee with His feathers." (Psalm xci, 3, 4).

In our last we considered the Divine response made to the formidable movement inaugurated by Jabin and his fellows. The Lord promptly took up the cudgels on behalf of His menaced people. He assured His servant that he need entertain no fear whatever about the outcome, promising him, "I will deliver them up all slain before Israel" (xi, 6). In like manner is the Christian to be assured, and therefore it is his holy privilege to enter upon and engage in the good fight of faith resting on the sure pledges of God, confident of a successful issue. "He is faithful that promised" (Heb. x, 23). The more we meditate upon the veracity of the Promiser, the more will faith be strengthened. In proportion as we truly realize that we have to do with One who cannot lie, the greater confidence shall we have in His Word. Instead of being so much occupied with the difficulties of the way (which will but engender doubts), we need to look above unto Him who has given us such "exceeding great and precious promises" (II Peter i, 4) to be the stay of our hearts, to cheer and gladden us. Those promises are to be treasured up in our minds, for they are both the food of faith to nourish and strengthen it and the fuel of faith to stoke and energize it, otherwise it will lack that which is necessary for its activity, as a fire will not burn without wood or coals—thus coldness of heart is due mainly to faith being deprived of its fuel!

There will be little or no success in our spiritual warfare unless we make much of the Divine *promises,* and still more of the Promiser Himself. The foes that have to be encountered are far too powerful to be overcome by any might of ours, and therefore must we look to Him whose soldiers we are. If we do so, no matter how great our weakness or formidable the task assigned, the Lord will not fail us. "Through faith also Sara herself received strength to conceive seed, and was delivered of a child when she was past age, because she judged Him faithful who had promised" (Heb. xi, 11). There were strong impediments in the way of her faith, and at first she was staggered by them, but as she regarded the immutability and fidelity of the Promiser her doubts were stilled, faith prevailed, and strength was given. As Manton well said, "Every Divine promise has annexed to it the challenge, 'Is anything too hard for the Lord?'" As in Sara's case, so with us, very often there is a fight with unbelief before faith is established on the promise. But instead of suffering obstacles to hinder faith, they should be made a help to it—arguing, Here is a grand opportunity for me to prove the sufficiency of my God. He never promises more than He is able to perform. His word never exceeds His power: "Faithful is He that calleth you, who also *will do it*" (I Thess. v, 24).

It should be duly considered that this massing of the Canaanites against Israel occurred not soon after they entered the land, nor did they encounter anything like such an opposing force either at Jericho or Ai. No, rather was this trial met with after they had made considerable progress in taking possession of their heritage. Thus it was too with the father of all them that believe:

each new test of Abraham's faith was more severe than the preceding ones. And so it is in the Christian life. Thus it is the mature and *aged warrior* to whom this word is most appropriate: "Be not afraid." Why should Joshua fear? Since God had so wondrously delivered Israel from the bondage of Egypt, overthrown Pharaoh and his chariots in the Red Sea, provided for them all through their wilderness journey, miraculously opened the Jordan for them to enter into Canaan, most certainly He was not going to abandon them now and allow them to perish at the hands of Jabin and his armies. No indeed, when God begins a work He never stops when it is but half done, but always completes and perfects it (Phil. i, 6). So it was with Israel under Joshua; and so it is with every elect vessel: "whom He justified, them He also glorified" (Romans viii, 30). Much takes place between the one and the other, but though death itself occurs (as has been the case with His people for the last six thousand years), the former guarantees the latter.

Let then the tried and aged pilgrim take comfort from the Lord's dealings with Israel, and give no place whatever to Satan's lie that God has tired of him. Like the fiend that he is, the Devil seeks to attack us most fiercely when much oppressed by circumstances or at our weakest physically. When natural vigour has abated and the increasing weight of years is felt, he will seek to inject the most God-dishonouring doubts into the minds of His people. Reject them with abhorrence, and rest on the Divine assurance, "I will never leave thee, nor forsake thee" (Heb. xiii, 5). He who has cared for His child all through the years most certainly will not forsake him or her in the time of old age. He who has responded to your cries in former days will not turn a deaf ear now that your voice has grown feeble. "He shall deliver thee in six troubles [has he not done so?]: yea, in seven [the final one] there shall no evil touch thee" (Job v, 19). Past deliverances are sure earnests of future ones. "And even to your old age I am He: and even to hoar hairs will I carry you: I have made, and I *will* bear; even I will carry, and will deliver you" (Isaiah xlvi, 4): those are the "I wills" of Him who is the Truth. Rest your whole weight on them.

But resting upon the promises does not mean that the saint may shirk any of his duties, or even relax in the performing of them. Rather do such Divine assurances involve corresponding obligations. That is clear from the two halves of the verses quoted in our opening paragraph: "Let us hold fast the profession of our faith without wavering; *(for* He is faithful that promised)" (Heb. x, 23). That "for" is very forceful, supplying us with a powerful motive unto steadfastness and diligence. Since God be faithful to us, we ought to be faithful unto Him. To hold fast the profession of our faith is a comprehensive expression which includes every aspect of the Christian life, and the knowledge that God will infallibly make good His word unto us is to animate unto fidelity in the carrying out of its engagements. The Divine promises are not only comforting pillows on which to rest our weary heads, but cordials to strengthen, spurs to move us, encouragements for us to press forward along the way, arguments for us to make use of in prayer. The Divine promises are the food of faith, and faith is for producing good works. That is the practical application which the apostle made of the Divine assurances in I Corinthians xv, 54-57: *Therefore*, my beloved brethren, be ye steadfast, unmoveable, always abounding in the work of the Lord, forasmuch as ye know that your labour is not in vain in the Lord."

So far from annulling the believer's responsibility or countenancing any slackness in the discharge of the same, spiritual privileges involve additional obligations. But alas, man is such a creature of extremes that even a Christian when he be deeply impressed with one aspect of the Truth is very apt to become so absorbed with it as to lose sight of and leave out of his reckoning the counter-balancing aspect of the Truth. Because *God* performs everything for us, it does not mean there is nothing for *us* to do. If we ascribe the glory unto Him to whom alone it is due, we shall freely own to the Lord, " for *Thou* also hast wrought all our works in us " (Isaiah xxvi, 12); nevertheless that does not alter the fact He has bidden us " work out *your own* salvation with fear and trembling " (Phil. ii, 12), yet that too is immediately followed with, " For it is God which worketh in you both to will and to do of His good pleasure." There the *two sides* of the Truth are placed in juxtaposition, and notice well the order in which they are set before us. First the enforcing of our duty, and then the encouraging motive to inspire us therein. The latter is not added to induce indolence, but in order to encourage effort. We have no scriptural warrant to expect that God will show Himself strong in our behalf unless we make conscience of His precepts and use the means He has appointed. Our bread is Divinely guaranteed (Isaiah xxxiii, 16), nevertheless it must be laboured for (John vi, 27).

The relation of Philippians ii, 13, to ii, 12, is a double one, being designed both to cheer and to humble us. The child of God is very conscious of his weakness, and knowing that the world, the flesh and the Devil are arrayed against him, and contemplating the tasks set before him—tasks which are spiritual and far above the compass of mere nature—he asks, How can I possibly accomplish them? The answer is, Divine assistance is assured. The believer is not left to himself, but the omnipotent God operates within as well as for him, and therefore is he to go forth in the confidence that Divine grace will be sufficient for him. Help is indeed needed by him, and if he conducts himself aright that help will certainly be given. On the other hand, he is required to work out his own salvation " with fear and trembling," that is in a spirit of humility and lowliness. But how is that possible unto those who are proud and independent? We are all of us Pharisees by nature—boastful and prone to self-glorying. How then can we be emptied of such a spirit? And again Philippians ii, 13, supplies the answer. From this consideration: since it be God who works in me all that is praiseworthy, then I have nothing to boast of. I am constantly to remind myself that it is God who makes me to differ from those of my fellows whom He leaves to themselves. The strongest inducement possible to produce a self-abasing spirit is the realization that apart from Christ we can do nothing (John xv, 5).

Above we have said that there will be little or no success in our spiritual warfare unless we make much of the Divine promises: let us now add that the same is equally true of the Divine *precepts*. That also is taught us in Joshua xi, 6, for immediately after assuring His servant, " Be not afraid because of them: for to morrow about this time will I deliver them up all slain before Israel," the Lord added, " *thou* shalt hough their horses and burn their chariots with fire." God's promises are not designed to further slothfulness, but to stimulate to the performance of duty. God does not work in us to promote idleness, but to " will and to do of His good pleasure." When the farmer sees God working by softening the ground with gentle showers, he is encouraged to plough and plant his fields. When the yachtsman perceives God working by stirring the becalmed air with a breeze, he is encouraged to hoist his sails. So it is spiritually. Grace is given the regenerate for them to *use*: " stir up the gift of God which is in thee " (II Tim. i, 6). We are to " work out" what God has wrought in us, yet in complete dependence upon Him. We must beware of abusing the truth of Divine operations and take to heart the warning of the lazy servant who hid his talent in the earth.

To be a successful warrior I must be able to say with David (and none obtained more military victories than he!): "Thy testimonies have I taken as an heritage for ever: for they are the rejoicing of my heart" (Psalm cxix, 111). We agree with C. Bridges that when "testimony" occurs in the singular number it has reference to the Bible as a whole—the entire revelation of God's will unto mankind—but when found in the plural it is chiefly the preceptive parts of Scripture which are in view. This is borne out by verse 138: "Thy testimonies that Thou hast *commanded*," and "I have *kept* Thy precepts and Thy testimonies" (168). David had chosen God's statutes or precepts as his "heritage" to live upon. Not the world did he select for his happiness, but a heritage of holiness and wisdom, one which would not fail in time and one that would endure for ever. He made this choice because he realized their value: that they are like their Author, namely "righteous and very faithful" (138), and because he loved them exceedingly (167). So too did the apostle bear witness: "I *delight* in the law of God after the inward man" (Romans vii, 22) —only then will our obedience be acceptable unto Him. "I have kept Thy precepts and Thy testimonies," and as Spurgeon said, "If we keep God's testimonies they will keep us—right in opinion, comfortable in spirit, holy in conversation, hopeful in expectation."

The Divine testimonies are as necessary and essential unto the believer in his spiritual warfare as are the Divine assurances. It is the fight of faith which we are called to wage, and as God's promises are its food, so His precepts are its *directors*. Faith has three great tasks to perform: to trust implicitly in God, to render obedience to His revealed will, and steadfastly to resist all that is opposed thereto. The promises provide encouragement for the first, the precepts light for the second, and the Lord Himself must be looked unto for strength for the third. So it was in Joshua xi, 6: the Divine promise there was immediately followed by a precept; Joshua was required to hough the horses of the Canaanites and burn their chariots with fire. Matthew Henry pointed out that this new campaign upon which Joshua was now entering "was a glorious one, no less illustrious than the former in the success of it, though in respect of miracles, it was inferior to it in glory. The wonders God then wrought for them, were to initiate and encourage them to act vigorously themselves. Thus the war carried on by the preaching of the Gospel, against Satan's kingdom, was at first furthered by miracles; but the warfare by then was sufficiently proved to be of God, and the managers of it are now left to the ordinary assistance of Divine grace in the use of the sword of the Spirit, and must not expect hailstones, or the standing still of the sun."

The order given to Joshua for the houghing of the horses of the Canaanites and the burning of their chariots involved, of course, the vanquishing of them in battle. Accordingly we are told, "So Joshua came, and all the people of war with him, against them by the waters of Merom suddenly; and they fell upon them" (verse 7). Though it was the Lord Himself who had accepted the challenge of Jabin and his confederates, and had assured His servant that He would deliver them up all slain before Israel on the morrow, this did not signify that he and his men were to remain passive—mere spectators of God's working. He was indeed about to act mightily *for* them, yet at the same time *by and through them*! This also needs to be made clear and emphasized in certain quarters today: not only where hyper-Calvinism or a species of fatalism holds sway, but also where a certain type of the "victorious life" teaching is misleading souls, for the one is as paralysing as the other. The Christian is informed that the reason why he so often yields to external temptations or is overcome by indwelling sin is because he is making the great mistake of trying to fight his foes personally; that they will never be conquered until he, "by faith," turns them over to Christ and counts upon His vanquishing them for him; that the battle is not his but the Lord's; that He triumphed over Satan and all his hosts at the cross; and that if we yield ourselves completely to Him His victory will be ours without any effort on our part.

There is just sufficient veneer of the Truth to give this line of teaching a plausible appearance, yet there is also more than enough repudiation of Scripture to convince all who are subject to God's Word of its error. Seemingly it supplies a blessed solution to the most distressing problem in the Christian life, and at the same time appears to honour Christ, but in fact it repudiates human responsibility, and falsifies the teaching of our Lord. Faith is not only to rest upon the Divine promises and rely upon what Christ has done for His people; it is also required to bring forth good works, run in the way of His commandments, follow the example He has left us. When one of the leaders of this modern movement declares, "As I trust Christ in surrender there need be *no fight* against sin, but complete freedom from the power and even the desire of sin," he not only inculcates what is contrary to the recorded experience of God's people in all ages, but he takes direct issue with Scripture itself. The Bible speaks of "striving against sin" (Heb. xii, 4), wrestling against principalities and powers (Eph. vi, 12), bids the believer "fight the good fight of faith" (I Tim. vi, 12), enjoins him to "endure hardness, as a good soldier of Jesus Christ . . . that he may please Him who has chosen him to be a *soldier*" (II Tim. ii, 3, 4), and calls upon him to "put on the whole armour of God, that ye may be able to stand against the wiles of the devil" (Eph. vi, 11).

It is obvious that the above references, and others of a similar nature, would be quite useless, meaningless, if the ideal state of Christian living were a merely *passive* thing, and if it be summed up in the catchword of one of its popular advocates, "Let go, and let God." Most assuredly the believer cannot gain the victory by his own powers; instead, he is to seek strength from the Lord, and then to use the same actively and strenuously. To speak of a *passive* "overcomer" is to employ words without meaning. To make the believer a mere onlooker of the Lord's exploits is to reduce him to something less than a moral agent. "Stand still, and see the salvation of the Lord" must not be so misunderstood and misapplied as to neutralize the exhortation "Let us run with patience [i.e. perseverance] the race that is set before us" (Heb. xii, 1). "Running," like "wrestling" and "fighting," is a figure which expresses the putting forth of vigorous endeavour. True, we are to be "looking unto Jesus" while thus engaged, yet *run* we must. True also that the Christian is to reckon on the blessed fact that his Saviour has triumphed over Satan, and yet that does not alter the fact that *he* is required to "resist the devil." True, God has promised to tread Satan under our feet shortly, yet he is not there now, any more than Christ's enemies have yet been made His footstool (Heb. x, 13). The ultimate victory is sure, yet it has to be *fought for* by each one of us.

Thus it was in Joshua xi. Divine assurance that Jabin and his army would be slain on the morrow had been given, yet that did not release Israel from performing *their* duty. God had made no announcement that He would destroy the Canaanites by fire from heaven, as He did the cities of the plain (Gen. xix), or that He would cause the earth to open her mouth and swallow them up as in the case of Korah and his company (Num. xvi). Instead, He had promised to " deliver them up all *slain* before Israel "—a word which imported, according to its common usage, being killed in battle. That His servant so understood it is evident, for we are told that he and all the men of war with him " fell upon them." Joshua did not seek a defensive position and dig trenches for the protection of his men, and then sit down and wait for the Lord to work. No, with full confidence in his Master's promise, he took the initiative, acted aggressively, and launched an attack upon the foe—boldly, suddenly, unexpectedly. God had said " to morrow I will deliver them up," and, taking Him at His word, Joshua delayed not. Probably *that* was the very last thing which the hosts of Jabin were expecting, and they would be thrown into the utmost confusion from the very outset.

The Challengers Vanquished

Our design in these articles has been to supply something more than a bare exposition of the book of Joshua, namely to point out some of the bearings which its contents have upon us today. A true understanding of God's Word is indeed of first importance, for unless its meaning be rightly apprehended, of what service will it be unto us? Yet it is *the use* to which we put it, the measure in which we appropriate its principles and precepts to the regulating of our daily walk, that is equally important. " If ye *know* these things, happy are ye if ye *do* them " (John xiii, 17), that is the test. Thus, to spare no pains in endeavouring to arrive at the meaning of God's Word, that he may give a sound interpretation of the same, is only a part of the duty resting upon the minister of the Gospel, and especially *the teacher* of God's people. Another part of his work, equally necessary and exacting, is for him to make practical application unto his hearers of each passage he takes up, to point out the various lessons it inculcates, to accommodate it unto the present condition and circumstances of those to whom he ministers. Only so will he emulate the example left him by the Divine Teacher of the Church: only so will he pursue the same course that was followed by His apostles: only so will he be of greatest service unto His needy, tried and often sorely perplexed people. It is not the elucidation of mysteries or light upon prophecy that they most need, but that which will comfort, strengthen and stimulate them.

Such a policy as just intimated will indeed slow down the speed of one who undertakes to go systematically through a whole book of Scripture, or even a single chapter thereof. But so far from speed being a virtue, it is more often a vice, as much in modern life tragically shows. " He that believeth shall not make haste ".(Isaiah xxviii, 16) holds good of the " opening up " of God's Word, as it does of everything else, and must be heeded if souls are to be really edified. But though such a method will not make for swiftness, yet by God's blessing (on much prayerful meditation) it will produce something far more substantial and satisfying than the superficial generalizations which now so widely obtain, both in the pulpit and in the religious press. As the old adage says, " Slow but sure is sure to do well." Instead of seeing how quickly we could race through the book of Joshua, we have endeavoured to ascertain and then point out the practical application of its contents unto ourselves and our readers. Particularly have we dwelt at length upon the many things in it which illustrate the various aspects of the Christian's spiritual warfare: the snares he must avoid, the rules he must observe, the means he must employ, in order to success therein. We have sought to call attention to the grand incentives and the real encouragements furnished by this book to "fight the good fight of faith," and to show how strength for the same is to be obtained.

In addition, we have endeavoured to remove those "stumblingblocks" (Isaiah lvii, 14) which various types of error lay in the path of the Christian warrior. Let us now add a few words to what was said at the close of our last concerning the misleading teaching of certain sections of what is known as "the victorious life" movement. While on the one hand we heartily concur with their deploring of the carnal and worldly walk of the rank and file of professing Christians, and agree that many of God's own people are living far below their privileges in Christ; yet on the other hand we neither endorse their language nor believe the remedy they prescribe is the true one. All of their leaders are decidedly Arminianistic, which at once evinces that they are unsafe guides to follow. It is scripturally warrantable to say that some believers are living Christ-dishonouring lives and acting contrary to God's revealed will; but that is very far from justifying the oft-made assertion that He desires to do this or that in and for them, but they will not let Him. That would connote a thwarted Redeemer, and obviously a *defeated* Christ could not be the Leader of any "victorious" followers! Such a "Christ" is very different from Him who is no less than "the mighty God" (Isaiah ix, 6). Verily "the legs of the lame are not equal" (Prov. xxvi, 7), and they who are proudest of their consistency are often the most inconsistent in their beliefs and conduct.

To contend for holiness of life is indeed praiseworthy, and to urge God's people to "possess their possessions" and enjoy now the rich heritage which is theirs in Christ is also a thing most needful; yet zeal requires to be tempered with knowledge, and if a spirit of fanaticism is to be avoided all must be tested by Holy Writ. Satan is never more dangerous than when he appears as an angel of light. To carnal reason it seems that Christ's acceptance of the Devil's challenge to cast Himself down from the pinnacle of the temple had been an outstanding act of faith in God to preserve Him from all injury; nevertheless, His reply shows that such had been an act of presumption and contrary t Scripture. Likewise, it may strike us as most honouring to Christ to say that He is ready to do all for us if we surrender wholly to His control; but the fact is that He will no more relieve us of personally contending with our foes than He would repent and believe for us in order to our being saved. Strengthen us He will, if we seek His grace aright; yet that strength will be given for the purpose of equipping us to fight the good fight of faith. As the apostle declared, "I also labour, striving according to His working, which worketh in me mightily" (Col. i, 29). Nor is there anything in that statement the least derogatory to His glory; but very much to the contrary.

Resuming our remarks upon Joshua xi. In view of the great preponderance of Jabin's forces over Israel's, and the weighty advantage he had in being possessed of so many horses and chariots, while they were on foot, there can be no doubt that he was not only fully confident of victory, but that he considered the initiative lay entirely in his own hands, and that there was not the least likelihood of their launching any attack upon him. Yet that was the very thing that happened. "So Joshua came, and all the people of war with him, against them by the waters of Merom suddenly; and they fell upon them" (verse 7). Therein we behold the confidence, the obedience, the daring and the promptness of faith. Joshua's confidence lay not in his own military skill, nor in the valour of his men, but in the sure promise of the One whom he served. The assault which he now made upon the Canaanites was not dictated by caprice, feelings, or carnal reason, but was in compliance with the orders which he had received from the Lord. His falling suddenly upon Jabin and his army was not due to any impatience or anxiety for the issue to be immediately determined, but was the result of laying hold of the Lord's " to morrow " in the preceding verse. His action was not a venturesome or foolhardy one, but a daring to rely upon his God when faced with what to sight appeared a hopeless situation—as the Hebrews, and later Daniel, feared not to defy the edicts of the king of Babylon.

"And the Lord delivered them into the hand of Israel, who smote them, and chased them unto great Zidon, and unto Misrephoth-maim, and unto the valley of Mizpeh eastward; and they smote them, until they left them none remaining" (verse 8). Thus did Israel's God make good His word through Moses (Deut. xx, 1), fulfil the promise made to His servant, and vindicate the faith of Joshua. Thus was provided yet another proof of how firm is the foundation on which has rested the faith of God's people in all generations. And thus too did He demonstrate His acceptance of the impious challenge of Jabin and his fellows, and make it clear that "There is no wisdom nor understanding nor counsel against the Lord" (Prov. xxi, 30)—another verse, by the way, whose language is not to be taken absolutely and where an interpreter is needed to bring out its sense. As a matter of fact all the wisdom of Satan and all the policy of the unregenerate is directed, immediately and actively, against the Lord; yet *all in vain*. He that sitteth in the heavens laughs at the most determined and concerted projects of men against Himself and His Anointed, and fulfils His pleasure despite them (Psalm ii, 1-6). As well attempt to stop the sun from shining or the ocean from moving as seek to nullify the decrees of the Almighty. All who make war with the Lamb shall most certainly be vanquished by Him (Rev. xvii, 14).

The total failure of Jabin's long-planned project demonstrated clearly that there is "no counsel against the Lord" which has the remotest possibility of succeeding. The best-contrived policy against Him comes to foolishness. "He taketh the wise in their own craftiness [not "ignorance"!]: and the counsel of the froward is carried headlong" (Job v, 13). Pharaoh's counsel to depress the Hebrews issued in their being increased (Exodus i, 8-12). Ahithophel's counsel was befooled at the very time when "it was as if a man had enquired at the oracle of God" (II Samuel xvi, 23; xvii, 7, 14, 23, with xv, 31). Ahab's attempt to falsify God's word by seeking to ward off the threatened stroke against his life (I Kings xxii, 30-34), Athaliah's deep-laid plot to exterminate the family of David and thereby frustrate the Divine promise (II Kings xi, 1), the blatant boast and wicked design of Sennacherib against Judah (II Chron. xxxii, 21; Isaiah xxx, 31), the strong and repeated efforts of the adversaries of Judah and Benjamin to prevent their building of the temple (Ezra iv, 6), and later the craft of Sanballat to oppose the erecting of the walls of Jerusalem (Neh.), the determination of Haman to slay all the Jews (Esther iii,), Herod's seeking to kill the infant Saviour (Matt. ii)—all came to naught, as inevitably they should do when opposing the decrees of heaven.

"And the Lord delivered them into the hand of Israel" (verse 8), thereby fulfilling the promise which He had given unto Joshua the day previously (verse 6). Blessed is it to learn from this, and many other passages, that the wicked, equally with the righteous, are in the hands of Him who made them and are entirely at His sovereign disposal. One of the chief designs of Scripture is to reveal unto us the several relations which God sustains unto His creatures.

He is not only their Creator, but their Lawgiver and Ruler, their King and Governor, and, ultimately, their Judge, to whom they must yet render an account of their deeds. Since the reprobate as well as the elect are represented as clay in the hands of the Divine Potter determining their eternal destiny (Romans ix, 21-24), then certainly He has full control of them and their actions while they be in a time state. This is a very real and substantial part of the believer's consolation, that his God "doeth according to His will in the army of heaven, and among the inhabitants of the earth: and none can stay His hand, or say unto Him, What doest Thou?" (Dan. iv, 35), and therefore that neither Satan nor any of his children can make the least move against one of the Lord's people without His express permission and the removing of His providential hindrances.

"And the Lord delivered them into the hand of Israel." What a commentary was that upon "The Lord bringeth the counsel of the heathen to nought: He maketh the devices of the people of none effect" (Psalm xxxiii, 10)! Not only are the wicked the subjects of God's government, but their every action is controlled by Him and made subservient to His eternal purpose, yet *without* His having any part in their wickedness. Was it not so in the cases of Pharaoh and Judas? And is it possible to select more extreme ones? If then the greatest of all rebels fulfilled the purpose of the Almighty (though quite unwittingly so far as they were concerned), then think it not strange that it is so with all lesser rebels. Nimrod and his fellows thought to erect a tower whose top should reach unto heaven, but God frustrated them. Abimelech king of Gerah sent and took Sarah unto himself, but God suffered him not to touch her (Gen. xx, 6). Balaam loved the wages of unrighteousness and hired himself out unto Balak to go and curse Israel, but the Lord so interposed that that prophet had to confess to his chagrin, "Behold, I have received commandment to bless: and He hath blessed; and *I cannot* reverse it" (Num. xxiii, 20). "Surely the wrath of man shall [be made to] praise Thee: the remainder of wrath shalt Thou restrain" (Psalm lxxvi, 10).

"The Lord hath prepared His throne in the heavens; and His kingdom ruleth over all" (Psalm ciii, 19)—over the evil and the good, over the demons and those they indwell as truly as over His Church. God rules in the decisions of the senate, the tumults of the people, the fury of battle, as really as in the ragings and tides of the sea. The plotting of kings, the ambitions of aggressors, the avarice of conquerors, are fully controlled by the Most High. He presides in their counsels, determines their decisions, decides which nations they shall attack, bending their minds to comply with His eternal decrees. Unmistakably, repeatedly, uniformly, is that the teaching of Holy Writ. Note well what the Lord said of that heathen monarch who was so filled with the lust of conquest: "O Assyrian, the rod of Mine anger, and the staff in their hand is *Mine* indignation. I will send him against an hypocritical nation, and against the people of My wrath will I give him a charge, to take the spoil, and to take the prey, and to tread them down like the mire of the streets. Howbeit *he meaneth not so* . . . but it is in his heart to destroy and cut off nations not a few" (Isaiah x, 5, 7). The Assyrian had other designs of a more ambitious scope, but God changed the direction of his thoughts, and caused him to be His instrument of retribution in inflicting judgment upon a people who had sorely provoked Him. God employed him, unknown to himself, as "the rod of His anger": thus he was in *God's hand* and his actions determined by Him.

"And the Lord delivered them into the hand of Israel . . . and they smote them, until they left them none remaining" (verse 8). See here the utter futility and madness of fighting against the Almighty! When He "delivered them up" unto their justly deserved death, what could they do? Nothing, they were helpless, unable to escape the due reward of their iniquity. "Though hand join in hand, the wicked shall not be unpunished; but the seed of the righteous shall be delivered" (Prov. xi, 21). Thus it was with Jabin and his hosts; their confederacy in evil came to naught. Their number, strength and unanimity availed them nothing now that God's hour of vengeance had arrived. Therein we have a solemn anticipation and adumbration of the judgment awaiting the world of the ungodly. The Lord has solemnly declared that He "repayeth them that hate Him to their face, to destroy them" (Deut. vii, 10); and again, "Thine hand shall find out all Thine enemies: Thy right hand shall find out those that hate Thee. Thou shalt make them as a fiery oven in the time of Thine anger: the Lord shall swallow them up in His wrath, and the fire shall devour them" (Psalm xxi, 8, 9). Out of Christ there is no protection from God's justice. When He appears to judge the world, the stoutest heart will melt in terror and the most obdurate will cry to the rocks, "Fall on us, and hide us from the face of Him that sitteth on the throne, and from the wrath of the Lamb: for the great day of His wrath is come; and who shall be able to stand?" (Rev. vi, 16, 17).

"And Joshua did unto them as the Lord bade him: he houghed their horses, and burned their chariots with fire" (verse 9). In the flush and excitement of victory Israel's leader failed not to comply with the orders he had received from his Master, and it is blessed to see how the Holy Spirit has taken notice of and recorded the same, thereby showing us the value which God places upon obedience. Not only so, but the chronicling of these details here is for our spiritual instruction, intimating as they do once more that *further victories* are not to be expected by us unless we remain in complete subjection to the Divine will. The continued blessing of God on our efforts to overcome our foes is dependent upon the maintenance of lowliness and submission unto Him, for if pride or self-will is allowed, then the Holy Spirit is grieved. Humility ever expresses itself in obedience to God. What is recorded here in verse 9 explains what follows to the end of the chapter, where we are shown how Joshua's progress remained unretarded. In what particular way this "houghing" was done we are not informed, so we cannot be sure whether the horses were only rendered powerless for warfare or completely destroyed. In view of burning the chariots, it seems more likely that they would be killed, so as to prevent other Canaanites from using them; the more so since they would be of no value to Israel.

"And Joshua did unto them as the Lord bade him: he houghed their horses, and burned their chariots with fire." What proof was this that "There is no king saved by the multitude of an host: a mighty man is not delivered by much strength. An horse is a vain thing for safety" (Psalm xxxi, 16, 17)! As God can save those who are without armies, so those with them are helpless if He be against them—as was clearly demonstrated at the Red Sea. It is a striking fact that the most glorious days of military victory for Israel were when the veto of Deuteronomy xvii, 16, was strictly regarded by them. In addition to their remarkable exploits in the time of Joshua, we may recall their victories over Sihon and Og (Num. xxi, 23-26, 33-35), their overcoming of Sisera and his nine hundred chariots of iron (Judges iv, 3-16), and David's victory over the king of Zobah, with his thousand chariots (II Samuel viii). On the other hand, it is equally noticeable that Israel's declension dates from their transgression of Deuteronomy xvii, 16 (I Kings iv, 26; x, 26), and that defeat came from the very quarter in which they foolishly placed their confidence (II Chron. xii, 2 9 and compare Isaiah xxxi, I): all of which goes to show "The horse is prepared against the day of battle: but safety [or "victory"] is of the Lord" (Prov. xxi, 31). It may also be pointed out that later, when Israel renounced this vain confidence, God healed their backsliding (Hosea xiv, 3, 4).

God and War

The title of this article may possibly shock some of our readers, thinking that "Satan and War" would be a more appropriate and accurate one. There are an increasing number today among churchgoers who repudiate the idea that God has anything to do, designedly and directly, with such calamities as tidal waves, earthquakes, or wars. Since *there are* such things, these people attribute them to and blame them upon the Devil. Their beliefs differ little from the religious conceptions of the ancient Persians and modern Parsees, for Zoroastrianism teaches that there are two Gods presiding over this sphere, a good and an evil one; that all blessings are to be ascribed unto the former and all our ills unto the latter. And just as that ancient system of philosophy and religion contains no definite statement as to *which* of the opposing deities will ultimately triumph, so these modern dualists have so little confidence in the true and living God, and are so determined to dissociate Him from the affairs of this scene, that they talk (and even write) about the likelihood of this earth being blown to smithereens by some devilish kind of bomb, instead of this world being (when it has served His purpose) destroyed *by its Creator* with fire (Psalm l, 3), as *He* did the antediluvian world by water.

It needs to be constantly pressed upon this sceptical generation that the One who made this world is now *governing* it; and that not merely in a vague and general way, but most definitely and specifically. The Lord God presides over all its affairs, regulates all its events, directs all its inhabitants. If He did not, if there be some creatures beyond His control, some happenings outside His jurisdiction, then there would be no guarantee that everything which transpires on earth (as well as in heaven) shall redound to His glory, and that all things are working together for good to them that love Him. Instead, all confidence in the future would be at an end, all peace of heart and tranquillity of mind an empty dream. But Scripture is far too plain on this matter to be misunderstood: "His kingdom ruleth over all" (Psalm ciii, 19), "who worketh all things after the counsel of His own will" (Eph. i, 11), "For of Him, and through Him, and to Him, are all things: to whom be glory for ever. Amen" (Romans xi, 36). So far from Satan being able to thwart Him, he could not lay a finger upon Job or any of his possessions until the Lord gave him permission to do so; and the demons could not enter the herd of swine without Christ's consent (Mark v, 12, 13). Nor can the Devil gain the slightest advantage over a saint without his own allowance, and if he resists him steadfastly in the faith, he is obliged to flee from him (James iv, 7).

Since "all things" are of God, then wars must not be excluded. So truly is this the case that His Word declares, "The Lord is a man of war" (Exodus xv, 3): thus Deity hesitates not to assume unto Himself a militant title. And again He declares, "The Lord mighty in battle" (Psalm xxiv, 8), which is illustrated and demonstrated again and again in the history of Israel, when He showed Himself strong in their behalf and slew their foes. "The Lord of hosts mustereth the host of the battle. They come from a far country, from the end of heaven, even the Lord, and the weapons of His indignation, to destroy the whole land" (Isaiah xiii, 4, 5). It may be objected that these are Old Testament references, and that the spirit of the New Testament denounces all war as now being unlawful. But the New Testament is far from bearing that out; its teaching thereon is in full accord with the Old. Thus, when the soldiers came to Christ's forerunner for instruction, asking, "What shall we do?" he did not say, Fight no more, abandon your calling, but gave them directions how to conduct themselves. When the centurion came to the Saviour and drew an argument from his military calling, our Lord did not condemn his profession or rebuke him for holding such an office; instead, He highly commended his faith (Luke vii, 8, 9).

When foretelling the destruction of Jerusalem, Christ declared that God would send forth *His* armies (Matt. xxii, 7), so that the Roman legions were but instruments in His hands, directed by Him to effect His judgment. When examined by Pilate, our Lord said, "My kingdom is not of this world: if My kingdom were of this world, then would My servants fight, that I should not be delivered to the Jews: but *now* is My kingdom not from hence" (John xviii, 36). Those words clearly imply that, though carnal means were then improper for advancing His spiritual kingdom, yet had not His state of humiliation precluded His assumption of the royal sceptre His followers might lawfully have fought to defend His title. Moreover, His qualifying "now" suggests that such a time *would* come, as Revelation xix, 11, plainly confirms. When the ten kings determine to make the mother of harlots desolate and burn her with fire, we are told, "For *God* hath put it in their hearts to fulfil His will" (Rev. xvii, 16, 17). How entirely different is the God of Holy Writ from the fictitious one of the sentimental dreamers of this effeminate age!

In our previous comments upon Israel's fighting in Canaan, our principal emphasis has been upon the application thereof unto the *spiritual* warfare in which the Christian is called upon to engage, but our articles would lack completeness if we failed to devote one unto the *literal* side of things. Much of human history consists of a chronicling of wars, and it is a matter of no little concern and importance that we should turn the light of Scripture thereon and ascertain *God's relation* thereto. Is He but a far-distant Spectator thereof, having no immediate connection with the horrible carnage of the battlefield, or is His agency directly involved in the same? To speculate upon such a matter is not only useless, but impious. War is ever a frightful calamity, the more so if it be a civil one, when one part of the populace is madly fighting against another; or when *many* nations become involved or embroiled. At such a time the suffering and anguish experienced rudely shake the belief of many in an overruling providence; and even God's own people find it difficult to stay their minds on the Ruler of the universe and trust in His goodness and wisdom, unless they be firmly rooted in the Truth.

Those who are familiar with history know how many sad proofs it contains that human beings are often more cruel than are the beasts of the jungle. Lions and tigers kill their prey in order to appease their hunger, but men destroy their fellows only to gratify their insatiable lusts of ambition and avarice. During the course of the centuries wild animals have killed thousands of mankind, but within the last few years literally millions have been destroyed by the restless wickedness of those who cared not what immeasurable suffering would result from the meeting of their greedy desires. We cannot sufficiently deplore the depravity of human nature which has made men beasts of prey, or rather devils to one another, seeking whom they may devour. The events of this "enlightened" century only too plainly confirm the teaching of Scripture on the thorough corruption of fallen human nature, that in their unregenerate condition men are "hateful, and hating one another" (Titus iii, 3). But let us not condemn the ferocity and wickedness of our fellows in any self-righteous spirit, but in the humbling realization that we too are clay of the same lump, and that if a spirit of benevolence now governs us, it is naught but sovereign grace which makes us to differ.

But while we contemplate with grief, shame and horror the vile works of men of the same vicious natures as our own, we must by no means overlook and ignore the place which Divine providence has in all those occurrences in which they are the actors. God is supreme, and all inferior agents are under His government, held by Him in such effectual control that they can do nothing without Him. In the most tremendous evils which they inflict, they are the ministers of His vengeance. Even when whole nations be destroyed, by whatsoever means, the hand of God is in that work of judgment. We briefly alluded unto this in our last, but deemed it necessary to supplement what was there pointed out. "I will set the Egyptians against the Egyptians: and they shall fight every one against his brother, and every one against his neighbour; city against city, and kingdom against kingdom. And the spirit [courage] of Egypt shall fail in the midst thereof; and I will destroy the counsel thereof . . . and the Egyptians will I give over into the hand of a cruel lord; and a fierce king shall reign over them, saith the Lord, the Lord of hosts" (Isaiah xix, 2-4)—words which ought to cause not a few people to revise their ideas on this subject. When cities are reduced to rubble, when civil war afflicts a country, when kingdoms are destroyed, the agency of God is to be acknowledged therein.

The worst tyrants, when inflicting the greatest outrages, are the instruments of God, accomplishing His will. In Jeremiah xxv, 9, we find Jehovah referring to Nebuchadnezzar as "My servant"—just as He spoke of "My servant Moses" (Num. xii, 7) and "David My servant" (Psalm lxxxix, 3). The king of Babylon was just as truly an instrument in effecting the Divine purpose as they were: they in delivering and building up, he in punishing and destroying. "Lo, *I will bring* a nation upon you from far, O house of Israel, saith the Lord . . . and they shall eat up thy harvest, and thy bread, which thy sons and thy daughters should eat: they shall eat up thy flocks and thine herds: . . . they shall impoverish thy fenced cities, wherein thou trustedst, with the sword" (Jer. v, 15, 17). God brings judgment upon a nation as surely as He gives blessing: uproots as truly as He plants. "Lo, *I raise up* the Chaldeans, that bitter and hasty nation, which shall march through the breadth of the land to possess the dwellingplaces that are not theirs: they are terrible and dreadful" (Hab. i, 6, 7). How clearly do those words show that heathen nations are under God's control and *used* by Him when it serves His purpose.

The Babylonians were employed by the Ruler of this world for the chastisement of His people and commissioned by Him to carry the Jews into captivity, yet in so doing they incurred great guilt and were made to reap as they had sown. Those things may seem utterly inconsistent unto carnal reason, yet they are not so in reality, for Nebuchadnezzar acted with no thought of fulfilling the Divine decrees, but rather to satisfy his own rapacity, and therefore was his kingdom providentially destroyed by Him with an unexampled destruction. Others were sent by God to execute His vengeance on Babylon, and though they in turn were incited by their own passions, nevertheless He it was who called forth their hosts and gave them the victory. "Behold, *I will stir up* the Medes against them, which shall not regard silver; and as for gold, they shall not delight in it. Their bows also shall dash the young men to pieces, and they shall have no pity on the fruit of the womb; their eye shall not spare children" (Isaiah xiii, 17, 18). How awful does Providence appear here! Even when savage idolators violate every dictate of humanity, they are the executors of the judgments of the Almighty. While their conduct is most horribly guilty, in the Divine sovereignty it fulfils God's will.

"The Lord of hosts hath purposed it, to stain the pride of all glory, and to bring into contempt all the honourable of the earth. . . . He shook the kingdoms: the Lord hath given a commandment against the merchant city, to destroy the strong holds thereof" (Isaiah xxiii, 9-11). The demolition of Tyre by the Chaldeans was not only the fulfilment of prophecy, but was accomplished by Divine agency. God did it, yet man did it. In unconsciously doing the work of the Lord, men act quite freely, and therefore are justly accountable for doing what it was eternally predestined they should do. Philosophy cannot plumb such a depth by its own line, but Scripture clears up the mystery.

Of Cyrus God declared, "Thou art *My battle axe* and weapons of war: for with thee will I break in pieces the nations, and with thee will I destroy kingdoms" (Jer. li, 20). What is there said of that mighty conqueror is equally true of all conquerors that ever lived, or shall live, on this earth. Conquerors regard themselves almost as gods, but the axes and saws with which men cut and cleave wood might with far better reason exalt themselves to the rank of human creatures. None of them can do anything but what God's counsel determined before to be done by their hands, and therefore it is our bounden duty to give God the glory for all the judgments which are done by them, and to adore His awful providence in all the miseries they inflict upon guilty kingdoms.

It is in the light of all that has been said above that the conquest of Canaan by Israel is to be viewed. Joshua x, 30, 42, makes it quite clear that the "sword" of Joshua was the sword of the Lord—compare "The sword of the Lord, and of Gideon" (Judges vii, 20). Equally so, it is in the light of various passages found in the Pentateuch that we must consider the severity of God's dealings with those whom His servant was commissioned to slay. The original inhabitants of Canaan were flagitious offenders, not only in being gross idolators, but in trampling underfoot the laws of morality and of humanity. If the reader turns to Leviticus xviii, 3, 27, 28, and then ponders what is recorded between verses 3 and 27, he will perceive the horrible depravity which the Amorites exhibited, for in those verses a black catalogue is supplied of the vile "abominations" of which they were guilty. Those heathen tribes were like a cankerous sore in the body politic, contaminating the surrounding nations, and therefore it was an act of mercy unto the latter, as well as a just punishment upon the former, that God ordered Joshua to destroy them root and branch. The Lord had borne long with them, but now that the iniquity of the Amorites had come to the full (Gen. xv, 16) naught but summary judgment suited their case.

Not only is no apology required for the Lord in connection with His solemn works of judgment, but He is to be owned and magnified therein. "O Lord, Thou art my God; I will exalt Thee, I will praise Thy name; for Thou hast done wonderful things; Thy counsels of old are faithfulness and truth. For Thou hast made of a city an heap; of a defenced city a ruin: a palace of strangers to be no city; it shall never be built. Therefore shall the strong people glorify Thee" (Isaiah xxv, 1, 2)—as Israel did when Pharaoh and his hosts were overthrown by the waters of the Red Sea, and as the inhabitants of heaven shall exclaim "Alleluia; Salvation, and glory, and honour, and power, unto the Lord our God: For true and righteous are His judgments, for He hath judged the great whore, which did corrupt the earth with her fornication, and hath avenged the blood of His servants at her hand" (Rev. xix, 1, 2). God is glorious in His works of providence as well as in His works of creation. As He made all things "good" at the creation of the world, so He doeth all things "well" in His government of it. He is to be revered and adored even of those works which He performs by the hand of His creatures. He is glorious in what He does by and through wicked men as well as by His saints: glorious in His acts of vengeance as well as in His acts of grace.

But if the balance of truth is to be preserved on this subject, due place must be given and full regard had to another class of passages, which show that when God deals in judgment—whether it be with individuals or nations —He does so because man's sinfulness calls for it, and not because He delights therein. This is clear from Ezekiel xiv, where, after announcing the "four sore judgments" which he would send upon Jerusalem, the Lord God declared, "And ye shall know that I have not done this without cause" (verses 21-23), for as Jeremiah xxii, 8, 9, informs us, "And many nations shall pass by this city, and they shall say every man to his neighbour, Wherefore hath the Lord done thus unto this great city? Then they shall answer, Because they have forsaken the covenant of the Lord their God, and worshipped other gods, and served them." How plain is the testimony of Lamentations iii, 33, "For He doth not afflict willingly [from His heart] nor grieve the children of men." Equally so is Ezekiel xxxiii, 11, "As I live, saith the Lord God, I have no pleasure in the death of the wicked; but that the wicked turn from his way and live." Therefore are we told that judgment is "His *strange* work . . . His strange act" (Isaiah xxviii, 21), for it is not as agreeable to Him as His works of mercy.

God approves of righteousness wherever it be found, and rewards the same with temporal blessings; but He ever disapproves of sin, and sooner or later visits His anger upon it (Prov. xiv, 34). Yet even when the dark clouds of His judgment are hanging over a kingdom or an evil system, calamity may be averted by national humiliation before God and reformation of conduct (Exodus ix, 27-29); Luke xix, 41-44; Rev. ii, 21, 22). How much to the point are those words of the Lord in Jeremiah xviii, 8: "If that nation, against whom I have pronounced [judgment], turn from their evil, I will repent of the evil that I thought to do unto them"—as was most definitely exemplified in the case of Nineveh. That verse has, of course, no reference to the alteration of His eternal decree, but instead enumerates one of the principles by which God *governs* this world, namely that He deals with nations as with individuals —according to their conduct, making them to reap as they have sown, for His judgment is ever tempered by His mercy (Judges iii, 8-10).

Now each of the two sides of our subject pointed out above was illustrated in Joshua xi. On the one hand we are told, "For it was of the Lord to harden their hearts, that they should come against Israel in battle, that He might destroy them utterly, and that they might have no favour, but that He might destroy them, as the Lord commanded Moses" (verse 20)—because they had filled up the measure of their iniquities and were ripe for judgment (compare Matt. xxiii, 32; I Thess. ii, 16; Rev. xiv, 7, 18). On the other hand we read that "But as for the cities that *stood still* in their strength, Israel burned none of them, save Hazor only" (verse 13), by which is meant those who remained passive and fought not against Israel. So that here too in wrath God remembered mercy. That is one of several passages which show that Israel did not massacre *unresisting* Canaanites (cf. Deut. xx, 10, 11)—Joshua xxiv, 11, shows that those in Jericho assumed a hostile attitude, and therefore we may conclude that those in Ai did so too.

Summary

Before turning to the next section of our book (chapters xiii-xviii), which treats of the apportioning of the land unto the tribes of Israel and their actual entrance into their inheritance, one more article is called for on chapter xi, with a few supplementary remarks upon the twelfth, where we have a breviate of Israel's conquests. A report is made of the protracted fighting which the complete subjugation of the Canaanites entailed, and this is followed by a list of the thirty-one kings who were vanquished by Joshua. There are a number of details in the former chapter which, despite the five articles we have already written thereon, have not yet been noticed, and which are much too important for us to pass over, for they are details which adumbrate and illustrate various aspects of that good fight which Christians are called upon to wage. They concern things which, if success is to crown our efforts, contain valuable lessons that we do well to take to heart. Since they be included in the "whatsoever things were written aforetime were written for our learning" (Romans xv, 4), we cannot afford to ignore them.

When our Lord had miraculously fed the multitude with the five barley loaves and two small fishes, we are told that He bade His disciples to "gather up the fragments . . . that nothing be lost" (John vi, 12)—a word that needs to be pressed much upon God's people today, for some of them are following the evil example of this wasteful and wanton generation by being guilty of throwing away much that could well be used or reused. It is in the spirit and according to the general principle contained in that precept of Christ's that we turn again to Joshua xi, for though we have, again and again, feasted from its contents in our more or less general survey of them, yet quite a few scattered "fragments" therein claim our attention, and these we shall now endeavour to "gather up" into this present article. Though we lack the ability to do as the apostles did and "fill twelve baskets" with the same, yet we trust that by Divine assistance we shall be able to provide sufficient to meet the needs of some hungry souls. The Lord graciously grant it.

"And all the cities of those kings, and all the kings of them, did Joshua take, and smote them with the edge of the sword, and he utterly destroyed them, as Moses the servant of the Lord commanded" (xi, 12). Most express orders had been given to him by his predecessor to do these very things (Deut. vii, 2; xx, 16, 17); he was to show no mercy and spare none, for they were drinking in iniquity like water is by the parched. And Moses, in turn, had received these instructions from the Lord Himself. Thus, in the slaughtering of the idolatrous and immoral Amorites, Joshua and his men were not actuated by a spirit of bloodthirstiness or malice, but instead were having regard to the Divine precepts. The practical application of this detail unto ourselves should be obvious. Some of God's statutes enjoin that which is painful unto flesh and blood (Matt. xvi, 24; Phil. iii, 10), yea, quite contrary to our fallen natures (Matt. v, 29, 30), yet we must not pick and choose only those which are agreeable to us, but conform to the most trying and disagreeable of them; and even though it involves antagonizing those nearest and dearest to us (Matt. x, 34, 35; Luke xiv, 26), we must, like David, "have respect to *all* God's commandments" (Psalm cxix, 6).

"As the Lord commanded Moses His servant, so did Moses command Joshua, and so did Joshua: he left nothing undone of all that the Lord commanded Moses" (xi, 15). That is to be regarded first as a general statement, summarizing his obedience unto such enactments as Exodus xxiii, 24; xxxiv, 11-13; Numbers xxxiii, 52; Deuteronomy xii, 3, in which he was bidden to overthrow their idols and quite break down their images, to destroy their altars and cut down their groves, to destroy all their pictures and pluck down all their high places, to break down their pillars and burn their groves with fire; in short, so thoroughly to make an end of all the monuments of their religion that the very names of their false gods should be "destroyed out of that place." Thus Joshua was not free to follow his own caprice, nor left to the exercise of his own judgment, but was required to carry out the detailed orders which he had received from his Master. How conscientiously and thoroughly he did so appears from this inspired record of the Holy Spirit: "he left nothing undone of all that the Lord commanded."

"Would we approve ourselves upright, then we must leave nothing undone which the Lord hath commanded: for though omissions are not so scandalous, either in the world or in the Church, as commissions, they are as certainly acts of disobedience and effects of a will unsubjected to the Divine authority" (Thomas Scott). As our Lord told the Pharisees, who were very punctilious in paying tithe of mint and anise, yet omitted the weightier matters of the Law— judgment, mercy, and faith—"these ought ye to have done and not to leave the other undone" (Matt. xxiii, 23). Sincere obedience is impartial. He who from a right principle obeys any of God's commandments will have respect unto all of them. Here is one of the radical differences between gracious souls and empty professors: the latter act for themselves and not for God, and will do no more than what they consider promotes their own interests or enhances their reputation before their fellows and, like the Pharisees, usually lay stress on the "least" commandments, especially those things which distinguish them from other denominations, and neglect those which relate to moral duties, attending to such externals as the "washing" of their hands, yet making no serious attempt to cleanse their hearts.

What a searching word is this for both writer and reader to measure himself by: "he left nothing undone of all that the Lord commanded"! Therein he conformed to that fundamental injunction, "What thing soever I command you, observe to do it: thou shalt not add thereto, nor diminish from it" (Deut. xii, 32). For men to *add* anything to the precepts of God, as binding upon the conscience or as being essential to personal piety, is an affront upon His wisdom, for it is tantamount to charging Him with an oversight. Equally so, to *diminish* aught from the Divine commandments, to ignore or render any of them void, is to despise God's authority and goodness. If we be wise, even a regard to our own interests will cause us to render unqualified obedience, for God has enjoined nothing but what is for our good, and therefore none of His commandments can be neglected but to our injury and loss. What a solemn word too is this to the preacher! Oh, that he may be able to look his congregation in the face and say truthfully at the close of a pastorate, "I kept back nothing that was profitable unto you" (Acts xx, 20).

"Joshua made war a long time with all those kings" (xi, 18). Though the account of his conquest of Canaan be a very brief one and his numerous victories are packed into a small compass, yet it is not to be thought that they were all obtained within a few days (or even weeks) as was the case at Jericho and in the campaign described in chapter x, but rather occupied a considerable period. Yet, after all, the expression "a long time" is a *relative* one, for the swiftness or slowness of time's passing is not always to be gauged by the clock. When its span is filled with stress and strain, its flight seems much slower— as it would to the mothers and wives more than to the fighting men of Israel themselves—hence in the Hebrew it reads "*many* days." But, as a matter of fact, that span of time comprised only seven years, as may be seen by a comparison of Joshua xiv, 1-10, with Deuteronomy ii, 14, for in the former we learn that Caleb was only eighty-five when Canaan was conquered and but forty when sent forth by Moses to spy out the land; while the latter informs us that thirty-eight of those years had been spent in the wilderness before Israel crossed the Jordan. Thus the whole of Canaan was subdued and occupied by Israel within the space of seven years.

Those words, "And Joshua made war a long time with all those kings," tell us of his *constancy,* and the stability of those who served under him. They did not take things easy after Jericho was captured, nor relax their efforts when Ai fell before them, but continued steadfast until they had completed the task assigned them. What a noble example for the Christian to follow in the prosecution of his spiritual warfare! Let him not be appalled by the obstacles confronting him, deterred by the number of enemies to be overcome, nor disheartened by his failures along the way. Patience and fortitude must be earnestly sought from above. Though the fight of faith lasts "a long time," for it is to be without any intermission while we are left in this scene, yet "Let us not be weary in well doing: for in due season we shall reap, if we faint not" (Gal. vi, 9). It is just because we are so prone to flag in our efforts during the performance of duty that this exhortation is addressed unto us and *repeated* in II Thessalonians iii, 13! Then let us watch and guard against this evil tendency and persevere unto the end.

"And at that time came Joshua, and cut off the Anakims from the mountains, from Hebron, from Debir, from Anab, and from all the mountains of Judah, and from all the mountains of Israel: Joshua destroyed them utterly with their cities" (verse 21). Apparently a special campaign was made against *them,* and particular notice is here made of the same. Nor is the reason for this far to seek. It will be remembered that when Moses sent forth the twelve men to spy out the land of Canaan and upon their return ten of them threw cold water upon the prospect of Israel's occupying it, they emphasized the formidable strength of its walled cities and made mention of the Anakims as being of "great stature," the descendants of the giants, being by comparison "as grasshoppers" in their own sight (Num. xiii, 28-33). But mighty as those men were, and taking refuge as they now did in their fastnesses, Joshua and his men—notwithstanding the difficulty of the mountain passes and attacking these giants in their caves—hunted them out and completely routed the very ones who had originally inspired their unbelieving fathers with such terror.

"Even that opposition, which seemed invincible, was got over. Never let the sons of Anak be a terror to the Israel of God, for even *their* day will come to fall. Giants are dwarfs to Omnipotence; yet this struggle with the Anakims was reserved for the latter end of the war, when the Israelites were become more expert in the arts of war and had had more experience of the power and goodness of God. God sometimes reserves the sharpest trials of His people, by affliction and temptation, for the latter end of their days. Therefore, 'let not him that girds on his harness boast as he that puts it off.' Death, that tremendous son of Anak, is the last enemy to be encountered, but it is to be destroyed (I Cor. xv, 26). Thanks be to God who will give us the victory" (Matthew Henry). The words "Joshua destroyed them utterly with their cities" are *not* to be understood absolutely, as the later Scriptures show, for both of the books of Samuel make it clear that the race of these giants had not been completely exterminated, that some of their number succeeded in escaping and either concealed their presence from Israel or took refuge in the surrounding countries. This is more than hinted at in the verse that follows.

"There was none of the Anakims left in the land of the children of Israel: only in Gaza, in Gath, and in Ashdod, there remained" (verse 22). This was one of the passages used by J. J. Blunt as an illustration of his striking book, *Undesigned Coincidences*. He pointed out that I Samuel xvii, 4, informs us that the Philistine champion whom David vanquished was "Goliath, of Gath," whose height was six cubits and a span—ten feet—and then bids the reader mark the value of that description, which though quite casual serves to authenticate its historicity. Next, he reminds us of the testimony of Moses in Numbers xiii, 32, 33, where we are told that certain of the original inhabitants of Canaan were "men of great stature . . . giants, the sons of Anak, which come of the giants." Those details are to be carefully borne in mind in connection with Joshua's final feat of arms, when, as we have seen, he "cut off the Anakims from the mountains," and none of them were left in the land of Israel "only [observe the exception] in Gaza, in *Gath*, and in Ashdod."

Thus, when we find in the book of Samuel that Gath is most incidentally named as the country of Goliath, that fact squares most unmistakably with the two other independent facts chronicled by two other authors, Moses and Joshua: the one that the Anakims were of gigantic size, the other that some of that almost-exterminated race, who survived the sword of Joshua, actually continued to dwell at Gath! Thus in the mouths of those three witnesses is the Word established, concurring as they do in a manner the most artless and satisfactory, in confirming one particular at least in that remarkable exploit of Israel's shepherd boy. Since this one particular, and that like a hinge upon which the whole incident moves, is discovered to be a matter of fact beyond all question, and in the absence of any evidence to the contrary, we have good reason to regard the other particulars of the same history to be authentic too. But there are also many providential circumstances involved in it which argue the invisible Hand by which David slew his adversary. His being on hand to hear and accept the haughty challenge, his bag with five small stones opposed to the helmet of brass and the coat of brazen mail and the spear like a weaver's beam, the first sling of a pebble, the panic of the whole host of the Philistines and their overthrow, combine to show that it was no ordinary event, and that "the Lord saveth not with sword and spear," but that the battle is the Lord's, and that *He* gave it into Israel's hand (I Samuel xvii, 47).

"So Joshua took the whole land, according to all that the Lord said unto Moses; and Joshua gave it for an inheritance unto Israel according to their divisions by their tribes. And the land rested from war" (xi, 23). It is clear from Joshua xiii and the book of Judges that those words are to be regarded as a *general statement*, probably meaning "the far greater and better part, all before described; all that he went against—he failed not in any of his attempts; no place stood out against him that he besieged or summoned; all yielded to him" (John Gill). Thus did God make good His promises unto the patriarchs (Deut. i, 8), to Moses (Deut. iii, 18), and to Joshua (i, 6). And now, for a season, the land "rested from war": those Canaanites who had escaped, fearing to attack and remaining quiet; the surrounding nations invading them not. The spiritual application of this unto ourselves is both apparent and blessed. However unpleasant and irksome the spiritual warfare of the Christian may be, his patience in tribulation should ever be encouraged by the joyful expectation of hope (Romans xii, 12), for ere long perfect rest above shall be his portion, and that not for a season, but for ever.

The twelfth chapter forms a fitting conclusion to the military campaigns of Joshua, containing as it does a summary of his numerous victories and a list of the thirty-one kings which were smitten by him. A short account is there given of the conquests made by Israel both in the times of Moses and of Joshua. The land which the Lord gave unto Israel consisted of two parts, for though it was but a single country, yet its terrain was divided by the Jordan. Thus the conquest of Canaan was a single enterprise, though it was actually accomplished in two distinct stages. That portion on the eastward side of Jordan was subdued by Moses, and given to the two and a half tribes, but the much larger half lay on the western side, and was subjugated by Joshua and allotted unto the nine and a half tribes. Typically, that probably has a threefold significance or application. First, *redemptively*, the fruits of Christ's mediatorial work: far more have benefited therefrom since His death (the Jordan) than those who were saved by Him during the days of His public ministry. Second, *dispensationally*, in connection with the Church and its members: most probably a much greater number of them being sinners taken out from the Gentiles than those who had formerly been from the Jews.

Third, *spiritually*, in connection with the believer's salvation: a portion of his inheritance is entered into and enjoyed by him before the Jordan is crossed, but the principal part of it lies on the farther side of death. But while looking for the mystical meaning of this, let us not overlook the practical lesson. " Them did Moses the servant of the Lord and the children of Israel smite: and Moses the servant of the Lord gave it for a possession unto the Reubenites, and the Gadites. and the half tribe of Manasseh. And these are the kings of the country which Joshua and the children of Israel smote on this side Jordan on the west . . . which Joshua gave unto the tribes of Israel for a possession according to their divisions " (xii, 6, 7). The linking together of those two things is instructive. " The enjoyment of present blessings should revive the grateful remembrance of former mercies, and the benefit derived from the labours of the living servants of the Lord should remind us to respect the memories of those who have hitherto served Him in their generation. The national covenant mediated by Moses engaged many temporal advantages to Israel " (T. Scott).

" And these are the kings of the country which Joshua and the children of Israel smote on this side Jordan on the west . . . all the kings thirty and one " (xii, 7, 24). It may be thought strange that there should have been so many kings in such a small country. In reality, it supplies evidence of the accuracy and veracity of this historical record, for it is in perfect accord with the ancient practice followed in various countries, namely that many of their principal cities had their own separate kings. Historians inform us that when Julius Caesar landed in Britain he found four kings in the single county of Kent— then how many more would there be in the whole island? How blessedly did Joshua's conquest of all those kings illustrate the truth that the more entirely our hearts be fixed upon the Lord our strength (xi, 6, 7), the more certainly will our foes—however powerful or numerous—be subdued before us! According to its gematria (the use of letters instead of figures—for our modern numerals were unknown to the ancients), thirty-one equals EL—the name of God. If then He be for us, who can be against us?

Chapter 15

THE SPOILS OF VICTORY

JOSHUA 13:1-33

The thirteenth chapter of Joshua is another chapter which offers very little scope for the commentator, for it consists largely of geographical details. After a brief but blessed word from the Lord to Joshua himself, the first six verses contain a list of those parts of the land which had not yet been possessed by Israel, together with an assurance from God that He would drive out from before His people the inhabitants of those sections also. In the next six verses the Lord gives orders concerning the dividing or apportioning of Canaan, naming some of the places therein and the bounds thereof. Then comes a reference to the portion which Moses had allotted unto the two and a half tribes on the eastward side of Jordan, with a detailed description of the same. Parenthetically, mention is made of Israel's slaying of Balaam, and twice over we are informed that Moses gave no inheritance to the tribe of Levi. Thus its contents admit of no unified treatment, its central subject being, perhaps, best described as the spoils of victory enjoyed by Israel and the respective portions therein assigned to her tribes.

Canaan was (as we have previously pointed out) at once a Divine gift, yet as to their occupying of the same it was the result of Israel's own prowess. It was bestowed upon them by free grant from God, nevertheless it had to be conquered by them. Therein there was an accurate shadowing forth of the Christian's inheritance. That too is wholly of Divine grace and mediatorial purchase, but it is not actually entered into by the heirs of promise without much effort on their part. It is at this point that theologians have so often gone wrong, by attributing either too much or too little unto the creature. Only by cleaving very closely to Holy Writ *as a whole*—and not by singling out detached fragments—are we preserved from serious error. On the one hand, we must see to it that we return right answers to the questions, "For who maketh thee to differ from another? and what hast thou that thou didst not receive?" (I Cor. iv, 7); on the other, we must give due place to such exhortations as "Strive to enter in at the strait gate" (Luke xiii, 24) and "Let us labour therefore to enter into that rest" (Heb. iv, 11); and not ignore such statements as "knowing that of the Lord ye shall receive the reward of the inheritance" (Col. iii, 24). Only thus will the balance of truth be preserved.

It is indeed true that the child of God has nothing good or spiritual but what the Lord has freely bestowed upon him. But does that mean he is as passive a "receiver" as the earth is when fructified by heaven's refreshing showers and genial sunshine? Great care needs to be taken in answering that question lest we contradict the Word of Truth. Certainly he is no co-operator with Christ in the work of his redemption. There is not the least warrant for us to say, "God will do His part if we do ours." There is no dividing of the honours: the glory is God's alone, and we have *no ground* for boasting. Most assuredly the elect have nothing to do with their election, for God chose them in Christ before the foundation of the world, and there is not a line in His Word to show that His choice was determined by anything praiseworthy which He foresaw in them. Those ordained to be vessels of honour were "clay of the same lump" as the vessels appointed to dishonour. Nor had they a thing to do with their redemption, for all that was required to make atonement for their sins and reconcile them to God was accomplished by Christ centuries before they existed. Nor had they anything whatever to do with their regeneration, for they were dead in trespasses and sins when the Spirit quickened them into newness of life.

But it is quite wrong to infer from the above that the regenerated soul remains a passive agent. Equally wrong is it to suppose that he is now possessed of any self-sufficiency, that his new nature empowers him to perform his duty. Though he has become a living branch of the Vine, yet he is entirely dependent upon the Vine's nourishing and fructifying. But we must not confine ourselves to *that* particular figure and relationship. The Christian is a moral agent, and grace has been given him to improve. Means of grace have been provided, and he is responsible to employ the same. He has a conflict to engage him, a race to run. There is a world for him to overcome, a devil to resist, a salvation to be worked out with fear and trembling. True, in and of himself he is quite incapable of accomplishing such tasks; nevertheless, through Christ he "can do all things" (Phil. iv, 13). He must tread the narrow way if he would actually enter into the fullness of Life, and is required to endure unto the end if he is to be finally saved. He must fight the good fight of faith if he is to enter into the eternal inheritance. These things are just as true and real as those mentioned in the preceding paragraphs.

It must not be forgotten that Scripture itself records, and without the least condemnation or criticism, such utterances as "by the word of Thy lips *I have* kept me from the paths of the destroyer" (Psalm xvii, 4), "I have refrained my feet from every evil way, that I might keep Thy word" (Psalm cxix, 101), "I keep under my body" (I Cor. ix, 27), "I have fought a good fight, I have finished my course, I have kept the faith" (II Tim. iv, 7). Those are not carnal boastings but true statements of fact, and due place must be given to them in our theological system, or our doctrinal beliefs are very defective. True indeed, it was by Divine grace that those men conducted themselves thus, yet *they* were active moral agents therein, and not passive ciphers. Thus also was Canaan a Divine gift unto Abraham and his descendants, but they had to fight —fight long and hard—in order to enter into possession of the same. True also that the Lord fought for them, and that their victories must be ascribed unto Him who so signally showed Himself strong in their behalf; nevertheless that altered not the fact that *they* fought and subdued their foes. Both the Divine and the human sides are to be recognized and owned by us.

In like manner our salvation has the same two sides unto it. God is indeed both the Alpha and the Omega thereof, yet He deals with us as rational creatures and enforces our responsibility in connection with the same. So far as we can discover, the plants in the garden and the trees in the orchard owe their growth and fertility entirely to the Creator. But it is otherwise with believers: they are required to use the means of grace which God has appointed, and look to Him to bless the same. The vegetables and trees are incapable of taking precautions against pests and tornadoes; but *we* are obligated to avoid evil, resist temptation, and take shelter from the storm. Eternal life is a Divine gift (Romans vi, 23), but we are to "lay hold on" it (I Tim. vi, 12). The celestial inheritance is "the purchased possession" of Christ for His people (Eph. i, 14), yet it is also "the reward" of service unto the Lord (Col. iii, 24). Grace is freely given, but we are to use it, and must improve the same if we would receive more (Luke viii, 18; Matt. xxv, 16). "Seek the Lord, and His strength: seek His face evermore" (Psalm cv, 4)—*there* is the meeting-place of the two sides! We have no sufficiency of our own, but if grace be duly sought (Heb. iv, 16) then "our sufficiency is of God" (II Cor. iii, 5).

"Now Joshua was old and stricken in years; and the Lord said unto him, Thou art old and stricken in years, and there remaineth yet very much land to be possessed" (xiii, 1). Unlike Moses, of whom it is recorded that at the close of a still longer life his eye was not dim, nor his natural force abated (Deut. xxxiv, 1), the strenuous life Joshua had lived took heavy toll of him, and the infirmities of old age had come upon him. Probably he had then reached the century mark, for he was one of the twelve originally sent forth by Moses to spy out the land, and therefore would be at least as old as Caleb, who was then eighty-five (xiv, 10), and most likely quite a few years more, for he was but 110 at the time of his death (xxiv, 29). But it is blessed to see that, despite his increasing bodily weakness, the Lord did not desert him in his old age, but now honoured him with a special visit and a most gracious communication. And that, dear reader, is recorded for the particular comfort and encouragement of His aged pilgrims. Unto them He has given the sure promise: "And even to your old age I am He [the unchanging One]; and even to hoar hairs will I carry you: I have made, and I will bear; even I will carry, and will deliver you" (Isaiah xlvi, 4), and that blessed assurance it is their holy privilege to rest upon day by day with childlike faith.

It is to be noted that after informing His servant that he was old and stricken in years—for the Lord never flatters man, nor withholds His Truth (except in judgment) from man—He did *not* say "but there remaineth yet very much land to be possessed": instead it was "*and* there remaineth." Thus He was not saying this by way of reproach. It appears to us that God so addressed Himself to Joshua on this occasion, first, to *instruct* Him: to let him know that He was no Egyptian taskmaster, who imposed burdens grievous to be borne; rather did He tenderly remember that Joshua was dust. By virtue of growing frailty he would be unfit to complete so vast a task as conquering the whole of Canaan—the major part of which remained to be done. Second, to *humble* him. While Joshua had much ground to be thankful for the considerable success with which the Lord had crowned his efforts, he had no reason to be elated, for the enemy was still in possession of the remoter sections of Israel's inheritance. Third, it was, as the following verses make clear, for the purpose of acquainting him with his immediate *duty*.

While the Lord took knowledge of the enfeebled frame of His servant, yet He did not for that reason encourage him to be slack. On the contrary, He assigned him a new though much lighter task. It is not the revealed will of God that His people should spend their old age in idleness. He does not preserve them through all the dangers of youth and the trials of maturity that they should be mere cumberers of the ground. He may well suffer them to become exceedingly tottery and perhaps bedridden and entirely dependent upon others; yet even so it is their privilege and duty to beg Him to make good in them that precious word, "They shall still bring forth fruit in old age: they shall be fat and flourishing" (Psalm xcii, 14). They may still commune with the Lord, and manifest the effects thereof. The decay of nature is no reason why grace should languish. Even when thoroughly helpless, the fruits of patience, meekness and gratitude may be borne, and they may carry themselves as the monuments of God's goodness and the memorials of His faithfulness, and thereby "*show forth* His praises." Though the strenuous efforts of earlier years be no longer possible, the *ministry of prayer* is available unto the very end, and who can say that more will not be accomplished therein for eternity than by any other spiritual activity?

As intimated above, one of the Lord's designs in now appearing unto Joshua was to make known unto him his duty; yea, this seems to have been His leading object. What that duty consisted of was revealed in verse 7: he was to superintend in the apportioning of the land unto the nine and a half tribes—the other two and a half having already been allotted their heritage by Moses. It was most essential that *he* should be the one to perform this task. Clothed as he was with Divine authority, called of God to be Israel's head, so markedly used by Him in vanquishing the armies of the Amorites and destroying their strongholds, none so well fitted as he now to divide the spoils of victory. Enjoying the confidence of the congregation, it behoved him to set about this important task while life and sufficient strength remained; and not leave unto some successor to do what could be far better and more appropriately done by himself. The decisions of the one who had in the hearing of the nation commanded the sun and the moon to stand still would not be challenged by the tribes; whereas it was not nearly so likely that they would freely accept the rulings of another. Joshua then must not delay.

"This is the land that yet remaineth [i.e. to be possessed]: all the borders of the Philistines, and all Geshuri" (verse 2). From there to the end of verse 6 follows a list of the more remote sections of Palestine which were still occupied by the heathen. Here, then, by clear implication, was another task assigned unto Joshua: to stir up the people unto further efforts, that while he could not personally take any further part in the fighting he must press upon the nation the duty still devolving upon *them*. Instead of now taking their ease and being satisfied with those portions of their inheritance which had already been secured, they must continue to "*possess* their possessions," and not miss God's best for them. It is highly probable that the great majority of Israel were quite ignorant of the extent of the land, unacquainted with the terms of the promise made by the Lord unto Abraham in Genesis xv, 18-21, etc. During their lengthy sojourn in Egypt their ancestors had lapsed into idolatry (see Lev. xvii, 7; Ezek. xx, 7, 8; xxiii, 3), and so unacquainted were they with the Lord Himself that when Jehovah commissioned Moses to lead His people out of the house of bondage he asked, "When I . . . say unto them, The God of your fathers hath sent me to you; and they shall say to me, *What is His name?* what shall I say unto them?" (Exodus iii, 13).

Sufficient attention has not been paid unto what has just been pointed out. While it be far from *excusing* the conduct of Israel under Moses—in view of the wondrous deliverance the Lord wrought for them and the signal favours shown by Him unto them at the Red Sea, at Sinai, and during the forty years that followed—yet it does supply the key which *explains* much that otherwise is altogether unaccountable. Their children had been reared in the wilderness, and now they had entered Canaan under Joshua it is likely that they knew little or nothing of its boundaries. Thus we consider it was for this reason that it was now necessary for the Lord to instruct Joshua by the details furnished in xiii, 2-5, that he might inform the people of the full extent of that land which had been given to them. The spiritual application of this unto ourselves is not difficult to perceive. Even after their regeneration, God's people are totally ignorant of the unsearchable riches that are theirs in Christ, until informed of the same from the Scriptures. " Eye hath not seen, nor ear heard, neither have entered into the heart of man, the things which God hath prepared for them that love Him "(I Cor. ii, 9). Nevertheless it at once follows, " But God *hath revealed them* unto us by His Spirit "—in His Word; and as we diligently search that Word we learn what those things are.

Matthew Henry pointed out three reasons why the Lord commissioned Joshua to acquaint Israel with the fact that " there remaineth yet very much land to be possessed," and to amplify that statement by announcing to them all the geographical details given in verses 2-5. First, that they might be more affected with God's goodness in giving them so extensive a portion, and thereby be engaged to love and serve Him. He would have them occupied with the Divine bounty, that their obedience to Him might be prompted by gratitude and not by a slavish fear. And thus it is to be with His people today: deep appreciation of His grace and goodness is to prompt them to run in the path of His commandments. Second, that they might not be tempted to make any league or contract any dangerous familiarity with those neighbours, so as to learn their ways; but might be jealous of them, as those who kept them out of their rightful inheritance. In like manner, Christians, as they contemplate the possession purchased for them, are to conduct themselves as strangers and pilgrims in this scene, keeping their garments unspotted from the world, walking with God in separation therefrom. Third, that they might keep themselves in a posture of war, and not think of putting off their harness as long as there remained any of the land to be possessed.

In closing this article, a final word upon the application of verses 1-5 to *the aged pilgrim*. You may, dear reader, be stricken in years, nevertheless the fact must be faced that " there remaineth yet very much land to be possessed." No matter what be your growth in grace or the extent of your progress in spiritual things, you are not as completely conformed to the image of Christ as you should be, nor have you as fully possessed your possessions (Obad. 17), as it is your privilege to do. Take a leaf out of the apostle's book. Near the close of his life he declared, " Brethren, I count not myself to have apprehended: but this one thing I do; forgetting those things which are behind, and reaching forth unto those things which are before, *I press toward* the mark for the prize of the high calling of God in Christ Jesus " (Phil. iii, 13, 14). Do thou the same. As for verses 2-5, we too should sit down and draw up a list of those parts of our heritage not yet experientially possessed by us—and note that verse 2 is headed by the most difficult one, for the later Scriptures show that Israel had most trouble from the Philistines. Do you ask, What good could that do? It should humble. It should prompt to more definite prayer. We read of " the meekness and gentleness of Christ " (II Cor. x, 1). Are those graces made good in you?

When Joshua had become old and more or less enfeebled, the Lord appeared unto His servant, and after informing him that there remained yet very much land to be possessed, and naming some of the places and peoples to be conquered, He declared, " them will I drive out from before the children of Israel: only divide thou it by lot unto the Israelites for an inheritance, as I have commanded thee " (xiii, 6). It had been so with Moses: under God he had begun the task of occupying Canaan (namely that part thereof which lay to the east of Jordan), but only a small beginning had been made. Joshua had been used to carry forward the enterprise considerably, yet it was far from being completed—others would be raised up later to effect the Divine purpose. And it has been the same ever since. A start was all that was made by the apostles in the evangelizing of the Gentiles, for when the last of them expired there remained yet very much land to be possessed. Calvin and Luther were mightily employed in delivering God's people from the deadly shackles of Rome, yet when the last of the Reformers was called home how much yet remained to be accomplished!

It is the same now. At the close of the most active and self-sacrificing life in the service of Christ, each succeeding minister of His leaves this scene with very much of the world still occupied by the enemy. But observe now the blessed consolation the Lord gave unto Joshua: "them will I drive out," *not* "from before *thee*," for he would not live to see it accomplished, but "from before the children of Israel." As he had carried forward the work begun by Moses, so others would be Divinely appointed and equipped to advance his efforts—the honour of laying the capstone thereon being reserved for David centuries later. A similar assurance should be the very real confidence of every aged minister of the Gospel. There is no statement in Scripture, so far as the writer can perceive, to show that a time will ever come when all upon earth will be saved, or even nominally receive the Truth: yet the Divine promise is given, "One generation *shall* praise Thy works to another" (Psalm cxlv, 4); yea, that some "shall fear Thee as long as the sun and moon endure, throughout *all* generations" (Psalm lxxii, 5). The words of Christ in Matthew xxviii, 20, make it clear that He will have some of His on earth till the last, and His "all that the Father giveth Me shall come to Me" (John vi, 37) proves that neither man nor devil will prevent the salvation of the entire election of grace. "The foundation of God standeth sure . . . The Lord knoweth them that are His" (II Tim. ii, 19) provides a grand haven of rest for every anxious heart.

"Them will I drive out from before the children of Israel: only divide thou it by lot unto the Israelites" (verse 6). We regard this statement as one with a clearly implied proviso attached to it, and as such addressed to their responsibility, presupposing *their concurrence*. Therefore we agree with Matthew Henry's comments thereon: "This promise that He would drive them out from before the children of Israel plainly supposes it as the condition of the promise that the children of Israel themselves must attempt and endeavour their extirpation, must go up against them, else they could not be said to be driven out before them. If afterwards, through sloth or cowardice or affection to these idolaters, they sat still and let them alone, they must blame themselves, and not God, if they be not driven out." Nor was that Puritan alone in so understanding those words of the Lord. Even the high Calvinist J. Gill remarked thereon, "Which the Lord would deliver into their hands, *providing* they were obedient to His will, for, because they were not, many of those places never came into their possession, though divided to them by lot"; and again (later), "that is on condition of their obedience, for it appears that not only the Sidonians but many others, even the chief, and most of those mentioned, were never possessed by them."

The same is true of Christians and their eternal inheritance: there are certain *conditions* which they are obligated to meet. "Conditions" not in the Romish sense, as con-causes with the Father's choice and the Son's atonement; nor in the Arminian sense, of an absolute power lying in their own wills and strength to comply therewith. But according to the order of things which God has established, for the enforcing of their moral agency—as there must be a sowing before reaping, the cross before the crown. Principal causes (God's grace and Christ's merits) do not exclude necessary means—grace must not be turned into lasciviousness nor Christ made the minister of sin. Scripture is unmistakably plain on this point: "For we are made partakers of Christ, *if* we hold the beginning of our confidence stedfast unto the end" (Heb. iii, 14, and note well the "if" in John viii, 51; I Cor. xv, 2; Col. i, 23). As remission of sins is promised to none but those who repent (Luke xxiv, 47; Acts iii, 19) and believe (Acts x, 43), so only he that endures to the end shall be saved (Matt. xxiv, 13). "Let us labour therefore to enter into that rest [the antitypical Canaan], lest any man fall after the same example of unbelief" (Heb. iv, 11), as the Israelites in the wilderness. That warning is a *real* one, which we ignore at our eternal peril.

"Only divide thou it by lot unto the Israelites . . . as I have commanded thee" (xiii, 6). This was the business in which Joshua was now to engage: to apportion *it*—the entire territory, both what was already subdued and those parts of it which still remained to be conquered. "Now *therefore* divide this land for an inheritance unto the nine tribes, and the half tribe of Manasseh, with whom the Reubenites and the Gadites have received their inheritance, which Moses gave them, beyond Jordan eastward" (verses 7, 8). Having received orders and authority from God, Joshua was to set about this task at once with all diligence. He was not to wait until all the tribes had actually secured their inheritance, but must define or mark out the portion allotted to each of them, so that they might know the particular section to which he had Divine title, and go forward, take and occupy the same. Thus Joshua was to act with full confidence in God. Though he should be called to leave the field of battle and enter his rest, others would be raised up to carry on the conflict until the Divine purpose was realized. *This,* we say again, needs to be borne in mind by the Lord's people in all generations, for considerable *unbelief* is often mingled with their grief when some much-used servant of His is removed from this world—as though the cause of Christ was jeopardized thereby.

Once more Joshua was to count implicitly upon Jehovah: to work while it was yet day for him, and to leave the outcome to his Master. Probably the major part of the land was then occupied by the Canaanites, yet he was personally to superintend the allotting of the whole of it to Israel. Thus was he called upon to trust in the Lord with all his heart, and lean not unto his own understanding (Prov. iii, 5), as had Noah and Abraham before him (Heb. xi, 7, 8). *That* is the principle by which every servant of God is ever to act. As Paul declared, "For we walk by faith, not by sight" (II Cor. 5, 7). The apostle and his fellow workers lived and laboured by faith, being inspired with courage and strength from having their hearts occupied with things invisible. Theirs was not a single act, but a constant course of trustfulness. To walk by faith is to conduct ourselves in the firm belief of those things we do not see, resting on the sure Word of God and being practically influenced thereby. It is to live in a steady expectation of things to come—the realities and glories of heaven. It is the opposite of being governed by our senses or regulated by visible objects, for "faith is the substance of things hoped for, the evidence of things not seen" (Heb. xi, 1), making them real and precious to the soul.

It was at this point that the predecessor of Joshua had failed; though, through not linking up parallel passages with Numbers xiii, 1-3, many have not perceived this—another case where Scripture must be compared with Scripture if we are to obtain the complete picture. "And ye came near unto me every one of you, and said, We will send men before us, and they shall search us out the land, and bring us word again by what way we must go up, and into what cities we shall come. And the saying pleased me well: and I took twelve men of you" and sent them forth (Deut. i, 22, 23). Those words seem to make two things quite evident. First, that this project originated with the people. Second, that Moses failed to discern the distrust which prompted their proposal —his approval thereof being a case of evil communications corrupting good manners. At a later date, when chiding the children of Gad and of Reuben, he said, "Wherefore *discourage ye* the heart of the children of Israel from going over into the land which the Lord hath given them? Thus did your fathers, when I sent them from Kadesh-barnea to see the land" (Num. xxxii, 7, 8), which shows they had a spirit of unwillingness to go up into it.

From the account given in Numbers xiii, 17-20, we learn that they questioned the value of the promised inheritance, as the language "see the land, what it is . . . whether it be good or bad . . . whether it be fat or lean" makes clear. Thus it was rank unbelief in the word of the Lord which lay behind their policy, while their "by what way we must go up" of Deuteronomy i, 22, showed their lack of confidence in being Divinely directed as to the best route to take. What need was there to go and examine the kind of land which the Lord had chosen for them, when He had already informed them that it was one "flowing with milk and honey" (Exodus iii, 8)? What occasion was there to investigate the approaches into it when there were the pillars of cloud and of fire to guide and show them the way? Nor have *we* any need to ask what God's will for us is, when He has already made known the same, or to inquire as to our path of duty, when we possess His Word as a lamp unto our feet. But alas, Israel had a better opinion of their own policy and judgment than of God's; and is it not often the same with us?

Though approving of the carnal suggestion of the people, before acting on the same Moses evidently sought confirmation from the Lord, and we are told that He said, "Send thou men, that they may search the land of Canaan" (Num. xiii, 2). In thus giving permission, God acted *in judgment*. Deuteronomy i, 6-8, makes it clear that a year previously Israel had received Divine orders to go forward and possess the land which had been given unto their fathers, but as soon as they left Horeb one sin after another was committed by them (Num. xi and xii). God had been provoked by their waywardness, and in order to make further manifest the hardness of their hearts He now gave them up to their lusts. The sequel at once demonstrated their unbelief and perversity. God also suffered their desire to be granted in order to serve as a solemn *warning* to His people in all generations. If we profit not from the recorded sins and punishments of others, then is our case indeed inexcusable. When God gratifies our self-will and suffers us to follow the schemes of our own devising, we pay dearly for it. If we have more confidence in our own wisdom or the representations of our senses than we have in the Divine counsels, we shall inevitably taste the bitterness of our foolishness.

It seems rather strange that, after a full description of the territory given to the two and a half tribes had previously been furnished in the closing verses of Numbers xxxii, the middle of Deuteronomy iii, a briefer reference in Deuteronomy xxix, and a fuller one again in Joshua xii, 4-6, a further account of the same should be *repeated here*. Matthew Henry suggested the following explanation. First, as the reason why the nine and a half tribes should now be assigned their portions: since their brethren had already been provided for, it was just and meet that they should be so too. Second, as the pattern for Joshua now to follow. He was not being ordered to do something unprecedented, for he had been personally present when Moses had distributed the eastern section of Palestine unto the two and a half tribes, and from his example he might well now act. Third, as an inducement unto Joshua to make no delay in performing this task, that the remaining tribes might no longer be kept out of their heritage. Thus the Lord who had provided for the former was equally solicitous about the welfare of the latter. Fourth, that the portion given to the two and a half tribes years before now being specified in detail signified a ratification of the original grant, thus obviating any disputes about the boundaries. Joshua was not free to make any alterations.

The account given of the portions allocated unto the two and a half tribes closes with the ominous statement, " Nevertheless the children of Israel expelled not the Geshurites, nor the Maachathites: but the Geshurites and Maachathites dwell among the Israelites until this day " (verse 13). This is the first time that anything of this nature is recorded of them, though if we are permitted to go through the book of Judges we shall see that other of the tribes were equally remiss at a later date. It reminds us of a similar and most regrettable failure on the part of Queen Elizabeth and those who succeeded her. Under the Reformation in the days of Luther and Calvin, the Protestant sections of Europe were delivered from the idolatries of the mass, Mariolatry and the worship of idols; but those who followed were found sadly wanting in purging themselves from other popish evils and superstitions. It is worthy of note that as the two and a half tribes were placed in their inheritance before their fellows, so (centuries later) they were displaced before the other tribes were, being carried captive to Assyria, and that because they " went a whoring after the gods of the people of the land " (1 Chron. v, 25, 26). Such a proportion does Providence often observe in the dispensations of prosperity and adversity, setting the one over against the other.

" Balaam also the son of Besor, the soothsayer, did the children of Israel slay with the sword among them that were slain by them " (xiii, 23). Nothing definite is known about the early life of this mysterious person. He is introduced abruptly in the Scriptures, being mentioned first in Numbers xxii, 5. A " soothsayer " was one who essayed to foretell the future and possess strange powers by means of the occult forces of evil. Balaam was a magician of renown and had, apparently, acquired some knowledge of the true God—probably by hearing of what He had wrought in Egypt and at the Red Sea (see Joshua ii, 10). Israel had then crossed the wilderness, and had arrived at the country of the Moabites—in the vicinity of the Jordan. Balak its king was afraid that Israel would destroy his people, and sent for Balaam to use his enchantments against them. Accordingly, his servants visited the prophet " with the rewards of divination in their hand," and invited him to return with them to their master, and pronounce such a curse on the Israelites that the Moabites might smite them (Num. xxii, 5-7). Balaam's character was at once revealed by his response to this temptation: he neither accepted nor refused. Instead of reprimanding them, he bade them lodge with him, and he would return his answer next morning.

During the night God appeared to him, and said, " Thou shalt *not* go with them; thou shalt not curse the people. Next morning Balaam informed his visitors, " The Lord refuseth to give me leave to go with you," and they departed without him—though he dishonestly failed to tell them *why* he must not accept their commission. Refusing to be discouraged by Balaam's repulse, Balak sent again to him, promising to promote him with very great honour if he would come and curse Israel. Though he knew the mind of the Lord, he temporized and invited the princes to stay with him that night. Prompted by the love of gain, he now mocked God by pretending to ask His permission—as though He might change His mind; and God now mocked him, giving him leave to go, but commanding him to utter only the word He gave him. This is evident from " And God's anger was kindled because he went," and from " the angel of the Lord stood in the way for an adversary against him." (Numbers xxii, 22).

Rebuked by the dumb ass and told by the angel, " I went out to withstand thee, because thy way is perverse before me," Balaam acknowledged his sin; yet when the word " Go with the men " was given to test him further, he was carried forward against all checks by the violent impulse of his lusts. When he arrived at his destination, so powerfully did the Spirit of God restrain that Balaam blessed Israel instead of cursing them. Nevertheless, so strongly did he love " the wages of unrighteousness " (II Peter ii, 15), and so determined was he to earn the same, that he now devised a method which promised to ensure the ruin of Israel (Num. xxxi, 16, and cf. Rev. ii, 14), and which had been completely successful had not God intervened (Psalm cvi, 28, 29). Thus did he definitely range himself against Israel and defy the Lord. Soon after he reaped what he had sown: linking his interests with the Moabites and Midianites, he died with them (Num. xxii, 7; xxxi, 8). Such is the doom of the double-hearted, and those who are in bondage to covetousness. None can serve God and mammon.

Chapter 16

THE DIVISION OF THE LAND

JOSHUA 14:1—16:10

Dividing the Land

"And these are the countries which the children of Israel inherited in the land of Canaan, which Eleazar the priest, and Joshua the son of Nun, and the heads of the fathers of the tribes of the children of Israel, distributed for inheritance to them. By lot was their inheritance, as the Lord commanded by the hand of Moses, for the nine tribes and for the half tribe " (Joshua xiv, 1, 2). Joshua was now old and stricken in years, and before the time came when no man can work the Lord had bidden him engage in the most important task of superintending the apportioning of Israel's heritage (xiii, 1, 6, 7). Invested with Divine authority to act as Israel's head, manifestly enjoying the favour of the Lord, possessing the full confidence of the people as their tried and faithful leader, none other was so well suited to perform this particular work. But like all the other duties which he had discharged, this one called also for the exercise of *faith*, for Joshua was now required to assign the entire country of Canaan which lay on the western side of Jordan : not only those portions of it which Israel had already conquered and taken possession of, but also the extensive sections which were still occupied by the Canaanites. This called for the most implicit confidence in the Lord—that He would grant the tribes possession thereof.

The land of Canaan had already been conquered, so far as its standing armies had been completely routed, its principal strongholds destroyed, and its kings slain. Yet much of its actual territory was still in the hands of its original inhabitants, who remained to be dispossessed. It is important to distinguish between the work which had been done by Joshua and that which still remained for Israel to do. He had overthrown the ruling. powers, captured their forts, and subdued the Canaanites to such an extent as had given Israel firm foothold in the country. But he had not exterminated the population in every portion of it, yea, powerful nations still dwelt in parts thereof, as is clear from Judges ii, 20-23, and iii, 1-4 ; so that much was still demanded from Israel. Therein we behold again the accuracy of the type. The antitypical Joshua has secured for His people an inalienable title to the heavenly Canaan, yet formidable foes have to be overcome and much hard fighting done by them before they enter into their eternal rest. The same is true of the *present enjoyment* thereof : faith and hope encounter much opposition ere there is an experiential participation of the goodly heritage which Christ has obtained for them.

The method appointed for the dividing of the land is deeply interesting and instructive. Two distinct principles were to operate, yet the giving place to the one appears to rule out the other. The first had been laid down by the Lord through Moses : " Unto these the land shall be divided for an inheritance according to the number of names. To many thou shalt give the more inheritance, and to few thou shalt give the less inheritance : to every one shall his inheritance be given according to those that were numbered of him " (Num. xxvi, 53, 54—

335

repeated in xxxiii, 54). There was the general rule which was to be followed in the dividing of Canaan and the quartering of the people : the size of the section allocated was to be determined by the numerical strength of the tribe to which it was given. Yet immediately after Numbers xxvi, 54, a second law was named : "Notwithstanding the land shall be divided by lot : according to the names of the tribes of their fathers they shall inherit. According to *the lot* shall the possession thereof be divided between many and few." That is to say, the disposition of the inheritance was to be determined by the sovereign will of God, for the lot was regulated by Him and made known His pleasure.

Those two principles seem to be mutually incompatible, and we are not acquainted with any attempt to show the agreement of the one with the other. It is the age-old problem of the conjunction of the Divine and human elements : in this instance, the human by the dimensions of the several tribes ; the Divine by God's determining their respective portions. Yet, in the case now before us, no real difficulty is presented : the larger tribes would still obtain the biggest sections, but the " lot " specified the *particular* situation in Canaan which was to be theirs. Neither Joshua, Eleazar, nor the heads of the tribes were free to dispose of the land according to their own ideas or desires : the final locations were reserved to the providence of God, to whose imperial will all must acquiesce, howsoever contrary to their thoughts and wishes. Such an arrangement not only accorded unto God His proper place in the transaction, but it also precluded the exercise of any spirit of partiality or favouritism on the part of Israel's leaders, and at the same time served effectually to close the mouths of the people from murmuring.

The more those two apparently conflicting principles be pondered, the more shall we admire the wisdom of Him who appointed the same. Obviously, it was most equitable and advisable that the larger tribes should be accorded more extensive quarters than the lesser ones, for their requirements would be the greater. Yet, fallen human nature being what it is, it is equally evident that had Israel been left entirely unto themselves the weaker tribes would have been deprived of their rightful portions : for if not entirely denied a separate heritage, they would most probably have been obliged to submit unto having the least desirable sections of the land Nor would there have been any redress, for in such a case (numerical) might would be right. It was therefore necessary for there to be a Divine supervision : not only in fixing the exact boundaries of each allotment, but also in determining their several locations, so that the mountainous sections and the fertile valleys should be fairly distributed. This is one of many examples where we see how the Divine legislation protected the welfare of the weak, and how the Lord ever manifested a concern for the poor and needy.

Side by side with Joshua xiv, 1, 2, should be placed Leviticus xxv, 23-28 : " The land shall not be sold for ever : for the land is Mine ; for ye are strangers and sojourners with Me. And in all the land of your possesion ye shall grant a redemption for the land. If thy brother be waxen poor, and hath sold away some of his possession, and if any of his kin come to redeem it, then shall he redeem that which his brother sold. And if the man have none to redeem it, and himself be able to redeem it ; then let him count the years of the sale thereof, and restore the overplus unto the man to whom he sold it ; that it may return unto his possession. But if he be not able to restore it to him, then that which is sold shall remain in the hand of him that hath bought it until the year of jubile : and in the jubile it shall go out, and he shall return unto his possession." That was the Divine law respecting the real estate of the Hebrews and the transferring of the same : a law by which the rights of rich and poor alike were fully and equitably safeguarded. In cases of need, property might be sold conditionally, but not absolutely so that the same should never again return to its original owner.

The above passages set forth a remarkable and unique *law of property,* displaying a wisdom wherein righteousness and mercy were blessedly intermingled, encouraging as it did individual enterprise, and yet also curbing greed. That disposition and arrangement was the very reverse of " State ownership," for the land was portioned out to the twelve tribes, and within the territory of each tribe the land was divided among its families. If hardship and poverty required a family to mortgage or sell its property, thereby an opportunity was offered unto the thrifty and ambitious to enlarge their holdings. But in the jubilee year that property reverted to its seller, and thus the cupidity of "capitalists" was restrained, and thereby were they prevented from taking undue advantage of the distress of others by a permanent acquirement of their estates. Thus the Bible not only teaches the right of the individual to own his own house (cf. John xix, 27) and possess real estate (Acts iv, 34), but, by clear and necessary implication, condemns State ownership, which is a manifest violation of the rights and liberties of the individual. How many-sided and far-reaching is the teaching of Holy Writ !

" The Israelites had acquired the land by conquest, but they were not allowed to seize upon what they could, nor to have it all in common, nor to share it out by consent or arbitration ; but, with solemn appeal to God Himself, to divide by lot ; for Canaan was His land, and Israel were His people. This was likewise the readiest way of satisfying all parties, and preventing discontent and discord " (Thos. Scott). Yet it should be pointed out that the basic law that operated here has also obtained all through human history. The Lord God is the Proprietor as well as the Governor of both heaven and earth, the sovereign Disposer of all the affairs of the children of men. He is the One who controls the courses of empires and determines the lives of dynasties, and has also decided the limits of each person's territory. That principle is clearly enunciated in Deuteronomy xxxii, 8, " When the Most High divided to the nations their inheritance, when He separated the sons of Adam, He *set the bounds* of the people according to the number of the children of Israel." And none of those nations ever has or will exceed those " bounds " which the Almighty originally prescribed.

As truly as the Divine " lot " assigned the particular parts of Palestine which the different tribes of Israel should possess, so has God predestined the precise portions of the earth which each nation shall occupy. " When He gave to the sea His decree, that the waters should not pass His commandment " (Prov. viii, 29), He gave a similar edict unto the nations. And military leaders impelled by the lust of conquest, and aggressive dictators aspiring to world dominion, have discovered that, like the restless sea (which is the scriptural symbol of the nations : Daniel vii, 2, and cf. Rev. xvii, 15), God has set a bound which they "could not pass," " and though the waves thereof toss themselves, yet can they not prevail ; though they roar, yet can they not pass over it " (Jer. v, 22, and cf. Job xxxviii, 11). Men like Napoleon, the Kaiser and Hitler might be dissatisfied with the allotments of providence, chafe against the restraints it had placed upon their greed, rage and roar against their neighbours, and attempt to acquire their Divinely given portions, but vain were their efforts. Thus will any present or future aspirant yet find out.

Deuteronomy xxxii, 8, informs us that God had before His mind the children of Israel when He divided to the nations their inheritance, for, as the apostle told his saints, " all things are for *your sakes* " (II Cor. iv, 5). Thus there was a partial reference to the seven nations whose place and portion were assigned them in Canaan, so that the Hebrews found it in a high state of cultivation, provided with towns and houses, all prepared for their use! In like manner, the favoured land in which the writer and the reader live, with all its natural and national advantages, and the temporal provisions we enjoy therein, is as much the special appointment and gift of God as Canaan was to Israel, and as truly demands our gratitude. God has the sole disposing of this life and the interests thereof, as truly as He has of the life to come. No man has a foot of land more than God has laid out for him in His all-wise providence : so whatever of this world's goods he obtains let him bear in mind, " thou shalt remember the Lord thy God : for it is *He* that giveth thee power to get wealth " (Deut. viii, 18). This world is not governed by blind chance, but by Divine wisdom. However possessions come to us, they are from God as the first cause

God " hath made of one blood all nations of men for to dwell on all the face of the earth, and hath determined the times before appointed, and *the bounds* of their habitation " (Acts xvii, 26) As Toplady remarked thereon, " The very places which people inhabit are here positively averred to be determined and fore-appointed by God. And it is very right it should be so, else some places would be overstocked with inhabitants, and others deserted. . . . Whereas by God's having fore-appointed the bounds of our habitations, we are properly sifted over the face of the earth, so as to answer all the social and higher purposes of Divine wisdom." God has appointed where each person shall reside : the particular country in which he should be born, and the very city, town, village, and house in which we shall dwell, and how long he shall remain there ; for our times are in His hand (Psalm xxxi, 15). A striking illustration of that is seen in connection with both the birthplace and the subsequent abode of the Saviour. It was ordained that He should be born at Bethlehem, and though circumstances appeared to prevent. God set in motion a Roman census throughout the whole of its empire, requiring Joseph and Mary to journey unto Bethlehem, (Luke ii, 1-6). Later, they resided at the appointed Nazareth (Matt. ii, 23).

The distribution of Canaan was *by lot*. To ascertain precisely what it consisted of and how the mind of God was made known therein, Scripture has to be carefully compared with Scripture, and even then we cannot be quite certain of the exact method followed. The first time (which is always of most importance) the lot is mentioned is in Leviticus xvi, 8, "And Aaron shall cast lots upon the two goats ; one lot for the Lord, and the other lot for the scapegoat " : i.e. to determine which of them should be used for the Godward side of the atonement (propitiation) and which the manward (the removal of sins). Thus the first occurrence of " the lot " associates it with Israel's high priest, and shows that it was employed in determining the will of God. So too " Eleazar the priest " is expressly mentioned both in Numbers xxxiv, 17, and Joshua xiv, 1, in connection with the transaction we are here considering. Likewise, when the claim was made by the daughters of Zelophehad to a portion of Canaan their case was determined before Eleazar the priest, Joshua, and the princes of the tribes (Joshua xvii, 3-6), because the use of the lot was there involved, as the word " fell," or more literally " came forth " (verse 5), indicates.

Personally we incline strongly to the view taken by the author of *The Companion Bible* (unprocurable today) that God's will in " the lot " was obtained by means of the mysterious " Urim and Thummim," which were probably two precious stones, for there was no commandment given to " make " *them*, and which were " put in the breastplate " of the high priest, (Exodus xxviii, 30).

Apparently they were " put '' in a bag in " the ephod " or robe of the high priest, which bag was formed by doubling a part of the garment—note " doubled " in Exodus xxviii, 16, and " inward " (verse 26). In Proverbs xvi, 33, we are told, " The lot is cast into the lap [Hebrew " bosom," which is put for the clothing covering it—cf. Exodus iv, 6, 7]; but the whole disposing thereof is of the Lord." Thus " the lot " was for the purpose of giving a judgment or infallible decision, and the breastplate is designated " the breastplate of judgment " (Exodus xxviii, 15), because by it God's judgment or verdict was given when the same was needed—compare I Samuel xxviii, 6, where the Lord refused to oblige the apostate Saul.

Thus it seems that when the lot was needed the high priest placed his hand in the bag or pocket behind his breastplate, and drew forth either the Urim or the Thummim, the one signifying Yes, and the other No, for in Joshua xviii, 11, we are told that the lot " came up," in xix, 1, that it " came forth," and in xix, 17, that it " came out." Joshua xix, 51, informs us that this important transaction took place at the entrance to the house of God : " These are the inheritances, which Eleazar the priest, and Joshua the son of Nun, and the heads of the fathers of the tribes of the children of Israel, divided for an inheritance by lot in Shiloh before the Lord, at the door of the tabernacle of the congregation." This casts light upon a number of passages treating of incidents in the later history of Israel. Thus, when they were uncertain as to whether or not they should go up against Benjamin again, they came to the house of God and inquired of the Lord, and it was Phinehas the high priest who obtained answer for them (Judges xx, 26-28). In Ezra ii, 61-63, no verdict could be given unless the high priest were present, with his breastplate of judgment, with " the lot," Urim and Thummim, which would give Jehovah's decision—guilty or innocent.

It is to be duly noted that, in addition to Eleazar the priest and Joshua himself, " the heads of the fathers of the tribes of the children of Israel " (xiv, 1) were also present when the official distribution of the land was made. This was in obedience to the Divine injunction given through Moses that " one prince of every tribe " (Num. xxxiv, 18) should be taken to serve as commissioners on this occasion. They were entrusted with the oversight, to be witnesses that everything had been conducted fairly and properly in the distribution of the land according to the size of the tribes and in the casting of the lot. Thus would they protect the rights of the tribes, preclude all suspicion that any partiality had been shown, and be qualified authoritatively to determine any controversy which might later arise. " Public affairs should be so managed, as not only to give their right to all, but, if possible, to give satisfaction to all that they have right done them " (Matthew Henry). It is very striking to note that God not only selected those commissioners during the lifetime of Moses, but actually *named* them all (Num. xxxiv, 19-29), which thereby guaranteed their preservation from death during the long interval, either from natural causes or from the fighting in Canaan.

The Inheritance

In our last we virtually confined our attention to a consideration of the method appointed by God for the distribution of Canaan among the tribes of Israel—that of Levi being exempted therefrom. That method was " the lot," and however casual and contingent the casting thereof might seem to man it was Divinely certain, for " the whole disposing thereof is of the Lord " (Prov. xvi, 33), so that His will was infallibly made known thereby. All important matters of order under the Divine theocracy were thus determined. Hence we find king Saul making request of the Lord God, "give a perfect lot" (I Samuel xiv, 41). The cities in which the sons of Aaron and their families were to dwell were determined by lot (I Chron. vi, 63), so too were the sacred singers of the divine worship (I Chron. xxv, 7, 8). Likewise, in Nehemiah's day, those who were to reside in Jerusalem were chosen by lot (xi, 1). In case of rival claims, the different parties agreed to abide by its decision, and thus " The lot causeth contentions to cease, and parteth between the mighty" (Prov. xviii, 18).

The practical application which is to be made unto ourselves of the above prniciple is that God does not leave secondary causes to their work as an idle spectator, but interposes and orders all the affairs of our lives. As an old writer quaintly expressed it, "Notwithstanding all our blowing, the fire will not burn without the Lord." "Except the Lord build the house, they labour in vain that build it: except the Lord keep the city, the watchman waketh but in vain" (Psalm cxxvii, 1). As the apportioning of Canaan was entirely by Divine determination, so are the bounds of our habitation fixed, and in whatever way our position and portion in this world be assigned or acquired by us, we should regard the same as coming from the Lord, and be thankful for and contented with it. One of the secrets of tranquillity of mind and happiness of heart is for us to be grateful and joyful for what God *has* so graciously given us, instead of lusting after and repining over those things which He wisely withholds. "Godliness with contentment is great gain . . . and having food and raiment let us be therewith content" (I Tim. v, 6, 8).

As the portion which Jehovah appointed, promised, and gave unto Abraham and his descendants, the land of Canaan has, all through this Christian era, been rightly regarded as figuring the heavenly Canaan, unto which the members of Christ are now journeying as they pass through this scene of sin and trial. Rightly so we say, for in the first place the New Testament refers often to the everlasting bliss of God's people as *an inheritance*. The evangelical commission which Paul received from the Lord unto the Gentiles was "to open their eyes, and to turn them from darkness to light, and from the power of Satan unto God, that they may receive forgiveness of sins, and inheritance among them which are sanctified by faith that is in Me" (Acts xxvi, 18). And therefore did he bid the Colossians give "thanks unto the Father, which hath made us meet to be partakers of the inheritance of the saints in light" (i, 12). In Hebrews ix, 15, he termed it the "eternal inheritance"; while Peter assured the saints that they had been begotten "to an inheritance incorruptible, and undefiled, and that fadeth not away, reserved in heaven for you" (I i, 4).

In the second place, Canaan was given to Israel *on the ground of the covenant* which Jehovah made with Abraham (Exodus vi, 4; Psalm cv, 9-11). In like manner, our heritage of blessing and glory is bestowed upon us in consequence of the everlasting covenant of grace. God and the Mediator agreed together in counsel for the accomplishment of a common end: to further the manifested glory of God and to secure the salvation of His people. In Zechariah vi, 13, we read, "And the counsel of peace shall be between Them both," the reference being to Jehovah and the Man whose name is the Branch of the previous verse. That "counsel of peace" signifies the compact between Them. Or the fulfilment of certain conditions by the Mediator, God stipulated to reward Him and His seed. That everlasting covenant is the foundation of all the good which God does to His people (Luke i, 68-72; Heb. xiii, 20, 21). His promises unto them were made to their Surety, on whose behalf He transacted. A remarkable proof of this is found in Titus i, 2, " In hope of eternal life, which God, that cannot lie, *promised* [not simply "purposed"] before the world began"—promised Christ that He would bestow eternal life (another name for the "inheritance"—Matt. vii, 14) upon all His seed.

In the third place, the everlasting portion of Christians is not only an "inheritance," but *an allotted one.* This is taught plainly in Ephesians i, 11, though a careful comparison of other passages is required in order to discern the real meaning and force of that verse. Since most of the Lord's people are unacquainted with the same, it will be necessary for us to enter into some detail In verses 3-9 the apostle had spoken of election, of adoption to glory (or an inheritance), of redemption, and of vocation. Then in verse 10 he stated that the design of the whole of the foregoing was that God should head up or gather together in one all things in Christ, both which are in heaven (the angels) and (the redeemed) which are on earth. In verses 11-13 this is amplified and explained. First he refers to Jewish believers, and says, "In whom [Christ, the Head] also *we* have obtained an inheritance," or a part in that grand "gathering together" into one in Christ. Then in verse 13 he alludes to the Gentiles: "In whom *ye also* trusted, after that ye heard the word of truth, the gospel of your salvation," for it is not until his conversion that any soul actually obtains either an interest in or meetness for the inheritance.

The "we have obtained an inheritance" is a single word—a compound one—in the original, and is derived from *kleros*, concerning which that eminent Greek scholar and exegete C. Hodge said, "The word *kleros* means to cast lots, to distribute by lot, to choose by lot, and, in the middle voice, to obtain by lot or inheritance or simply to obtain." Our own study has confirmed that, first, *kleros* signifies a part or portion in a thing, to be a partaker with others therein, and it is so rendered in Acts i, 17, 25. Thus the saints have a part in that gathering together of all things in Christ. Second, *kleros* signifies an inheritance, and is so rendered in Hebrews i, 4—"heritage" in I Peter v, 3. Third, *kleros* signifies a lot, being so translated seven times: Matthew xxvii, 35, etc.; Acts i, 26. Thus by combining those three meanings we get a part or portion, which part or portion is an inheritance, and this inheritance comes to us by lot, as did that of the Hebrews: "Ye shall divide the land by lot for an inheritance" (Num. xxxiii, 54, and see Ezek. xlv, 1), and therefore it is called "the lot of our inheritance" (Num. xxxvi, 3).

It is also to be observed that the verbal noun of Ephesians i, 11 (for a verb it is) is a *passive* one, importing that the inheritance has been *bestowed upon* us, and is not something actively acquired by us. The word is used in the passive voice when we say a man is *disinherited,* but we have no English word that answers thereto to say a man is *inherited,* so we supply a word and say he is *endowed with* an inheritance. The Christian's inheritance is not something he has earned by his own efforts, nor is it even sought by him, but is conferred upon him gratuitously. We obtained an inheritance in Christ, were made joint heirs with Him, before we were aware of it. In some cases this is much more evident than in others, as with those who are utterly unconcerned about their souls' eternal welfare being suddenly and quite unexpectedly apprehended by Christ—like Saul of Tarsus. Yet in reality it is so in *every* case, for Christ took the initiative in seeking out and working upon the ones who became anxious seekers after Him, for did not God first quicken the dead in sins, none would ever make a movement towards Him; yet they know no more about that quickening than a man asleep would of obtaining an inheritance then bequeathed to him.

Thus it turns out under the preaching of the Gospel and those who hear the same: the lot falls on some and passes by others. One may attend out of idle curiosity and be arrested by God the first sermon he hears; as Zacchæus, being little, climbed up into a tree, that he might get a glimpse of the miracle-worker who was passing that way, yet Christ said unto him "make haste, and come down. . . . This day is salvation come to this house"; while regular attenders are left to themselves. "Go ye therefore into the highways, and as many as ye shall find, bid to the marriage" : every saint is Divinely ordained, yet to human perception things are carried out casually, as if grace comes to them by lot—even as Saul merely went forth to seek his father's asses, but before he arrived back home had been anointed king of Israel. The hearers of Christ's forerunner went to view a novelty, as they would go to a show (Luke vii, 24, 25), yet under his call to repentance many of their hearts were turned to God.

The above remarks receive definite confirmation in II Peter i, 1, where the apostle addresses himself to "them that have *obtained* like precious faith with us," for the Greek word there used also signifies "to obtain by lot" (Young's Concordance), being the same one as is rendered "*his lot was* to burn incense" (Luke i, 9). By using that term, Peter would remind his readers that if they had really believed to the saving of their souls they were indebted for their faith not at all to their own superior sagacity but solely to the sovereign dispositions of Divine grace. In the distribution of His favours, that blessed portion had fallen to their share. Thus II Peter i, 1, is one of many verses which teach us that saving faith is a *gift* from God, and not a product of the creature's will: all room for boasting is excluded (I Cor. iv, 7): it is the Divine lot which makes believer differ from unbeliever!

It is not simply predestination which gives a soul a right to the Divine inheritance, but a Divine work—a work of grace on the heart—which is the effect of predestination. So teaches the apostle in Ephesians i, 12-14: it was *after* they heard the Gospel, "after that ye believed," that they were sealed by the Holy Spirit of promise, "which is the earnest of our inheritance." It is not until we are converted that we obtain a personal interest in the inheritance." This is clear from Acts xxvi, 18, for Christ sent forth Paul to preach in order to turn men "from darkness unto light . . . that they may receive forgiveness of sins, and inheritance among them which are sanctified [set apart from unbelievers] by faith that is in Me." Simon Magus was told frankly, "Thou hast neither part nor lot in this matter." And why? because he was an impenitent and unpardoned soul (Acts viii, 21, 22). We have to be made meet by the gracious operations of the Spirit before we become partakers of the inheritance (Col. i, 12). Likewise does I Peter i, 3, 4, expressly inform us that we must be begotten of God ere we have a saving and experiential interest in the heavenly inheritance.

After stating that those who are converted have obtained an inheritance or "part" in the gathering together into one of all things in Christ, the apostle then traced this unspeakable blessing back to *its source*: "being predestinated according to the purpose of Him who worketh all things after the counsel of His own will" (Eph. i, 11). God has sent forth the Gospel on no uncertain mission, but whenever and by whomsoever it be preached it shall not return unto Him void, but accomplish that which He pleases and prosper in the thing whereto He sent it—all the forces of evil being powerless to prevent it. It is not left to human caprice, the wills of those who hear it, and though it comes to men by "lot" (which to the eye of man appears to be wholly a matter of chance), yet that lot is directed by God's eternal predestination; and though the favoured ones on which the lot falls be by nature as alienated from God and as dead in sin as those whom the lot passes by, nevertheless their effectual calling and conversion is accomplished by Him who works all things after the counsel of His own will.

Many of God's people rejoice and give thanks unto Him for His bringing them from death unto life, working repentance and faith in them, and granting them a saving interest in Christ; but fail to perceive that those acts of the Divine mercy are the consequents and fruits of God's eternal choice and foreordination of them unto eternal life and glory (Acts xiii, 48 ; II Thess. ii, 13, 14). The order of the Divine procedure is clearly stated in Romans viii : " For whom He did foreknow, He also predestinated to be conformed to the image of His Son, that He might be the firstborn [chief] among many brethren " (verse 29). Foreknowledge there is the knowledge of approbation, as in " The Lord knoweth the way of the righteous " (Psalm i), " you only have I known of all the families of the earth " (Amos iii, 2, and see Romans xi, 2). The distinction between foreknowledge and predestination is this : the Divine foreknowledge is of the *persons* selected and approved ; the predestination is the appointing of the *blessings* designed them. The next verse shows how that grand purpose of God is accomplished : " Moreover whom He did predestinate, them He also called : and whom He called, them He also justified : and whom He justified, them He also glorified."

Thus, God's electing grace and sovereign purpose are the ground and root of all that follows. Many other passages teach the same thing. " I have loved thee with an everlasting love : *therefore* with lovingkindness have I drawn thee " (Jer. xxxi, 3)—all of God's dealings with His people in time are the outworking of His decrees concerning them in eternity past. " God hath from the beginning chosen you to salvation through sanctification of the Spirit and belief of the truth " (II Thess. ii, 13) : He who determined the end also appointed and provided the means thereto. " Who hath saved us, and called us with an holy calling, not according to our works [either actual or foreseen, for we have no good ones except those which He produces in and through us], but according to His own purpose and grace, which was given us in Christ Jesus before the world began " (II Tim. i, 9). Now observe how strong and emphatic is the language of Ephesians i, 11 : " In whom also we have obtained an inheritance, being predestinated according to the purpose of Him who worketh all things after the counsel of His own will." Not only predestinated to that inheritance, but according to Divine purpose, which expresses the certainty and immutability thereof ; and that the decree of Him who effectually works all things after the contrivance of His own pleasure, none being able to withstand Him.

In the fourth place the allotment of Israel's inheritance was conveyed through the exercise of *the priest's office*. " And these are the countries which the children of Israel inherited in the land of Canaan, which Eleazar the priest, and Joshua the son of Nun, and the heads of the fathers of the tribes of the children of Israel, distributed for inheritance to them " (Joshua xiv, 1). Since a solemn appeal was to be made unto God for the knowledge of His will, the presence of the high priest with his Urim and Thummin was necessary. Accordingly, Eleazar, the son and successor of Aaron (Deut. x, 6), is here mentioned, and that *before* Joshua. By thus giving him the precedence, signal honour was placed upon the priesthood. Therein we behold once more the beauty and the accuracy of the type, though ours is an age of such spiritual ignorance that few today perceive this. The careful student of the New Testament will have observed that the priesthood of Christ is there given a prominence which is accorded unto neither His prophetic nor His kingly office. Nor is that in the least surprising, for it was the very end of His incarnation " that He might be a merciful and faithful high priest in things pertaining to God, to make reconciliation for the sins of the people " (Heb. ii, 17).

There was obviously no necessity for the assumption of human nature by the Son of God if the only results to be achieved thereby were the publication of truths undiscoverable by the efforts of human reason and the promulgation of laws invested with the authority of God, for prophets and apostles were quite competent (by Divine enduement) to perform such offices. But the mediation of Christ rendered it requisite and fitting that it should assume the peculiar form of *priesthood*, so that His death might be not only a satisfaction unto justice, but a sweet-smelling sacrifice—a free-will offering unto God. It is most important to recognize that Christ's redemptive work was a priestly one. This has been denied by Socinians, and it is sad to find some who believe in Christ's deity adopting the vain reasoning of "Unitarians" concerning the sacerdotal nature of the Saviour's oblation. The New Testament represents Christ not only as priest, but as the great High Priest of His people, and if the character, purpose and scope of that office be interpreted in the light of the Old Testament types (as it must be) there is no room left for doubt as to the meaning of the antitype.

Now it is in the epistle to the Hebrews that the functions of Christ's priesthood are most fully made known. There we are shown that both Aaron and Melchizedek were needed to foreshadow completely its various aspects : the design of God in appointing Aaron was to typify the person and work of Christ, as is clear from " as was Aaron . . . so also Christ " (v, 4, 5)—an unmistakable parallel. Hebrews ii, 17, makes it quite plain that Christ acted as Priest here on earth, for He made "reconciliation for the sins of the people "—as Aaron was priest *before* he entered the holiest, so also was Christ. Hebrews vii, 26, exhibits the qualifications and excellences which fitted Christ to discharge this office, describing what He was here when brought into contact with sin and sinners. " Such an high priest became us " : was requisite for and suited to fallen creatures —none other could expiate our sins, procure acceptance with God, or purchase eternal redemption. Hebrews viii, 3 ; ix, 11-15, 25-28 ; x, 10-12, also prove that Christ discharged His priestly office *on earth*, offering Himself as a sacrifice to God. Conclusive proof of this was furnished by God's rending of the veil, thereby setting aside the whole system of the Levitical order, His priestly oblation having superseded theirs.

As might well be expected from their relative positions in the Sacred Canon, Hebrews takes us farther than Romans (wonderful as that epistle is) in the revelation of God's manifold wisdom and the unveiling of His amazing grace. In Romans the scene is laid in the law court ; in Hebrews, within the temple. In the former, the righteousness of God is displayed ; in the latter, His holiness shines forth. In the one, justification is the outstanding provision of the Gospel ; in the other, sanctification is the product of Christ's sacrifice. In Romans Christ is seen as the covenant Head and federal Representative of His people ; in Hebrews as their great High Priest. In the former, believers obtain a secure standing before God's throne ; in the latter, they are privileged to draw nigh as worshippers before the mercy seat. As both Aaron and Melchizedek were needed to set forth the sacrificial and royal functions of Christ's priesthood, so both Phinehas and Joshua were required (xiv, 1) to exhibit Him as the Bestower of our inheritance— the Lamb-Lion of Revelation v, 5, 6. As Priest (and Lamb) Christ *purchased* the "eternal inheritance" (Heb. ix, 11-15), as the antitypical Joshua (and Lion) His *power* conducts the heirs into it.

In our last we pointed out some of the principal respects in which the distribution of the land of Canaan unto the tribes of Israel adumbrated the blessings and glory which the spiritual Israel obtain in and by Christ. We saw that, in the first place, our eternal portion is distinctly termed an " inheritance " (I Peter i, 4). Second, that our inheritance is bestowed upon us on the ground of a covenant

(Luke i, 72). Third, that our inheritance too is an allotted one (Eph. i, 11), and that the very faith which is necessary to give us a personal and saving interest therein is bestowed upon us by Divine lot (I Peter i, 2). Fourth, that our glorious heritage is conveyed to us by the exercise of Christ's priesthood (Heb. ix, 11-15). Continuing to ponder the analogies between type and antitype, we note, in the fifth place, that responsible princes of Israel's tribes attended when Canaan was divided, for there were present with Eleazar the priest and Joshua "the heads of the fathers of the tribes of the children of Israel" (Joshua xiv, 1). Nothing is told us of the particular part they played in that important transaction, but it appears that they were appointed to act as overseers or supervisors on that occasion.

"And Jesus said unto them, Verily I say unto you, That ye which have followed Me, in the regeneration when the Son of man shall sit in the throne of His glory, ye also shall sit upon twelve thrones, judging the twelve tribes of Israel" (Matt. xix, 28). That, in our opinion, is what answers to and corresponds with that particular detail in Joshua xiv, 1. If "the saints shall judge the world," yea, "judge angels" (I Cor. vi, 2, 3), we need not be surprised to learn that the twelve shall sit upon thrones judging the tribes of Israel. The apostles were closest to Christ and shared most in His humiliation, and therefore in the day of His manifested glory they will be distinguished from and honoured above all their brethren. Since they were so fiercely persecuted by the Jews, they will be Christ's assessors in their judgment. A further dignity is bestowed upon them by the names of the twelve apostles of the Lamb being in the twelve foundations of the new Jerusalem (Rev. xxi, 12). In each instance—Joshua xiv, 1 ; Matthew xix, 28 ; I Corinthians vi, 2, 3—the bare fact is stated without any explanation or amplification, and therefore any attempt to speculate thereon is not only useless but impious.

In the sixth place, our inheritance is *a reward*. As we have so frequently pointed out in these articles, while Canaan was the land of promise, Israel had to *fight* for it : even Jacob spoke of one portion therein "which I took out of the hand of the Amorite with my sword and with my bow" (Gen. xlviii, 22). It was bequeathed unto Abraham and his seed, nevertheless it became theirs only by their own prowess. Notwithstanding its being theirs by Divine donation, in a subordinate but very real sense their actual entrance into and possession thereof was the result of their own efforts. Whether or not we can perceive the "consistency" and congruity of those different principles, they are the plain facts of the case. Nor should they present any difficulty to us, for they are complementary to each other, and not contradictory. God's sovereignty lies at the foundation of all things, yet in His dealings with men—His own people not excepted—He ever treats with them as moral agents, enforces their accountability, and causes them to reap as they have sown, whether it was evil or good seed.

Now what pertained to the bestowment and acquirement of the earthly Canaan holds good in connection with the heavenly Canaan. It could not be otherwise, for God made the type to shadow forth accurately the antitype, therefore we read, " And whatsoever ye do, do it heartily, as to the Lord, and not unto men ; knowing that of the Lord ye shall receive *the reward of the inheritance* : for ye serve the Lord Christ" (Col. iii, 23, 24). Nothing can be more free or a matter of bounty than an inheritance. Then since it be an inheritance, with what propriety term it a "reward"? If a reward, how can it be, at the same time, an "inheritance"? The two things seem to be quite incompatible, especially since the inheritance is also designated "the purchased possession" (Eph. i, 14)—bought with the blood of Christ. Yet such language is no more antithetical than that of the Saviour when He exhorted the Jews to "labour not for the meat which perisheth, but *for* that meat which endureth unto everlasting life," and then added, " which the Son of man shall *give* unto you" (John vi, 27); nor that of His apostle, who declared, "For we which have believed *do enter* into rest," and then enjoined, "let us labour therefore *to enter* into that rest" (Heb. iv, 3, 11).

There is much in the Scriptures which appears to the infidel to be contradictory : as that "the Lord our God is one Lord" (Deut. vi, 4), yet is three distinct persons; that "His mercy endureth for ever" (Psalm cxxxvi, 1), yet that He will send many of His creatures to everlasting punishment; that Christ should affirm "I and Father are one" (John x, 30), yet also declared "My Father is greater than I" (John xiv, 28). And though the Christian perceives the perfect harmony of those statements, yet there are some things which greatly puzzle him. As for instance, that since God has predestinated everything which comes to pass, what room is left for free agency and the discharge of human responsibility ? If the fall has deprived men of all spiritual strength, how can they be justly held blameworthy for failing to perform spiritual duties ? If Christ died for the elect only, how can He be freely offered to every creature ? If the believer be Christ's "free man," then why is he required to take upon him His yoke ? If he has been set at liberty (Gal. v, 1), how can he be "under the law" (I Cor. ix, 21) ? If he be preserved by God, then how can his own perseverance be necessary in order to the attainment of eternal bliss ? If sin does not have dominion over him (Romans vi, 14), why do "iniquities prevail against" him so often (Psalm lxv, 3) ?

Whatever difficulties may be involved, the fact remains that Scripture has not a little to say about God's rewarding the obedient and crowning the overcomer. " In keeping of them there is great reward" (Psalm xix, 11). "To him that soweth righteousness shall be a sure reward" (Prov. xi, 18). "Then He shall reward every man according to his works" (Matt. xvi, 27). "Well done, good and faithful servant; thou hast been faithful over a few things, I will make thee ruler over many" (Matt. xxv, 23). "They [the poor] cannot recompense thee : for thou shalt be recompensed at the resurrection of the just" (Luke xiv, 14). There are other declarations that God will take special note of the fidelity of His servants, and amply compensate them for the sufferings which they have endured in His behalf. "Blessed are ye, when men shall revile you, and persecute you, and shall say all manner of evil against you falsely, for My sake. Rejoice, and be exceeding glad : for great is your reward in heaven" (Matt. v, 11). "Be thou faithful unto death, and I will give thee a crown of life" (Rev. ii, 10). Now all such passages as these must be allowed their obvious and legitimate force, and be given a due place in our hearts and minds.

In a brief and incidental statement on this subject, Calvin beautifully preserved the balance. "The Scripture shows *what* all our works are capable of meriting when it represents them as unable to bear the Divine scrutiny, because they are full of impurity. And in the next place what would be merited by the perfect observance of the Law if this could anywhere be found, when it directs us, 'when ye shall have done all those things which are commanded you, say, We are unprofitable servants' (Luke xvii, 10), because we shall not have conferred any favour on God, but only have performed the duties incumbent upon us, for which no thanks are due. Nevertheless, the good works which the Lord has conferred on us, He denominates *our own,* and declares that He will not only accept, but also reward them. It is our duty to be animated by so great a promise, and to stir up our minds that we ' be not weary in well doing,' and to be truly grateful for so great an instance of the Divine goodness. . . . Good works, therefore, are pleasing to God and not unprofitable to the authors of them, and they will moreover receive the most ample blessings from God as their reward : not because they merit them, but because the Divine goodness has freely appointed them this reward " (*Institutes*, book 3, chapter 5).

If it were " inconsistent " with the Divine perfections for God to bestow any *future* rewards on His people both for Christ's sake (primarily and meritoriously) and because of their own obedience (according to the terms of the new covenant and the governmental principles of God), then it would be equally so for Him to grant any *present* ones, for no difference in time or place can make any change in the essential nature of things. That He does richly recompense them in this world is clear from many passages. " Great peace have they which love Thy law " (Psalm cxix, 165, and cf. Isaiah lviii, 13, 14). The peace and joy which are the believer's now flow originally from the meditation of Christ, but subordinately from his own obedience and fidelity—if he pursues a course of disobedience, then peace of conscience will not be his. Those who deny themselves for Christ's sake and the Gospel's are assured of a grand reward : " an hundredfold now in this time," as well as " in the world to come eternal life " (Mark x, 30). " Godliness is profitable unto all things, having promise of the life that now is, and of that which is to come " (I Tim. iv, 8).

He who was outstandingly the apostle of grace declared, " I press toward the mark for *the prize* of the high calling of God in Christ Jesus " (Phil. iii, 14) : whatever that " prize " may consist of, the fact remains that the Holy Spirit moved him to use that term. Nevertheless, it is evident that our rewards, whether present or future, are not due to us as a wage is to a hired servant who has properly fulfilled his duty ; rather are they entirely a matter of Divine bounty. This is clear from the following considerations. First, it is Divine grace which alone *produces* our good works : " Thou also hast wrought all our works in us " (Isaiah xxvi, 12). Second, it is Divine grace which *approves* of them, despite their defects, for our gifts or benevolences (Phil. iv, 18) and our worship are " acceptable to God by Jesus Christ " (I Peter ii, 5) ; yea, our prayers are heard by God only because of the " much incense " of Christ's merits being added to them (Rev. viii, 3, 4). Third, there is no proportion between our performances or sufferings and the " exceeding and eternal weight of glory " (II Cor. iv, 17) which they " worketh for us."

Rewards are in no sense the recognition of personal worthiness, for we can deserve nothing good at the hands of God. Therein they differ radically from the punishment which shall be meted out unto the reprobate. The penalty inflicted on the wicked is an act of strict justice, the paying to them the wages of sin ; but the rewarding of the righteous is entirely a matter of Divine bounty, and therefore all room for boasting is excluded. It is impossible for any creature to bring God under obligation to him or make Him in any wise his debtor. Nevertheless, He is graciously pleased to recognize, own and recompense all that is done with an eye to His glory. Promises of reward are among the incentives to industry (Psalm cxxvi, 6), the encouragements of fidelity (Heb. xi, 26), and the motives to inspire us in unwearied well doing (Gal. vi, 9)—it was for " the joy set before Him " that the Lord Jesus endured the cross (Heb. xii, 2). Finally, it is to be pointed out that in signifying His approval of the services of the saints, God, at the same time, is owning the Spirit's work in them, for they are the " fruits " of His gracious operation.

In the seventh place, there will be *degrees of glory* among the saints when they enter into their final inheritance, though there are those who call this into question. It is objected that, since all believers are clothed with the righteousness of Christ and are equal in that respect, all have title to an equal inheritance. But that does not follow: varying degrees or measures of grace are bestowed upon one and another of them in this life. But since they all stand in the same relation to God, and are His dear children, will they not enjoy the same honours and dignities? Not necessarily, for even in this world they are not all of the same spiritual stature. Some are babes in Christ, while others are young men and fathers (I John ii, 12-14), and, no matter how long they be left here, some of the first-mentioned never attain unto the level of the others. Some argue that since all be of *grace*, distinctions could not obtain. All *is* of grace, and every crown will be cast at the feet of Christ, yet it does not follow that they shall be in all respects alike. Paul's crown of rejoicing will greatly consist in the salvation of those among whom he laboured (I Thess. ii, 19), yet that will not be the case with every inhabitant of heaven.

Others insist that the saint's title to eternal life is the meritorious work of the Mediator, being "the gift of God . . . through Jesus Christ our Lord" (Romans vi, 23), and that since all of His redeemed have His obedience imputed to them, that must ensure equality in glory. Not so, for Revelation xiv, 13, tells us that, from henceforth, blessed are the dead which die in the Lord, that they may rest from their labours, and then adds, "their works do follow them." Note, *not* "precede" as the ground of their justification, but "follow" as intermediate causes of their felicity. Since the amount of their works varies, so will they contribute to different degrees in augmenting their bliss. But since all be loved with the same love, called by the same calling, and are heirs of the same inheritance, it must be concluded that all will possess it in the same degree. If that reasoning proves anything, it "proves too much," for in such case all would be on a spiritual equality now; whereas it is an incontrovertible fact that God distributes His gifts and graces unevenly among His people.

All of the redeemed will be entirely content and perfectly happy in heaven, rejoicing with joy unspeakable and full of glory; yet while every cup of bliss will be full, they will not all be of the same size. All the saints will participate in celestial and eternal felicity, but not on an equality, "otherwise there would be no suitableness in God's dispensations. . . . There are higher degrees of glory for those who have done and suffered most" (Matthew Henry). This too was definitely foreshadowed in the distribution of Canaan. Joshua did not divide the land into twelve equal parts, for the Lord had given orders, "To many thou shalt give the more inheritance, and to few thou shalt give the less inheritance: to every one shall his inheritance be given according to those that were numbered of him" (Num. xxvi, 54); and so it came to pass. That also had a spiritual significance and application to us. "A believer's *state* of happiness is determined by his faith, but the *measure* of his happiness in that state depends upon the fruits of faith. Faith alone saves a Christian, but his crown is brighter according as his faith works more abundantly by love" (John Berridge, 1774).

As we have shown above, Scripture repeatedly informs us that the services and sufferings of the saints shall be rewarded in the day to come: though that reward be not of debt, but of grace, yet it *is* a "reward"—which could not be if what is enjoyed in the life to come had no relation to and bore no proportion to what was done in this life. As the different portions allotted Israel were determined by the size of their tribes, so that of the saints will be regulated by the number of their good works, in proportion as they use their talents. "Every man shall receive his own reward according to his own labour" (I Cor. iii, 8): according to the extent to which he exercised his grace and holiness here. As there are different measures of fruitfulness among believers, some thirtyfold, some sixty-fold, and some a hundredfold (Mark iv, 8), so there will be differences of reward. Though an eternity of bliss will be the portion of both the repentant thief and the apostle Paul, it is inconceivable that the latter will receive no more from the hands of Christ than the former. " To deny degrees in glory is to say that God wil! not suit men's wages to works " (Thomas Brooks, 1606-1680).

" But this I say, He which soweth sparingly shall reap also sparingly ; and he which soweth bountifully shall reap also bountifully " (II Cor. ix, 6). "As there is a difference in the kind of crop according to the kind of seed (Gal. vi, 7, 8), so according to the degree. Some well, others better ; so some fare well, others better, are more bountifully rewarded ; for God will deal more liberally with those who shall accordingly with greater diligence acquit themselves in well doing. There is a proportionate observance " (Manton). " Knowing that whatsoever good thing any man doeth, the same shall he receive of the Lord " (Eph. vi, 8), " that is, shall be particularly and punctually considered by God for it. He shall receive the same, not for kind, but for quantity and proportion " (Manton). The moral government of God will thus be honoured, and the equity of His procedure manifested. All will be of grace, yet then too shall it be seen that grace works " through righteousness " (Romans v, 21). " Ye shall receive the reward of the inheritance : for ye serve the Lord Christ " (Col. iii, 24), who is not only a bounti-ful Master, but a faithful one. " For God is *not unrighteous to* forget your work and labour of love, which ye have showed toward His name, in that ye have ministered to the saints, and do minister " (Heb. vi, 10).

It is in His office as moral Governor that the Lord will act in the day to come, and therein He will display not only His benevolence, but His righteousness. It will become Him to exhibit His approbation of holiness, put honour upon virtue, and crown fidelity. " If heavenly bliss bear any relation to the labours and suffer-ings of the present life on behalf of Christ, which the Scriptures assure us it does, there being diverse, that must also be the same " (Andrew Fuller). Different degrees of glory accords most with God's ways in creation, which is everywhere marked by diversity rather than uniformity. There are differences and disparities in every-thing among men : in wisdom and rank, in abilities and riches. Among the angels also there are " principalities and powers, thrones and dominions." It accords with God's dealings with His saints here : He gives the greatest spiritual blessings to those who most eminently glorify Him. Various measures of glory accords too with different degrees of punishment for the wicked (Matt. xi, 22 ; Luke xii, 47, 48 : Heb. x, 29). " Heavenly bliss will consist in ascribing glory to God and the Lamb : but this can be proportioned only in proportion as we have glory to ascribe. When Paul acknowledges ' by the grace of God I am what I am,' there is a thousand times more meaning in the expression, and a thousand times more glory redounds to God, than in the uttering of the same words by some men, even though they be men of real piety " (A. Fuller).

Individual Portions

Our previous articles upon the distribution of Canaan were confined almost entirely to the typical side of things, adumbrating as it did that blessed heritage which God decreed and Christ purchased for His people. But we must now con-sider briefly some of the *literal* features connected with the same. The orderly dividing of the land was not only a wise provision, but a necessary arrangement, so that the particular section of each tribe should be clearly defined. In Joshua xiv-xix a full and detailed description is recorded of the boundaries of each one. That was done by the immediate appointment and direction of God, and not by any human sagacity and prudence, still less by the dictates of partiality and greed. All was regulated by " the lot." This was done long before the whole of Canaan was actually conquered and possessed by Israel. There was to be no waiting until all the tribes had secured their respective portions : instead, they were now informed of the exact section to which they had been given a Divine title, so that they might go forward and possess their possessions. Thus were they called unto the exercise of *faith* and full confidence in God as they set about the performing of their respective tasks.

In our last we saw that the method which God selected for the allocating of Canaan unto Israel combined the principles of grace, sovereignty and righteousness : of grace, inasmuch as Israel's inheritance was a Divine gift ; of sovereignty, for all was done by lot or submitting to the Divine will in the dispositions made ; of righteousness, for the numerical strength of the tribe was taken into account in the size of the portion allotted it. The plan followed was thus the very opposite of what would be euphemistically termed a " Welfare State," for there was no dividing of the land into twelve equal parts. The whole of Scripture makes it plain that it is the Divine will that there should be distinctions both among nations, in the territory which they occupy, and among individuals, in the property which they possess. Likewise, it is required that each shall be contented with what the Lord has assigned them and him. " Thou shalt not covet " is as much a part of the Divine law as " Thou shalt not kill." When the antitypical Joshua was asked to appoint two of His disciples to the chief places of honour in His kingdom He replied, " to sit on My right hand, and on My left, is not Mine to give, but it shall be given to them for whom it is prepared of My Father " (Matt. xx, 23), thereby acknowledging the sovereignty of the Father.

The benefits to be derived from the dividing of Canaan to Israel by Divine lot should at once be apparent. Not only did such an arrangement exclude the exercise of human avarice and injustice, but it also precluded any occasion for strife and wrangling between the several tribes, determining as it did the precise location assigned unto each of them, with the limits thereof. Thus all ground for jealousy, misunderstanding and law-suits about their respective territories was obviated. But more : Israel were thereby taught to submit themselves to the good pleasure of the Lord. Therein lies the chief practical lesson which *we* should draw from this transaction : to surrender ourselves wholly to the Divine will and beg God to choose for us—whether it be in the matter of our earthly vocation, the selection of a life-partner, or the measure of temporal prosperity which will be most for His glory and our good. As an old writer truly remarked, " Such as refer themselves unto God to choose for them, will never find cause to repent of their lot." No, it is when we leave Him out, lean unto our own understanding, act by carnal impulse, that we bring trouble upon ourselves. How we should pray daily, " work in me both to will and to do of Thy good pleasure."

Before the lot was cast for the determining of the portions of the respective tribes, Caleb appeared before those who had charge of that business, and presented his claim unto Hebron for his own possession. A brief allusion was made to the same at the end of our October 1951 article, but a closer examination of the incident is now called for. Ere so doing, it should be pointed out that Joshua xiv, 5, is a general statement, which is amplified in xv, 1, and onwards, the narrative being interrupted by what is now to be before us. " Then the children of Judah came unto Joshua in Gilgal : and Caleb the son of Jephunneh the Kenezite said unto him, Thou knowest the thing that the Lord said unto Moses the man of God concerning me and thee in Kadesh-barnea " (verse 6). Observe here the gracious humility of the man ! Caleb was himself one of those who had been Divinely appointed to serve as one of the commissioners, to see that the lot was carried out in a proper manner (Num. xxxiv, 17-19) ; yet, lest it might appear that he was seeking unduly to use his authority in furthering his own interests, he brought with him some of his brethren to act as witnesses. How careful was he to " abstain from all appearance of evil " (I Thess. v, 22) ! Equally circumspect should we be in all of our public transactions.

" Forty years old was I when Moses the servant of the Lord sent me from Kadesh-barnea to espy out the land ; and I brought him word again as it was in mine heart " (verse 7, and cf. Num. xiii, 30). Those last words are very expressive and blessed. It was in Caleb's heart that God was fully able to give what He had promised : that the gigantic Amorites with their chariots of iron were nothing to Him. Caleb was strong in faith, and therefore he was quite sure that Jehovah would make good His word. It was the Lord Himself who had put such a firm persuasion in his heart : just as at a later date, when faced with a task that was formidable unto flesh and blood, Nehemiah declared " neither told I any man what my God had *put in my heart* to do at Jerusalem " (ii, 12) : that too was something which burned within and sustained him through heavy trials. David also had " found it in his heart to build the house of the Lord." How that language of Caleb's made it evident that his heart was set upon the Promised Land ! His " treasure " was there, and so was his heart also. That was his animating hope all through the forty years he had to spend with his unbelieving fellows in the wilderness. And so it should be with each Christian : his affections set upon things above as he journeys through this world to the antitypical Canaan.

" Nevertheless my brethren that went up with me made the heart of the people melt : but I wholly followed the Lord my God " (verse 8). His fellows walked by sight instead of faith, and consequently they were occupied with and appalled by the obstacles which stood in the way. Full of distrust themselves, they infected the whole of the congregation with the same, intimidating and discouraging them so far that their spirits sank. But Caleb refused to be influenced by them, yea, boldly withstood them. " I wholly followed the Lord my God " was not the language of presumption, but a plain declaration that he was neither daunted by the power of the enemy nor swayed by the scepticism of his brethren. It signified that on that occasion he had faithfully discharged his duty, remained steadfast in his faith in God, assured that He would enable His people to overcome the mighty sons of Anak. That meaning of his, " I wholly followed the Lord," is made clear by the contrast of Numbers xxxii, 11, where the Lord complained of his unbelieving fellows, " they have not wholly followed Me," and from the fact that He there predicated the same fidelity and perseverance of Joshua. The great value which God set upon His servant's steadfastness appears in His having recorded it in His Word no less than six times : Numbers xiv, 2 ; xxxii, 12 ; Deuteronomy i, 36 ; Joshua xiv, 8, 9, 14.

" And Moses sware on that day, saying, Surely the land whereon thy feet have trodden shall be thine inheritance, and thy children's for ever, because thou hast wholly followed the Lord my God " (verse 9). The sure word of prophecy he had hid—held fast, treasured—in his heart throughout the lengthy interval. It is to be considered that probably most of that generation of Israel would be ignorant of the Divine grant which had been made unto him and his descendants so long before, and therefore Caleb quoted the Lord's promise thereon for their benefit more than Joshua's, so that it might appear that he was not now making any selfish or unreasonable demand. The Divine promise was recorded in Deuteronomy i, 36, and treasured in the mind of Caleb. His object was to prevent this particular part of Palestine being put in the lot with the other portions of the country. He had a definite and valid claim upon the same, and he here insisted upon his right. Since God's own mind concerning it had been plainly made known, then it would be useless to appeal unto His will respecting it via the lot, as in the case of the sections for the tribes.

"And now, behold, the Lord hath kept me alive, as He said, these forty and five years, even since the Lord spake this word unto Moses, while the children of Israel wandered in the wilderness : and now, lo, I am this day fourscore and five years old" (verse 10). What a God-honouring testimony was this ! Passing through all the vicissitudes of Israel's wilderness wanderings, during which so many of his fellows were removed from this scene, engaged in the five years of fighting in Canaan, when no doubt there was often but a step betwixt him and death, Caleb here ascribed his preservation not to " good luck " or " fortune " (heathen terms !), but unto Him " which holdeth our soul in life " (Psalm lxvi, 9). Caleb had something more than a general realization that his times were in God's hands (Psalm xxxi, 15) : his faith had laid hold of a special promise, as his " as He said " plainly shows. He was resting on the word of One who cannot lie—as David, at a later date, relied upon God's changeless veracity : " do as Thou hast said " (II Samuel vii, 25). We are on both sure and comfortable ground, my reader, when we take our stand upon God's promise, *expecting* a fulfilment. Caleb's repeated " and now " was tantamount to his saying, The time has at last arrived for the Lord to make good His engagement.

"As yet I am as strong this day as I was in the day that Moses sent me : as my strength was then, even so is my strength now, for war, both to go out, and to come in" (verse 11). In those words he was forestalling an objection which might be made against his appeal. Should the demurrer be advanced, But you are much too old for such a difficult and dangerous venture as the dispossessing of the giants from the mountainous district of Hebron, that such a strenuous and hazardous task called for a much younger man. Caleb here pressed his physical fitness for the same. The One who had preserved his life throughout the years had also renewed his youth like the eagle's (Psalm ciii, 5). Ah, my reader, God does nothing by halves : when He appoints a man for any particular work, He also equips the worker and furnishes him with everything needful. Not only so, He sustains and animates the heart for the task. Faith inspires resolution and courage, and He who had enabled His servant to hold fast for so long to His promise also removed all hesitation and fear, so that Caleb was just as ready and eager to set about the task which lay before him as he was in the prime of life.

"Now therefore give me this mountain, whereof the Lord spake in that day ; for thou heardest in that day how the Anakims were there, and that the cities were great and fenced : if so be the Lord will be with me, then I shall be able to drive them out, as the Lord said " (verse 12). The second half of this verse is very lovely, yet some have quite misunderstood its force. Though Caleb still retained his vigour, it was not *that* upon which he relied, nor yet upon his military ability and experience ; but instead, upon the Lord. Thus his " if so be the Lord will be with me " was not the language of doubting, but of self-renunciation. He had no confidence in the flesh and felt his own insufficiency. There will not be faith in God, nor even a sincere looking to Him, my reader, while we retain faith in ourselves. Trust in the Lord is ever accompanied by distrust of self. No, Caleb was conscious that the successful accomplishment of the work before him was quite beyond his own powers, but he counted upon the faithfulness of God to undertake for him. Proof was this that the Divine promise was no empty theory to him, but a precious reality. Therein he differed sharply from his unbelieving companions : they were occupied with the power of the enemy and their own impotence ; he with the omnipotent One and the sureness of His word.

"And Joshua blessed him, and gave unto Caleb the son of Jephunneh Hebron for an inheritance" (verse 13). Thus was the promise of God through Moses made, good *by Joshua*. This is very blessed, for it causes us to look beyond the shadow to the substance : the fulfilment of all the Divine promises is in and through the antitypical Joshua. "For all the promises of God in Him [Christ] are yea, and in Him Amen, unto the glory of God by us" (II Cor. i, 20). Since Christ Himself is the end and chief object of all the promises, He has become by His mediatorial character both the channel of supply to all who receive the grace of God in truth and the medium of their responsive praise. To the certified promises thus declared to God's elect, in the person of His Son, the Church now sets the seal of her Amen, affirming thus adoringly to the glory of the Father what the lips of Christ have first spoken to her heart. In Christ we now have by an everlasting covenant of grace whatever good things God spoke aforetime. In the Lord Jesus the very fullness of God dwells, and in that holy humanity which He took upon Him for our sakes. The concentrating of God's mercies in the living and effective Vindicator of His promises—"the Amen, the faithful and true witness" (Rev. iii, 14)—is declared to be "to the glory of God *by us*," because of the praise which He receives from His people as they realize that all is summed up for them in God's Beloved and in their Beloved.

"Hebron therefore became the inheritance of Caleb . . . unto this day, because that he wholly followed the Lord God of Israel. And the name of Hebron before was Kirjath-arba ; which Arba was a great man among the Anakims. And the land had rest from war" (verses 14, 15). Hebron signifies "fellowship," and may have been so named because of the wonderful communion which Abraham had with God there (Gen. xiii, 18, first mention). This is the place above all others which the enemy of souls s eks to prevent God's people occupying. What a suitable place was Hebron for Caleb ! How appropriate an inheritance for the one who (we are once more told) "wholly followed the Lord God of Israel"— who persevered in the performing of his duty, though opposed by ten of his companions and menaced by the whole congregation ; which shows us that the ones and twos who are out and out for God must not expect to be popular, no, not with their brethren. Nevertheless, Hebron or the place of intimate fellowship with God is ever the portion of such. Finally, let it be duly noted that upon Caleb was conferred the honour of the hardest task of all—the overcoming of the mighty sons of Anak. The next chapter tells us, "And Caleb drove thence the three sons of Anak" (xv, 14). Of course he did ! God never fails such a one.

In Joshua xvii, 3, 4, another case is recorded of claim to an individual portion being laid before Joshua, which is in some respects similar to that of Caleb. It was made by the five daughters of Zelophehad, who belonged to the tribe of Manasseh. Those women had received promise through Moses that when Canaan was divided among Israel they should have an inheritance, and now they came before those who had charge of the allotting, making request for the implementing of the same. God's commandment and promise by Moses is recorded in Numbers xxvii, 1-11. These women appeared before what might be termed the supreme court, pointing out that their father was dead and had left no son. Up to that time no legal provision had been made where the male issue had failed, and thus these daughters of Zelophehad, having neither father nor brother, found themselves destitute. Instead of murmuring and mourning over their hard lot, they wisely came before God's servants and asked for arrangement to be made for them to have a portion of their tribe's section. Moses did not presume to answer their inquiry personally, but brought the case before the Lord, and He declared, " thou shalt cause the inheritance of their father to pass unto them."

In Numbers xxxvi we learn that the case of those five women was brought again before Israel's high court. This time it was the chief fathers of the families of Gilead, to which Zelophehad belonged, who appeared. A difficulty was anticipated : should these five women intermarry with other tribes, then their portion would pass out of Manasseh's possessions unto another's, and that would probably occasion future strife and confusion. In reply thereto, a more specific law was enacted : " Let them marry to whom they think best ; only to the family of the tribe of their father shall they marry. So shall not the inheritance of the children of Israel remove from tribe to tribe " (verses 6, 7). It is very blessed to see how the Lord honoured the faith of those women by protecting their interests. At the time when they first appeared before the judges, Israel was in the wilderness ! Canaan had not then been entered, still less conquered and possessed, yet so sure were these women that God would fulfil His promise to give that land unto His people that even then they put in their claim to a portion thereof. As Matthew Henry wittily remarked, " they were *five wise virgins* indeed."

In a striking address made in 1918 on the Virgin Birth, Dr. A. T. Schofield (not the editor of the Scofield Bible) pointed out that but for the above scriptures an insuperable difficulty had stood in the way of Christ's being " the King of the Jews." " Therefore in any case it seems our Lord could not be the inheritor of the throne of David, either through Joseph, for he was not born of Joseph, or through Mary, because a woman could not inherit it ; and but for one remarkable circumstance it would be impossible for Him to be King of the Jews. In fact, the virgin birth in itself would appear to bar Him from the throne." Then the doctor went on to show that the " remarkable circumstance " which removed all difficulty was found in Numbers xxvii, 8, " If a man die, and have no son [as in the case of Heli, the father of Mary], then ye shall cause his inheritance to pass unto his daughter." Thus our Lord, according to the flesh, *had* legal title to inherit the throne of David, while Numbers xxxvi, 6, shows why it was necessary for Mary to be espoused to Joseph. From which we may see that not only in the ceremonial law, but in the civil law of Israel also, God ever had *Christ* before Him !

Tribal Portions

We turn now to those chapters (xv-xix) which offer the least scope to the expositor, the presence of which has probably deterred not a few from attempting to write a connected commentary on this sixth book of the Word. Those chapters contain, for the most part, a geographical description of the different portions of Canaan which were allotted unto Israel's tribes. They consist largely of a list of places, many of which are never referred to again in the Scriptures, and which cannot now be identified ; nor can we be sure, in the majority of instances, of the precise meanings of the names of those towns and villages ; though in those cases where such is obtainable the typical and moral significance thereof is more or less apparent. That nothing has been recorded in the Bible without Divine design must be believed by every reverent heart—the genealogies of I Chronicles i-ix not excepted—and that all is of real value to the people of God is not to be questioned ; yet, so far as we are aware, the Holy Spirit has not yet " opened " their purport and spiritual contents to the Church. Acknowledging our ignorance and refusing to speculate thereon, we can but single out a few of the more prominent details found in this section, and offer some remarks thereon.

" This then was the lot of the tribe of the children of Judah by their families " (xv, 1). The first two of the tribes to have made known to them their allotments were Judah and Joseph : that being detailed here, the other in the next chapter. Upon which Matthew Henry said, " Judah and Joseph were the two sons of Jacob on whom Reuben's forfeited birthright devolved. Judah had the dominion entailed on him, and Joseph the double portion, and therefore the two tribes were first seated : Judah in the southern part of the land of Canaan, and Joseph in the northern part, and on them the other seven did attend, and had their respective lots as appurtenances to these two ; the lots of Benjamin, Simeon and Dan were attendant to Judah, and those of Issachar and Zebulon, Napthtali and Asshur to Joseph. These two were first set up to be provided for, it should seem, before there was such an exact survey of the land as we find afterward [xviii, 9].

" It is probable that the most considerable parts of the northern and southern countries, and those that lay nearest to Gilgal, and which the people were best acquainted with, were first put into two portions, and the lot was cast upon them between these two principal tribes, of the one of which Joshua was, and of the other Caleb, who was the first commissioner in this writ of partition ; and by the decision of that lot the southern country fell to Judah, of which we have an account in this chapter ; and the northern to Joseph, of which we have an account in the two following chapters. And when this was done, there was a more equal dividend (either in quantity or quality) of the remainder among the seven tribes. And this, probably, was intended in that general rule which was given concerning this partition : ' to the more ye shall give the more inheritance, and to the fewer ye shall give the less inheritance : every man's inheritance shall be in the place where his lot falleth ' (Num. xxxiii, 54) : that is, ' Ye shall appoint two greater portions, which shall be determined by lot, to those more numerous tribes of Judah and Joseph, and then the rest shall be lesser portions, to be allotted to the less numerous tribes.' The former was done in Gilgal, the latter in Shiloh." It should also be pointed out that, as the injunction was given that when Israel were on the march " these [i.e. Judah] shall first set forth " (Num. ii, 9), so the assigning of Judah's portion *first* was a prophetic intimation of the future pre-eminence of this tribe.

It is to be observed that the description given of Judah's heritage is broken into at xv, 13, by mention being made of Caleb (who belonged to this tribe) receiving Hebron for his personal portion. This was before us in our last, but a further detail is here recorded which claims our attention. After informing us that he drove thence the three sons of Anak we are told that " Caleb said, He that smiteth Kirjath-sepher, and taketh it, to him will I give Achsah my daughter to wife " (verse 16). This should not be understood as an exhibition of any personal sloth on Caleb's part, still less of fear, but rather as his affording an opportunity for another to obtain some laurels as well as himself. It is to be borne in mind that in the East the father is regarded as having the right to dispose of his daughter, and it is the regular custom for him to select her husband without consulting her—compare I Samuel xvii, 25. Kirjath-sepher was a fortress of the Anakims, one that was difficult of approach, being situated on a hill (note " went up " in verse 15). The offer made by Caleb was an incentive to bravery : he knew that only a man of faith and courage would attack such a place.

In the above we obtain a further insight into Caleb's character and see what a well-balanced one it was : he was not only a man of strong faith, an intrepid warrior, but a dutiful father as well. It was not only that he desired to stir up Israel generally to set about the tasks which still required performing (xvi, 10, shows that some of them had already become slack in their duty), but that he desired to make sure that his daughter obtained a worthy husband. Caleb's challenge was accepted by his own nephew, for we read : "And Othniel the son of Kenez, the brother of Caleb, took it " (verse 17). It is noteworthy that, years later, this same Othniel who acted so admirably and valiantly on this occasion became both a deliverer and a judge in Israel (Judges iii, 9), and, in fact, the first person who presided over the nation after Joshua's death. " It is good for those who are setting out in the world to begin betimes with that which is great and good, that, excelling in service when they are young, they may excel in honour when they are old " (Matthew Henry).

" And he gave him Achsah his daughter to wife " (verse 17). It is to be borne in mind that there was nothing in the Mosaic Law which forbade the marrying of cousins. As others before us have suggested, it is highly probable that Othniel was in love with Achsah before her father made this proposal. It is also likely that Caleb was aware of it and looked favourably upon him, but decided thus to put him to the test before finally committing himself. It was both an honour to wed the daughter of the man who was the chief of his tribe and a great privilege for Othniel to marry into a family so marked by faith and piety, and to be united to one who we cannot doubt had been brought up in the nurture and admonition of the Lord : such a woman is to be desired far above one who is endowed with the riches of this world, or possesses little else than a pretty face.

" And it came to pass, as she came unto him, that she moved him to ask of her father a field : and she lighted off her ass ; and Caleb said unto her, What wouldest thou ? " (verse 18). Here we behold some of the becoming traits which marked the character of Caleb's daughter. The " as she came unto him " means to her husband, her father accompanying them from his house where they would be married. First, her meekness appears in the owning of Othniel as her head—desiring that he should be the one to present her request unto Caleb. Apparently Othniel considered that the request would come better from her direct ; and though contrary to her own inclination she deferred to her husband's judgment. Second, her getting down from her mount betokened her respect and reverence for her father (compare Genesis xxiv, 64, where Rebekah did the same when Isaac approached her), which showed that marriage had not " turned her head " ; she was as ready to honour her parents now as formerly.

Perceiving that his daughter desired to ask him for some favour, Caleb said to her, " What wouldest thou ? " And she answered, " Give me a blessing ; for thou hast given me a southland ; give me also springs of water " (verse 19). We do not understand from the first clause that she meant the paternal benediction, or that he should supplicate Jehovah for a blessing upon her, but rather an inheritance over and above what he had already given her. She desired this bounty because it would add to the comfort of her settlement : teaching us thereby that it is no transgression of the commandment " Thou shalt not covet " to desire those conveniences and comforts which may be obtained in an honest and honourable way. Caleb had already given her some land which was much exposed to the sun and poorly watered : having married according to his orders, she felt he would the more readily grant what she now petitioned him for. Her modesty appears in the simplicity of her request, namely some field with springs of water in it. She might have asked for jewels to adorn her person, or servants to make her lot easier in the home ; instead, she confined herself to bare necessities, for land without water could not be very productive.

"And he gave her the upper springs, and the nether springs," probably bestowing upon her more than she had asked. Plain is the celestial lesson illustrated for us here : if earthly parents are ready to bestow upon their children that which is good for them, how much readier is our heavenly Father to give both spiritual and temporal blessings when we ask Him in faith ! This is indeed a lovely domestic picture, and each of its features claims our admiration and imitation. Here we see the wife in subjection to her husband, and he declining to take advantage of his authority. When husbands and wives mutually advise and jointly agree about that which is for the common good of the family, the domestic machinery will run smoothly. Here we see a married woman despising not her father when he was old, and she lost not by honouring him. Here we see how wise parents will not deem that lost which they bestow upon their children for their real advantage, especially when they are dutiful ones. " When the character of parents, the education of their children, and the children's consequent prudent and pious conduct combine, there is the fairest prospect that they will be settled in life to the mutual comfort and advantage of all the parties concerned " (T. Scott).

There is one other detail recorded here of the tribe of Judah, and it is in marked contrast with the above. "As for the Jebusites the inhabitants of Jerusalem, the children of Judah could not drive them out : but the Jebusites dwell with the children of Judah at Jerusalem unto this day " (xv, 63). It is to be recalled that in the tenth chapter we saw how that the king of Jerusalem persuaded four of his fellow monarchs or chieftains to join him in launching an attack upon Gibeon (which made peace with Israel), and how that Joshua completely vanquished their combined forces, slew the five kings (verse 26), and took all their land (verse 42). Judges i, 8, supplies an additional detail, informing us. " Now the children of Judah *had* fought against Jerusalem, and had taken it, and smitten it with the edge of the sword, and set the city on fire." However, it would appear that during the next few years, while Israel were occupied in conquering other parts of the country, the Jebusites recovered the fort of mount Sion at least, which remained in their hands till the time of David (II Samuel v, 7). Matthew Henry suggested : " It may, therefore, be justly looked upon as the punishment of their neglect to conquer other cities which God had given them, that they were so long kept out of this." So today, if the Lord's people be slack in performing their duties, they need not be surprised if some important centres of Christendom remain under the control of the enemy, having the management of the same—how many of the denominational boards, seminaries, etc., are now governed by modern Jebusites !

" And the lot of the children of Joseph fell from Jordan by Jericho, unto," etc. (xvi, 1). The order of procedure among the tribes of Israel was always Judah first, the sons of Joseph second, which is in full accord with that parenthetical but important statement in I Chronicles v, 1, 2. " Now the sons of Reuben the firstborn of Israel (for he was the firstborn ; but, forasmuch as he defiled his father's bed, his birthright was given unto the sons of Joseph the son of Israel :

and the genealogy is not to be reckoned after the birthright. For Judah prevailed above his brethren, and of him came the chief ruler ; but the birthright was Joseph's)." As Ellicott pointed out, " Accordingly, in the division of the land of Canaan under Joshua, there are three successive stages. First, the settlement of the tribe of Judah in the strongholds in the south of Palestine. Second, the estating of Ephraim and Manasseh in the centre of the country, and in some strong positions in the north. Third, the settlement of the remaining tribes, so as to fill up the gaps between Judah and Joseph, and also upon the outskirts of their territory, so as to be, as it were, under the shelter of their wings."

Reuben's portion was much inferior to that of Joseph, for it lay on the wilderness side of the Jordan (xiii, 7, 15-21), separating them from the tribes on the western side, thereby exposing them to be attacked more easily by enemies. As a matter of fact, this tribe, with that of Gad. (which adjoined it) was sorely stricken by Hazael (II Kings x, 32, 33), and afterwards carried into captivity twenty years before the general seizure of the ten tribes by the king of Assyria (I Chron. v, 26) ; whereas Joseph and his posterity were highly favoured in their lot, for their position lay in the very heart of the land of Canaan, extending from the Jordan in the east to the Mediterranean in the west. It is therefore very striking indeed to note how that on the one hand we behold in Reuben's heritage and its history a solemn demonstration of God's " visiting the sins of the fathers upon the children unto the third and fourth generation of them that hate " Him ; and on the other hand we see in the case of Joseph's posterity a blessed exemplification of the Divine promise " showing mercy unto thousands of them that love Me and keep My commandments " (Exodus xx, 4, 5). The disposings of Divine providence are not capricious or arbitrary, but regulated by moral and spiritual considerations which accord with the principle of sowing and reaping.

" And the separate cities for the children of Ephraim were among the inheritance of the children of Manasseh, all the cities with their villages " (xvi, 9). This was because the tribe of Ephraim was now much more numerous than that of Manasseh. Matthew Henry appropriately called attention to the fact that "though when the tribes were numbered in the plains of Moab, Manasseh had got the start of Ephraim in number, for Manasseh was then fifty-two thousand and Ephraim but thirty-two thousand (Num. xxvi, 34, 37) ; yet, by the time they were well settled in Canaan, the hands were crossed again (Gen. xlviii, 13, 14) and the blessing of Moses was verified : ' They are the ten thousands of Ephraim, and these are the thousands of Manasseh.' " Since the Ephraimites were much more plentiful than the Manassites, additional cities were given them besides " the lot " which fell to them. Those cities were in the heritage of Manasseh, God having assigned them more than their own needs required. No doubt that was to *test them,* to afford an opportunity of showing kindness to their brethren, by giving of their abundance to those who lacked. This is one reason why Providence so orders things that " ye have the poor always with you " (Matt. xxvi, 11) : note that " always "—sure intimation that Socialism, the Welfare State, will never become universally and permanently established.

" And they drave not out the Canaanites that dwelt in Gezer " (xvi, 10), which marked the boundary of this tribe, and was close to the sea (verse 3). Their failure to do so was much worse than that of Judah to recapture Jerusalem (xv, 63), for *they* made an attempt to do so, whereas *these* did not. No specific reason is given for their wanting in duty, whether it was because of cowardice, slothfulness, or something else ; but the fact remains that they disobeyed the commandment in Deuteronomy xx, 16. There is no intimation that these

Canaanites renounced their idolatry and became worshippers of Jehovah. But the second half of the verse seems plainly to indicate that their disobedience was due to the spirit of greed : " But the Canaanites dwell among the Ephraimites unto this day, and serve under tribute." Since the Emphraimites were strong enough to subject the Canaanites and compel them to play tribute, no excuse can be made for allowing such to live with them. They considered their financial gain more than submission to God or the good of their country, which was in keeping with their general character—compare Hosea xii, 8. They soon followed the ways of those heathen, and became idolators themselves (Judges xvii, 1-5). The Canaanites continued to dwell in Gezer until the days of Solomon, when the king of Egypt took and gave it to his daughter who had married Solomon (I Kings ix, 16, 17).

Chapter 17

INDOLENCE IN FINAL POSSESSION
Joshua 17:1—19:51

The Danger of Partial Victory

Before turning to the next chapter an incident recorded in Joshua xvii requires our attention. It may be recalled that the fourteenth chapter closed with the words, " And the land had rest from war." At first sight that seems to be a blessed statement, but in view of several later ones it should rather be regarded as the striking of an ominous note. The fact is that Israel had, temporarily at least, become weary of well-doing, and were resting on their oars, for they had failed to complete the task which God had assigned them. There were many places yet unsubdued, numerous companies of the Canaanites which were still unconquered. That resting from war was fraught with evil consequences, for soon after we are told, "As for the Jebusites the inhabitants of Jerusalem, the children of Judah could not drive them out " (xv, 63). And again, it is recorded of the Ephraimites, " they drave not out the Canaanites that dwelt in Gezer : but the Canaanites dwell among the Ephraimites unto this day, and serve under tribute " (xvi, 10). And once more, " yet the children of Manasseh could not drive out the inhabitants of those cities ; but the Canaanites would dwell in the land " (xvii, 12). Sad blemishes were those in the account given of the general success of the nation.

The above failures are to be accounted for by God's *withholding* of His power and blessing upon their efforts. And why did He not show Himself strong on their behalf ? Because they had failed in their duty, for, instead of finishing the work which the Lord had given them to do, they became slack and took their ease, and later, like poor Samson when he awoke out of his sleep, said, " I will go out as at other times," but " wist not that the Lord was departed from him " (Judges xvi, 20) ; thus it happened with them—they were shorn of their strength. For God to have given success unto those Israelites would be countenancing their indolence. Never does He place a premium upon slothfulness, but, instead, leaves those who yield thereto to suffer the painful effects thereof. The lessons *for us* to learn therefrom are obvious. God grants His people no furloughs in the " good fight of faith " (I Tim. vi, 12) to which He has called them, and should they take one, then their enemies will inevitably prove too strong, nor will the Captain of their salvation fight their battles for them. Our commission is, " Watch ye, stand fast in the faith, quit you like men, be strong " (I Cor. xvi, 13), and if we heed not, most unpleasant will be the outcome.

It is important to note carefully *the order* of those four precepts, for the first three must be obeyed in order to the realization of the fourth. Unless we be vigilant in guarding against the temptations and dangers on every side, are faithful in holding the truth of the Gospel both doctrinally and practically, are undismayed and undaunted by those who oppose us—conducting ourselves boldly and bravely—we shall have no strength with which to overcome our foes. Nor is there to be any cessation in the discharge of those duties : the Divine command is " always abounding in the work of the Lord " (I Cor. xv, 58) i.e. striving against sin, resisting the Devil, bringing forth the fruits of holiness. But note well the precise point at which the great failure of Joshua xiv, 15, occurred : it was immediately following the most notable successes which had attended their arms, so that they probably thought they were now entitled to a respite. Here too the lesson is plain for us : it is right after some signal victory which grace has given us over our lusts that we are most in danger—tempted to relax our efforts. Ah, my reader, forget not that it is the " *fool* " who says " take thine ease " (Luke xii, 19), whereas God enjoins us, " Let not thine hands be slack " (Zeph. iii, 16).

In xvii, 14-18, an incident is recorded which afforded a further opportunity for Joshua to display yet another striking quality of his character. There we read of the children of Joseph coming to Israel's leader with a complaint : " Why hast thou given me but one lot and one portion to inherit, seeing I am a great people, forasmuch as the Lord hath blessed me hitherto ? " (verse 14). The tribe of Joseph was, of course, a *double* one, comprising the descendants of both Ephraim and Manasseh, nevertheless we consider that avowal of their greatness had reference to something more than their numerical strength, namely their honourable parentage—their being the descendants of the man whom Pharaoh had made lord of Egypt—and thus it was the breathing of pride. This is borne out by the subsequent history of this tribe, in the light of which their complaint unto Joshua was thoroughly characteristic of the haughty spirit that possessed them. Thus we behold their arrogance again in their murmuring against Gideon (Judges viii, 1), in the conduct of Jephthah (Judges xi, 9, 30, 31), and later still in the days of David they were constantly asserting their claim to superiority in Israel without exhibiting any qualification for it.

"And Joshua answered them, If thou be a great people, then get thee up to the wood country, and cut down for thyself there in the land of the Perizzites and of the giants, if mount Ephraim be too narrow for thee " (verse 15). Thus did Joshua turn their argument against themselves, rebuking their pride and discontent, as well as their unbelief and indolence, for there was plenty of room for their expansion if they possessed the necessary enterprise and courage. Ellicott pointed out that it is plain from what is here stated that a large part of the country of Palestine then consisted of uncleared forest, that the inhabitants of that district were far fewer than those in the valley of Esdrealon and of the territory assigned to Judah in the south. Also that this fact justifies the strategy of the attack of Israel upon *the centre* of the country, so that the forces of the Canaanites were necessarily divided, and thus Israel could strike first with their whole force at the southern armies, and then turn round upon the enemies in the north. This serves to explain the ease with which they set up the Law at Ebal (viii, 30) at the commencement of the invasion, and the selection of Shiloh for their capital afterwards.

" And the children of Joseph said, The hill is not enough for us : and all the Canaanites that dwell in the land of the valley have chariots of iron, both they who are of Beth-shean and her towns, and they who are of the valley of Jezreel " (verse 16). Here we behold their covetousness, for xvii, 5, informs us that " there fell ten portions to Manasseh, beside the land of Gilead and Bashan, which were on the other side Jordan," while another and separate inheritance had been allotted unto their brethren the Ephraimites. But though they had been given the largest share of Canaan they were not satisfied, while the reference they made unto the " chariots of iron " possessed by the Canaanites, who occupied the adjacent valleys, at once revealed the unbelief and timidity of their hearts and disproved their pretensions to being " a great people." See here again, my reader, the evil results of allowing ourselves an intermission from the warfare to which the Christian is called : as surely as he ceases therein and takes his ease, so will a spirit of discontent with his lot come upon him, and so too will unbelief occupy him with the might of his enemies and dispirit him.

" And Joshua spake unto the house of Joseph, to Ephraim and to Manasseh, saying, Thou art a great people, and hast great power ; thou shalt not have one lot only : but the mountain shall be thine ; for it is a wood, and thou shalt cut it down : and the outgoings of it shall be thine : for thou shalt drive out the Canaanites, though they have iron chariots, and though they be strong " (verses 17, 18). We do not regard that as the language of satire, but rather as pressing upon them the discharge of their responsibility, and calling upon them to trust in the Lord and go forward in His name. Joshua pointed out that there were extensive tracts of wooded country which could be cleared for agricultural use, so that, if they continued to multiply, land would be available for their families. True there was the menace of the powerfully armed Canaanites in the immediate vicinity, but if they bestirred themselves and performed their duty, looking to the Lord for protection and help, they might assuredly count upon His enabling them to drive out those who then possessed that land which He had given unto the seed of Abraham, and be granted strength to vanquish all their enemies. Thus from Joshua's reply it is clear that they were lacking in diligence and enterprise.

There can be little doubt that the Ephraimites and Manassehites expected to receive preferential treatment from Joshua, since he himself belonged to the tribe of Ephraim (Num. xiii, 8) ; but Joshua refused to show partiality unto his brethren, thereby demonstrating his fidelity unto the commission Jehovah had given him. Blessed is it to behold in that refusal still another adumbration in the character of his Antitype, for when the Saviour was asked to assign the seats on His right hand and on His left unto those who were nearest and dearest to Him (James and John), He declined to show any favouritism (Matt. xx, 20-23). In his *Practical Observations* on this passage Thomas Scott well remarked, " Alas, professing Christians are often more disposed to murmur, envy and covet, than to be content, thankful, and ready to distribute. Indeed, we are more prone to grasp at what belongs to others, than to manage our own to the best advantage ; and many complain of poverty, and encroach upon the benevolence of others, because they rebel against the sentence of Divine justice, ' Thou shalt eat thy bread in the sweat of thy brow.'

" Men excuse themselves from labour on any pretence, and nothing serves the purpose better than having rich and powerful relations, though by providing for them, these are often partial and unfaithful in disposing of those funds with which they are entrusted for the public benefit. But there is more real kindness in pointing out to men the advantages within their reach, that they may be excited to improve them, than in gratifying their indolence and profusion. True religion gives no sanction to these evils : ' we commanded,' says the apostle, ' that if any man would not work, neither should he eat ' ; and many of our *cannots* are only the language of sloth, which magnifies every difficulty into an impossibility, and represents every danger as inevitable destruction. This is especially the case in our spiritual work and warfare ; but even our professed relation to the Captain of the Lord's host will not avail us if we be indolent and self-indulgent. Our very complaints that comforts are withheld, frequently result from negligence and fear of the cross ; and when convinced that we can do nothing, we are apt to sit still and attempt nothing." Such has been poor human nature throughout the ages : either spurred on by the feverish energy of the flesh, so that we run without being sent, or lazing and repining instead of doing with our might what God has bidden us to do.

"And the whole congregation of the children of Israel assembled together at Shiloh, and set up the tabernacle of the congregation there. And the land was subdued before them " (xviii, 1). The commentators are unanimous in supposing that this moving of Israel's camp and headquarters was by Divine appointment. They surmise that Joshua had received some message from Jehovah, either direct or through the Urim and Thummim of the high priest, bidding him remove the tabernacle from Gilgal to Shiloh ; and they also point out the advantages of this new location. Gilgal was at the extremity of Palestine, being situated on the bank of the Jordan ; whereas Shiloh was in the heart of the land, and thus would be much more handy for the males to visit (Deut. xvi, 16) after the tribes had departed to their separate sections. Personally, we consider that is assuming too much. There is not the slightest hint that God had given any orders for them to leave Gilgal, where they had been encamped ever since their supernatural entrance into Canaan, and we regard the absence of any record of God's revealing His will for them to do so as ominous. It seems to us much more likely that this move was dictated by what the flesh terms " prudential considerations "— their own convenience. " Shiloh was in the lot of Ephraim, the tribe to which Joshua belonged, and it was expedient that the sanctuary should be near the residence of the chief governor " (Scott). But if *that* was the reason which prompted Joshua to act, then he was leaning to his own understanding, instead of having his paths directed by the Lord (Prov. iii, 5, 6).

Gilgal was the place of circumcision (v, 9)—typically the mortifying of the flesh and separation from the world—and so long as Israel returned thither after each campaign the power and blessing of the Lord rested upon them. They should, therefore, have been very slow in leaving Gilgal, even though what it signified spiritually was very unpleasant to nature. Nothing is said of their waiting upon the Lord for guidance, no mention made of their seeking His mind via the high priest. Let it be carefully borne in mind that what is here said in xviii, 1, follows right after the record of a number of sad failures. Observe too that the Holy Spirit does not here designate the sacred tent " the house of the Lord " as He did in vi, 24, or " the Lord's tabernacle " as in xxii, 19, but merely " the tabernacle," as though to indicate that He did not endorse or associate Himself with the move made—cf. " the Jews' passover " and " a feast of the Jews " (John ii, 13 ; v, 1), rather than " the Lord's passover " (Exodus xii, 11) and a feast " of the Lord " (Lev. xxiii, 2). It is also solemnly significant that in the opening chapters of Judges (which record Israel's failures after the death of Joshua) we are told " there arose another generation after them, which *knew not the Lord* " (ii, 10), so apparently they had forsaken the angel of His presence, who had remained at their true base.

During several generations of Israel's spiritual poverty and powerlessness the tabernacle remained at Shiloh (I Samuel iv, 3), but in centuries later, when God through Elijah and Elisha was granting a revival unto Israel, those prophets made Gilgal and not Shiloh their headquarters (II Kings ii, 1), the Holy Spirit thereby intimating that if in a dark day of declension we make the place of circumcision (devotedness unto God) our camping ground or centre, then the Divine blessing will be upon us. But *Gilgal* is not at all popular, making demands which are unwelcome to flesh and blood. Thus in the type itself : Gilgal lay at the very extremity of the land, a long and tiresome journey being entailed for the men of war to return to camp, and therefore a more convenient headquarters— easy to the flesh—would be far more acceptable. The commentators dwell upon the fact that " Shiloh " was one of the names by which the Messiah was fore-announced (Gen. xlix, 10), and conclude that it was with an eye to Him that Israel so designated the place to which the tabernacle was now taken and erected. But we very much question such a view, for xviii, 1, reads as though this place was already known as Shiloh when they arrived there, and not that *they* gave it such a name on this occasion. The word itself means "rest," and *that* was what appealed to them now that so much of Canaan had been subdued.

We have pointed out above that what is recorded in xviii, 1, comes right after several marked failures on the part of three of Israel's tribes, and now immediately following it we find Joshua upbraiding seven of the other tribes, saying " How long are ye slack to go to possess the land, which the Lord God of your fathers hath given you ? " (verse 3) ! Thus, the whole context is directly *against* a favourable construction being placed on this mention of moving their headquarters to Shiloh. Instead, we consider that they acted precipitately, that they walked by sight instead of by faith, and consulted too much their own convenience. Viewed thus, there is pointed another practical lesson unto which *we* do well to take heed. Not only is it our bounden duty, but also for our good both spiritually and temporally, that we heed the Divine precept " he that believeth shall not make haste " (Isaiah xxviii, 16). To act by impulse or passion is unworthy of a rational creature, yet it is only by definite prayer, constant watchfulness and strict self-discipline that we shall be preserved from the frenzied spirit of this foolish generation, which makes a god of speed.

More specifically, the above incident cautions us to be slow when contemplating *a change of our location*. Only too often the Lord's people are regulated in this matter by material considerations rather than by spiritual ones, thinking more of improving their position than of glorifying God ; and many of them are made to smart for their pains. " Ponder the path of thy feet " (Prov. iv, 26) is wisdom's counsel, and failure to do so results in many a fall. Those who act hastily usually have reason to repent at their leisure. " The prudent man looketh well to his going " (Prov. xiv, 15). The Christian should do more than that : " Commit thy way unto the Lord ; trust also in Him ; and He shall bring it to pass ! " Nor is that all : " Rest in the Lord, and wait patiently for Him " (Psalm xxxvii, 5, 7) to make His way plain before your face, and remember that He guides us a step at a time, rather than making evident the whole of our path at once. Lean not unto your own understanding, nor confer with flesh and blood : instead, beg the Lord to work patience in you, and let your attitude be that of David's, " My soul, wait thou *only* upon God ; for my expectation is from Him " (Psalm lxii, 5). " The way of the righteous [the one whose heart is right with God] *is made plain* " (Prov. xv, 19) : until it be so, remain where you are.

Indolence

Not a very appealing title for an article ! Quite so, but the Bible does not flatter human nature, nor should God's servant do so. However unpleasant, realities should be faced, and not shunned or denied. But though our theme be unattractive, it is surely a timely one. Does not indolence stare us in the face on every side ? Is there not a spirit of sloth and apathy apparent in all classes ? Has there ever been such a generation as ours for loathing work and loving pleasure ? The expression " organized labour " has become almost synonymous with " the shirking of duty " : it is a holding out of the nation to ransom in order to extract the maximum amount of money for the minimum expenditure of energy. On the other hand, any fair-minded man who is really acquainted with the social and economic conditions which prevailed a century ago must acknowledge that, because of the merciless greed of far too many employers, labour was virtually forced to organize itself to secure bare justice. But human nature being what it is, the pendulum has now swung to the opposite extreme, so that in many cases the employer can no longer obtain a fair day's work for a fair day's pay.

As the Lord God informed man at the beginning, one of the consequences of his falling into sin was, " in the sweat of thy face shalt thou eat bread, till thou return unto the ground " (Gen. iii, 19)—a sentence from which men have sought to escape by their " labour-saving " devices : generally to the promotion of indolence, the impairing of health, and often the loss of life. Yet it is a mistake to suppose that all work has been entailed by the fall : not so. In his sinless condition man was put into the garden of Eden " to dress it and to keep it " (Gen. ii, 15). Whereas work was then a pleasure and easy, now it is distasteful and burdensome. Never more so than in our day, when shorter hours and bigger pay is the demand—much of the pay being spent not in wholesome re-creation, but in injurious dissipation. And how few there are who realize and recognize that this manual and industrial blight is traceable to a spiritual and *religious evil*. As we have pointed out more than once, social conditions are the repercussions of ecclesiastical ones ; the state of the world is largely a reflection of the state of the churches. As the breakdown of parental authority in the home was preceded by lack of discipline in the assembly, the disregard of law in the state by the jettisoning of God's Law by the pulpit, so the apathy of artisans is but a shadowing forth of the indolence of the majority of professing Christians.

It is true that perfection has never been found among the Lord's people, yet a relative healthiness and vigour *have* frequently marked them. But during the past century there has been a steady and noticeable deterioration in spirituality and a sad decline in practical godliness. Power has diminished, love has cooled, less and less of the fruit of the Spirit and works of righteousness has been produced. Instead of " always abounding in the work of the Lord " (rendering universal obedience unto Him), the majority of those bearing the name of Christ were " at ease in Zion." Instead of going forth to meet the Bridegroom with lamps trimmed and burning, the wise virgins, equally with the foolish ones, slumbered and slept. Instead of running the way of God's commandments (Psalm cxix, 32), too many sat still; waiting for God to " apply " the promises to their hearts. Instead of engaging in aggressive evangelism, most of the churches petted and pampered their own members. Instead of contending earnestly in the world for the Faith, other churches turned aside to bitter wrangling and profitless contentions among themselves. The Lord's cause languished, and Satan was well pleased.

Among the contributing causes which have produced and promoted a generation of spiritual sluggards may be mentioned the following. First, the slackness of preachers. An ever-increasing number of men who sought a soft and easy job were attracted to the ministry, and few indeed burned the midnight oil in their studies and spent themselves in the service of Christ. Second, unfaithful preaching, where there was an entirely one-sided emphasis : a concentrating upon blessings and privileges and a neglecting of duties and obligations, a magnifying of the gifts of Divine grace, but a minimizing of the requirements of God's holiness. Third, the inculcation and encouragement of a spirit of fatalism, through failing to preserve the balance of truth between God's sovereignty and man's responsibility, between human ability and accountability, with the result that a race of do-nothings was produced—waiting for God to give them more grace, instead of using what He had already bestowed. Fourth, being too readily discouraged by the difficulties in the tasks assigned by God, walking too much by sight rather than faith, their zeal abating because they could perceive so little fruit produced. It is not without good reason that the Holy Spirit repeated in II Thessalonians iii, 13, the exhortation of Galatians vi, 9 : " *Be not weary* in well doing " !

"And there remained among the children of Israel seven tribes, which had not yet received their inheritance " (xviii, 2). Why was this ? Because some Divine decree had blocked the way ? Because " God's time " for them to do so had not yet arrived ? No indeed, from a very different cause. It was due to their own indifference. The immediate sequel makes it very evident that there was no unwillingness on God's part : the indisposition was in them. Thus, this statement is more than an explanatory reference, namely a word of reproach. In view of what is recorded in xv, 63, and xvi, 9, 10, we see how infectious is the spirit of sloth : the evil which affected Judah and Ephraim had spread to the remaining tribes. "A little leaven leaveneth the whole lump," more especially so where the leaders are involved : when the principal tribes of men be dilatory, those of lower rank will quickly emulate them. These tribes were heedless of their privileges, too unconcerned to avail themselves of their advantages.

"And Joshua said unto the children of Israel, How long are ye slack to go to possess the land, which the Lord God of your fathers hath given you ? " (verse 3). Thus did their leader reprove them for not bestirring themselves and securing their portions of Canaan. Such a reproof supplies confirmation of our remarks on the previous verse : it was due entirely to their own laziness, and not to anything in God, that they were not yet in happy possession of their possessions. True, the language of Joshua did not signify that those tribes could have occupied their portions before the same had been assigned them by the lot, but rather that they were to blame for not applying to the high court of Israel for the same. They had witnessed the allotments of the other two and a half tribes, yet had been too unconcerned to ask for theirs. This laxity was not confined to a single tribe, but had, like a dry rot, spread through the body politic. Not only is such an evil very contagious, but when it has gripped a person or people it cannot be easily and quickly thrown off, as Joshua's " how long ? " shows.

How like the vast majority of modern church members were those Israelites ! They had crossed the Jordan and set foot in Canaan, but they had become slack and failed to make their own the fair prospects before them. In like manner, countless thousands make a profession, join the Church, and, imagining that their sins have been forgiven and their souls delivered from the wrath to come, are satisfied with their case and complacently rest on their oars. They make no conscience of mortifying their lusts, no serious efforts to perfect holiness in the fear of the Lord, no progress in the Christian life. They are drones, yea, stumbling-blocks to those who seek to be diligent in making their calling and election sure. They are deceived by Satan. Persuaded that they were saved some time in the past, they delude themselves into thinking that, however slack they be in resisting the Devil and overcoming the world, they are eternally secure. They shirk the cross, yet imagine the crown is sure. They engage not in the good fight of faith, yet suppose they have laid hold of eternal life. They do not make the pleasing and obeying of God their daily concern, yet think to obtain the reward of the inheritance.

The fatal mistake made by so many is to think that, once assured their names are written in heaven, they may, with complete safety to themselves, lapse into a state of utter carelessness. Whereas, so long as he remains in this world, the Christian is required to " continue in the faith grounded and settled, and be not moved away from the hope of the gospel " (Col. i, 23), to take heed that there be not in him an evil heart of unbelief in departing from the living God, and be on his guard against being hardened through the deceitfulness of sin (Heb. vi, 12, 13), to work out his own salvation with fear and trembling (Phil. ii, 12), and to hearken unto the solemn warning of Christ, " No man, having put his hand to the plough, and looking back, is fit for the kingdom of God " (Luke ix, 62). It is he who " endureth unto the end " that shall be saved (Matt. xxiv, 13), and not those who yield to their lusts and tempt Christ (I Cor. x, 10, 7-9). Christians are called upon to build up themselves on their most holy faith (Jude 20), and that is a work which demands labour and industry. "' For if ye live after the flesh, ye shall die : but if ye through the Spirit do mortify the deeds of the body, ye shall live " (Romans viii, 13).

" How long are ye slack to go to possess the land ? " No longer meeting with any open opposition, they had settled down to rest, though more than half of Israel had not yet obtained their inheritance. Those Israelites were " too well pleased with their present condition, liked well enough to live in a body together, had no mind to be scattered abroad. The spoil of the cities they had taken served them to live plentifully for the present, and they banished the thoughts of time to come. They were slothful : it may be they wished the thing done, but had no spirit to set about it or move toward the doing of it, though it was so much for their own advantage. The countries that remained to be divided lay at a distance, and some parts of them in the hands of the Canaanites. If they go to take possession of them, the cities must be built or repaired, they must drive their flocks and herds a great way, and carry their wives and children to strange places ; and this will not be done without great care and pains, and breaking through hardships " (condensed from Henry). Again we say, how we like unto their religious descendants : more than fifty per cent of professing Christians fail to fix their affections on things above and continually set themselves to the appropriation and enjoyment of them.

And Joshua said, " Give out from among you three men for each tribe, and I will send them, and they shall rise, and go through the land, and describe it according to the inheritance of them ; and they shall come again to me " (verse 4). Once more we see that there was a human side, as well as a Divine one, to this important transaction. This detail also serves to illustrate, and in a clear definite manner, the important truth that the fact of God's sovereignty (in the " lot ") does not set aside the exercise of human responsibility : *they* were required to discharge their moral agency and act intelligently. Alas, how many hyper-Calvinists have sought to excuse their apathy by perverting and sheltering behind the Divine decrees ! How fearfully deceitful is the human heart in persuading not a few that they are displaying a commendable spirit of humility and meekness in " waiting God's time " before they act, when instead they are guilty of shirking their duty. There is a terrible amount of humbuggery under a seemingly pious guise. There is no unwillingness on God's part to give : the unwillingness to seek and take is always on our side. Then let us be honest, and place the blame where it belongs.

Joshua did not wait for a reply from the people to his reproving question, " How long are ye slack ? " but at once set them upon their duty. In the injunction which he gave them we may perceive again that blessed *balance* which marks all the ways of God and of His servants when directed by Him—in this instance, between the exercise of *their* freedom and the discharge of their responsibility (in " give " [or " choose "] out from among you three men for each tribe ") and the acting of *his* authority : " and I will send them." The spiritual lesson for us therein is that the Christian is not to engage in any self-appointed tasks, but be directed in his service by the authoritative instructions of the antitypical Joshua. Their leader did not take it upon him to appoint the different individuals who were to serve in this matter, but left the selecting of them to the tribes ; but when chosen, *he* gave them their commission. The same principle is to be observed under Christianity : " look *ye* out among you seven men of honest report, full of the Holy Spirit and wisdom, whom *we* may appoint [by setting them] over this business " (Acts vi, 3).

Though Joshua set these men to work, yet it was far from being either a difficult or an unpleasant task which he assigned them : " they shall rise and go through the land, and describe it according to the inheritance of them ; and they shall come again to me. And they shall divide it into seven parts : Judah shall abide in their coast on the south, and the house of Joseph shall abide in their coasts on the north. Ye shall therefore describe the land into seven parts, and bring the description hither to me, that I may cast lots for you here before the Lord our God " (verses 4-7). It was virtually an appeal to their cupidity, a stirring of them up to recognize their advantages and privileges. It was a project by which they might behold for themselves what a goodly inheritance God had given them : By thus surveying the same, they would obtain a better knowledge of what awaited them, and then they would be more disposed, to bestir themselves and take possession thereof. If the believer's faith were more occupied with the " far more exceeding and eternal weight of glory," then he would be less dispirited by his " light affliction, which is but for a moment " (II Cor. iv, 17). They were not to encroach upon the portions of Judah and Joseph, but rather to confine their attention unto what was available to them. Thus a spirit of covetousness was disallowed.

"And the men went and passed through the land, and described it by cities into seven parts in a book, and came again to Joshua to the host at Shiloh. And Joshua cast lots for them in Shiloh before the Lord : and there Joshua divided the land unto the children of Israel according to their divisions " (verses 9, 10). Aroused from their stupor, shamed by their leader's rebuke, they performed his bidding. As he had given them orders (verses 4, 8), they delivered the results of their commission not to their tribes, but to himself—just as the disciples made their report unto Christ (Luke x, 17), and as each of us must yet render an account unto Him (Romans xiv, 12). From this incident it seems clear that while the relative positions or general locations of the tribes were determined by the " lot," yet the proportion of land assigned to each one was decided (in some measure) by other considerations : as xvii, 17, 18, shows, the lot did not preclude the exercise of individual enterprise and industry to improve the same—as everlasting glory is sure to all the redeemed, yet the degree thereof will be decided by their own zeal and fidelity.

Final Possession

In our last we dwelt upon the rebuke by Israel's leader unto those seven tribes which were slack in going up to possess that land which the Lord God of their fathers had given them. How that he bade them appoint three men of each tribe to go and make a thorough survey of those sections of Canaan which had not yet been distributed. They were required to furnish something after the order of a map, supplying a detailed description of the country, fully sectionalized, and return unto the commander with their report. They duly performed their task : " the men went and passed through the land, and described it by cities into seven parts in a book, and came again to Joshua to the host at Shiloh." And we are told, " And Joshua cast lots for them in Shiloh before the Lord : and there Joshua divided the land unto the children of Israel according to their divisions " (xviii, 9, 10). The order of their allotments accorded neither with their seniority nor with their numerical strength.

It is to be borne in mind that two and a half of the tribes, namely the Reubenites, the Gaddites, and half of Manasseh, had been assigned their places and portions by Moses on the eastern side of the Jordan (Num. xxxii, 33), and in Joshua xiii the boundaries of the same had been carefully defined and stated. After Caleb had put in his lawful claim to mount Hebron, and had been granted the same, the tribes of Judah, Joseph, and the second half of Manasseh were given their allotments, a full enumeration of the places which they were to occupy being furnished in Joshua xv, xvi and xvii ; at which we have already glanced. What was done for them by Eleazer and Joshua at Gilgal was now done for their fellows at Shiloh. We shall not attempt any detailed examination of their respective territories, for there is little in the geographical description which lends itself to the making of edifying comments thereon. On the other hand, it would be improper for us to ignore the same entirely. We shall therefore content ourselves with an occasional remark thereon.

First, "And the lot of the tribe of the children of Benjamin came up according to their families : and the coast of their lot came forth between the children of Judah and the children of Joseph " (xviii, 11). Two striking predictions had been made concerning this tribe, which, though the one almost appears to clash with the other, were manifestly fulfilled, as the verses now before us and the subsequent history of this tribe demonstrate. The earlier one was made by dying Jacob : " Benjamin shall ravin as a wolf ; in the morning he shall devour the prey, and at night he shall divide the spoil " (Gen. xlix, 27). It is evident from this language that the patriarch followed not his natural inclinations on this occasion, for Benjamin was his youngest and most dearly beloved son. No, it was under Divine impulse that he uttered this remarkable prophecy. Yet it is to be observed that while the wolf is characterized mainly by its ferociousness it is also marked in its fortitude and courage. Benjamin was indeed the fiercest and most warlike of the tribes. The reference to what he should do " in the morning " and " at night " intimates that there is a distinct reference here to both the earlier and later history of the tribe.

The fierceness and cruelty of the men belonging to this tribe appeared conspicuously in the horrid treatment which they meted out to the Levite's concubine. Their warlike character and ability and tenacity in fighting were seen in their singly withstanding the combined forces of all the other tribes in two pitched battles, in one of which 20,000 of them defeated the opposing army of 400,000, and later refused to yield until they were almost completely destroyed (Judges xix, 14-30 ; xx, 12-14). King Saul, who so fiercely persecuted David, was of this tribe. Other examples of their fierceness and valour are found in II Samuel ii, 15, 16 ; I Chronicles viii, 40 ; x, 2 ; II Chronicles xvii, 17. In their later history Benjamin allied himself to Judah, and thus " divided the spoil," sharing in their privileges. Esther and Mordecai were also of this tribe, and through them the enemies of Israel were destroyed. But the most renowned and honourable of them all was Saul of Tarsus (Phil. iii, 5), and most remarkably were the terms of Jacob's prophecy made good in him, for in the morning of his career, when persecuting the early Christians, he ravened as a wolf ; but at the close, by his evangelistic labours, he delivered the Devil's prey.

The later prediction concerning this tribe was made through Moses : " Of Benjamin he said, The beloved of the Lord shall dwell in safety by him ; and the Lord shall cover him all the day long, and He shall dwell between his shoulders " (Deut. xxxiii, 12), which had reference chiefly to the favoured and honoured position or portion which that tribe would occupy. As others before have pointed out, it was here intimated that the temple, in which Jehovah would dwell, would be situated within the territory of this tribe. And such was indeed the case, for Jerusalem, the holy city, was in the lot of Benjamin (Joshua xviii, 28)—" though Sion, the city of David, is supposed to belong to Judah, yet mount Moriah, on which the temple was built, was in Benjamin's lot. God is Himself said to dwell between his shoulders ' because the temple stood on that mount as the head of a man upon his shoulders " (Matthew Henry). Thus Benjamin was under the protection of the Divine sanctuary, adumbrating the grand truth that " As the mountains are round about Jerusalem, so the Lord is round about His people from henceforth even for ever " (Psalm cxxv, 2).

" The coast of their lot came forth between the children of Judah and the children of Joseph " (Joshua xviii, 11). Herein we behold the gracious ruling of Divine providence in arranging for " little Benjamin " (Psalm lxviii, 27) to be located between two of the most powerful of the tribes. It is to be observed that in the prophetical benedictions of Moses that of Benjamin came right after that of Judah and immediately before Joseph's (Deut. xxxiii, 7-17)—Levi having no separate portion or lot in Canaan—so that there may be (" as frequently in Scripture) a *double* meaning in the words " He shall dwell between his shoulders " (verse 12)—the place of strength (Isaiah ix, 6) and of security (Luke xv, 5). There was also a peculiar propriety in this appointment, for Benjamin was Joseph's own brother, and later was the tribe which united with Judah in adhering to the throne of David and the temple at Jerusalem. Finally, we see in this arrangement the wisdom of God in the lot, for nothing was more likely to secure a *united Israel* than to make Benjamin the link between the two most powerful and naturally rival tribes—it was through the mutual affection of Judah and Joseph for Benjamin, as their father's youngest and dearest son, that the brethren were reconciled in Genesis xliv, 18—xlv, 24.

"And the second lot came forth to Simeon, for the tribe of the children of Simeon according to their families : and their inheritance was within the inheritance of the children of Judah " (xix, 1). The portion which had been given to Judah was more extensive than was required by that tribe. " It seems that, without murmuring, Judah renounced his claim, at the instance of Joshua and those who had been nominated to the work of dividing the land " (Scott). This is borne out by what is stated in verse 9, " Out of the portion of the children of Judah was the inheritance of the children of Simeon : for the part of the children of Judah was too much for them ; therefore the children of Simeon had their inheritance within the inheritance of them "—there were more cities than they could fill, more land than they could cultivate. It is worthy of note that this is the only recorded instance of their portion being too large for any of them, and it is surely significant that it was *Judah's* which proved to be the exception, for it was the tribe from which according to the flesh our Lord sprang. Thus we have here adumbrated that grand truth of the *fullness* of Christ, that in Him there is an abundance of grace, inexhaustible riches available for the saints to draw upon !

It is striking to note that this second lot fulfilled the prophecy of Jacob. He had linked together Simeon and Levi in judgment, who earlier had been united in wickedness (Gen. xxxiv, 25), saying, as God's mouthpiece, " I will divide them in Jacob, and scatter them in Israel " (Gen. xlix, 5-7). Because of his noble conduct subsequently, the curse upon Levi was revoked and displaced by the blessing of the Lord, and he who was originally joined to his brother in sin and cruelty was eventually joined to the Lord in grace and honour, so that there was made with his seed " the covenant of an everlasting priesthood ; because he was zealous for his God, and made an atonement for the children of Israel " (Numbers xxv, 6-13). Nevertheless, the terms of the patriarch's prediction were accomplished, for the Levites had as their portion in Canaan forty-eight cities, which were scattered throughout the inheritance of the other tribes (Num. xxxv, ,8 ; Joshua xiv, 4 ; xxi, 3). So too in the case of Simeon : his descendants received not a separate territory in the promised land, but had their portion within the allotment of Judah, and, as Joshua xix, 2-8, shows, the tribe of Simeon was widely " scattered," being dispersed among many different cities.

"And the third lot came up for the children of Zebulun according to their families " (xix, 10). The part played by Zebulun in the history of the nation was not a prominent one, but though referred to rarely as a tribe, each time that mention *is* made of them it is of a highly creditable nature. First, we read of them in Judges v, where Deborah celebrates in song the notable victory over Jabin and Sisera, and recounts the parts played therein by the different tribes. In verse 18 we read, " Zebulun and Naphtali were a people that jeoparded their lives unto the death in the high places of the field." In I Chronicles xii, where we have enumerated those who " came to David to Hebron, to turn the kingdom of Saul to him," we are told, " Of Zebulun, such as went forth to battle, expert in war, with all instruments of war, fifty thousand, which could keep rank : they were not of double heart " (verses 23, 33). So too they were among those who brought a rich supply of provisions for the feast on that occasion. But that which mainly characterized it was the *maritime* nature of this tribe.

Jacob foretold, " Zebulun shall dwell at the haven of the sea ; and he shall be for a haven of ships ; and his border shall be unto Zidon " (Gen. xlix, 13). Moses also, "And of Zebulun he said, Rejoice, Zebulun, in thy going out ; and Issachar, in thy tents. They shall call the people unto the mountain ; there they shall offer sacrifices of righteousness : for they shall suck of the abundance of the seas, and of treasures hid in the sand " (Deut. xxxiii, 18, 19). And so it came to pass, for Joshua xix goes on to say of the lot of Zebulun " and their border went up toward the sea "—a statement of seemingly little importance and easily overlooked by the casual reader ; yet one which announced the literal fulfilment of prophecies made centuries before. The expressions " thy going out " and " they shall suck of the abundance of the seas " received their accomplishment in their ocean life and trading in foreign parts.

But that which is of interest to the Christian in connection with Zebulun's portion is the honourable place which it receives in the New Testament, for if the character of the people was praiseworthy, even more notable was the *position* they occupied in Palestine. Matthew iv, 15, 16, informs us that " the land of Zebulun and the land of Naphtali " (which adjoined it) was none other than " Galilee of the Gentiles," concerning which it is said, " The people which sat in darkness saw great light ; and to them which sat in the region and shadow of death light is sprung up." Nazareth, where the Saviour spent so much of His time when He tabernacled here among men, was in its borders, and it was also on the shores of its sea that He did so much of His preaching and wrought so many miracles. Well might the voice of prophecy bid Zebulun " rejoice " (Deut. xxxiii, 18). Therein also we may perceive the deeper and spiritual allusion in the words " Rejoice in thy *going out.* . . . They shall call the people unto the mountain," i.e. the kingdom of the Messiah (Isaiah ii, 2), which was done by the preaching of Christ and His *apostles*—which means those who *go out* It is remarkable that, with the lone exception of Judas, all of the twelve apostles were men of Galilee ! Zebulun was also " for a haven," and it was in its borders that Joseph and Mary, with the Christ child, found a haven after their return from Egypt, and it afforded Him shelter when the Jews sought to kill Him in Judea (John vii, 1).

"And the fourth lot came out to Issachar " (xix, 17). Since this tribe was united with Zebulun in blessing (Deut. xxxiii, 18, 19), there is the less need for us to offer separate remarks thereon. The " in their tents " was in apposition to the " ships " : they would be a pastoral people rather than a sea-going one cultivating the land. Their inheritance was the fertile plain of Jezreel, with its surrounding hills and valleys, afterwards known as lower Galilee—it extended from Carmel to the Jordan, and in breadth to mount Tabor. Shunem (I Kings iv, 8, etc.) was one of its cities, and Naboth's vineyard was within its lot. Matthew Henry pointed out how that we may see both the sovereignty and the wisdom of Divine providence in appointing not only the bounds of men's habitations, " but their several employments for the good of the public ; as each member of the body is situated and qualified for the service of the whole. Some are disposed to live in cities, some in the countryside, others in sea-ports. The genius of some leads them to the pen, some to trading, others to mechanics. ' If the whole body were an eye, where were the hearing ?' (I Cor. xii, 17) "

"And the fifth lot came out for the tribe of the children of Asher " (xix, 24). It was pointed out in the opening paragraph that the order in which the tribes are here mentioned is not that of seniority : rather is it a spiritual one, according to the meaning of their names as given in Genesis. Benjamin signifies " the son of the right hand " (xxxv, 18), Simeon " hearing " (xxix, 33), Zebulun " dwelling " (xxx, 20), Issachar " hire " or " reward " (xxx, 18), Asher " happy " (xxx, 23), Naphtali " wrestling " (xxx, 8), Dan " judging " (xxx, 16). Combined we get : The son of the right hand (the place of honour and power) is the hearing one (the new birth precedes believing !), dwelling (no longer tossed about like the restless sea) in Christ ; great is his reward, for he is happy or blessed. Such a one is marked by wrestling against (instead of submitting to) the powers of evil, and by unsparingly judging himself. And of what does the happiness of the spiritual Asher consist ? The meanings (taken from Young's concordance) of the towns mentioned in xix, 25, 26 (omitting the second, " Hali," which is unknown), are : portion, height, dedicated, the king's oak (strength and durability), a station, depression (mourning for sin), fruitful place, glass river (Rev. xxii, 1).

"And the sixth lot came out to the children of Naphtali " (xix, 32). This is also of most interest to us because of its New Testament connections. Its territory adjoined that of Zebulun (Matt. iv, 13), yet each had its own distinct interest. Jacob likened Naphtali to " a hind let loose " and foretold, " he giveth goodly words " (Gen. xlix, 21) ; while Moses spoke of him as " full with the blessing of the Lord " (Deut. xxxiii, 23). In the title to Psalm xxii our Lord is likened to " the hind of the morning," because of His swiftness to do His Father's will and work. The cities of Capernaum and Bethsaida were in the borders of Naphtali, which were indeed filled with the blessing of the Lord, for it was there that Christ and His apostles did most of their preaching and gave forth " goodly words."

" And the seventh lot came out for the tribe of the children of Dan " (xix, 40). Genesis xxx, 1-6, records his lowly origin. As this tribe brought up the rear of the congregation when they were on the march, so they were the last to receive their inheritance. Jacob likened Dan to a serpent, Moses to a " lion's whelp." Samson was of this tribe, and in him both characters were combined. Dan was the first tribe to fall into idolatry (Judges xviii, 30), and apparently remained in that awful condition for centuries, for we find the apostate king Jeroboam setting up his golden calves in Bethel and Dan (I Kings xii, 28, 29, and cf. II Kings x, 29).

" When they had made an end of dividing the land for inheritance by their coasts, the children of Israel gave an inheritance to Joshua the son of Nun among them : according to the word of the Lord they gave him the city which he asked, Timnath-serah in mount Ephraim ; and he built the city, and dwelt therein " (xix, 49, 50). Blessed is it to see that, though the greatest and boldest among them, the one who had led Israel to the conquest of Canaan, instead of seeking first his own portion, he waited till all had received theirs. Thus did he put the public good before his private interests, seeking theirs and not his own. " Our Lord Jesus thus came and dwelt among us, not in pomp, but in poverty, providing rest for us, yet Himself not having where to lay His head " (Matthew Henry). Nor did Joshua seize his portion as a right, but, like his grand Antitype, " asked " for it (Psalm ii, 8). And as Christ built the Church and indwells it, so Joshua built his city.

Chapter 18

THE CITIES OF REFUGE

JOSHUA 20:1-9

" The Lord also spake unto Joshua, saying, Speak to the children of Israel, saying, Appoint out for you cities of refuge, whereof I spake unto you by the hand of Moses : that the slayer that killeth any person unawares and unwittingly may flee thither : and they shall be your refuge from the avenger of blood. And when he that doth flee unto one of those cities shall stand at the entering of the gate of the city, and shall declare his cause in the ears of the elders of that city, they shall take him into the city unto them, and give him a place, that he may dwell among them. And if the avenger of blood pursue after him, then they shall not deliver the slayer up into his hand ; because he smote his neighbour unwittingly, and hated him not beforetime. And he shall dwell in that city, until he stand before the congregation for judgment, and until the death of the high priest that shall be in those days : then shall the slayer return, and come unto his own city, and unto his own house, unto the city from whence he fled " (Joshua xx, 1-6).

In that passage we are furnished with a condensed account of the statutes with regard to murder which the Lord gave to Israel for the maintenance of righteousness in their midst. On the one hand, there must be a strict enforcing of justice ; on the other, the exercising of mercy. The guilty were not to be cleared ; the innocent must not be executed. Due and orderly investigation must be made, and each case tried on its own merits before a court of law. Where guilt was established, malice aforethought being proved by witnesses, the death penalty was to be inflicted upon the murderer. But when a neighbour had been inadvertently killed extreme measures were not to be taken against the one occasioning his death. Nor was the next-of-kin to the one slain permitted to take matters into his own hands and wreak vengeance upon him who by misadventure had tragically terminated his life. Instead, there was a sanctuary provided for the innocent, to which he could fly, shelter afforded for one who had involuntarily committed homicide.

The original statute pertaining to the subject was, " Whoso sheddeth man's blood, by man shall his blood be shed : *for* in the image of God made He man " (Gen. ix, 6). There is nothing whatever " Jewish " about that injunction, for it was given centuries before the nation of Israel had any existence. It needs emphasizing today that capital punishment as the penalty for murder was ordained by God Himself long before the giving of the Mosaic law, and, since it has never been repealed by Him, that precept is binding until the end of time. It is important to observe that the reason for this law is not here based upon the well-being of human society, but is grounded upon the fact that man is made " in the image of God." That expression has a twofold significance ; a natural and a moral— the moral image of God (inherent holiness) was lost at the fall, but the natural still exists, as is clear from I Corinthians xi, 7, and James iii, 9. Thus, the primary reason why it is sinful to slay a man is because he is made in the image of God.

" To deface the king's image is a sort of treason among men, implying a hatred against him, and that if he himself were within reach, he would be served in the same manner. How much more heinous, then, must it be to destroy, curse, oppress, or in any way abuse the image of the King of kings ! " (A. Fuller).

Whereas that original statute of God has never yet been repealed, it has been more fully explained, amplified, and safeguarded in later passages ; and to them we now turn. The first one having a direct bearing upon our present subject is found in Exodus xxi, 12-14 : " He that smiteth a man, so that he die, shall be surely put to death." There is the general principle, but it is *qualified* thus : "And if a man lie not in wait, but God deliver him into his hand, then I will appoint thee a place whither he shall flee. But if a man come presumptuously upon his neighbour, to slay him with guile ; thou shalt take him from Mine altar, that he may die." A sharp distinction was thus drawn between deliberate murder and involuntary manslaughter. In the former instance, when one smote his fellow intentionally, whether from premeditated malice or in the heat of sudden passion, so that he expired from the injury, then the deed must be regarded as murder, and the death penalty be enforced. But where one unwittingly and unwillingly inflicted an injury upon another, even though it proved to be a fatal one, he was not to be executed for the act. Instead, there was a place appointed by God to which he might flee, and where he could be sheltered from any who sought vengeance upon him.

We have been much impressed by the fact that the above passage is found in the very next chapter after the one which records the Ten Commandments. Let those who have such a penchant for drawing invidious and odious comparisons between that which obtained under the old covenant and that which pertains to the new take careful note that this gracious provision was made by God under that very economy which dispensationalists are so fond of terming " a forbidding and unrelieved regime of stern law." It was nothing of the kind, as any impartial student of the Word is aware. In all ages God has tempered His justice with mercy and caused His grace to reign through righteousness. Let it not be overlooked that such declarations as the following are found in the *Old Testament* scriptures. " Like as a father pitieth his children, so the Lord pitieth them that fear Him " (Psalm ciii, 13). " Great are Thy tender mercies, O Lord " (Psalm cxix, 156). The putting forth of His wrath is spoken of as His " strange work " (Isaiah xxviii, 21). " Thou art a God ready to pardon, gracious and merciful, slow to anger, and of great kindness " (Neh. ix, 17). " He restraineth not His anger for ever, because He delighteth in mercy " (Micah vii, 18), and most evidently did the cities of refuge testify to that fact.

Ere passing on from Exodus xxi, 13, 14, let us also duly attend to the wording of verse 13. It is *not* "And if a man lie not in wait, but *accidentally* slay another," but instead, "And if a man lie not in wait [having no intention to injure his neighbour], but *God deliver him* into his hand." In full accord with the uniform teaching of Holy Writ concerning the Divine superintendence of all events, such a calamity as is here supposed is not ascribed to " chance " or " ill fortune " (for there is nothing fortuitous in a world governed by God), but instead is attributed to an act of God—i.e. the Lord being pleased to take away in that manner the life which He had given. " Unto God the Lord belong the issues from death " (Psalm lxviii, 20). The gates of the grave open unto none except at the command of the Most High, and when He gives the word none can withstand it. " My times [to be born and to die : Eccles. iii, 2] are in *Thy hand* " (Psalm xxxi, 15), and not in my own. " Seeing his days are determined, the number of his months are with Thee, Thou hast appointed his bounds that he cannot pass "

(Job xiv, 5). Not only is the hour of death Divinely decreed, but *the form* in which it comes. "Then the Jews took up stones again to stone Him" (John x, 31), but in vain, for God had ordained that He should be crucified. No matter in what manner death comes, it is the Lord who kills and "bringeth down to the grave" (I Samuel ii, 6).

"And the Lord spake unto Moses, saying, Speak unto the children of Israel, and say unto them, When ye be come over Jordan into the land of Canaan ; then ye shall appoint you cities to be cities of refuge for you ; that the slayer may flee thither, which killeth any person at unawares" (Num. xxxv, 9-11). That which is mentioned in Exodus xxi had reference to God's merciful provision for Israel during the time they remained in the wilderness. There was, even then, "a place" appointed by the Lord to which the manslayer might turn for sanctuary. We are not told where that place was. Some of the ancient Jewish writers suppose that it was located "outside the camp," but, since all the cities of refuge were cities which pertained to *the Levites,* we consider it more in keeping with the Analogy of Faith to conclude that the "place" was within that part of the camp assigned to the priests. That temporal provision was to give way to a more permanent arrangement after the children of Israel became settled in their inheritance.

"And of these cities which ye shall give six cities shall ye have for refuge. Ye shall give three cities on this side Jordan, and three cities shall ye give in the land of Canaan, which shall be cities of refuge" (Num. xxxv, 13, 14). Two and a half of the tribes, namely the children of Gad, the children of Reuben, and half the tribe of Manasseh, had been assigned their place and portion on the eastern side of the Jordan (Num. xxxii, 33), in the fertile valley which had been occupied by Sihon king of the Amorites and Og king of Bashan, who, refusing Israel's request to pass through that country, had been slain in battle and their territory seized by the conquerors (Num. xxi, 21-31). The remaining three were to be situated in convenient sections in Palestine, where they would be accessible at short notice unto those who might have need of the same. Nor was their use restricted to those who were of the natural seed of Abraham : "These six cities shall be a refuge, both for the children of Israel, and for the stranger, and for the sojourner among them : that every one that killeth any person unawares may flee thither" (verse 15). Thus, even under the Mosaic economy, Divine mercy was extended unto those who threw in their lot with the people of God !

In the verses that follow various cases are described in detail, so that there might be no miscarriage of justice when the magistrates were adjudicating thereon : "And if he smite him with an instrument of iron, so that he die, he is a murderer : the murderer shall surely be put to death. And if he smite him with throwing a stone, wherewith he may die, and he die, he is a murderer : the murderer shall surely be put to death. Or if he smite him with an hand weapon of wood, wherewith he may die, and he die, he is a murderer : the murderer shall surely be put to death. The revenger of blood himself shall slay the murderer : when he meeteth him he shall slay him. But [or "and"] if he thrust him of hatred, or hurl at him by laying of wait, that he die ; or in enmity smite him with his hand, that he die : he that smote him shall surely be put to death ; for he is a murderer : the revenger of blood shall slay the murderer, when he meeteth him" (verses 17-21). Thus those cities of refuge were not meant to afford shelter for murderers as such. Therein they differed noticeably from the sacred precincts of the heathen gods, which provided a safe asylum for any violent or wicked man. The Divine statute insisted on the sanctity of life and the inflexible maintenance of righteousness.

Equally express were the instructions on the other side. " But if he thrust him suddenly without enmity, or have cast upon him any thing without laying of wait ; or with any stone, wherewith a man may die, seeing him not, and cast it upon him, that he die, and was not his enemy, neither sought his harm : then the congregation shall judge between the slayer and the revenger of blood according to these judgments. And the congregation shall deliver the slayer out of the hand of the revenger of blood, and the congregation shall restore him to the city of his refuge, whither he was fled : and he shall abide in it unto the death of the high priest, which was anointed with the holy oil " (verses 22-25). Shelter and security were provided only for one who had brought about the death of another without deliberate design, yea, with no intention of inflicting any injury upon him. Murder, strictly speaking, involves more than the overt act : it includes the spirit behind the act, the motive prompting it. If the act be performed " without enmity " and with no desire to harm another, then it is a case of involuntary manslaughter and not of murder.

To prevent any guilty one taking advantage of this provision for the innocent, the accused must " stand before the congregation in judgment " (Num. xxxv, 12) : that is, he was to be brought before a court of justice, where the magistrates were to give him a fair trial. Full and formal investigation was to be made, so that the accused had every opportunity to prove his innocence. " Then the congregation shall judge between the slayer and the revenger of blood according to these judgments." Once the manslayer had been received into the city of refuge, the avenger of blood could act only as prosecutor (previously he had the right to be the executioner—verse 19), and his case had to be determined by the rules God had specified. If it were proved that death had ensued where no malicious attempt upon life had been made, but, instead, the injury had been inflicted casually, " unawares," then the death penalty was not to be visited upon him.

It is highly important in the administration of law that that no innocent person should be made to suffer, and equally so that the guilty should not be exempted from the due reward of his iniquities. In the case of murder, the Divine law required proof of previous malice, a laying in wait to slay the victim, deliberate measures taken to encompass his death, an assault with some weapon of violence to accomplish the fell deed. " Whoso killeth any person, the murderer shall be put to death by the mouth of witnesses : but one witness shall not testify against any person to cause him to die. Moreover ye shall take no satisfaction for the life of a murderer, which is guilty of death : but he shall be surely put to death " (Num. xxxv, 30, 31). Thereby did the Lord manifest His abhorrence of this crime : no atoning sacrifice was available for it, nor could any ransom be accepted for its perpetrator. Justice must be administered impartially, the law strictly enforced without fear or favour. Very solemn and impressive is it to note what follows.

" So ye shall not pollute the land wherein ye are : for *blood it defileth the land* : and the land cannot be cleansed of the blood that is shed therein, but by the blood of him that shed it. Defile not therefore the land which ye shall inhabit, wherein I dwell : for I the Lord dwell among the children of Israel " (Num. xxxv, 33, 34). Such shedding of blood not only defiles the conscience of the murderer, who is thereby proved not to have eternal life abiding in him (I John iii, 15), but also pollutes the land in which the crime was committed, being abominable to God and to all good men. Nor can that land be cleansed from the blood of murder but by executing condign judgment upon the murderer himself. Thus we are informed that there was far more involved in the enforcing of these statutes than the maintenance of righteousness between man and man. As another has pointed out, " the glory of God, the purity of His land, and the integrity of His government, had to be duly maintained. If those were touched, there could be no security for anyone."

The same things are taught, substantially, in the New Testament, particularly in Romans xiii, 1-4. There the civil ruler or magistrate is twice denominated " the minister of God " : first, in protecting the law-abiding ; second, in penalizing the law-defiant. He is Divinely appointed to maintain civic righteousness, for if the restraints of government be removed, a state of anarchy and bedlam at once ensues. The "sword " is the symbol of the ultimate power of life and death (Gen. iii, 24 ; Zech. xiii, 7), and the " he beareth not the sword in vain " signifies that God has invested him with the authority to inflict capital punishment—the common method of which in olden times was by decapitating with the sword. It is an essential part of the governor's office to be " a revenger, to execute [God's] wrath upon him that doeth evil." Nothing is said about its being his duty to reform criminals, rather is it his business to redress wrongs and to instil fear into those who contemplate doing wrong. Romans xiii, 1-4, is silent upon any efforts being required to reclaim the refractory, the emphasis being placed upon his alarming them and imposing the full penalty of the law : compare I Peter ii, 14. It is a sure sign of a nation's moral degeneracy, and a dishonouring and incurring of God's displeasure, when capital punishment is abolished, or magistrates become lax and yield to sentimentality.

Reverting to the case of the one who is not guilty of deliberate murder, there are four other details which require to be noticed. First, when one unintentionally killed a neighbour, there must usually have been in such cases a culpable degree of carelessness, and therefore, though his life was spared, his freedom was curtailed. Second, accordingly he was required to leave his home and family, and take up residence in the city of refuge. Third, if he forsook that city, he forfeited legal protection, and then, should the revenger of blood find him without its borders, he was entitled to kill him (Num. xxxv, 27). Fourth, it was required that he remain within the city of refuge until the death of the high priest, and then he was free to return to his home and reside there unmolested (verse 28). By limiting the time of his banishment by the high priest's death, honour was put upon the priesthood—as it had been in selecting those cities, for they all belonged to the Levites. " The high priest was to be looked upon as so great a blessing to his country, that when he died their sorrow upon that occasion should swallow up all other resentments " (Matthew Henry).

Further reference is made to our subject in Deuteronomy iv, 41-43, wherein we see illustrated the law of progressive development. First, bare mention of an unspecified " place " is referred to (Exodus xxi, 13). Next, instructions are given for the appointing of six cities of refuge, without stating more than that three of them are to be on the wilderness side of the Jordan, and three within Canaan (Num. xxxv, 14, 15). Then the first three are actually named (Deut. iv, 43), while in Joshua xx, 7, 8, the locations of all six are given. In Deuteronomy xix, more definite instructions were communicated as to the precise situations of those cities ; the land was to be divided into three parts, so that one of them would be the more readily accessible for those in any particular section (verses 2, 3). A " way " which led to each city was to be prepared (verse 3) so as to guide the fugitive who was fleeing unto it. Joshua xx, 4, supplies the additional information that when the manslayer arrived at the gate of the city of refuge he received a preliminary hearing from the elders ere he was admitted, which was followed by a fuller and more formal investigation of his case in a court of justice (verse 6).

In his comments upon Numbers xxxv T. Scott well remarked, " This remarkable law, expressive of the deepest detestation of murder, yet providing most effectually against the innocent being punished with the guilty, is likewise an instructive typical representation of the salvation of the Gospel. ' The wrath of God is revealed from heaven against all ungodliness and unrighteousness of men (Romans i, 18). If it is appointed unto men once to die, and after death the judgment, with the eternal consequences, in the meanwhile a Refuge is provided and revealed in Christ Jesus. His ministers warn sinners to flee from the wrath to come, and instruct and exhort them to ' flee for refuge to lay hold upon the hope set before them.' All things are prepared for the reception of those who obey this call. By faith they discern both their danger and refuge. Then fear warns and hope animates. Should death, like the avenger of blood, find them *without*, destruction is inevitable." The fact that the cities of refuge are described at more or less length in no fewer than *four* of the Old Testament books—Exodus, Numbers, Deuteronomy and Joshua—denotes the importance of them, as well as adumbrating the delineation which we have of the antitypical Refuge in the *four* Gospels.

When we bear in mind how much the Holy Spirit delighted in shadowing forth the Lord Jesus under the Old Testament, in type and figure, and when we observe how closely and strikingly the various things said of the cities of refuge point to the Saviour, we must conclude that they were Divinely designed to foreshadow Him. In seeking to understand and interpret the types, two dangers need to be guarded against : first, the giving way to an unbridled imagination ; second, ultra-caution and conservatism. On the one hand, we must not indulge in the fanciful allegorizing of Oregon ; on the other, we must eschew the rationalizing of the Higher Critics. In the past, too many have been chargeable with the first : but today, when the Divine element is either denied or pushed into the background, the pendulum has swung to the opposite extreme. To assume that we are unwarranted in regarding anything in the Old Testament as possessing a spiritual significance unless the New Testament expressly says so is as unjustifiable as to insist that there are no prophecies there except those specifically termed such in the New Testament—for instance, Genesis iii, 15.

Concerning the subject now before us there are, in the judgment of this writer, at least two passsages in the Epistles which confirm the view that the cities of refuge are to be regarded as having a spiritual meaning and reference. The first is in Philippians iii, 9, where the apostle, after announcing and then renouncing all his natural advantages as a Hebrew, counting them but loss for the excellency of the knowledge of Christ Jesus his Lord, expresses the desire that he might be " *found in Him,* not having mine own righteousness, which is of the law, but that which is through the faith of Christ, the righteousness which is of God by faith." There the proud Pharisee forsook his own righteousness, which was condemned by the law—as the manslayer fled from the avenger of blood— and he betook himself to the righteousness of Christ as the homicide did within the city of refuge from the sword of justice. The second passage is a still more manifest allusion to this Old Testament figure, for there the heirs of promise are assured that God has provided strong consolation unto those who have " *fled for refuge* to lay hold upon the hope set before us " (Heb. vi, 18), i.e. in the Gospel : reminding us of the prayer of David, " Deliver me, O Lord, from mine enemies : I *flee unto Thee* to hide me " (Psalm cxliii, 9)

The manslayer is an apt representation of the sinner, who is a soul-slayer : " thou hast destroyed thyself " (Hosea xiii, 9). But more particularly : he sets before us *the awakened sinner*. Previously, the man had lived in quietness and comfort, but when he slew another, though unintentionally, his peace was shattered. Everything was suddenly changed : there was danger without, and fear within. He now discovered himself to be in a very evil case. There lies the body of another, dead by his own carelessness. Who can conceive the distress and dismay which overwhelm his mind ? He knows that the next of kin has the right to take vengeance and slay him. He is no longer safe in his own home ; he is unable to find security in any building of his own hands ; he must perforce flee for his life. Thus it is with the unconverted. In his natural condition, a false serenity is his, and he finds contentment in the things of this world and the pleasures of sin. Then, unawares, the Holy Spirit arouses him from the sleep of spiritual death, convicts him of sin, makes him realize that the wrath of God is upon him, and his soul exposed to eternal death. Oh, what unspeakable anguish is his as he now realizes himself to be a rebel against the Most High, lost and undone.

Intolerable dread now fills him as the fire of hell is felt in his spirit and the undying worm gnaws at his conscience. What must I do ? How shall I escape ? are his urgent inquiries. Proud reason can furnish no answer. His outlook appears to be hopeless, his case beyond the reach of mercy. Now it is that the message of the Gospel receives welcome attention. He has heard it, perhaps, many times before, but without any personal interest or deep concern. So with the manslayer. Hitherto he gave little or no thought at all to what he had read or heard about the cities of refuge : having no need of them, they possessed no special interest for him. But matters are very different with him now. Having become a homicide, those places become of the utmost importance in his esteem, and he is greatly relieved by the knowledge that a merciful provision has been made with God to meet his desperate case, that shelter is available from the avenger. Thus it is with the sinner. He may be informed about·God's way of salvation, but he never sets his heart upon it, labours to understand it clearly, and appropriate it unto his own deep need, until he is made sensible of his ruined condition.

" Men do not flee for refuge when they are in no distress. The vessel puts not into the harbour of refuge when winds and waves all favour her. A man does not escape out of a city, like Lot from Sodom, unless he be persuaded that the city is to be destroyed, and that he is likely to perish in it. Ah ! Indeed, we who are saved confess with gratitude to Him that has delivered us that we were once in danger. In *danger,* my brethren ; is the word strong enough ? In danger of eternal burnings ! It was worse than that, for we are brands plucked out of the fire ; we already burned with that fire of sin, which is the fire of hell " (Spurgeon). It is one thing to be in deadly danger—as are all who lie under the condemnation and curse of God's broken law—but it is quite another to have a feeling sense of the same in our souls. A man is satisfied with his condition until he sees his vileness in the light of God's holiness. He has a good opinion of his own character and righteousness until his eyes be Divinely opened to perceive that he is a moral leper. He is self-complacent and self-confident until he is given a terrifying sense of the wrath of God pursuing him for his sins, and that there is but a step between him and eternal death.

But mark it well, my reader : it is not sufficient for the manslayer to recognize his peril, nor to have the knowledge that God has provided relief for him : he must flee to the city of refuge and personally avail himself of its shelter. Not until he actually passed within the portals of that sanctuary was he safe from the avenger of blood. His case was so desperate that it admitted of no delay. If he valued his life he must flee in haste. A dilatory and trifling spirit would evince that he had no real sense of his peril. So it is with the sinner. No matter how deep or long-protracted be his convictions, until he really betakes himself to Christ and closes with His gracious offer he is a lost soul. He is either under the wrath of God or under the atoning blood of Christ. There is no middle place between the two. He is this very day " condemned already " (John iii, 18), waiting for execution, or he is absolved, so that vengeance cannot strike him. As it was something more than a momentary alarm, which could easily be shaken off, that seized the manslayer—deepening in its intensity the more he pondered it—so something more than a temporary fright that soon passes away is required to make the sinner come to Christ.

" The manslayer left his house, his wife, his children, everything, to flee away to the city of refuge. That is just what a man does when he resolves to be saved by grace : he leaves everything he calls his own, renounces all the rights and privileges which he thought he possessed by nature ; yea, he confesses to having lost his own natural right to live, and he flees for life to the grace of God in Christ Jesus. The manslayer had no right to live except that he was in the city of refuge, no right to anything except that he was God's guest within those enclosing walls. And so we relinquish, heartily and thoroughly, once and for ever, all ideas arising out of our supposed merits ; we hasten away from self that Christ may be all in all to us. Fleeing for refuge implies that a man flees from his sin. He sees it and repents of it " (Spurgeon). There has to be a complete break from the old self-pleasing life. Sin must be made bitter before Christ will be sweet. Fleeing for refuge implies earnestness, for the manslayer dared not dawdle or saunter : he ran for his life. It implied unwearied diligence, so that he loitered not till shelter and safety were reached.

It is just at this point that the convicted sinner needs to be most careful. When Satan cannot prevail with a person to reject wholly the imperative duty of his fleeing to Christ, his next attempt for the ruination of his soul is to prevail with him at least to put off the performing of it. Many who have been shaken from their unconcern are easily persuaded to defer a wholehearted seeking of Christ until they have taken their fill of the things of this world, until they are warned by serious illness or the infirmities of old age that soon they must leave it, hoping that a season of repentance will be given them before they die. But such postponing shows they are unwilling to repent and believe until they be forced by necessity, and that they prefer the world to Christ. Thus they unfit themselves more and more for this urgent duty by continuing in sin and wasting the time which is now theirs. Others persuade themselves they are not yet sufficiently convicted of sin, and must wait till God assures them more fully that the Gospel is suited to their case ; and thus those who are wrongly termed " seekers " misspend their day of grace.

It is quite evident from what has been before us that in this type there is an enforcing of *the sinner's responsibility*. A merciful provision had been made to meet the dire need of the homicide, yet *he* was required to exert himself in order to benefit thereby. The city of refuge was graciously available for him, but he must flee thither and enter it if he would be safe. If under any pretext he failed to do so, and was slain by the next of kin, his blood was upon his own head. As another has said, " It is not at all likely that anyone would be so blind or so infatuated as to fold his arms in cold indifference and say, If I am fated to escape, I shall escape : *my efforts* are not needed ; for if I am not fated to escape, I cannot escape, my efforts are of no use. We cannot fancy a manslayer using such silly language, or being guilty of such blind fatuity as this. He knows too well that if the avenger could but lay his hand upon him all such notions would be of small account. There was but one thing to be done, and that was to escape for his life—to flee from impending judgment, to find his safe abode within the gates of the city of refuge."

The cities of refuge were a manifest type of Christ as He is presented and offered to sinners in the Gospel. 1. They were *appointed by God Himself.* They were not of man's devising, as the Gospel is no human invention. They were an expression of the Divine mercy : and how rich the grace thus evidenced, for it provided not merely one, but no less than six, of these cities ! They anticipated the urgent situation. The Lord did not wait until an Israelite had unwittingly slain one of his fellows, and then arrange for his deliverance from the sword of justice. No, He is ever beforehand in supplying what we lack. Those cities were available ere they were made use of. In like manner, God's appointing of Christ to be the Saviour of sinners was no afterthought to meet an unlooked-for emergency : in the Divine purpose and plan Christ was the Lamb "slain from the foundation of the world" (Rev. xiii, 8).

2. Those cities were given *to provide shelter from the avenger.* That was the outstanding feature in this lovely evangelical picture. Sought by one who was determined to execute judgment upon him, the manslayer turned unto this haven of peace. To attempt to brazen things out was futile : equally so is it for the sinner to imagine he can successfully defy Him whose justice is even now pursuing him. Thus there was no other alternative but death. In like manner " Neither is there salvation in any other : for there is none other name under heaven given among men, whereby we must be saved " (Acts iv, 12). To delay was madness : " he shall flee unto one of those cities, and live " (Deut. xix, 5) was the peremptory requirement. It was dangerous for Lot to linger in Sodom, lest fire and brimstone destroy him (Gen. xix, 17). So God bids us, " Today if ye will hear His voice, harden not your hearts " (Heb. iii, 7, 8).

3. Those cities were *placed on an eminence,* being built upon hills or mountains, as several of their names and the locations of others plainly intimate. This made them the more readily seen and kept in sight by those who were fleeing to the same. As such they blessedly prefigured Him whom " God exalted with His right hand to be a Prince and a Saviour, for to give repentance to Israel, and forgiveness of sins " (Acts v, 31). So too when the Gospel is faithfully preached the antitypical Refuge is held forth, so that it may be said of the hearers, " before whose eyes Jesus Christ hath been evidently [plainly] set forth " (Gal. iii, 1). For the same reason, the ministers of Christ who lift Him before their congregations are likened to " a city that is set on an hill " (Matt. v, 14).

4. The road to the city was *plainly marked out.* " Thou shalt prepare thee a way . . . that every slayer may flee thither (Deut. xix, 3). Jewish writers say it was a law in Israel that one day in every year there were persons sent to repair the roads leading to them, to remove all stumbling-stones which might by time have fallen in the way, and to see also that the signposts which were set up at every corner leading to the city were carefully preserved, and the name *Miklac* (that is, refuge) legible upon them. Whether or not that was the case, certain it is that in the Gospel God has fully and plainly made known the way of salvation, so that " wayfaring men, though fools, shall not err therein " (Isaiah xxxv, 8). See also Romans x, 6-8.

5. They were *easy of access.* Those cities were so situated that when a person had need of such, one was near at hand. Express instructions were given that

they were to be " in the midst of the land " (Deut. xix, 2, 3), and not in remote corners which had been difficult to approach. The land had to be divided " into three parts," one city of refuge in each, so that it could be reached within a single day's journey, no matter where the manslayer resided—what a touching proof of God's tender mercy ! Everything was done to facilitate the homicide's escape. The application is obvious : " The Lord is nigh unto them that are of a broken heart " (Psalm xxxiv, 18). Unto such He says, " My righteousness is near " (Isaiah li, 5). The way to Christ is short : it is but a simple renunciation of self and a laying hold of Him to be our all in all.

6. The city of refuge provided *protection only for the homicide* from the revenger of blood. The deliberate murderer was excluded, to teach us that there is no salvation in Christ for *presumptuous* sinners who still go on deliberately in their trespasses. Those who persist in wilful sin, and continue to defy God and trample upon His law, bar themselves from His mercy. There is no shelter in a holy Christ for those who are in love with sin, but unto those that flee to Him *from* their sins there is " plenteous redemption." In Christ the penitent and believing sinner is secure from the curse of the broken law and the wrath of God, for the Lord Jesus endured them in his stead. In Christ he is safe also from the fury of a raging Devil and is delivered from the accusations of a guilty conscience.

7. Nevertheless, the one who took refuge in that city *had to remain there*. If he was foolish enough at any time to forsake its bounds, the revenger of blood had the right to slay him (Num. xxxv, 26, 27). As it was his duty to flee into it, so he was obliged to continue therein. That imports the responsibility of the believer to make use of Christ not only at the time of his conversion, but all through his life. There is as much emphasis placed upon our abiding in Christ as there is upon our coming to Him (John viii, 31 ; Col. i, 23 ; Heb. iii, 6, 14 ; 1 John ii, 28).

8. They were *available for Gentiles* as well as Jews (Num. xxxv, 15) How thankful we should be that " there is no difference between the Jew and the Greek : for the same Lord over all is rich unto all that call upon Him " (Romans x, 12).

9. It was *the death of the high priest* which secured full and final deliverance (Joshua xx, 6). It is indeed striking to observe how the procuring cause of the believer's redemption was prefigured in this many-sided type, though some expositors experience a self-created difficulty in connection therewith. All the days that Israel's high priest lived and the manslayer abode within the city, no condemnation could come upon him ; and since the Christian's High Priest is " alive for evermore," they are eternally secure. Still, it was upon the death of Aaron or his successor that the homicide was made free, as we owe our emancipation to the death of Christ—thus the double figure of the city (safety) and the high priest's death (propitiation) was necessary to set forth both aspects, as were the two goats of Leviticus xvi, 7, 8. There may also be a designed dispensational hint here : saints were saved of old, but not until the death of Christ was the full liberty of sonship enjoyed (Gal. iv, 1-7).

10. *The names of* these cities (Joshua xx, 7, 8) spoke of what the believer has in Christ. Kadesh signifies " holy," and Jesus Christ, the Holy One of God, is made unto the believer sanctification as well as righteousness (I Cor. i; 30)— how deeply suggestive that this is the first mentioned, that in the Redeemer we have a sanctuary of holiness. Shechem means " shoulder," which is the place of strength (Isaiah ix, 7) and of safety (Luke xv, 5)—under the government of

Christ the believer finds security. Hebron means "fellowship," and through Christ His people are brought into communion with the Father and with the holy angels. Bezer means "a fortified place" and "The Lord is good, a strong hold in the day of trouble" (Nahum i, 7); therefore "I will say of the Lord, He is my refuge and my fortress: my God; in Him will I trust" (Psalm xci, 2). Ramoth means "height" or "exaltation": in Christ we are elevated above the world, made to sit in heavenly places (Eph. ii, 6). Golan means "exultation" or "joy," and "we also joy in God through our Lord Jesus Christ" (Romans v, 11).

Chapter 19

THE LEVITICAL CITIES

Joshua 21:1-45

The residence of the Levites. On this occasion it will be *the cities* which were Divinely appointed them for residence which will engage our attention. Since it has pleased the Lord to devote a whole chapter, and a lengthy one, to the subject, it is evident that—whether or not we can discern it—there must be that in it which is of spiritual importance and practical value for us today. Nor shall we experience any difficulty in ascertaining its central message if we bear in mind that the *ministers of the Gospel* are the counterparts of the Levites of old. In that chapter we find it recorded that the heads of the tribe of Levi came before the assembled court of Israel and presented their claim for suitable places where they might settle with their families and possessions. Their petition was received favourably, and their request was granted. Forty-eight cities with their suburbs were assigned them—appointed by the " lot," as had been the case with all the other tribes.

" Then came near the heads of the fathers of the Levites unto Eleazar the priest, and unto Joshua the son of Nun, and unto the heads of the fathers of the tribes of the children of Israel ; and they spake unto them at Shiloh in the land of Canaan, saying, The Lord commanded by the hand of Moses to give us cities to dwell in, with the suburbs thereof for our cattle. And the children of Israel gave unto the Levites out of their inheritance, at the commandment of the Lord, these cities and their suburbs " (xxi, 1-3). Aaron was a descendant of Levi, and in his official capacity as the high priest of Israel he foreshadowed the Lord Jesus, who now, as the Son of God consecrated for evermore, is " a minister of the sanctuary, and of the true tabernacle which the Lord pitched, and not man "(Heb. vii, 28—viii, 2, and cf. Rev.xv, 3-5). The sons of Aaron, by natural generation, are types of Christians who are given to Christ to serve Him (Num. iii, 63), the brethren of Christ sharing by grace His double title of both king and priest (Rev. i, 6, 7). The priestly sons of Aaron and the ministering Levites were also a figure of the public servants of the Lord in the present dispensation, as is clear from I Corinthians ix : " Do ye not know that they which minister about holy things live of the things of the temple ? and they which wait at the altar are partakers with the altar ? Even so hath the Lord ordained that they which preach the gospel should live of the gospel " (verses 13, 14).

In stating that ministers of the Gospel are present-day counterparts of Israel's priests and Levites, it must be borne carefully in mind that (in keeping with the radical differences which characterize the old and the new covenants) there are marked features of dissimilarity as well as resemblance between them. It was the failure, or refusal, to recognize that fact which laid the foundation for the Judaizing and paganizing of public Christianity and the erection and development of " mystery Babylon," with all its sacerdotal and ritualistic pretensions.

385

While there is, as I Corinthians ix, 13, 14, shows, an analogy in the *provision* made for the support of the ministers respectively in both dispensations, there is none whatever in the *services* they render. The priests had no commission to go forth and evangelize (that fell more to the lot of the prophets—Jonah i, 2, etc.), nor is the preacher today called of God to act as an intermediary between others and himself, or in any way to offer satisfaction for their sins—only on the *essential* ground of his being a Christian (and not in an official character as a clergyman) may he intercede for his brethren or present a sacrifice of praise on their behalf.

Israel's priests and Levites were, by their birth and calling, nearer to God than were those for whom they acted, and by virtue of their office holier than they. But both nearness to God and sanctification are conferred in Christ, without any distinction, upon all who are called of God unto the fellowship of His Son, so that, fundamentally, saved ministers and the believers to whom they minister are equal before God. " There is neither Jew nor Greek, there is neither bond nor free, there is neither male nor female [and we may add, there is neither clergy nor laity] : for ye are all one in Christ Jesus " (Gal. iii, 28). Whatever vital privilege and spiritual dignity Christ purchased for one He secured for all His redeemed alike. It is most important that we should be quite clear upon this point, for it gives the death-blow to all priestcraft. There is absolutely nothing of a sacerdotal character in true Christian ministry, and therefore the whole system of Romanism is antichristian. Again, the Jewish priesthood was restricted to the limits of a single family—the Aaronic—whereas in the selection of those whom He calls to preach the Gospel of His Son God is no respecter of persons, but acts according to His sovereign grace and power.

Stating it in its simplest terms, Joshua xxi sets forth the gracious provision which Jehovah made to meet the temporal needs of the Levites. They were the ones who served Him in the tabernacle and ministered to the congregation in holy things, and as such suitably adumbrated the Divinely called ministers of the Gospel, whose lives are devoted to Christ and His churches. Unlike all the other tribes, no separate portion of Canaan was allotted to the Levites upon the distribution of the land (Deut x, 8, 9 ; Joshua xiii, 14). In like manner, the good soldier of Jesus Christ is forbidden to entangle himself with the affairs of this life (II Tim. ii, 3, 4), for it would ill become one who was the messenger of heaven to occupy his heart with earthly avocations. He is called upon to practise what he preaches, to be a living exemplification of his sermons, denying all fleshly and worldly lusts, and be " an example of the believers, in word, in conversation, in charity, in spirit, in faith, in purity." He is required to walk in entire separation from the world, and give himself " wholly " to the things of God and the welfare of souls, that his profiting may appear unto all (I Tim. iv, 12, 15). What mortification of corrupt affections and inordinate desires of earthly things and what spiritual mindedness are necessary if the preacher· is to give a just representation of Him in whose name he ministers.

But though no separate portion of Canaan was to be apportioned to the Levites, that was far from signifying that they must in some way secure their own interests, or that they were left dependent upon the capricious charity of their brethren. It was not the Divine will that they should earn their living by the sweat of the brow, or that they should beg their daily bread. Not so does the Lord treat His beloved servants. He is no Egyptian taskmaster, demanding that they make bricks but refusing to provide them with straw ; instead, He is " the God of all grace," who has promised to supply their every need. Thus it was with the Levites. Full provision was made for their temporal sustenance. The Lord had not only appointed that a liberal part of the heave and wave offerings was to be their food, as well as the best of the oil, and the wine, and the first-fruits, with the tithes of the children of Israel (Num. xviii, 9-19, 24) ; but He had also given a commandment that the other tribes should give unto the Levites, out of their own inheritance, cities to dwell in and the suburbs round about them (Num. xxxv, 2-5). In like manner, God has stipulated that those of His people who are indebted to the spiritual ministrations of His servants should, in turn, minister to their temporal subsistence. This is clear from I Corinthians ix, 13, 14, and, though it may be somewhat of a digression, we will take a closer look at that passage.

In I Corinthians ix, Paul was vindicating his apostleship (verse 3), which his traducers denied. They objected that he had not personally seen Jesus Christ (verse 1), as had the twelve. That he did not live like other men, going without the ordinary comforts of life (verse 4), being unmarried (verse 5). That he and his companion Barnabas were obliged to support themselves by their own manual labours (verse 6), and therefore that he knew they were not entitled to count upon the gifts of believers for their sustenance (verse 12). The main drift of his reply was that, though he acted voluntarily on the principle of self-denial, yet that by no means disproved that he was sent of God, or that he had not a right to be maintained by the saints. So far from that being the case, he was clearly and fully warranted in claiming their support. This he demonstrates by a number of plain and irrefutable arguments, educed from a variety of cogent considerations. Those arguments lay down principles which are applicable to the servants of Christ in all generations, and therefore are pertinent for today, making known as they do the revealed will of God on this practical matter. It therefore behoves the Lord's people carefully to weigh the same and be regulated by them.

He began by asking, " Have not we power to forbear working ? " (verse 6). The word " power " there signifies right or authority, being used in the same sense as it is in John i, 12. Though in the interrogative form, it has the force of an emphatic affirmative : such is our legitimate prerogative, if we choose to exercise it—to abstain from earning our own living, and to count upon the saints ministering to our bodily needs. This he proceeded to prove by three obvious analogies. First, this accords with the universally recognized rule : " Who goeth a warfare at any time at his own charges ? " (verse 7) : as it is the bounden duty of the State to provide for its defenders, equally so of the churches to care for the soldiers of Christ. Second, this is in keeping with the well-established principle that the workman is entitled to remuneration : " Who planteth a vineyard, and eateth not of the fruit thereof ? " Third, this is exemplified by the law of nature : " Or who feedeth a flock, and eateth not the milk of the flock ? " (verse 7) : the husbandman by virtue of his calling has a right to a livelihood from the same. But, conclusive as was such reasoning, the apostle did not conclude at that point.

Paul then proceeded to show that the duty he was contending for—the temporal maintenance of Christ's servants—was not only required by the law of nations, and the dictates of nature, but was urged by the law of God : " For it is written in the law of Moses, Thou shalt not muzzle the mouth of the ox that treadeth out the corn (cf. Deut. xxv, 4)—an example,of the humanity which marks the statutes that God gave to Israel (cf. Exodus xxiii, 19, twice repeated ; Deut. xxii, 6). Labouring for its owner, the ox was worthy of its food, and must not be deprived thereof. Upon which the apostle asks, " Doth God take care for oxen ? Or saith He it altogether [i.e. assuredly] for our sakes ? " (verse 9). If He be so solicitious about the welfare of animals and requires that they be treated justly and kindly, is He indifferent as to how His honoured servants be dealt with ? Surely not. " For our sakes, no doubt, this is written : that he that ploweth should plow in hope, and that he that thresheth in hope should be partaker of his hope " (verse 10). The Mosaic precept was designed in its ultimate application to enforce the principle that labour should have its remuneration, so that men would work more cheerfully. In the next verse the obvious conclusion is drawn.

" If we have sown unto you spiritual things, is it a great thing if we shall reap your carnal things ? " (verse 11). If it be right and meet that those who cultivate the earth should be encouraged to do their work diligently by the assurance that they shall themselves be permitted to enjoy the fruit of their labours, then surely those who engage in the far more important and exacting task of toiling in Christ's vineyard, endeavouring to advance His cause, proclaim His Gospel, feed His sheep, should be recognized and rewarded. The same precept is enforced again in II Timothy ii, 6, " The husbandman that laboureth must be first partaker of the fruits." Still more plainly is the exhortation given, " Let him that is taught in the word communicate unto him that teacheth in all good things. Be not deceived ; God is not mocked : for whatsoever a man soweth, that shall he also reap " (Gal. vi, 6, 7). Thus it is laid down as an unchanging principle that spiritual benefits demand a temporal return. Not that any price can be put upon the invaluable ministry of the Gospel, but that those whom God has set apart to preach it have a just claim for generous compensation. And that not in the way of charity or gratuity, but as *a sacred debt*—a debt which professing Christians fail to discharge at the peril of their souls. For let none be deceived : if they fail to support the Gospel, God will severely chastise them.

Such a statement as that in verse 11 rebukes and shames any spirit of miserliness or stinginess on the part of those who participate in the privileges of a Gospel ministry but fail to do their fair part in supporting the same. If God's servants have been used of Him to bestow one class of benefits, is it unreasonable or unequal that they should receive another class of benefits in return ? Why, there is no proportion between the one and the other. They dispense that which is spiritual and concerns the eternal interests of the soul, whereas you are required to contribute only that which is material for the needs of the body. If they have faithfully executed their office, will you consider it burdensome to discharge your obvious obligations ? Shame on you if you feel that way. Instead, it should be regarded as a holy privilege. " On every principle of commutative justice the minister's right to a subsistence must be conceded " (Hodge). But the apostle did not conclude his appeal even at this point, but clinched his argument by citing scriptural proof that God had ordained this very thing.

" Do ye not know that they which minister about holy things live of the things of the temple ? and they which wait at the altar are partakers with the altar ? " (verse 13). Here the testimony of God's own institution is quoted, linking all that has been before us in I Corinthians ix with the theme of Joshua xxi, for the reference has directly in view the provision made by the Lord for the maintenance of Israel's priests and Levites. They were supported in their work by the offerings of the people, being Divinely permitted to eat a portion of the animals which had been presented to God in sacrifice. " The priests the Levites, and all the tribe of Levi, shall have no part nor inheritance with Israel : they shall eat the offerings of the Lord made by fire, and His inheritance " (Deut. xviii, 1, and cf. Num. v, 9, 10). "A part of the animal offered in sacrifice is burned as an offering to God, and a part becomes the property of the priest for his support ; and thus the altar and the priest become joint participators of the sacrifice. From these offerings the priests derived their maintenance " (A. Barnes, to whom we are indebted for not a little of the above). Thus, that for which the apostle was contending was sanctioned by Divine authority.

" Even so hath the Lord ordained that they which preach the gospel should live of the gospel " (verse 14). Here, by Divine inspiration, the apostle declares that Christ has made the same ordinance for this dispensation as obtained under the old one. He who provided that those who served Him in His earthly temple should be partakers of the altar has also willed that those who minister His Gospel should be duly cared for. This is not optional, but obligatory. It is a Divine command, which demands obedience. If on the one hand the minister is entitled to support, on the other hand his hearers are not at liberty to withhold the same. It is both a duty and a privilege to comply. It is not a matter of charity, but of right, that the preacher should be compensated for his labours. " The maintenance of ministers is not an arbitrary thing, left purely to the good will of the people, who may let them starve if they please ; no, as the God of Israel commanded that Levites should be well provided for, so has the Lord Jesus, the King of the Church, ordained, and a perpetual ordinance it is " (Matthew Henry). Devotion to the Lord, the spirit of gratitude, the claims of love, and the work-ings of grace should make the duty a delight. The honour of Christ's cause, the usefulness of His servants, yes, and the happiness of His people (Acts xx, 35), are bound up in heeding this rule.

A beautiful illustration of compliance with the Divine requirement is found in Philippians iv. There we have the apostle expressing his appreciation and gratitude unto an assembly of the saints for the practical way in which they had manifested their love to him and their fellowship in the Gospel : " But I rejoiced in the Lord greatly, that now at the last your care of me hath flourished again ; wherein ye were also careful [solicitous], but ye lacked opportunity " (verse 10). They were not among that large class of professing Christians who deem themselves willing to profit from a Gospel ministry, but who have very little concern for the temporal welfare of Christ's servants. On the contrary, they had been mindful of His minister, and as occasion arose and opportunity was afforded they had sent of their substance to him while he was away labouring in other parts. This brought back to his memory similar kindnesses which they had shown him years before : " Now ye Philippians know also, that in the beginning of the gospel [when he commenced his evangelistic career], when I departed from Macedonia, no church communicated with me as concerning giving and receiving, but ye only. For even in Thessalonica ye sent once and again unto my necessity " (verses 15, 16). So far from being a case of " out of sight, out of mind," he was constantly in their thoughts.

During Paul's extensive travels the Philippians had lost touch with him—though not their interest in him, as the " wherein [i.e. during the lengthy interval] ye were also careful " attests, but they had no " opportunity " to communicate with him. But now that they learned that he was a prisoner in Rome for the Truth's sake, they sent to him a further token of their affection and esteem by Epaphroditus (verse 18). Most blessed is it to mark the spirit in which the apostle received their gift. First, while gratefully acknowledging their present (verse 14), he looked above them to the One who had put into their hearts the desire to minister unto him : " I rejoiced *in the Lord* greatly (verse 10). Second, he was made happy too on *their* behalf : " Not because I desire a gift : but I desire fruit that may abound to your account " (verse 17)—it furnished proof of the workings of the spirit of grace within, evidencing that they were in a healthy condition spiritually. Third, he declared that their gift met with the approval of his Master, that it was " an odour of a sweet smell, a sacrifice acceptable, wellpleasing to God " (verse 18). Fourth, he assured them that they would be no losers by caring for him : " But my God shall supply all your need according to His riches in glory by Christ Jesus " (verse 19).

" Then came near the heads of the fathers of the Levites unto Eleazar the priest, and unto Joshua the son of Nun, and unto the heads of the fathers of the tribes of the children of Israel " (xxi, 1). There are one or two details here which call for a brief word of explanation. First, each of the tribes was divided into or was grouped under its leading families : they being the descendants of the original sons—the heads, or chiefs, being designated " fathers." Second, Eleazar is mentioned here because this transaction involved the use of " the lot," and he was the one who bore the sacred bag containing the Urim and the Thummim, by which the Divine will was made known. Joshua was also present as Israel's commander, to see that all was done in an orderly manner. Third, the additional reference to " the heads of the fathers of the tribes " clearly intimates that they were now formally assembled as a court, to examine the petitions of claimants and determine their cases.

The careful reader will observe that the chapter opens with the word " Then." That time-mark is more than a historical reference, pointing an important practical lesson which we do well to heed. Historically, the incident recorded here occurred " when they had made an end of dividing the land for inheritance by their coasts," and when " the children of Israel gave an inheritance to Joshua the son of Nun " (xix, 49). Then Joshua was bidden by the Lord, " Speak to the children of Israel, saying, Appoint out for you cities of refuge, whereof I spake unto you by the hand of Moses " (xx, 2). Now the Lord had previously given orders that those cities of refuge (six in number) were to be " among the cities which ye shall give unto the Levites . . . and to them ye shall add forty and two cities. So all the cities which ye shall give to the Levites shall be forty and eight cities : them shall ye give with their suburbs " (Num. xxxv, 6, 7). Those cities of refuge had now been specified (xxi, 7, 8), but as yet the remaining forty-two had not been assigned them.

"And they spake unto them at Shiloh in the land of Canaan " (verse 2), for that was where the tabernacle was now situated, and therefore the place where the mind of the Lord could be authoritatively ascertained. It is blessed to see that the Levites deferred their appeal until all the other tribes had been provided for, thereby setting an admirable pattern before all the official servants of God, to suppress everything in themselves which has even the appearance of covetousness. How incongruous and reprehensible it is for those who profess to be the ministers of grace and truth to exhibit a mercenary or greedy demeanour ! It was " an instance of their humility, modesty, and patience (and Levites should be examples of these and other virtues) that they were willing to be served last, and they fared never the worse for it. Let not God's ministers complain if at any time they find themselves postponed in men's thoughts and cares, but let them make sure of the favour of God and the honour that comes from Him, and then they may well enough afford to bear the slights and neglects of men " (Henry)

It should also be carefully noted that these God-honouring Levites made known their claim openly and publicly, instead of secretly and privately. They did not engage in a " whispering campaign," going around sowing the seeds of dissension among their brethren, or of criticism of Joshua, complaining at their being neglected—for as yet no provision had been made where they should reside with their families and flocks. No, they applied in an orderly and frank manner before the Divinely appointed court, saying, " The Lord commanded by the hand of Moses to give us cities to dwell in, with the suburbs thereof for our cattle " (verse 2). Their petition was brief and to the point ; their language firm but reverent. They came not as beggars, and asked for no favours. Their appeal was neither to charity nor to equity—as being due them on the ground of fairness. They used no claim of worthiness or fidelity to duty. Instead, their appeal was made to *the word* of God, that which He had commanded by Moses ; and thus they acted on the basis of a " Thus saith the Lord."

It is quite evident, then, that on this occasion the Levites were far from being actuated by a spirit of either discontent or covetousness. Had they been moved by avarice they had not waited until now, but had either taken matters into their own hands or had put in their claim much earlier. No, it was an orderly request that they should now receive that to which they were entitled by Divine grant. Most commendable was their meekness and patience. How different the character and conduct of so many ecclesiastics during the Christian era, whose love of money and lust for power knew no bounds, scrupling not to employ the most tyrannous measures and heartless methods to impoverish their members while they lived in luxury and resided in their " palaces " ! And the same spirit is by nature in every preacher, and against its least indulgence he needs to be on his guard. Unspeakably solemn is it to note that the oft-quoted words, " For the love of money is the root of all evil : which while some coveted after, they have erred from the faith, and pierced themselves through with many sorrows," occur in one of the *pastoral* epistles ! They are succeeded by, " But thou, O man of God [i.e. servant of Christ], flee these things ; and follow after righteousness, godliness, faith, love, patience, meekness " (I Tim. vi, 10, 11).

Nor is it without reason that the injunction " having food and raiment, let us be therewith content " is found in *the same epistle* (vi, 8), immediately preceding the above warning and exhortation. Few realize the sinfulness of discontent, which is nothing but a species of self-will, a secret murmuring against Providence, a being dissatisfied with the portion God has given us. Contrariwise, contentment is a holy composure of mind, a resting in the Lord, a thankful enjoyment of what He *has* graciously bestowed. Hence, contentment is the spiritual antidote to covetousness : " Let your conversation be without covetousness ; and be content with such things as ye have " (Heb. xiii, 5)—the former vice can be avoided only by assiduously cultivating the opposite virtue. If the preacher is to magnify his office and glorify his Master, he needs to mortify his fleshly lusts and carnal ambitions, abstaining from all extravagance, and living frugally ; evidencing that his affections are set upon things above and not on things below. When Socrates the pagan philosopher beheld a display of costly and elegant articles for sale, he exclaimed : " How many things are here that I need not ! " Such ought to be the attitude and language of every child of God as he passes through this " Vanity Fair," pre-eminently so in the case of His servants.

" Giving no offence in any thing, that the ministry be not blamed : but in all things approving [commending] ourselves as the ministers of God " (II Cor. vi, 3, 4). What an exalted standard of piety is that ! Yet nothing less is what the Holy One requires of His representatives. The unbelieving are ever ready to charge the Gospel itself with having a strong tendency to encourage the carnalities which disgrace the character of so many professors, and especially if the same appear in the lives of those who preach it. Nor is that a thing to be wondered at. What can be expected from those who have no experiential acquaintance with the things of God than to conclude that those who preach salvation by grace through Jesus Christ are the products of the same ? In their judgment, the daily life of the preacher either commends or condemns his message. Hence it is that, among other reasons, the minister of Christ is bidden : " In all things showing thyself a pattern of good works : in doctrine showing uncorruptness, gravity, sincerity, sound speech [and not the slang of the world], that cannot be condemned ; that he that is of the contrary part may be ashamed, having no evil thing to say of you " (Titus ii, 7, 8).

Returning more directly to the Levites in Joshua xxi. In their " The Lord commanded by the hand of Moses to give us cities to dwell in " they were, in reality, *pleading a Divine promise* ! It was recorded in Numbers xxxv, 1-8, that Jehovah issued definite orders to that end, and therefore they were asking only for that to which they had a right by Divine authority. Here too they have left an example, which needs to be followed not only by God's servants but by all of His people, for it is *the use* which we make of His promises that, to a considerable extent, regulates our spiritual prosperity, as well as the peace and joy of our hearts. First, we should labour to become well acquainted with the same, for while we remain in ignorance no benefit can be derived from them. Those Levites were informed upon that which concerned their interests. So should we be. We should daily search the Scriptures for them, and make an inventory of our spiritual wealth. The Divine promises are the peculiar treasure of the saints, for the substance of faith's inheritance is wrapped up in them. Second, they should be carefully stored in our minds, constantly meditated upon, and every effort of Satan's to rob us of the same steadfastly resisted.

Third, God's promises are to be personally appropriated and pleaded before His throne of grace. This is one reason why He has given them to us : not only to manifest His lovingkindness in making known His gracious intentions, but also for the comfort of our hearts. Had He so pleased, our Father could have bestowed His blessings without giving us notice of His benign purposes ; but He has ordained that we should enjoy them twice over : first by faith, and then by fruition. By this means He weans our hearts away from things seen and temporal, and draws them onward and upward to things which are spiritual and eternal. Thus are we to make His promises the support and stay of our souls. Not only are they to be the food of faith, but the regulators of our petitions. Real prayer is the making request for those things which God is pledged to bestow : "And this is the confidence that we have in Him, that, if we ask any thing according to His will, He heareth us " (I John v, 14) : that is, according as His will is made known to us in His Word—anything other than that is self-will on our part (James iv, 3).

While on the one hand God has promised to bestow, on the other hand we are required to make request—that He may be duly owned and honoured, that we express our dependence upon Him. "Ask, and ye shall receive " is the Divinely appointed way. In Ezekiel xxxvi, 36, God makes most definite promise to His people, adding, " I the Lord have spoken it, and *I will do it.*" Yet immediately after, He declares, " Thus saith the Lord God ; I will yet [nevertheless] for this be enquired of by the house of Israel, *to do it* for them." Such inquiry is designed for the strengthening of our faith, the quickening of our hope, the development of our patience. Cities had been Divinely assured unto the Levites, yet they received them not until they appealed for them by pleading God's word to them through Moses ! And that has been recorded for our instruction. One wonders how often it is the case that " ye have not, because ye ask not " (James iv, 2)—always so when faith be not in exercise (James i, 6, 7). Observe well how Jacob pleaded the Divine promise in Genesis xxxii, 18 ; Moses in Exodus xxxii, 13 ; David in Psalm cxix, 58 ; Solomon in I Kings viii, 25, and go thou and do likewise.

"And the children of Israel gave unto the Levites out of their inheritance, at the commandment of the Lord, these cities and their suburbs " (xxi, 3). Thus was the priestly tribe fully provided for through its brethren by Divine ordinance ; and it is blessed to mark how particularly the Holy Spirit has placed it upon record that they discharged this obligation as an act of obedience unto God. They might have demurred at being called upon to relinquish some of the places which they had fought hard to obtain, but they raised no objection and duly performed their duty when reminded of the Divine will. In like manner, Christians are bidden to communicate unto those who care for their spiritual interests, and to do so at God's commandment. Equally striking is it to observe how that the portion received by the Levites was a *gift*—so referred to in both verses 2 and 3. This act of giving was designed by the Lord to counteract that selfish spirit and attachment to a present world which is common to all of us. The same principle is illustrated again in Romans xv, 27 : " their debtors they are. For if the Gentiles have been made partakers of their [Israel's] spiritual things, their duty is also to minister unto them in carnal things."

The principle which was to regulate the allocating of the Levitical cities by their brethren was clearly defined in Numbers xxxv, 8, "And the cities which ye shall give shall be of the possession of the children of Israel : from them that have many ye shall give many ; but from them that have few ye shall give few ; every one shall give of his cities unto the Levites according to his inheritance which he inheriteth." Thus was each tribe accorded the opportunity of making grateful acknowledgment unto the Lord of what He had so graciously bestowed upon them, for what they gave unto the Levites was accepted as given to Him, and thereby were their possessions sanctified to them—some of the best and largest of the cities being freely donated. The several tribes were not assessed uniformly, but according to the extent of their possessions. The equity of such an arrangement is at once apparent. The same was duly executed, for out of Judah's and Simeon's lots (the most extensive) nine cities were given, whereas out of the other tribes only four cities were taken from each (Joshua xxi). In like manner, New Testament saints are exhorted, " Upon the first day of the week let every one of you lay by him in store, as God hath prospered him " (I Cor. xvi, 2), i.e. a definite proportion of his income.

If it be true on the one side that a mercenary priesthood has been notorious for its greedy grasping of wealth and temporal power ; on the other side, only too frequently many of the most devoted and self-sacrificing of Christ's servants have received the scantiest acknowledgment. As Barnes remarked, " The poor beast that has served the man and his family in the days of his vigour is often turned out in old age to die ; and something like this sometimes occurs in the treatment of ministers of the Gospel. The conduct of a people, generous in many other respects, is often unaccountable in their treatment of their pastors ; and one of the lessons which ministers often have to learn, like their Master, by bitter experience, is the ingratitude of those in whose welfare they have toiled and prayed and wept." Yet that is far from being always the case, as this writer can thankfully testify. For upwards of forty years the Lord has moved His stewards to minister freely and liberally to his temporal needs ; so that we too can reply to His question "lacked ye anything? Nothing" (Luke xxii, 35). No good thing has He withheld from us.

The method followed by Israel in selecting the Levitical cities appears to have been something like this. First, the court, after duly considering the size of its inheritance, appointed how many cities should be taken out of each tribe. Then the "fathers of the tribes" agreed among themselves which cities were most suitable. After that had been settled, the forty-eight cities were divided into four groups, for the four branches of the Levitical tribe. Lots were cast to determine the distribution of them. The sons of Levi were Gershom, Kohath, Merari. From Kohath descended Moses, Aaron and Miriam (I Chron. vi, 1-3). The "children of Aaron" (Joshua xxi, 4) were not only Levites, but priests too, whose more immediate work was to serve at the altar. It should be duly noted that though this was the least numerous of the four branches, yet, in keeping with the prominence of the priesthood throughout the book of Joshua, "the first lot" (verse 10) was for the children of Aaron, and thus was honour placed again upon this Divine institution. It is further to be observed that more cities were assigned unto them than to any other branch of Levi.

It should perhaps be pointed out that the term "city" in Scripture does not signify (as it does with us today) a large town having a corporation, but simply "an inclosed space"—see Genesis iv, 17, for the first mention. The "suburbs," as pastures for the cattle, extended for nearly a mile in every direction (Num. xxxv, 5). In appointing the larger number of cities for the children of Aaron we see a proof of the Divine foreknowledge, for those who have made a thorough study of this detail judge that they increased more than any of the other three families, therefore larger accommodation would be required for their descendants in the future. That their cities were taken from that part of Canaan which had been given to the tribes of Judah, Simeon and Benjamin (Joshua xxi, 4) was also profoundly significant, illustrating as it did the wise disposings of Providence, for that was the territory which lay nearest *to Jerusalem*, which centuries later was to be the site of the temple, and the headquarters of Judaism. That was the place which had been chosen in the Divine counsels where God should put His name. "Known unto God are all His works from the beginning of the world" (Acts xv, 18)!

In verse 8 the statement is repeated, "And the children of Israel gave by lot unto the Levites these cities with their suburbs, as the Lord commanded by the hand of Moses." This is to intimate that all was done by Divine appointment and in obedience unto God's will. There is a touching detail recorded in verse 11 which we must not overlook, for there we are told that the city of Hebron became the possession of the children of Aaron. It will be remembered that this was the city which had been given to Caleb by the commandment of the Lord (Joshua xv, 13). It seems, then, that he had personally made it a voluntary present unto the priests, thereby setting an example before his fellows of noble generosity and devotion to the cause of Jehovah. How he puts to shame many church members of today who are so neglectful of the maintenance of Christ's servants! Those who are indifferent to the temporal welfare of His ministers cannot be in communion with Him who notices the fall of every sparrow, or recognize the holy privileges of being "fellowhelpers to the Truth" (III John 8). May writer and reader ever act in this manner "according to the commandment of the Lord."

Chapter 20

DEMOBILIZATION

JOSHUA 22:1-34

Pledges Honored

"Then Joshua called the Reubenites, and the Gadites, and the half tribe of Manasseh" (xxii, 1). The opening "Then" looks back to xxi, 43-45, where there is a brief but blessed summing up of all that is recorded in the foregoing chapters : "And the Lord gave unto Israel all the land which He sware to give unto their fathers ; and they possessed it, and dwelt therein. And the Lord gave them rest round about, according to all that He sware unto their fathers ; and there stood not a man of all their enemies before them ; the Lord delivered all their enemies into their hand. There failed not ought of any good thing which the Lord had spoken unto the house of Israel ; all came to pass." Therein thankful acknowledgment was made of the inviolable integrity of Jehovah, for there had been an exact performance of everything He had promised. Therein we behold His unchanging faithfulness : notwithstanding their wilderness provocations, He brought them into Canaan. Therein we have exhibited the perfect harmony which there is between God's words and His works, which are wonderful not only in contrivance, but equally so in their execution. Therein we learn how sure is the fulfilment of Divine prophecy ; every detail predicted was literally accomplished.

The Lord had promised to give the land of Canaan unto Abram's seed for a possession (Gen. xii, 7), and He had now done so. He promised to make Abram's seed a prolific and numerous one (Gen. xiii, 16), and they " multiplied and grew " (Exodus i, 12), so that by the time they left Egypt a single family had become " about six hundred thousand on foot that were men, besides children " (Exodus xii, 37). The Lord promised to preserve them in all places whither they went (Gen. xxviii, 15), and He had done so—in Egypt, at the Red Sea, and throughout all their wilderness journeyings. He promised to bring into Canaan the fourth generation of Abram's descendants after their sojourn in Egypt (Gen. xv, 16), and a close examination of Exodus vi, 16-28, proves that so it came to pass. The Lord promised to give them success in their fighting : " I will send My fear before thee (cf. Joshua ii, 9), and will destroy all the people to whom thou shalt come, and I will make all thine enemies turn their backs unto thee . . . for I will deliver the inhabitants of the land into your hand " (Exodus xxiii, 27, 31), and so their sons acknowledged (Psalm xliv, 3). He promised to deliver " kings " into their hands (Deut. vii, 24), and Joshua x, 24, 40, attests that He did so. He promised to give them " rest " in the land (Deut. xii, 10), and we are told " the Lord gave them rest " (Joshua xxi, 44).

There were indeed some of the original inhabitants still left in the land to test and try God's people ; but at the close of the seven-year campaign all open conflict had ceased. The whole of Canaan had now been given by Divine lot unto Abram's descendants : the greater part of it was then occupied by the different tribes, and they were peacefully settled in their heritage. If they continued to obey the Lord and count upon His enablement, they should still more completely possess their possessions. " There failed not ought of any good thing which the Lord had spoken unto the house of Israel." Such will be the triumphant testimony of the whole Church collectively and of every Christian individually. In due season shall all that God has promised the spiritual Israel come to pass, with regard both to their present comfort and future felicity. All will be accomplished, exactly and perfectly, as God has declared, for all His promises are in Christ yea and amen (II Cor. i, 20). At the last, when the whole company of the redeemed will have entered their eternal rest and inheritance, they will bear joyous witness that " He hath done all things well."

" Then Joshua called the Reubenites, and the Gadites, and the half tribe of Manasseh " (xxii, 1). The passage which opens with those words contains the sequel to what is recorded at some length in Numbers xxxii. There we read, " Now the children of Reuben and the children of Gad had a very great multitude of cattle : and when they saw the land of Jazer, and the land of Gilead, that, behold, the place was a place for cattle . . . came and spake unto Moses, and to Eleazar the priest, and unto the princes of the congregation, saying . . . the country which the Lord smote before the congregation of Israel, is a land for cattle, and thy servants have cattle ; wherefore, said they, if we have found grace in thy sight, let this land be given unto thy servants for a possession, and bring us not over Jordan " (verses 1-5). They referred to the land which had formerly been occupied by Sihon and Og, whose forces Israel had, under God, completely destroyed, and whose territory they then seized by right of victory (Num xxi, 21-35). Lying in the Jordan valley, the ground was well watered, and ideal for pasturage.

For several months the camp of Israel had remained stationary on the plains of Moab : looking backward to the house of bondage from which they had been delivered ; looking forward to the land of Canaan which had been promised them for their inheritance. Behind them lay the dreary desert, before them was the river of Jordan. In view of the mentioning of " the princes of the congregation " in addition to Eleazar, it would appear that an official conference of the Sanhedrin, or chief counsel of the nation, was being held—perhaps over the disposing of the territory which had been acquired by their recent victory. The language used by the spokesman of the two tribes also conveys the impression that their request was of the nature of a formal petition. It was to the effect that they should be given the title to settle in the luxurious valley of Jazer and Gilead. There was nothing underhand or stealthy in the appeal which they. made, but an honourable and open approach unto the heads of authority ; and in a meek and modest spirit, as their " if we have found grace in thy sight " evinces. Notwithstanding, the commentators generally condemn their action.

It is concluded by some that their conduct was very blameworthy : that they showed contempt of Canaan, or, if not that, were following the line of least resistance in wanting to remain where they were, and thus escape the hardships and fighting which the crossing of the Jordan would involve. Others see in their proposal a display of covetousness, a greedy desire to make this fertile portion their own. Still others charge them with being lacking in public spirit, putting their own private interests before the common good of the nation. Personally, we see nothing definite in the narrative to support such views, but rather some things to the contrary. Had their request been as reprehensible as these critics make out, they had been promptly informed of its *unlawfulness,* and there the matter would have terminated. Most certainly the Lord had never confirmed it ! God had already delivered this land into the hands of Israel, and someone must inherit and inhabit it. It was particularly suited for pasturage, and *that* was what these tribes, with their " very great multitude of cattle," most needed. Nor were they despising the Lord's inheritance, for the boundary of Canaan was not the Jordan, but rather the mountain-range of Gilead, which separated it from the desert lying beyond. Thus, as Joshua xxii, 9, shows, the section desired by these tribes was as much *within* Canaan proper as was the land on the farther side of the Jordan.

Moses was thoroughly displeased with their suggestion, placing the worst construction upon it. He supposed that their request proceeded from a spirit of cowardice and sloth. He considered that they were giving way to unbelief, distrusting God's power, seeking to shelve their responsibility (Num. xxxv, 6). In any case, it would mean the weakening of Israel's army by a reduction of at least one fifth of its manpower. Moreover, they were asking him to establish a dangerous precedent, which others might desire to follow (verse 7). He recalled the faint-heartedness of their fathers, and the disastrous sequel which had attended the same (verses 8, 9). He feared that their attitude would bring down the Lord's wrath upon the whole congregation (verse 14). But his suspicions were unwarranted, and his fears unnecessary.

"And they came near unto him, and said, We will build sheepfolds here for our cattle, and cities for our little ones : but we ourselves will go ready armed before the children of Israel, until we have brought them unto their place : and our little ones shall dwell in the fenced cities because of the inhabitants of the land. We will not return unto our houses, until the children of Israel have inherited every man his inheritance. For we will not inherit with them on yonder side Jordan, or forward ; because our inheritance is fallen to us on this side Jordan eastward " (Num xxxii, 16-19). Thus did they show how grievously Moses had misjudged them, and how unfounded were his surmisings. They had no intention of sitting still while the other tribes went to war. Without murmuring or disputing, they expressed a willingness to share their brethren's burden. So far from being afraid to enter the field against the enemy, they were prepared to take the lead and go " before the children of Israel." They would remain with their fellows until all of them were duly settled. Nor would they require any compensation or expect to receive any share of the spoils.

Satisfied with their explanation and assurances, Moses conditionally granted their request. Holding them to their promises, he agreed to the proposal on their fulfilment of its terms. If they carried out their part of the contract, the land of Jazer and Gilead should be their " possession before the Lord " (Num. xxxii, 22). But if they went back upon their word, then they would be offending against God Himself, and in such an event their sin was certain to find them out (verse 23), which signifies that bitter and inevitable would be the consequences, and not discovered or brought to light. " Thy servants will do as my lord commandeth " (verse 25) was their ready response and solemn vow. Thereupon the agreement was formally and publicly ratified before Israel's supreme court, Joshua (who was to succeed him) being expressly informed of the compact (verse 28), according to the terms of which the coasts and cities of Sihon and Og became the possession of the two and a half tribes (verse 33). Thus did they strikingly prefigure the Old Testament saints, who entered into their spiritual inheritance during the Mosaic economy.

When Joshua took over the leadership, he addressed himself to the two and a half tribes thus : " Remember the word which Moses the servant of the Lord commanded you, saying, The Lord your God hath given you rest, and hath given you this land," and then detailed the stipulated conditions of this provisional arrangement (i, 12-15). As we pointed out in the ninth article of this series, Joshua was acting here not on the ground of natural prudence, but in obedience to his Master's will. The Lord had bidden him to " observe to do according to all the law, which Moses My servant commanded thee " (i, 7), and *this* was one of those things (Num. xxxii, 28) ! Thus, the new head of the nation did not take it for granted that they would carry out their agreement, but definitely reminded them of the same and held them to it. It is blessed, too, to observe the ground upon which he appealed to them : it was neither as a personal favour to himself for their co-operation nor as an encouragement unto their brethren, but as an act of obedience : " Remember the word which Moses the servant of the Lord commanded you."

Equally blessed is it to hear their response : "And they answered Joshua, saying, All that thou commandest us we will do, and whithersoever thou sendest us, we will go. According as we hearkened unto Moses in all things, so will we hearken unto thee : only the Lord thy God be with thee " (i, 16, 17). Thus did they solemnly and explicitly renew their agreement ; and, as the sequel demonstrates, it was no idle boast that they made. It is ever God's way to honour those who honour Him : Joshua had given Him His proper place by complying with his commission and magnifying God's Word, and now the Lord graciously inclined these two and a half tribes willingly to serve under him. In his " until the Lord have given your brethren rest . . . and they also have possessed the land " (verse 15), he expressed his unwavering faith in the successful outcome of the campaign ; and here the Lord moved these men to give him their full support. They averred their willingness to accept him as their commander and yield full obedience to his authority.

Faithfully did they fulfil their part of the agreement : "And the children of Reuben, and the children of Gad, and half the tribe of Manasseh, passed over armed before the children of Israel, as Moses spake unto them : about forty thousand prepared for war passed over before the Lord unto battle, to the plains of Jericho " (iv, 12, 13). How the Holy Spirit delights to record the obedience of saints ! And now we come to the happy sequel to the whole of the above : " Then Joshua called the Reubenites, and the Gadites, and the half tribe of Manasseh, and said unto them, Ye have kept all that Moses the servant of the Lord commanded you, and have obeyed my voice in all that I commanded you : ye have not left your brethren these many days unto this day, but have kept the charge of the commandment of the Lord your God " (xxii, 2, 3). A real tribute of praise was that, and a signal proof of the magnanimity of the one who paid it. Though they had only discharged a manifest obligation and fulfilled their part of the contract, it cost Joshua nothing to acknowledge their fidelity and commend their obedience, and such a word from their general would mean much to them.

They had given further proof of the sterling quality of their character by submitting to the authority of Joshua. They might have pleaded that their agreement had been made with *Moses,* and that, since death cancels all contracts, his decease relieved them of their engagement. But having put their hand to the plough, they refused to look back (Luke ix, 62). Or, to change the figure, they conducted themselves in a manner that was in every respect the very opposite of that of the Ephraimites at a later date, of whom we read that they " turned back in the day of battle. They kept not the covenant of God, and refused to walk in His law " (Psalm lxxviii, 9, 10). Alas, how the courage of many who enlist under the banner of Christ fails them in the day of testing, so that they retreat before the foe ; and in the hour of temptation prove false to their good resolutions and solemn promises and vows. Different far was it with these Reubenites and Gadites. Not only did they begin well, but they also endured unto the end ; yea, their wholehearted devotion to the cause of God and His people *increased,* for a comparison of Joshua i, 16, with Numbers xxxii, 31, reveals that the promise which they made unto Joshua went beyond that which they had pledged unto Moses.

For seven years they had served obediently under Joshua, had disinterestedly put the welfare of the nation before their own private comforts, had made no attempt to rejoin their families, but had remained by the side of their brethren until Canaan was conquered. Most commendable was their meekness in waiting for their dismissal. They did not chafe at the delay, but were submissive to their leader's will. Instead of seeking out Joshua and complaining that it was high time for them to return to their homes, they quietly tarried for Him to take the initiative in the matter. As another remarked, " Like good soldiers they would not move till they had orders from their general. They had not only done their duty to Joshua and Israel, but, which was best of all, they had made conscience of their duty to God : ' Ye have kept the charge,' or, as the word is, ' Ye have kept the keeping,' that is, Ye have carefully and circumspectly kept the commandments of the Lord your God : not only in this particular instance of continuing in the service of Israel to the end of the war, but in general, you have kept up religion in your part of the camp—a rare and excellent thing among soldiers, and which is worthy to be praised " (Matthew Henry).

"And now the Lord your God hath given rest unto your brethren, as He promised them : therefore now return ye, and get you unto your tents, and unto the land of your possession, which Moses the servant of the Lord gave you on the other side Jordan " (verse 4). How careful was Joshua to place the crown of honour where it rightly belonged, and ascribe the glory of their victory unto the Author of the same ! At the same time, he considered it meet that thankful acknowledgment should be made to those who had assisted him therein. " God must be chiefly eyed in our praises, but instruments must not be altogether overlooked " (Henry). Equally definite was Joshua in here magnifying the fidelity of Jehovah, reminding Israel that the successful outcome of their military efforts, and the resultant rest for the whole nation, was the fulfilment of the sure word of the Lord. Having faithfully performed their part of the contract by sharing the hardships and dangers of their brethren, Joshua now made good the assurances which Moses had given to the two and a half tribes, publicly and solemnly granting them an honourable discharge from the army and authorizing them to rejoin their families.

" But take diligent heed to do the commandment and the law, which Moses the servant of the Lord charged you, to love the Lord your God, and to walk in all His ways, and to keep His commandments, and to cleave unto Him, and to serve Him with all your heart and with all your soul " (verse 5). Ere dismissing the two and a half tribes, Joshua gave them salutary counsel. No instructions were furnished for the fortifying of their cities or for the cultivation of their land, the whole emphasis being placed upon the regulating of their spiritual lives. Nor was there any lowering of the rule to meet their " moral inability," but a strict maintaining of God's claims upon them. " Perfect obedience to the Divine Law was no more practicable in the days of Joshua than at present, yet his exhortation takes no notice of this, for the standard of obedience cannot be too high (Matt. v, 43-48), nor our aim too high, as we are sure to fall very far short of what we propose for ourselves. But the consciousness of our imperfections subserves the purposes of humiliation, and the feeling of our insufficiency dictates prayers for forgiveness and assistance " (Thomas Scott). It is not sufficient that we know God's Law, we are required to *do* it : in order to obedience, we must " take diligent heed " : we shall only walk in God's ways to the extent that we serve Him wholeheartedly, for love to Him is the spring of all acceptable obedience and worship.

Demobilization

Attention has been called to the conflicting opinions relative to the actions of the Reubenites, the Gadites, and the half tribe of Manasseh in seeking their inheritance on the wilderness side of Jordan. The opinion of some is that they did wrong; while, of course, the opposite opinion is shared by others. In these studies this second opinion has been sustained. Where in Scripture there is no direct statement to clarify a matter, it is well not to dogmatize but to love as brethren and to be courteous (I Peter 3:8). One thing is sure, they returned to their possessions on the east side of Jordan with the commendation and blessing of Joshua.

Frequently the Apostle Paul opens his epistles to the churches, as did Joshua his address to the two and a half tribes, with a word of praise. To the saints with the bishops and deacons at Philippi, he wrote, "I thank my God upon every remembrance of you, Always in every prayer of mine for you all making request with joy, For your fellowship in the gospel from the first day until now" (Phil. 1:3-5). Christians should seek to maintain the attitude of "honour to whom honour is due, and all the glory to God."

While Joshua released the two and a half tribes from present military obligations, he imposed upon them other obligations of both a spiritual and a material character; they were to be mindful of the Lord and of their brethren.

Joshua reduced the content of the divine commandment to five important statements: to love the Lord, to walk in His ways, to observe His commandments, to cleave to Him and to serve Him. These would engage the entire personality and demand an unreserved response of the whole being to the divine claims. Their meaning to those for whom they were intended would be very similar to that of the Apostle's words to the saints at Corinth and, of course, to us: "Ye are not your own. For ye are bought with a price: therefore glorify God in your body, and in your spirit, which are God's" (I Cor. 6:19-20).

It would be difficult for these faithful war veterans not to feel a sense of pride in their accomplishment, especially after the eulogy of Joshua; and to feel that the much riches, much cattle, silver, gold, brass, iron, and very much raiment, with which they returned were their own, the remunerative spoils of the battles they had fought and won, their possessions purchased with blood. Notwithstanding, Joshua instructed them, saying, "Divide the spoil of your enemies with your brethren" (v. 8), those that had remained at home to guard their belongings.

Moses had set a precedent years before when he had avenged the children of Israel of the Midianites. The Lord spoke to him, and said, "Take the sum of the prey that was taken, both of man and of beast, thou, and Eleazar the priest, and the chief of the fathers of the congregation: And divide the prey into two parts; between them that took the war upon them, who went out to battle, and between all the congregation" (Num. 31:26-27). Centuries later this was the principle upon which David commanded his men, "As his part is that goeth down to the battle, so shall his part be that tarrieth by the stuff: they shall part alike" (I Sam. 30:24).

While this is not the only principle underlying David's song of triumph, Psalm 68, it is one of them. The victor who had led the former captor into captivity gave gifts unto men, apparently from the spoils of the battle (v. 18), sharing his victory with others. The Spirit of God applies this conception to our Lord Jesus in Ephesians 4:8, 11: "When he ascended up on high, he led captivity captive, and gave gifts unto men. . . . And he gave some, apostles; and some, prophets; and some, evangelists; and some, pastors and teachers." As the men who remained on the east side of Jordan were enriched by the spoils of the war fought by their brethren, even so the Church has been enriched by the spoils of Calvary where Christ, "having spoiled [stripped] principalities and powers, . . . made a shew of them openly, triumphing over them in it" (Col. 2:15). Our blessed Lord shares with His Church His glorious victory.

The Memorial Altar

"Let him that thinketh he standeth take heed lest he fall" (I Cor. 10:12). God's people must learn to act in the spirit of Hezekiah, who said, "I shall go softly all my years" (Isa. 38:15). There is always need of caution lest, having earned a commendation, we imprudently and inadvertently bring upon ourselves and others unnecessary troubles. God would have His own abstain from every appearance of evil (I Thess. 5:22). The plans we formulate and execute may veil the true intention of the heart, and result in misunderstandings.

Shiloh had become the headquarters of Joshua (Joshua 18:8-9). Gilgal was the place associated with the conquest of the land (Joshua 5); it was from his military position there that Joshua directed the invasion of Canaan. When the conquest was assured, obviously he moved to Shiloh, a good choice because of its central location, and from there supervised the distribution of the territory. It was from here that these heroic soldiers were demobilized and sent back to their families.

A memorial marked that earlier extraordinary episode in the history of the nation, the crossing of the Jordan. Moses had built it when first they entered the land. Representatives of these very tribes had carried the stones out of the river and piled them as a cairn on its bank (Joshua 4), stones which were to be a sign to future generations. They had carried out the instructions of the Lord, "This may be a sign among you, that when your children ask their fathers in time to come, saying, What mean ye by these stones? Then ye shall answer them, That the waters of the Jordan were cut off before the ark of the covenant of the LORD; when it passed over Jordan, the waters of Jordan were cut off: and these stones shall be for a memorial unto the children of Israel for ever" (vv. 6-7).

The Reubenites, the Gadites, and those from Manasseh apparently felt that as a memorial witnessed before their posterity to the miraculous entering into Canaan, so a memorial should also witness to their children why they recrossed the Jordan, and why they had their inheritance on the east side.

No matter how plausible the argument for the altar seemed, there was a great difference between the cairn of stones and the altar as they stood on the bank of Jordan; the one was there in obedience to the Word of God, the other because of human reasoning and planning. Any departure from the divine will as it has been revealed, whether by an addition to it or a subtraction from it, must ultimately involve us in difficulties.

The intention of the two and a half tribes may have been sincere enough, but the appearance of the altar certainly seemed to violate the Word of God given by Moses, "And it shall be on the day when ye shall pass over Jordan unto the land which the LORD thy God giveth thee, . . . there shalt thou build an altar unto the LORD thy God" (Deut. 27:1-10). Their brethren viewed it in that light. The motive may not have been wrong, but the method was not right.

From the reading of Joshua 22:11 in the King James Version, it would appear as if the two altars were very close together; but since the phrase, "at the passage of the children of Israel," might also be rendered "at the side of them" the actual position of this second altar is not given.

This memorial of sacred appearance might easily have been a trap for future generations instead of a witness. The brazen serpent which brought life to many dying in Israel (Num. 21), eventually became a snare and the people worshiped it. Good King Hezekiah destroyed it along with other idolatrous objects when he instituted his reforms in the nation (II Kings 18:4).

We read that it was "a great altar to see to"; that is, to look upon. It was large so as to attract attention. How very human! An accomplishment by man generally results in a large celebration and display, an ostentatious reminder of successful performance. The classic example of this is Nebuchadnezzar and his massive image through which he sought worship. With pride he exclaimed, "Is not this great Babylon, that I have built for the house of the kingdom by the might of my power, and for the honour of my majesty?" Even as he thus spoke, divine judgment was decreed against him (Dan. 4:30-31). Surely, "a man's pride shall bring him low" (Prov. 29:23). "Whosoever shall exalt himself shall be abased; and he that shall humble himself shall be exalted" (Matt. 23:12).

Alarm spread quickly among the other tribes. "When the children of Israel heard of it [the building of the altar], the whole congregation of the children of Israel gathered themselves together at Shiloh, to go up to war against them" (v. 12).

Shiloh, as we have noticed, was the centre of government. Israel met there in a general and solemn assembly. This was not a movement resulting from mass psychology, nor was it a rash act that might burst into mob violence. The Lord through Moses had legislated already how apostasy was to be punished. Israel, therefore, in formal assembly gathered for consultation and investigation. This wise and firm action stands in vivid contrast to that of the men of Gilead who indiscriminately slew forty-two thousand of the tribe of Ephraim (Judges 12). The rash words of the Ephraimites on that occasion indubitably were provocative, but the harsh and cruel deeds of Jephthah and his followers were not justifiable.

The Spirit of God differentiates between righteous indignation and cruel anger and malice. Of the first He says, "Be ye angry and sin not: let not the sun go down upon your wrath"; but of the second He says, "Let all bitterness, and wrath, and anger, and clamour, and evil speaking, be put away from you, with all malice" (Eph. 4:26, 31).

The thoroughness with which the governing body of Israel, probably the Sanhedrin, studied the matter is admirable. They conducted their investigation according to the will of the Lord which stipulated, should certain men arise and attempt to lead the people of their city into idolatry: "Then shalt thou enquire, and make search, and ask diligently; and, behold, if it be truth, and the thing certain, that such abomination is wrought among you; Thou shalt surely smite the inhabitants of that city" (Deut. 13:12-18).

The procedure they were to follow required both caution and patience. They were to enquire; that is, seek the answer to the difficulty. They were to search; that is, more intensely examine the evidence for proof. They were to ask diligently; make direct interrogations. They were to adopt a process of justice which would lead them to a righteous decision. Spiritual discretion and discernment will "prove all things; hold fast that which is good" (I Thess. 5:21). The church at Ephesus was commended by the Lord because she "tried them which say they are apostles, and are not, and found them liars" (Rev. 2:2). It was the failure in the Corinthian church to practice a judicial caution, a failure to investigate certain discrepancies, that brought upon them the severe reproof: "Do ye not know that the saints shall judge the world? and if the world shall be judged by you, are ye unworthy to judge the smallest matters? . . . I speak to your shame. Is it so, that there is not a wise man among you? no, not one that shall be able to judge between his brethren?" (I Cor. 6:2-5).

This enquiry in Israel revealed certain fundamental principles which should be observed in dealing with rumours of a detrimental nature: consultation, representation, declaration, and recommendation. When these are strictly adhered to, they will result either in exoneration or condemnation.

At the solemn assembly the elders of Israel decided to make representation to their brethren: "The children of Israel sent unto the children of Reuben, and to the children of Gad, and to the half tribe of Manasseh, into the land of Gilead, Phinehas the son of Eleazar the priest, And with him ten princes, of each chief house a prince throughout all the tribes of Israel" (vv. 13-14). A large degree of wisdom is evinced in the choice of Phinehas. It was during a sad period of apostasy that he first distinguished himself. The Lord said concerning him: "Phinehas, the son of Eleazar, the son of Aaron the priest, hath turned my wrath away from the children of Israel, while he was zealous for my sake among them, that I consumed not the children of Israel in my jealousy. Wherefore say, Behold, I give unto him my covenant of peace" (Num. 25:11-12). Their sending Phinehas was the outcome of his forceful resistance to apostasy and the consequent confidence this produced in the minds of his brethren. They knew that without doubt Phinehas would maintain the honour of Jehovah's name, and that he would defend the monotheistic testimony of the nation. Furthermore, no more favourable choice could have been made for the two and a half tribes. To be exonerated by so zealous an individual as Phinehas would be a complete justification of blamelessness, and would result in an immediate restoration of confidence and national unity. The entire course of action proves the truth of the thrice repeated proverb, "In the multitude of counsellors there is safety" (Prov. 11:14; 15:22; 24:6).

Phinehas and the princes which accompanied him, with candour and concern stated their suspicions of idolatry and rebellion, and from the bitterness of national disaster at Peor presented the case from the perspective of the tribes gathered at Shiloh. If such sins were permitted, the entire congregation would suffer. Since "a little leaven leaveneth the whole lump," and there were still some among them so tainted (v. 17), all would be implicated and exposed to divine displeasure. Had the men of Reuben, of Gad, and of half Manasseh forgotten? "Did not Achan the son of Zerah commit a trespass in the accursed thing, and wrath fell on all the congregation of Israel?" (v. 20).

Nevertheless, with this stern reprimand of what to them seemed a grievous error, there was a gracious recommendation for peaceful settlement. "If the land of your possession be unclean, then pass ye over unto the land of the possession of the LORD, wherein the LORD's tabernacle dwelleth, and take possession among us: but rebel not against the LORD, nor rebel against us, in building you an altar beside the altar of the LORD our God" (v. 19). There are those who see in this appeal an allusion to indiscretion on the part of the two and a half tribes choosing to remain on the east of Jordan. They look upon the altar as another instance of indiscreet action arising from a selfish and covetous attitude.

The carrying out of the advice given by the heads of Israel might cause considerable inconvenience, might require reallocation of territory, might result in overcrowding in some areas within the original boundaries. Whatever a recrossing of Jordan might involve, it would be an insignificant consideration if only the secession be abandoned and the nation be spared. The words of the princes were mellowed by grace and truth; they spoke the truth in love (Eph. 4:15). Truth alone will make one too intolerant; love alone will make him too tolerant. Where these are properly combined, they produce a maturity that will express itself in vigour and kindness, in discernment and sympathy, in righteousness and compassion, in stability and flexibility. The firm yet gentle manner in which the men from Gilead were treated probably helped them to be courteous and humble.

As there were serious internal difficulties within Israel, early in her history, there were also internal difficulties within the Church in her early history. The same firm and gracious principles which led to the solution in Israel were applied in the Church. Errors in practice, like those propagated in Antioch, led to a council at Jerusalem where, after a careful and prayerful examination of the difficulties under the guidance of the Holy Spirit, proper recommendation was made to Gentile believers, a recommendation made by capable representatives (Acts 15). The Church would have been spared many a heartache had she followed the example set by the apostles and elders on that occasion.

The reply and the denial of the men of Reuben, Gad, and Manasseh were characterized by simplicity and sincerity. Their appeal to the witness of God (v. 22) as a proof of their blamelessness is forceful. In this they employed three distinct names: El, Elohim, and Jehovah, God in His power, in His trinitarian nature, and in His eternal essence. Furthermore, there is a suggestion in this appeal that God alone, as He had revealed Himself, was acknowledged by them, and that they claimed Him as their covenant-keeping Lord. God was their witness, and should they be prevaricating, so they asserted, then let God require it of them, let Him not spare them.

In their repudiation of all evil intentions, they made reference to the anxiety that had motivated their action: "For fear of this thing, . . . In time to come your children might speak unto our children, saying, What have we to do with the LORD God of Israel?" (v. 24). Whether or not some in Israel had manifested an attitude that caused them this concern is not known. It may have been the product of evil surmisings on their own part. Many of the fears of the human heart are self-imposed. In spite of the excellent arrangement made between Moses and themselves (Num. 32), they may have experienced a guilt complex over deflecting from the original plan.

Their fear was not over the attitude of their own posterity but that of others. If they had doubts about the behaviour of the descendants of the other tribes, they seemed quite self-assured. The future history of these two and a half tribes (I Chron. 5:25-26) leads to the conclusion that they had more to fear in their self-complacence then they had in the imaginary attitude and action of others. "The heart is deceitful above all things, and desperately wicked: who can know it?" (Jer. 17:9).

Apparently unconscious of self-complacence, these men from Gilead presented their explanation with sincerity and clarity. Yes, they had built an altar patterned after the brazen altar in the Tabernacle, only larger. They may have thought that the pattern itself would have been a link between them and their brethren on the west side of Jordan. They may also have thought that in an altar of such shape, they would have a reminder of God's demands, the demands of the one and only true God. They may likewise have thought that its presence would confirm in their lives, and in those of future generations, that God could be approached only on the basis of atonement. One thing was sure, it was not to be used for animal sacrifices. They averred their plan: "Let us now prepare to build us an altar, not for burnt-offering, nor for sacrifice: But that it may be a witness between us, and you, and our generations after us" (vv. 26-27).

Following their explanation they disclaimed any attempt to rebel against the Lord, or to depart from the service of the Tabernacle at Shiloh.

The reply of Phinehas expressed pleasure, not in that they had built an altar, but in that they had not trespassed against the Lord, and consequently the nation had been saved from God's wrath against apostasy. The absence of any reference to the altar by Phinehas at this time might be interpreted as a disapproval. It was the fact that the two and a half tribes had not transgressed that pleased the children of Israel when Phinehas and his associates on their return reported the matter. A civil war to extirpate the evil from the congregation had been averted. The joy that was Israel's through this clear understanding expressed itself in worship. "The children of Israel blessed God." Open strife and armed conflict had been avoided, and so praise ascended to the Lord.

"And the children of Reuben and the children of Gad called the altar Ed: for it shall be a witness between us that the LORD is God" (v. 34). How long the altar Ed remained is not stated, but in little more than four centuries, its witness to God was forgotten. We read: "And they transgressed against the God of their fathers, and went a whoring after the gods of the people of the land, whom God destroyed before them. And the God of Israel stirred up the spirit of Pul king of Assyria, and the spirit of Tilgathpilneser king of Assyria, and he carried them away, even the Reubenites, and the Gadites, and the half tribe of Manasseh, and brought them unto Halah, and Habor, and Hara, and to the river Gozan, unto this day" (I Chron. 5:25-26).

Such are the good intentions of men. They do not have the strength to implement their good resolutions. The tendency of man is downward. The very generations for which the altar was intended despised its testimony and plunged into idolatry. Apart from the grace and power of God deterioration is stamped on all human plans.

A New Priest

Any scriptural reference to the believer's walk is an allusion to his public habit of life; his walk is his manner of living before men by whatsoever influence directs him. According to the New Testament various powers control the walk of the child of God. He may walk after the flesh (Rom. 8:4), and thus be directed by sensual desires; or he may walk in darkness (I John 1:6-7), and thus respond to ignorance. Instead, he may walk after the Spirit (Rom. 8:4), and follow the inward impulses of God the Holy Spirit; and he may walk by faith (II Cor. 5:7), and live in reliance upon the Lord. Furthermore, he may walk in light (I John 1:6-7), and enjoy the atmosphere of purity and holiness; and he may walk in truth (II John 3; III John 4), and be guided by divine revelation. It is true that at times he may be called upon to walk through fire (Isa. 43:2), and experience in the trial the presence of the Son of God as did the three Hebrew youths (Dan. 3). The highest form of public living is a demonstration of the results of constantly walking with the Lord. To walk with God would be to hold communion with Him, and that communion would result in pleasing Him personally and glorifying Him publicly.

This high plane of spiritual living apparently is a very rare experience among men. As far as actual biblical records are concerned only a very few men have received commendable mention in regard to this form of intimate, enjoyable, and spiritually successful living. The life of Enoch is summarized in these words: "Enoch walked with God: and he was not; for God took him" (Gen. 5:24). Noah received a similar commendation: "Noah was a just man and perfect in his generations, and Noah walked with God" (Gen. 6:9).

David is given credit for walking before the Lord (I Kings 3:14), but there seems to be a difference. Walking before the Lord would involve the ideas of walking in His presence under His scrutiny and fulfilling His will. It lacks the thought of companionship and pleasure expressed by the use of the preposition "with."

In Malachi 2:6, the Lord declared of a descendant of Levi, "He walked with me in peace and equity, and did turn many away from iniquity." The prophet, in the immediate context, deplored the carnal state of the priesthood in his day. When its incumbents should have been the living exponents of the law, alas, such was their sin that God's curse had descended upon them. In contrast to what they were, a reference is made to one of their ancestors, presumably Phinehas. (Compare Numbers 25:12 with Malachi 2:5.) It is believed by many that the Lord here recalled the zeal of Phinehas in the matter of Zimri and Cozbi (Num. 25).

Phinehas was the man who walked with God in peace and equity; consequently, the absence of inward conflict was well reflected in the uprightness of his behaviour. In his relationship with God's people, this man who walked with God in peace and equity was strict in discipline and keen in discretion. In all probability he had learned of the divine discipline that had consumed his two uncles, Nadab and Abihu, in their sin (Lev. 10:1-7), and had been thereby warned. At any rate, he did not hesitate to vindicate the holiness of God with a javelin (Num. 25:7). With him the wages of sin were death. Righteousness demanded the punishment of evil, and justice the execution of the guilty, so in his zeal he justified the character of God.

Phinehas was not only a severe disciplinarian, but he was a discreet negotiator; that we saw in his plenipotentiary work for Israel as they dealt with the two and a half tribes which made the great altar. How true are the proverbs, "Most men will proclaim every one his own goodness: but a faithful man who can find? The just man walketh in his integrity: his children are blessed after him" (Prov. 20:6-7). Phinehas was a humble and faithful man of much ability.

The name Phinehas suggests one of bold countenance; if this trait is to be added to what has been already noticed, he was a man of courage, peace, and uprightness. How much are men of this type needed in the Church today! He was the third high priest of Israel in the line of direct descent, and some historians claim that he functioned as such for nineteen years.

While we admire zeal, it becomes necessary, notwithstanding, that we differentiate between spiritual and carnal zeal. Phinehas drew a javelin, and was approved of God; Peter drew a sword and in the flesh sought to defend his Master, and suffered the Lord's rebuke (John 18:10-11).

The Book of Joshua closes with a reference to the death and burial of Eleazar, the high priest of Joshua's day. His natural successor was Phinehas. It is recorded, "And Israel served the LORD all the days of Joshua, and all the days of the elders that overlived Joshua, and which had known all the works of the LORD, that he had done for Israel" (Joshua 24:31). Phinehas would be the high priest to these elders. From what has been learned of his character and actions, his influence would be beneficial.

Attention is frequently called to the progressive spiritual deterioration evident in certain family lines. In the case of Eleazar and his son Phinehas the opposite is obvious. Aaron, their father and grandfather, was influenced by the people for ill (Exod. 32:19-24) ; Phinehas, conversely, influenced the people for good (Joshua 22:32-34).

Chapter 21

FAREWELL AT SHILOH

JOSHUA 23:1-16

The Council Called

Inasmuch as the negotiations recorded in the preceding chapter were directed from Shiloh, it seems reasonable, in spite of the fact the exact location is not stated, to assume that the summons which called together the elders of Israel instructed them to meet there. Gilgal was the point at which the reproach of Egypt had been rolled away and the place at which were established the army headquarters from where the invasion of the land was conducted. Shechem was the centre for national convocations; but Shiloh, where the tabernacle stood, was the seat of government in Joshua's day (Joshua 19:51).

There are noticeable differences between the events narrated in chapters 23 and 24; the places of gathering apparently were not the same, nor were the audiences.

Joshua, first of all, called for Israel representatively in the nation's leaders: elders, heads, judges, and officers. He sent for the entire parliament. The elders would be the successors to the seventy men chosen by Moses (Exod. 18:13-26; 24:1-11), the forerunners of the Sanhedrin, eventually established at the time of the Maccabees. The name *elder* may have been a generic one for all, and the others may merely indicate the respective offices these filled in a declining gradation as suggested in Exodus 18:13-26, "Rulers of thousands, and rulers of hundreds, rulers of fifties, and rulers of tens."

At the time Israel was encamped around Sinai, Joshua, servant to Moses, was called "a young man" (Exod. 33:11). About eighteen months later Israel reached Kadesh-barnea from where Joshua and others were sent to search the land of Canaan (Num. 13). When the people listened to the evil report of the other ten men, and talked about returning to Egypt, "Joshua the son of Nun, and Caleb the son of Jephunneh . . . rent their clothes: And they spake unto all the company of the children of Israel, saying, The land, which we passed through to search it, is an exceeding good land. If the LORD delight in us, then he will bring us into this land, and give it us; a land which floweth with milk and honey" (Num. 14:6-8). In making reference to that experience, Caleb said, "Forty years old was I when Moses the servant of the LORD sent me from Kadesh-barnea to espy out the land" (Joshua 14:7). From these particular statements, it is assumed that Caleb probably was senior to Joshua by several years.

In view of this deduction it is very interesting to contrast Joshua's physical condition as reported in chapter 13 with that of Caleb stated in chapter 14. "Now Joshua was old and stricken in years; and the LORD said unto him, Thou art old and stricken in years" (Joshua 13:1). "Caleb the son of Jephunneh the Kenezite said unto him, . . . I am this day fourscore and five years old. As yet I am as strong this day as I was in the day that Moses sent me: as my strength was then, even so is my strength now, for war, both to go out, and to come in" (Joshua 14:6-11). What made the great difference in the appearance of these two former spies of Israel? Why does the younger look older, and the older seem stronger? There is no doubt that God had promised to keep Caleb alive (Joshua 14:10), but he was very much more than just alive. Could it be that the weight of responsibility, the burden of government, the duties of administration, had all so aged Joshua?

The Apostle Paul was called "a young man" at the time of Stephen's death (Acts 7:58), but in the year A.D. 64, he wrote to his friend Philemon and called himself "Paul the aged" (Philemon 9). At the time he could not have ·been more than sixty years of age, but because of toil and suffering in his service, and because of solicitude and anxiety toward the churches of the saints, he possibly felt and looked as he described himself, "Paul the aged." Suffering for the Lord, bearing responsibility in His service, pastoring the saints of God, supporting the testimony of Christ before the world, and patiently enduring the trials and the disappointments and disillusionments of life, all take their toll on both physical health and appearance. No doubt, there have been some who so expended their strength in the work of the Lord, they, humanly speaking, filled a grave prematurely. How many years had passed between the Lord's statement in chapter 13:1 and Joshua's admission of the fact at the opening of chapter 23, we do not know; but definitely, age and his approaching decease prompted this heroic leader to call the elders of Israel to him at Shiloh.

Had this aged warrior wished to speak of himself to the august gathering, he could have employed the language of Samuel, who on a similar occasion said: "Behold, here I am: witness against me before the LORD, and before his anointed: whose ox have I taken? or whose ass have I taken? or whom have I defrauded? whom have I oppressed? or of whose hand have I received any bribe to blind mine eyes therewith? and I will restore it you. And they said, Thou hast not defrauded us, nor oppressed us, neither hast thou taken ought of any man's hand" (I Sam. 12:3-4).

The purposes of Joshua in calling this council at Shiloh in certain aspects correspond to the intentions of the aged Peter when he wrote to them of like precious faith: "Wherefore I will not be negligent to put you always in remembrance of these things, though ye know them, and be established in the present truth. Yea, I think it meet, as long as I am in this tabernacle, to stir you up by putting you in remembrance; Knowing that shortly I must put off this my tabernacle, even as our Lord Jesus Christ hath shewed me. Moreover, I will endeavour that ye may be able after my decease to have these things always in remembrance" (II Peter 1:12-15). Joshua's primary interests were in the people of God and their safety.

The time at which the summons was sent forth is most interesting: "And it came to pass a long time after that the LORD had given rest unto Israel from all their enemies round about." It is gratifying that Joshua was permitted a period of rest, God-given rest. He had fought and won many battles; he had faced difficulties in the distribution of the territories, as he did in the previous chapter; he had arranged the execution of the guilty like Achan; he had smarted under defeat as well as exulted in victory; but, eventually, God gave his faithful servant rest, and with him the entire nation.

From the Epistle to the Hebrews, it is learned that this rest is the symbol of the believer's present rest in Christ, not, of course, his rest in Heaven. "There remaineth therefore a rest to the people of God" (Heb. 4:6-9). It is well, therefore, to examine the facts and features of this rest in Canaan in the light of New Testament Scripture.

That this rest of Israel in the land of Canaan was given divinely is distinctly stated (Joshua 23:1), and that God instrumentally through Joshua guided the nation into it is also clearly obvious (Heb. 4:8). Furthermore, from a careful reading of the valedictories of Joshua and the details of the subsequent history of the nation, it is seen that this rest was only temporary and conditional; there were several factors which could disturb it. In many parts of the land there still existed numbers of opposing, idolatrous Canaanites. Moreover, Phinehas himself was apprehensive of deep-rooted evils which could quickly develop and disrupt the peace of the nation. According to the Epistle of the Hebrews the most disquieting element did not lie in their enemies nor in their compatriots, but within themselves; "They . . . entered not in because of unbelief" (Heb. 4:6).

Christ is both the rest and the guide into rest for all in this present day. He offers rest to the sinner, "Come unto me, all ye that labour and are heavy laden, and I will give you rest" (Matt. 11:28). He also offers rest to the saint, "Take my yoke upon you, and learn of me; for I am meek and lowly in heart: and ye shall find rest unto your souls. For my yoke is easy, and my burden is light" (Matt. 11:29-30). To the one He offers rest in conversion, and to the other He offers rest in consecration. Of the first, we read, "We which have believed do enter into rest" (Heb. 4:3); and, of the second, we read, "Let us labour therefore to enter into that rest, lest any man fall after the same example of unbelief" (Heb. 4:11).

While expositors differ in their interpretation of Hebrews chapter four, some claiming that the rest refers to a present experiential rest, and others that it refers to a full and final rest, a keeping of an eternal sabbath, there is no question but that both aspects begin with conversion. The rest of the Christian in verse nine is called "a Sabbath of rest" in the Greek in order to identify it with God's rest on the seventh day (Gen. 2:2). Such a rest does not denote inactivity, but rather the completion of labour, a cessation from toil. It should be remembered that even God's rest on that first sabbath was broken by man's sin; it cannot, therefore, picture an eternal rest. Disobedience on the part of a believer not only mars the tranquility of the soul but produces in its stead inward conflict and distress.

Joshua's Appeal

The spirit in which Joshua addressed this council of national representatives and the text of his speech remind one of Paul's discourse before the elders from Ephesus: "Take heed therefore unto yourselves, and to all the flock, over the which the Holy Ghost hath made you overseers, to feed the Church of God, which he hath purchased with his own blood. For I know this, that after my departing shall grievous wolves enter in among you, not sparing the flock. Also of your own selves shall men arise, speaking perverse things, to draw away disciples after them. . . . And now, brethren, I commend you to God, and to the word of his grace, which is able to build you up, and to give you an inheritance among all them which are sanctified" (Acts 20:28-32).

The warnings, admonitions, and counsel of Israel's great military commander seem to be echoed in the words of the Church's great Apostle.

The rulers of the people whom Joshua soon expected to leave were certainly cast upon God. In his discourse, Joshua made some twelve references to the Lord in His dual distinction of Jehovah (LORD) and Elohim (God). Let us consider briefly these two names in order that we ascertain just what Joshua sought to emphasize in this farewell speech.

The name Jehovah is a derivative of the Hebrew verb "to be," and implies that God is the "I Am," He who always is, the absolutely existent One (Exod.

3:14). It was the name by which God made Himself known especially to His ancient people. "And God spake unto Moses, and said unto him, I am the LORD [Jehovah] : And I appeared unto Abraham, unto Isaac, and unto Jacob, by the name of God Almighty, but by my name JEHOVAH was I not known to them. . . . Wherefore say unto the children of Israel, I am the LORD [Jehovah], and I will bring you out from under the burdens of the Egyptians, and I will rid you out of their bondage, and I will redeem you with a. stretched out arm, and with great judgments : And I will take you to me for a people, and I will be to you a God: and ye shall know that I am the LORD [Jehovah] your God, which bringeth you from under the burdens of the Egyptians" (Exod. 6 :2-7). As Jehovah, God kept to them the covenants He had made with their forefathers.

Eventually, this name was considered by the Jews as too sacred to express in the public reading of the Scriptures. The reader, consequently, on encountering this name, either substituted or remained silent.

The name Elohim is the plural form of the Hebrew word *Eloah,* meaning God. When it appears with a singular verb, it expresses not only greatness and supremacy but also triunity. Furthermore, in such a construction it emphasizes that God is one in the divine unity of a threefold distinction: Father, Son, and Holy Spirit (See Deuteronomy 6 :4 and Mark 12 :29).

This is the name of God which occurs almost thirty times in Genesis chapter one. It is used of the Lord in His creative power and infinite wisdom.

Joshua, conscious of an imminent, inevitable change, directed the attention of all those who ultimately would have to assume leadership to the Lord as the great "I Am" who fulfilled His covenants, and as God who performed all His works. These very names that he employed were in themselves reminders of divine grace and divine power.

In this important message, the aged speaker not only focuses the minds of his hearers upon the Lord their God, but he commends to them a consideration of God in His many activities on their behalf. He mentioned God's actions in the past (v. 3) ; he predicted God's actions in the future (v. 5) ; and he noticed God's actions in the present (vv. 9-11).

Joshua called upon these elders as witnesses of God's grace to their nation throughout the past : "Ye have seen all that the Lord your God hath done unto all these nations because of you." The words "because of you" cannot fail to arrest interest. Some might expect to read, "All that the Lord your God hath done unto these nations because of their wickedness." Did the Lord not predict in His promise to Abraham a time when the iniquity of the Amorite would be filled (Gen. 15 :16) ? Was not Israel's presence in the land a proof of the fulness of the wickedness of the former inhabitants? It surely was.

The command against the Canaanites was clear : "When the LORD thy God shall bring thee into the land whither thou goest to possess it, and hath cast out many nations before thee, the Hittites, and the Girgashites, and the Amorites, and the Canaanites, and the Perizzites, and the Hivites, and Jebusites, seven nations greater and mightier than thou; And when the LORD thy God shall deliver them before thee; thou shalt smite them, and utterly destroy them; thou shalt make no covenant with them, nor shew mercy unto them : . . . But thus shall ye deal with them; ye shall destroy their altars, and break down their images, and cut down their groves, and burn their graven images with fire" (Deut. 7 :1-5).

The total war, the complete extermination of these peoples, were because of their grievous sin. It was the execution of God's punitive government. Not only is there a proof of divine government over the nations (Dan. 4 :32), but also an evidence of divine patience and grace. He expelled from Canaan a people whose idolatrous iniquity was full, and repeopled that land with Israel in her monotheistic testimony to Himself. It was because of Israel in that regard that the Lord had expelled the Canaanites. Joshua's retrospect demonstrated both God's government and God's grace upon the nations.

As Joshua contemplated the future and the certain fulfilment of God's promise, he reviewed in one verse his own service of many years. He did not indulge in self-eulogy, nor did he seek the praises of men. In his allusion to the dividing of the land, he spoke of "these nations that remain" and "the nations that I have cut off." Apparently, the thought here is "even all the nations that I have cut off," those that remained as well as those that had been exterminated. All alike were cut off and had no national status. There were pockets of resistance, but all opposition on a national level had been overcome. Consequently, the entire land, whether occupied or otherwise, was a divine inheritance from the Lord. Their responsibility was to possess this inheritance in full accord with the promise of the Lord: "I will set thy bounds from the Red Sea even unto the sea of the Philistines, and from the desert unto the river: for I will deliver the inhabitants of the land into your hand; and thou shalt drive them out before thee. Thou shalt make no covenant with them, nor with their gods. They shall not dwell in thy land, lest they make thee sin against me: for if thou serve their gods, it will surely be a snare unto thee" (Exod. 23:31-33). God would, little by little, expel, drive out, dispossess the enemies in order that they claim all territories as the fulfilment of His promise. Such was the future before them. What they had witnessed of the power of God in the past was sufficient to strengthen their faith for the future.

Since the past cannot be retrieved and the future cannot be revealed by man, the present is of paramount importance, for in it the mistakes of the past may be amended and the actions of the future be arranged. The greater part of Joshua's speech had to do with the time then present. His appeal to the elders was to each in his particular capacity and position. It was as if, like Paul to Timothy, he were saying, "Take heed to thyself, . . . For in doing this thou shalt both save thyself, and them that hear thee" (I Tim. 4:16). Personal faithfulness to the Word of God does not assure one of only individual preservation, but it wields a beneficial influence upon those committed to one's care. Furthermore, an elder, in fact a Christian leader in any capacity, ought to be the living example of God's Word.

In his appeal to the elders before him, Joshua gave three forceful exhortations. The first was, "Be ye therefore very courageous to keep and to do all that is written in the book of the law of Moses" (v. 6). The word *courageous* suggests more than bravery; it intimates that which makes one brave. The word in its various usages implies the confirmation of truth that produces strength of conviction. These elders were to derive strength by observing and performing all that was written in the law of Moses, what would be called the Pentateuch.

Courage is frequently thought of by some as the absence of fear in the presence of danger. By others it is looked upon as the act of bravery in spite of a sense of fear. In this exhortation courage is the manifestation of a strength derived from an adherence to the law of God. The divine Word when it is kept and obeyed builds a spiritual fortitude into character.

The second imperative exhortation by Joshua is found in verse eight: "But cleave unto the Lord your God, as ye have done unto this day." The verb "to cleave" used here means to adhere, not to cling. There are times when in his weakness the believer cleaves, clings, to the Lord for support. Such is not the idea here as will be seen by taking notice of the alternative. In verse eight the elders are exhorted to cleave to the Lord; in verse twelve, they are warned of the consequences of cleaving to the remnants of the idolatrous nations about them.

The exhortation of Joshua embraced an appeal to the elders that they firmly attach themselves in willing practical obedience to the Lord, and that they detach themselves from the immoral and idolatrous peoples not yet expelled from the land.

The third exhortation appeals to the affections. "Take good heed therefore unto yourselves, that ye love the Lord your God" (v. 11). "Now these are the commandments, the statutes, and the judgments, which the Lord your God commanded to teach you, . . . Hear, O Israel, The Lord our God is one Lord: And thou shalt love the Lord thy God with all thine heart, and with all thy soul, and with all thy might" (Deut. 6:4-5). The Lord demanded the supreme place in the hearts of His people, especially in the hearts of the elders among His people.

The bridegroom in the Song of Solomon (chap. 8:6-7) asked that he might seal the heart of his bride against all intruders. The reason for his request was the character of his own love for her. He indicated that his love was as strong as death in that it overcame every obstacle to make its claims. His jealousy (the zeal of a husband for his wife) was as the grave in that it refused to relinquish what it once had possessed. Furthermore, he added, his love burned as a fire kindled by the flame of Jehovah; therefore, it was unquenchable.

To love the Lord with all the heart is to reciprocate. "We love him because he first loved us." Such should be the character of our love that it will close the heart to every object unworthy of the Lord Jesus.

Throughout his appeal, Joshua with tender warmth reasons with these elders of Israel as to why they should cleave to the law and love the Lord. There seem to be at least four reasons, the first of which might be considered the snare of the enemy. "Turn not aside therefrom to the right hand or to the left; that ye come not among these nations, these that remain among you; neither make mention of the name of their gods, nor cause to swear by them, neither serve them, nor bow yourselves unto them" (vv. 6-7).

Idolatry has been defined as the worshipping of a material image which is held to be the abode of a superhuman personality. The wisdom of this world asserts that idolatry was one of the stages through which religion passed in its evolution. The Word of God declares that idolatry with its resulting immorality is the evidence of man's departure and decline from God. "Because that, when they knew God, they glorified him not as God, neither were thankful; but became vain in their imaginations, and their foolish heart was darkened. Professing themselves to be wise, they became fools. And changed the glory of the uncorruptible God into an image made like to corruptible man, and to birds, and fourfooted beasts, and creeping things" (Rom. 1:21-23).

God called Abraham from such idolatry. "Your fathers dwelt on the other side of the flood [the river] in old time, even Terah, the father of Abraham, and the father of Nachor: and they served other gods" (Joshua 24:2), Joshua told Israel. God called Abraham to Himself that he might become a testimony to the one and only true God. Such is the depravity of the human heart that it does become ensnared by heathenism. Throughout its early history, Israel was constantly falling into this evil. In fact, the nation was not finally cured from this tendency until the Babylonish captivity. Since then the Jews have resisted all encroachments of idolatry, their house has been swept and garnished (Matt.

12:43-45), but when the Beast will set up his image in the future temple, most will bow and worship it (Rev. 13:14-15); and the last state of the nation will be worse than the first.

Joshua realized that preservation from such evil lay only in obedience to God's law: "Thou shalt have no other gods before me. Thou shalt not make unto thee any graven image, or any likeness of anything that is in heaven above, or that is in the earth beneath, or that is in the water under the earth: Thou shalt not bow down thyself to them, nor serve them: for I the Lord thy God am a jealous God, visiting the iniquity of the fathers upon the children unto the third and fourth generation of them that hate me" (Exod. 20:3-5).

The Apostle John declared that God is fully revealed in Jesus Christ. He closed his first epistle with a most emphatic affirmation to the effect that God, whom Christ has revealed, is the true God. He then exhorts the children in the faith to reject all superstition and all carnal opinion in regard to God; yea, and to reject everything and anything which may divert the heart and mind from God and His Son, Jesus Christ our Lord. He ended that epistle with the terse admonition, "Little children, keep yourselves from idols."

The second reason Joshua gives for his insistence upon loyalty and love to God is seen in the propensities of human nature: "Take good heed therefore unto yourselves, that ye love the Lord your God. Else if ye do in any wise go back, and cleave unto the remnant of these nations, even these that remain among you, and shall make marriages with them, and go in unto them, and they to you: Know for a certainty that the Lord your God will no more drive out any of these nations" (vv. 11-13).

There are some who feel that there is a constant struggle between a lower self and a higher self, and they become discouraged because that victory is seldom on the side of righteousness. It is difficult for man to face realistically his own moral state. Only occasionally in despair does he raise the question, "How can he be clean that is born of a woman?" (Job 25:4). Or state honestly, "I know that in me (that is, in my flesh,) dwelleth no good thing" (Rom. 7:18). There is in each an evil heart of unbelief that ever departs from the living God (Heb. 3:12). And the sooner man acknowledges that and admits his own weakness, the sooner is there hope of blessing and stability.

There is only one deterrent from this proneness to wander away from God, and that is occupation with God and His Word. The Psalmist realized this and wrote, "Thy word have I hid in mine heart, that I might not sin against thee" (Ps. 119:11).

The child of God today must recognize that the Word of God is "profitable for doctrine, for reproof, for correction, for instruction in righteousness: that the man of God may be perfect, throughly furnished unto all good works" (II Tim. 3:16-17). It should also be remembered that these statements relative to the value and benefit of the Holy Scriptures were made in direct reference to the Old Testament; the New Testament canon had not yet been formed.

Joshua alluded to the faithfulness of God as another reason why they should love and serve Him. How could they possibly depart from Him and resort to the vain idols of the heathen remnants? Joshua declared, "Ye know in all your hearts and in all your souls, that not one thing hath failed of all the good things which the Lord your God spoke concerning you; all are come to pass unto you, and not one thing hath failed thereof" (v. 14).

He made reference to the kindness of God in the next chapter as he addressed the entire nation. He reviewed some of these kind acts of the Lord which in His grace He had bestowed upon the tribes of Israel. His mercy spared them repeatedly from the punishment they deserved, and His grace lavished upon them the kindnesses that they did not merit. The words of I Corinthians 13:4 could be written over their entire history: "[Love] suffereth long, and is kind."

His statement also emphasized the faithfulness of God. "Not one thing hath failed of all the good things which the Lord God spake concerning you." "Great is Thy faithfulness," wrote Jeremiah (Lam. 3:23); and David said, "Thy mercy, O Lord, is in the heavens, and Thy faithfulness reacheth unto the clouds" (Ps. 36:5).

God's mercy and God's faithfulness were in full evidence because of His power. "All are come to pass unto you, and not one thing hath failed thereof." What He had promised, He was able also to perform (Rom. 4:21). How could they possibly turn their backs upon God, and turn to gods who had eyes but could not see; ears, but they could not hear; and mouths, but they could not speak? Oh, the wickedness of the human heart! How quickly man forgets! "And Joshua the son of Nun, the servant of the Lord died, . . . And also all that generation were gathered unto their fathers: and there arose another generation after them, which knew not the Lord, nor yet the works which he had done for Israel. And the children of Israel did evil in the sight of the Lord, and served Baalim" (Judges 2:8-11).

The fourth persuasive argument Joshua advanced in his appeal for steadfastness in the law and fidelity to God was that of divine discipline. Do we not read, "Whom the Lord loveth he chasteneth"? (Heb. 12:6). As Moses at the close of his life blessed Israel, he expressed himself thus in regard to God's attitude toward the nation: "Yea, he loved the people; all his saints are in thy hand: and they all sat down at thy feet" (Deut. 33:3). Earlier in his ministry he had told them, "The Lord did not set his love upon you, nor choose you, because ye were more in number than any people; for ye were the fewest of all people: But because the Lord loved you" (Deut. 7:7-8).

Such was God's love for Israel that He could not allow them to wander away from Himself. Centuries later than the point of their history now under consideration, He lamented over them, "Why should ye be stricken any more? ye will revolt more and more." There had been strong resistance against His disciplinary actions. Notwithstanding, He pled with the nation, saying, "Come now, and let us reason together, saith the Lord: though your sins be as scarlet they shall be as white as snow; though they be red like crimson, they shall be as wool" (Isa. 1:18).

Such, then, is God's love for Israel that He will, even through discipline, draw her back to Himself: "I will heal their backsliding, I will love them freely: for mine anger is turned away from him. I will be as the dew unto Israel: he shall grow as the lily, and cast forth his roots as Lebanon" (Hos. 14:4-5).

How solemn were the words of Joshua to these elders! How gratifying to know that these elders who overlived Joshua responded to these words of warning! Joshua charged the elders over the people; he encouraged them, counselled them, and admonished them, in order that not only they themselves might be preserved, but that through them the entire nation might be guarded from and sanctified in the presence of evil influences.

Chapter 22

VALEDICTORY

Joshua 24:1-33

Shechem

Three geographic points were of vital importance to Israel during their early years in the Land of Promise: Gilgal, Shiloh, and Shechem. Gilgal was the military headquarters of the invasion; Shiloh, the religious centre of the people; and Shechem, the political cradle of the nation. These might illustrate different periods in the life of a Christian, periods not altogether consecutive, for what these represent may transpire also concurrently. They illustrate the stages of spiritual preparation, revitalized devotion, and progressive consolidation.

GILGAL: This military bridgehead where Israel raised the memorial of twelve stones was near Jericho. It was not only used as a headquarters by Joshua in the early days; it became a centre of administration some 350 years later, and was thus used by Samuel. We read, "He went forth from year to year in a circuit to Bethel, and Gilgal, and Mizpeh, and judged Israel in all these places" (I Sam. 7:16). It was there that Samuel anointed Saul as king (I Sam. 10:1), and there he slew Agag (I Sam. 15:33).

During the Israelitish invasion of the land, Gilgal was the place to which Joshua frequently returned to reorganize his forces, to replenish his supplies, and to strengthen his men. This place may illustrate for us the many privileges and experiences of the child of God in the heavenly places. "God, . . . even when we were dead in sins, hath quickened us together with Christ, . . . And hath raised us up together, and made us sit together in heavenly places in Christ Jesus" (Eph. 2:4-6). Israel had entered into her promised possessions by descending into and ascending out of Jordan; Gilgal, therefore, figuratively speaking, was *the place of resurrection,* illustrating the present spiritual position of the believer as risen with Christ and seated in heavenly places.

Gilgal was not only the place of resurrection, it was also *the place of responsibility.* The enemy was near, and any apparent failure of his strength was only temporary (Joshua 5:1). He soon mobilized his military strength and presented a united resistance to Israel (Joshua 11:1-5).

The Christian faces an array of invisible offensive powers. "We wrestle not against flesh and blood, but against principalities, against powers, against the rulers of the darkness of this world, against spiritual wickedness in high places" (Eph. 6:12). We need therefore to put on the whole armour of God and to stand and withstand in an evil day.

The reproach of Egypt was rolled away at Gilgal for it was to the nation *a place of recovery.* There Israel accepted again the sign of the Abrahamic covenant, circumcision. This act was by the law of God (Gen. 17:10-14; Lev. 12:3). It became a rite so distinctive of Israel that their oppressors tried to prevent its observance. There is a reference in the writings of the Maccabees to this wickedness of Antiochus Epiphanes, who decreed that every one in his realm should forsake his former laws, as these were keeping the people apart and from acting as one. He forbade the Jews the right to offer burnt offerings, and sacrifices, and drink offerings, in the temple. He decreed that they should profane the sabbath and feast days, and that they should also leave their children uncircumcised. It may have been that the Egyptians did likewise, and that this humiliation was rolled away on a national basis at Gilgal.

During the years in the wilderness, circumcision, for one cause or another had not been practiced; it was, therefore, necessary in order to claim the promises and presence of God in a fuller measure to comply with His law. "Joshua made him sharp knives and circumcised the children of Israel." According to Jewish tradition, these knives were buried with Joshua. Some, considering the highly spiritual and typical significance of circumcision (Deut. 10:16; Rom. 2:27), make the burying of these knives the symbolic cause of the spiritual decline and lawlessness recorded in the Book of Judges.

SHILOH: How deeply emotions are stirred by the very mention of the name Shiloh! This city situated east of the main road from Jerusalem to Bethel, and about nine miles north of Bethel, was the place chosen for the sanctuary. The religious life of the people revolved around this centre all during the years of occupation, and throughout the days of the Judges. It was there that Israel replenished their spiritual strength, and, so it seems, it was there that they eventually lost it.

Since the sanctuary was at Shiloh, God's people resorted there to enjoy His presence; the godly Elkanah "went up out of his city yearly to worship and to sacrifice unto the LORD of hosts in Shiloh" (I Sam. 1:3). Furthermore, in the early days of national life with its difficulties, it was there that Israel sought the mind of the Lord (Joshua 22). As has been suggested, it may have been at Shiloh that Joshua addressed the elders, heads, judges, and officers of the nation as he anticipated his departure from them (Joshua 23:1).

Young Samuel was given to the Lord at Shiloh, and served Him there in his youth; his prophetic ministry actually began there.

Apparently the ark was taken there shortly after the occupation of the land by Israel, and it remained there until it was carried into the camp of Israel from whence it was captured by the Philistines. Eli's wicked sons lived at Shiloh and by their deeds profaned the place where the Lord had put His name.

Excavations by archaeologists at the site of Shiloh sustain the contention that at the time the Philistines captured the ark, they destroyed the city and the sanctuary. Such evidence explains why the ark, when returned to Israel, was not set up at Shiloh. This destruction of Shiloh, while probably carried out by the Philistines, was the disciplinary act of God because of the sin and declension of His people. Of this the Psalmist wrote centuries later, "When God heard this, he was wroth and greatly abhorred Israel: So that he forsook the tabernacle of Shiloh, the tent which he placed among men; And delivered his strength into captivity and his glory into the enemy's hand" (Ps. 78:59-61).

The Word of the Lord through Jeremiah recalled the spiritual departure which characterized Israel in the early days of Samuel, the weakness of Eli, the gross sins of his sons, and the consequent judgment of God upon the nation at large and upon the place of the ark and the tabernacle, Shiloh. Furthermore, in this way the Lord draws a parallelism with conditions in Jeremiah's day, and refers to the destruction of Shiloh as a warning of impending doom (Jer. 7:12-15; 26:6-7).

Shiloh was indeed the spiritual pivot of national life. God's grace, guidance, and power had all been manifested there. The devout of the people had made pilgrimages to the sacred city, and their leaders had received indications of divine purposes at the sanctuary within its area; but, alas, there had been at

Shiloh so great a departure from God, that seven centuries later, it was remembered and used to warn God's apostate people.

Similar spiritual conditions, with the corresponding punishment, have been seen in the lives of more than one professed believer. Where grace has been abundantly bestowed, responsibility is increased; where this responsibility is not assumed in all humility, where indolence and neglect result in a conformity to the things of this present evil age, nothing can be expected but acts of divine displeasure.

SHECHEM: This ancient city was situated on the floor of a valley near its entrance, Mount Gerizim and Mount Ebal forming the respective walls. The contour of the land resulted in a natural amphitheatre, the acoustics of which were so good that the human voice carried to exceptional distances. Shechem was not only the geographic centre of Canaan; it was in some respects the moral heart of the nation. It was at this city that Abraham built the first altar to the Lord within the land, and it was here that God appeared to him, and promised, "Unto thy seed will I give this land" (Gen. 12:7).

Near this same city the patriarch Jacob purchased a field (Gen. 33:18-20), and settled there for a while on his return to his father's home. His two sons, Simeon and Levi, displayed their subtlety and cruelty here, acts which forced him to withdraw in shame and fear from the area.

Not only had the two great patriarchs of the nation been there but the nation itself had previously visited this vicinity. Joshua, after final victory at Ai and in compliance with the prediction of Moses, in faith called the nation together. As they stood, six tribes on Mount Gerizim and six tribes on Mount Ebal, he raised a cairn of stones, upon the plaster of which he wrote the law. Moreover, he read to the nation the curses and the blessings of the law to which the nation replied, "Amen." In that manner he renewed the covenant of God with Israel.

Now at the close of his full and active life, Joshua calls all the tribes back again to Shechem, to present themselves there before the Lord.

It may have been that the gathering together of the representatives of the nation at Shiloh was a regular administrative council and that he took that occasion to address himself to the national leaders; but the mighty convocation gathered before God at Shechem was extraordinary. Thirty years before, the same people had gathered in the same place in order to renew their covenant with God; they now gather to say farewell to the talented and noble leader, and to listen to his last words of encouragement and admonition.

A mental picture of Joshua addressing the tribes of Israel positioned on the slopes of Gerizim and Ebal suggests similar scenes. One is reminded thereby of aged and grieved Samuel, disappointed by the behaviour of his own sons, and displeased by the desires of Israel for a king, standing among the elders of the nation praying to the Lord on their behalf, and repeating in their hearing the divine message of God to them (I Sam. 8:1-10).

A New Testament scene in like manner comes to mind. Peter, an aged apostle, sitting in a room away in the city of Babylon, dictating a letter to the churches of the saints, passes on to their younger leaders the commission which he had himself received from the Lord: "Feed the flock of God which is among you, taking the oversight thereof" (I Peter 5).

Joshua was a soldier and an administrator; Samuel a judge and a prophet; and Peter a servant and an apostle of the Lord Jesus; but all had one burden in common: the welfare of the people of God. In Joshua's case the opposing influence was mostly external; in Samuel's case, it was mostly internal; but, in the case of Peter the adverse influences were both external and internal.

The voice of Joshua that resounded throughout the valley and over the slopes of Gerizim and Ebal was not the last to be heard in the great amphitheatre. Jotham stood on the top of Gerizim and told his parable to the men of Shechem. His attitude was one of defiance and fear, for we read, "And Jotham ran away, and fled, and went to Beer, and dwelt there, for fear of Abimelech his brother" (Judges 9:21). In the case of Joshua at Shechem there is dependence upon God, not defiance; there is quietness, not fear; there is authority, not weakness; there is clear instruction, not parabolism. With authority "Joshua gathered all the tribes of Israel to Shechem . . . they presented themselves before God" (Joshua 24:1). Oh, that Israel had remained submissive to divine authority, and receptive to the Word of God! This they were throughout the period of the elders that overlived Joshua (Joshua 24:31); but lawlessness and idolatry invaded their hearts. We read, consequently, "There was no king in Israel, but every man did that which was right in his own eyes" (Judges 17:6; 21:25). Hope for a theocracy in the nation vanished with the upsurging disregard of authority and the disrespect of divine revelation.

The Church of God might well learn from the sad history recorded in the Book of Judges. Departure resulted in discipline; reprobation in partial recovery. In spite of the deterrents placed in the way, the decline was progressive until Eli's daughter-in-law exclaimed, "The glory is departed from Israel!" The Lord apparently withdrew His presence and allowed His people to suffer the consequence of their own folly. In this Laodicean period of the Church's history when the Lord seems to be on the outside, on the outside appealing to the individual, oh, that wills might be brought into subjection to divinely constituted authority, and hearts made receptive to the Scriptures of Truth!

There is a belief among some Christians that the gifts of the apostles and prophets have forever passed away, and that these gifts have no important influence upon the Church of God today. True, the persons who were the embodiments of those gifts have gone home to Glory and, unlike the other three public gifts—the evangelist, the pastor, and the teacher—these were not transferable from one generation to another. When a great evangelist dies, God raises up another; when a pastor or teacher passes away, these gifts are entrusted to other persons. This was not so with the two important gifts, the apostle and the prophet. These men in the early Church were fitted for a special ministry, and when that ministry was fulfilled, they were removed and not replaced. Undoubtedly, there is a succession of evangelists, pastors, and teachers; certainly not of apostles and prophets.

While this is true, we must maintain a proper and scriptural perspective. The apostles themselves have passed to their eternal reward, but we have their authoritative writings. In these writings we still hear the apostles speaking with a power which was invested in them exclusively. No man today possesses the authority of, say, the Apostle Paul. Only such an one could write to the church of God at Corinth and say, "What will ye? shall I come unto you with a rod [a sceptre of authority], or in love, and in the spirit of meekness?" (I Cor. 4:21). The divine authority conferred upon Paul (and of course the same is true of all the other apostles) ended with his death.

In contrast to the temporary investment of the persons, the sacred Writings given by inspiration through them possess a permanent authority. "For the prophecy came not in old time by the will of man: but holy men of God spake as they were moved by the Holy Ghost" (II Peter 1:21). The words of the

New Testament possess for the Church of God today all the authority of faraway apostolic times.

There are four important verbs used in apostolic writings which emphasize the divine authority of the New Testament Scriptures. These are: "to command," "to charge," "to ordain," and "to will." There, no doubt, are others, but these will suffice for our present consideration. These verbs do not all possess the same force and power; in fact, their power seems to decrease in the order in which they have been listed. "To command" is to demand obedience. This verb is used in connection with the words of Christ and with the words of His apostles. Both Paul and Peter use it. Paul's commands are given in connection with domestic affairs (I Cor. 7:10); public ministry (I Cor. 14:37); church fellowship (Col. 4:10); and personal holiness and behaviour (I Thess. 4:2). Peter uses it in relation to the entire ministry of all the apostles (II Peter 3:2).

The attitude of lawlessness so prevalent in the world frequently infiltrates the congregations of the Lord's people. Such a spirit resents authority and refuses all commands. While the verb "to charge" is weaker than the previous one, nevertheless, it imposes responsibility. Paul not only did this himself, but he authorized Timothy to do likewise. Paul charged the elders at Thessalonica to read his epistle to the entire church (I Thess. 5:27). He charged Timothy to observe the instruction concerning the qualifications of elders (I Tim. 5:21); to keep the divine command relative to moral standards (I Tim. 6:13-14); and to perform the ministry that he had received from the Lord (II Tim. 4:1).

"To ordain" suggests the making of an appointment or arrangement with some authority. The idea of ordaining or appointing was used by the Lord, by His apostles, and by certain apostolic delegates. Paul used this verb in regard to marital relationships (I Cor. 7:17), certain abuses existing within the church at Corinth (I Cor. 11:34), and overseers (Titus 1:5). It was also used by Paul and Barnabas at Galatia (Acts 14:23), and by the elders and apostles at Jerusalem in connection with Christian liberty (Acts 16:4).

The last verb suggested, "to will," while being the weakest of the four, expresses the idea of a preference made by conviction. Paul thus uses the word asserting that the males should pray publicly (I Tim. 2:8); that younger women should marry (I Tim. 5:14); and that believers should maintain good works (Titus 3:8).

Jesus marvelled at the humility of the Roman centurion who said, "I also am a man set under authority, having under me soldiers, and I say unto one, Go, and he goeth; and to another, Come, and he cometh; and to my servant, Do this, and he doeth it" (Luke 7:8). While possessing authority to command others, he himself was under superior authority. In reading the New Testament, we must ever remember that while the apostles with authority commanded, charged, ordained, and willed, they were under the supreme authority of Christ. As the authority of the Roman centurion, an officer over one hundred men, was only the expression of the authority of his general; even so, divine authority expressed in the writings of these holy men is but the transmission through them of the absolute authority of the risen Christ and Lord, the supreme authority to be obeyed.

May the Lord's beloved people learn from the history of the nation of Israel that "to obey is better than sacrifice, and to hearken than the fat of rams" (I Sam. 15:22).

Joshua's Review of Israel's History

We are not much concerned with the actual mechanics of this meeting at Shechem. Whether Joshua was able to make himself heard, or whether he relayed his message to each tribe through an elder, is not important for our purpose. The acoustics of the valley are reputedly good, and it is wonderful what the human voice accomplishes under favourable circumstances. Benjamin Franklin asserts that on one occasion, with ease and comfort, he listened to George Whitefield preach in the open air to an estimated crowd of twenty thousand persons.

Our primary concern is with the speaker himself. His first words are very important, for they indicate the actual source of the message. We allude frequently to this chapter as being Joshua's valedictory speech, but literally this was a direct word from God. "Joshua said unto the people, Thus saith the Lord God of Israel." This great national leader was only a mouthpiece for God.

One recalls the timidity of Joshua's predecessor, Moses, and his acknowledgment of inability to speak in public: "O my Lord, I am not eloquent, neither heretofore, nor since thou hast spoken unto thy servant: but I am slow of speech, and of a slow tongue. And the Lord said unto him. Who hath made man's mouth? or who maketh the dumb, or deaf, or the seeing, or the blind? have not I the Lord? Now therefore go, and I will be with thy mouth, and teach thee what thou shalt say" (Exod. 4:10-12).

Forty years before, Moses had learned how ineffective were his persuasive powers. He no doubt recalled the challenge of his fellow Hebrew, "Who made thee a prince and a judge over us?" (Exod. 2:14). Moses had learned the futilty of human endeavour exerted without divine sanction. How gracious the Lord was with His servant! He, first of all, assured him that all the functions and capabilities of the human senses: speech, sight, and hearing, were fully known to Him, their Creator. He was not, therefore, assigning to Moses an unreasonable task. In second place, He allayed the fears which beset Moses' heart, stating, "I will be with thy mouth, and teach thee what thou shalt say." Joshua in all probability did not have such an experience of fear and timidity. From the opening words of his speech we learn he knew that God was merely using him as a mouthpiece to accomplish His own purpose.

Moses was possessed by a feeling of inability; Jeremiah with a sense of immaturity. Said Jeremiah, "Ah, Lord God! behold, I cannot speak: for I am a child" (Jer. 1:6). Although probably forty-five years of age, Jeremiah lamented his limitations and inexperience.

In the case of Moses the ability apparently already existed, but required stirring. Moses was encouraged to use what God had already given him. In the case of Jeremiah the Lord put forth his hand, and touched his mouth, and said, "Behold, I have put my words in thy mouth" (Jer. 1:9). Here a divine impartation seems to be implied. Similar language is used in connection with Daniel, who had gone through such an experience that his mouth was closed, his lips sealed. Daniel records, "Behold, one like the similitude of the sons of men touched my lips: then I opened my mouth, and spake" (Dan. 10:16). Whether in the servant of the Lord it is as in the case of Moses, the sanctification of some latent ability; or, as in the case of Jeremiah, the endowment of special powers; or, as in the case of Daniel, the recovery of lost capabilities; one and all must result from divine intervention and imposition. It was only when so fitted that a prophet could write, "Thus saith the Lord." Furthermore, it was only after such an experience from the Lord that the Apostle Paul could write, "I command, yet not I, but the Lord" (I Cor. 7:10).

If it were necessary that these holy men of old needed the divine touch upon their lips and personalities, how much greater is the requirement today! "If any man speak, let him speak as the oracles of God" (I Peter 4:11). The Old Testament Scriptures are called the oracles of God (Acts 7:38; Rom. 3:2), and without doubt the New Testament may thus be described; it is referred to as a sacred writing (II Peter 3:16). Men who profess to be servants of Christ today must speak in perfect accord with what has already been written in that which is acknowledged as "the oracles of God." There is an imperative need in the Church for men who like Joshua can face the congregation of the Lord and solemnly assert, "Thus saith the Lord God."

Joshua, like many of the great orators of Israel, began his speech with a review of national history: Israel's divine call, preservation, establishment, and hope. Moses reviewed their history as he anticipated their entrance into the land of promise, and he did so to impress upon them the grace of God that had elevated them from a very lowly origin (Deut. 26). Here Joshua follows this usual method, but does so to manifest God's determined intention to firmly implant Israel as a nation in Canaan. The Psalmist in like manner examines the details of national history for the proof of divine immutability in the fulfilling of the covenants made by God to His people (Ps. 78). In the days of Nehemiah a great and holy convocation met for the reading of the law and for prayer. At that time the entire history of the nation was considered from its beginning to demonstrate the mercy of God. Israel had declined and had departed from the Lord and because of this spiritual and moral defection had endured His discipline. As a nation His people were obliged to confess, "Nevertheless for thy great mercies' sake thou didst not utterly consume them, nor forsake them; for thou art a gracious and merciful God" (Neh. 9:31). It would be difficult to think of the history of Israel without recalling Stephen's brilliant address before the Sanhedrin, an address through which the accused became the judge, and the judges became the accused.

Stephen surveyed the different stages of the national story from its earliest days to indicate the rebellious spirit against the Lord that had always characterized Israel, a rebellion that had reached its climax in the rejection and crucifixion of the Messiah (Acts 7). What tremendous lessons may be learned from history: lessons of God's faithfulness, lessons of man's complete failure!

The many activities of the Lord since the beginning of His dealings with Israel are here set down in order. Such clauses as the following prove the power of God to accomplish what He had intended: "I took," "I gave," "I sent," "I brought," "I have brought," "I have done," and "I destroyed."

When Pharaoh and his taskmasters increased the burdens of the Israelites and made them serve under greater rigour, God made promise to His people saying, "I am the Lord, and I will bring you out," "I will rid you out," "I will redeem you," "I will take you to me," "I will be with you," "I will bring you in" (Exod. 6:6-8). God is not using here the simple future of our grammar; these promises are predetermined by the sovereign fiat of God. Through Joshua God is asserting that what He purposed to do for the nation, He has done. Israel now possessed the land of Canaan, not because of their own strength, nor because of wise leadership. The Lord claims the credit of the mighty accomplishment for Himself. "I brought you into the land of the Amorite, . . . I gave them into your hands. . . . I destroyed them before you."

A contrast is seen between the words of Jethro to Moses and those of the Apostle Paul. Said Jethro, "Thou art not able to perform it thyself alone" (Exod. 18:18). The Apostle wrote of Abraham's attitude toward the Lord, that he was fully persuaded "what he [God] had promised, he was able also to perform" (Rom. 4:21). All this illustrates what Paul had in mind when he wrote to the Philippians, "Being confident of this very thing, that he which hath begun a good work in you [ten years previously] will perform it until the day of Jesus Christ" (Phil. 1:6).

In this review of their history the Lord refers to their call in Abraham and his descendants, their redemption at the Red Sea, their preservation in the wilderness, and their inheritance of the land.

The purpose of God in directing their minds to their ancestor Abraham, whom He had called from a land of idolatry, was to remind them of His abhorrence of this wickedness, and that, in the separation of their forefathers from such an environment and from such a practice, they were to consider themselves separate from it as well. "Your fathers dwelt on the other side of the flood [beyond the river Euphrates] . . . and they served other gods." They who thus sat in darkness saw a great light. Stephen says, "The God of glory appeared unto our father Abraham, when he was in Mesopotamia, before he dwelt in Charran" (Acts 7:2). The conversion of Abraham from polytheism to monotheism was complete. The former idolater became a worshipper of the only true and living God. He left Ur of the Chaldees, a great political and religious centre in which Sin, the moon-god, was worshipped, to look for "a city which hath foundations, whose builder and maker is God."

During his pilgrimage between these two cities, God led him through a land in which he was a stranger, and gave him Isaac. And to Isaac, God gave Jacob, and multiplied his seed. Thus the foundation of the nation was laid in God's calling of Abraham, and in His gift of Isaac and Jacob. There was nothing here that happened by chance; all was according to the sovereign will of God.

Many events in Israel's history are not referred to in this address; it is the high points only that the Lord would employ in the farewell of Joshua.

God plagued Egypt through the hands of Moses and Aaron. Here again the Lord reminds His people of His disdain for the gods of the heathen; these are the evidence of departure from Himself. "Professing themselves to be wise, they [men] became fools, And changed the glory of the uncorruptible God into an image made like to corruptible man, and to birds, and fourfooted beasts, and creeping things" (Rom. 1:22-23). Part of Moses' message in regard to the passover was, "Against all the gods of Egypt I will execute judgment: I am the Lord" (Exod. 12:12). The objects venerated by Israel's oppressors fell under the judgment of God; He destroyed them one by one. Since idolatry was a snare into which Israel might fall, she would not be seduced without warning; she would know God's concept of this grave sin, and his hateful judgment upon it. The last word of the speaker in this connection refers to the overthrow of the idolaters, and possibly their deified king, Pharaoh. "When they [Israel] cried unto the Lord, He put darkness between you and the Egyptians, and brought the sea upon them, and covered them; and your eyes have seen what I have done in Egypt" (Joshua 24:7).

Almost every object was considered the habitation of some spirit; consequently, reptiles, insects, animals, birds, and humans became deities in the life of the Egyptians. They considered many of their pharaohs as the incarnation of one of their favourite gods. "Upon their gods also the Lord executed judgments" (Num. 33:4).

The many years spent in the wilderness are passed over in silence. The Lord is not narrating the events of human failure, "the provocation in the wilderness." He, rather, is stating His own glorious exploits. In Hebrews chapter 11 much of the sin and failure in the lives of the heroes of faith is eliminated in order to magnify the grace of God in responding to their confidence in Him; but here the deletions are to demonstrate the mighty power of God in the important events of history.

The next reminiscence is that of the defeat of the Amorites and the experience with Balak, king of Moab, and Balaam. What is recorded in the Book of Numbers, chapters 22 to 24, might not be considered as war by some. But God declares, "Balak the son of Zippor, king of Moab, arose and warred against Israel." There are different methods of conducting a war. We are well acquainted with the expression "the cold war," which in reality is a war on the nerves of the opponent rather than against his military force. Balak's strategy was the use of divination by means of demon power. In the law, God insisted, "There shall not be found among you any one . . . that useth divinations, or an observer of times, or an enchanter, or a witch, Or a charmer, or a consulter with familiar spirits, or a wizard, or a necromancer" (Deut. 18:10-11). These were the very means which Balak tried to employ against Israel. The Lord through Joshua says, "I delivered you out of his hand."

The closing part of Joshua's review of their past treats the crossing into the land of promise and the resistance they encountered at that time. The entire confederacy of seven nations is mentioned, not only to remind them of the forces of opposition they had faced, but to prove again that not with their own accoutrements had they gotten the victory. How true the assertion of Joshua at his earlier meeting with the representatives of the people, "Ye have seen all that the LORD your God hath done unto all these nations because of you; for the LORD your God is he that hath fought for you" (Joshua 23:3).

What an encouragement for the Christian! A great array of enemies would hinder him in the enjoyment of his inheritance in Christ. There are principalities and powers, the rulers of the darkness, and spiritual wickedness (Eph. 6:12) to hamper his progress. Israel armed herself with obedience and faith and followed the instructions of the Lord; with the result that God delivered these enemies in Canaan into her hand; she relied upon the power of God's might, not upon her army and strategy.

In the struggle against opposing powers in heavenly places, those powers would rob the Christian of his spiritual possessions. May he, yea all of us, be strong in the power of God's might, and put on the armour He has graciously provided, every whit of which speaks of our blessed Lord Jesus, Christ-imputed and Christ-imparted. Let us ever remember that we have an adversary the devil as a roaring lion walking about seeking whom he may devour. We are enjoined to resist him stedfastly (I Peter 5:8-9), and if we do, God affirms, "Resist the devil, and he will flee from you" (James 4:7).

The hornets to which Joshua refers were one of the means the Lord employed in this fierce combat against the Canaanites. There are different viewpoints in regard to these. Some Bible students believe that the hornets may have been literal plagues of stinging creatures, of which there seem to be different species in Palestine. It is believed that these scourges infested certain areas and attacked the Canaanites. If we are to accept them as literal, then we must also believe that the Lord wrought a miracle in protecting the people of Israel from similar attacks.

There are other Bible students, equally careful in their exegesis, who believe that the reference here and in Exodus 23:28 and Deuteronomy 7:20, is to figurative hornets; that the Lord is referring metaphorically to the stinging terrors which gripped the Canaanites as they watched the advance of the children of Israel into their territories. The promise of the Lord in the Exodus passage would rather substantiate this contention: "I will send my fear before thee, and will destroy all the people to whom thou shalt come, . . . I will send hornets before thee."

God fulfilled His prediction. He drove out the Canaanite. Whether by literal hornets or merely figurative ones is not too important; His was the victory.

The final statement in this immediate context suggests to the reader the words of Jeremiah: "Thus saith the LORD, Let not the wise man glory in his wisdom, neither let the mighty man glory in his might, let not the rich man glory in his riches: But let him that glorieth glory in this, that he understandeth and knoweth me, that I am the LORD which exercise lovingkindness, judgment, and righteousness, in the earth" (Jer. 9:23-24). Israel could not boast of her prowess; she could not correctly speak of her conquest of the land; but she could glory in her God who gave her richly all these things to enjoy: a beautiful country, established cities, and fruit-bearing vines and olive trees which they had never cultivated.

Joshua's Exhortation

The Apostle Paul generally in the first part of his epistles teaches doctrine, and, then, in the second part exhorts to corresponding duties. He first gives the reason for Christian conduct, and then logically insists upon commendable behaviour. There is something similar here, not that Joshua was teaching doctrine, but he was reviewing the grace and goodness of God throughout their past in order to appeal to the hearts of the people for an attitude of holiness, fear, and love toward God.

Nothing moves the heart, and therefore the will, like recollections of the grace of God in hours of need, like the guidance of the Lord in difficulties, the power of God in victories, and the patience of God in periods of weakness and temptation. These in themselves are sufficient to produce a response to the claims of God upon us.

The Spirit of God makes an entreaty to the saints at Rome, and, of course, likewise to us. "I beseech you therefore, brethren, by the mercies of God, that ye present your bodies a living sacrifice, holy, acceptable unto God, which is your reasonable service" (Rom. 12:1). This appeal rests upon the tracings of the mercies of God in the earlier chapters. In these it is demonstrated how patiently and mercifully God deals with man who has come short of glorifying Him, and how He so changes this unregenerate man and eventually glorifies him. Man, who fails, because of his depravity, to glorify God, by God in His mercy is ultimately glorified. What tender mercies! Well might the Spirit, on the ground of the grace that justifies and glorifies, appeal for unreserved devotion and sacrificial living for the Lord. Through Joshua the Lord in like manner entreats Israel on the ground of His wonderful accomplishments and benevolence.

The appeal of Joshua was primarily against idolatry. Obviously he had reason to fear further and deeper defection. Among them there were some who venerated the gods which Abraham once served on the other side of the

Euphrates, some who still worshipped the gods of the Egyptians, and some who seemed very susceptible to the worship of the gods of the Canaanites. The leaven of pagan idolatry was already at work.

One cannot think of this appeal by Joshua without recalling the earnest pleadings of Elijah some centuries later: "How long halt ye between two opinions? if the LORD be God, follow him. . . . And the people answered him not a word" (I Kings 18:21). It was only after the dramatic proof that Baal was nonexistent, and that the Lord was indeed the living and true God, that the people fell on their faces, and said, "The LORD, he is the God; the LORD, he is the God" (I Kings 18:21-39).

Until the seventy years' captivity in Babylon, the inclination on the part of Israel, and of Judah as well, was toward idolatry. Since then the house has been swept and garnished, but in the future days of the antichrist, this evil will return with sevenfold intensity, and the last state will be worse than the first (Matt. 12:43-45). Thank God, the day will come when under the benign rule of the true Messiah, Ephraim shall say, "What have I to do any more with idols? I have heard him, and observed him" (Hos. 14:8).

The aged Apostle John knew the tendencies of the human heart to depart from the living God. He closes his first epistle with the exhortation, "Little children, keep yourselves from idols." There is not the danger of a Christian indwelt by the Holy Spirit of God falling into the wicked practices of heathen worship; but there is the danger of his esteeming altogether too highly some much-liked object, and allowing it a place in his affections which the Lord asks for Himself alone. As Israel was admonished to put away all strange gods, and to fear and serve the Lord alone, so the Christian is responsible to rid from his heart all carnal idolatrous love; to keep himself from idols (I John 5:21), and to keep himself in the love of God, looking for the mercy of our Lord Jesus Christ unto eternal life (Jude 21).

With the background of a national weakness and a propensity toward idolatry, Joshua avers his own determination. "Choose you this day whom ye will serve; whether the gods which your fathers served that were on the other side of the flood [beyond the Euphrates], or the gods of the Amorites, in whose land ye dwell: but as for me and my house, we will serve the LORD" (Joshua 24:15). These were words of knowledge and wisdom. Joshua knew the futility and degeneracy of idolatry, and, furthermore, he knew the reality and supremacy of God. Observation and experience fully equipped him to so challenge the nation. Idolatry was obnoxious to him, but God was very personal and true.

That the whole nation felt the impact of these words is obvious in their reply. They were also to feel the force of other charges by Joshua before they were finally dismissed. To this challenge based upon the reality of God, "The people answered and said, God forbid that we should forsake the LORD, to serve other gods; . . . therefore will we also serve the LORD; for he is our God" (vv. 16-18). How little they knew of the wickedness of their own hearts! They would be influenced for good throughout their own generation by the example and power of Joshua. Consequently we read, "Israel served the LORD all the days of Joshua, and all the days of the elders that overlived Joshua" (v. 31). Notwithstanding, we read of a sad change: "And also all that generation were gathered unto their fathers: and there arose another generation after them, which knew not the LORD, nor yet the works which he had done for Israel" (Judges 2:10).

How miserably that first generation had failed! Had they served the

Lord, had they obeyed the command of Moses, such dreadful ignorance would not have prevailed. Before Israel had crossed the frontier of Canaan Moses had said, "Only take heed to thyself, and keep thy soul diligently, lest thou forget the things which thine eyes have seen, and lest they depart from thy heart all the days of thy life: but teach them thy sons, and thy sons' sons; . . . The LORD said . . . Gather me the people together, and I will make them hear my words, that they may learn to fear me all the days that they shall live upon the earth, and that they may teach their children" (Deut. 4:9-10).

Joshua received their reply, but such was his knowledge of this insidious evil that he declared the infinite holiness of God and the sure and dire consequence of their sin. God would not forgive "the great transgression," as David called idolatry. To indulge further in this evil would only result in the severest possible divine punishment. For presumptuous sin there would be no remedy.

This solemn assertion of divine holiness might well be thoughtfully considered. "The LORD . . . he is an holy God; he is a jealous God" (v. 19). The Apostle Peter made an impressive appeal to the strangers of the dispersion, and, of course, makes it also to us: "As he which hath called you is holy, so be ye holy in all manner of conversation [mode of living] ; Because it is written, Be ye holy; for I am holy. And if ye call on the Father, who without respect of persons judgeth according to every man's work, pass the time of your sojourning here in fear" (I Peter 1:15-17).

The second reply of the people reveals how vain they were in themselves and, at the same time, how ignorant they were of the true character of God. The words of the Decalogue had not deeply impressed them. "Thou shalt not bow down thyself to them, nor serve them: for I the LORD thy God am a jealous God, visiting the iniquity of the fathers upon the children unto the third and fourth generation" (Exod. 20:5).

The words of Joshua on this occasion remind one of the words of Paul to the Corinthians as he draws lessons from the behaviour of Israel in the wilderness. He describes how many of them fell under the disciplinary hand of God because of sin, and asserts, "Now all these things happened unto them for ensamples," and then gives the word of warning, "Wherefore let him that thinketh he standeth take heed lest he fall." That is, let him be careful lest he too fall under divine discipline. The congregation gathered before Joshua thought that it stood well, but their leader knew them thoroughly, and for them he feared lest eventually they too would fall under punitive measures by the Lord.

There had been a time in the life of their forefather Jacob when he said unto his household, "Put away the strange gods that are among you, and be clean, and change your garments: And let us arise, and go up to Bethel; and I will make there an altar unto God, who answered me in the day of my distress, and was with me in the way which I went. And they gave unto Jacob all the strange gods which were in their hand, and all their earrings which were in their ears; and Jacob hid them under the oak which was by Shechem" (Gen. 35:2-4).

On this occasion his descendants did not follow the example of Jacob. There was no such practical response to the appeals, warnings, and admonitions of Joshua. He therefore took them at their word, and made a covenant that day. Alas for their self-confidence! It has been pointed out that Joshua actually made a covenant for the people rather than with the people. What he wrote in the Book of the Law is not certain, but one might assume that he recorded the proceedings of the day: the instructions, entreaties, and warnings, as well as the bold answers of the people. Moreover, he set up a stone as a witness of all the transactions of the convocation.

This means of preserving the evidence of an agreement was very common in patriarchal times. Jacob used a heap of stones to mark the arrangement between himself and his uncle Laban (Gen. 31:43-55). We have noticed in chapter 22 that the tribes of Reuben and Gad erected an altar as a witness between themselves and the other tribes. Here Joshua uses a great stone as the evidence of the promise of Israel to God.

It is rather interesting to notice that the first time we see Joshua in service with Moses was during the battle with Amalek. At the close of the conflict we read, "And the LORD said unto Moses, Write this for a memorial in a book, and rehearse it in the ears of Joshua: for I will utterly put out the remembrance of Amalek from under heaven. And Moses built an altar, and called the name of it Jehovah-nissi" (Exod. 17:14-15). The public service of this remarkable soldier and administrator closes, as it had opened, with the keeping of factual records and the sealing of these by a permanent witness in stone.

Throughout the life and service of Joshua the influence of Moses may be traced. Typically there are some contrasts. Moses represents the law which cannot give the believer that liberty in Christ that is his through faith; Joshua typifies our Lord Jesus in whom we are seated in heavenly places and through whom we enter into our inheritance. Notwithstanding, as historical characters, we see how the elder influenced the younger. Joshua, like his worthy predecessor, was a very humble man; he sought little for himself; he was a faithful man and executed the will of God as he understood it; and he trusted the Lord implicitly. Furthermore, like Moses, he kept records, and made covenants, and used means to permanently fix these in the minds of the people. It would seem that God fits a younger man through association with an older one. This is seen in the case of Timothy. The Apostle Paul wrote to him saying, "Hold fast the form of sound words, which thou hast heard of me, in faith and love which is in Christ Jesus" (II Tim. 1:13). "Continue thou in the things which thou hast learned and hast been assured of, knowing of whom thou hast learned them" (II Tim. 3:14).

The work for which Joshua was so well trained and equipped, the service which he endeavoured to do in faithfulness for God, had come to an end. "So Joshua let the people depart, every man unto his own inheritance."

Chapter 23

IN MEMORIAM

There have been various conjectures as to what Joshua wrote in the Book of the Law of God. Some assume that he added the book that bears his name to those already prepared by Moses, and that the Book of Joshua forms a necessary link between the Pentateuch and the historical books of the Old Testament. In one sense at least, it is the complement to the Pentateuch, for it demonstrates the power of God to bring the children of Israel into the land as He had promised when He brought them out of Egypt. This Book of Joshua received divine endorsement through the writer of the Epistle to the Hebrews. There is in that epistle a direct reference to Joshua himself (chap. 4:8), and another to the history recorded in his writings (chap. 11:30-31).

It seems logical that Joshua be considered the author of this work. Many military leaders and many governors have sketched for future generations the events and details of battles in which they had directed the main movements. Nevertheless, there is some reasonable doubt as to his writing the entire book on the occasion referred to in this the last chapter. The amassing of all the details, the organizing of the material, and the compilation would require much more time. It could have been commenced at Shechem and completed after Joshua reached his home. This work of history could have been the last service he performed for the Lord and his beloved people.

Because of his character and service, Moses, the servant of the Lord, earned for himself the distinctive title, "Moses the man of God" (Psa. 90). Joshua in like manner seems to have earned the appellation, "the servant of the Lord" (Joshua 24:29; Judges 2:8). Both of these remarkable men had lived a God-centred life. In fact, the Lord was the circumference as well as the centre; He controlled the entire area of daily experiences. In language similar to that of the Apostle Paul, both of them could have said, "Be ye followers of me, even as I also am a follower of the Lord."

Obviously, the closing two paragraphs of the book were not written by the hero. Who appended the account of Joshua's death and burial we do not know, but they seem a necessary close to the work.

In his death he was ten years younger than his predecessor, Moses; but of Moses at the time of his death it is written, "His eye was not dim, nor his natural force abated" (Deut. 34:7). But of Joshua it is recorded, "Joshua waxed old and stricken in age" (Joshua 23:1). Whether the Lord preserves a man in a miraculous way, as in the case of Moses, until his service is completed; or whether He allows nature to take its course, as in the case of Joshua, is entirely within His own wisdom and power. May we learn to say, as suggested by James, "Ye ought to say, If the Lord will, we shall live, and do this, or that" (James 4:15).

It was a sad day when the nation gathered to honour and bury their great warrior governor. They gathered in the city which he had asked and which they had given him according to the word of the Lord (chap. 19:50). We have noticed the influence that Joshua had wielded during his lifetime; it is gratifying to notice also that the beneficial influence remained upon that generation. "Blessed are the dead which die in the Lord from henceforth; yea, saith the Spirit . . . that they may rest from their labours." "Surely . . . the righteous shall be had in everlasting remembrance." That Joshua should have been honoured by the nation, and that the people he had taught, and before whom he had been such an example, should have walked in the ways of the Lord, all will agree. But do all practice this proper attitude? There are leaders among the congregations of the saints today. Do we revere their name, and do we emulate their exemplary lives? The writer to the Hebrews admonishes to remember the leaders of the past as well as those of the present: "Remember them which have the rule over you, who have spoken unto you the word of God: whose faith follow, considering the end of their conversation." "Obey them that have the rule over you, and submit yourselves: for they watch for your souls, as they that must give account, that they may do it with joy, and not with grief: for that is unprofitable for you" (Heb. 13:7 and 17).

Two other burials are mentioned here: that of Joseph and that of Eleazar. Joseph died in Egypt, but under oath the children of Israel arranged to carry his bones with them when they left Egypt. Joseph did not want to remain in a permanent grave until his people had a permanent rest in the land of promise. His final resting place was in the area where his father Jacob had bought a property from Shechem's father for an hundred pieces of money (Gen. 33:19-20), and where Jacob built an altar after his return to the land from Haran.

It is assumed by many that the bones of Joseph were buried much earlier than the time covered by this chapter, probably at the time of the renewing of the covenant mentioned in chapter 8:30-35. They were laid to rest near to the place where his grandfather Abraham first entered the land, and where he built his first altar, and where God appeared to him—the place of Shechem and Moreh.

The other burial mentioned is that of the high priest Eleazar. He had succeeded to the office on the death of his father Aaron, and had been very closely associated with Joshua during the conquest of the land and the administration of the tribes. In fact, he had conducted the inaugural ceremony for Joshua. Furthermore, he had assisted Joshua in the division of the land among the tribes. Scripture is silent as to the time of his death. Josephus, the Jewish historian, says that he died about the same time as did Joshua.

The account of the burial of these three wonderful leaders forms a very befitting close to this Book of Joshua. One by one they had served their generation and had fallen asleep, but their very names direct the attention to the One who remains forever. The name Joshua means "Jehovah is salvation"; Joseph, "Jehovah may add"; Eleazar, "God is help." History is ever in the making; times change as do conditions and people. Amidst all that is mutable, how stabilizing and strengthening to know that there is One who never changes, and to hear His own word, "I Jehovah change not" (Mal. 3:6), and the New Testament revelation, "Jesus Christ the same yesterday, and today, and for ever" (Heb. 13:8).